DEALING WITH DICTATORS

DEALING WITH DICTATORS

THE UNITED STATES, HUNGARY, AND

EAST CENTRAL EUROPE, 1942–1989

LÁSZLÓ BORHI

TRANSLATED BY JASON VINCZ

INDIANA UNIVERSITY PRESS
Bloomington & Indianapolis

This book is a publication of

Indiana University Press
Office of Scholarly Publishing
Herman B Wells Library 350
1320 East 10th Street
Bloomington, Indiana 47405 USA

iupress.indiana.edu

Translation funded by the László Tetmájer Fund of the Hungarian Studies Program, Department of Central Eurasian Studies, Indiana University–Bloomington.

First paperback edition 2018
© 2016 by László Borhi
All rights reserved

No part of this book may be reproduced or utilized in any form or by any means, electronic or mechanical, including photocopying and recording, or by any information storage and retrieval system, without permission in writing from the publisher.

The paper used in this publication meets the minimum requirements of the American National Standard for Information Sciences—Permanence of Paper for Printed Library Materials, ANSI Z39.48–1992.

Manufactured in the United States of America

Cataloging information is available from the Library of Congress.

ISBN 978-0-253-01939-4 (cloth)
ISBN 978-0-253-01947-9 (ebook)

ISBN 978-0-253-03371-0 (paperback)

1 2 3 4 5   22 21 20 19 18

*For my boys, Dániel and Marcell
and for my wife, Csilla*

CONTENTS

Acknowledgments ix

Introduction 1

1 Peace Overtures, the Allies, and the Holocaust, 1942–1945 12

2 *Cuius Regio, Eius Religio*: The United States and the Soviet Seizure of Power 50

3 Rollback 84

4 1956: Self-Liberation 117

5 Reprisals and Bridge Building 138

6 The Dilemmas of External Transformation 184

7 "The Status Quo Is Not So Bad": Détente 219

8 Nixon, Carter, and the Kádár Regime 265

9 "Love Toward Kádár": Reagan and the Myth of Liberation 323

10 1989: "Together We Liberated Eastern Europe" 364

Conclusion 434

Notes 443

Bibliography 527

Index 541

ACKNOWLEDGMENTS

I wish to express my appreciation to the Institute of History of the Center for Humanities of the Hungarian Academy of Sciences and the Department of Central Eurasian Studies at Indiana University for providing a stable support and a stable background while I was writing and researching this book. My research in the National Archives and Records Administration was generously funded by the Cold War International History Project of the Woodrow Wilson International Center for Scholars and Hungarian-American Scholarship and Enterprise Fund. I wish to take the opportunity to express my gratitude. I also wish to thank the Scowcroft Institute of International Affairs for funding my research in the George Bush Presidential Library. Last but not least I am grateful to the László Tetmájer Fund at Indiana University for funding the translation of this volume.

I owe an intellectual debt to a long list of peers and professors. They share in everything that is positive about this volume. I take full blame for its faults.

I wish to thank the following who generously shared their experience and expertise with me in interviews: Robert Hutchings, János Nagy, the late Mark Palmer, General Brent Scowcroft, Thomas Simons, Ferenc Somogyi, and John Whitehead.

DEALING WITH DICTATORS

Introduction

This is a book on the impact of one country on the other. At first sight the selection of this topic may seem a bit odd in light of the fact that it describes the relationship of two geographically distant countries: the United States, the most powerful state of the times, and Hungary, a weak client state in the middle of Europe. It is the history of how the framers of American policy sought to exploit this small but strategically well-located state to further America's strategic interests and how Hungarians, caught in the net of aggressors, first Germany, then the Soviet Union, tried to use the United States as a counterbalancing force. Even though American influence in East Central Europe was not decisive, at certain junctures U.S. policies impacted Hungary profoundly. Although Hungary was rarely the focus of American foreign policy, developments there influenced the overall U.S. strategy toward Eastern Europe.

Only a few historians have dealt with the bilateral relations between the United States and a small state under foreign domination. *Dealing with Dictators* provides an in-depth case study of Cold War history that more general accounts of the Cold War cannot address. The case-study approach makes possible an exploration of the bilateral relations between the United States and Hungary from two sides. The book addresses a number of important questions. What works better, isolating enemy states or building contacts with them? Did communist states speak with one voice on foreign policy matters? How did Soviet hegemony affect the foreign policy of its client states in various periods of the Cold War? How did the

U.S. attempt to influence the weak states of East Central Europe for its strategic objectives? How did American objectives and strategy toward the region change over time? Was the relationship between the United States, Hungary, and the other client states strictly one way, or did the weak states affect America's strategy in the Cold War? How profound was, after all, the impact of American foreign policy on the countries behind the Iron Curtain?

Perhaps the main argument of this book is that engagement through economic, cultural, and humanitarian contacts can be more successful in transforming the political system and foreign policy of hostile dictatorships than can policies of embargo and isolation. In addition, it will be argued, the weak states of East Central Europe were by and large unable to influence their position in the international arena after the start of World War II. This does not mean that they were always entirely powerless. Although they were unable to rid themselves of the consequences of Soviet hegemony until 1989, some Soviet satellites such as Romania were able to manipulate Cold War rivalries in their favor. In 1989, however, the Soviet satellite states launched the avalanche that ended communism and reunited Europe.[1]

For this study, I analyze – from the perspective of both states – the relationship between the United States and a small state in East Central Europe, from the start of World War II to the end of the Cold War. Focusing on the policies of the two states as they interacted allows us to see how the initiatives of one state shaped and affected the responses of the other. Policymakers in Washington may have devised strategies toward Eastern Europe, but these strategies had to be implemented on the ground. Political strategies can be disconnected from reality, and this is especially the case when policymakers at the highest echelons of power are poorly informed of the conditions in the countries they are trying to engage. In general, a state is able to attain its objectives in foreign policy only if the intentions of the other state are properly appraised and understood. This level of understanding can be achieved only by a well-trained diplomatic corps that is well-versed in the historical and cultural heritage and political customs of the host country and therefore is able to properly interpret its intentions. Initiatives failed in the Cold War when the intentions of the target state were misinterpreted.

The proper interpretation of scarce intelligence was particularly hard in the highly secretive communist political settings, where even official data were rendered unreliable by politically and ideologically motivated manipulation and where credible information on the functioning and aims of the opaque political system was almost impossible to come by. American diplomats stationed in Budapest found it particularly hard to gauge the true intentions of their interlocutors. Oftentimes, functionaries posing as party liberals claiming to be constrained only by intransigent Soviet masters were in reality members of the state security apparatus with a mission to curry unreciprocated favors from the United States.

Paradoxically, the United States was able to exert strong influence on Hungarian politics in World War II, when there were no official contacts between the two states. In order to improve the chances for the planned invasion of Europe, the Joint Chiefs and the State Department sought to exploit Hungarian (and Romanian) efforts to quit the war. The idea was that if Germany found out about its allies' intrigues and moved to occupy Hungary, Romania, and Bulgaria, it would be forced to redeploy troops that could otherwise be used to repel the Normandy invasion. In Hungary's case the ploy worked. Hitler did order its occupation, citing the country's impending treason. This occupation, in turn, had catastrophic consequences for the last intact Jewish community in Europe.

In the early phase of the Cold War, American foreign policy had little influence on the actions of the Soviet Union in its sphere of occupation in Eastern Europe. American property was confiscated; U.S. citizens were arrested and incarcerated with impunity. Moscow pursued two simultaneous policies: gradual Stalinization and imperial penetration. These policies were interrelated. Soviet military and economic penetration helped the process of political and economic Sovietization; the installation of pro-Moscow communist regimes ensured the almost unconditional satisfaction of Soviet imperial needs.[2] In Hungary, the introduction of the dictatorship of the proletariat was announced in May 1946. Hungarian democratic political elements sought American support against the onslaught of the Soviet-backed Communist Party. While the U.S. diplomatic mission in Budapest was well aware of the scope and depth of Sovietization and Soviet imperial penetration and thought it detrimental to American interests, intervention on behalf of the Hungarians was nevertheless rejected. Washington referred to the principle of nonintervention, believing in any case that the democratic elements were too complacent and caved in too easily to communist pressure. Those in Hungary who were ready to resist lost heart because they could not count on external support. Washington also remained inactive because the British failed to support even modest diplomatic measures against Moscow on behalf of the Hungarians. Washington did present a démarche in Moscow demanding that the Soviets cooperate with the West in Hungary's economic reconstruction, but to no avail. If it came to a choice between the full control of their zone and continued cooperation with the West, the Soviets opted for control. Ultimately, however, the retention of Hungary (or Bulgaria or Romania) was not a priority for American politics. President Truman held out hope for the possibility of cooperation with the Soviets even after the war, but mainly, as the historian Günter Bischof has shown, Austria was the key state for Western security.[3] Hungary was highly significant strategically for the Soviets, so the strategic dividing line between East and West was the Austro-Hungarian border.

In February 1948 the communists seized power in Prague. President Edvard Beneš hoped to build a bridge between East and West, but his bridge, as the historian Vít Smetana observed, was trampled on. That same month the Soviets imposed a treaty of friendship on Finland, but as far as incorporation into the Soviet sphere was concerned, Helsinki was off the hook. In response to the Soviet-sponsored coup in Czechoslovakia, the Truman administration gave up its policy of accommodating the Soviets in East Central Europe and gradually introduced a policy of economic and psychological warfare intended to subvert the newly installed communist regimes and to weaken the Soviet bloc's military capabilities. Policymakers in Washington reasoned that the instability of the Soviet-controlled regimes enhanced Western security. Everything from ball bearings to penicillin were barred from crossing the Iron Curtain, and America's allies were also obligated to comply with the economic embargo. Propaganda broadcasts were transmitted to encourage passive resistance and to nurture the hope of liberation from communist and Soviet domination; agents were introduced to recruit volunteers for armed resistance.

Despite the skepticism of the State Department and the Department of Commerce, the Joint Chiefs of Staff and the Department of Defense expected the collapse of the communist systems under the weight of economic embargo and from massive unrest encouraged by American propaganda. Even though these policies caused economic hardship and did impede the military preparedness of the satellite states, the optimistic hopes attached to quarantining the Soviet bloc failed to materialize. In fact, it can be argued that the policies intended to hurt the communist regimes were instead harmful for the population.

Policies designed to undermine Soviet power and the reigning communist regimes met with limited success. Moscow did not perceive American policies toward Eastern Europe as particularly threatening and understood that Washington feared the Soviet nuclear deterrent too much to take military action. Indeed, American analysts had concluded that the Soviets would resort to war if their vital interests, including their hold on Eastern Europe, were threatened. Economic warfare succeeded in exacerbating shortages and technological backwardness but did not come close to causing a political crisis sufficient to topple any regime. Hare-brained schemes that were hatched for subversion, such as flooding government offices with phone calls in a country where hardly anyone had a private telephone, were even less effective. The isolation of communist regimes was a rigid policy that left little room to adjust to change. After Stalin's death in 1953, prime minister Imre Nagy introduced a new course in Hungary, a modest but significant relaxation of domestic terror and economic reforms, which encouraged agricultural production at the expense of heavy industry. U.S. analysts, however, misinterpreted Nagy's reforms as sham, and Washington made no effort to take advantage of them.

During the Hungarian revolution of 1956, the Soviet Party Presidium did not even consider the possibility of an American response to the Soviet military intervention in Hungary. Rightly so, because despite American propaganda that there could be no lasting peace in Europe until the liberation of Eastern Europe, the United States was left with few options to support anti-Soviet unrest. The rollback of Soviet power was the priority of U.S. policy in Europe, and the self-liberation of the Hungarians would have realized this goal, so Washington tolerated the strident line broadcast by Radio Free Europe that encouraged the Hungarians to fight. This decision undermined any hope of a negotiated settlement, since the harder the Hungarians fought the less chance remained for the Soviets to settle the crisis peacefully. Many Hungarians, thinking that external armed assistance was forthcoming, fought the Soviets and died.

The spectacular failure of the policy of liberation in Hungary led to a slow and protracted re-evaluation of U.S. policy toward the Soviet bloc. From the late 1950s into the 1970s, the goal of rollback was shelved, and the division of Europe into two opposing and hostile blocs was gradually accepted as an unalterable fact. Rather than reunifying the continent, Washington's goal was now "re-association," bringing the two parts of Europe closer together.

As the goals changed, so did the strategy. From the early 1960s, the United States pursued, even if in fits and starts, a policy of evolutionary transformation that helped to erode the communist monopoly of power. This policy was most successful when the sensibilities and weaknesses of individual countries were taken into account. Even communist states were sensitive about national sovereignty and did not tolerate overt American intervention in their domestic affairs. In making concessions to American demands, they wanted to maintain the semblance of acting of their own accord. Political and economic reforms in some Soviet bloc countries were conducive to the changes in the American approach. The odd man out was Hungary, where Kádár's Soviet-installed regime conducted massive reprisals against its political opponents.

The policy of gradually constructing cultural, economic, and humanitarian ties with the Soviet bloc was introduced on the basis of the liberal tenet that more ties lead to more openness and more democracy. President Kennedy called it peaceful engagement; his successor, Lyndon B. Johnson, called it bridge building. The new approach was fraught with difficulties. It involved the normalization of relations with regimes supported by the Soviet Union and convinced of their moral superiority. Cultural and scientific contacts offered an alternative to Marxist indoctrination, the Beatles rather than the Communist International. Visits to Western capitals convinced even faithful party members that life was better outside the communist paradise. The economy turned out to be the Achilles heel of the Soviet Union's Eastern European allies. Economic dependence on the West forced closer contact with the West, and the extension of economic favors allowed the United States the best opportunity to affect changes in communist politics.

The mainstay of the doctrine of bridge building was the use of trade as a means to shape events behind the Iron Curtain. It is an irony that the president who embraced the policy most decisively was the most anticommunist of them all, Richard Nixon. Yet even Nixon moved slowly because members of his administration were divided over the policy. Beside the long-standing concern that unbridled trade would strengthen the enemy, there were other reservations as well. Secretary of defense Melvin Laird believed that internal liberalization would come about as economic problems intensified rather than as a result of the relaxation of external pressures. Henry Kissinger, on the other hand, was convinced that the communist states would be willing to give up something for the privilege of trading with the United States. The question was only whether trade policies should be extended as a reward for political concessions already granted or as a carrot in the expectation of a communist political reward. Eventually Nixon moved forward with the expansion of trade when, in the midst of economic difficulties at home, the Soviet zone was seen as a potential market for American exports.

Each communist state required an individual approach. Bridge building required a process of "normalization" with each, which meant addressing outstanding financial claims and a host of other issues. In order for incentives to work, it was necessary for U.S. diplomatic missions to be able to understand domestic political processes and "read" the intentions of the hosts. This was not always possible. Hungary's case was especially difficult because of the legacy of 1956. The Hungarian leadership bore a grudge against the United States for its alleged part in the outbreak of the revolution and for putting the Hungarian question on the United Nations' agenda. There was also the question of financial claims and the return of the Crown of Saint Stephen, the symbol of Hungarian statehood, which had been in U.S. protective custody since the end of World War II. Hungary's motivation to settle with the Americans was purely economic, but this was a powerful driving force. For the emerging reform wing of the party, the consolidation of political power after the failed revolution necessitated economic modernization to elevate living standards. The first impediment to normalization was removed in 1963, when, in exchange for the renewal of the Hungarian mandate in the UN and the removal of the Hungarian question, the regime declared a political amnesty for the persecuted revolutionaries. Normalization talks started, only to be halted by the escalation of the war in Vietnam.

Party conservatives and the security apparatus were unhappy with opening to the West anyway; they feared that Western creeping "subversion" would destroy the country's ideological integrity and eventually undermine the political system itself. The controversy between party "liberals" and "conservatives" was not about the ends but the means. Both worked for the regime's consolidation. The first favored getting Western loans in return for minor political concessions; the second was convinced that loosening the system was counterproductive and dangerous. Cultural contacts were a case in point. Reformers believed that Western-trained specialists were needed to modernize the economy. But the possibility of sending specialists to study in the United States forced the communists to accept "subversive" specialists in the humanities in return. The expansion of contacts generated pro-American feelings among the population at large that outweighed the governments' anti-American campaigns. Even convinced communists returned home with a highly positive image of the United States. On the other hand, people who attended events organized by the Americans in Budapest took some risks: the Hungarian employee of the British library was an operative of the state security services and reported the names of attendees to the Ministry of Interior. Appearing in the ministry's records could adversely affect careers and the ability to travel abroad. Eventually the deployment of soft power, despite all its controversies, contributed to the restoration of cultural and intellectual diversity behind the Iron Curtain.

Besides appreciating the risks involved in more contacts, the state security services also saw possibilities for information gathering and recruitment on the expansion of exchange programs. In the early 1970s, they hatched a plan to fund a Hungarian position at an American university, where the holder of the chair would be a clandestine operative of the counterintelligence service tasked with identifying possible recruits. The survival of cultural exchange programs was to some extent at the mercy of the state security services. For example, when an exchange scholar was abruptly expelled from Hungary in 1973, the sponsoring institution, IREX, threatened to shut down all exchange programs. The State Department, however, was more prudent and decided that such a countermeasure would only assist the forces that were opposed to Western contacts.

In the final analysis, the expansion of trade and economic relations did the most to undermine communist power. Poland, Hungary, and Romania incurred huge Western debts to modernize their economies in the hope that increased exports would pay for the debt. This never materialized; most of the money was squandered. Romania tried to pay off its debt with disastrous consequences. Hungary ended up in a cycle of debt and hovered on the brink of bankruptcy from 1982. The country's debt crisis helped rock the regime's foundations. Even though Hungary was a member of the Comecon and the Warsaw Pact, the regime depended on Western loans for survival.

Bridge building was not without pitfalls. First, it was easy to go overboard in throwing support behind undeserving dictators. A case in point was Romania's Nicolae Ceaușescu, who achieved a quasi-ally status and most favored nation treatment from the United States for the foreign policy services he rendered to the United States. But well into the 1980s the United States turned a blind eye to Ceaușescu's tyrannical rule and perverse personality cult. Hungary under Kádár was a police state that nonetheless led the West to believe it was implementing far-reaching economic reforms while the basic structure of the Stalinist economy remained untouched. The United States held up Kádár's morally corrupt, economically failing government as a model for other communist states to follow.

The onset of the 1980s saw the resurgence of Cold War hostility. While President Ronald Reagan publicly labeled the Soviet Union an evil empire, recent scholarship has shown that the president was more reasonable toward the Soviets than his strident rhetoric suggested. By the early 1970s there was a consensus in government circles that the status quo in Europe was not unacceptable, signified by the signing of the Helsinki Agreement and the return of the Holy Crown to Hungary in 1978. American diplomats did not hesitate to disclose to their Soviet bloc colleagues that Washington did not wish to cause them problems with the Kremlin. The Reagan administration continued to recognize the Soviets' sphere of influence in Europe and had no intention of challenging the political realities. On the other hand, the president was open to rewarding the more autonomous and more liberal states such as Hungary. By then Budapest was in such dire economic straits that the leadership refused to cut back its contacts with Western states despite a Soviet warning to do so, thereby decoupling bilateral relations with the United States from relations between the superpowers. And if relations remained adversarial, on balance Hungary emerged as one of America's favorites behind the Iron Curtain.

In an unpublished private letter to Mikhail Gorbachev, President George H. W. Bush claimed that "together we liberated Eastern Europe and unified Germany." In reality, the "miraculous" transformation in Eastern Europe did not result from an act of liberation from either of the superpowers. For the first time since the Second World War, the states of East Central Europe had agency in domestic and foreign policy. Although Bush claimed that his administration wedded itself to the notion of "Europe whole and free," the rapidly changing scene met with an ambivalent American response. Although the president asserted that Eastern Europe was the priority, the record shows that keeping Gorbachev in power was the chief concern. The Soviet Union's loss of its sphere of influence could have been inimical to this goal. In addition, some American officials were concerned that the retraction of Soviet power could lead to local hostilities. As democratization rapidly unfolded, the survival of the Warsaw Pact began to be questioned, which, paradoxically, could be seen as a security challenge. If the Soviet alliance disappeared would there be a raison d'être for NATO?

It was clear that political and economic catastrophe could ensue unless profound changes were allowed to happen behind the Iron Curtain. Nonetheless, Washington accepted the Soviet position that such changes should not challenge the "post war realities." Gorbachev created the environment in which the regime change could take place, but the collapse of communism and the subsequent reunification of the continent originated in Poland and Hungary. This is not to say American politics did not contribute to this outcome. The events of 1989 were in large part caused by the debt crisis generated by the policies of bridge building, but that policy, as opposed to those practiced in the first half of the 1950s, did not envision either regime change or the end of the European system that had been in place since Yalta.

1

Peace Overtures, the Allies, and the Holocaust, 1942–1945

In a forgotten episode of World War II, the United States and Great Britain chose to provoke a German invasion of Hungary (and Romania) in order to "spread the Germans thin" in Western Europe and facilitate the Allied landing in France in 1944. This decision appears to have been made without concern for the last remaining Jewish community in Europe, then numbering 825,000 people, or for Hungarian democratic elements. Allied planners expected that the Germans would need ten to fifteen divisions to occupy Hungary, troops that would thus be rendered unavailable for the fighting in Normandy. No calculation seems to have been made, however, to determine whether the removal of these divisions would actually make a difference in the success of the landing and the future course of the war, or whether these expected gains would outweigh the potential murder of almost a million people. According to Allen Dulles, the calculus was a callous one: for the sake of victory, "a few hundred thousand lives would not make a difference." In January 1942, under strong German pressure, the Hungarian government had agreed to send a Hungarian army to the eastern front. Shortly thereafter, the Hungarian regent, Miklós Horthy, appointed a new prime minister, Miklós Kállay, in hopes of restoring Hungarian independence from Germany, and later that year they made secret peace overtures to the British and Americans. Soon Romania was sending peace emissaries as well, and by refusing to take advantage of these overtures the Allies missed a chance to disrupt the Axis and thereby to bring the war to an earlier end. The geopolitical consequence of this wartime diplomacy was, in the words of the historian Frazer Harbutt, that "Soviet domination of Eastern Europe ... had in substance been accepted by the governments of Britain and the United States by 1945."[1]

Through an in-depth analysis of Hungary's secret peace talks with the Allies, this chapter will explore the relationships between Allied war strategy and the final phase of the Holocaust, the dilemmas of weak states in the definition of their national interests, and the moral choices great powers face in the coercion of smaller states. In Hungary in 1943 and 1944, American policymakers faced a dilemma that would recur in 1956: the defeat of a powerful aggressor, they believed, could be achieved only by placing a foreign population in mortal danger.

Small states in the international arena are like bottles floating in the sea: they may surface for a moment on a wave of history, only to disappear after the wave has subsided. Weak powers had their moments in shaping the history of World War II. Yugoslavia's anti-German stance forced Hitler to delay operation Barbarossa, which cost the Germans precious months of good weather and contributed to the German failure. In 1944 and 1945, the Red Army was held up in Hungary for eight months, which spared Austria the full brunt of Soviet occupation. Had Stalin been able to occupy Austria alone, the Soviet bargaining position in the Cold War would have been vastly enhanced. Yet the perspectives of small powers hardly ever figure into the "big picture" of international history, even though those perspectives may significantly modify our view of it.

Accounts of World War II do not mention the clandestine peace talks between Hitler's satellites and the Allies that took place in the neutral capitals of Europe. Had these talks, which held out the prospect of disrupting Germany's southern flank, been pursued with more vigor in early 1943, the war might have been brought to an earlier and possibly different end. We will never know for sure. Logically, these peace overtures ought to have been welcomed in London and Washington. With the exit of Hungary, Romania, and Bulgaria, Hitler would have been deprived of crucial war materials including oil, bauxite, manganese, coal, and foodstuffs, not to mention the loss of the Balkans and much of Central Europe. Yet Hungarian and later Romanian and Finnish peace feelers were either not taken seriously or rejected outright. Numerous doubts arose. In order not to arouse Hitler's suspicion, the Hungarians chose obscure envoys whose identities were hard to verify. British and American officials were often unsure whether these envoys genuinely represented their governments or were instead spies or provocateurs anxious to sow seeds of doubt among the Allies. Was the enemy using these secret peace overtures to stay in power? And what if Stalin found out? Negotiating a surrender behind the Soviets' backs might prompt Stalin to seek his own agreement with Germany, a prospect that in light of the Hitler-Stalin pact remained distinctly plausible. The first peace feelers were thus coolly received.

In March 1942, Regent Horthy, a former admiral in the Austro-Hungarian navy, realizing that Germany might lose the war, dismissed his pro-German prime minister, László Bárdossy, and charged Miklós Kállay, known for his moderate political views and firm anti-German stance, with "restoring" Hungary's "freedom of action." Hungary was the first of the German satellites to move slowly and cautiously toward extricating itself from Hitler's alliance. Its example would soon be followed by Finland, Romania, and Bulgaria. The stakes were no less than national survival. Ending another war on the losing side could lead to a repetition of the disastrous Treaty of Trianon, which had deprived Hungary of two-thirds of its prewar land and population. The only way out of this predicament was to surrender to the British or the Americans. Initially, Hungarian leaders ruled out the option of surrender to the Soviet Union, since they, like the vast majority of Hungarians, considered the prospect of Soviet occupation as undesirable as an invasion by the Nazis. Kállay and the few others who were privy to the plans for defection, however, were playing a dangerous game. Hungarian territory had to that point escaped the fighting, but betraying Hitler could provoke an invasion by Germany and all that German occupation had meant elsewhere on the continent. Nevertheless, the anti-German segment of the country's elite favored a withdrawal from the war, an option that despite all its dangers and pitfalls seemed essential to the country's survival as an independent entity. Hungarian leaders hoped to convince the Anglo-Saxons that they had had no other choice than to align with Germany, and that Hungary would be useful in the upcoming struggle against Bolshevism, which the West could not afford to lose. By surrendering to the British and the Americans, the Hungarians sought to avoid invasions by the Germans and the Soviets, as well as to hold onto the territories they had recovered in the early stages of the war. Such hopes were fueled by a rumor that the British and the Americans were about to open a second front in the Balkans, allowing them to beat the Red Army into central Europe.

These Hungarian secret maneuvers were to end in disaster. On March 19, 1944, German tanks rolled into Budapest and removed its relatively independent government. Deportations of Jews, which Kállay had refused the Germans, soon began; democratic elements were rounded up. Hitler designated Hungary *Festung Europa* and ordered the Wehrmacht to fight to the death in order to protect the Reich from the Bolshevik onslaught. In the last year of the war, one out of every ten Hungarians was killed. Whether this tragic ending was inevitable has been disputed ever since. Kállay has been reproached for his alleged vacillation and even duplicity in dealing with the Allies. He has been portrayed as a weak, irresolute leader whose personal failures led to his country's tragedy. But research done in British archives in the 1970s suggests that London's dealings with the peace feelers from Eastern Europe may have concealed ulterior strategic calculations that were inimical to the survival of large numbers of people. Evidence from U.S. archives is even more revealing in this respect. Had the Hungarians known the Allies' purpose in negotiating with them from mid-1943, these talks might have not have been pursued. In fact, the story behind the secret talks reveals what could turn out to be a highly controversial chapter of Allied diplomacy in World War II.

"A BASKET OF ORCHIDS":
THE AMERICAN IMAGE OF HUNGARY

Under German pressure, Hungary declared war on the United States on December 12, 1941. Nevertheless, the head of the American diplomatic mission to Hungary, Herbert Claiborne Pell, believed that many Hungarians remained sympathetic toward the United States and viewed it not as an enemy but as a friend. Horthy surprised Pell's spouse with a basket of orchids, which the State Department took as a gesture of open sympathy toward the United States and an act of defiance toward the Axis. Pell later recounted that he and his wife were showered with manifestations of kindness.[2] Pell's predecessor, the Roosevelt appointee John Flourney

Montgomery, had been impressed with the baroque ways of the Hungarian ruling classes and described his post as a bastion of Western civilization to which the West owed much of its security.[3] Not all agreed with such flattering views: Allen Dulles, who headed the American intelligence service (OSS) in Switzerland and was in charge of dealing with Hungarian envoys (even procuring gas for his car from one of them), was irritated by the Hungarians' tendency to demand exceptional treatment by virtue of the fact that "their table manners were better" than their neighbors'. At the same time, he acknowledged that they were past masters of obstruction and passive resistance, which could provide the Allies with important military benefits.[4]

U.S. intelligence assessments of Hungarian attitudes found that aside from most of the Christian middle classes, the Schwabian segment of the peasantry, and a large part of the officer corps, the majority of Hungarians disliked the Germans, while many in the aristocracy and the higher clergy were pro-British and anti-Russian.[5] In German-controlled Europe, Hungary enjoyed by far the greatest internal liberties. The OSS pointed out that although the country was kept under supervision and control, liberal and socialist opposition parties continued to function, British and American books continued to be translated and sold, people were still allowed to listen to foreign radio stations, and domestic press reports on developments in enemy countries were still available.[6]

"THE ANNIHILATION OF USEFUL ELEMENTS":
THE UNITED STATES AND THE DILEMMA OF SECRET TALKS

The first cautious steps to establish contact with the Allies were made in 1942. Horthy, who was known for his profound antipathy toward the Soviet system,[7] feared a communist conspiracy to overthrow all existing institutions.[8] His entourage shared his views, thus the option of surrendering to the Soviet Union was ruled out. Dulles, who understood the Hungarian dilemma, noted that the Hungarians did not want to risk a German invasion, but feared Russian occupation even more than another Trianon.[9]

The Hungarian leadership assumed that the West understood their difficult predicament and would count on Hungary's help in the inevitable struggle against Bolshevism. But a key figure in the effort to break with the Axis, Aladár Szegedy-Maszák, who would become Hungary's first minister to the United States after the war, wrote that Hungarian diplomacy had overestimated the importance of the Danube Basin for the Western powers. The Hungarian minister in Lisbon, the wealthy industrialist Andor Wodianer, thought that his country would be in the first line of defense,[10] while Tibor Eckhardt, the highly influential Smallholder politician who was sent to the United States in 1940 to assure Roosevelt of Hungary's pro-American sentiments, claimed to have convinced his American friends of the need for a powerful Hungary to help "balance the Soviet Union."[11]

The misperception that the British were interested in beating the Soviets to the Danube was rooted in flawed assumptions about Hungary's geopolitical significance. Dulles's regular interlocutor, the diplomat György Bakách-Bessenyey, took for granted that the Anglo-Americans would not allow the Soviets to control "this geographically important area, the gateway to Western Europe," because to do so would be more inimical to their security than German domination.[12] Hungary's influential minister in Stockholm, Antal Ullein-Reviczky, led himself to believe that his country was in a "key position from the perspective of the British Empire[;] its survival and security was a British interest."[13] Long after the war had ended, Kállay argued that British and American influence would have prevailed in the Balkans had Hungary been used as a base.[14]

Hungarian peace feelers first approached the Americans in the fall of 1942, mainly through Turkey. They carried the message that the Hungarian army would not resist an Anglo-American invasion.[15] The OSS and the State Department differed in interpreting these overtures. Whereas the OSS tended to take them seriously and was ready to take advantage of the opportunity they presented, the State Department refused to deal with them. Dulles was eager to explore the proposals for informal U.S.-Hungarian talks to "foil the Nazis," although he was aware that a variety of perspectives had to be considered in the U.S. response, including the general policy toward Eastern Europe and, more importantly, U.S.-Soviet relations. Therefore, with OSS director William Donovan's support, he sought policy guidance from the State Department regarding these peace feelers.[16] It is important to point out that the OSS was not in a position to pursue foreign policy without the explicit approval of the State Department, and that the State Department was ultimately guided by the military considerations of the Joint Chiefs of Staff (JCS).

In January 1943, the Second Hungarian Army was destroyed near Voronezh, which gave Hungary a strong impetus to explore the possibility of exiting the war. Unfortunately, the Allies adopted at precisely this moment the principle of unconditional surrender, which made it all but impossible for a German satellite to defect from the Axis. This formula was meant to signal to the Soviets that the United States and Great Britain would not enter into a separate deal with Hitler or any of his allies and to drive home to the Germans that there would be no promises or commitments to them this time.[17] Moscow also insisted on this inflexible formula, but only while there was still a realistic chance for the Western powers to occupy Eastern Europe. Stalin wanted to make sure that Hitler's satellites surrendered to no one but Moscow. Dulles had personal experience of how the Conference of Casablanca had made it difficult to subvert the Axis; he therefore recommended that U.S. propaganda should differentiate between the main Axis powers and the ones that had cooperated with the Germans under constraint. He believed that while unconditional surrender should be required of the former, the lesser satellites should be allowed to negotiate in case they were ready to scale down their military and economic cooperation with the Axis. They were not then in a position to turn against Berlin, but, he argued, they might soon be able to sabotage the German war effort.[18]

The American stance on unconditional surrender was more rigid than the British stance. In December 1942, Hungary had offered to send a government official to Ankara to discuss terms of surrender with the United States. And though the American embassy there was eager to follow up on this proposal, which they believed to be sincere,[19] the State Department refused to do so because of the presumed sensitivities of the Kremlin. Although assistant secretary of state Adolph Berle supported the idea on the grounds that the British secret service was also conducting talks, he was overruled. A Romanian sounding in early 1943 was also disregarded out of deference to the Soviets. The industrialist Max Auschnitt informed the OSS that if Romanian independence was guaranteed by the Russians and that guarantee were backed by the United States, the Romanian Conducător, Ion Antonescu would be willing to join the United Nations.[20]

The State Department stopped U.S. representatives from dealing even with Nobel Prize winner Albert Szent-Györgyi, who was clandestinely negotiating with the British in Turkey. The U.S. embassy in Ankara was instructed to avoid doing or saying anything that could damage the joint war effort,[21] a stricture that applied to U.S. intelligence representatives as well. It was not that Kállay's overtures were considered insincere or insufficiently daring. An Abwehr agent informed the OSS that Hitler, who had found out about Budapest's maneuverings, was "mad" at the Hungarians and believed that once he could get rid of Kállay he would be able to deal with the "traitors."[22]

This inflexible attitude was motivated primarily by the fear that the Soviets would defect from the alliance if they found out that separate deals were being made with minor German satellites. Moreover, the State Department feared that Hungarian and Romanian peace overtures were driven by the desire to extract political advantages and might even have been aimed at subverting the alliance.[23] The State Department's caution was underscored by the fact that in March 1943 Stalin had rejected a proposal by the U.S. ambassador in Moscow for mediation between Finland and the Soviet Union, allegedly because he was skeptical of the Finnish desire for peace. Few if any in the U.S. administration shared Berle's notion that the quickest way to Germany's surrender was the defection its southeast European allies and a simultaneous Allied landing in the Balkans.[24]

Still, the precarious relationships among the Allies were not the only considerations militating against negotiations between Hungary and the West. Defecting from Germany would have potentially adverse effects on Hungary itself. A premature break with the Axis would be dangerous, if not impossible. A volte-face could lead to the "annihilation of the elements" that would be "more useful for the United Nations," if such a move could be carried out with a chance for success. Moreover, the British suspected the Hungarians of trying to salvage their existing regime for the postwar period.[25] The American minister in Helsinki, who was then working on extricating Finland from the war, understood the contradiction inherent in U.S. policy. He believed that if the goal was to break up the Axis, the prevailing policy of threats and warnings was inappropriate.[26]

The U.K. Foreign Office attempted to convince the State Department to alter its inflexible stance in light of the fact that the small Axis powers were positioning themselves for a German defeat. In light of the conflicts between Germany's satellites, the Foreign Office believed it was inexpedient or even impossible to take an undifferentiated stance toward the satellites' peace feelers or in the propaganda directed at them. The British wanted the Soviet Union to be responsible for separate peace talks with Romania and Finland. Hungary, on the other hand, showed more signs of independence. Relatively significant opposition had surfaced, including a right-wing movement fueled by nationalist and anti-German sentiments that deplored the country's foreign-directed course. British reports suggested that the lot of the Jews had improved; Hungary's Catholic primate, Archbishop Serédi, openly deplored Nazism. Therefore the Foreign Office proposed to tell the Hungarians that His Majesty's government had no wish carve up the country or to punish her people for the folly of their government. Hungary was to be judged by its efforts to promote Allied victory and its own self-liberation. Nevertheless, the British took only one peace envoy seriously: Albert Szent-Györgyi. The others were rebuffed, including the former Hungarian minister to London, György Barcza, who approached the British in Bern. On behalf of the Hungarian prime minister, the commercial attaché in Ankara offered to withdraw Hungarian troops from the eastern front and to improve the lot of the Jewish population, but he too was rejected.[27] For the time being, the State Department showed no interest and would not consider more lenient terms for Budapest. The decision that Hungary would survive as an independent sovereign state behind its 1938 boundaries was not made until August 1944.[28]

"TOTAL SOVIET INFLUENCE WILL PREVAIL":
THE DILEMMAS OF BREAKING WITH HITLER

Even though Kállay had certain apprehensions concerning Western designs and feared that the British were out to provoke a German invasion of his country, he felt he had no other option than to approach the Western Allies.[29] He was convinced that Soviet victory would lead to his country's demise, the disappearance of Hungarian identity into the Slavic sea.[30] Surrender to the British seemed to be the optimal solution for avoiding the evils of a German or a Russian occupation. Thus in July 1943, the former president of the Hungarian National Bank, Lipót Baranyai, informed

Dulles that Hungary would pledge de facto neutrality if the Allies would not surrender it to the Soviet Union and if no territorial commitments were made at Hungary's expense.[31] Dulles recommended replying that Hungary would be judged by the extent to which it broke with Germany. He was willing to promise the Hungarians that no territorial assurances would be made behind their backs, but he also suggested emphasizing to them the "cold realities" of the war.[32]

Questions of less significance than the postwar territorial settlement remained unresolved as well, which meant that this peace initiative could not be brought to fruition. Berle understood that if the Allies were to tell the Hungarians what they expected of them, there was a chance those expectations would be satisfied. After the Quebec conference, at which the Allies decided to open the second front in Normandy, Berle recommended that the Hungarians be directed to undertake actions that would aid Allied military operations. As an inducement, the Hungarians were to be assured of their survival as a sovereign state without any territorial commitments. Berle regarded the Hungarian army as a crucial factor in the struggle for the Balkans, ready to be used against the Germans when the time was ripe.[33]

The likely cost to Hungary of premature defection from the Axis was German occupation with all its potential consequences. On the other hand, procrastination could result in the loss of Allied sympathy and a consequent loss of favor at the peace conference. At the same time, the Allies would make no commitments regarding Hungary's territorial integrity and sovereignty, even if Budapest were to comply with Allied demands. Dulles saw a parallel between Romania and Hungary in that any rash move on either's part could have invited German reprisals. The Allied dilemma, as Dulles saw it, was the reverse of the satellites'. Would it be worth overthrowing the Hungarian and Romanian regimes and provoking their occupation by the Germans at a relatively low cost? Their withdrawal from the war would almost certainly hasten the German collapse.[34] Eventually the Allies concluded that they would benefit from a German invasion of the satellites because it would draw troops away from the western theater of war.

The choice between fence sitting and immediate surrender was difficult; the Allies were sending mixed signals as well. A British diplomat explained that Britain did not expect Hungary to provoke a German invasion, and, in light of the consequences, he could not imagine Hungary's defection from the Axis. Only three months later, though, the same diplomat urged Hungary to follow the Italian example and shoulder the risks. If the Hungarians failed to draw upon themselves the necessary consequences, it would mean that they had sided with the Germans again and all hope of being treated differently from Germany would be lost. Hungary was obliged to make this move even at the risk of temporary German occupation.[35] When it was pointed out that a German occupation would destroy Hungary's social fabric, the British intelligence chief in Bern, Frederick Vanden Heuvel, retreated. He was clearly testing the Hungarians to see how far they would go.

Prior to the Moscow conference of October 1943, Hungarian intelligence reports had suggested that the country would be occupied by British and American forces. After lengthy negotiations, a Hungarian representative, László Veress, signed a secret preliminary armistice with the British ambassador in Turkey. Because the British assumed that Kállay would not surrender unless he was given acceptable guarantees against German intervention, the parties were not to make their agreement public until British troops had entered Hungary.[36] The memorandum indicates that Winston Churchill and the U.S. Joint Chiefs stipulated the terms of surrender.[37] On September 7, Churchill declared that the Hungarians' defection from the Axis would be invaluable to the Allies, but should be carried out at the appropriate time.[38] An immediate surrender would be detrimental if it were to provoke Hitler to invade and install a puppet government. This preliminary armistice fit nicely into Churchill's plans for an Anglo-American drive into the Danube Basin, but his position on defection was still in a state of flux. In a speech delivered to the House of Commons on September 27, 1943, the prime minister declared that the satellites should be given the opportunity to "work their way home" – that is, to oppose the Germans actively in return for better treatment.

U.S. intelligence had been working in earnest on decoupling the satellites since the summer of 1943. The OSS launched a "grandiose" operation code-named "Dogwood," the mission of which was to penetrate the satellites, gather military intelligence, and work with resistance groups to overthrow their pro-German governments.[39] On August 28, peace envoy György Bakách-Bessenyey had a lengthy conversation with an OSS representative named Royall Tyler, a noted expert in Byzantine studies who knew Hungary intimately from his days as the League of Nations' financial commissioner there. Tyler was anxious to convince his interlocutor that Hungary should jump out of the war alongside the Italians. Bakách-Bessenyey got the feeling that Washington had directed Tyler to emphasize this point.[40] Sensing an ominous shift in Washington's attitude, Hungarian deputy minister of foreign affairs Andor Szentmiklósy (who would soon die in a German concentration camp) instructed Bakách to call Dulles's attention to the danger a German occupation would pose to Jews and to the approximately one hundred thousand Poles who had found refuge in Hungary since 1939. He also stressed that Hungary hoped to pursue a policy of "successive dissociation" from Germany.[41]

In the meantime, a Soviet diplomat who was sounded out for Moscow's peace conditions warned that there was only one option open to Hungary: to break with Germany. He believed that the most appropriate and least risky moment to do so would be during the landing in Normandy.[42] Considering that Italy's defection had ended in disaster and that Germany had occupied Rome on September 12, the Italian example was hardly inspiring to Budapest. Perhaps this is why the Hungarian minister in Lisbon was warned that the Hungarian government should take no precipitate action that could prematurely strain its relations with Germany.[43] The adverb "prematurely" is notable: withdrawal from the Axis was to be carried out when it most suited the Allies. In August 1943, Churchill and Roosevelt agreed to open the second front on May 1, 1944, bringing about a fundamental shift in their policies toward the satellites. All of a sudden Hitler's Eastern European allies mattered; their defection from Hitler gained urgency. U.S.-Hungarian talks intensified when Washington broke with the policy of neglecting the peace overtures. American diplomatic and military personnel were allowed to establish contact with the Hungarians, and the Kállay government became increasingly decisive in communicating its willingness to break with Berlin when the Western Allies decided the time was right.

On September 14, 1943, the American military attaché in Lisbon met with Sándor Hollán, a counselor at the Hungarian legation. Introduced by the Portuguese diplomat Saldanho de Gama and authorized by the U.S.

minister to Portugal, George F. Kennan, the military attaché told Hollán that he would have to answer political and military questions without expecting any promises from the United States or any discussion of the restoration of the Habsburg dynasty. Hollán declared that his government was ready to break with the Germans at the first opportunity and that the Hungarian army would be ready to cooperate with Allied troops as soon as they approached.[44] A few days later, Bakách-Bessenyey delivered Kállay's message to Dulles urging the Allies to trust him and pledging that Hungary would be ready to make the necessary sacrifices and to assist them at the appropriate moment.[45] On October 5, Hollán received a reply from the Americans. Acting under the assumption that Budapest accepted the principle of unconditional surrender, the U.S. government informed Hollán that his approach would be taken seriously only if a Hungarian plenipotentiary were to offer to surrender to all three allies simultaneously.[46] No mention was made (here or in any other known U.S. document) of the preliminary armistice Budapest had concluded with the British. American officials either had no knowledge of it or chose to disregard it.

The American attitude toward the satellites remained rigid, suggesting that Washington was not yet interested in subverting the Axis's southeastern flank. On October 2, the Romanian military attaché in Ankara delivered to his British counterpart a message from Marshal Antonescu. Seeking to avoid a Soviet occupation of Romania, the Conducător signaled his willingness to cooperate with any Anglo-American forces that might land in the Balkans and to put at their disposal a significant amount of oil, gold, cash, and trained pilots. The British ambassador was skeptical of the offer, thinking the idea smacked of German propaganda that the Romanians had adopted for their own purposes.[47] The British then informed Bucharest that Romania would profit from jumping out of the war even at the cost of German occupation. The State Department objected to the idea of a German invasion of Romania,[48] but the American position continued to change. On October 14, Dulles sent word to Budapest that Hungarian troops should be withdrawn from the eastern front without regard to the consequences. He also demanded that Hungary accept an American telegrapher,[49] a provision Bakách-Bessenyey strongly recommended that his government comply with. His argument revealed that this way out of the Hungarians' hopeless situation was illusory: the Germans would not be able to defend the country from the Russians, thus their only solution was the "Anglo-American" line. Bakách-Bessenyey argued that the Americans had not demanded anything that would "ineluctably" lead to a German invasion and that bringing the troops home was in Hungary's interest anyway.[50] His advice was, in part, heeded: in mid-November, the Hungarian government agreed to receive an American officer. Thus a decisive shift in Allied policies seems to have occurred sometime in October.

In December 1943, the Hungarian Foreign Ministry learned that the Western Allies would not be landing in the Balkans. After the Teheran conference, the Hungarian embassy in Stockholm informed foreign minister Jenő Ghyczy that Hungary would end up in the Soviet sphere: "Total Soviet influence will prevail . . . in the Danube Basin and the Balkans."[51] From Ankara, János Vörnle predicted that in Eastern Europe "every country will be Bolshevized."[52] Similar opinions were expressed by other diplomatic missions. This led to a partial shift in foreign policy: Hungary approached the Soviet Union for separate peace terms in early 1944, though even then Hungarian leaders were still entertaining the notion of an "Anglo-Saxon" invasion.

"GIVEN TO THE WOLVES": ALLIED DIPLOMACY
AND THE FATE OF EASTERN EUROPE

British and American military planners did not envision operations in the Danube Basin. On March 28, 1944, the Joint Chiefs of Staff declared that the United States would assume no responsibility for the Balkans.[53]

Already by 1941, Stalin had asserted to British foreign secretary Anthony Eden that the eastern part of the continent would belong to the Soviets: "the role of the USSR shall be taken into consideration as a power waging a great war of liberation . . . and as the greatest factor in the cause of preserving a lasting peace in Europe and the prevention of new acts of aggression by Germany."[54] Control of adjacent space and enhanced industrial and military capacities were key components of Soviet thinking about the postwar world.[55] Neither Eden nor anyone else seriously contested Stalin's plans. Sir Orme Sargent was perhaps the only influential British official to suggest a Balkan expeditionary force by the Western Allies as a way to counter Soviet penetration in the region after the war."[56]

The British foreign secretary hoped that the USSR would play a positive role in postwar Europe, and he wanted to win the Soviet government's friendship and confidence. William Bullit had warned Roosevelt in 1943 that the Soviet Union aimed to dominate all of Europe, and that Stalin put out "pseudopodia like an amoeba rather than leaping like a tiger. If the pseudopodia meet no obstacle the Soviet Union flows in."[57] Roosevelt, who also hoped that the Soviet Union would help preserve European peace, was not convinced by Bullit's argument. The United States would not fill the vacuum left by Germany's collapse.

At the Teheran conference, Churchill broached his pet idea of attacking the Reich from southern Europe, either by reinforcing the Italian front or by landing on the Adriatic coast. The Hungarians attached their greatest hopes to the latter possibility, not knowing that Churchill "never wished to send an army to the Balkans, but only agents, supplies and commandos to stimulate the intensive guerilla activity there" in the hope of yielding "measureless" results.[58] The British chiefs of staff and their planners never produced any specific plan for operations in the Balkans.[59] This issue divided the Allies. Stalin and Roosevelt favored a second front in Normandy with a complementary operation in southern France. Churchill hoped that an Allied landing in the Balkans would draw Turkey into the war on the side of the Allies and induce Bulgaria, Hungary, and Romania to defect from the Axis. He also acknowledged that a Mediterranean campaign would delay Operation Overlord, which had received a green light at the conference in Moscow in October 1943. Roosevelt feared that Churchill's proposal would alienate the Russians. The United States wanted to stick to the priorities decided at the Quebec conference and warned against transferring resources to the Mediterranean. Roosevelt insisted on holding only the existing positions in order to tie down an adequate number of German troops. At the Cairo conference, the United States had opposed military operations in the Balkans, but Churchill managed to postpone the final decision to Teheran. There he pressed for accelerating the Italian campaign to reach Rome and advocated the seizure of a bridgehead on the Dalmatian coast. From the Pisa-Rimini line, Allied forces would be able to turn toward the Danube countries through the Ljubljana gap.

At the first plenary session of the Teheran conference, Roosevelt unexpectedly proposed "a possible operation at the head of the Adriatic to make a junction with the Partisans under Tito and then to operate north-east into Romania in conjunction with the Soviet advance from the region of Odessa."[60] Churchill seized the opportunity and proposed a committee to study the plan, but Stalin thought it unwise to scatter the Allied forces in the Mediterranean and backed landing them in southern France to support Overlord. There was nothing surprising about the Soviet position. Eden had tried to gauge Stalin's stance on the second front in October and concluded that the Soviet leader was "completely and blindly set on our invading northern France and there is absolutely nothing that we could suggest in any other part of the world which could reconcile them to the cancellation of or even a postponement of 'Overlord.'"[61] Stalin's unequivocal stance in Teheran allowed Roosevelt to reiterate his earlier position, that nothing could delay Overlord, which is precisely what the Mediterranean operations would do.[62] Furthermore, Roosevelt thought that a plan should be developed for future operations in southern France. The fate of the Balkan project was apparently sealed, and the campaign in Italy was also in danger.

The purpose of the Italian campaign was not to penetrate the Danube Basin but to knock Italy out of the war and to tie down the German forces that would be needed to replace the Italians.[63] The British military agreed that the campaign should reach the Pisa-Rimini line, but the commander in chief of the Allied forces in Italy, Sir Harold Alexander, wanted to extend operations toward Yugoslavia, an idea that the chief of the British Imperial Staff, Alan Brooke, did not support. Even so, Churchill planned to divert ten divisions designated for Operation Anvil to the Adriatic to take Trieste by the end of September. Roosevelt countered by citing the views of Generals Bernard Montgomery and Dwight Eisenhower, both of whom favored Anvil. In a message to Churchill on July 1, 1943, the president claimed that he would not survive politically if Overlord suffered even the slightest delay.[64] Churchill appreciated Roosevelt's predicament but still hoped to reach Vienna through Yugoslavia. Eventually, he concluded, the terrain would make operations impossible beyond the River Piave.[65] Thus a combination of political and military arguments doomed whatever hope the nations of the Danube Basin might have had of being subsumed into the Western sphere of influence.

To preserve British interests, Churchill moved to divide Eastern Europe into spheres of "responsibility." U.S. officials indicated they had no intention of assuming responsibility for Europe after the war, and thus

Churchill was initially forced to deal with the Soviets alone. In March 1944, the U.K. offered the Soviet Union a free hand in Romania in return for the same in Greece. The offer did not come out of the blue. In February 1943, secretary of state Cordell Hull had received a top-secret document from the U.S. Embassy in London indicating that the British Foreign Office had been preparing to subordinate East Central Europe to global British-Soviet relations and was therefore ready to recognize the primacy of Soviet interests in Romania – which, as the document put it, would be "given to the wolves" – and adjacent countries.[66]

London had always founded its attitudes toward Eastern Europe on the principle of stability. By the late 1920s, British politicians had concluded that the "pauper states" of Eastern Europe were economically hopeless, incapable of political stability and populated by culturally backward inferiorities.[67] In the 1930s, British governments had been willing to see much of eastern and central Europe fall under German hegemony. A similar Soviet sway over postwar Europe was acceptable to the British, provided their interests in Western Europe and the Mediterranean were not endangered.[68] Although Churchill was initially wary of Eden's eagerness to include Eastern Europe in a territorial deal with Stalin, the necessities of war brought the prime minister around. "The increased gravity of the war has led me to feel that the principles of the Atlantic Charter ought not to be construed so as to deny Russia the frontiers she occupied when Germany attacked her," even though "it would be a disaster if Russian barbarism overlaid the culture and independence of the ancient states in Europe."[69] Still, the British political establishment was concerned that if the West did not take the Soviet position into account, "we should be laying the foundation of another world war in a generation."[70]

At the first conference in Moscow in October 1943 Eden had proposed a "declaration regarding general European responsibility," hoping to extract a Soviet pledge of nonintervention into the internal affairs of liberated countries. He received no support from Hull, and deputy commissar of foreign affairs Maxim Litvinov refused to commit the Soviet Union to such a declaration on the grounds that it would "give rise to the belief that there had been such an intention" on the part of the Allies.[71] By then it seemed logical to Churchill that Britain and the USSR should try to crystallize the *geopolitical arrangements* that they had been moving toward since 1941.⁷² He was aware of the consequences: "Great evil may come upon the world," he wrote to Eden. "The Russians are drunk with power and there is no length they may not go."⁷³ On May 31, Churchill informed the president of his proposal to the Soviets to exchange Romania for Greece: "The Soviet government would take the lead in Romanian affairs while we would take the lead in Greek affairs."⁷⁴ Churchill claimed that Stalin wanted to be sure the United States consented to the proposition. He attempted to convince Roosevelt by arguing that the arrangement "would be a natural development of the existing situation since Romania falls within the sphere of the Russian armies and Greece within the Allied command." Somewhat disingenuously, Churchill alleged that the Balkans would not be "carved up into spheres of influence" and that the arrangement would not "affect the rights and responsibilities which each of the great powers will have to exercise at the peace settlement and afterward in regard to the whole of Europe." This agreement, the prime minister explained, was devised to maintain Soviet-British harmony in the Balkans. Roosevelt saw through Churchill's intentions and was concerned that the Stalin-Churchill deal would lead to the division of the Balkan region into spheres of influence, despite the parties' declared intentions to limit their involvement to military matters.⁷⁵ Churchill's response reveals the real motive behind his insistence on the deal: his desire for a free hand in suppressing the Greek National Liberation Front. British influence in Greece could be preserved, and because the Red Army was about to invade Romania, Soviet leaders "would probably do what they wanted anyhow." To placate Roosevelt, Churchill proposed a trial period of three months.⁷⁶ At the end of June, Roosevelt, against Hull's advice and at Stalin's insistence, gave the British initiative a green light.

At the second Quebec conference, Churchill told Roosevelt that "we must forestall the Russians in Central Europe ... it is important we retain a stake in Central Europe."⁷⁷ By then, Foreign Secretary Eden was preparing for a permanent arrangement. In a Cabinet Office paper presented on August 9, he affirmed that "the foundations of our postwar European order must be the Anglo-Soviet alliance." Eden argued that Britain should consolidate its position in the European countries with which it had been traditionally "close and intimate." On the other hand, Britain "should avoid any challenge to Soviet interests" in states adjacent to or near the

USSR, including Poland, Czechoslovakia, Yugoslavia, Hungary, Romania, and Austria.[78] He reiterated the position the Foreign Office had already expressed in a memorandum to Hull in January 1943. In October 1944, Churchill relinquished Bulgaria, Hungary, and Romania to the Soviet sphere, while agreeing to share Yugoslavia on an equal basis. Churchill got what he wanted: Moscow agreed that Britain would enjoy predominant influence in Greece. This deal with Stalin reflected British thinking on Eastern Europe. Churchill was ready to make concessions because the eastern and middle parts of the continent were slipping out of British reach anyway. In June 1944, the British Post-Hostilities Committee predicted that Soviet influence would extend to Poland, Czechoslovakia, and Hungary after the war.[79] The percentage agreement that the prime minister concluded with Stalin thus reflected the traditional British notion that London was entitled to decide the fate of unimportant small states for the sake of European order. In October 1944, Churchill gave Stalin something Hitler had refused him in November 1940: control of the Balkans, as well as the strategic key to consolidating his holdings in Eastern Europe: Hungary. As the specifics of the arrangement were being discussed in the Kremlin, Molotov was in another room of the palace hammering out the details of the first postwar Hungarian government.

When Churchill met Stalin on October 9, 1944, he indicated that Britain's chief interest was holding onto Greece. Britain was striving to remain the leading power in the Mediterranean region, and Churchill hoped to ensure that the British would "have the first say in Greece in the same way as Marshal Stalin about Romania." Stalin agreed, and Churchill produced his infamous "naughty document," expressing Soviet and British influence in the Balkan area in percentages. Churchill explained that "it was better to express things in diplomatic terms, and not to use the phrase 'dividing into spheres' because the Americans might be shocked if they saw how crudely he had put it."[80] Churchill prepared the notes of the meeting for Roosevelt, describing each country in terms of the varying degrees of responsibility the great powers would assume toward it. The next day at lunch, in front of Averell Harriman, Stalin crossed out the sentence referring to spheres of responsibility. The ambassador thereupon remarked that Roosevelt would no doubt be pleased that the sentence in question had been deleted, since he thought that such questions should be dealt with by the three powers together. At that point, Stalin reached behind Churchill's back and shook hands with Harriman.[81] After reaching this initial agreement with Churchill, Stalin asked to change the fifty-fifty deal on Hungary, a country in which, according to Churchill, the Soviets had shown "great interest." Molotov claimed that Hungary "bordered Russia not Great Britain." This might have been a Freudian slip of the tongue: Carpathian Ruthenia, which had belonged to Czechoslovakia from 1918 to 1939, was about to be annexed to the Soviet Union, giving it a common border with Hungary for the first time. Eden, who saw risks in abandoning Bulgaria,[82] agreed to grant the Soviets predominance in Hungary in return for a slightly stronger British influence in Bulgaria. In the end, the Soviets seized control of both countries. And although Churchill was upset by Eden's horse-trading with Molotov, he was happy about the final outcome of his talks with Moscow, which allowed Britain "to save Greece."[83] Although Churchill talked about spheres of influence, Eden explained that the agreement assigned each power relative responsibilities for helping the individual countries solve their problems.[84]

Without having been fully apprised of the details of Churchill's agreement with Stalin, Roosevelt assured Churchill that "it is most pleasing to know that you are reaching a meeting of your two minds as to international politics." Roosevelt's acceptance of the arrangements even before he received the full details suggest a lack of interest in the topic. He probably did not suspect foul play on Moscow's part, or if he did, he likely figured he could do nothing about it.

"ADOLF AND HIS BOYS": SPREADING THE
GERMANS THIN IN THE WEST

The British and the Americans did not intend to risk the coalition for the sake of the lesser Axis powers. The significance of the latter, however, was temporarily elevated by the fact that their defection from the war could spread the Germans thin and thereby help the Allied forces landing in Normandy.

In a memorandum dated August 22, 1943, the British Joint Planning Staff Committee theorized that a German invasion of Hungary would suit British interests well. During the time it would take Germany to prepare the necessary forces and occupy the country, it would receive no benefit from Hungary and would be hard-pressed to maintain its forces in the Balkans. "Moreover the diversion of German forces for the invasion and occupation of Hungary might result in a dangerous weakening in the German position elsewhere."[85] The next day, Britain's deputy chief of staff offered a similar argument to Sir Alan Brooke. Hungarian capitulation could cause political and military complications for the Germans. If Romania followed Hungary's example, Hitler would be confronted by a crisis that he could solve only by invading Hungary. If Germany took the risk and pulled troops out of other areas to keep the Hungarians at bay, her position in these other theaters of war would be weakened to the Allies' advantage. The deputy chief acknowledged that in this case Hungary could not count on external help.[86] Churchill was also well aware of the advantages a break between Germany and its allies would bring. On October 7, he wrote to Roosevelt that the Germans obviously attached great importance to the eastern front and would not hesitate to divert a major part of their strategic air force to maintain their position there. Germany feared Hungary's and Romania's desertion and a "violent schism" in Bulgaria. "When we remember what brilliant results have followed from the potential reactions in Italy induced by our military efforts," Churchill continued, "should we not be short-sighted to ignore the possibility of a similar or even greater landslide in some or all the countries I have mentioned? If we were able to provoke such reactions and profit by them, our joint task in Italy would be greatly lightened."[87]

Lewis Namier, a Polish-born historian in the policy-planning division of the U.K. Foreign Office, was concerned about the possible consequences of a premature break with Germany. He warned that if the Hungarian government broke with the Germans while they were still in a position to react, it would spell the end of the last Jewish community in Europe. On October 14, Dennis Allen, another planner in the Foreign Office, responded that this consideration had always played an important role in not encouraging the Hungarians to take drastic action, although he believed that the chance of a German invasion was low.[88] (Allen knew what he was talking about. He was one of the few who were privy to the German messages decoded in Bletchley Park that revealed the Germans' systematic mass murder of Jews in Europe.[89]) On the same day, Dulles urged Hungary's defection from the war without regard to the consequences and told Romania to do the same. At the foreign ministers meeting in Moscow in October, Molotov complained about the British government's half measure in not making public the provisional armistice signed with the Hungarians, which he thought was contrary to the principle of unconditional surrender. Eden added that the Soviets should have the deciding voice in the formulation of Allied policies in Hungary.

While the Big Three were warming to the idea of provoking a schism between Germany and its allies, pro-Western circles in Budapest were bringing themselves around to a break with Berlin. On October 23, Ullein-Reviczky met the OSS representative in Stockholm, R. Taylor Cole, on behalf of Prime Minister Kállay and Foreign Minister Ghyczy. The Hungarians, Ullein-Reviczky declared, were well aware that they had to do as the Allies told them. All they wanted were terms of surrender that omitted the term "unconditional" – terms Reviczky and his superiors in Budapest had no way of knowing had not yet elaborated by the Allies. The U.S. minister in Stockholm supported the idea of forgoing unconditionality and wanted to establish a committee composed of representatives from the U.S. legation, the OSS, and the military attaché. This committee would convey to the Hungarians the specific military measures they would have to carry to expedite an Anglo-American invasion of Hungary.[90] Even though the proposal was discussed at the highest levels, it was rejected. The JCS argued that they were not in a position to offer terms of surrender until they had been formulated by the European Advisory Committee, which was not even functioning.[91]

Secretary of State Hull doubted Ullein-Reviczky's good will and seriousness of purpose, perhaps because the British embassy in Washington had warned the State Department not to trust him.[92] Hull also assumed that the "unconditional surrender" formula precluded Ullein-Reviczky's attempts to negotiate.[93] Still, Regent Horthy's British-oriented son, Miklós Horthy Jr., who ran what was called the "Defection Office," informed Dulles on December 18 that if the Allies expected the Hungarians to capitulate, he would see to it that they did so. His envoy, György Ghika, added that Budapest was waiting for the Allies to give the signal.[94]

In his worst moments, Kállay suspected that the British wanted to provoke Hitler to invade. On November 2, 1943, JCS chairman William Leahy informed the head of the State Department's European division, Freeman Matthews, that "the Joint Chiefs of Staff are of the opinion that from a military standpoint the Allied cause would be advanced by the withdrawal [of] either or both of these countries [Hungary and Romania] from the war, regardless of whether or not such action would be likely to entail full German occupation of these countries." Hull's memorandum of March 16, 1944, reveals that this formula was adopted as the joint policy of the United States and Great Britain and was extended to Bulgaria.[95] This decision was likely made even earlier, since William Donovan instructed Dulles to implement this policy only one day after Leahy's memorandum was sent out, on November 3. Donovan stated that hitherto Kállay and his circle had received ambiguous instructions. For Dulles's "exclusive information," Donovan revealed that the JCS "had approved specifically to detach H[ungary] and the other satellites from Axis immediately. JCS directive should govern your attitude. Adolf aware of this decision and informing his boys."[96] Did "Adolf" refer to Berle or to Hitler? The available evidence regarding U.S. policy toward Hungary does not allow the latter possibility to be ruled out. German intelligence may have learned of the Hungarians' maneuvers from their sources in the Hungarian government; it is also possible that U.S. officials recklessly leaked Hungary's impending betrayal to the Nazis in order to ensure the success of Operation Overlord. Whatever the case may have been, the Joint Chiefs instructed Donovan to "explore possibilities for influencing Hungary to withdraw from the war." The JCS also instructed the OSS to "make no commitments on behalf of the U.S." Romania was also to be urged to defect: "immediate unconditional surrender by Romania would be desirable even if such surrender were to entail immediate German occupation of the country." Because "military considerations" had prevailed in policymaking, the State Department "has now taken the foregoing as its own."[97] The State Department was instructed to pursue this new line. Berle noted, "On the second of November we informed our representative in Bern that the JCS had instructed us to do what we could to detach the satellite countries ... immediately from the Axis. We are wiring Dulles ... that the JCS order applied to all three nations."[98]

A memorandum found in Harriman's papers reveals the military motive behind detaching the satellites: to draw German forces away from the Allied operations in France, as well as from the eastern front. Operation Bodyguard, a deception plan adopted in Teheran, was intended to convince the enemy to deploy its forces in areas where they would not be able to influence the second front. "The enemy will do its utmost to hold Southeast Europe.... It should be possible to contain German forces in the Balkans. Germany's armed forces are dangerously overstretched by current operations and provided we can induce her to retain surplus forces in Scandinavia, Italy, the Balkans, she will find it difficult to simultaneously provide forces for Russia, France and the Low countries. The attitude of the neutrals and the satellites may move further in favor of the Allies compelling Germany to dispose reserves to meet unfavorable developments."[99] Several months before the second front was opened, an article in the Soviet press similarly emphasized the military significance for the Allies of Germany's occupation of Eastern Europe. "Germany's 'victory' over its unfortunate Allies does not in the final analysis solve Germany's difficulties, but on the contrary, increases them. Additional transfer[s] of German troops to the territories of the occupied 'Allies' further weaken the already thin German reserves in the West. Thereby the possibilities for a blow at the common enemy from the West becomes more favorable."[100] The Germans, according to U.S. intelligence, badly needed the ten to fifteen divisions that would be required to occupy Hungary.[101]

To hinder the German war effort, the OSS encouraged the Hungarians to cut the German army's logistical lines when the Soviets reached the Carpathians, thus severing Germany's southern army groups from their northern counterparts. Allied deception plans were designed to convince Hitler that the second front would be opened in the Balkans in the hope that the Germans would divert forces from Western Europe.[102] Hitler seems to have believed the rumors about an Allied landing in the Balkans, even though such plans were never seriously considered. Churchill did toy with the idea of auxiliary military actions in southern Europe and even Scandinavia, but neither was ever treated as a site from which to launch the final offensive on Germany. A British intelligence report seemed to confirm that Hitler was uncertain about Allied designs: German troop concentrations prior to the invasion of Hungary revealed German anxiety about the general military situation in southeastern Europe rather than increasing suspicions concerning Hungarian reliability. This intelligence turned out to be wrong.

German military leaders do seem to have expected the second front to be opened in the south. Initially the Wehrmacht General Staff devised a plan for the occupation of western and central Hungary up to the river Tisza, which portions they wanted to isolate from the eastern part of the country. No invasion of eastern Hungary was ever planned, even though the two Hungarian armies there could have opened the Hungarian border to the Red Army, which was then rapidly advancing through Romania and the Carpatho-Ukraine. All this suggests that fear of an Allied landing in the Trieste area may have been one of the motives for the German invasion. Eastern Hungary was to be occupied in the second phase of the operation in order to defend the Carpathians.[103] Later reports suggested that Hitler pulled three of his best SS Panzer divisions out of France as a result of this deception; Hitler claimed that if these divisions had been deployed in the West on the day of the invasion, the landing never would have happened.[104]

LANDING OF THE SPARROW: ALLIED PRESSURE TO WITHDRAW FROM THE WAR

By the late fall of 1943, as the push to make Hungary take the precipitous step was gaining urgency, the British became frustrated by what they saw as Hungarian procrastination. Senior Foreign Office officials attributed the Hungarian reluctance to accede to an unconditional surrender to Italy's discouraging example. Allied troops were too far off, making it unreasonable to expect sudden developments in Hungary. At the same time, W. Harrison, an official of the U.K. Foreign Office, approved of the arguments Churchill and his chiefs of staff had originally advanced for delaying Hungary's defection from the Axis until it could be fit into Allied military plans.[105] In Harrison's view, the Hungarians' withdrawal from the war would be most effective if it were to coincide with the Allied landing in Normandy.[106]

While the British did not want to play the Hungarian card prematurely, the United States was more eager to provoke immediate action.[107] Roosevelt, who according to Ambassador Harriman displayed little interest in matters relating to Eastern Europe,[108] told Otto von Habsburg that Hungary, by rapidly changing sides, could secure favorable terms including cobelligerent status and the acquisition of Transylvania,[109] both of which were highly coveted by the Hungarians. The U.S. government, however, refrained from any such commitments in their official contacts with Hungarian personnel. And though Hungarian leaders reserved the right to determine the best time to make the final move, or "jump" as they called it, the Allies continued to press Hungary and Romania to take action. On November 21, Dulles sent a message to Iuliu Maniu of the Romanian democratic opposition informing him that Romania would have to accept an unconditional surrender even though it might result in "Romania's occupation by Germany," adding that this was the official policy of the United States.[110]

Unaware of the hidden agenda behind Anglo-American policies, György Bakách-Bessenyey shared his doubts with Dulles. He complained that Budapest was slow and indecisive and suggested he would resign if no "realistic steps" were taken. To his superiors, Dulles expressed skepticism about early action from the Hungarians: the United States had not encouraged them with more lenient terms of surrender, Budapest thought the Allies supported their neighbors' territorial claims, and, moreover, the Hungarians were not prone to heroic acts. He also pointed out that they were more afraid of the Red Army than of the Germans and that the Soviets were more hostile toward them than even toward the Romanians. The situation would change if the Allies appeared in the Balkans, but as Dulles noted this was not going to happen.[111] His doubts may have been what prompted him to ask Washington to reaffirm that the policy of detaching the satellites applied to Hungary. He received an affirmative answer.[112]

After the conference in Teheran, detaching Hitler's allies became a priority. Secretary of State Hull issued a warning to the satellites that because of their "ruthless" participation in the war they would have to share Germany's fate in the consequences of defeat. In its own way the declaration was meant to accelerate defection from Germany even though policy papers recognized that Kállay was in dire straits. Breaking with Hitler should not occur so soon as to provoke a German invasion, nor so late as to exhaust the Allies' patience. After Italy's collapse, Hungary was in a difficult position, and although Horthy tried to act like Pietro Badoglio, he wanted to keep his country from becoming a German battlefield.[113]

The British Foreign Office complained that the Hungarians were procrastinating, were not heeding calls for sabotage, and would not receive a Special Operations Executive (SOE) group. Harrison recommended a tougher line, adding that Hungary's unconditional surrender should be announced to coincide with the landing on the continent. F. K. Roberts agreed with the British Chiefs of Staff that Hungary's defection should be delayed until it suited Allied military plans. Another senior British official proposed bombing Budapest to expedite Hungary's withdrawal from the war. Only permanent undersecretary Alexander Cadogan disagreed, arguing that Hungarian and Romanian defection would be inconceivable until "we can defend them." He insisted it was unrealistic to expect unconditional surrenders from nations that were in no position to heed the Allied call,[114] but no one else shared his view. The British wartime intelligence service (the SOE) also accused the Hungarians of biding their time and wanted them to receive a small parachute detachment as well as to accept unconditional surrender.[115] The Foreign Office eventually intervened to cancel the parachute operation. In the meantime, the United States, which had been more understanding of Hungary's difficult situation, took over the British role as Hungary's main negotiating partner.

By the end of 1943, OSS goals in Hungary were growing increasingly ambitious. The agency sought to force Hungary's immediate defection from the war, to foster tension and hostility between Budapest and Berlin, and to construct an intelligence network in Hungary. The OSS saw no sign of anti-British or anti-American sentiment among the Hungarians, who hoped only to survive, to withdraw from the war, and to hammer out an agreement with the Allies that would enable them to preserve some degree of independence. Hungary's pro-German officer corps was first and foremost "Hungarian nationalist"; their attitude toward the Allies would be determined by what they thought to be in their country's best interest. If Germany turned against their country, they might well turn against the Germans.[116]

At the end of November 1943, the U.S. Joint Chiefs instructed the OSS to extricate Hungary from the war without offering anything in return.[117] An opportunity presented itself when a Hungarian staff officer, Ottó Hatz, approached the OSS in Turkey. Hatz had been a world-champion fencer and may have been a double agent working for the Germans. In 1944, he began cooperating with the Soviets, only to be arrested by the NKVD (the Soviet intelligence service) in 1945. (Sentenced to twenty-five years of forced labor, he was released in 1955 and died in Budapest in 1972.) In September 1943, an OSS intelligence network code-named "Dogwood" established contact with Hatz, who agreed to arrange negotiations between Hungarian chief of staff Ferenc Szombathelyi and U.S. officials.[118] In accordance with an OSS request, the Hungarians appointed Hatz military attaché to Turkey. Hungary's key strategic position, the prospect of anti-German cooperation with Hungarian military intelligence, and the fact that Hungary was willing to express its sympathy toward the Allies prompted the American intelligence service to contemplate dispatching a "small but highly powered group" to Hungary.[119] With Kállay's authorization, the Hungarian General Staff offered to provide detailed military intelligence on the German army and its operations in return for recognition of their contribution to an Allied victory. They neither asked for nor received any political or military concessions. Pro-Western Hungarians saw Anglo-American occupation as deliverance. They were willing to accept an American officer disguised as Hungarian and even offered military assistance to the invading forces. In return, the OSS offered unconditional surrender and an "acknowledgment" of Hungarian assistance to the Allied cause. OSS director William Donovan then asked the JCS to concur with OSS participation in the talks. Donovan added that the Hungarians had turned down a British approach and would not let them in on the talks, even though the British wanted back in.[120] By the end of 1943, Hungary was providing the OSS with military intelligence through Swedish, Turkish, and Swiss channels.[121]

The JCS found the Hungarian approach "sincere" and agreed to conduct peace negotiations in the near future, or when Germany's collapse was imminent. The Hungarians, the Joint Chiefs believed, wanted to demonstrate that they had cooperated with Hitler only to avoid a German occupation tantamount to "national slavery." The JCS also believed that the Germans no longer trusted their allies and therefore that the intelligence offered by the Hungarian leadership would come from Hungarian, not German, sources. Finally, the JCS told Donovan that Hitler had made Hungary part of his *Festung Europa* and that talks with Hungary were thus of higher political and military importance than other Balkan countries.[122] This piece of intelligence shows that military leaders in Washington were receiving solid information about Hitler's plans. The Führer did in fact make Hungary part of his Fortress Europe, which explains the utmost ferocity of the German resistance there and the huge losses the Red Army suffered to take it. In any case, the OSS was hatching plans for cooperation with Hungary. An American staff officer would be dispatched to Budapest with the passport of a Hungarian look-alike. Hungarian diplomatic couriers would be used to send and receive messages, Hungarian intelligence services would share information with the OSS,[123] and Budapest would become one of the most important American centers of communication with Germany and German-occupied Europe.

Hatz hoped to negotiate an eleventh-hour defection to the Allies, allowing Hungary to distance itself morally from the Axis without risking its relations with Berlin. Every form of collaboration short of open military and political cooperation was envisioned, including the American use of Hungarian diplomatic resources. Nothing concrete was offered in return, only a vague promise of possible future membership in the United Nations, depending on Hungary's contribution. Hatz would have liked reassurances regarding territorial gains, but no such prospect was held out.[124] (Although Hatz did later claim, under interrogation by the Hungarian state security services after the war, that the United States had offered territorial concessions in return for Hungarian cooperation.[125]) The OSS learned from a mole in the German Foreign Ministry that the Germans had learned of the Hungarians' preparations to defect from the war,[126] but the negotiations were pursued nonetheless.

Although U.S. intelligence reports implicated Hatz and his superiors in the leak, the OSS continued to discuss possible military cooperation with the Hungarians at a meeting on January 22, 1944. The United States would negotiate with any group that was ready to resist, irrespective of ideological conviction.[127] On the basis of these talks, the OSS concluded that Hungary was ready to renounce all political and territorial demands. Hatz had promised Hungarian military assistance when the moment was right, and in return he asked only that Hungary be deemed a liberated country, like Austria, and not to be saddled with a government unsupported by popular will. He accepted unconditional surrender. To promote anti-German cooperation, the OSS recommended the relaxation of the formula of unconditional surrender, arguing that the United States was already receiving Hungarian assistance in covert actions and communications.[128] In his interrogation after the war, Hatz claimed that the United States had asked for sabotage operations against the Germans and for Hungarian armed forces to be pulled from the eastern front. These conditions confronted Kállay with hard choices. Accepting them could entail a German occupation; refusing them could result in an Allied bombing.[129]

In the meantime, the OSS and the Hungarians, unaware that similar negotiations were underway in Turkey, held talks in Bern concerning an American military mission to Hungary. These talks revealed that the Hungarians had still not faced up to the full severity of their situation. Bakách-Bessenyey was anxious to find out whether the Red Army would stop at the Carpathians if Hungary denied the Germans the use of its territory for military purposes or turned against them, but Dulles declined to ask Moscow about it.[130] In February 1944, the JCS drafted the terms of the Hungarian surrender on the basis of the German model, suggesting that the conditions were to have been strict even in case of a break with Hitler. Hungary would be administered by an Allied-controlled (that is, Soviet) military government for an unspecified period of time. That government would be obliged to implement the instructions of the Allied (Soviet) High Command, and its diplomacy would be controlled by the Allies. More importantly, Hungary would be obliged to withdraw from the "occupied territories" without prejudice to the final territorial settlement. The JCS wanted the existing government to sign the capitulation so that Hungarian nationalists would not get a chance to blame democratic elements for the severe terms.[131]

The Soviets' conditions were also harsh. Success or failure in deserting the Germans made no difference in their provisions for surrender. Hungary's break with Hitler would contribute to the defeat of the Third Reich, but the Soviet draft for Romania reveals that Moscow had already made up its mind on possibly the most significant regional issue, Transylvania. The contentious territory would be given to Bucharest. The Soviet-Romanian border would be re-established along the lines of the bilateral agreement of 1940, while the Second Vienna Award, which had partitioned Transylvania, would be declared unjust and therefore invalid. The draft also mentioned that the Soviet Union would wage war with Romania against Hungary and Germany so that Romania could retrieve Transylvania or "the greater part thereof." The Soviets did not offer the Hungarians the prospect of joint struggle even when Horthy sent an armistice mission to Moscow in the fall of 1944. Churchill accepted the Soviet draft with the proviso that the arrangement for Transylvania would be settled at the peace conference. The United States agreed to accept the Soviet formula with the reservation that the final decision on the issue would be left to a general settlement.[132] The terms show that military considerations played a role in the Soviet position on Transylvania. At that point, Romania's surrender was far more pressing for the Soviet military campaign than Hungary's. In addition, Transylvania may have been intended as compensation for the territory the Romanians would lose to the USSR. Stalin had told Edvard Beneš in December 1943 that in order "to save Romanian democracy," Transylvania would go to Romania. Molotov added that Northern Bukovina and Bessarabia, territories assigned to the USSR by the Stalin-Hitler pact, would belong to the USSR after the Germans were driven out.[133]

On February 13, 1944, the OSS presented the American provisions to Hatz, but the Hungarian reply proved unsatisfactory. The United States expected an unequivocal approval or rejection. Only then could an officer or "politician" be sent to Hungary. Because the precise details of these discussions are not available, there is no way to know what was meant by "politician." The message to Hatz now carried a sense of urgency: rejection of the U.S. terms would mean an end to the talks and the immediate start of hostilities.[134] On February 14, the Hungarian government presented two letters. The first reiterated that precipitate action would invite German occupation and reaffirmed that Hungary would offer no resistance if U.S. or British troops were to enter the country. Hungarian soldiers would not fight Soviet forces if they stopped at the Carpathians but would vigorously resist Soviet attempts to penetrate into Hungary. The second Hungarian letter requested an American officer with knowledge of the local conditions in Hungary, such as the former military attaché to Budapest, Lanning McFarland. Finally, the letter asserted that no country would accept such severe conditions without knowing what to expect.[135]

U.S. officials sought to reaffirm the Hungarians' intention to withdraw. In January 1944, Frances Deak, who claimed to be negotiating on behalf of the State Department and the American "High Command," told the Hungarian minister in Lisbon that Washington wanted to keep Transylvania under Hungarian sovereignty but that this required the Hungarians to break with Hitler. Deak declared that the formula of unconditional surrender was flexible, but that changing sides would be worthless if Hungary acted too late. Past a certain point, "our American friends" would not be able to help.[136] American officials always avoided saying anything that could be construed as a territorial guarantee and rigidly insisted on unconditional surrender. Deak's authorization and legal status were and are unclear, but if he did have the authority to make such statements, they were aimed at expediting a break with the Axis by dangling bait the Hungarians would swallow.

A U.S. military mission to Budapest was an important part of the discussions. The idea was raised in October 1943 and Dulles embraced it enthusiastically. He wanted to send an "Aryan," "robust, intelligent American specimen" with no foreign traits.[137] The OSS originally selected a well-qualified Jewish officer, but Dulles vetoed him on the grounds that his "Jewish appearance" made him unsuitable to carry out the mission.[138] Dulles regarded this mission as a unique opportunity to which the Hungarians attached great significance, and he hoped it would be implemented as quickly as possible.[139] Thus a senior officer was appointed to lead the mission, code-named "Sparrow."[140] When the British found out about Sparrow, they protested that they had not been informed. The Americans responded that the JCS had authorized the OSS to carry out intelligence operations on enemy territory without the approval of foreign governments. They denied that the mission was designed to negotiate a separate peace and pointed out that the British had kept the United States in the dark about similar operations of their own. The U.S. government thus refused to disclose the identity of Sparrow's leader to their British allies.[141]

The Hungarians seem to have believed that the American mission was being sent to discuss the terms of a separate peace. The Hungarian officials who dealt with the Americans were taken into German custody. They told their German interrogators that after the arrival of the Americans, "Hungary was going to jump out of the war, which was foiled by the German occupation."¹⁴² The head of Hungarian military intelligence, General István Ujszászy, claimed that Col. Florimond Duke, Sparrow's leader, told him he had discussed the mission with President Roosevelt. Ujszászy also said that Duke presented the armistice terms: Hungary was to turn against the Germans, place its airspace at the disposal of the Allies, return to its 1938 borders, and accept Allied occupation.¹⁴³ These were basically the same surrender terms worked out by the JCS, minus some of the stricter conditions. Moreover, having decided that the United States would not participate in military operations in the region, the JCS seems to have envisaged a Soviet occupation of Hungary. American documentation of the Sparrow mission emphasizes that the officers were sent to Hungary exclusively to gather intelligence and to organize sabotage operations; they were not authorized to discuss political matters.¹⁴⁴ Ujszászy's memory, though, is probably accurate. His later admission, in communist captivity, that he was negotiating with the Americans during the war, did not serve him well; by then, cooperation with the United States at any time was considered an act hostile toward the Soviet Union. Immediately after the war, in his own recollection of these events, Duke claimed that when the Hungarians asked about terms, he told them that their surrender would still be unconditional. The true aims of Operation Sparrow were later further obscured when Duke changed his story. In the mid-1960s, he decided to write his memoirs, and because he had no access to government documents, he queried his erstwhile superior Allen Dulles. A memorandum of a 1965 conversation between the two men notes that the Duke mission was meant to install a pro-Allied government in Hungary.¹⁴⁵ It is not inconceivable that Ujszászy's version is closer to the truth. Duke may have been instructed to present the Hungarians with more favorable terms than they were to get in reality. The Hungarians were known to want to hear that the Allies would occupy Hungary; they would make sacrifices in return. On March 15, Washington was informed that the Hungarian army would offer no resistance to a British-American invasion of Hungary.¹⁴⁶

Only three days after the Americans landed in Hungary, the German army carried out Operation Margarethe II. Was this what the Allies had wanted? Shortly before Sparrow got under way, one participant complained that he had received no information about the purpose of the mission and that nobody seemed to care what was accomplished. Even though the mission was designated a top priority, the intelligence division of the OSS did not receive full information about it either.[147] This may suggest that the mission had no goal other than to get the Hungarians to make their move immediately. This possibility is supported by the fact that the OSS wanted the mission to achieve maximal results, to put an end to Hungary's procrastination.[148] The United States, like the other Allies, threatened the satellites with the loss of their sovereignty and even of their national existence if they failed to break with Germany. The longer they held out, the worse it would get for them. After the German occupation, the Hungarians were warned that only by resisting the invaders would they be entitled to independence. Romania, on the other hand, was offered cobelligerent status for switching sides.

After the war, Duke considered the possibility that his mission had been designed to provoke the Germans' invasion of Hungary. As we have noted, as early as November 1943 the JCS had instructed the OSS to detach the satellites, even if doing so resulted in their invasion by Hitler. And how better to persuade Hitler of Hungarian perfidy than the arrival of an American colonel? It was no coincidence that Sparrow was delayed until 1944; the month of March was chosen because of weather conditions. At that point, D-Day was planned for May 1. Although there is no direct evidence linking the U.S. mission to the German invasion, such a response had to have been foreseeable. After the war, Wilhelm Höttl, the controller of the SS political security and counterespionage service in Budapest in 1944, claimed that Sparrow played a crucial role in Hitler's decision by convincing him that the Hungarians were traitors.[149] The Führer's order for Operation Margarethe did, in fact, emphasize the Hungarians' impending defection, which had to be prevented by military action. The Hungarians were expecting to negotiate a surrender with the arriving American detachment, and since the Germans were aware of the Americans' presence, it seems likely that Berlin understood the point of their being there. In Nuremberg, Ribbentrop claimed that the invasion was caused by Allied deception. Dulles assumed that the Germans knew about the secret talks and did not want another Badoglio in Hungary, where one million Jews lived.[150] Did Operations Sparrow and Bodyguard hasten – or even cause – Hitler's invasion of Hungary? No definitive answer is possible. The desired outcome of Allied efforts, German occupation, may have been predictable as military strategy, but among its tragic consequences was the extension of Hitler's "final solution" to the Jews of Hungary.

MORAL CHOICES

Hungary's aims and interests were incompatible with the Allies'. Hungary wanted it both ways: to win Allied sympathy while avoiding the catastrophe of being overrun by the Nazis. This mission was almost impossible in itself, and the attitude of Hungary's desired partners put it in a no-win situation. Though well informed, the pro-Western Hungarian elite were living in a political dream world. Convinced of their country's strategic significance in a presumed Western struggle against Bolshevism, they expected an "Anglo-Saxon invasion" of the Danube Basin. They thus neglected, although did not completely disregard, the Soviet Union as a negotiating partner and stretched Hitler's tolerance to the limit. They hoped that by deserting Hitler they could preserve Hungary's territorial integrity, avoid another disastrous loss of territory, and forestall a Soviet takeover. Myths, illusions, and prejudices, however, are seldom good guides to the terrain of international affairs. Although well-intentioned, Kállay may not have chosen the most appropriate responses to the complex, almost hopeless challenges his country confronted.

The United States and its allies came to see in these peace initiatives an opportunity to provoke a German invasion of Hungary and Romania, which would necessarily spread Hitler's forces thin and facilitate the Allied landing in Normandy. Initially, the Allies reckoned that the danger of breaking with Hitler was too great for these countries; they did not press the issue until October of 1943. They spared scant concern for the immediate fate of this faraway, momentarily unimportant, German-dominated part of Europe. The Allies had not even decided whether Hungary should survive as an independent sovereign state. The OSS was aware of Hungary's dilemma: deserting Hitler too early could mean occupation; waiting too long might mean squandering the Allies' sympathy. Only after deciding to land in Normandy did the Allies begin to apply pressure: postwar independence for Hungary and Romania was made contingent on their sabotaging the German war effort and breaking with the Axis. The Allies were simply pursuing their political and military interests against the enemy; the occupation of Hungary would draw German troops away from the site of the invasion as well as from the eastern front. This idea was – at least in part – behind Churchill's plan to apply more military pressure in the Mediterranean.[151] But were the military benefits of these plans to the Allies outweighed by the resultant destruction of a large mass of enemy civilians? A similar dilemma arose in October 1956, when U.S. declarations about rolling back communism helped spark a brief Hungarian war of liberation from the USSR. Though the local population initially embarrassed the Red Army, none of the pledged Western aid materialized, allowing the Soviets to counterattack, killing, imprisoning, and exiling hundreds of thousands of people. The United States had to weigh the benefits of supporting the Hungarian revolution against the risks of a larger war with the Soviet Union.

On May 23, 1943, a representative of the Foreign Office informed a Hungarian envoy that Britain did not expect anything of Hungary that might provoke a German occupation, and in light of the dire consequences "[could not] conceive" of Hungary's defection from the war. Three months later, the same person told Barcza that Hungary would have to follow Italy's example in leaving the war and suffering the consequences, including German occupation.[152] When Lipót Baranyai, the former president of the Hungarian National Bank, tried to alert Dulles's associate Royall Tyler to the possible consequences of a German invasion, he was told that there was a war on, that "we are up to our elbows in blood, [and] a few hundred thousand lives here or there do not count."[153]

Hungarian historiography has described the failure to defect from the Axis as a missed opportunity and attributed it to the weakness, even duplicity, of Hungary's leaders, especially Kállay. Kállay's former envoy, György Barcza, claimed that "Kállay ... was sitting on the fence but forgot that he could run out of time ... herein ... lies his personal tragedy which at the same time became Hungary's tragedy."[154] Szegedy-Maszák depicted Kállay as representative of the "Transylvanian school," waffling between partners not because he believed that the Nazis, whom he despised, would win the war, but because he imagined that the war would end with a compromise peace.[155]

Though Barcza later lambasted Kállay for failing to break with Hitler, at the time he considered such a step drastic and undesirable. On May 21,

1943, he wrote to Foreign Minister Jenő Ghyczy: "He [Frederick Vanden Heuvel, Barcza's British contact in Switzerland] did not even mention what on the other side amateur politicians recommend so often, that we should turn our backs to the Axis and leave the war because this is the only way we can show our goodwill. Since I know that this view is quite widespread I noted that those that recommend this to us are not aware of the consequences of such a step. If we jumped out of the war the Germans would immediately occupy the country." The democratic opposition would be "arrested perhaps even executed," Barcza wrote, and "tens, perhaps hundreds of thousands of Jews would be killed." At this point Vanden Heuvel interjected that he "could not conceive" of a break with Hitler.[156]

Accepting Allied demands may not have been in Hungary's interest given the threat Germany posed and that little if anything was offered in return. Kállay and the country's pro-Western elite overestimated Hungary's significance and its role in the anti-Bolshevik struggle. In January 1944, Foreign Minister Ghyczy expressed hope that the United States and Britain would understand that Hungary's military collaboration with the Germans had been directed against the Bolshevik menace.[157] That the Hungarians' services would soon be crucial against "the Bolsheviks" was an illusion of which the Allies took advantage. Inducements were more productive than threats.[158] The methods – psychological warfare, subversion – prefigured the tactics the United States would use in the 1950s in trying to roll back Soviet power in Eastern Europe. The military benefits to the Allies of the German occupation of Hungary, however, were ambiguous at best. Around one hundred thousand Wehrmacht and SS troops, amounting to almost ten divisions, marched into Hungary on March 19, 1944. This invading force included men from some of the most battle-hardened units in Hitler's army, including the 5th SS Panzer Division "Wiking," the Panzergrenadier Division Grossdeutschland, the Panzerkorps Feldherrnhalle, and the 16th SS Panzergrenadier Division. This contingent was on the small side of the U.S. estimate of ten to fifteen divisions, and by the time of the invasion in Normandy, as many as half of these German occupying forces had been pulled back out of Hungary.

Small states are often limited to a small number of choices. Sometimes they are able to manipulate stronger allies and thereby augment their own power and security,[159] but often their fates are merely the by-products of great powers' policies. Hungarians were unable to use foreign policy to improve their position in the international arena; even if they had broken with the Axis, the peace terms would likely still have relegated them to the Soviet Union's sphere of influence. The fact that Hungary sought to negotiate a separate position, the risks of which threatened its most basic interests, demonstrates the power the Western Allies exerted, even in Germany's *Festung Europa*. But this particular route to victory, over one of the most evil powers in history, included a moral tradeoff.

2

Cuius Regio, Eius Religio: *The United States and the Soviet Seizure of Power*

Historians have taken for granted that the Cold War originated at least partly in the fatal discord between the Soviet Union and the United States over the future of Eastern Europe. Scholars also tend to have narrowed the debate to the timing of and motivations behind the introduction of Stalinist regimes in Eastern Europe, generally focusing on whether the Sovietization of Eastern Europe was the predetermined result of Soviet foreign policy or a reaction to American assertiveness. This chapter will suggest that American policies had little or no influence on the course of events in Hungary. There is no evidence that the Soviets were responding to challenges from Washington; in fact, the United States was mostly cooperative with Soviet desires in Hungary, offering only slight resistance to the drastic process of Sovietization there. Like the British in the 1930s, Washington was not displeased to see a large power stabilizing a region that had been a cockpit of hostilities in the prewar period. It was only after 1948 that President Harry Truman came to regard Eastern European independence and the rollback of Soviet power as prerequisites for European security. Thus the axiom that Soviet-American discord over Eastern Europe was a cause of the Cold War may need to be revised. The traditional focus of Cold War historiography, Bolshevization, may have been secondary in significance to the interrelated process of military and economic colonization, in the face of which the United States was equally passive.

There is no need to separate the ideological and imperial aspects of Soviet expansionism. The two were intertwined. Soviet colonization of Eastern Europe went hand-in-hand with the introduction of Stalinist terror and the liquidation of democratic leaders there. These processes had nothing to do with American foreign policy, which was fairly complacent. When Soviet leaders were faced with the choice of cooperating with adjacent states that had been German allies, they instead chose to dominate these neighbors utterly. Eastern European sources reveal that Soviet policy toward the vassal states was not a response to American actions. The communist tactic of moderation lasted only until the peace treaties with the former German satellites were concluded. The introduction of proletarian dictatorships was announced well over a year before the Marshall Plan; military and economic colonization had begun even before the war in Europe ended.[1]

"THIS IS OUR TERRITORY": SPHERES OF INFLUENCE

In 1947, a Hungarian official got a glimpse of the world as viewed from Moscow. A vast map, covering an entire wall of the office occupied by Anastas Mikoyan, the economic czar of the Soviet Union, represented the Eurasian landmass from a northern projection. The overwhelming portion of the map was occupied by the Soviet Union; Western Europe was just a small protuberance at the left, while America was reduced to a principality on the right.[2] Eastern Europe was invisible, a true reflection of the region's place in geopolitics. Two agreements governed the territorial distribution of hegemony there. The 1939 Hitler-Stalin pact had guaranteed Soviet influence in Poland and the Baltic states, while the Stalin-Churchill pact had extended Soviet control into the Balkans and Hungary. Only Czechoslovakia was left out. Like other territories conquered by the Red Army, Hungary became a Soviet possession – militarily, economically, and politically – as soon as Soviet soldiers crossed the Carpathians in late 1944. The extent of their control is demonstrated by one relatively minor episode. In 1946, when Prime Minister Ferenc Nagy conveyed to the Soviets President Truman's desire to obtain Hungarian landing rights for U.S. civilian airlines, Georgi Pushkin, the Soviet minister in Budapest, told him it would be easier for the Americans to get permission to land in the Soviet Union itself. As Marshal Kliment Voroshilov put it, "This is our territory and we shall determine who can enter."

Some historians claim that the USSR introduced communism into Hungary as a response to Western policies, notably the Marshall Plan. In fact, American policies do not seem to have influenced the Soviets' approach to Hungary. In May 1946, well over a year before the Marshall Plan was announced, Mátyás Rákosi, the leader of the Hungarian Communist Party, pledged that every measure would be taken to install a proletarian dictatorship, "with no regard for internal and external conditions." In the same speech to a select audience of high communist functionaries, Stalin's self-described "best disciple" revealed Moscow's plans to revive the communist international and announced that his party would merge with the Social Democrats whether they liked it or not. A few weeks before that speech was delivered, the Soviet State Agency for Property Abroad (Gusimz) had seized a dominant position in the Hungarian economy, adding Hungary's most important firms to an economic empire that stretched from North Korea to East Germany. Thus it will be argued that the United States bears little responsibility for the Soviet takeover of Hungary. Moscow, given the choice between Western reconstruction aid and unbridled power over Eastern Europe, opted for the latter.

Hungarian democrats expected the United States to assist them against the Soviet-backed Communist Party, but the Americans' already limited willingness to do so was further dampened by the Hungarians' apparent lack of resolve in resisting communist pressure. In turn, Hungarian democrats saw little point in wrestling the Soviets without external help, and this vicious circle of mutually reinforcing hesitations facilitated the Soviets' takeover. It will be argued that political calculations, ideology, and deeply ingrained prejudices were at play in Washington's approach to the Hungarians. And while the Truman administration did pressure Moscow for joint action in Hungary's economic rehabilitation, the Soviet leadership sacrificed cooperation with the United States for absolute control.

Nothing revealed the United States's impotence in Eastern Europe like the Soviets' gradual expulsion of American investors from Hungary. This process went hand-in-glove with the Soviet colonization of the Hungarian economy, and by 1948, trials involving American business leaders were under way. They provided insights into Stalinist police procedures and the role show trials would play in communist statecraft, but the United States was unable to protect its citizens. The proceedings against Robert Vogeler especially showed that the United States was virtually powerless behind the Iron Curtain.

AMERICAN VISIONS OF POSTWAR EUROPE

Roosevelt envisioned a Europe in which the Soviet Union and Great Britain would safeguard peace. If necessary, the national independence of small states would be subordinated to stability; in fact, the principles of independence and stability seem to have been mutually exclusive. Churchill's deal with Stalin fit neatly into the president's concept of a postwar peace. In the final phase of the war, it became apparent that the Soviet Union could stabilize the eastern part of the continent by liberating and occupying the smaller countries there. Even if Moscow was likely to curtail those countries' independence by imposing a form of its political system on them, at least the Soviet security umbrella would neutralize a hitherto unstable part of the continent. The region's relative political and economic insignificance to the Americans and the British made this tradeoff easy to make. The best the West could hope for was an open-door economy, allowing free trade and investment while recognizing Moscow's political and military supremacy.

It was not until 1948 that the Truman administration began to see the restoration of Eastern European sovereignty as a prerequisite for Western security. In the crucial intervening period when the Soviets were taking military, economic, and political control of their satellites, Western governments tended to see the Soviet Union as a necessary counterbalance to German power in central Europe and a stabilizing factor in an area plagued by persistently nasty rivalries.[3] Many in Washington believed in a middle ground between full independence and total domination. Some in American government circles (and not only there) hoped that the Soviets had changed and that Moscow was no longer driven by a relentless and dangerous ideology. The hope was that messianic Bolshevism had faded and given way to the pragmatic motivations of traditional powers. After his talks with Stalin in December of 1943, the head of the Czechoslovakian government-in-exile, Edvard Beneš, became convinced that the Soviets had given up their revolutionary principles and the imperative of spreading communist ideas abroad.[4] He was not alone. The visionary George F. Kennan hoped that friendly governments would not necessarily mean Bolshevized ones.[5] Roosevelt thought there were grounds for hope. He assured Czechoslovak foreign minister Jan Masaryk that "Russia wants to and will cooperate." Churchill's ambassador to Moscow, Stafford Cripps, had anticipated that the Kremlin would "determine the future of Europe." Cripps did not think this would matter because, in his view, the Russians had no desire to impose their system abroad. The historian E. H. Carr shared Cripps's perspective that Moscow sought only security. He argued that Stalin would not use his military success to promote communism and did not think that Moscow had any "aggressive design in Europe."[6] It may be noted that in 1940 Carr advocated a Soviet-German condominium of Europe, and during the war he wrote articles in the *Times* arguing that Eastern Europe should be surrendered to the Soviets. The *New York Times* opined that Marxist thinking had disappeared from Soviet Russia.[7] Stalin's personal charm doubtlessly played a role here: people with backgrounds and persuasions as varied as Churchill's, Truman's, and Hungarian premier Ferenc Nagy's were all taken in by it. Liberals and Republicans alike believed that cooperation with the Soviet Union was not only possible, but desirable. *Life* magazine claimed that Russians were just like Americans. Even in 1947, Truman thought that Stalin had a heart and only the Politburo was preventing him from using it.[8]

The State Department was divided over the prospect of postwar cooperation with the Soviets. Washington's first ambassador in Moscow, William Bullit, warned that the Soviets filled every vacuum in which they met no resistance. Initially he had been eager to expand Soviet-American relations, but by the end of the war he concluded that there was little to differentiate Stalin from Hitler: each wanted to extend his influence to the end of the world. On the other hand, Charles Bohlen, the State Department official in charge of the USSR (and whose career would cross paths with Hungarian history at a critical juncture of the Cold War), claimed that Marxism-Leninism had lost its relevance for Soviet foreign policy. Kennan had no fear of a Soviet invasion of Western Europe, but Harriman expressed reservations regarding Stalin's good will. In September 1944, when the Soviets were about to break through the Carpathian Mountains onto the Hungarian plain, Harriman warned Roosevelt that it would be harder to work with the Soviets than they had previously imagined. The ambassador, who was finding his work in the Russian capital increasingly frustrating, still thought that the most important people in Moscow wanted to be friends. Soviet foot-dragging on the UN, however, led Secretary of State Hull to think that they had changed their minds about cooperation.[9]

Despite manifestations of Soviet ill will in matters large and small, cooperation still formed the basis of U.S. policy in Eastern Europe. After having briefed the president on regional problems, Harriman observed that except for its effect on domestic politics, Eastern Europe did not arouse Roosevelt's interest. He saw it as part of a larger picture, a rearrangement of the European scene on the basis of balanced power and cooperation between Great Britain and the USSR. William Bullit advocated an Anglo-American line of defense in Eastern Europe to keep the Soviets out of the rest of the continent. Roosevelt would not reject the replacement of nation-states with larger federations and was ready to sacrifice national self-determination to Soviet interests in Eastern Europe if necessary. Even the potential Bolshevization of Soviet-occupied territory was a reasonable price to pay if Soviet-British cooperation would preserve European peace. Kennan recognized that the region's fate hinged on Soviet good will. He advocated recognizing the Soviets' desire to control the areas adjacent to their western border and supported a division of the continent to realistic spheres of influence so as to facilitate cooperation among the great powers.[10] His reading of Gibbon suggested that an overextension of the Soviet Union's power would eventually lead to its collapse or at least a significant weakening. The influential Walter Lippmann agreed, arguing that there was no point in establishing a Versailles-style *cordon sanitaire* around Russia. The United States had no interest in the region, and, lacking military means, there was nothing it could do to roll the Soviets back. Those who thought that European peace should rest on cooperation between East and West accepted the principle *cuius regio, eius religio* ("whose realm, his religion") and hoped for the best.

The American military had surrendered the region by rejecting any participation in its occupation. Moreover, the Joint Chiefs of Staff (JCS) were aware that the Soviets were the preponderant military power in central Europe and could not be challenged with any realistic hope of success.[11] The State Department imagined that Moscow would allow Eastern Europeans democratic, pro-Soviet governments open to the West, that the Czechoslovakian model would be adopted in Poland and elsewhere.[12] If the Kremlin's security concerns could be alleviated, perhaps they would not feel constrained to curb Eastern European freedoms. Moscow and Washington did, in fact, reach an agreement on mutual withdrawal from Czechoslovakia. Eventually, though, this appraisal of Soviet domination proved generous to a fault. In Eastern Europe, the Soviets' military, economic, political, and ideological objectives were woven into the same fabric.

The prospect that Eastern Europe could function as an open, nonexclusive portion of the Soviet sphere motivated American involvement in alleviating the financial burdens the Soviets wished to impose on the former German satellites. Ambassador Harriman was able to reduce reparations for Romania and Hungary, although Moscow rejected the original American proposal that reparations be adjusted annually to the capabilities of those economies. It is a different matter that the Soviets eventually collected many times the amount fixed in the agreements. Washington predicted that oversized reparation payments would allow the Soviets to dominate the economies of the states in question, a fear that turned out to be precisely correct. Crippling debt would impede economic reconstruction in Eastern Europe, which in turn would hinder the political stabilization of the continent. Europe had formed an organic economic unit and its reconstruction would be harder without its normal flow of east-west trade.[13] The Western ideal was to keep the Soviet-controlled areas economically attached to the rest of Europe; healthy Eastern European economies were to help revive the West and save it from communism.

The Allies agreed that Hungary needed profound social transformation and democratization for the region to achieve stability. At that time, however, the obvious may not have been apparent: the two sides had fundamentally different notions of democracy, a difference of opinion that was never clarified. For Moscow, "democratization" meant a dictatorship of the proletariat, under which the "minority" – in reality the majority – was to be dominated by a new ruling class. The United States even supported the Soviets' version of land reform in the hope that Soviet control might be compatible with some form of democracy. In sum, Washington wanted to see these countries as friends of, and even as formal allies to, the Soviet Union, but also hoped they would remain constitutionally democratic states, allowed to pursue open-door policies in trade, raw materials, and access to investments. Eastern Europe's fate, however, was entirely in Soviet hands.

Unlike Romania or Bulgaria, Hungary was not immediately written off; the dividing line between East and West seemed to be Austria. Mussolini once remarked that one who has breakfast in Vienna will dine in Milan: Austria was the key position in Central Europe not just for Italy, but also for another bastion of the West, southern Germany.[14] Hitler had declared Hungary *Festung Europa* and launched an offensive in Western Hungary as late as March 1945.[15] The Soviets had gotten bogged down in Hungary in the last phase of the war, which ultimately deprived them of a forward position in western Austria. Because Austria's location on the Danube River was of vital strategic importance to the British, they considered a Soviet invasion of Austria a potential catastrophe for Czechoslovakia, Germany, and Italy.[16] Some specialists at the State Department regarded Czechoslovakia as the test case of Soviet intentions and urged the United States to hold firm in the country, which was the "master key to Europe."[17] American analysts, on the other hand, understood that Hungary was as vital to the Soviets as occidental Austria was to the West. Hungary was a Danubian state linking Romania, Czechoslovakia, and Yugoslavia to the Ukraine. Perhaps most importantly, Hungary was a traditional route for the Germans' Drang nach Osten and was therefore pivotal to Soviet security.[18] Moreover, once the Soviets were on the Hungarian plain, western Austria, with its gateways to northern Italy and Bavaria, was just a hop away. Later the Soviet break with Yugoslavia would further augment Hungary's importance: it became the launching pad for a potential invasion of Yugoslavia, just as it had been for the Germans in 1941. At minimum, it became the tool with which Moscow applied political and military pressure to the South Slav state. Hungary would be the only nation in the region the Soviets were to leave out of the conventional arms reduction talks for Central Europe in the early 1970s. Thus the discrepancy between the Soviets' and the Americans' stakes in Hungary was vast. Austria turned out to be the state Washington and London could not afford to lose; only Austria was able to rely on the full support of the United States and Great Britain in staying out of the Soviet sphere.

PARALLEL TRAGEDIES: HUNGARY IN U.S. POLICY TOWARD EASTERN EUROPE

After nine months of intensive fighting in which the Red Army spent eighty thousand men to capture the capital city alone, the Soviets took firm control of Hungary. Motivated by deprivation and revenge, brutalized Russian troops went on a rampage of unbridled destruction, including murder, rape, and looting. The writer Sándor Márai ascribed the Soviets' indiscriminate looting and confiscations to their "abject poverty." Even in its ruins, Budapest preserved its prewar glory; its shops, coffee houses, and grand boulevards radiated bourgeois affluence. The contrast to the Soviet home front was striking, and the Red Army expressed its frustrations by demonstrating an utter disdain for local culture. Buildings were wantonly destroyed even when they served the needs of the Soviet military, and, as in Austria, private book collections were defecated on. Rákosi, the leader of the Communist Party, alarmed that the Red Army's heavy-handedness was vindicating the worst predictions of Nazi propaganda, protested to the Soviet leadership, but to no avail. There was neither internal nor foreign restraint on Soviet practices in their own political space. Hundreds of thousands of civilians, including as many as 10,000 Holocaust survivors, were hauled off to Soviet labor camps. As many as 80,000 to 150,000 of them perished in Soviet camps. Ethnic Germans, as identified by family names, were particular targets for deportation. To satisfy Stalin's quotas for prisoners of war, the military captured civilians at random, many of whom were elderly or female. Well-trained detachments searched public and private collections for art treasures to be confiscated as spoils of war. Disregarding their allies' protests, the Soviets filled wagons with the machinery and inventories of dismantled factories, facilities often fully or partially owned by American, British, French, Swiss, or Austrian companies. Violating both the letter and the spirit of the armistice agreement, the Soviets fixed reparation prices unilaterally, nullifying the concessions given to Harriman in Moscow. Formerly German assets, often falsely identified as such, were seized by the Soviets, and within a year Hungary was virtually an economic colony. Military agreements allowed the Red Army unrestricted use of Hungarian territory at Hungarian expense. The cost of this extension of the Soviet military border to Austria and Yugoslavia, including pay for Soviet military personnel, doubled Hungary's reparation burden. Setting a pattern for the decades to come, economic and military services were intertwined. After only a year of occupation by the Soviets, Hungary was a client state, directed by Moscow to perform financial, political, and military service.

Because Hungary was a highly important asset to Moscow, America's hopes there could be expressed only in the negative: that Hungary's economy should not become entirely dependent on the Soviet Union.[19] But nobody in the U.S. mission in Budapest knew any Hungarian, not even the intelligence officer. Thus, the means to achieve U.S. aims were lacking. In May 1945, the Truman administration refused to recognize the governments of Romania and Bulgaria on the grounds that they were undemocratic. In Hungary, though, Washington offered to recognize a provisional government headed by the former general Miklós Dálnoki Béla, who had switched sides to the Soviets in October 1944. This might have signaled that Washington attached greater significance to Hungary than to Romania or Bulgaria; recognition by Washington could also have been intended to strengthen the hand of Hungary's noncommunist political forces. Prime Minister Dálnoki, however, had been appointed by Moscow and would not risk infuriating the Soviets. He sounded out Voroshilov, whose "friendly advice" was to wait until Moscow had recognized Hungary. Dálnoki lacked the daring and self-confidence to take advantage of the American initiative.

As the country was preparing for elections, U.S. officials at the American mission in Budapest were optimistic about the future. As a result of recent British and American statements on Eastern Europe, Hungarian democratic forces had regained some enthusiasm and were resisting communist penetration, which gave hope that the country could withstand the communists' drive for unilateral power and avoid being Bolshevized.[20] In reality, the leadership of the largest political party, the Smallholders, was caving in. Voroshilov, as chairman of the Allied Control Commission (ACC), proposed applying the Bulgarian model to the Hungarian elections (ensuring a communist victory), but because of U.S. opposition he dropped the idea. At this point, Zoltán Tildy, the president of the Smallholder Party, suggested to Voroshilov that they establish a coalition government no matter how the election turned out. As it happened, Tildy's party won a landslide victory, with almost 60 percent of the vote. The communists received 17 percent, which, given the widespread anticommunist sentiment in the country, was not a bad result. Still, through this premature commitment to a coalition government, the communists found their way into the government, whereupon they opened a Pandora's box of Stalinist encroachments, eventually seizing every significant position of power. Some members of the Smallholders Party sought American financial support on the grounds that the Soviet Union was providing funds to its radical-leftist clients. The U.S. minister in Budapest, Arthur Schoenfeld, claimed that interference in domestic matters was inconsistent with American political traditions, which held that every nation must win its freedom and democracy through its own efforts.[21]

Schoenfeld was conflicted. He was aware of Soviet abuses and the sway the Soviet members of the ACC held over Hungary, thus he expected from the Hungarians a strongly anti-Soviet stance without his having to offer even modest support for their cause. Minister Schoenfeld, who had served in Helsinki during the Finns' life-and-death struggle through the winter war and supported Budapest in its diplomatic battle to save the Hungarian minority in southern Slovakia from expulsion, had a jaundiced view of the Hungarians. He compared their "rabbit squeals" to the courageous stand taken by the "sturdy" Nordic Finns.[22] Assistant secretary of state Robert Lovett held a similar view: all too often, the Hungarians sought outside help without comprehending that democracy requires personal sacrifices.[23] And while he was right about the feeble resolve of some Hungarian politicians, he failed to appreciate that their situation was more complicated than Finland's had been. There the calculus had been simple: victory or defeat and the loss of national independence. In Budapest, the Soviets were more insidious. There was no open talk of a Soviet takeover, no clear choice to be made between giving in to communist demands and obliteration. The winds of Stalinism were already blowing: communist leaders ordered the subversion of political parties from within, tapped their phones, and arrested their officials on trumped-up charges. Occasionally, democratic politicians were beaten or even lynched as the communists whipped up mass hysteria against the "capitalist" classes.

Schoenfeld's claim that Hungary was already a Soviet economic colony may have played a role in the United States's rejection of a loan to the Hungarians in 1946. It is revealing of Schoenfeld's views of the Hungarian political elite that he found Rákosi to be the most intelligent on the political scene and the only one who knew what he wanted.[24] Only Minister of Supply Bárányos resisted the communist pressure; even Prime Minister Ferenc Nagy was doing the bidding of the Russians.[25] The OSS representative thought that the Hungarians were, without exception, rooting for a war between Russia and the West and doing their utmost to increase tensions.[26] Washington's seeming indifference and the Hungarians' apparent paralysis were mutually reinforcing: democratic Hungarians felt that the Americans were not doing enough to keep the communist tide at bay, which inclined them to give in to the Soviets' ever-increasing demands, which resulted in a seemingly endless string of compromises that dampened the Americans' eagerness to help.

Schoenfeld's colleague in Prague, the vain but energetic Lawrence Steinhardt, a lawyer who had also served as the U.S. ambassador in Moscow, was more sympathetic to Budapest's predicament. He didn't think the Soviets understood Western ethics or morals and were to be treated accordingly. Steinhardt hoped to make Prague the pillar of an American presence in East Central Europe, imagining that by taking strenuous countermeasures in Czechoslovakia, Washington could curb Soviet penetration there and possibly improve the situation in other Soviet-dominated states as well. By the fall of 1946, several prominent members of the Truman administration had concluded that there was no point in supporting the Czechoslovakian democrats; they had already lost their battle with the communists. Czechoslovakia was undermining its position in Washington by supporting the Soviets in their open criticism of American aid policy. President Beneš had staked his country's future on an unequivocally pro-Soviet line, which he hoped would guarantee Czechoslovakia's independence and democratic political system. His calculations proved to be as mistaken as the Hungarians', who hoped that feigning acceptance of communist dictates would forestall full Sovietization. Moved by his host country's suffering in the war, Steinhardt supported all "legitimate" Czechoslovak demands, including the expulsion of Germans and Hungarians.[27] In Romania, U.S. minister Burton Y. Berry, an art historian by training who specialized in eastern textiles and numismatics, promoted active opposition to Soviet policies. When not at work to enrich his collection of ancient rarities, he was pushing Romanians to stand up to communist pressure. In August 1945, he urged King Michael to oust Petru Groza, the prime minister who had been imposed by Soviet deputy foreign minister Andrei Vishinsky in March. Again, there was a large discrepancy between American and Soviet interests in Romania. In 1941, Romania had served as one of the main launching pads for the Germans' invasion of the Soviet Union, an attack Bucharest supported with significant forces. In addition, it sat on the Danube Delta, a spot the Soviets had coveted since 1938.[28] Moreover, in return for Bessarabia, which Romania had been forced to return to the Soviets, Romania had reacquired Northern Transylvania and thus taken command of some of the mountain passes down to the Great Hungarian Plain, from which access into the heart of Europe was easy. Washington would begin to compete for influence in Romania only under Nixon. In 1945, the Americans attached no strategic significance to a presence there, ceding to the Soviets full control of the Balkans. In November 1945, President Truman dispatched a fact-finding mission to Romania, which confirmed that it was under Soviet domination. Even so, in February 1946, the Truman administration recognized Romania in return for a pledge to hold elections, which no one expected to be kept.

Whenever American diplomacy intervened on Hungary's behalf, it was always through Moscow. Local politicians were seldom directly encouraged to defy Soviet demands. In August 1945, without his government's authorization, Ernő Gerő, the communist minister of the economy, initialed an agreement in Moscow that would reorient Hungary's trade toward the Soviet Union and confer ownership of important branches of the Hungarian economy on the Soviets. This agreement clearly violated the nondiscrimination clauses of the armistice and mocked the notion of Hungarian economic sovereignty. Strongly criticized by the Hungarian cabinet, the bill was never sent to parliament; it was ratified only by a select, politically controlled body of the legislature. And instead of supporting the domestic opponents of this pro-Soviet agreement, U.S. diplomats worked through Moscow to accommodate it to the nondiscrimination clause of the armistice. Although its wording was altered somewhat, no practical changes were made, and this agreement thus served as the legal basis for the Sovietization of the Hungarian economy. And while U.S. officials protested the Soviets' economic onslaught, they were unwilling to sign a trade agreement of their own. The United States had never been an important trading partner, but the situation in 1945 was unique: Hungary's traditional partners, Austria and Germany, had collapsed. Soaking up Hungarian commodities became a weapon with which to extract political concessions. Washington was buying all of Austria's trade surplus in order to preserve its independence from the Soviets,[29] but it excluded the Hungarians' chief export, meat products, because of an outbreak of foot-and-mouth disease back in 1938. While the State Department was working to keep Hungary economically open, with equal opportunities for Western powers, and was willing to confront the Soviets on the issue, the Department of Commerce did not rescind the trade restrictions on former German satellites until 1947. Whatever its other defects, American trade policy was not well coordinated by the government agencies charged with its implementation.

Supporting anticommunist forces in Hungary might have been the only way to curb Soviet influence. Washington had no leverage in Moscow, where its interventions were ineffective and may only have served to damage Soviet-American relations. In a note delivered by George F. Kennan in March 1946, the United States demanded that the Soviet members of the ACC in Budapest cooperate with the British and American representatives in rehabilitating Hungary's economy, otherwise Moscow would not be allowed to benefit from the new international financial regime then being established under the aegis of the United States.[30] Nothing could have been further from Molotov's mind. It was then that the details of Soviet-Hungarian joint companies were being finalized, which among other things were to provide the Soviets control over one of the largest bauxite deposits in the world, including processing facilities, at a time when the Soviets had no source of aluminum for their military-aircraft industry. Reparation shipments went into full swing, leading to the worst hyperinflation in history. This in turn allowed the Communist Party to impose a program of economic centralization in the guise of stabilization.

The president of the Hungarian National Bank was removed for providing a U.S. representative of the ACC with data on the economy. Deputy Foreign Minister Andrei Vishinsky rejected American allegations that the Soviet Union played a role in Hungary's economic malaise and, not unexpectedly, refused any cooperation. As the Novikov telegram, a Soviet appraisal of world politics, would put it, Eastern Europe was a buffer zone, a line of defense against the imperialist threat.

The Hungarians soon signed the agreements for the joint-stock companies that would extend the Soviets' economic empire from Manchuria through the Balkans and into Austria. The Communist Party then provoked a political crisis that threatened the coalition as Rákosi ordered a full-fledged assault on the right wing of the Smallholder Party. Secretary of State James F. Byrnes suggested that the United States would not insist on maintaining the coalition,[31] but given that Nagy and President Tildy were being regularly summoned and instructed by the local Soviet potentates, getting rid of the communists was not a feasible option. American diplomacy could have helped the Smallholders in the reallocation of Transylvania, a national question of the utmost importance to both Hungary and Romania. The Soviets understood how crucial this issue was to the success of the Communist Party, and Stalin led the Hungarians to believe that he would support at least a minor rectification of the prewar border with Romania (though by 1943 he had decided to let Bucharest have it all). Byrnes was not inimical to minor changes in favor of the Hungarians if an ethnically more just border would help stabilize the region politically, but he was not willing to challenge the Soviets on it. Decisions regarding territorial arrangements in Eastern Europe were to be made in Moscow.

Still, the United States had not completely surrendered in Hungary. Prime Minister Nagy was invited to Washington for an official visit, followed by a trip to London and Paris. The Soviet ambassador, Georgi Pushkin, reminded the Hungarians to keep the "geographical realities" in mind; the Hungarians gave him a list of the topics they would discuss in Washington. No other government in the Soviet zone was invited to the United States. President Truman returned the Hungarians' gold reserves to facilitate the stabilization of their new currency. The Czechoslovakians, by contrast, would not get their American-held gold back until the middle of the 1970s. President Truman asked that American civilian airlines have Hungarian landing rights, but Prime Minister Nagy was unable to comply.

Hungarian airspace was still under Soviet military control; Ambassador Pushkin declared that "it would be easier for the Americans to get landing rights in the USSR itself." The atmosphere of the talks was congenial. Even Rákosi put a good face on it. Only he knew that Stalin had already given him the go-ahead for the Bolshevization of Hungary. Rákosi, a stocky man nicknamed "Potatohead," harbored ruthless instincts. Having divested himself of the capacity for human emotion, he dedicated his life to the triumph of communism. He was unimpressed by what he saw in the United States, including the Tennessee Valley Authority, which he was doubtlessly shown in an effort to demonstrate that capitalism was compatible with state action in the economy. He reported his experiences to Stalin, who may have read with some interest Rákosi's account of meeting the Hungarian-born David Lilienthal. Rákosi later ridiculed the United States, describing people he met there as fools and warmongers, but the early appraisals he offered Stalin were relatively positive. He was satisfied with the economic concessions and with the fact that American "official circles did not try to turn them against the Soviet Union." He remarked that American economic strength – which he attributed to its having escaped extensive damage in the war – made a good impression on the Smallholders in the delegation.[32] Ferenc Nagy, a quintessential peasant politician of humble stock, returned home with mixed impressions. His meetings were successful, but the profit-oriented culture on the other side of the ocean, particularly commercialized animal husbandry, was alien to him. This ambiguity toward capitalist culture, so characteristic of his class, may explain why he never earnestly sought American assistance against the Soviets. The ultimate irony of his personal history was his emigration to the United States, where he spent the last decades of his life farming.

Rákosi was not so sentimental. Shortly after his return from the United States, he secretly announced the new political line: the dictatorship of the proletariat would be introduced. He noted that his party's initial "moderation" was dictated by tactical considerations. Hyperinflation had been the single largest impediment to the consolidation of the communists' power until the Truman administration inadvertently helped the communist cause by returning the Hungarian gold reserve.

When, in February 1947, the general secretary of the Smallholder Party, Béla Kovács, was taken into Soviet custody (where he would remain until

1956), Washington protested and offered $15 million in economic aid, a fraction of what was offered to Austria. This aid was announced in three stages to amplify the impact.[33] The Department of Commerce belatedly lifted the export controls on Hungary, enabling it to receive commodities in short supply.[34] John Hickerson of the State Department urged the establishment of a tripartite or UN committee to investigate the Kovács affair. The new secretary of state, George C. Marshall, protested the Soviets' failure to consult with the British and American authorities. Marshall declared that the charges against Kovács were unfounded and served the introduction of a dictatorship. He accused the Soviet high command of direct and unjustifiable intervention and of triggering a crisis in Hungary. Marshall announced that the United States would oppose Soviet ambitions and demanded a tripartite investigation with the participation of the Hungarian government and the president of the National Assembly, but he made no mention of a UN investigation.

On March 5, the U.S. representative of the ACC presented a note to the committee's acting chairman, Vladimir Sviridov, who had replaced the disgraced but more pliant Voroshilov in Budapest as a show of support for Nagy.[35] It came as no surprise when Moscow rejected the accusations and the motion for tripartite investigation, alleging that these would create a semblance of "interference in Hungary's domestic affairs."[36] Moscow's unusually swift response indicated that the Soviets were on the defensive. At the same time, the State Department was unhappy with the way the Smallholders were handling the situation. John Hickerson considered the prime minister unable to bear the pressure and incapable of providing adequate support if the Kovács affair were to be taken up at the UN. Schoenfeld complained that under its present constitution, the Hungarian government was unable and often unwilling to resist pressures put on it by minority factions.[37] The New York Times accused Nagy and President Tildy of full cooperation with the communists and appeasement of the Soviets. Tildy did in fact predict, with remarkable prescience, that the Soviets would not leave for fifty years; those who opposed the radical left were subjected to harassment and abuse without any hope of effective external assistance.[38] Nevertheless, Nagy was grateful for the American intervention, which had enabled him to compromise. A secret clause in the agreement prohibited the intimidation of civil servants, pledged to put a stop to the campaign of terror against centrist and right-wing politicians, promised these groups proportionate representation in police forces and local administrations, and curbed press attacks on party leaders. That none of these pledges were observed is another matter.

Kovács's arrest by Soviet authorities focused attention on Hungary, where Moscow's interference had thereto been kept quiet, executed with secret diplomacy and pressure behind the scenes. The *New York Times* likened events there to the Greek civil war, speculating that the Americans' rapid response to events in Greece, along with their protests against Soviet interference in Hungary's domestic matters, suggested that Washington would not accept spheres of influence in Europe. Assistant secretary of state Dean Acheson told the British ambassador that the preservation of Greek and Turkish independence was closely linked to common concerns for other countries, one of which was Hungary.[39]

London showed no enthusiasm for Washington's "energetic" steps on behalf of Hungary. British reluctance may have been one of the reasons why Hungary was not put on the list of countries in which communism was to be contained, although it was certainly not the only one. The U.S. ambassador in Moscow, Walter Bedell-Smith, opined that the conspiracy in Hungary was real and that some Smallholders were taking part in it.[40] Schoenfeld's pessimistic assessment of the ability of Hungarian democratic forces to stand up to the communists may also have helped to make the loss of Hungary acceptable.[41] In the final analysis, Washington was not in a position to challenge the Soviets there. Stalin had demonstrated that he was willing to sacrifice the alliance in order to assert absolute control in his sphere of influence.

In the midst of this domestic turmoil, Hungary, along with Bulgaria and Romania, signed the peace treaty of Paris on February 10, 1947, an agreement that would define the political future of these countries for almost half a century. With the international status of the former German satellites thus settled, the final obstacle to a full Soviet takeover had been removed. American officials had hoped that the conclusion of the treaties would remove the pretext for Soviet occupation, but a British proposal allowed Soviet troops to stay in Romania and Hungary in order to secure their logistical lines for the Soviet occupation army in Austria. There is no doubt that the Soviets would have stayed even without this unfortunate clause; through bilateral treaties, they had already secured the unrestricted use of Hungarian territory for military purposes. The United States wanted to insert into the Romanian and Hungarian treaties a clause governing the restoration of their sovereignty,[42] but the Soviets rejected this proposal on the grounds that the peace treaties were already a sufficient guarantee of their independence.[43]

Inexplicably, as an antirepublican conspiracy was destroying his party, Nagy left the country for a vacation in Switzerland. While Nagy was away, Rákosi received a summons from the Soviet ambassador in Budapest to proceed to the border town of Arad, Romania. The matter was urgent; half an hour later, Rákosi was sitting in a Soviet ZIS limousine with a high-ranking Soviet official authorized to cross the Red Army's checkpoints along the Hungarian-Romanian border. There Rákosi received a handwritten letter from Stalin instructing him to get rid of Nagy while he was gone; otherwise, he was warned, "it will be very hard for [you]."[44] The supreme communist leader also announced that on the basis of Kovács's interrogation by the NKVD, Nagy may have been implicated in a plot to overthrow the republic. In return for the safe passage of his four-year-old son to Switzerland, Prime Minister Nagy agreed to resign. The boy was handed over along with a gift from Rákosi, a black, Soviet-made limousine. A few days later, speaker of the Parliament Béla Varga, a Catholic priest who had saved tens of thousands of Poles during the war, also left the country. Perhaps it was a coincidence that Nikola Petkov, the peasant leader of the Bulgarian opposition, was arrested on June 4. On that very same day the president of the Hungarian Republic approached the U.S. legation in Budapest to help him escape abroad.[45] His request was not granted. Rákosi, whose reputation in Moscow had been tarnished by his electoral defeat in 1945, had every reason to highlight his role in the removal of the communists' chief political opponent. "We accelerated the crisis," he boasted, "because we had cause to worry that procrastination will enable our opponents to launch their attacks."

Nagy's resignation led the *New York Times* to announce that the "Reds" had come to power and that the abdication of the premier signaled the beginning of a "Communist police state." There was panic in the business world as not a single transaction was processed at the Budapest stock market.[46] Szegedy-Maszák, Hungary's ambassador to the United States, requested that the Hungarian question be taken up at the UN. A member of the ultra-secret Pond network, Szegedy-Maszák had been one of the key figures at the Hungarian Foreign Ministry charged with his country's withdrawal from the war. His diplomatic activities and contacts, along with his aristocratic descent, made him a "class alien," anathema to the representatives of the new regime in Budapest. They made sure he would not return. One of his former subordinates at the legation in Washington, the Hungarian president's son-in-law, Viktor Csornoky, who was also working with the Grombach organization, made the mistake of leaving his post in Cairo and going back to Budapest after the communists had seized power. He was arrested, tried on charges of espionage, and executed.

The Hungarian ambassador's initiative was supported by Senator James Eastland of Mississippi, who urged the head of the State Department's Office of Special Political Affairs, Robert McClintock, to explore the possibility of a UN Security Council resolution. McClintock agreed, believing that such action would be worthwhile even if a Soviet veto was inevitable. The acting director of the Office of European Affairs, John Hickerson, thought along similar lines. He suspected that the Russians were behind Prime Minister Nagy's sudden resignation and considered such intervention a "clear cut act of political aggression." Hickerson therefore drafted a note that underlined the USSR's responsibility and recommended that the three powers represented in the ACC send a joint fact-finding mission to Hungary. If the Russians failed to comply, the matter would be taken up at the Security Council and pursued with "utmost persistence" until it could be addressed in the General Assembly. He pressed for action, possibly even a general indictment of Soviet political action in Eastern Europe.[47]

Officials in Washington planned to send a strongly worded note, but they first consulted the British Foreign Office about the possibility of concerted action. The response illustrates the different approaches the Europeans and the Americans would take over the next fifteen years or so. While the United States would eventually come to consider the Soviet occupation of Eastern Europe immoral and dangerous, and therefore to be dislodged, Western Europeans tended to be satisfied with Soviet hegemony and the conservation of the continental status quo. The British thus shunned forceful action and disagreed with an emphasis on Soviet responsibility. Moscow's complicity in the political developments would be hard to prove, thus London chose not to support a protest initiative in the ACC. Behind the formal excuse, there were more profound reasons for this failure to oppose the Soviets in Hungary.

The Labour government was sympathetic to the Soviets. U.K. foreign secretary Ernest Bevin hoped that the "Left would be able to speak to the Left." Few in the Labour government were prepared for a showdown with the communists. Many thought communism suited countries that lacked democratic traditions. Reports about labor camps were dismissed as slanderous fabrications, and some blamed Western statesmen for their failure to get along with Stalin.[48] British strategy was concentrated on the retention of Britain's role as a world power and its dominant position in the Middle East; thus the British concern was not the Soviets' expansion into Eastern Europe, but the extension of their reach to the west and south. London had grown disenchanted with the states of Eastern Europe well before World War II. "All these states," permanent undersecretary of state for foreign affairs Robert Vansittart had written in 1930, "like France, are obsessed by anxiety to keep what they got out of the war and to preserve the status quo against those neighbors whom the war despoiled ... their peppery weakness and local brawls have been a disappointment (they are) unreliable allies in the pursuit of this haunting and evasive 'security.'"[49] Britain's strategic interests were the security of the Commonwealth and the protection of Middle Eastern oil, and given that British diplomats had written Hungary off by the early 1930s, their assumption in 1945 that the Soviets would gain predominance in Hungary is not surprising. Even though the Labour government had repudiated Churchill's spheres-of-influence approach, the Foreign Office believed that Hungary and Romania had no bearing on the British position in the eastern Mediterranean and were thus countries where decisive Soviet influence would be allowed, even if that meant communization.[50]

It made no sense to entangle Britain in this pointless affair. The Americans would only be "making fools of themselves." Although Foreign Secretary Bevin publicly denounced the Soviet Union's imposition of dictatorships and declared that the policy of "appeasement" was over, he took no further action against either. London was satisfied with Molotov's assurance that his government would not impede normal Anglo-Hungarian relations and made known that Britain would not take part in the tripartite investigation the Americans had proposed.[51] Given British reservations, the United States backed down, referring only mildly to Soviet interventions and omitting any mention of the Security Council. The tripartite committee and the notion of further action were touched on only vaguely.[52] And the Soviets rejected even this modest proposal on the grounds that it constituted inadmissible interference in domestic affairs, a formula the Soviets would abuse throughout their occupation of Eastern Europe.

In Poland, these roles were reversed. There, Great Britain encouraged a tougher stance against the Soviets, which the United States opposed. When the Polish government postponed elections in March 1946, the British proposed joint action against the Polish government and the suspension of loans to Poland. Washington, however, rejected the call to action and continued to provide loans to the Poles. London refused to sign any new Anglo-Polish loan agreement.[53]

Although Truman was outraged by the Hungarian situation and made a public pledge not to sit idly by, Washington gave up the push for a UN investigation. It would be hard to muster sympathy for a former German satellite against the victorious Soviet Union, and Hungary's new, communist-dominated government was unlikely to take a stand against the Soviets. It was also inadvisable to put the freshly established UN to a hard test over a former enemy.[54] Finally, and perhaps most importantly, Washington wanted to concentrate on Greece, which was then threatened by an armed communist insurgency. Thus the putsch in Budapest would not be discussed in any international forum, even though international sanctions offered the last dim hope of arresting Hungary's slide into single-party dictatorship. A recent convert to internationalism, Senator Arthur Vandenberg of Michigan, summed up the U.S. position: "they are parallel tragedies, but cannot have parallel treatment."[55]

The dividing line between East and West would be Austria. London had concluded that a Soviet occupation of Austria would have disastrous effects, especially on Czechoslovakia, Germany, and Italy. In Austria, Red Army units would be positioned to outflank all of Central Europe, even Italy. The British Defense Department agreed that Austria's central location on the Danube made it strategically vital to Great Britain. The Truman administration regarded Austria as a test of Anglo-American resolve to resist Soviet intimidation, listing it as an American priority along with other countries where communist takeovers seemed imminent, including

Greece, Turkey, Italy, and France. And thus the United States shored up the struggling Austrian economy, reoriented its trade toward the West, and assumed responsibility for Austria's trade deficit. Budapest was a three-hour train ride from Vienna, but in terms of geopolitical importance, the two capitals were a world apart.

Though the Senate considered severing diplomatic relations with Hungary, the State Department opposed the move, as well as the establishment of a government-in-exile.[56] Szegedy-Maszák also pushed for a termination of diplomatic relations, but he was the only Hungarian who made a serious effort to garner U.S. support. The Hungarians were not eligible for support, but they also made little effort to ask for any. Perhaps they were right: the State Department did not wish to cause problems for Hungary's newly established puppet government. The Soviets selected a Smallholder fellow traveler, Lajos Dinnyés, to replace Nagy, but his inclusion was only a crude ruse concealing the fact that the new government would be a pliant tool of the communists. In addition to his pro-Soviet leanings, the new prime minister was also in dire financial straits related to a gambling problem, a weakness of character that provided the communists with a welcome lever by which to guide his activities. In a futile gesture, the Hungarian minister in Washington joined several colleagues in other capitals in resigning from their diplomatic duties and refusing to recognize their new government. Their actions most likely pleased the new masters of Budapest; it spared them the trouble of having to make more arrests. President Tildy's son-in-law, Viktor Csornoky Bun, was an attaché in the Hungarian diplomatic mission in Cairo and later Washington. After the communists took power in 1947, he was summoned to Budapest, arrested, and sentenced to death. Tildy made no effort to save him, and his farewell letter to his spouse was not delivered. Szegedy-Maszák entertained the hope that Washington would continue to recognize him as the representative of his *country*, or at least that Schoenfeld's successor would not be sent to Budapest, but he was disappointed on both counts. "As planned," Selden Chapin proceeded to his new post. In the absence of diplomatic relations, the State Department argued, there was nothing they could do for Hungary. Still, as the Hungarian minister pointed out, diplomatic contact could have been maintained without recognizing the new government immediately. The legation could have functioned without a head of mission and the United States would still have been represented on the ACC.⁵⁷ But not even the slightest diplomatic gesture was made to censure the government the Soviets appointed in Budapest. The new Hungarian minister to the United States, Rusztem Vámbéry, scion of the brilliant orientalist Ármin Vámbéry, received his *agrément* without delay. Thus the claim of left-wing critics, that American policy was too tough on the Soviets in Eastern Europe, holds no water.

The new American minister in Budapest was a less keen observer than his cynical, well-informed predecessor. Like Schoenfeld, Chapin had a jaundiced view of the Smallholder leaders, among whom the most valuable were either under arrest or in exile by then. Although Chapin had no illusions about Moscow's intent to incorporate the country into the Soviet sphere, he was unduly optimistic in predicting that Hungary's social and economic structures would not be immediately and entirely Sovietized. Chapin thought that Hungary's lack of democratic traditions meant it would not have sufficient moral strength to resist. In addition, the Hungarians overestimated America's capabilities, even if Washington had failed to do all in its power to preserve Hungarian independence. Chapin was not the only U.S. diplomat in Eastern Europe who was appalled by Washington's unwillingness to counter the Soviets. The ambassador to Poland, Arthur Bliss Lane, resigned in protest. And yet Chapin did not link Hungarian defeatism to American inaction; he explained it as a lack of character stemming from an absence of democratic traditions, implying that Hungarians were not worthy of protection. Even so, he recommended action in the UN Security Council and a rapid ratification of the peace treaty, believing that these steps would make it harder for the Soviets to claim a legal basis for their interventions into domestic affairs. Obviously ignorant of the depth of Soviet and communist entrenchment in all positions of power, Chapin advocated economic assistance, as well as cultural and information programs, to influence the people. More in tune with present realities, he also urged the State Department to help evacuate opposition figures whose lives were in danger.⁵⁸

A diplomat far more experienced with the Soviets than Chapin, the American ambassador in Prague, Lawrence Steinhardt, was optimistic about the outlook for Czechoslovakia. At the time of Ferenc Nagy's resignation, Steinhardt still hoped that United States had not given up completely. Even in November 1947, he considered the situation in Prague different from those in the rest of Eastern Europe. In Steinhardt's view, the communists in Czechoslovakia were 80 percent patriots, and he expected the situation there to improve, if slowly. Small wonder, then, that the United States was caught off guard by the putsch in February.[59] As the historian Igor Lukes put it, the communist coup in Prague had far-reaching consequences: it weakened Washington's stature, intensified the rivalry between the United States and the Soviet Union, and contributed to the militarization of the Cold War by providing the impetus for NATO a year later.[60]

Washington seldom followed the advice that emanated from its diplomatic posts in Eastern Europe. Neither the Social Democrats nor the Smallholders were able to secure American financial support. The former were looking for American assistance in establishing a new party because the communists and their fellow travelers had hijacked their original organization. These requests were rejected on the grounds that the United States did not interfere in the internal affairs of other countries.[61] Hungary was written off by the State Department, which considered severing diplomatic relations. Eventually this possibility was discarded, lest it be construed as a lack of American interest in the plight of the Hungarian people. Appearances mattered. Hungary could also be a listening post, a setting in which to establish an intelligence network. Both the British and the Americans operated networks there, even during the war. The Americans had contacts in the upper echelons of the Hungarians' Foreign Service, intelligence, and general staff, through whom they procured data on German military activities. These same arguments would justify maintaining relations with other Soviet bloc states as well. Bulgaria, with which Washington broke off relations in 1950, would be the only exception.

Chapin continued to advocate active opposition to the Soviets in Eastern Europe and was open to any means short of a direct military clash. He was told that Hungary would not be the focus of U.S.-Soviet relations.[62] At that point, the basic Western conception of Eastern Europe had not yet changed. European stability and Soviet hegemony in Eastern Europe were not seen as contradictory conditions. It was only after 1948 that the Truman administration would start to see Soviet domination there as a threat to Western security.

THE DESTRUCTION OF AMERICAN INTERESTS IN EASTERN EUROPE

American and Soviet economic goals were incompatible. Washington wanted open doors in trade and investment, while Moscow worked to erect a self-contained economic bloc in the territories under its control. Hungary lost its most important traditional partners, Austria and Germany, as well as a flourishing trade with the United States, especially in imports. Hungarian exports were growing modestly, partly due to wartime restrictions that were still in place, but America had quickly become the largest source of Hungarian imports, largely because of the significant amount of aid it was sending. By 1949, this exchange of commodities was to plummet to a negligible level.[63] Extensive trade with the Western world was not one of Moscow's objectives. The economic agreement of August 1945 had given the Soviet Union a preponderant role in Hungary's foreign trade, the first step toward the establishment of a self-contained, Eastern European economic bloc.

The economic viability of the small states in East Central Europe had been problematic ever since the region's political map had been redrawn in the wake of the First World War. After 1918, the single market of Austria-Hungary dissolved into a number of economically vulnerable, politically hostile entities – "pauper states," as the British called them. Already in 1920, Montagu Norman, then the governor of the Bank of England, realized that economic fragmentation would lead to political strife and instability and toyed with the idea of restoring the economic unity of the Monarchy. Later, various plans for regional economic cooperation and integration were devised, but all foundered on the mutual hostility and suspicion that plagued the region, along with German intransigence. Germany eyed the former Habsburg territories as its exclusive domain, eventually filling the power vacuum in Eastern Europe and using its economic essentials for the Nazi war effort. The economic reorganization of Eastern Europe was thus a necessary measure, but few in Eastern Europe envisioned it the way the Soviets did. The USSR rapidly integrated the former Axis satellites on its peripheries into an economic empire stretching from North Korea to East Germany. The Potsdam Declaration, the terms of which were interpreted liberally, allowed Moscow to seize formerly German, Italian, and Japanese assets. In Hungary, hundreds of companies came to be fully or partially owned by a Soviet government agency, which among other things gave the Soviets unrestricted access to vital natural resources like coal, manganese, and aluminum. Simultaneously, Western-owned companies were either liquidated or gradually pushed out of business. The most effective but politically costliest method was to declare properties German assets even if their German owners' stake had been minor or nonexistent. American-, British-, French-, Austrian-, and Swiss-owned firms were taken over during this process, and diplomatic protests rarely helped. Even more drastically, the Soviets simply seized certain enterprises as war trophies. Despite a flurry of protests, the Hungarian subsidiary of General Electric was dismantled in 1945, all its machinery shipped back to the Soviet Union as spoils of war.

Some firms, on the other hand, were producing for reparation payments to the Soviet Union. These were squeezed financially but allowed to stay in business as long as they were useful. By far the largest U.S. investment in Hungary was a subsidiary of Standard Oil New Jersey, the Hungarian-American Oil Company (MAORT). Starting in the 1930s, Standard Oil had taken the lead in exploring for and exploiting oil and natural gas in Eastern Europe, and MAORT owned Hungary's largest known field, in the southwestern part of the county. Even though it was American-owned, the company had produced oil for the German war effort. Its production had reached a peak in excess of 600,000 tons in 1944. When the Germans lost the oil fields of Ploesti in Romania, Hungarian oil became their last natural source of fuel. Even though the Germans had wanted to seize the company, the Hungarian Treasury sequestered it for the duration of the war. This made it harder for the Russians to seize because it could not be construed as having been German-owned. The Soviets had expressed interest in Eastern European oil reserves as early as 1944, including Hungarian and Austrian fields. American ownership of the company would be a nuisance, but not an insurmountable obstacle to the Soviets' seizure of its output, and eventually of ownership of the company itself. The company's management would soon be accused of sabotage so that MAORT could be nationalized and integrated into the Soviet-Hungarian oil company established shortly after the war. The hapless victims were subjected to a show trial designed and staged with the intention of shattering the old professional elite by exposing its representatives as foreign spies. Their "treason" would justify severing Hungary's remaining contacts with the Western world.

Once Soviet military authorities took over oil production and refining, they refused to pay for the products. In July 1945, oversight of the company was returned to its American general manager, but by then the Communist Party was planning its nationalization. The government appointed a plenipotentiary to oversee production. István Timár, a communist colonel of the political police, was tasked with collecting compromising materials to be used against the company. Predictably, his methods would include sabotage. In order to satisfy Soviet demands for reparation deliveries, the company was obligated to increase production to a level that threatened to compromise the field. Overproduction under the Germans had already depleted the field's natural gas reserves, and though the company's management ordered a 10 percent reduction in output, it was not implemented and soon the Soviets seized control. The price the Hungarian government received for the company's deliveries did not cover its production costs. The other U.S. oil company, a subsidiary of Socony Oil, was in a similarly difficult situation. Its inventory of refined oil had been seized by the Soviets as a war trophy; it was then forced to produce at levels well below capacity, which sharply reduced its revenues.[64] Despite American protests, these oil fields remained under Soviet control. Both the Ministry of Industry and the communist-led Supreme Economic Council suggested that production levels needed to be cut to preserve the oil field, but to no avail. Lacking adequate revenue, MAORT was unable to update its equipment. Nevertheless, encouraged by the Smallholders' victory in 1945, MAORT placed an order for new machinery, but only a fraction of it ever arrived. No firm, with the exception of Soviet companies, was allowed to receive convertible currency for its products. When General Electric complained about the situation, Prime Minister Nagy assured the American legation that American economic interests would be respected, a promise he was not in a position to keep. The Ministry of Industry opined that the government was not responsible for the profits of foreign investors; "capital must take risks." The United States pointed out that these restrictions did not apply to Soviet companies, which enjoyed preferential treatment. Eventually, Standard Electric was allowed to keep 30 percent of its income in convertible currencies. It still did not receive payment for its reparation deliveries to the USSR, and unlike Soviet companies, it was not allowed to transfer dividends. The Hungarian division of Ford Motor Company was bankrupt by 1947; unable to import motor vehicles, it confined its activities to repair. Most Western companies were allowed to continue functioning only as producers of replacement parts.

Washington's position on nationalization was clarified in 1947. Revisionist historians have claimed that the United States was attempting to construct an economic empire in Eastern Europe and endangering the Soviet Union's economic interests there. In reality, Americans were unable to protect even the interests and assets they already had behind the Iron Curtain. Washington declared that the nationalization of foreign companies in Hungary would be a domestic affair, insisting only on the immediate, adequate compensation of former owners. This was hardly a robust program of economic expansion. Bilateral talks on compensation ended inconclusively, in part because the Hungarian government twisted the definition of U.S. citizenship for potential creditors. On paper, nationalization was not to involve companies whose ownership was more than half foreign, but in practice this was disregarded when the owner had been naturalized after 1931. No agreement was reached on compensation for war damages to American property, as stipulated by the armistice. By 1957, the USSR received payments of $150–180 million under a similar pretext, but the Hungarian government declined to honor any of its obligations to the United States, including American financial claims related to the land reform of 1945. Washington, in return, halted the restitution of Hungarian property.

ANTI-AMERICAN SHOW TRIALS

In 1948, a state supervisor was appointed to oversee MAORT. The company's managers were accused of being "agents of imperialism" and of deliberately sabotaging exploration for new oil reserves. In September, the government confiscated the company's properties and took over its management, allegedly to curb sabotage and to "secure normal production." Simultaneously, the political police took MAORT's American managers,

Paul Ruedemann and George Bannantine, into custody. The head of the political police, Gábor Péter, attended the arrest, which was not without difficulty: it was reported that an "American of huge stature" appeared on the scene and "threw one of the detectives a distance of three meters." The American version of the same event makes no mention of an altercation, recounting only that a pistol was aimed at a legation employee and that the two individuals had been taken away in handcuffs. The participation of Péter, a slow-witted psychopath who took personal pleasure in torturing his helpless victims, underscored the political significance of the arrest; by that point, he was one of the most powerful members of the country's political establishment. Foreign Minister László Rajk, whom the State Department would later mistakenly identify as a "national communist," informed the U.S. diplomatic mission that they had been taken into custody because MAORT's Hungarian managers had confessed to having sabotaged MAORT's production at "the instruction of and with the active participation of the two Americans" in order that "the Hungarian state receive less oil." Rajk pointed out that the Americans had confessed to acting on the instructions of their superiors at Standard Oil. Rajk refused to disclose where they were being held and violated diplomatic norms by refusing to allow the American consul to see them. Repressive measures, like this isolation from the outside world, were typical of the Stalinists' treatment of their victims.

The proceedings against MAORT, which fused the motive of class struggle with anti-Americanism, revealed that the Stalinist machinery of repression was in place even before the one-party dictatorship had been officially installed. Preparations for the takeover, including arrests and the scripting of bourgeois sabotage trials, had started much earlier. MAORT's former president and director, the geologist Simon Papp, had been arrested the month before, along with other Hungarian members of the company's management. One person committed suicide rather than go into custody. Under duress, Papp confessed that he had wanted to minimize production from the beginning because he had not wanted to produce for the Russians. Ruedemann, he claimed, wanted to see a reduction of oil output in Hungary because it "was in the United States' political and national interest." Bannantine affirmed that he had received instructions from Standard Oil to cut Hungarian production for political reasons, given that "in the future Hungary might participate in a new world war." He also admitted to having caused more harm to the Hungarian economy than natural fluctuations in oil production would have. Ruedemann confessed that he had intended to cut production, but denied having given instructions to that effect. He also denied Papp's claim that they had intentionally chosen test drilling spots where no oil deposits could be expected.

In response to the arrests, the United States suspended the restitution talks, threatened to close the Hungarian consulates in New York and Cleveland, and considered banning American citizens from Hungary. It mattered little; the two Americans were soon released and expelled. Both withdrew their confessions as soon as they reached safety, claiming that they had offered them under duress. The Hungarians were sentenced at a political show trial that forced them to confess to acts they did not commit and to claim they saw events that had never happened. Papp was condemned to death, a sentence later commuted to life in prison. He was forced to work in captivity, helping Soviet experts find new oil deposits until he was amnestied in 1955. His trial lacked any basis in fact. The communist-led Supreme Economic Council had advocated the reduction of output "as an unavoidable necessity" to save the oil field from destruction and suggested that domestic and international obligations could be met despite a 10 percent curtailment. This report had been sent to the communist leadership. Moreover, even the Communist Party members at MAORT had failed to notice any signs of sabotage. Rákosi admitted as much at a meeting of the Political Committee: "party members kept repeating that there was no sabotage and that the constant plummeting of production was justified from the national economy's perspective." Communist Party membership was no guarantee for immunity. Geologist György Kertay, MAORT's Communist Party secretary, was also arrested, even though he denied the possibility of sabotage. Sabotage did not have to be proven; it was taken for granted, as was the Americans' role in it. Westerners, bourgeois managers, and experts were presumed to be working together to undermine the new regime. Their alleged deeds were used as pretexts for getting rid of them. Even before Ruedemann and Bannantine were arrested, Papp's interrogation officer reported to Rákosi that "after sabotage is proven there will be no legal obstacle to MAORT's nationalization."[65] The colonel of the political police was aware that the proceedings served political purposes. Besides extracting evidence to be used against the company, Papp's interrogators also tried to force him to divulge information about new oil deposits Soviet experts had failed to find. The Communist Party, renamed Hungarian Workers' Party (HWP), wanted the judicial procedure to be wrapped up within a month so they could proceed with nationalization and the expropriation of the company's oil concession. The verdict, of course, was ready before the trial began.

This was only the beginning of a series of Stalinist trials aimed at political and economic crimes like bourgeois sabotage. The deputy director of IT&T in Hungary, an MIT graduate named Robert Vogeler, was taken into custody in November 1949 as he tried to cross the border into Austria. This, along with the subsequent arrest in Budapest of Israel Jacobsen, a representative of the Jewish relief agency JOINT, prompted the State Department to advise American citizens that their safety could no longer be guaranteed in Hungary and to leave at once. Vogeler, whose memoir recounts his torment, would not get away as easily as Ruedemann and Bannantine. After having a confession extracted from him, he was convicted of espionage and received fifteen years. His Hungarian codefendants, Zoltán Radó and Imre Geiger, were convicted of Trotskyism and treason and executed. The proceedings served as a pretext for nationalizing the company and as an opportunity to unmask "the mean and predatory nature of imperialism"[66] and its "bourgeois hirelings," like members of the former ruling elite, aristocrats, Jews, Germans, and foreigners. By demonstrating that a wide array of "hostile" elements would be mercilessly rooted out, these masquerades intimidated society. Ultimately, though, this trial was intended to show that foreign companies were little more than nests of spies serving no useful purpose. Isolation from the "hostile" West, according to this logic, was in the country's interest, and compliance with this new political system was achieved through the institutionalization of state terror.

Unlike MAORT's, General Electric's fate may not have been a foregone conclusion. It had signed an agreement that would allow it to survive in exchange for its sale of modern telecommunications and airport equipment to Hungary. The State Department, however, vetoed the agreement. Arrests followed;[67] Vogeler confessed to all charges, including espionage, the collection of intelligence related to Hungarian oil, gas, and uranium deposits, as well as the smuggling of Romanian officials into Austria. His confessions sounded absurd that the U.S. press speculated that he had been given drugs. Vogeler, like the other victims of the political police, was isolated from the outside world, denied contact with the American consul, and refused the right to hire his own lawyer. As the State Department reminded the Hungarian Foreign Ministry, even the National Socialists had allowed the Bulgarian communist Dimitrov to hire a lawyer for his trial in 1935. Though Vogeler played his part in the trial flawlessly, he fared worse than Ruedemann and Bannantine. The legation worked to get him released after the trial, but this time Rákosi insisted on political concessions including the return of the Crown of Saint Stephen, a relic that had been seized by U.S. authorities in the last days of the war in Austria, where it had been taken by Crown Guards to save it from the Russians. Vogeler would not be released until 1951, but his imprisonment served little useful purpose. In return for his release, the United States merely canceled measures that had been put into effect against Hungary *because of* Vogeler's incarceration. They met only one of Rákosi's further demands – changing the wavelength of Radio Free Europe's Hungarian broadcast,[68] which did nothing to curb RFE's influence. Although it is easy to explain why Vogeler was arrested, it is harder to understand his not having been released after sentencing. On this count, Hungarian sources are silent.

Vogeler later published the tale of his sufferings in Budapest, a memoir that confirmed the Cold War narrative of a struggle between good and evil. The arrest of Cardinal József Mindszenty on Christmas Day 1948 also reaffirmed the Americans' image of Stalinism as an evil system. The State Department expressed outrage and disgust, but its harsh rhetoric was not accompanied by action. The president was advised not to intervene in the case of a Roman Catholic primate for whom nothing could be done.[69] Mindszenty was charged with an absurd range of crimes including treason, conspiracy, espionage, and currency speculation. The communists implicated the American minister Selden Chapin in these alleged crimes and declared him persona non grata.

The historian Geir Lundestad has argued that between 1945 and 1947, Washington was encroaching on the other power's sphere of influence. A universalist concept of foreign policy had led the United States to assume obligations across a large portion of the globe. Although the United States had no imperialist designs on Eastern Europe (as some experts have claimed), American interference was too pronounced for Moscow to overlook. Inadvertently, Lundestad has argued, Washington pushed the Soviet Union to dominate its adjacent states without having any means to offset Soviet policies there. The best course would have been to take Kennan's advice and allow Soviet ambitions to flow freely.[70] Others have held the Marshall Plan responsible for the communists' seizure of power in Hungary, which is alleged not to have been "planned" for another ten or fifteen years. Eastern European archives had not yet been opened, however, at the time these books were written. To uphold the argument that the Soviets' seizure of power was a reaction to American policies requires one to overlook a large body of documentary evidence[71] suggesting that Hungary became the Soviet Union's exclusive political, military, and economic space immediately after it was conquered. Washington had no real influence there at all. As Communist Party leader Mátyás Rákosi explained in May 1946, the relative moderation of the communist takeover had lasted only until the peace treaties had been signed. After that, the "liberation of the proletariat," also known as the "dictatorship of the proletariat," was given a green light.[72] Recently, a Polish historian has concluded that Poland and Czechoslovakia lost their independence because the United States did not allow the more assertive British line to prevail. Americans had little interest in Eastern Europe and thus pursued a conciliatory line, a theory that directly contradicts the claims of generations of Western historians. Thus, as this line of thinking goes, the weaker British were unable to win American support for their proposals, including the democratization of the Lublin government and the maintenance of U.S. occupation troops in parts of Germany that had been assigned to the Soviet zone.[73] It is hard to imagine that political conditions like these could have been set at a time when the Red Army was still in a death struggle on the eastern front. The German Army had been capable of launching a major counteroffensive in western Hungary as late as March 1945. It also stretches the imagination to think that a British-Czechoslovak treaty, or the international observation of a Polish election, could have changed the outcome. Decisions about Eastern Europe were to be made in Moscow alone, without regard to what Washington did or did not do.

3

Rollback

The year 1948 saw a basic shift in American policymakers' attitudes toward Soviet control of European territory. The idea of peaceful cooperation, nurtured up to then by many British and American politicians and diplomats, was shattered. The last Eastern European democracy, Czechoslovakia, had been amalgamated into the Soviet camp and closed off, although, almost miraculously, Finland was released from Moscow's grasp. Washington no longer saw Soviet control as a stabilizing factor in Eastern Europe. Instead, the restoration of independent states and the rollback of Soviet military power became the prerequisites of a secure and lasting continental peace. The goal thenceforth would be to destabilize the communist regimes of Eastern Europe in the hope of depriving the Soviets of reliable launching pads for a war against the West. The principles of national independence in Eastern Europe and Western security were now mutually reinforcing. This was a clear break with the policy London and Washington had pursued at least as far back as 1942, which was to divide the continent into Soviet and Western spheres of influence.[1]

In themselves, the nations of Eastern Europe were of secondary importance. Their significance derived from their status as the Soviet Union's "political and military allies" and their effective "[extension of] Soviet power to the heart of Europe." Washington aimed to check Soviet influence over these lands and to reduce Moscow's control to a "normal" level. In 1948, the USSR ostracized Yugoslavia from its bloc of fraternal nations, thus pitting "the peoples' democracies" against a new enemy, Belgrade. The Soviets imposed an economic blockade and staged military exercises that led to skirmishes on the Hungarian-Yugoslav border. After a brief period of hesitation, the United States decided to "keep Tito afloat" by providing economic and military aid to the southern Slav state, helping to deny the Soviets complete hegemony in the Balkans. American officials considered Tito a "national communist" who had broken with the Soviets in order to pursue a domestically directed, anti-Soviet variant of socialism. László Rajk's show trial in Budapest was also misunderstood. Rajk, though not among the communist leaders who had returned from Moscow, was a staunch Stalinist. This led observers to believe that the Soviets had disposed of him because he represented a "nationalist" alternative to the prevailing slavishly pro-Soviet line. Therefore, American officials chose to promote "national communist deviation" as a method of undermining the Sovietized governments of Eastern Europe. In the summer of 1950, the National Security Council (NSC) authorized practically all forms of clandestine warfare against the Soviet bloc. The Truman administration went beyond its publicly espoused policy of containment in envisioning the liberation of the Soviet Union's "satellites."

The Korean War was to change America's foreign and security policies. Stalin supported Kim Il Sung's revolutionary war to insulate the Soviet Union from a perceived imperialist threat on the Korean peninsula. Instead of more security, he ended up with less: the United States responded by launching a crippling arms race that would eventually contribute to the downfall of the Soviet empire. Viewed as an arena in which Stalin was pursuing a quest for world mastery, Eastern Europe gained prominence. The satellites gave Moscow a forward position from which to put pressure on, and possibly even attack, the West, and the Eastern Europeans' rapidly growing military might only added to the Soviet threat. In January 1950, the Central Intelligence Agency (CIA) estimated that the combined military forces of Hungary, Romania, and Bulgaria numbered 346,000 troops,[2] and after 1951, military preparations in the Eastern bloc began to intensify. Paul Nitze, who took over from George F. Kennan in leading the State Department's policy planning staff, was convinced that the USSR was animated by a fanatical creed and was striving for world domination.

Some in his office feared that the Soviets would be able to launch an overpowering attack by 1954.

In intensifying psychological and economic warfare in Eastern Europe, U.S. officials encouraged unrest in strategically important satellites to impede the consolidation of their leadership. The consequences hardly mattered, because war with the Soviets seemed inevitable. Stalin, too, assumed a military conflict between the two blocs, possibly as soon as 1953, the year he would die. In January 1951, Stalin instructed the satellites to prepare for war. Their economies were militarized and their industrial production raised to absurd levels, causing huge economic distortions and social dislocations. Moscow and its satellites would both pay a price: the frantic heavy industrialization of this military buildup virtually destroyed other segments of the economy. Shortages of food and consumer goods caused standards of living to drop at a rate unprecedented in peacetime, and the Soviets responded to the resultant revolutionary unrest with a campaign of terror that would shake the foundations of their Eastern European empire.

American observers were perplexed and appalled by the show trials of Cardinal Mindszenty and László Rajk. Nathaniel Davis, the U.S. minister in Budapest, was one of the very few who understood the hidden truth behind these trials. Rajk, he reported, spoke as if he had learned his lines by heart. Behind the Iron Curtain, the discourse sounded increasingly Orwellian; honest declarations, even in sworn testimony, were unwelcome in public spaces.

By the time the American businessman Robert Vogeler was finally released (escorted to the Austrian border in a black Chevrolet sedan), Hungarian-American relations had already hit rock bottom. The closed Hungarian consulates had been reopened only to be closed again in 1952. In retaliation for America's having put them on the spot for human rights abuses, the Hungarians sought and received Moscow's permission to close the American library in Budapest, then barred the American legation from carrying out any information activities. The last, tiny American foothold was thus eliminated. Since their physical safety could not be guaranteed, Americans were forbidden from visiting Hungary. Trade declined from $8 million in 1948 to a mere $100,000 in 1951. By then, Stalin had announced that exchanges with the "capitalist" world would be impermissible, even though the Soviet economy was unable to compensate the satellites for the loss of Western trade.

Hostilities escalated. U.S. authorities barred the shipment of 356 trucks the Hungarians had bought in the American zone of West Germany; the Hungarians protested against an alleged plot to kill a member of their legation in Washington; both sides' diplomats were expelled. A few days after Stalin revealed his expectation that war would break out by 1953, the Hungarian government limited American officials' travel to an eighteen-mile radius around Budapest; Washington soon reciprocated. On November 19, 1951, a U.S. military aircraft flew into Hungarian airspace and was forced to land by Soviet fighter jets. Its crew was taken into custody and charged with espionage, an accusation available documents cannot confirm. After an inconclusive exchange of diplomatic notes, the Hungarian government announced that the crew would stand trial. The day after Christmas, Washington agreed to pay the Hungarians a "fine" ("ransom," the United States called it) for the release of the defendants, who finally returned home in May 1952. The amount was added to the list of American financial claims against Hungary, which would be settled in 1973.

In February 1953, the U.S. Senate discussed a motion to sever diplomatic relations with Hungary and Czechoslovakia. From May of that year, U.S. passports were not valid for the Soviet bloc without the preapproval of the State Department. Relations with other satellites, including Romania and Czechoslovakia, deteriorated similarly. Shortly after Vogeler's release, Czechoslovakian security agents arrested the Associated Press correspondent in Prague, William Oatis. The Pentagon pushed for a break in diplomatic relations, but the State Department insisted on maintaining them on the grounds that Prague was an important observation post.[3] Even Stalin's death in March 1953 failed to improve the situation; U.S. passports continued to be invalid for Eastern Europe without State Department consent.

Passive steps like this would not suffice. Communism in Eastern Europe had to be strangled, or at least destabilized. Beyond the morally outrageous human rights abuses behind the iron curtain, for which the Soviets had been indicted by the UN, the Soviet domination of Eastern Europe posed an unacceptable security threat to the West. Some interpret communism as a distorted attempt at modernization, an illustration of the historical metaphor of "catching up" with the developed West. But the economic blockade put into place after 1947 to contain the Soviets would deprive the Soviet satellites of the financial and technological resources they would need to do that "catching up."

ECONOMIC WARFARE

Even though the United States had been publicly proclaiming the principle of free trade since at least 1948, it also introduced a series of severe restrictions on trade with Eastern Europe,[4] amounting to an economic blockade. These measures were designed to diminish the military capabilities of the Soviet Union and to impede the consolidation of the communist regimes sustained by Moscow. It was also conjectured that the Soviets would not be able to furnish their allies with substitutes for Western consumer products and that these shortages would increase tensions within the communist camp.[5] High hopes were attached to fomenting discord between Moscow and its allies, and these restrictive measures caused significant tension within the western group of states. Washington's allies, especially the French, felt they were being deprived of business opportunities and were incurring more losses than the United States, whose trade with the nations of the Soviet bloc had always been negligible. Paradoxically, the embargo meshed with Soviet interests. Moscow had prescribed a policy of economic isolation for the satellites, banning all trade with the Western world to preclude the infiltration of hostile influences. As it soon turned out, though, the satellites could not do without Western European trade, and the policy of economic autarchy was rescinded.

Averell Harriman, who as ambassador to Moscow had been an enthusiastic supporter of expanding trade relations with the Soviet Union, was the first to propose trade sanctions against the Soviet bloc. In a letter to the National Security Council, Harriman argued that by rejecting the European Recovery Plan, Moscow and its satellites were hindering Europe's rehabilitation and therefore posed a threat to U.S. security and to world peace. His solution to the problem was to suspend shipments to the Soviets and their satellites of any commodity in critically short supply in the United States or that might be of use to the Red Army.[6] This was to be done without overt discrimination against Eastern Europe. To hinder the growth of the Soviets' military capabilities, Congress pushed for the stringent application of trade controls, passing two amendments to this effect in 1951. A coordinating committee (CoCom) was established to compile a list of commodities to be embargoed by the European allies. Military and financial aid would be suspended for any country that violated the embargo, although in practice this sanction was never applied. For security reasons, the Pentagon and the Department of Commerce supported stringent measures, while the State Department argued for a more liberal approach. A significant reduction of East-West trade would hamper economic reconstruction in Western Europe as well, making it more susceptible to Soviet subversion. Countries receiving Marshall Plan aid had exchanged $1.5 billion worth of goods with Soviet-controlled nations. A drastic curtailment of this trade could mean diverting Marshall Plan dollars toward commodities that were no longer available from behind the Iron Curtain because of the trade blockade. This was counterproductive since the Marshall Plan was intended in part to alleviate the shortage of dollars. It seemed the embargo might do more harm than good.[7]

Thus Secretary of State Marshall wanted the trade embargo to accommodate conflicting principles: it needed to curtail the shipment of strategic commodities to the Soviet zone without hampering the normal flow of East-West trade or the American import market for rare metals from the Soviet Union.[8] To prevent a damaging, all-out economic war, export licenses were approved on an individual basis and commodities were ranked according to military and strategic significance.

Government agencies continued to differ on the most efficient way to implement the economic blockade, and the question of whether to impose this policy on allies lingered throughout the 1950s. The Joint Chiefs of Staff (JCS) argued that an "economic iron curtain" would paralyze the Soviet economy within five to ten years.[9] Secretary of Commerce Charles Sawyer was eager to get the Europeans involved, fearing that Western European businesses would be at an advantage over their American counterparts if U.S. restrictions were more stringent than the ones under which Europeans operated. He was supported by business representatives who saw their overseas competitors getting deals from which they had been excluded.

The Korean War occasioned a review of existing policies. Some agencies, including the Department of Defense, wanted to see national security determine priorities for trade policy.[10] The National Security Council opined that the trade restrictions had already significantly hampered the growth of the Soviets' military capabilities. In addition, the European allies were on their way to economic recovery and were therefore less dependent on East-West trade. Thus more radical measures could be incorporated into the blockade of the Soviet zone.[11] The Canon Amendment, passed in September 1950, barred economic assistance to countries that traded with the Soviet Union as long as U.S. troops were fighting in Korea. From 1951, all exports to the Soviet bloc required a license, though shortly after the Korean War ended, the National Security Council asserted that a Soviet-American war was no longer imminent and recommended the relaxation of trade controls.[12]

Gradually, the State Department's more moderate approach gained the upper hand. Western economic interests were accorded more significance, and fewer illusions were harbored about the ability of trade controls to influence Soviet behavior. The NSC concluded that the Soviet economy was becoming less reliant on external resources. A 1954 CIA appraisal suggested that a relaxation of controls would be of some small benefit to the Soviet military but would have little impact on economic growth behind the Iron Curtain. On the other hand, a partial relaxation of controls could improve relations within the Western world; perhaps the allies would adhere to the controls with more enthusiasm.[13] President Eisenhower's Foreign Policy Commission recommended strengthening the Western economies by allowing East-West trade in peaceful goods. The obstruction of such trade had led to an increasing reliance on American aid.[14]

After his election, President Eisenhower followed the State Department's approach and decided to relax the controls.[15] He did so partly because the American pressure for stringent controls had caused tension within the alliance and partly because he was not convinced the policy was working. Rather, he thought that the satellites could be lured away from the Soviet Union with the promise of more trade. As a weapon, trade could be used in various ways. In July 1953, the president decreed a "gradual and moderate" relaxation of trade controls. As a result, a number of commodities were taken off the U.S. and CoCom lists. The JCS opposed the president's decision because they thought it too difficult to draw a line between strategic and nonstrategic items. They also believed the embargo was causing bottlenecks in Soviet production.[16] It took a while for Eisenhower's new approach to be implemented. In 1956, the National Security Council again called on Congress to relax trade controls for the nations of the Soviet bloc and to confer most-favored-nation status on them.[17]

If the implementation of the president's new directive was slow and gradual, it was also ill-timed. In 1954, the Soviet Union reduced its exports of raw materials to Eastern Europe, which then grew increasingly dependent on Western sources. The Council for Mutual Economic Assistance (Comecon) was forced to rescind its policy of self-reliance and authorize member nations who "were out to do so themselves" to intensify their trade relations with capitalist states. The ruling only codified what was already happening. Hungary's economic dictator, Ernő Gerő, had already announced in 1952 that trade with the Western world was a necessity. The Hungarian legation in Washington received instructions to find ways of increasing trade with the United States and to determine which "circles" would need to be won over for this cause.[18]

Using trade as a weapon in the president's sense was more easily said than done. American government agencies did not see eye-to-eye about how, or even whether, to implement the new guidelines. Negotiations with Poland started in 1957. Due to a chronic shortage of convertible currency and a lack of products marketable to the United States, communist countries needed commodity credit to purchase American goods. Hungary was already running a high trade deficit; its minister of finance had ordered a drastic curtailment of Western imports, with little success.[19] The situation worsened when the Soviet Union drastically cut its shipments of raw materials. If Hungary had not made up the difference with imports from the "capitalist" world,[20] its heavy industry and the economy based on it could have collapsed.

The State Department considered barter arrangements for raw materials,[21] which might have worked for Hungary. It had large deposits of bauxite and uranium, but the Soviet Union was the only country allowed to buy them. Hungarian products were increasingly hard to sell on

Western markets because they were outdated and of low quality. In the course of one year, 1.7 billion forints' worth of items were returned from Austria, Belgium, Holland, Sweden, and Switzerland because of quality issues. Certain Hungarian goods were so shoddy even the Soviets returned them.[22]

Trade controls impeded the modernization of production, but this was only a part of a large and intractable problem with which all centralized, command economies struggle. In 1955, Hungary attempted to purchase wheat and cotton from the United States, but because of the tense relations between the two countries and the outstanding American financial claims, it could not secure the credit it needed to do so. Under American pressure, West Germany also rejected a similar Hungarian deal.[23]

There was no agreement in Washington about the effectiveness of trade controls. According to one view, the embargo limited the economic and military potential of the Soviet bloc; restrictions on technology transfers forced the Soviets to use largely obsolete equipment and production methods. Even so, trade controls would not be enough to put an end to Soviet rule in Eastern Europe.[24] Clearly, the system was not working as intended. Information from Budapest suggested that the Hungarian economy was suffering greatly from the lack of modern technology but remained operational at least partly because Hungary had been able to circumvent trade controls.[25] One way of doing so was to establish trading companies abroad whose purpose was to acquire listed goods and re-export them to Hungary.[26] Rákosi revealed that profit motives had led U.S. allies to assist Hungary in defying the embargo.[27] Israel was supplying ball bearings in return for Jewish emigration on the basis of a head quota, and Sweden had been willing to supply them as well. The American embassy in Vienna reported that Austria, Finland, and Egypt were the main routes by which Hungary was circumventing the trade controls and acquiring listed commodities.[28] France also sold Hungary ball bearings and steel alloys as part of a Franco-Hungarian trade agreement.[29] Romania was able to procure Jeeps by having them shipped to Syria, from where they were taken in Italian vessels to the Romanian port of Costanza.[30]

While they were insufficient to overthrow the communist system, the punitive economic measures implemented in the 1950s did cause serious and lasting harm to the Hungarian economy. In theory, a perfect blockade might be capable of toppling a regime, but in practice a perfect blockade was impossible. U.S. allies chafed under the trade restrictions and were perfectly willing to profit from circumventing them, but this does not mean the embargo was a wholly useless tool. On one occasion, during a talk about the alleged benefits of the embargo to socialist states, Rákosi claimed that it had spurred economic growth by encouraging cooperation among the Comecon states and wiser exploitation of domestic resources.[31] In reality, as Lavrenty Beria acknowledged, the Comecon was not working at all and trade controls were causing serious harm.[32] Severe shortages were registered in products badly needed by the country's military and heavy industries, such as ball bearing gauges, spiral drills, instruments to measure the hardness of steel, and the like.[33] Ernő Gerő, the man in charge of the Hungarian economy, acknowledged that the country was unable to sell abroad because its products were obsolete and shoddy. To earn badly needed hard currency, the government was forced to sell agricultural goods like wheat, even though they were in short supply due to the collectivization drive and an attendant, ideologically motivated persecution of the peasantry. The resultant shortage of food and the low quality and short supply of consumer goods intensified popular dissatisfaction. Western imports resulted in a trade imbalance and depleted the country's gold reserves. This increasing pressure on the national economy led to tensions with Moscow. The Soviet leadership was growing wary of Hungary's indebtedness to the capitalist world, which it saw as heightening the bloc's vulnerability to unwanted foreign influence.[34] Later, in the 1980s, Hungarian leaders acknowledged that the denial of advanced technology had caused immense harm to the Hungarian economy and that they had made desperate efforts to get themselves exempted from at least some of the American coordinating committee's restrictions.

While not unsuccessful, the U.S. trade embargo raised questions. Besides causing hardship to the ruling parties, trade restrictions also added to the suffering of populations already facing immense hardships. Restricted items included new medications such as Sabin drops and penicillin. Grain shortages resulting from industrialization and persecution could have been alleviated by selling wheat. And while the CIA fed undernourished East Germans in 1953, some former victims of Nazism were left to fend for themselves, denied humanitarian food aid as part of a quixotic effort to defeat communism through trade restrictions.

THE STRUGGLE FOR HEARTS AND MINDS

In the Cold War, propaganda was a weapon of crucial importance. In the interwar period, when it first gained prominence, it was still regarded as a subsidiary of military operations. After the war, the term came to cover all activities meant to influence public opinion in the service of foreign policy goals. It encompassed traditional political propaganda, economic aid, cultural exchange programs, and clandestine activities including covert warfare.[35] The "struggle for hearts and minds" was also meant for Americans. U.S. media presented most social, cultural, and political developments through the prism of the crusade against communism, an ideology that was portrayed as an infectious disease that threatened the foundations of American culture.[36] In this struggle between good and evil, Americans were asked to help the victims of communism. The Iron Curtain Refugee Campaign sent donations to Eastern Europe.[37] The Crusade for Freedom, a movement founded in 1950 to protect Western values by condemning communist expansion, highlighted the dangers looming over the United States. It sought to awaken the defensive reflexes of American messianism, self-determination, and freedom,[38] to strengthen American patriotism and anticommunism, and to frame the Cold War as a struggle to liberate the "captive peoples" of Eastern Europe.[39] As Gordon Gray, president of the Psychological Strategy Board, put it, psychological warfare channeled all available resources into the service of U.S. foreign policy.[40] Although the home front was important for mustering the nation's resources and support for the long haul ahead, the central theater of combat in America's virtual war against communism and Soviet expansion was Eastern Europe.

Though the communist regimes combined forces against the penetration of hostile propaganda, they were waging a losing battle. After the consolidation of the communist regimes in 1948, wireless sets capable of receiving foreign signals were taken off the market. People risked punishment by listening to Western broadcasts on old wireless sets, usually the same ones they had used during the war to tune in to alternatives to Nazi propaganda. The unabashed aim of these broadcasts was to increase Western security by destabilizing the governments behind the Iron Curtain. John Foster Dulles explained that Eastern Europe was to be liberated without the use of force. The Soviet Union was overextended, thus its empire could be brought down by exposing its latent weaknesses. By carrying a message of truth and hope, as well as an American commitment to freedom, the United States would be able to weaken the Soviet Union to the extent that Eastern Europe could regain its independence.[41] As with economic warfare, the high hopes attached to psychological warfare were not realized. Nevertheless, Eastern European regimes were to put great effort into combating subversive propaganda.

For people living under Stalinist dictatorships, Western radio broadcasts were the sole link to the world beyond the Iron Curtain. As the Soviet Union imposed its political system on Eastern Europe, it applied one rule to the region's dealings with the allegedly hostile outside world: borders were sealed. The resultant thirst for alternative sources of information provided American propagandists with an opportunity to target disparate social groups that agreed on one thing only: the rejection of domination by foreign communists. The barrage of words aimed to nurture a spirit of protest. Communist subjects were encouraged to resist their governments in hopes of rendering Moscow's satellites unreliable in case of war. The U.S. legation in Budapest cautioned that it would be impossible to create a resistance movement capable of toppling the Hungarian regime in the "near future."[42] Nevertheless, schemes to paralyze communist governments by means of nonviolent mass action were discussed. All forms of resistance were to be supported: sabotage, work slowdowns, passive resistance, embarrassing demands, overburdening the bureaucratic machinery, and any other kind of activity that could be carried out without incurring grave personal risk.[43] The question was whether grave personal risk could be avoided in a region where "crimes" like collecting enemy leaflets and hoarding a few loaves of bread were punishable by imprisonment.

Shortly before the 1956 revolution, the U.S. chargé in Budapest wondered whether the Hungarian people would be able to offer any meaningful resistance to a wholly unpopular government without external assistance. He believed that a recommendation for mass action could be worked out abroad and then communicated to millions of people within a short time. It would be possible to coordinate mass action (even in the era before Facebook) without having to make direct contact with the participants, thus minimizing the risk to individuals. "Trivial" acts that could be undertaken by anyone – throwing away torn pieces of paper, for instance – were preferred. If thousands of bits of paper were to appear in the streets daily as proof of the people's hatred of the system, the prestige and perhaps even the stability of the regime could be upset. Spencer N. Barnes, the American chargé in Budapest, recommended similar "attacks" on the economy and the bureaucracy. One idea was for Hungarians to flood government offices with thousands of calls, thus obstructing the work of the government and revealing their discontent[44] – a plan that obviously did not take into account the almost total lack of private phone lines in Hungary. Barnes advocated caution in the implementation of such plans; nevertheless, some of his recommendations reveal the more reckless side of psywar.

Efforts to sow discontent fell on fertile ground. America was highly popular. In 1945, Hungarians (or a vast majority of them, at least) had hoped to be liberated by American or British troops, and many never lost faith that it would happen someday. The American legation's Buick Century was surrounded by large crowds of admirers whenever it appeared in the streets of Budapest, and the crowd sometimes grew so large that the traffic police needed to step in.[45] In the town of Cegléd, the local cooperative decided to sell children's clothing that had belonged to the Jewish congregation and had been lying in a local warehouse for almost a decade. A rumor, that the clothes had in fact been sent by the Americans for victims of the 1954 flood and still had the original U.S. labels in them, spread like wildfire. A crowd stampeded the cooperative and shattered windows to get hold of the clothing. The tumult forced the local party secretary to suspend the sale for having "occasioned hostile propaganda and agitation."[46] American movies were equally popular, which did not escape the attention of the Soviet ambassador, Yevgeny Kiselev, who complained that while Soviet movies were playing in front of half-empty houses, U.S. pictures were attracting crowds. Rákosi was forced to say that the Soviets should learn to make better movies. Shortly before the revolution, Barnes organized a reception for an American film industry delegation headed by the chief of Paramount Pictures. The pleasant evening expected by the guests from the Hungarian Foreign Ministry was "ruined" by an embarrassing incident. Barnes approached deputy foreign minister Károly Szarka on behalf of workers from the Ministry of People's Education, who hoped to be allowed to attend the screenings the Americans had organized. After soliciting Barnes' intervention, the ministry workers were reported to have "grouped together" to await a reply.[47]

Radio broadcasts were most efficient in influencing foreign populations. They could manipulate religious and nationalist sentiments, point out grievances, and hold out hope that the communist regimes would eventually disappear. Concerns that nationalism was a potentially destructive force, which would later mitigate some anticommunist propaganda, had not yet arisen. Radio broadcasts were not supposed to promise the overthrow of communist governments or of American intervention for this purpose. The legal basis for the anticommunist campaign was provided by the 1948 Smith-Mundt Act. Both Radio Free Europe (RFE) and the Voice of America (VOA) were instructed to use harsh anti-Soviet language; RFE was assigned the mission of contributing to the liberation of the nations behind the Iron Curtain.[48] Its messages were supposed to confirm that the "tide of Soviet imperialism" would be turned back and that there could be no lasting peace until the fate of Eastern Europe had been resolved. None of this was to be construed as a promise of military intervention.[49] The Hungarian Revolution of 1956 would show that the line between keeping hope alive and raising unjustified expectations was a fine one. Instructions to broadcasters were ambiguous, making it possible for some to go too far. Some Hungarians believed that liberation was coming and tended to interpret every allusion to freedom as a pledge that it would happen soon. Many did not find the broadcasts anticommunist enough. Thus, as liberation continued not to materialize, some began to hold the American government and its radio stations responsible.[50] Some went so far as to hope that the United States would liberate their country even at the price of war. A nineteen-year-old who fled Hungary in 1956 claimed the Hungarians were aware that Western intervention would mean war, and although they were certainly conscious of war's horrors, he insisted they preferred them to "slavery." They feared that the United States had accepted their satellite status and that only the Americans could force the Russians to compromise.⁵¹ Another refugee claimed that the people were eagerly listening to Western and particularly American news and were still hoping for a war, which they thought the Americans would win.⁵²

It is hard to tell how widespread this sentiment was. A survey conducted in 1957 revealed that before the revolution, half of a group of 620 refugees headed to the United States had expected the Americans to intervene. Many of those who had been charged by the security police with antigovernment conspiracy confessed that their acts had been inspired by foreign radio programs, although these records need to be handled with a great deal of caution. Béla Halász, who had been accused of spying, told his interrogator that he and his group believed "the news and propaganda from imperialist radios and expected a regime change."⁵³ In 1951, state security agents had arrested an unskilled worker called Győző Flossmann, who declared that he had listened to Western radio stations regularly and "particularly to the Voice of Radio Free Europe [sic]."⁵⁴ Based on the programs he heard, he had concluded that there would be a war and that the Americans would occupy Hungary. An associate of his claimed they were working to expand their conspiracy, to awaken the country with explosions, and to paralyze industrial production with terrorist acts when the war broke out. In another alleged plot, a Catholic priest planned to install a new government with American military aid.⁵⁵

These "conspirators" – it is often hard to separate facts from the fictions contrived by the political police – often worked out elaborate plans to attack their government with American help. Kálmán Horváth was accused of organizing a plot on behalf of a right-wing émigré Hungarian military organization, the MHBK, which was then cooperating with U. S. military intelligence and the West German spy agency known as the Gehlen organization.⁵⁶ Horváth was firmly convinced that Hungary would be invaded by forces deployed from the Federal Republic of Germany and that his organization would be supplied by airlift with arms, clothing, and other military equipment. During his interrogation, he claimed that American propaganda had led him to believe that a regime change was imminent.⁵⁷ Encouraged by RFE, Gedeon Ráth's group distributed flyers and tried to acquire arms with which to support the troops they hoped would invade.

In May 1950, Ráth had expected to receive military equipment from "Tito" or the Americans, to launch an overthrow of the existing regime, and to support Western occupation troops.[58]

The Hungarian authorities were highly concerned about the influence of RFE and the VOA over the population. In his indictment speech at the Flossmann trial, Judge Vilmos Olti, a former national socialist, accused American propaganda of stirring up panic and counterrevolution, of circulating the false news that war would soon break out, that U.S. troops would occupy Hungary, and that the old regime would be restored.[59] Some surely believed the United States would intervene. György Alföldy requested explosives from the American diplomatic mission in Budapest on behalf of a "Hungarian People's Party." Legation experts concluded that Alföldy was a specialist in the field and had specific plans to use the munitions.[60] Though Hungarian security services inflated the size and significance of underground organizations, they did exist. Some may have been promised external assistance by Western agents; most were probably encouraged by Western propaganda.

The main significance of foreign broadcasts was that they broke the communists' monopoly on information. Without them, Hungarians would have had a more "distorted picture" of the outside world.[61] Ernst Halperin, a correspondent for the *Neue Züricher Zeitung* who visited Budapest in 1954, claimed that public opinion in international affairs there was shaped more by editors of foreign radio broadcasts than by Hungarian newspapers, which "nobody reads."[62] Foreign broadcasts impeded communist indoctrination; many believed that without them, the Hungarians would lose hope for their future.[63] The local audience had limited access to printed information, but the United States Information Agency (USIA) still handed out two thousand bulletins and three thousand newspapers, magazines, and flyers annually.[64]

In 1950, the CIA launched an operation in which devices disguised as meteorological balloons released propaganda over Soviet-controlled areas. The United States employed this technique until 1956, dropping about three hundred million leaflets containing images of the United States, cartoons and photos of Western statesmen, and inflammatory political slogans like "The regime is weaker than you think. Hope is in the people."⁶⁵ Flyers dropped over Hungary were entitled NEM, which means "no" in Hungarian, and was also the acronym for Hungary's National Resistance Movement.

The messages from the sky met a mixed reception. Some people complained that they did more harm than good because they gave the police a pretext to intensify their "persecution of class alien elements and one more reason to search peoples' homes." People were persecuted and harassed even where no leaflets fell; the inhabitants of Nyögér village considered the balloon operation a failure because the police had searched their homes as soon as they had seen the balloons coming.⁶⁶ Moreover, the balloons rarely carried any information that they had not already heard "ages ago" on the radio.⁶⁷ Many of the balloons crashed close to the border – Hungarian authorities often claimed to have brought them down – and the fliers reached far fewer people than did radio broadcasts.⁶⁸ Still, some people considered them effective weapons against the regime because they raised people's spirits. The leaflets also "encouraged people to oppose the regime and weakened communist power."⁶⁹ They constituted valuable reading material, reassured people that they had not been abandoned to their oppressors, and put the authorities on the defensive.⁷⁰ A Radio Free Europe survey in 1957 suggested that the balloons were a source of information for 15 percent of the population. In 1955, the Hungarian authorities collected 2.6 million flyers, which the Political Committee regarded as a mobilizing influence on "hostile elements."⁷¹ Although the political police threatened prison for people who kept leaflets, quite a few took the risk of sharing them with others. One refugee claimed that even though officials had encouraged an intimidating whisper campaign about the prospect of incarceration, nobody was ever actually sent to jail for the possession of illegal leaflets.⁷² A sixteen-year-old high school student was forced to defect to Austria after being caught sharing the forbidden (and therefore highly sought after) flyers at his school. According to eyewitness accounts, even the policemen who collected them sometimes slipped some into their pockets.⁷³ Other accounts suggest that border guards who had been ordered to pick up the leaflets would pass them around and read them.⁷⁴

The balloon operation irritated local authorities. Czechoslovakia and Hungary both used their air forces to hunt them down. Hungarian diplomats protested several times, calling the leaflets "slanderous and filthy writings" and contending that they constituted interference in the country's domestic affairs. Foreign Minister Endre Sík, an acclaimed specialist in African history and an old guard Bolshevik who had lived through the Great Terror in Moscow, claimed that the balloons had caused a civilian aircraft to crash, for which damage he demanded compensation and the termination of the operation.[75] The United States rejected the accusation, falsely claiming that the balloons had been sent by private organizations or served genuine meteorological purposes. In response, Budapest threatened to ground international civilian airlines, suggesting that the balloon operations were hindering the improvement of bilateral relations and warning the United States that they could cause a catastrophe.[76]

Despite their best efforts, the communist authorities found no antidote to hostile propaganda. Even though the people's democracies cooperated in jamming foreign broadcasts, RFE technicians were able modulate their frequencies to keep the programs audible.[77] In the year before the Hungarian Revolution, state security agents intercepted twelve thousand "hostile" letters, brochures, and illegal publications. Party leader Rákosi was forced to admit that his functionaries were finding it increasingly difficult to defend the party line "against the enemy."[78]

This stridently subversive propaganda campaign, however, was not an unqualified success. Radio Free Europe and other stations did help Hungarians keep in touch with the forbidden world. The relentless communist propaganda, indoctrination, and hate mongering disguised as Hungarian news was offset by alternative accounts of events in Hungary and the world. For some, these broadcasts were a lifeline to sanity. And the communists' refusal to allow access to Western broadcasts and publications, not to mention the consumerist lifestyle advertised in the Americans' propaganda, stirred up resentments and further diminished the regime's already low popularity. Still, picking up leaflets and listening to "enemy" radio stations was risky, a cost of the rollback that Hungarians would have to bear. As the surveys taken after the revolution suggest, American propaganda had led people to expect American intervention or even an all-out war against the Soviet Union, and this notion contributed to their willingness to fight the Red Army in 1956.

COVERT OPERATIONS

America's strategy to subvert the Soviet bloc in the early 1950s included covert operations conducted by the ultra-secret Office of Policy Coordination. In Poland, an effort was made to revive the Home Army in 1951–1952.[79] Border incidents were provoked in Czechoslovakia, and its airspace was violated; radio transmitters were dropped to outlaw agents. In the two years before Stalin's death, Czechoslovakian authorities arrested twelve hundred "Western agents"; seventy-nine assassinations were attributed to foreigners between 1951 and 1956.[80] Various groups were trained to illegally penetrate the Iron Curtain, conduct espionage, and organize paramilitary units capable of fighting the Soviets. Several hundred foreign agents were sent in to support anticommunist resistance groups.[81] In October 1953, sixteen "terrorists and agents" were tried in Romania on charges of parachuting to Romanian territory with the help of American personnel.[82] Covert operators also coordinated underground resistance, either by encouraging active guerrilla warfare or by organizing detachments to be available for the coming war. U.S. authorities tried to make sure these operations could be plausibly denied if uncovered.[83]

Shortly before his demise, Rákosi bragged that Hungarian security organs uncovered an average of two "counter-revolutionary conspiracies" with links to the "imperialists" every month. In the first half of 1956 alone, thirty-seven alleged spies smuggled into the country from Austria were taken into custody.[84] According to official figures, between 1949 and 1953, Rákosi's regime investigated 120 cases related to foreign intelligence services, 41 of which involved the United States. In the same period, the members of fourteen spy rings, all with American ties and allegedly organized before 1949, were arrested. More than 60 percent of the alleged spies apprehended in 1955 were Americans. After interrogating agents of the CIC (the Counter Intelligence Corps, U.S. military intelligence), the Ministry of the Interior concluded that the United States was organizing an anticommunist resistance and supporting sabotage actions in Hungary.[85]

These accusations may not have been unfounded. In 1949, an agent named George Mason was parachuted into Romania to contact resistance groups in Transylvania and incite mass unrest. Mason's network allegedly cultivated resistance groups in areas where they could cause problems for the Soviets in a war. Two years later, agents were sent to the Fogaras region of Transylvania, where they were supposed to collect intelligence and organize local resistance groups. They were carrying a radio transmitter, arms, gold, and local cash when they were apprehended.[86] An émigré from Czechoslovakia, Vladimir Komarek, was sent back from the United States in 1948 to organize an anticommunist resistance network and was arrested in 1950.[87] Similar arrests took place in Hungary. In the dungeons of the political police, individuals arrested for spying often claimed that the United States intended to organize groups capable of carrying out terrorist attacks and joining a war against the Soviets if the need arose. These alleged agents sometimes confessed to having organized armed groups on behalf of the CIC and to preparing for an invasion of Hungary. János Weissengruber claimed that the CIA was planning to plant guerrillas in Transylvania who would cross into Hungary and commit acts of terror. If a war were to break out, they would cut logistical lines. Sándor Dudás, another person arrested for leading a resistance group, claimed to have received similar assignments.[88] Hungary's vegetation and topography were considered unsuitable for guerrilla activity, which may explain why such groups were expected to infiltrate the country from the mountains of Transylvania.

Covert warfare thus revealed the more reckless side of U.S. policy toward Eastern Europe. Given the strength of Eastern European security establishments and their commitment to hunting down and destroying domestic and foreign "enemies," any locals recruited into resistance groups there faced mortal danger. Those arrested for espionage and conspiracy on behalf of "imperialist" intelligence services faced harsh prison sentences, confiscation of wealth, and death. In addition, given the Soviets' military strength and America's inferior strategic position in Central Europe, the establishment of such "resistance" groups served no practical purpose.

STALIN'S DEATH

Even though there was an almost palpable sigh of relief at Stalin's death, there was virtually no change in the hostile relationship between Hungary and the United States. Initially, this could be attributed to the Soviets' rigid position: the Kremlin's aspiring new leader, Lavrenty Beria, allegedly harshly reprimanded Rákosi for accepting an American offer to negotiate (an episode that probably never took place). This incident occurred when Hungarian leaders appeared in Moscow for "consultations" in June 1953, at which point the situation in the Soviet bloc was critical. There was unrest in East Germany resulting from forced Bolshevization, and in the judgment of the Soviet diplomatic and security establishment in Hungary, the excesses of the Hungarian Communist Party were making Soviet control there precarious. All this led the Kremlin to instigate reforms in Eastern Europe and to install the reformer Imre Nagy as Hungary's prime minister. Even though he was opposed to the worst excesses of Stalinism, Nagy had spent fifteen years in Moscow and was considered by the Soviets to be reliable. Nagy chose not to make a drastic opening to the "capitalist world," even though his country was economically reliant on it, but he did introduce domestic reforms that were extensive by Soviet bloc standards. These stemmed from his personal beliefs and were not merely the dictates of the imperial center. Nagy may have feared for his reforms, which were strongly attacked by his arch-rival, Rákosi. He was also genuinely convinced of the correctness of a unilaterally Soviet line in Hungarian foreign policy. In contrast, in neighboring Romania, the otherwise Stalinist Georghiu-Dej set out to improve his country's relations with the United States and to offset Soviet influence. This would be the political pattern for these two allied but hostile communist neighbors: Romania would stray from the Soviet line in foreign policy, while Hungary would test Moscow's patience with its political and economic reforms. Diversity began to appear behind the Iron Curtain almost as soon as Stalin passed away.

There was virtually no change in Hungarian-American relations. Unlike his Romanian counterpart, Nagy made no attempt to improve bilateral relations, even though East-West tensions had subsided some. This was not a question of the two leaders' ideological convictions. Georghiu-Dej was an orthodox Stalinist who ruled with an iron fist; Nagy was disgusted with Stalinist methods, mitigated terror, decentralized power, and moved the economy toward satisfying popular needs (though he did not introduce any structural changes to the Stalinist model). In the coming decades, Romania would always make manifest its opposition to the USSR and flirt with the West, while Hungary would push domestic reforms as Moscow's unwavering foreign policy ally. Georghiu-Dej hoped he could reduce the Soviets' influence by normalizing his country's relations with the Americans, and he was ready to introduce token reforms to that end. His ambitions meshed with American diplomats' intentions to be more flexible in dealing with the satellites and to "drive a wedge" between Bucharest and Moscow.[89]

Washington did not appreciate Nagy's domestic reforms, which they thought were of a tactical nature designed to win over the population. Like the Soviets, American observers thought Nagy's economic policies could lead to catastrophe. Nevertheless, relations began to thaw. Hungary accepted American aid to victims of the flood that hit in 1954; a year later, the idea of trade talks was broached. Deputy Foreign Minister Károly Szarka "almost pleaded for the trade talks to begin."[90] The Hungarian economy was on the verge of collapse because Moscow had refused to furnish the commodities necessary to keep its heavy industry going and Hungarian gold reserves were being depleted by payments for Western imports. Budapest hoped to raise hard currency by marketing exports, which may have been unrealistic in view of the fact that the country produced literally nothing it could sell in North America. The Hungarians also hoped that American commodity credits would allow them to purchase wheat and cotton. In itself, this need for American wheat illustrates a tragic decline. Hungary had been one Europe's chief suppliers of wheat since at least the sixteenth century and had never experienced a shortage of this basic commodity until Rákosi's regime began destroying its producers and exporting their remaining crops to finance the production of iron and steel. Hoping to facilitate a trade agreement, Deputy Foreign Minister Sík offered to ease travel restrictions on American diplomats.[91] Hungary frequently offered political concessions for economic gains. The Foreign Ministry's ideas were at odds with the Ministry of the Interior, which suggests that the communist bureaucracy was not monolithic. Later, as Hungary's economic woes worsened, the pressure to open up to the capitalist world intensified and this conflict between ministries grew even more pronounced. It was not that the Foreign Ministry and the interior establishment differed about the consolidation of the political system. They simply wanted to do so by different means. The former hoped to uphold the integrity of the regime by making use of external resources, while the latter wanted to shut out hostile external influences. Thus the trade initiative never got off the ground. In 1956, the security establishment arrested two employees of the American legation in Budapest, and in retaliation the United States banned its citizens from traveling to Hungary. Even though Washington officially encouraged an intensification of trade relations with the world behind the Iron Curtain, it was not yet ready to move decisively in that direction.

Nagy was eventually removed from power, but in May 1956 the improvement of bilateral relations came up again. The most important American condition was that the Hungarian regime curb the power of the political police, which had become a "state within the state."[92] The American minister, Christian Ravndal, was told that the secret police would be reined in and that the government was willing to discuss mutual grievances with an eye toward opening a new chapter in bilateral relations.[93] Péter Kós, Hungary's minister in Washington, was told that the first step would be the resolution of the cases of any American citizens who had been arrested in Hungary.[94] Even the Foreign Ministry failed to achieve unanimity in choosing a course, split between the diehard anti-Americans and the foreign policy realists who understood the importance of normal ties with the United States. In June, the Advisory Council of the Ministry of Foreign Affairs produced a proposal for a diplomatic "initiative" and a "review" of any outstanding cases involving American citizens. The council recommended that the Ministry of the Interior "consult" the Foreign Ministry about diplomatic missions and the relaxation of the travel restrictions it had imposed on American diplomats. The mere fact that such a memorandum was prepared was a sure sign of change, not to mention the recommendation for a Hungarian diplomatic initiative. Negotiations over the settlement of outstanding financial claims and the regulation of commercial and cultural affairs were expected to commence shortly.[95] The foreign minister, however, a hardliner named János Boldóczki, rejected these recommendations on the grounds that any initiative for talks should come from the United States; anything else would constitute a victory for American "power politics." Boldóczki chastised the author of the recommendations, László Helmeczi, accusing him of taking the Americans' side. A real debate then developed in which several functionaries, including the future chargé in Washington, took Helmeczi's side, arguing that "several socialist states including the Soviet Union maintained better contacts with the U.S. than Hungary." In addition, they argued that Hungary was not a large power and therefore was not in the same league with the Americans and the Soviets.[96] Shortly thereafter, Estes Kefauver, a U.S. senator from Tennessee and one of the few American lawmakers who ventured into Hungary at that time, was received by Mátyás Rákosi, who expressed his desire to expand trade relations and to visit the United States as soon as the occasion arose.[97] Rákosi was ousted in July 1956, and his successor, Ernő Gerő, was invited to observe the American election process. The Ministry of Foreign Affairs put together a list of people who would accompany Gerő, but the revolution canceled their travel plans.

Relations were hostile, but they still allowed for small personal gestures, though some of these also illustrate Hungary's decline under the Stalinist dictatorship. Some of the country's leading pianists complained to the American minister that their only Steinway piano was in such a poor state of repair that practicing on it had become very difficult. In an unusually relaxed conversation with an American desk officer at the Foreign Ministry, Ravndal promised to replace the old Steinway with a brand new piano without any publicity. His negotiating partner, Károly Szigeti, was eager to take advantage of the offer since he had no suitable piano available for an upcoming concert featuring works by Bartók and Liszt.[98] The noted tenor Mihály Székely was treated with medication provided by Ravndal's spouse.[99] Hungary's new representative Péter Kós, a dual Hungarian-Soviet citizen, assured assistant secretary of state Herbert Hoover that his "main mission" was to improve relations with the United States.[100] In early 1956, with Soviet consent, travel restrictions were eased for diplomatic and official personnel and the number of restricted areas was reduced. In return, Hungary was allowed to expand its information activities in the United States. Hoover told Kós that in order to lift the travel ban, which would have allowed cultural and trade delegations to visit Hungary, the Americans held in Hungary would have to be released. Foreign Minister Horváth, a veteran Bolshevik, was willing to do so. He asked László Piros, minister of the interior and a general of state security, to review the cases of the arrested Americans. Piros did not respond, so Horváth returned to the question on October 23, emphasizing that he had wanted to be able to reply at the opening session of the General Assembly, but the events of the day made the issue irrelevant. It would take a decade for this diplomacy of small steps to be reinitiated.

"BIOLOGICAL ANNIHILATION": EISENHOWER, DULLES, AND LIBERATION

The Eisenhower administration pledged that its policy in Eastern Europe would be more active than its predecessor's. John Foster Dulles talked about an "explosive and dynamic" policy of liberation, yet the Eisenhower administration never developed a coherent policy to deal with the areas under Soviet control. Public and private pronouncements on Soviet matters diverged radically. Recently, historians have differentiated *rhetorical* and *confidential* diplomacies in explaining the distances between public and private utterances. As the historian Chris Tudda has explained, Washington reverted to "fiery rhetoric" in condemning Moscow's policies; privately, however, U.S. diplomats pursued the policies of peaceful coexistence. "Rhetorical diplomacy overwhelmed their confidential diplomacy, intensif[ying] conflict between Washington and Moscow."[101] In other words, rhetoric and foreign policy were two sides of the same coin. Even though the president and Dulles were often conciliatory in private, their peaceful intentions were sometimes undermined by their public utterances. Still, the president and his secretary of state were not making cautious private and reckless public pronouncements simultaneously. In fact, there tended to be gaps in time between their seeming reversals. Their public rhetoric was not invariably strident, but their public pronouncements nevertheless made Dulles and the president seem more belligerent than they really were.

Shortly before the end of the war, Dulles had been ready to face the fact that Eastern Europe would end up in the Soviets' sphere of influence. He accepted the continental division even in 1949. In 1944, Eisenhower had predicted that the larger part of the Balkans would end up under Soviet control and that only the use of force would be able change such a state of affairs. During the 1952 election campaign, both American candidates promised to liberate the Eastern European satellites, although the future secretary of state assured the British in confidence that despite the fiery rhetoric, nothing reckless would be done to liberate the peoples behind the Iron Curtain.[102] Still, right after Stalin's death he instructed American diplomatic missions to sow the seeds of discord, confusion, and uncertainty about the new Soviet regimes, both within the Soviet bloc itself and in other communist parties as well.[103] Although the president was skeptical of schemes for liberation, some of his advisors, like C. D. Jackson, a propaganda specialist who helped launch Crusade for Freedom in 1950, were anxious to implement the new line as soon as possible.[104] The occasion arose when Walter Ulbricht's reckless Bolshevization campaign triggered an uprising in East Berlin in 1953. Although Dulles saw a chance for the West to seize an advantage over the Soviet Union, he was incapable of capitalizing on the situation. The president would have intervened gladly had the movement spread to China or had there been a genuine chance at victory, but he eventually concluded that the opportunity to roll the Soviets back "for keeps" had not yet arrived. C. D. Jackson initially wanted to send arms to the protesters, which, given the Soviets' determination to suppress the revolt, would have had tragic consequences; he was forced to admit that the United States would be unable to drive the Soviets out of Germany.[105] Washington's response to the East German uprising was part of a strategy of containment, not the loudly proclaimed platform of aggressive liberation. Instead of sending troops to combat the German Democratic Republic's security forces, the CIA delivered a large volume of food for distribution among the famished population of East Berlin. This was undoubtedly a public relations success, but not exactly a tool of liberation.[106]

The CIA's food project for East Germany reflects history's failure to serve justice. Only a decade earlier, Germans had implemented a hunger plan over a large part of Eastern Europe and the Soviet Union, a monstrous quest to colonize the East by starving millions of innocent civilians to death.[107] Thus in 1953, while the Soviet Union's erstwhile ally was serving free food to Germans, millions of others behind the Iron Curtain, many of whom had fought alongside the Americans in the war, were suffering from food shortage, at least partly due to the United States's politically driven refusal to ease their shortage of grain.

Operation Solarium, an exercise commissioned by the president in the wake of the German crisis, confirmed that liberation would not be a viable option for U.S. policy. "Rollback" was dropped. U.S. leaders instead adopted a policy of gradual transformation, making clear that the United States would not take responsibility for any consequences of a mass revolt in Eastern Europe.[108] In December 1953, the National Security Council officially renounced the policy of aggressive liberation behind the Iron Curtain.

Historians generally argue that U.S. policy softened at that point, but documentary evidence of the activities of the Operations Coordinating Board (OCB), the organization that took over from the Psychological Strategy Board in planning and implementing covert operations, suggests that American goals remained ambitious. Washington continued to offer assistance to the peoples of Eastern Europe who "resisted" communist rule and strove to keep alive the hope that a "liberation" was coming, sooner or later. Policy recommendations included undermining Soviet power and the authority of the "puppet governments," as well as slowing the growth of the Soviet economy and military. The Soviet Union was to be forced into a negotiated settlement. Resistance movements were not meant to become mass uprisings, and the authorities charged with the implementation of these programs were to make sure that the "spontaneous" nature of these movements not be compromised. Top-secret resolutions were couched in the harsh "newspeak" of the Cold War. There were now two languages, one public, meant to rally support, and another for private use. The ideological struggle between the communist and Western worlds was to transform the language of political discourse. There was no room for compromise in the conflict between the two world systems: Soviet power threatened the survival of American institutions. "Communism" was understood as worldwide movement committed to "overthrowing" every noncommunist government in the world. Americans tended to paint the fate awaiting the rest of the world in almost apocalyptical colors; the communist governments were dedicated to and already capable of achieving the goal of world mastery. Coexistence with such a movement could only be a temporary tactic. Nothing could stop the "communist offensive." Nuclear parity and the growth of the Soviet bloc's industrial might meant communist aggression could no longer be deterred.

All this made the subversion of the Soviets' satellites important, and despite claims to the contrary, U.S. officials kept the policy of covert aggression behind the Iron Curtain on the agenda. There were plans to obstruct communist bureaucracies, making it impossible for them to exercise power and to induce the satellite regimes not to fight alongside the Soviets. To achieve these objectives, U.S. officials proposed to organize, train, and equip organizations that would be *capable of protracted resistance* within the communist bloc.[109] Even though mass uprisings were not supposed to be encouraged, guidelines for fomenting unrest referred to this possibility. Shortly after the events in East Berlin, the Psychological Strategy Board affirmed that despite all efforts to avoid a "premature rebellion," such a rebellion could occur, and if it were to spread to Ukraine and Belorussia and the Baltic states, bold and daring action, like sending U.S. "military aid" to the rebels, could "change the course of history."[110] Thus the United States needed to be ready to take advantage of any chance to reduce Soviet territory in the near future."[111] Liberation was still on the table. To "detach an important satellite" from the Soviet Union would "undermine" communism. And even though Washington disavowed "premature" rebellion, it never clarified what that term meant. The OCB offered several options for implementing the National Security Council's recommendations. One was to train leaders and make plans for shipping arms and equipment into the satellites for use in a potential revolt. A related proposal envisioned secret operations to organize underground groups through "satellite leaders" who would be able to carry out a "coup d'état" in the event of an uprising, or at least mount a significant resistance against communist forces. The OCB did not accept these recommendations in the expectation of a separate memorandum on these matters from the CIA.[112] Even though the National Security Council did not formally recommend the liberation of the satellites, the claim that the NSC rejected the policy of aggressive rollback[113] may require revision, as might the notion that Dulles's policies as secretary of state and U.S. government actions toward the Soviet bloc were equivalent.

Dulles grew skeptical of the wisdom of liberation, regarding it as an expensive and risky option for reducing the Soviet danger, which in the worst case could destroy the "free world."[114] Although he is remembered as an archetypal cold warrior, Dulles expressed more moderate ideas as time passed. In 1955, he acknowledged that tensions had diminished and declared that the Soviet danger was becoming less acute. The United States and the Soviet Union were getting closer to something resembling a friendly relationship.[115] When Eisenhower's opponent in the 1952 and 1956 presidential campaigns, Adlai Stevenson, referred to "liberation" as a Republican promise, Dulles retorted that there had been no such pledge. The State Department did not endorse the policy of liberation. After Stalin's death, when the idea of a "rollback" was still alive, State Department officials told Polish émigrés that it would be impossible for captive nations to liberate themselves through their own efforts. Only a significant change in international relations could liberate Eastern Europe,[116] an appraisal of the situation that, in light of future developments, was realistic and honest. The Policy Planning Staff (PPS) excluded the use of force in defining the doctrine of liberation as keeping the spirits of liberty and hope alive.[117] The caution of the foreign affairs establishment became apparent when the Hungarian émigré leader and former prime minister, Ferenc Nagy, requested that a high-level State Department official speak at a commemoration of the tenth anniversary of Hungary's 1945 national elections. His request was declined because the State Department had no desire to identify "publicly and officially" with the attitudes exiled Hungarians were likely to express.[118] State Department officials, in their routine responses to queries about American policies toward Eastern Europe, always avoided giving the impression that liberation was a realistic possibility.[119]

The danger of a nuclear confrontation ruled out the forceful liberation of Eastern Europe, and the president was firmly convinced that any confrontation with the Soviets would be a nuclear one. The secretary of state and other high-level functionaries continued to make ambiguous statements about the relationship between rollback and massive retaliation, which made it hard for foreign audiences to get a realistic picture of Americans' foreign policy aims. This may have resulted from a lingering assumption in the U.S. military and intelligence establishments that Eastern European resistance was not completely "hopeless" after all.[120]

FINLANDIZATION

While Stalin's former cronies struggled for power in the wake of his death, a number of outstanding international issues were resolved. A 1955 treaty granted the Austrian state full independence and neutrality. This agreement, reached on the western segment of the former Austro-Hungarian Empire, could have been an opportunity to renegotiate the status of Eastern Europe, but whatever hope it held out was dashed when Soviet troops withdrawn from Austria were redeployed in Hungary. Fearing that the USSR might pull out of Hungary, the Hungarian Political Committee petitioned the Kremlin to avoid such a catastrophe and let the occupation army stay. No such petition was necessary. Shortly after Stalin's death, his heir apparent, Lavrenty Beria, explored the possibility of striking a deal on the GDR, whose incompetent regime had made it a trouble spot and a political liability for the Soviets. In the meantime, Beria summoned Rákosi, Hungary's dictator – or "Jewish king" as Beria touted him – to Moscow to be dressed down and demoted for allegedly selling out to the Americans.

By then, the idea of a negotiated settlement was floating around Washington. Dulles recommended a mutual withdrawal of forces from Europe and a mutual understanding on international controls for missiles and nuclear weapons.[121] Although the secretary of state soon changed his mind, the Policy Planning Staff of the State Department worked out ideas for a negotiated settlement of the East-West conflict. In retrospect, these concepts were stillborn, but they remain noteworthy because their argumentation reveals American thinking about the motives behind Soviet expansionism and formed the basis of Washington's policy toward the 1956 Hungarian revolution. PPS member Louis Halle, an international scholar known for his musings on the arrival of spring, argued that the power struggle in Moscow had weakened the Soviets and that they might thus be willing to give up much in return for small American concessions. Perhaps the Iron Curtain might be raised by a promise not to extend the European Defense Community to the Soviet border.[122] The underlying idea was that Eastern Europe served as the Soviet Union's buffer zone against the capitalist world. Charles Bohlen, a leading expert on the Soviet Union, was convinced that the Soviet occupation of Eastern Europe was motivated primarily by strategic considerations and less by ideology.[123] In fact, Soviet foreign policy was an amalgam of ideological, economic, and political concerns. Some members of the Policy Planning Staff concluded that the Soviets would be willing to retract the Red Army to their borders in return for adequate security guarantees. A memorandum prepared in

July 1953 argued that the region from the Baltic to the Black, Aegean, and Adriatic Seas constituted a defense perimeter for the Soviet Union. If the United States insisted on free elections, and governments hostile to Moscow could be voted into power, legitimate Soviet security concerns would have to be taken into account, including guarantees that countries adjacent to the USSR would not be allowed to participate in open hostilities or any other activity detrimental to Soviet security.[124] In return, Moscow was expected to withdraw and to return only at the invitation of freely elected governments. Existing administrations would be disbanded and internationally supervised elections would be held. Each new government would be allowed a free hand in formulating its domestic and trade policies, but would be obliged to subordinate its security policies to the interests of the Soviet Union. In short, the satellites' status would resemble Finland's.[125] For the sake of an agreement, the West might have provided further security guarantees including a pledge not to unify Germany.[126] Hence, not even the boldest conception envisioned the full and unconditional restoration of European unity. Even these (by the standards of the times) utopian proposals did not suggest an extension of Western security arrangements into Eastern Europe, which in this respect was to remain in the Soviet sphere. In spite of the risks, the PPS urged an agreement on the quantity and placement of armaments in Europe as compensation for expected Soviet concessions.[127] In late 1954, the NSC discussed the possibility of talks, and while the Joint Chiefs urged a more assertive policy, Dulles recommended walking the fence between military liberation and completely abandoning the Eastern Europeans. Since the Soviets had shown flexibility in resolving the Austrian question, the State Department hoped similar agreements could be reached in other countries under Soviet occupation. Negotiations, the OCB conjectured, offered the only real chance to decouple a satellite.[128]

Austria became the showcase for the Soviets' new slogan, "peaceful coexistence." But while Moscow had plenty of incentives to agree to Austria's neutralization, it had none for doing so with the fully Sovietized satellites of Eastern Europe. Most contemporary analyses reduced the complexities of Soviet interests in their ring of satellites to security and ideology. Another kind of domino theory seemed to apply to the Soviets as well: if they were to lose one satellite, they might lose the rest. Nevertheless, the summit in Geneva offered an occasion to raise the subject with the Soviets. It was important, however, not to give the impression that Washington was dealing with Moscow behind the Eastern Europeans' backs or planning to abandon them. The PPS urged the State Department to raise the issue of German unification and a subsequent Soviet pullout from the GDR.[129] Shortly before the summit, the NSC affirmed that the Austrian treaty would be taken as a model for other agreements.[130] Plans for Eastern Europe were connected to new ideas about Germany. Dulles was attracted to the idea of decoupling Germany from the United States and unifying it outside NATO. In 1955, he was ready to allow a unified, neutral Germany under some form of international supervision that included the participation of the Soviet Union. He even toyed with a war game in which the Soviets were attacked and the United States assisted them. Both Dulles and the president played with the idea of pulling American troops out of Europe with preconditions being the reunification of a neutral Germany and Western Europe's paying for its own defense.[131] An American withdrawal would have been facilitated by the Soviets' pulling out of Eastern Europe, and thus the vague outline of a new European order was taking shape; perhaps the independence of the states under Soviet domination and the security of all the continental powers could be restored simultaneously. Nothing came of it. Both the secretary of state and the president raised the question of Eastern Europe in private conversations with Soviet prime minister Nikolai Bulganin in Geneva. Bulganin was told that the Americans attached great significance to the region because of the influence of émigré groups in the United States. He was reassured that they had no intention of surrounding the Soviet Union with a ring of hostile countries. Dulles recommended the Finnish model but offered nothing in return, and, as could be expected, Bulganin refused even to discuss the matter.[132] The problem of Eastern Europe would not be the subject of international political debate again until 1989. In 1955, it was no longer timely. Khrushchev was convinced that the Soviets' expansion into Eastern Europe had fulfilled the dreams of communism and freed the locals from the "yoke of capitalism," and considering the aftermath of 1989, his fears that NATO would march eastward were not unfounded. Thus the consolidation of the empire in Eastern Europe was still an important goal for Soviet policymakers.[133]

In June 1956, the National Security Council discarded the possibility of negotiations, aiming instead at splitting the Soviet bloc. Two approaches to the Soviet satellites remained: to destabilize them, thereby weakening the Soviet Union's position of power, or to reach consensus on a redrawn map of Europe. The year 1956 would prove that these two approaches were mutually exclusive.

1956: Self-Liberation

On October 23, 1956, Hungary exploded. Although it is hard to pinpoint why one country remains docile under tyrannical rule while another revolts, historians have dedicated years of research to identifying the specific factors that led to the only armed uprising against Soviet rule. Because virtually all segments of Hungarian society had suffered various forms of repression, unrest was not confined to the capital city. Centrally engineered "circular social mobility" failed to satisfy even the social groups whose aspirations the regime had privileged.[1] Grievances included foreign military occupation, state terror that sometimes exceeded even the limits of Soviet tolerance, serious shortages of basic consumer goods, social dislocations caused by heavy industrialization and conscious attacks on traditional rural ways of life, economic injustices including unequal trade terms and Soviet exploitation of Hungarian resources, the suppression of national culture, and a ban on the free flow of information and commerce. Communist rule was widely considered alien to the country's traditions and had to lean on Soviet military power for survival. It has been argued that Imre Nagy, the bespectacled, jovial communist reformer, could have prevented the escalation of a mass protest into an armed revolution if had he been able to soothe the crowd that had gathered in front of the Parliament balcony. Instead, his unemotional, detached address was so disappointing it managed to whip the crowd's sentiments up even more.[2] And this was not a miscalculation or oversight on Nagy's part. He knew no other language than the invented, bureaucratic parlance of Soviet communism. He had never been required to speak to a crowd; he had been socialized not by a parliamentary bureaucracy where skill with words was indispensable in winning elections, but among communist functionaries. He was accustomed to reading carefully scripted statements in front of a sham parliament that expressed its gratification with compulsory storms of applause. More importantly, it is hard to see how a single speech could have halted such an overflow of powerful emotions. That crowd had been guided to the steps of Parliament by the lodestar of 1848, the Hungarians' cherished revolution against the Habsburgs. Once they had taken to the streets en masse, no magic spell was going to force them back into the Soviets' bottle.

TO MINIMIZE BLOODSHED

Although policymakers had been preparing for it for years, the revolution caught Washington off guard.[3] The Eisenhower administration wanted to respond, but it ruled out military intervention. The political options were limited by a lack of effective leverage on the Soviet Union. Negotiations along the lines suggested in 1953 were one option. Proponents hoped that the Soviet Union would be willing to withdraw from Eastern Europe and allow it to have a status like Finland's in return for Western guarantees of Soviet safety. Western security would be enhanced by eliminating Eastern Europe as a potential springboard for Soviet aggression.[4] President Eisenhower claimed that European tensions would not diminish as long as the Soviet Union occupied the satellites.[5] Therefore if the United States could reduce Soviet influence on the satellites, the risk of war would be greatly lessened.[6] Soviet domination in adjacent areas, the National Security Council (NSC) opined, posed a grave threat to European, and by extension U.S., security. There were ethical considerations as well. American political traditions prescribed the recognition of a nation's right to independence and its right to choose its own form of government. Thus the liberation of the satellites was a basic American goal.[7] A few days after the revolution erupted, Dulles described it as the hitherto greatest threat to Soviet dominion over its satellites.[8]

Washington opted for caution in view of the possible consequences of aggressive action, a stance that was at odds with the Eisenhower administration's belligerent rhetoric and some of the more reckless aspects of its campaign of psychological warfare. The underlying logic behind Eisenhower's response was that American reserve might convince Moscow to alter Hungary's international status to something resembling the Finnish or Austrian model. Had American leaders known that the Soviet Party Presidium was split over its course of action, they might have offered concessions in support of a peaceful solution. Instead, decision makers were forced to guess at Soviet intentions, and these guesses often turned out to be highly inaccurate. Surprisingly, the Soviets did not worry about American intervention; the United States was hardly mentioned in their deliberations. This suggests that U.S. rhetoric was unconvincing and the Kremlin understood American fears of Soviet nuclear deterrence.[9]

Analysts had expected dissatisfaction to intensify in the Soviet bloc, but they did not anticipate an open, armed rebellion. The State Department was convinced that any uprising was doomed to failure and could potentially result in the "biological annihilation" of the rebellious nationality. Thus the United States should avoid inciting dissidents to "premature" rebellion with unfulfillable promises that could result in their "destruction."[10] But with the word "premature" left undefined, the door remained open to reckless schemes. From these statements, it is clear that the State Department never intended to participate in a military liberation of the satellites. If they were brave enough to rise against their foreign rulers, they would be left to their own devices. Hence the costs of liberation were to be left to others. The dire prospects facing the rebels led Dulles to declare that the United States should support Hungary's peaceful transformation. In a telegram to the U.S. ambassador in Belgrade, Dulles outlined his position: "As in Poland we welcome all steps by any people towards national independence and freedom from Soviet domination.... Nevertheless it is difficult to see how unarmed people no matter how heroic can overcome Soviet tanks. In circumstances therefore we desire to minimize bloodshed, keep the Nagy-Kádár regime from taking reprisals ... and encourage it to proceed with rapid democratization."[11] Eisenhower's thoughts on Poland may also have been valid for Hungary: where military force renders protest suicidal, the day of liberation must be postponed.[12] In a televised speech on October 21, the president ruled out military intervention in Poland.

Eisenhower condemned the Soviets' intervention and expressed his sympathy to the Hungarian people on October 24. The use of the world "deplore" may have softened the edge of the president's message to Moscow; perhaps it was read as an expression of mere disapproval.[13] Dulles was elated that the United States had succeeded in keeping the spirit of freedom alive in the Soviet bloc, which he imagined was on the verge of collapse.[14] American officials had no reliable information on the events in Hungary or the Soviet response to them; they hoped only to dissuade the Soviet Union from crushing the rebels. The president and Dulles were also concerned about creating an impression among Eastern Europeans that the United States was selling them out or bargaining behind their backs with their "hated masters."[15] On October 26, the National Security Council was convened to work out an appropriate strategy. Presidential advisor Harold Stassen proposed informing Moscow without delay that the independence of Hungary and other parts of Eastern Europe would in no way endanger Soviet security.[16] He was rebuffed, but Stassen's supporters were able to convince the president that the United States should propose to apply the Austrian model to Hungary, guaranteeing both Hungary's independence and Soviet security.[17] The notion that Moscow's safety concerns were the key to the liberation of Eastern Europe was based on the tacit but false assumption that Eastern Europe was merely Moscow's security zone. The Policy Planning Staff agreed, though, arguing that if Washington were to recognize "legitimate Soviet security interests in this region," Soviet intervention could be averted and Hungarian independence restored.[18] In retrospect, Stassen explained the American position as an attempt to let the Russians grant the Hungarians sovereignty by ruling out Hungarian membership in NATO. He felt, however, that Moscow would be unable to "swallow" the removal of the Red Army from Hungary.[19] He assumed that Zhukov, the Soviet minister of defense, would welcome such a proposal. Zhukov had to be reluctant to keep large numbers of troops deployed in the Balkans to keep the local populations at bay, but he would be unable to prevent the deployment of Soviet troops if his domestic opposition could raise the specter of NATO bases in Hungary or the "Balkan" countries.[20] Stassen was concerned that Dulles's statements about Soviet security were not clear enough. Eisenhower wanted Dulles to draft a declaration to the effect that the United States would respect Soviet security, but Dulles was unwilling to make such a clear statement. He said that the United States would not regard the countries of Eastern Europe as potential allies,[21] but added that the United States wanted to see the independence and sovereignty of these peoples restored.[22] While Eisenhower would have accepted nonaligned status for Eastern Europe, Dulles did not find this possibility attractive. Nevertheless, the ambassador in Moscow, Charles Bohlen, was instructed to call Soviet leaders' attention to the key part of Dulles's speech, namely that the satellites were not seen as potential American allies. Bohlen did so at a Kremlin reception on October 29. The next day, after a heated discussion, the Communist Party of the Soviet Union (CPSU) Presidium decided to negotiate with the Nagy government, and it is conceivable (although not provable) that Bohlen's statement influenced their decision.[23] Finally, in an address on October 31, the president repeated Dulles's statement and offered only modest economic aid to Hungary.[24] It is unclear why the president deferred to Dulles on the wording of this message to the Soviets, but discussions among Soviet leaders suggest that American statements did little to influence the final outcome.

On October 27, the UN Security Council discussed the first Soviet intervention on the basis of article 34 of the UN charter. Hungary's representative, Péter Kós, a citizen of the Soviet Union, protested against the discussion. Soviet representative Arkady Sobolev justified his government's action by claiming that Hungary had not carried out its obligation to extirpate "fascist movements," as required by the peace treaty of 1947. This statement was blatantly false: all noncommunist organizations had been banned in Hungary since 1946 and the Soviets had previously acknowledged Hungarian compliance. The British and the Americans referred publicly to violations of UN principles but failed to specify them. The British representative, Sir Pearson Dixon, cited the clause in the peace treaty that guaranteed democratic rights for the Hungarians, but a lack of concrete evidence of violations of those rights undermined his charges. Sobolev dominated the debate, accusing the Americans of siding with "Hitler's collaborators." At this point, the U.S. ambassador to the UN, Henry Cabot Lodge Jr., lost his calm. He "found it unacceptable that the murderers of women and children [were] pointing fingers at those [who] send Christmas packages."[25] Eventually, sentiments calmed down, and the meeting ended on an inconclusive but more optimistic note: it was reported that Soviet troops were filing out of Budapest. On October 30, the Soviet Presidium resolved to pull its forces out of Budapest and initiate talks with the Hungarian government regarding its status in the Warsaw Pact. The situation in Moscow, however, remained volatile. At a Kremlin reception immediately before the presidium meeting, Marshal Zhukov discussed the Hungarian situation with Western ambassadors and in the course of the conversation made an ominous reference to the Poles. In a manner that seemed to refer to Hungary, Zhukov stated that Moscow had showed restraint in Poland; "he could have crushed them like flies."[26] In the presidium debate, the marshal supported a withdrawal from Budapest, and at a late-night reception he informed Bohlen of the decision to pull out.[27] Some observers were convinced that this announcement, along with the Politburo's decision on October 30 to renegotiate the Soviet Union's presence in Eastern Europe, would usher in a new age. The Indian government "firmly believed" that the Soviets' announced troop withdrawal signified a complete pullout.[28] The French Embassy in Moscow was even more optimistic, claiming that the October 30 declaration demonstrated the Soviet Union's readiness to renounce its economic and, "under certain conditions," even its military empire in Eastern Europe.[29]

It looked as though Washington's approach to the crisis was working. The day Khrushchev offered to negotiate with the Hungarian government, Eisenhower told the newly designated U.S. minister to Hungary, Edward Wailes, that Eastern Europe's neutrality and independence would mark a new and more constructive phase in world politics.[30] Referring to a report by the American diplomatic mission in Budapest, a State Department memorandum announced that the Soviets were leaving Budapest. The State Department pointed out that all this had happened without Western pressure, an illustration of the immense strength of the popular movement and its *influence* over Soviet politics; it was "obvious" that the Soviets were considering leaving Hungary shortly.[31] This passage suggests that the ideological biases of Soviet thinking were not properly understood in the United States. Internal Soviet documents reveal that Moscow attributed the Hungarian uprising to "imperialists," Hungarian "reactionaries," and the "class enemies" that did their bidding. Their ideological biases had blinded Soviet decision makers to the actual causes of the Hungarian popular movement, hence their response to it was flawed from the outset. And the State Department was not the only agency that saw the future in bright colors. The Joint Chiefs of Staff opined that the Russians would leave without American intervention. And even two days after the Soviet decision to crush the Hungarian Revolution, Charles Bohlen did not think the Soviets were buying time to plan their military intervention. On the basis of what he had heard from Zhukov and foreign minister Dmitri Shepilov, Bohlen concluded that the Soviets would stand by the Nagy government to the end and avoid a full military occupation of Hungary.[32]

Relieved that the crisis in Hungary was approaching a positive resolution, the NSC spent most of its November 1 meeting on the more pressing crisis in the Middle East. At a secret conference in Sèvres, the home of the finest French porcelain, Great Britain and France agreed with Israel that the latter should attack Egypt, allowing the two European powers to exploit the resultant chaos and restore their control over the vital Suez Canal, which had been nationalized unexpectedly by Egypt's nationalist leader, Gamel Abdul Nasser. Israel had technically been at war with Egypt since 1948; it launched the first attack of its most recent battle against Egypt on October 29. Then, as had been scripted in advance, London and Paris sent a joint ultimatum to Israeli and Egyptian leaders threatening them with invasion unless they retreated. In line with the choreography, they then bombarded Egypt to facilitate their seizure of the canal. Dulles was outraged: just when the "Soviet bloc was crumbling" and the United States could have pointed to a difference between the East and the West, the West was now committing a similar aggression.[33] Precisely as the Soviets were deciding to intervene, the NSC was operating under the assumption that "national communist governments" would come into being in Eastern Europe. It saw three ways to encourage such a movement in Hungary: to exert pressure on the Soviets in the UN and in public, to support the insurgents by supplying them openly or clandestinely with arms, and to achieve Soviet troop withdrawal and a neutralization of Hungary according to the Austrian model.[34] On November 2, however, the situation changed for the worse. Herbert Hoover Jr., undersecretary of state, remarked that the "Hungary situation" [sic] was being lost.[35]

Later Hungarian propaganda would accuse the United States of having furnished clandestine military aid to the rebels. In 1958, its Foreign

Ministry would organize and heavily publicize an exhibition proving this claim and justifying Hungary's virulently anti-American stance. As far it is possible to know, no such aid was ever provided, even though doing so would not have contradicted Operations Coordinating Board (OCB) guidelines. And Radio Free Europe did disseminate military advice to the rebels. Eagerly awaiting the chance to roll back the Soviets, to liberate Eastern Europe, and to alleviate a shortage of personnel in the U.S. armed forces, cold warriors toyed with the idea of setting up a "Volunteer Freedom Corps" in each of the Eastern European nations, which would serve as the future vanguard in any American-directed liberation of their respective homelands.[36] The plan was never implemented. Eastern European refugees were trained near Munich as part of Operation Red Sox/Red Cap, which the Office of Policy Coordination (OPC) had devised as a way to send paramilitary units behind the Iron Curtain in support of national uprisings against Soviet occupation. Reckless as the project was, OPC director Frank Wisner had been ready to activate these units for the Hungarian Revolution, but nothing came of it.[37] The project's existence demonstrates that although national uprisings were considered suicidal, Cold War agencies did prepare to exploit such eventualities. Nevertheless, Washington rejected a Spanish proposal for joint military aid to Hungary,[38] which would have been inexplicable if the United States had been considering such aid. Otto Habsburg, who had learned the craft of clandestine diplomacy during World War II in an effort to help the Hungarians leave the war, contacted the Spanish dictator Francisco Franco through an intermediary who delivered his plea for help for the revolutionaries. Franco was eager to seize the opportunity to participate in an anti-Soviet crusade, and Madrid decided to dispatch a unit under the former commander of the Spanish Blue Division.[39] On November 6, Spanish foreign minister Alberto Martin Artajo told Lodge that his government was ready to send armed forces to Hungary. He proposed that the United States send two military planes to be loaded with arms in Spain and sent to Budapest. Lodge rejected the proposal outright: the United States would extend neither open nor clandestine assistance to a Spanish military intervention in Hungary. The State Department warned against precipitate action, defined as any action taken without consulting the United States. U.S. officials assured the Spanish dictator that all the necessary steps for "preserving international peace" would be taken at the UN.[40] Given that Moscow was ready to restore its control over Hungary at any cost, this was a wise step. Arming the rebels from abroad would have made the fighting much worse and, with little likelihood of increasing the rebels' chance of success, would probably have resulted in even more needless bloodshed. Even though the OCB had prepared for coups against communist leaders if revolution were to break out anywhere in Eastern Europe, the State Department's more moderate approach prevailed. Hoping to prevent an invasion of Hungary, the NSC recommended that the Soviet Union be assured that the United States did not see Hungary as a potential ally. On October 31, it accepted a proposal by the PPS for an offer of mutual troop withdrawals from Europe.[41]

It was too late for any of these schemes. On November 1, upon learning that Soviet forces were entering the country, Imre Nagy, whom Washington had dismissed as a sham, declared Hungary's neutrality in the hope of buying time for negotiations. In their eagerness to divert attention from their actions in Egypt, London and Paris supported Nagy's initiative enthusiastically. The U.K. Foreign Office instructed the British ambassador to the UN, Sir Pearson Dixon, to work toward the acceptance of Hungary's neutrality without guarantees. Because of the Suez "difficulties," Dixon was instructed to push his American colleague to take the initiative while providing close and firm support.[42] His French counterpart, Cornut-Gentile, received similar instructions: support Hungarian neutrality and the Hungarian peoples' right to express their notions of the future through free elections.[43] Lodge, however, was receiving conflicting orders. Washington's relations with its two chief European allies were highly strained because they had undertaken military action against Egypt against the explicit wishes of U.S. leaders. Dulles cabled Lodge that he should do everything possible to dissuade the French from introducing a motion on Hungarian neutrality at the evening session on November 2.[44] If this was impossible and the French were to introduce the motion, Lodge was to make sure that a vote on it was postponed on the grounds that there was insufficient evidence available on the situation in Hungary. In Dulles's cable, he refers to "obvious" reasons, though one can only wonder what those were. One explanation may be the secretary's abhorrence of neutrality.[45] Perhaps he did not wish to put Moscow on the defensive at a time when relations with U.S. allies were tense; Washington had condemned France and the U.K. simultaneously (though not jointly) with the Kremlin. It was also conceivable that Hungarian neutrality would have led to a discussion of German neutrality, which the secretary of state wanted to avoid.[46] This episode supports the view that the president and Dulles rejected neutrality,[47] even though they may have been willing to discuss it for Eastern Europe in direct talks with Moscow. The subject was not discussed even though it was becoming increasingly obvious that the revolution was being "lost"; the pressure to direct public attention toward the events unfolding in Budapest was increasing.[48]

On November 4, Soviet tanks entered Budapest and installed János Kádár as prime minister of Hungary. The previous day, KGB chairman Ivan Serov had arrested every member of the Hungarian military mission charged with negotiating the withdrawal of Soviet troops from Hungary. This turn of events shocked even Soviet military men. Kádár's government was organized from Moscow, just as the provisional Hungarian government of 1944 had been. Nagy fled to the Yugoslav Embassy, which would soon release him to the Soviets. State minister István Bibó went to the American legation early that morning to beg U.S. administrators to call on the Soviet Union to halt its aggression. They did so that afternoon. Lodge condemned the Soviets' aggression in harsh language, then introduced a motion calling on Moscow to refrain from intervention, particularly of the military sort, into Hungarian domestic affairs. His motion also demanded that Soviet armed forces leave the country without delay. It called on the UN secretary-general to investigate and report to the General Assembly on the subject of halting the intervention. Even though pleas to halt Soviet aggression remained ineffective, establishing UN responsibility would make it possible to exert diplomatic pressure on Hungarian authorities, which eventually forced Kádár to terminate reprisals.

THE TWO FACES OF U.S. POLICY

Ultimately, Washington took no effective action to roll back Soviet power in Eastern Europe. A lack of reliable information has been cited as one reason for American hesitation, but this explanation is hardly satisfactory. Robert Murphy pointed a finger at the intelligence community, which, as he said on November 2, had failed to predict any of the three recent crises,[49] including Poland and the Suez. In the midst of the political crisis in Budapest that summer, the NSC had ruled out the possibility of an open mass uprising in Hungary, and they were not the only ones. The Quai d'Orsay had also discounted this possibility, asking whether the Hungarians would be as courageous as the Polish workers in Poznan.[50] The Suez crisis was another problem. It may not have "diverted" attention to a "more important" international issue,[51] but it certainly made diplomatic challenges to the Soviets more difficult. Dulles remarked at a State Department staff meeting that he did not want the events in the Middle East to divert attention from "the critical importance" of taking the necessary steps in the Hungarian case.[52] Richard Nixon later remembered that it was hard to complain about Soviet intervention when the British and the French had chosen that precise moment to take action against the Egyptians.[53]

Another factor influencing U.S. policy toward the Hungarian Revolution was that the Americans were unsure of the Hungarian leaders' motives. More precisely, Imre Nagy was not the person they wanted to see in power. Not because he was a communist; Washington had no problem dealing with his Polish counterpart, Władysław Gomułka. Their aversion toward Nagy dated back to his earlier term as prime minister and would change only after November 4. His "new course" was seen as a tactical ploy that failed to improve the economy or to win over the population. In 1955, the U.S. legation in Budapest reported that the Hungarians were just as hostile to Nagy's regime as to the previous one and were ready to voice their antipathy or to resist the state passively just as they had before.[54] Unlike Romania, Hungary did not show even the slightest sign of wanting to improve relations with the Americans, and Washington had few regrets when Nagy was removed in early 1955, though they did recognize that he represented a more liberal and independent line than Rákosi's. In a telephone conversation on October 29, Dulles explained that the Nagy government was not one "we wanted much to do with."[55] Unlike Gomułka, Nagy was considered insufficiently anti-Soviet.[56] Austrian "observers" were reported not to trust Nagy.[57] Thus it came as no great surprise when the newly designated minister to Hungary, Edward Wailes, was instructed not to present his credentials to the Nagy government.[58]

This order reflected a measure of premature optimism in Washington about the possible outcome of the revolution. On the one hand, the United States was ready to deal with "national communists," and Nagy was the only leader in Hungary in this category. If Nagy had been dismissed as a negotiating partner, Dulles must have expected the revolution to go beyond its national-communist phase and produce a different political system. Otherwise it would not have made sense for Wailes to make the trip at all. It was another matter that Nagy did not seek any contact with the U.S. legation in Budapest. On November 3, Wailes was finally instructed to contact the highest circles of the Hungarian government. American officials explained this move by saying that Soviet actions had driven Nagy to the UN and the United States and that he had accepted popular demands for freedom and independence.[59] The administration's divergent views of Nagy and Gomułka reflected broader patterns in U.S. foreign policy that impeded U.S. action during the Hungarian Revolution. In almost every respect, Poland took priority over Hungary in U.S. calculations.

The fact that there was no communication between Washington and Nagy would have tragic consequences. Nagy could have been advised that no external help was coming and that Hungary's place in the Warsaw Pact was not to be questioned. This would have been highly significant: Nagy's public remarks about Hungary's place in the alliance contributed to the Kremlin's rationale for invasion. Poland's pre-eminence on Washington's agenda is confirmed by the fact that the NSC ordered a feasibility study of a NATO or American-led military intervention there, while no such study was ordered for Hungary. Poland was also more significant for the Soviets: Khrushchev had stormed into Warsaw to negotiate with Polish leaders, but sent only minions to Hungary. By then, he was unquestionably in charge of the Soviet leadership, *primus inter pares* in the presidium. The debates there were genuine, with factions like in any decision-making body, but Khrushchev had the final word in the deliberations. It is also true that Poland got off the hook because the events in Hungary spiraled into violence on October 23, making the deployment of Soviet troops to Budapest essential.

The NSC called for "studies immediately to be made to determine whether, if the U.S.S.R. used military force to suppress the Gomułka regime or to reverse a future trend toward national independence, and if the Polish regime resists and makes timely request to the U.N., the U.S. should be prepared to support any U.N. action, including the use of force, necessary to reimposing its control."⁶⁰ On November 23, 1956, the assistant secretary of defense instructed the Joint Chiefs of Staff to prepare a feasibility estimate of UN military intervention in Poland and to gauge the risk of global conflict.⁶¹ The Joint Chiefs' response suggested that if the United States resorted to these measures, it would incur the risk of a general war,⁶² which ruled out the possibility of military action on Poland's behalf. Interestingly, the Joint Chiefs reckoned that the Polish army would participate on the Western side. This appraisal harmonized with the Muscovite view that Soviet military action in Poland would spark a civil war between the pro-Western Polish army and the pro-Soviet Polish security forces. The chief of staff of the U. S. Air Force estimated that with the contribution of the Poles, NATO and the U.S. air command would be sufficient to defeat Soviet bloc forces, as long as the goals were limited.⁶³ Under NSC directive 5612/2, any attempt by the Soviet army to restore its control over Poland would require the administration to inform Moscow that the UN would immediately take steps to reverse the situation. The Joint Chiefs of Staff drafted a message to inform the Kremlin that the United States was ready to use force against the USSR in restoring Polish national independence.⁶⁴ Although the message may not have been sent, it reveals American military thinking about conflicts behind the Iron Curtain. The possibility of military aid to Hungary was discussed at a much lower level of the bureaucratic hierarchy and was then discarded altogether. American diplomatic staff members in Budapest told the crowds that gathered in front of the legation in Szabadság tér (Liberty Square) that the revolution was a matter for the "U.S. government and the United Nations" to resolve.⁶⁵ In a conversation with the president, CIA deputy director Robert Cutler broached the dropping of an atom bomb on Soviet logistical lines in the Carpathians to stop Soviet troops from entering the Hungarian plain. Records do not reveal whether this was an off-the-cuff idea or something that the intelligence agency had given serious thought. Either way, Eisenhower rejected it outright, saying that the United States could not risk destroying the people it wanted to save. It was widely held in political circles that a conventional military conflict in Europe would escalate into a nuclear confrontation. Eisenhower was certainly convinced of this.⁶⁶ American intelligence agents had gleaned that the Soviets would go to any length to keep Hungary within the bloc, thus military action on behalf of the Hungarians could escalate into an all-out war.⁶⁷ Khrushchev had said as much immediately before the revolution erupted. On October 30, the PPS asserted that effective measures were likely to lead to hostilities with the Russians.⁶⁸ In connection with the Spanish offer to send arms to Budapest, Deputy Secretary of State Hoover responded that they could not do so without provoking an armed conflict with the Soviet Union.⁶⁹ The sheer logistical difficulties also militated against such efforts. No supplies could be sent in without violating Austrian, Czechoslovakian, or Yugoslavian airspace or territory. For obvious reasons, those states would never have agreed to the Americans' use of their territory for military purposes.⁷⁰ Vienna regarded even the presence of Hungarian refugees on Austrian territory as politically risky and asked for Washington's mediation in removing them.⁷¹ Hungary was inaccessible to conventional forces, which practically excluded military help. West German foreign minister Heinrich von Brentano admitted that it was impossible to provide military help to the rebels.⁷² Robert Murphy remembered that Dulles and everyone else in the State Department were terribly distressed but that nobody had enough imagination to come up with a solution.⁷³

Nor could the United States count on support from its allies. Great Britain was apprehensive about the events in Hungary. In London's view, the Warsaw Pact and the Soviet Union's domination of Eastern Europe threatened NATO, and tensions between the communists' client state governments and their populations posed a threat to European security. Yet it was feared that a mass uprising could lead to a clash between NATO and the USSR. And the British were not concerned solely with the risk of war. A sudden collapse of communism might cause interwar nationalism and ethnic strife to flare up again. In addition, there was the concern that Germany could seek to restore its hegemony over its eastern neighbors.⁷⁴ In its policies toward central Europe, Great Britain had traditionally placed stability ahead of national self-determination, and it would be guided by a similar calculus when the prospect of Soviet collapse there finally became a reality in 1989.

Was this concern with escalation a pretext for inaction or a real fear? Given that the Soviets were willing to use force to defend their vital interests – including Eastern Europe – and that the Kremlin had suggested it would go to any length to keep Hungary in the fold, there was little reason to doubt that an armed intervention would lead to a large-scale war. Eisenhower was convinced that both sides would give it all they had, including their stocks of nuclear arms. In such a war, national survival would be endangered[75] even if influential scientists considered the damage estimates for a nuclear war to be exaggerated.[76] The president was in a dark mood; his conception of the situation was shaped by his experiences of World War II. "In view of the serious deterioration of their position in the satellites, might they not be tempted to resort to very extreme measures and precipitate a global war? This [is] a situation which must be watched with extreme care. After all Hitler had known . . . that he was licked. Yet he had carried on to the very last and pulled down Europe in his defeat. The Soviets might develop some desperate move such as this."[77]

Lacking other viable alternatives, Washington hoped that assuring Soviet leaders of the peaceful intentions of the West would convince them to let the Hungarians go. The strategy was clear to the British ambassador in Washington: "It is evident that the American administration is anxious to dispel any Soviet fears that the U.S. intends to exploit the present situation in the Satellite area to the point of creating a strategic threat to the USSR. Foster Dulles made this quite clear in his speech in Dallas."[78] It has been argued that the Soviet intervention could have been avoided if Washington had pushed the Soviets to the limit and accepted something less than a restoration of Hungarian independence. Records reveal, however, that the United States *was* willing to compromise on the outcome in Hungary and even to offer something in return. Moreover, there is nothing in the Soviet deliberations to suggest that the Kremlin's decisions were influenced in any way by American policies.[79] U.S. foreign policy was not responsible for all outcomes.

Henry Kissinger has criticized the Eisenhower administration for not raising the price tag on aggression and for not seeking the advice of such specialists on Soviet foreign policy as George F. Kennan, Charles Bohlen, and Llewelyn Thompson.[80] Bohlen sent messages reaffirming the American course of action. Given Kennan's position on containment, it was hardly likely that he would have proposed a more assertive line. In return for their moderation, U.S. officials expected the same from the Soviets.

The president is usually praised for his reserve in the crisis, although the Hungarians felt let down. The historian H. W. Brands has written that at some points in time and in places such as Hungary, Eisenhower's propensity not to interfere in the course of affairs served the cause of world peace well. Even though these events did not constitute a victory for American foreign policy, the president appraised the risks of an activist foreign policy and decided to accept a lesser failure rather than risk a catastrophe.[81]

In working on the principles of foreign intervention in the nineteenth century, John Stuart Mill had drawn on the lessons of the failed Hungarian war of independence in 1848 and 1849. Mill believed in the ideals of self-help and nonintervention, but he thought these principles could be suspended if intervention on behalf of a democratic movement could be justified, that is, if a foreign power had already interfered in the domestic affairs and self-determination of a community. A similar situation arose in 1956. But in the nuclear age, Michael Walzer argued, the situation was not so simple. Political prudence required that the intervening power weigh the dangers to itself and to the international community. That power would have to, "for moral reasons[,] weigh the dangers its actions will impose on the people it is designed to benefit and on all other people who may be affected. An intervention is not just if it [exposes] third parties to terrible risks: the subjection cancels the justice. . . . And clearly, an American threat of atomic war in 1956 would have been morally and politically irresponsible."[82]

John Lewis Gaddis pointed to an important contradiction: "American nuclear superiority [was] useless in the crisis. Eisenhower's caution . . . illustrated very clearly the limits of nuclear superiority. Indeed, fear of the Soviet Union's wholly inferior nuclear capability had convinced Eisenhower of the need to reassure the Russians, rather than to deter them."[83] This reassurance may not have been immoral, as many argue. Rather than giving the Russians a blank check to put down the revolution in their sphere of interest, it may have been designed to buy time for a political solution to the crisis. Eastern Europe was thus the captive of Soviet nuclear deterrence. Paradoxically, the revolution may have strengthened, rather than enfeebled, the Soviets' hold on the satellites. As it turned out, no power on Earth could wrest it from them.

One final question remains: did the United States unfairly encourage the Hungarians to revolt? As far as covert operations were concerned, CIA director Allen Dulles declined to recommend any steps for NSC approval. On the other hand, Cord Meyer, the chief of the CIA's psychological warfare division, ordered Radio Free Europe (RFE) to support the Hungarian rebels, though he later denied having tried to incite a revolution.[84] Meyer's actions were questionable if judged by the guidelines of the NSC's 1956 report, which stipulated that the United States was to avoid inciting actions that could lead to reprisals or other consequences detrimental to U.S. foreign policy goals. Although spontaneous manifestations of dissatisfaction and anticommunism could not be prevented by public statements alone (even if individual lives were endangered), the RFE broadcasts encouraged them.[85] After the crisis ended, the CIA acknowledged that "RFE occasionally went beyond the authorized factual broadcasting... to provide tactical advice to the patriots as to the course the rebellion should take and the individuals the best qualified to lead it." Although the CIA claimed that the RFE broadcasts before the revolution "could not be construed as inciting armed revolt," that conclusion contains only a part of the truth.[86]

"THE SOVIETS ARE NOT INVINCIBLE"

American propagandists were not in an easy position. Eisenhower had rejected military intervention and thus the rebels could not be "encouraged." At the same time, it would have been unacceptable for the revolutionaries to portray their sacrifice as "needless." Thus the Voice of America was left to support the rebels' aspirations and condemn Soviet intervention. Transcripts of Radio Free Europe's Hungarian-language broadcasts from 1956 reveal how incautious, and even reckless, some of the programming was, though a meeting of the State Department's Special Committee on Soviet and Related Problems had concluded that RFE should not provide the Hungarian rebels with instructions.[87] In one instance, a broadcaster assured listeners that "The Soviet forces deployed against Hungary are not invincible. The troops available [to the Soviets] have been used up... the Hungarian forces are superior to these.... Every weapon that is not being used now will turn against its holder. Every weapon that procrastinates will be victim of the Nagy government's deceptive tactics." In an even more reckless broadcast transmitted on November 28, a speaker using commentator Julián Borsányi's pseudonym "Colonel Bell" advocated a full-blown war against the Soviets, to be fought by regular formations of the Hungarian People's Army. The broadcaster claimed that "if the Hungarian national forces are clever and their leadership is quick-witted, then the Soviet reinforcements... will not even reach the Danube line within three or four weeks."[88] "Borsányi" invoked the tactics used by Serbian partisans against the Germans in 1943.[89] "Borsányi" himself had refused to relay these messages, but they still went out attached to his pseudonym. And this was not the only program to convey such advice. Gyula Litteráti-Loótz, alias Gyula Patkó, a former member of the Vannay Brigade, a Hungarian unit made up of military cadets who had fought staunchly on the German side in the bloody siege of Budapest in 1945, used the radio to disseminate tricks for making Molotov cocktails. Such broadcasts were allegedly conceived by William Griffith, a senior official at RFE/Radio Liberty.[90] Defectors later remembered such programs well and had considered them effective encouragement to revolt. In 1953, at least some East Germans had expected "Western tanks [to] come to their aid"; many Hungarians did so as well. One rebel later claimed that "the demands of Hungarian insurgents grew because RFE broadcasts encouraged the belief that decisive aid would come from the West," although he admitted that "RFE made no specific promises to this effect."[91] This former rebel insisted that "the mere reiteration of the need to continue the fight convinced the Hungarian populace that they would not be fighting for long.... RFE would have better served Hungary's cause by frankly informing the Hungarian people that the only aid the West was able to supply was food and medicine."[92] Listeners found Bell's programs among the easiest to recall[93]; after the revolution, only the program "Reflector," hosted by "Gallicus," was remembered as more damaging.[94] Looking back on these events, one rebel asserted that the West should have used the radio to explain why intervention on their behalf was *not* possible.[95]

Radio Free Europe's programming was hard to reconcile with the long-standing notion that an unassisted armed uprising against the Soviets could lead to the annihilation of the rebellious nation. Reckless programming was also at odds with the strategy of avoiding Soviet intervention and negotiating Hungary's independence. Listeners were not informed of Dulles's view that they had no chance of victory, even though this might have convinced them of the futility of their efforts. In fact, precisely the opposite was broadcast, and the rebels were not called on to lay down their arms even after Marshal Konev's forces had launched their offensive on November 4. This was not the first occurrence of its kind, either. During the rebellion in Poznan that summer, Dulles had stated that the U.S. government should not encourage anything, but RFE had been allowed to broadcast encouraging propaganda to the Poles.[96] By contrast, the response to the Berlin uprising in June 1953 was very different. Frank Wisner, then deputy director of the CIA, suggested that the United States should do nothing to encourage the East Germans to further actions that might endanger their lives, and CIA director Allen Dulles shared these views. Accordingly, on June 17, RIAS, the propaganda station transmitting to East Germany, exhorted the rebels to obey the Soviets and to avoid clashes with Soviet forces.[97] No such effort was made to stop the Hungarians,[98] even though the British Foreign Office told the State Department, perhaps cynically, that "it was important not to encourage the Hungarians to needless self-slaughter because we need that kind courage alive behind Iron Curtain ... [and] it is important not to encourage Russians to be rougher and tougher than they already are."[99] As early as 1953, U.S. officials had concluded that the Soviets would not tolerate the secession of a satellite; the United States would be able to liberate them only by force, which was impossible.[100] Self-liberation may have been risky, but it was the only way Eastern Europeans could roll the Soviets back. RFE broadcasts may have been tolerated because they were part of an alternative strategy, one that actively encouraged armed revolt and could be plausibly denied later on.[101]

In the final analysis, U.S. policy was torn between activist desires and a fear of their consequences, and thus sent mixed messages both to the rebels and to leaders in Moscow. On the one hand, Washington hoped to reassure the Kremlin about U.S. intentions, to insist that the revolution would not be exploited at the Soviet Union's expense, and thus to start talks regarding Hungary's status in the Soviet bloc. On the other hand, no effort was made to curb RFE's reckless propaganda campaign, which aimed at subverting the Nagy regime by giving hope to the rebels and encouraging them to fight as hard as they could. This contradictory approach undermined the basic strategy: the harder the Hungarians fought, the smaller the chance for a peaceful outcome. The fact that the West ruled out an armed response to the Soviet invasion made their struggle suicidal. The policy of liberation may have been pursued at the cost of others' lives. Although there was hardly any hope that the uprising would succeed, it may have been promoted as a low-cost effort to destabilize the Soviet bloc. If the effort failed, the American role in it could be denied.

It has also been argued that the United States "sacrificed" Hungary for a détente with the Soviet Union because the existing situation was better than a change in the balance of powers.[102] Western passivity has been seen as a de facto recognition of the division of Europe.[103] It is equally likely, however, that American options were held in check by the fear of escalation.[104] Washington believed that the Soviets intended to keep their sphere of vital interest in Eastern Europe at any price, from which follows that any measure short of war would be ineffective. The historian Bennett Kovrig has argued that a rapid recognition of Hungarian independence by the United States and the sending of an international observation committee could perhaps have delayed the Soviets' decision and thereby helped to consolidate the achievements of the revolution.[105] Given what we know of the Soviets' decision-making processes and subsequent events, this seems unlikely.

Even though the U.S. abandoned the Hungarian Revolution, it did not remain completely inactive. By keeping the memory of the uprising alive and on the UN agenda, Washington was able to put pressure on Kádár's Soviet-installed government. This was not easy. Already on November 8, Indian premier Jawaharlal Nehru declared that he could no longer make sense of the events in Hungary. Americans footed much of the bill for the Hungarian refugees in Austria and covered the costs of transporting them to their final destinations. Perhaps most significantly, the United States waived its Hungarian immigration quota and accepted more than thirty-eight thousand people, including top scientists, engineers, scholars, and experts on the Soviet bloc, some of whom it recruited.

The bloody suppression of the 1956 Hungarian Revolution led to some soul searching in Washington. The lessons would restrain Washington from encouraging other oppressed populations to rise against their rulers.

This became obvious in Czechoslovakia in 1968, when U.S. propaganda organs were explicitly barred from encouraging the Czechoslovakians to fight. President Bush's caution in 1989 can also be explained in part by the ghosts of 1956. Both containment and liberation had failed. The Soviets' hold in Eastern Europe was reinforced, and oppressive regimes in Romania, East Germany, and elsewhere were strengthened by the Soviets' willingness to restore order. The aims and methods of American policy were transformed as the policies of containment and isolation came to seem impotent and even immoral. Instead, policies of "peaceful engagement" and, later, "bridge building" were adopted. In the 1950s, the United States had sought to *destabilize* the satellite region for the sake of Western security, but from the 1960s onward, Washington desired to *consolidate* the region for that same purpose. The 1950s made clear that Eastern European independence could not soon be restored. Instead of full independence, the United States began to work toward the autonomy of the Eastern Europeans, toward distancing them from their hegemon.

5

Reprisals and Bridge Building

The failure of the 1956 revolution shattered the notion that the European status quo could be changed without the consent of the Soviet Union. Washington was forced to take a hard look at the European situation, and over the course of a decade they concluded that there was nothing they could do to reverse the continental division. The calculation that Europe would remain divided for the foreseeable future was not based solely on the United States's inability to influence the power structure behind the Iron Curtain. The domestic and foreign policies of communist states like Poland, Romania, and Czechoslovakia also seemed to be changing for the better. Romania in particular showed strong signs of autonomy in pursuing its self-interest. The likelihood that these adjacent states would act as marionettes in a hostile Soviet action was diminishing. Romania and Poland seemed just as likely to promote American interests by mediating crises that embroiled the United States. In addition, the hardest pillar of political power, economic strength, depended on openings to the West, which in Poland, Hungary, and Czechoslovakia were becoming more and more pronounced. Although the Comecon survived until the final curtain fell on communism in Eastern Europe, the economic and financial survival of the communist states came increasingly to depend on the Western world, including the United States. As time went by, this hitherto troublesome region appeared to be stabilizing. Rather than diminishing the security of the Western world, Soviet hegemony might even have served to enhance it by holding national antagonisms in check. In a dramatic reversal of the policies of the late 1940s and 1950s, Eastern Europe ceased to be an area of conflict between the Soviet Union and the United States. Washington hoped to remain a nuisance and to keep the satellites from becoming mere Soviet proxies, but they also recognized that Soviet power seemed to have brought balance to the Eastern European region. The painful experiences of 1956 demonstrated the Soviets' ruthless determination to cling to their empire, exposed American weaknesses, and raised questions about the dangers of promoting radical, revolutionary change.

Washington's goals and strategies in Eastern Europe changed. A reduction of hostility and an increase in cooperation between East and West were now to be achieved through a cautious and gradual process of evolution. The United States would no longer put other peoples at risk. It was in no one's interest to do so: stability and predictability were valued by both the East and the West. The United States would thus build bridges of human contact through culture and trade and would avoid provoking the Soviets. The Eastern Europeans would be left to decide how far they would go. Stability prevailed over national self-determination as a result of strategic calculations and a measure of callousness regarding the plight of the subjugated states. They could become *more autonomous*, but not sovereign and independent. While in the 1950s U.S. officials had thought destabilizing the Eastern European regimes would enhance Western security, in the 1960s American policymakers aimed at the *consolidation* of the communist systems for the same purpose. Eventually, the dire domestic records of countries like Hungary and Romania were doctored in official U.S. documents to excuse the decision to support them. Washington preferred autonomy in foreign policy over domestic liberality (in the communist sense); hence, the United States supported Romania's repressive regime almost to the very end. In the early 1970s, a high-level functionary at the National Security Council (NSC) wrote that the status quo in Eastern Europe was not so bad for the United States. International systems are not changed according to the intentions of bureaucrats, whatever their level. Policies begin to live their own lives. Subject to the interpretations of the functionaries who implement them, they are changed by situations on the ground in the countries in which they are enacted. This policy of engaging Eastern Europe through trade and propaganda, through cultural, scientific, and humanitarian exchanges, backfired in Hungary. Rather than promoting domestic change within the limits of the existing power structure, it helped undermine the political system. Interestingly, American policies were mirror images of the Hungarian, thus Hungarian communists and American liberals unintentionally reinforced each other's approach.

Deep changes took place in Hungarian policies, too. After a ruthless period of consolidation that cost hundreds of lives, the Soviet-installed regime in Hungary gradually began to open to the West, hoping that an economic consolidation would produce political tranquility. János Kádár, the new Hungarian leader, had to contend with a number of conflicting forces: recurrent fears of another massive uprising, domestic opposition on his left and right, the Soviet Union's interests, and American pressure for change. After prevailing over isolationist forces in the party and the state security apparatus, Kádár came to rely on these organizations' more enlightened members to help him open Hungary to closer economic ties with the West. Their purpose was simple: to finance economic modernization and growth with foreign credits while making small concessions at home. Neither Kádár nor his diplomats nor his foreign trade representatives envisioned a democratic transformation or the subversion of the Soviet bloc. Their purpose was the same as that of the communist diehards: to strengthen the regime, if by different means. The opening of Hungary would have come more quickly were it not for the ups and downs of superpower relations, and in particular the Vietnam War. Eventually, Hungary's financial desperation led it to wriggle free of external constraints on its economic policies. Even the state security apparatus went along with the financial logic of this opening up. The Hungarian thirst for capital, especially technology, scientific knowledge, and management skills, led it to liberalize access to certain Western markets. In the 1960s, these processes were just beginning, and Hungary's outstanding disputes with the United States and the international community would make it one of the hardest cases with which the United States had to deal. But it was also in Hungary that U.S. diplomats would score their first significant victory of the Cold War: American political pressure contributed to a relaxation of postrevolutionary terror and the granting of political amnesty to the majority of the people who had been imprisoned for their participation in the 1956 uprising.

IDEOLOGY AND PRAGMATISM IN HUNGARIAN FOREIGN POLICY

After 1956, Hungarian leaders were concerned with one overriding goal: keeping 1956 from ever happening again. The question was how to do it. After the initial restoration of order, a massive terror campaign of heavy-handed policies lingered for years, and Hungarian officials realized that a lasting consolidation would require the appeasement of the population. Economic and cultural incentives would be offered in return for political tranquility. Many resented this opening to the hostile capitalist world and doubted the newfangled policy of appeasement through economic growth. There was concern that external influences would erode the system instead of stabilizing it. Slowly and gradually, and never entirely unequivocally, the proponents of engaging with the West would win this debate. They did not surrender their ideological beliefs or become liberal democrats, but they did lose their irrational fears of the West. Their goal was the same as the conservatives': a lasting consolidation of the system called socialism, but with new methods. This would require communists to demonstrate pragmatism and conceal their ideological motivations in exchange for short-term gains. All this took place in the wider context of the Cold War, a fluctuating set of relationships between and among the United States, the Soviet Union, and the Soviet satellites. Pragmatists worked toward the long-term goals of communism by calling for a rapprochement with the United States, which would make it possible for Hungary to finance an export-oriented growth policy.

It was assumed that the communist satellites (with the exception of Romania) did not have their own foreign policies. They worked for the purposes of the Soviet Union and were allowed to pursue their national interests only if they did not conflict with the Soviets'. As will be seen, this was true for Hungary, although with some qualifications. It is also true that the communist bureaucracy was not monolithic. As in a liberal democracy, communist government agencies sometimes differed over the means of arriving at an outcome even when they agreed on a strategic objective. Behind these debates was the search for a balance between pragmatism and ideology. No decision maker wholly rejected one or the other, though the increasing prevalence of pragmatic concerns and external constraints would eventually undermine the foundations of the dictatorship.

In general, Hungarian foreign policy, including its stance toward the United States, was governed by two main considerations. One was the status of U.S.-Soviet relations. The second was the widely, though not evenly, shared ideological conviction that the struggle between progressive and reactionary forces extended into the international arena. Thus Hungarian leaders never left any doubt: as a result of proclaimed ideological principles and unannounced reasons of power politics, the interests of the Soviet Union would take precedence over whatever might be best for Hungary. Eventually, one area would be exempted from this subordination: economic foreign policy, where Hungarians were increasingly free to take their own interests into account.

Romania's example showed that the USSR might have allowed more room for foreign policy maneuvering than Hungary created for itself. This could be explained by several factors. One is Romania's relatively lesser strategic significance, which had allowed the Soviets to pull their troops out in 1958. Second, the internationalist convictions of Romanian leaders were less pronounced than the Hungarians'. The third was an intangible, almost sublime element of foreign policy: historical experience. Continuous failures throughout the twentieth century – lost wars and territorial truncations – made Hungary a less self-confident state than its larger neighbor to the east. Hungarian leaders were explicit about international constraints. Shortly after the 1956 revolution, Ferenc Münnich, a veteran of the Spanish Civil War and an old-guard Bolshevik, declared that "by virtue of its position Hungary cannot take the initiative in international politics, which is Moscow's prerogative."[1] Kádár, who as prime minister gradually emerged as his country's undisputed leader, asserted that Hungarian-Soviet "friendship" was based on an ideological communion, adding that Hungary's interests coincided with the Soviet Union's.[2] Referring to the Sino-Soviet conflict, Kádár explained that "Hungarian communists always avowed that the cornerstone of internationalism was and still is the ideological-comradely relationship with the Soviet Union. There exists no anti-Soviet communism and never will."³ Soviet imperial domination was thus coupled with ideologically motivated loyalty.

The historian Csaba Békés has argued that "right from the outset the guiding principle of Hungarian foreign policy was to walk the middle of the road, which meant the unceasing emphasis (and practice) of unconditional loyalty to the Soviet Union with the increasingly effective exploitation of maneuvering space, the assertion of national interest (or what the leadership took as national interest) given that this did not collide with the Soviet Union's interests."⁴ Yet relative independence was not an objective condition that a satellite could exploit or not. Rather it was created by the desire to be independent, as Romania showed. With the passage of time, Hungary enjoyed more and more freedom to formulate bilateral relations, and as Soviet oversight became less stringent, Moscow's power position in Eastern Europe mellowed from domination to a softer form of control, hegemony.⁵ This should not be confused with independence; in every question of global significance to Moscow, Hungary took the Soviets' side. A case in point was the issue of the Hungarian minorities in neighboring people's democracies. Prior to the communist takeover, this subject was the focal point of Hungarian foreign policy. After 1948, however, Budapest was willing to forgo clashes with Prague or Bucharest for the sake of bloc cohesion, even though it was aware that the minorities' situations remained critical and the passivity of the Hungarian government was undermining whatever popular support it had. In international forums, Hungary always espoused the Soviets' position, sometimes expressing even harsher views of the "capitalist world" than did the Kremlin itself. Occasionally, this kowtowing to the Soviets subverted other Hungarian goals. While the great pressure of financing its economy was forcing Budapest into strenuous efforts to normalize relations with the United States, the Hungarian foreign minister delivered a viciously anti-American speech in the UN that impeded the normalization process for a significant period. When required to, the Hungarians adopted Soviet positions even in contacts with individual states, the best example of which would be their economically crucial relationship with the Federal Republic of Germany (FRG). The establishment of Hungarian diplomatic relations with Bonn was delayed because Moscow wanted it tied to

German concessions on Poland and Czechoslovakia. This would change slightly in the 1980s, when contacts with Western states were intensified despite expressions of Soviet displeasure; by then, the Hungarian regime's survival depended on its ability to get Western loans.

Hungary's aspirations defined only a part of its relationship with the United States. It was largely a function of Soviet-American relations as they stood on the chessboard of world politics. Hungary never toyed with the option of expanding its leeway by playing the Americans or the Chinese against the Soviets, as Romania did. The memory of Soviet invasion would stay with Kádár for the rest of his life. In 1958, the Foreign Ministry asserted the primacy of Soviet needs: "our relationship [with the Americans] is a function of changes on the international scene and of the extent to which the successes of Soviet policy, to which we must give all support possible, force the United States to alter its anti-socialist stance."[6] In 1960, for example, the Political Committee stressed that progress in relations with the United States would be contingent on the success of the Khrushchev-Eisenhower summit. Later, the Vietnam War would stand in the way for an entire decade, even though the Soviets privately blamed China for protracting the war. Kádár's stance on Vietnam is revealing. He, too, put some of the blame on China, and even on the intransigence of the North Vietnamese. And yet he supported Hanoi, not just because Moscow desired it, but also because he genuinely thought of the conflict as the struggle of one nation against imperialism. Kádár may have been ready to open up to the West and normalize relations with the United States as early as 1963. The Kennedy administration's policy of peaceful engagement would have been conducive to such a move, but the crisis in Indochina and the Soviets' role in it cut this path short. Thus the cycle of debt that finished off Hungarian communism in the 1980s could have come a decade earlier. In that case, the agony might have been prolonged, or the collapse in Hungary accelerated, with all the potential consequences for the rest of the Soviet zone.

The coupling of superpower relations with Hungarian policy was not a well-guarded secret. An official at the Hungarian Foreign Ministry explained to his American counterpart that the problems in U.S.-Hungarian relations "are caused on two levels, because of American aggression against Vietnam, U.S. policy in the Middle East and Cuba, etc." and only secondarily by bilateral issues.⁷ This equation may apply to other states that are dominated by a more powerful neighbor. Though external control may be crucial to such a state's behavior, domestic components like inner power struggles and ideological convictions should not be disregarded either.

Hungary was caught in a nutcracker. On the one hand, Soviet expectations had to be met. On the other, the vital importance of external economic relations made it essential to accommodate the West, at least to some degree. This would in turn strain relations with Moscow, as Hungary did in disregarding Moscow's wishes and joining the International Monetary Fund. When the communist regime was in its final agony, this conflict could no longer be resolved. Soviet demands in foreign policy and intelligence were incompatible with the Hungarian economy's American and Western European life-support system.

Ideology remained an important component of foreign policy even though Kádár, whose influence in this field was decisive, liked to stress his pragmatism. He even called himself a practitioner of realpolitik. Nevertheless, he saw pragmatism as a means of promoting the victory of socialism, though not at any price. He repeatedly stated that averting war was more important than the worldwide victory of Marxism-Leninism. Shortly after the third Arab-Israeli War in 1967, Kádár asserted that his government accepted the principle of peaceful coexistence, which "may have been impossible only twenty years ago when the power of ideology was a lot stronger, but currently the greatest challenge is to avert a nuclear war between the two superpowers."⁸ Of course, it is possible that he was just repeating Soviet slogans. Brezhnev condemned his predecessor's brinkmanship (although he would soon fall victim to the same vice) in lamenting that the Cuban missile crisis had "almost led to nuclear catastrophe." In a debate about the first round of Strategic Arms Limitation Talks (SALT) in the Soviet Defense Council, he argued against depleting the Soviet economy for the sake of military expenditures.⁹ Yet for Kádár, the threat of war became a fixation on which he would reflect again and again. In 1978, he was willing to act as a go-between for a Carter-Brezhnev meeting and told Averell Harriman that a nuclear war would annihilate the Hungarian nation. In 1965, he told the Political Committee that "peaceful coexistence and [the] struggle against imperialism exist side by side ... [either there will be] a Third World War or we must tolerate each other, exist side by side."[10]

While Anastas Mikoyan was predicting to American leaders that communism would triumph in the United States one day, Kádár, in a confidential discussion with U.S. officials, offered a declaration possibly intended for the higher echelons in Washington: "I must say we have no illusions about the victory of socialism or communism in the United States. We Hungarian Communists are realists."[11] Still, he walked a tightrope between realism and ideology. In 1972, he would receive William Rogers, the first secretary of state ever to visit Budapest, but only after a personal plea from President Nixon, this after the superpowers had just agreed on arms limitations. Kádár took his obligations to North Vietnam seriously and mentioned Saigon in passing in his talks with Rogers. It should be remembered that even though SALT I was among Brezhnev's priorities, Moscow had almost canceled Nixon's visit at the last moment in response to American bombings in North Vietnam.[12] In his dealings with the United States, the first secretary of the Hungarian party tried to appear as a dedicated communist who took the correlation of powers seriously. In dealing with Americans, he consciously used the term "realpolitik," adding that he used the word despite his dislike of Germans. At the same time, he wanted his political system recognized as a fait accompli. Readers of the deliberations of the Hungarian Politburo may get the impression that its members were not aware of Hungary's insignificance in international politics. Particularly in the first few years after the revolution, they showed arrogance in dealing with Western states, an attitude for which Moscow was the gold standard. Prime Minister Ferenc Münnich declared that if the Americans "have a problem," they could "go home." Kádár seems to have been one of the few who had a clear notion of his country's place in the world, often calling it a "tiny louse" (U.S. translators may have been puzzled by his word choice, which they translated as "flea").

Hungarian leaders wanted de facto American recognition of their government as well as a lasting Soviet presence in Eastern Europe. Dictatorships require external threats to legitimize their rule, and Hungarian propagandists cast the United States in the role of relentless and cruel enemy almost to the end. Initially, Washington refused to recognize Hungary's postrevolutionary government, and later the Hungarians would refuse to acknowledge U.S. gestures. Eventually, Kádár came to understand that the United States would not extend armed assistance to realize its goals in Eastern Europe and therefore had "no interest in the outbreak of revolutions." He believed that the Americans were "trying to improve their positions in the people's democracies to widen their influence on the masses – to drive a wedge between them and the Soviet Union if they can – and as in the case of Poland to extend economic aid with the intention of promoting a more independent policy."[13] Why did the Hungarian party leader still wish to normalize relations with a state that questioned the very existence of his regime? Between 1957 and 1963, he had no other choice; only Washington was in a position to relieve Hungary of its international isolation. Most of the other European communist states enjoyed closer relations with the United States than Hungary did, which the Soviets tolerated.

In the final analysis, the United States took the front seat in the relationship. Under Eisenhower, the United States had had no choice but to put up with the communist regimes, even though Washington was actively promoting regime change. After the failed revolution, the president wrote Marshal Tito that European tensions would not subside until the Soviet Union withdrew behind its own borders and released Eastern Europe from its grip.[14] This position would change gradually but fundamentally. The strident ideological content of the U.S. approach all but disappeared, replaced by a more pragmatic intention to reward or punish what Washington considered good or bad behavior. Washington followed its allies' lead in accepting Soviet hegemony for the sake of European stability, while promoting liberalization and greater autonomy from the Kremlin. Eventually, Hungary emerged as a model for domestic change, while Romania pursued the kind of foreign policy Washington wanted to see. Ideological dogma captivated the minds of communist leaders and guided their actions. Such blinders did not obscure the views of planners and decision makers in Washington, who drew pragmatic conclusions from the failed revolt of 1956. Émigré groups from Eastern Europe would come to support more moderate policies toward the communist regimes, and the conservatives were never strong enough to force Washington's hand.

The first steps in the new direction were taken under Eisenhower, when U.S. officials recommended that export controls be relaxed, rather than made more stringent, in order to promote the satellites' national self-determination and independence. While U.S. allies in Europe had long urged such a move, American businessmen also resented stringent controls that disadvantaged them in competition with European firms. In 1958, the secretary of commerce introduced important changes to export-control regulations.[15] In May, the NSC replaced the doctrine of liberation with a policy of "gradual change."[16] There were other factors as well. The Eisenhower administration came under strong domestic and international fire for its encouragement of the Hungarian rebels in 1956 and for the inaction that left Hungary without any hope of Western help. Most importantly, Washington seemed finally to be settling down into the post-1948 world order. Eastern European regimes were being re-evaluated. Their consolidation and lasting survival was no longer an unlikely prospect. The passing of time, it seems, inured people to the endurance of the regime, eventually making it acceptable to them. Economic conditions would improve, Soviet occupation would become less blatant, and communist education was impressed particularly on the youth, who had no experience of any other lifestyle. Thus this rapprochement between the regimes and their societies made American attempts to isolate the satellites superfluous.[17] For several years the State Department persisted in the assumption that the majority of the people behind the Iron Curtain did not accept the communist system.[18]

PEACEFUL ENGAGEMENT

The process of re-evaluation would drag on for years as American government officials failed to see eye-to-eye on the course to be followed. The battle lines would remain the same, except that the hard-line stance of the military establishment was becoming harder to justify. The Joint Chiefs of Staff insisted that independence behind the Iron Curtain would never be restored peacefully. They therefore advocated support for passive resistance and unrest, with calculated guerrilla activities only when the United States was ready to face a Soviet counterstrike. The wording remained relatively cautious since it was evident that the United States would not soon be ready to oppose the Soviets in Eastern Europe. Dulles recommended that this passage be stricken from the policy paper. The

NSC also affirmed that the United States would not use force to end the Soviet occupation of Eastern Europe and would not support uprisings either. Recognizing that the isolation of the Soviet bloc had failed to bring about the collapse of the communist regimes and had done nothing to curb the growth of Soviet military power, as some in American military circles had expected, the NSC advocated an expansion of contacts with those states that were willing to alter their position of subjugation to the USSR. The United States would seek to drive a wedge between the Soviets and their satellites because efforts to expand communism still posed a threat to U.S. security. The elimination of communist regimes remained the long-term goal, but it was now acknowledged that this would happen only gradually. "Subjugated peoples" would be advised to approach their goals slowly. Even the restoration of their independence would not mean that the United States would surround the Soviet Union with a ring of hostile states. Prewar relations with Eastern European countries would be restored on an individual basis.

The harsh reprisals that had followed the 1956 revolt made this more conciliatory approach impractical for Hungary. Improvements in the relationship between the two countries could not be allowed to compromise the worldwide symbolic value Hungary had acquired by struggling against communism. The new U.S. policy of engagement would focus on Romania, whose leaders were particularly eager to mend fences with the West so as to acquire American technology and justify their legitimacy to the Romanian people.

Economic issues were the focal point of this debate. Since his election, Eisenhower had argued for the expansion of trade, which he regarded as the "politician's best weapon." He now argued that trade expansion would serve the purpose of peaceful transformation, but not necessarily of profit. The president resented congressional restrictions on his administration's ability to change policies of trade with the Soviet bloc. Lawmakers curbed the administration's efforts to sell surplus grain to the Soviet Union, although in 1957 they were willing to make an exception for Eastern Europe. On the other hand, Dulles opposed a generally worded statement on economic relations and the secretary of commerce's proposal to encourage U.S. business deals with the Soviet bloc. Eventually, it was decided that the United States would normalize commercial relations on an individual basis in order to expand trade and reduce the economic dependence of the "captive nations" on the Soviet Union.[19] Although liberation was rejected for the time being, Washington did not recognize "Soviet domination" in Eastern Europe and still nurtured hopes for the restoration of "independent national existence."[20] In 1960, the State Department was still insisting that "the United States was not ready to recognize the status quo in Eastern Europe."[21] At the same, it suggested that Eastern Europe's significance would diminish for future administrations.

The Kennedy administration termed its approach "peaceful engagement." In 1962, President Kennedy declared that differences existed even within the communist world. He said the United States would eventually take the initiative in Poland and elsewhere and warned that the United States should never acknowledge the permanence of Soviet domination in Eastern Europe.[22] In his State of the Union address, the president signaled that he would seek congressional approval for an expansion of trade with the satellites on a selective basis. The State Department's Policy Planning Staff asserted that the flexible use of the trade weapon would enhance the ability of the United States to shape events behind the Iron Curtain.[23] The Department of Finance also advocated the use of U.S. products and services in an aid program aimed at helping the Poles balance their budget.[24] Senator Charles Vanik of Ohio expected "the individual missions of American citizens" who visited these countries (which he assumed were pro-American) would do more to restore hope in democracy than covert operations.[25] At Radio Free Europe, the policy of persuasion replaced messages of subversion. Central oversight of its broadcasts was enhanced, and commentators who had come under fire for their incendiary language in 1956 were laid off. Instead of liberation programs, the station now supported gradual liberalization and sought to provide its listeners with credible information. A special committee set up by President Kennedy stated that the best way to reach people behind the Iron Curtain was to provide them with information and ideas. Knowing that their lies could be debunked would force communist leaders to strive more for truth. The committee recommended programming that would shed favorable light on the United States and proposed that brazen interference in the domestic affairs of the target countries should be avoided.[26]

In the early 1960s, the focus of Washington's new policy toward Eastern Europe was Poland, which was considered the most pragmatic satellite. Poland was thought to provide its citizens with more freedoms than other Iron Curtain states, which made it an "acceptable model" for the other satellites. Poland, however, owed only a part of its prominence in U.S. policy to its internal reforms. Situated between the FRG and the USSR, Poland straddled lines of communication that the Soviets would need to exploit in order to conduct hostilities in Western Europe. American officials therefore found it expedient to "diminish the degree of Soviet control over this strategic area." In addition, the United States wanted to demonstrate that more independent communist states would be able to count on American assistance. The policy of engagement allowed the administration to show its interest in the Polish people and, it was hoped, to exert limited influence on the policies of the Polish government. This intention was encouraged by the fact that economic difficulties had opened the Poles' minds to an intensification of relations with the West. Human contacts were to be promoted by a relaxation of visa procedures; trade concessions were expected to mollify the Poles on other issues. The sale of agricultural surpluses would demonstrate capitalist "plenty."[27]

This engagement of the communist regimes through expanded commercial and cultural contacts took place largely on paper. All American attempts to liberalize and intensify trade relations with the communist world were blocked either by Congress or by government bureaucracies. Conservative representatives insisted that trading with communist states constituted support for the enemy. In 1961, the Department of Commerce hoped to permit the sale of state-subsidized agricultural products to communist states for hard currency, but Ohio representative Delbert Latta moved to curb this deal in Congress. That same year, Romania, which was trying to assert its independence from the Comecon, tried to purchase U.S. equipment for ten of its factories, but the Department of Commerce denied the export licenses.[28]

Throughout the later 1940s and 1950s, the chief purpose of American policy in the Soviet bloc was to transform communist regimes into full-fledged democracies and to put an end to the Soviets' domination there. In the political calculus of the times, no other solution seemed as likely to ensure lasting peace and prosperity on the old continent. In the early 1960s, all this began to change, and debate over the desired direction for Eastern Europe was reopened.

In the year of Kennedy's death, the State Department dramatically rephrased U.S. policy toward the Soviet bloc. It reiterated that "our stake in Eastern Europe is generally that of our security.... The United States is threatened by the intrusion of Soviet power, through occupation and domination of this region, into the heart of Europe." On two crucial points, however, the State Department deviated from earlier positions. Up to then, instability in Eastern Europe had been considered *conducive* to European security, but now the opposite would be argued. "The *instability* of these regimes ... also acts as an unsettling factor in Europe [,] *jeopardizing* the general security" (emphasis mine). Secondly, the restoration of full independence no longer seemed a likely prospect. "The present realities of Soviet power in Eastern Europe hold out little if any prospect for an early rollback of Soviet domination there.... The United States seeks to promote ... *national autonomy* ... the U.S. nevertheless does not accept the moral legitimacy of the East European regimes or the permanence of Soviet domination in the region" (emphasis mine). A complete break with the policies of the Eisenhower and Truman administrations was necessary: "a policy of quarantine by the West ... is passive, sterile and defeatist."[29] Not everyone agreed with the State Department's new principles, which seemed to imply acquiescence to a permanent division of Europe into two spheres of influence. Undersecretary of State Averell Harriman represented continuity with the Truman era in hoping "to see E[astern] E[uropean] peoples fully independent, prosperous and restored to their natural relationship with the rest of Europe and the Free World ... [for these] peoples to be able freely to determine their own form of government and achieve independence ... Europe cannot enjoy full security and prosperity until Eastern Europe is drawn back into historical relations with the rest of Europe."[30] Such voices would soon fade; the division of Europe would be accepted as an accomplished fact. At this point, however, the new approach had not yet crystallized. Ambiguities persisted. The State Department affirmed that it would not accept permanent Soviet occupation of Eastern Europe, but that seemed to conflict with its statement that the long-term objective in Poland was a "larger degree of independence" from the Soviet Union.[31] This was hardly a restoration of sovereignty.

Progress toward autonomy would be achieved by establishing contacts with the people behind the Iron Curtain, but this approach would require the communist regimes there to pursue different tactics as well. Thus the break with the American policies of the first decade of the Cold War, which required the full isolation of the Soviet-sponsored governments, was complete. Slowly, more intensive contacts were established with most of the Soviet-bloc states, the prerequisite for which was the settlement of outstanding issues such as debts to the United States. This would not be possible in Hungary, where mutual hostility rooted in post-1956 reprisals and the U.S. decision to provide refuge to Archbishop József Mindszenty was acute. Hungary would demonstrate that dramatic changes planned at the top were difficult, if not impossible to implement. In fact, American policy would be determined more from the bottom up than by decision makers at higher levels.

THE POWER OF DIPLOMACY

Democratic powers have always faced recalcitrant rogue states and have often presumed that the right set of policy pressures could force these contrarian nations to comply with civilized codes of conduct, domestically and internationally. It is often forgotten that even such states have domestic, bureaucratic struggles, disagreements between agencies and decision makers with divergent agendas. Such states are often nationally self-conscious entities that demand respect from the international community and thus whose actions are conditioned by foreign pressures and unforeseen events. Accordingly, there is no single, "correct" policy for any regime. Transformations require patience, flexibility, and the quickness to adapt to changing circumstances. When to give in and when to tighten the reins, how much to expect in a given situation, how to sound out the vulnerabilities of the opponent, and how to avoid to blackmail: these are problems and dilemmas that are rarely recognized as factors in international affairs.

The United Nations had been conceived as a supranational organization that would transcend narrow national interests to uphold international harmony. Instead, it became a forum in which the interests of the two superpowers and the blocs they represented were to collide. The UN was incapable of stopping Soviet aggression in Hungary, but, perhaps surprisingly, it became an efficient tool with which to exert pressure on the Kádár regime to bring its bloody rampage of terroristic reprisals to an end.

Shortly after Marshal Konev launched the final assault on Budapest, the UN decided to suspend its decision on the Hungarian mandate in the world organization. Subsequently, on January 10, 1957, the General Assembly formed a fact-finding committee to explore the Hungarian situation in the hope of sending a UN mission to Budapest. A separate proposal, to reject the Hungarian mandate (which would have meant the country's ejection from the world organization), was not accepted due to fears it could serve as a precedent for excluding Taiwan, which the USSR had refused to accept as the legitimate representative of mainland China. Nevertheless, domestic opponents accused the Eisenhower administration of a double standard, of doing less against the aggressor in Eastern Europe than the ones (Israel, France, and Great Britain) in the Middle East.

Even so, the taking up of the Hungarian question and the suspension of the Hungarian mandate isolated the Kádár regime. In the international arena, Kádár's government was forced to concentrate on resolving the Hungarian question, restoring its full status in the UN, and breaking out of its status as an international pariah. This was not a new predicament for Hungarian foreign policy: the country had experienced similar situations in the aftermath of both World Wars. For the United States, the question was whether the Hungarian government was willing to take concrete steps toward a domestic détente. To maximize the pressure, Washington questioned the Soviet-installed regime's legitimacy. In addition to the impasse in the UN, Hungarian-American relations were also complicated by a number of other, interrelated issues, which meant that U.S. contacts with Hungary took place at a lower diplomatic level than its relations with other people's democracies. One such issue was the seemingly intractable problem of Cardinal Mindszenty. Until the problem of his presence in the U.S. embassy in Budapest was resolved, talks on the settlement of financial claims could not even begin. Such efforts were already under way with Romania. Moreover, diplomatic contacts were stuck on the legation level. The new minister, Edward Wailes, had arrived at his post as Soviet tanks were rolling into the Hungarian plain. He had had no time to present his credentials to the Nagy government before it was overthrown, and he did not do so afterward. When the U.N. General Assembly acted on a U.S. proposal to suspend Hungary's mandate, the Hungarian Foreign Ministry asked Wailes to present his credentials or leave the country. Wailes opted for the latter and departed within four days. Nobody suspected that a decade would pass before his successor was appointed. Thus bilateral relations had again reached a nadir. Almost all contact ceased, even at the grass-roots level. Diplomats avoided each other in the corridors of the United Nations; "contacts" were restricted to the mutual expulsion of military attachés; the Hungarian chargé was not received at the State Department for months. Political pressures drove the business community to boycott Hungary, which led Paprikás Weiss, a popular delicacy store in New York, to seek State Department approval to import Hungarian salami. American passports were invalid for Hungary, thus almost no one embarked on the trip across the ocean.

In their own way, the Hungarians also created tensions, sometimes seemingly ready to take things to the breaking point. In reality, Budapest would stop at the edge of the precipice, just short of breaking off relations. In May 1957, at the instigation of the Ministry of Interior and the counterintelligence service, the Hungarian Foreign Ministry demanded that the U.S. legation reduce its staff of diplomats and administrative personnel.[32] The pretext was that "the American employees are illegally collecting intelligence instead of nurturing relations."[33] The Hungarians then offered to exchange ministers,[34] but to nobody's surprise this offer was rejected. Dulles would allow minor gestures only to support steps toward the relaxation of tensions and to nurture the peoples' spirit of resistance. This included the relaxation of travel restrictions and a token expansion of cultural exchanges.[35] The chargé in Budapest opposed the exchange of heads of mission on the grounds that it would entail the acceptance of the Hungarian mandate and the easing of economic controls; at the same time, he saw no chance for UN resolutions to be implemented in Hungary.[36] Austria's foreign minister, the future chancellor Bruno Kreisky, who would eventually build a special "K und K" relationship with Kádár, offered to mediate negotiations with the regime in Budapest. When Kreisky asked what conditions they would have to fulfill for the sake of normalization, he was told that the Hungarians needed to comply with UN resolutions, admit UN representatives to the country, grant safe passage to Mindszenty, and make peace with the Hungarian people, conditions the chargé in Hungary considered exaggerated.[37] By the end of 1957, tensions partly subsided when it became apparent that the regime in Hungary would last.

Kádár managed to eliminate the Central Workers' Council, his main rival for the hearts and minds of the working class. Meanwhile, his Stalinist foe Rákosi was kept in Moscow, and the chief ideologist of Hungarian Stalinism, József Révai, was neutralized. Most importantly, Kádár won Khrushchev's firm support.[38] The head of the State Department's Bureau of East European Affairs pointed out that the regime in Budapest was on its way toward domestic and international consolidation. Internationally, the revolution was fading into oblivion, and it was doubtful whether international pressure could do anything to liberalize the system. He therefore recommended a more flexible course, one more readily adaptable to existing conditions.[39] On the first anniversary of the revolution, Eisenhower made it clear that no one in the higher echelons of power had contemplated any radical changes in U.S. policy. In response to the president's address, Hungarian Foreign Ministry officials recommended that diplomatic relations with the United States be severed, but Kádár rejected such a drastic measure. Instead, a harshly worded note was drafted calling on U.S. leaders to refrain from supporting "counter-revolutionary elements." The Soviets, however, prevented the message from being sent.[40] Moscow exercised restraint, an approach Washington did not expect.

Another push toward normalization came from an unexpected quarter. The Hungarian chargé in Washington, Tibor Zádor, a relatively junior diplomat who had distinguished himself in his proclamations of support for Kádár, now advocated "steps towards normalization of relations" with the United States in order to "reduce the intensity of the hostile campaign and improve relations with other Western states." He recommended the release of the Hungarian employees of the U.S. legation and a "revision" to the quantitative controls on American personnel. This diplomat was also in favor of further steps, including an exchange of statements by high-level functionaries; he primarily recommended diplomatic channels and the use of the legation in Washington in pursuing a policy of normalization.[41]

On his own initiative, Zádor met Senator George W. Malone of Nevada with the intention of expanding trade relations.[42] Zádor used the modest means at his disposal to break out of his isolation, although some of his efforts may have done more harm than good, such as film screenings at the legation. One of his movies was meant to show that "the situation is quite normal and the traces of the counter-revolution were disappearing," but since such a film "obviously" did "not exist," the legation staff pieced one together from some older footage and borrowed a screen from the Romanians. This short film was named *Hungary 1957*, but the Hungarian desk officer at the State Department had good reason to doubt its authenticity. It was also subject to question whether an audience of American businessmen, lawyers, and diplomats would appreciate scenes like "Workers' Meetings in Budapest," "The Formation of the Workers' Militia," "Ho Chi Minh's Visit," and the like. "Unforgettable April," a film about the visit of "the Soviet Party and Government Delegation" to Budapest, screened on a different occasion, was probably equally successful.[43]

In 1958, the Hungarian Foreign Ministry, which had showed at least some interest in improving relations with the United States, perceived a positive shift in the American attitude toward Hungary, which they hoped to exploit. For the sake of improvements, they made a list of possible measures taking into account mutual grievances. On the Hungarian side these included the closing of the consulates in 1951, the "propaganda campaign" against the Hungarian government including Radio Free Europe, and the lack of economic contacts. The foreign ministry recommended that the Hungarian government make known that it would be receptive to an overture and simultaneously release the U.S. legation's imprisoned employees.[44] The Hungarian security apparatus won this round of the contest; as soon as the employees in question were released, they were immediately relocated to the countryside. At that point the Foreign Ministry was under the close direction of the Hungarian Socialist Workers' Party's (HSWP) Department of International Relations, so there is no doubt that its recommendations represented the ideas of at least some top leaders.

The international climate favored improvements. Khrushchev launched a peace offensive, and although he made it clear that he would not negotiate on Eastern Europe, he pulled Soviet troops out of Romania and at least one division out of Hungary. Romania made good use of this window of opportunity. Party leader Gheorghe Gheorghiu-Dej invited Americans to observe Romanian elections, and in 1958 his government announced that it would purchase $100 million worth of industrial equipment from the United States. The National Security Council noted that Romania was prepared to expand its commercial ties and to arrange limited cultural, scientific, and technical exchange programs. In 1960, the Battle Act was modified to allow the president to extend economic aid to communist countries if it could be justified by national security, and in March of that year, Romania concluded an agreement to settle outstanding financial claims with the United States. An exchange of notes would launch exchange programs between the two countries in 1962, by which time Washington was no longer treating Romania like the "most Sovietized" satellite.[45]

On January 25, 1958, the Political Committee of the HSWP discussed the normalization of Hungarian-American relations and the settling of the Hungarian question at the UN. Foreign Minister Sík gave a speech in Parliament on April 2 in which he announced that he would take an initiative to repair ties with the United States. On May 8, he told the American chargé, Garret Ackerson, that he had been thinking of exchanging ministers but that the initiative had been cancelled. Ackerson knew Hungary well. He had worked at the U.S. legation in the 1930s and had compared the current state of Hungarian affairs unfavorably with the country he had known under Horthy. Sík had studied in Moscow in the 1930s and lived through the Great Terror, which left an indelible imprint on his psyche. His memoir, published in the 1970s, recounts that while he was third secretary in the Hungarian legation in Washington, he made a trip to New York during which the police stopped his car in Central Park after dark. Sík was terrified of the American authorities, convinced he would disappear and lose his life. Now the foreign minister was claiming that his initiative had been rescinded because the Hungarian mandate had been rejected during the Maritime Law Conference in Geneva and because the U.S. representative to the UN, James Wadsworth, had demanded information on the whereabouts of the leaders of the Hungarian Revolution. Ackerson pointed out that both events had occurred after Sík had announced his diplomatic initiative.[46] Its cancellation was all the more surprising since

Sík had informed Soviet foreign minister Andrei Gromyko of his proposed action on April 7, and Gromyko had approved it.[47] U.S. diplomats suspected that Khrushchev might have been behind the cancellation of the initiative, but in light of the foregoing this seems unlikely. The minutes of the Khrushchev-Kádár talks contain no reference to it. In his conversation with Ackerson, Sík hinted that the Foreign Ministry had had nothing to do with the relocation of the legation's employees, and the fact that Sík needed minister of interior Béla Biszku's permission to relax travel restrictions suggests that the Ministry of the Interior may have intervened. Ackerson recorded that during their conversation, Sík nodded toward the Interior Ministry building on the opposite bank of the Danube. This would indicate that the process of formulating foreign policy was more complicated than the Americans suspected. The Soviets did not interfere in relatively minor matters; the two rival ministries were simply pursuing the same goal by different means. In the 1950s, the Ministry of the Interior would win battles like this even though the foreign minister was part of the old guard that had returned from Moscow.

The Foreign Ministry suspected that the State Department no longer considered felt justified in "punish[ing] the Hungarians for the Soviet intervention" and in continuing to reject overtures.[48] If this idea had any real basis, it would be soon dispelled. The execution of Imre Nagy and his associates on June 16, 1958, put an end to the lukewarm and sluggish process of improvement. These executions outraged the administration, and U.S. diplomats made it clear that relations would turn for the worse. This also meant that the Hungarian question would be kept in the limelight at the UN. On July 11, State Department officials consulted with their British and French ambassadors on the rejection of the Hungarian mandate and possibly even the rupture of diplomatic relations with Budapest.[49] The drastic step was not ultimately taken, but the latest American offensive at the UN caused a great headache in Hungary. The Political Committee prepared an offensive of its own: they wanted simultaneously to "unmask" American espionage and to show that Nagy's execution was the outcome of legal proceedings against the participants of the 1956 revolt. In this debate, prime minister Ferenc Münnich called the American legation a "spy center" and declared they could "go home if they want." The éminence grise of

Hungarian foreign policy, a party historian named Dezső Nemes, did not think it "useful" to sever diplomatic relations.[50] The anti-American campaign would include two more steps. There would be a government press conference on September 12 to denounce American espionage against Hungary. Then Budapest would present a diplomatic note offering to participate in a dialogue if the United States "ceased hostile propaganda and spying against the country."[51] Hungarian leaders were trying to legitimize their terror campaign by alleging threats from a dangerous foreign enemy. The Foreign Ministry's unveiling of an American "spy center" in front of a large audience invoked the atmosphere of the show trials, though now the "defendant" was a foreign state.

The State Department was in no hurry to reply. Six months passed before the Hungarians were told that normalization would occur if they were to adhere to their commitments to the UN and to the terms of the peace treaty.[52] In the meantime, U.S. diplomacy was working feverishly to reject the Hungarian mandate, even though China's membership in the organization would require a two-thirds majority. In this critical situation, the foreign minister initiated the second part of his "diplomatic offensive," announcing to the General Assembly that judicial proceedings against "counterrevolutionaries" had been closed and terminated. U.S. ambassador to the UN Henry Cabot Lodge Jr. immediately declared that to his knowledge, four other leaders of the uprising had just been convicted.[53] The "offensive" was thus defeated and the Hungarian question was inscribed on the agenda of the Thirteenth General Assembly. By rejecting the Hungarians' mandate, the State Department wanted to draw world attention to communist reprisals there and thereby to deal the Soviet Union a psychological defeat.[54] Eisenhower did not want to proceed all the way to a rejection of Hungary's membership, so the original situation remained: the Hungarian mandate was merely suspended. The General Assembly did condemn the Hungarians for the executions (although the Americans erroneously held the Soviets responsible) and asked Leslie Munro to report on the implementation of the UN resolutions on Hungary.

As if this were not enough, another time bomb exploded, fraying the U.S.-Hungarian relationship. Cardinal Mindszenty, the archbishop of Esztergom and primate of the Hungarian Catholic Church, had been held under house arrest until a Hungarian army unit – the head of which was later executed for this act – briefly liberated him in 1956 and brought him to Budapest to deliver a radio message. Sensing that he was running out of luck, he appeared at the entrance of the U.S. legation in the small hours of November 4, just as the Soviet offensive on Budapest was beginning. He was admitted and, after consultations with Washington, given asylum, even though legation personnel feared that doing so might cause the premises to be attacked. Béla Kovács, whose arrest in 1947 became a symbol of the Soviets' ill will behind the Iron Curtain, also appealed for refugee status but was denied. Kovács spent a number of years in Soviet captivity before serving in Imre Nagy's revolutionary government. The Hungarians understood that it was against international law and U.S. government regulations to use diplomatic missions for asylum, but Mindszenty's presence at the U.S. mission eventually provided unforeseen opportunities to influence Hungarian politics, the likes of which did not exist in any other Iron Curtain state.

Initially, there were only difficulties. Legation employees prepared for an assault on the building by the Hungarian police they expected would try to abduct the cardinal. In order to minimize risks, he was barred from all correspondence other than discussions of his personal life. Nevertheless, the aged prelate would bombard senior U.S. officials and even presidents with letters. He criticized their foreign policy. He thought it too conciliatory toward the Soviets, too accepting of the status quo in Eastern Europe, and unprincipled in its compromises with communism, a system he detested passionately. He was rarely answered. His views were taken into account in the controversy over the return of the Crown of Saint Stephen. Mindszenty also caused problems for the communist authorities. He was regarded as a political criminal, but charging him seemed undesirable because of the public outcry it would likely cause. Both sides took the most convenient course: they kept silent about it for as long as possible. But Mindszenty's fate was to become interlocked with Cold War politics.

The day of reckoning arrived with the death of Pope Pius XII on October 9, 1958. That afternoon, the U.S. Embassy in Rome recommended that the State Department ask the Sacred College of Cardinals to summon Mindszenty to the papal election. Even though the State Department did not like the idea, the embassy took the necessary steps without waiting for an answer.[55] The Vatican saw a chance to get Mindszenty out, so the State Department instructed the American legation in Budapest to negotiate with the Hungarian government on behalf of the Sacred College of Cardinals.

Leaders in Budapest hoped so much to extract political concessions that it took them a long time to realize that there was no chance for any. Mindszenty himself was fairly unenthusiastic about the prospect of leaving his refuge and agreed to go only after lengthy persuasion. The Hungarians were not even willing to explore the possibility at that point. They pointed out that their authorities had condemned the cardinal to a life sentence for "political and other crimes" in 1956, including his escape from custody and his carrying out "criminal activity against the political order of the Hungarian People's Republic." It was also noted that the cardinal's asylum constituted a violation of international law and U.S. government regulations, as well as an attempt to interfere in Hungary's internal affairs. Mindszenty's fate was a Hungarian matter, not "subject to Hungarian-U.S. talks." Finally, the note made it clear that the government would "pay more attention to [the] Mindszenty question in the future."[56] The legation concluded that the Hungarians were happy with the situation, or at least less uncomfortable than the United States. They emphasized that their "guest" was not making things any easier and should therefore be advised to seek the pope's "spiritual leadership."[57]

The Foreign Ministry saw no link between Hungary's intransigence and the poor state of its relations with the Americans. This was attributed to the "sharply antisocialist stance of [American] leading circles," due to which only slow improvements could be expected. The resolution of the Hungarian question and the normalization of ties were expected in the longer run.[58] By this time, however, there were debates in the higher echelons of the party about economic reform. This would require financial and economic assistance from the United States, but it was well-understood that Washington would not agree to expand economic ties until its outstanding financial claims were settled. The balance would favor the Americans. Even if Washington were to accept all Hungarian claims, including frozen assets, the restitution of Hungarian commodities, and compensation for the property lost on the "Gold Train" – Jewish valuables seized by the Nazis – it would not match the amount owed by Hungarians for war damage to U.S. property and nationalizations of American companies.[59] Although the "Polish model" presented itself, the Foreign Ministry counseled procrastination. Poland had agreed to a financial settlement with the United States using income derived from increased trade resulting from commercial incentives and long-term loans. Romania had increased its trade with the United States threefold between 1956 and 1960 and had agreed to settle U.S. claims. The Hungarians must have known that Romania had signed to pay only a fraction of the original claims against it, and that Hungary could expect a similar deal, but the necessary pragmatism and political will seems to have been missing from Budapest.[60]

IMAGE MAKING IN U.S. POLICY

Foreign policy is formulated not according to some objectively existing reality in the external world, but on the basis of images in the minds of the leaders of one power or another. Eventually this dependence on perception would work in favor of Kádár's Hungary. Hungary came to be pictured as the most liberal state behind the Iron Curtain, even though, to paraphrase the Nobel Prize–winning author Imre Kertész, it was "so horrible we did not even notice it." In an analysis of Eastern European satellites prepared in 1959, the CIA noted that Hungary had been consolidated to a considerable extent since 1956, and although the CIA had been grossly mistaken three years earlier, it predicted again that mass rebellion was unlikely.[61] Stability was discussed in a positive light, even though prior to 1956 it would have been seen as an unwelcome development, and pro-American sentiment was taken for granted. Senator Charles Vanik wrote that "penetration might be made in this part of the Soviet-dominated world to preserve and keep alive well-developed but silent affection for America. The hope for the restoration of democracy in this part of the world will be strengthened as a result of individual missions of American citizens visiting their relatives."[62] The second secretary of the legation in Budapest, however, warned American citizens traveling to Hungary that tourism behind the Iron Curtain was different from a trip to Western Europe. Tourists and people visiting family were to be aware that they were coming to a "police state," where, if they met with difficulties, they might end up at the mercy of capricious bureaucrats.[63]

A correspondent for ABC television named George Bailey traveled across Hungary in 1960 and claimed to have spoken with "hundreds of people." His overall impression was "depressing"; he found that people had lost faith and did not wish to get into trouble. Most of the people with whom he had spoken were initially suspicious, but after a while they tended to loosen up and begin condemning the Kádár regime and the country's foreign occupation. He visited the once-upscale holiday resort of Siófok on Lake Balaton, where he saw hotels for workers so depressing that they evoked Orwell's *1984*. It seemed as if everyone were wearing the same uniform and taking part in group activities like building roads. Later in Tihany, Bailey met others more like the Hungarians who lived in his memory, teachers, writers, and intellectuals who openly lambasted the regime. In the agricultural town of Makó, Bailey found beautifully kept farm animals and buildings, "but the cows were better groomed and happier than the people."

While Bailey saw the dreariness of life there, National Geographic deputy director Francis Shor focused on Hungary's standards of living. Shor randomly selected ten families, and since there were two wage earners in each, every one of them was able to maintain "a tolerable standard of living." Shortages of goods were "annoying," but nothing that would lead to "unrest." He found housing conditions poor but thought that people tolerated it "philosophically." Shor found, "somewhat to his surprise" (one may wonder why he would find this surprising), "a fairly substantial intellectual middle class – unhappy and by no means enthusiastic about the regime, but tending to accept it for the present." A freelance writer, Lance Wiley, found evidence that standards of living were higher than in Romania and thus opined that the Hungarians "did win a partial victory in 1956." In contrast to Bailey, one legation officer found that the middle-class way of life had not disappeared. Hungarians went on vacation to "enjoy themselves"; only a few attended the almost compulsory lectures that had become a part of what was called "vacationing" in other bloc countries. He found "much greater resistance [in] the Hungarians to forced indoctrination" than in other communist countries. When the officer, Nicholas Feld, visited the scenic resort of Tihany, he thought it "still preserve[d] some of its upper bourgeois atmosphere." The intense, purposeful flow of motorized traffic to Lake Balaton evoked the "decadent" pursuits of people in the free world.

The *Wall Street Journal* reported on manifestations of a "bourgeois lifestyle" in Romania, where communists "could enjoy the merry-go-round of night clubbing, sailing and opera recitals." Later, the *New York Times* would celebrate changes in Romania in a small press campaign. The U.S. legation in Budapest reported in 1961 that the number of American visitors to Hungary had grown significantly and that many were surprised by the courteous treatment they received from Hungarian authorities. A *Christian Science Monitor* correspondent was pleasantly surprised by the significant changes that had taken place in Hungary since 1956, but an American conductor of Hungarian descent, László Halász, found a different reality in 1962. Halász had once thought that changes for the better had occurred in Hungary, but two visits convinced him he had been mistaken. "There is general fear, cultural stagnation and except in showcase Budapest, a serious food shortage."[64] Dissent notwithstanding, a narrative was being constructed to improve the image of satellites in hopes of earning them better treatment by the United States. They were no longer depicted as mortal dangers to American values, but as places that were assuming more human qualities. The psychological barriers to accepting the communist regimes, and to accepting that Soviet control of Eastern Europe was a more or less permanent phenomenon, were falling.

Czechoslovakia was a favored spot in the 1960s. Many Americans found reality there far more pleasant than the nightmarish image presented by anticommunists. Journalists found it to be a prosperous country even by Western standards, the only country where "Marx was right," although some remarked that Prague was just a showcase that hid a less happy truth. Even so, Czechoslovakia was considered the most flourishing state behind the Iron Curtain.[65] Prague had begun to open up in the mid-1950s; Czechoslovakia's renowned spas in Karlovy Vari and Marianske Lazne were reopened in 1955. Six thousand Americans visited the country in 1958, and the motivation for allowing them to do so was twofold: an urgent need to earn hard currency and a desire to display the "human face" of socialism.⁶⁶ Hungary also seemed to be on its way to more prosperity. In the view of the American legation in 1960, Kádár had "every reason" to be satisfied with the performance of his economy. In spite of a claim in the *New York Times* – which would later champion the cause of "goulash communism" – there was no shortage of food in Budapest.⁶⁷ And despite its political pronouncements, the Hungarian government was making cautious overtures to the West, and there was interest in increasing the number of visitors. American Express included Hungary in one of its package tours: three nights in Budapest's *art nouveau* Hotel Gellért, or at the Royal, complete with sightseeing, wine tasting, and a night at the opera.⁶⁸ Such images evoked not communist drudgery but a more upscale and colorful middle-class existence.

Hollywood was making a comeback behind the Iron Curtain as well, though not to the same extent in every country. In 1961, two American movies were among the most popular motion pictures in Hungary. *Cinderella* averaged 339 moviegoers at 3,800 (!) screenings, while *Around the World in Eighty Days* was enjoyed by an average of 555 viewers per show. These numbers far exceeded the averages for Hungarian (206) and Soviet (174) films. Hollywood was equally popular in neighboring Czechoslovakia, where authorities considered cinema a potential tool for political subversion and cultural penetration. The first American film to be shown in Czechoslovakia in the communist period was screened only in 1960, and U.S. movies would seldom appear there after that, although some were allowed into the Karlovy Vary film festival to raise its international prestige.⁶⁹ Thus in this regard, Hungarian practices were more liberal. In his study of "soft power," Joseph Nye has pointed out that while American films may make the United States look attractive in some countries, they may have the opposite effect elsewhere. Hollywood images could also attract one segment of the population while repelling others.⁷⁰ Thus showing American movies behind the Iron Curtain was a double-edged sword. Some carried messages critical of the United States and underscored communist propaganda. So, on the basis of a "gentleman's agreement," an expert on motion pictures and propaganda in the U.S. legation in Budapest, Turner Shelton, "censored" whatever products the U.S. movie industry intended to show behind the Iron Curtain. Disney went so far as to negotiate with the Hungarian state film company Hungarofilm to produce a movie in Hungary for distribution in the United States. The State Department disapproved, fearing unwanted publicity for Hungary.[71]

Washington imagined Eastern Europe as a pro-American region, a dubious assessment as there were no public opinion surveys to prove or disprove the assertion. Other evidence was circumstantial and sometimes hard to interpret. An attraction to American-made automobiles, for instance, does not automatically signify approval of U.S. foreign policy. State Department assessments optimistically concluded that "the US in Eastern Europe can draw upon considerable assets of goodwill. . . .This fund of resources is perhaps unique throughout the region and unmatched by any Western country." America "has the most prestige of any Western nation in Eastern Europe," and therefore the American presence there had to be increased.[72] Hungarians had been considered mostly pro-American ever since World War II. Lacking reliable statistics, surveyors depended on meta-communication and signs to measure American popularity, such as the reactions of people on the street to an automobile flying a star-spangled banner.

In 1961, the chargé in Budapest perceived a drop in American popularity. He noted that he never saw any signs of hostile sentiment; in fact, people were ready to show their interest and friendship in many ways, including semihidden smiles, waves, hearty welcomes, and even gestures of agitation. He attributed the decreasing frequency of such friendly signs to the Berlin crisis and to Titov's space flight, which had showed that Soviet successes were real. This slide in popularity was also a part of a healthy maturing process, as the image of America as a romantic "white knight" shrank back to reality.[73] In spite of the tensions, the U.S. legation sought to maintain contact with the Hungarian intelligentsia, which was not easy. Some, like the celebrated actress Éva Ruttkay and her spouse, for instance, rejected an invitation to a party organized by a foreign national and claimed that attendance "would not be wise." Still, the influential poet and translator István Vas did show up, and he asserted that "the most exciting and most productive contemporary theater existed in the United States." The remarks of another poet of national recognition, Ágnes Nemes Nagy, were more characteristic of the paucity of knowledge in Budapest about American culture. Nagy had no idea that Ezra Pound had been born American, had never heard of Robert Frost, and declared that "only the British produce good poetry in the English language."[74]

AMNESTY FOR 1956

While tensions between the two superpowers were receding, the United Nations became the scene of a dramatic confrontation between the Western bloc and the East over censuring the Soviets and their now staunch allies in the Hungarian government. This would be American diplomats' first real success behind the Iron Curtain and would demonstrate the usefulness of diplomacy and the strength of the United Nations in exerting pressure on tyrannical governments. While international interest in Hungary was waning, not a single outstanding issue between Hungary and the United States had been resolved. As long as there was no improvement, the United States would not be able to exert any influence, thus American diplomats in Budapest recommended a favorable response to Hungary's overtures on trade expansion and a readiness to drop the Hungarian question at the UN.[75] While the diplomatic mission was closer to the real world in its day-to-day dealings with the communist government and often closer to the truth in arguments with the State Department, this time Washington's harsher approach turned out to be more productive. There was an impasse; the Hungarians were waiting for an American initiative in a diplomatic game of patience. Only Tibor Zádor, the Hungarian minister, took the initiative to find out the Americans' conditions for reconciliation. He told the State Department that while Hungary stood ready for talks, the government would not consider any negotiations directed toward "changing Hungary's social order or provid[ing] unilateral advantage to the opposing political forces in the current international situation."[76] In response, Livingstone Merchant, the head of the State Department's Office of East European Affairs, confided that what mattered for Washington was not the domestic order of an individual country, but its relationship to the Soviet Union. Ceaușescu's Romania would go on to become the best example of this initially rigid, but later more flexibly interpreted, formula. In Hungary, there was no apparent sign of autonomy from Moscow or even a domestic ideological thaw. International relations were still seen through the prism of Marxist ideology as a struggle between the "forces of progress" and imperialism. The Hungarians' "main question" was whether the expansion of American imperialism could be halted.[77]

Referring to the spirit of Camp David and the imperative of reducing international tensions, Soviet deputy foreign minister Vasili Kuznetsov tried to convince the Fourteenth Assembly of the UN to drop the Hungarian question for good, but to no avail. At Lodge's initiative, the world organization once again condemned the Soviet Union and the Hungarian regime for failing to implement UN resolutions in Hungary.[78] Budapest was thus forced to revert to diplomacy and the politics of "small steps," moving from easily resolved problems to more difficult ones.[79] They began negotiating economic issues such as animal health, hoping to be allowed to sell meat in the United States for the first time since the war.[80] Their main purpose was the "liquidation" of the Hungarian question.[81] Hungarian leaders were willing to make an offer on Mindszenty but affirmed that no "compromise of principle" would be made, and they required that any formula take into account the "prestige and sovereignty" of the Hungarian People's Republic, a condition they would take very seriously.

Budapest wanted to be viewed as an independent entity on the international scene. The Political Committee, the country's highest decision-making organ, concluded that an offer for "normalization" should be made if the four-power summit scheduled for May 1960 was successful. This initiative included an offer to resolve the Mindszenty problem.[82] The conditions set by the Politburo were wholly unrealistic, betraying an ignorance of the possibilities for Hungarian (and even Soviet) foreign policy. Up to that point, the party had regarded an exchange of ministers as the precondition of normalization talks; now it was meant to be a "reward" for the Americans if they would stop "spying," cease giving refuge to Mindszenty, and terminate their economic embargo against the socialist bloc. It was as though the Political Committee did not take its own initiative seriously. The best solution for the Hungarians would have been house arrest for Mindszenty, with his release from the country dependent on "international conditions."[83] That meant the United States would have had to guarantee that the cardinal would not publicize his political views, a condition that was not unacceptable to the United States.

The Hungarians seemed to forget that any solution would require the approval of the Vatican and of the cardinal himself. Budapest insisted that the Vatican remove Mindszenty from his position as head of the Hungarian Catholic Church, and the affair thus grew into a quadratic equation the chief variable of which was an obstinate individual who had made it his personal mission to combat communism.[84] In the meantime, the Political Committee hoped that the United States would take the first step. The Hungarian Foreign Ministry may have had a small degree of independence from the country's leadership; the minister in Washington seems to have acted independently in using a Swiss mediator to inform the State Department that the government in Budapest was willing to take into account whatever recommendations the United States administration might make, or to make specific recommendations of its own, if it would contribute to a normalization of relations. The mediator, Joseph Milleger, added that he and Zádor had discussed the possibility of releasing Mindszenty to Switzerland. He also claimed that the Hungarian foreign minister was ready to approach the U.S. minister in Budapest to discuss the Mindszenty question, which was then considered the main impediment to a restoration of relations. The State Department refused the Swiss mediator's services, questioned his authenticity, and affirmed that they would keep the Hungarian question on the UN agenda in order to preserve the prestige of the UN and remind the "free world" of the Soviet Union's behavior in world politics.[85] Hungarian records contain no trace of this strange episode, thus it is hard to say what may have motivated it. Given that it was the most sensitive issue in contemporary Hungarian international relations, it could hardly have been the initiative of a single diplomat. Perhaps it was a trial balloon meant to sound out the State Department. This would indicate that an agreement was more important to Hungary's leaders than the transcripts of the Political Committee's meetings suggest.

The whole thing came to naught as an ill-timed U-2 spy mission wrecked the 1960 summit.[86] Thus, seemingly because of world politics but more probably because neither side was ready for substantial compromise, the Hungarians dropped their grander schemes for normalization. The Foreign Ministry pointed out that Soviet-American relations had deteriorated and that the U.S. administration was not in a position to relax economic controls without congressional approval.[87] In 1961, Kádár went to the UN, setting foot in the United States for the first – and last – time in his life. On the way there, he enjoyed Khrushchev's company on the ocean liner *Baltica*, playing cards and his favorite game, chess. In New York, he asserted that Hungary was ready to discuss normalization, but he also attached a warning: "if possible we would like to avoid severing diplomatic relations with your country."[88] The American minister in Budapest commented that relations between his government and Kádár's "turncoat" regime had never shown any real signs of change. The State Department's short-term goal in 1961 was to encourage peaceful progress toward a larger measure of national independence and internal freedom for Hungary. Full independence and the free choice of government would remain aims to be achieved in the future, but as was noted then, almost no progress had been made since 1956. U.S. officials believed that communist rule in Hungary rested on Soviet power, police terror, and the suppression of civil rights, but given the tensions between the two countries, American goals had to be modest. They would begin by letting go of the Hungarian question and restoring the legation's ability to function, thus increasing American influence.[89] It was added that though the Hungarian question was already losing currency, the worst was still to come. Despite the standoff, it was thought that the "average non-official Hungarian" still respected the United States.[90]

As the memory of 1956 faded, the Kennedy administration grew eager to "engage" Eastern Europe. The State Department was anxious to get over 1956, instructing the U.S. ambassador to the UN to drop the Hungarian question as soon as possible so that the United States could make contact with the "Hungarian people."[91] This coincided with a new Hungarian initiative: Foreign Minister Sík, probably inspired by the forthcoming meetings between Kennedy and Khrushchev, wished to make a "significant" overture to the Americans. He considered eliminating travel restrictions, but since this was a security issue, he would need the consent of the Ministry of the Interior.[92] In the meantime, the head of the State Department's Office of Eastern European Affairs declared that the United States would regard it very favorably if the travel restrictions imposed on U.S. official personnel were lifted, and suggested such a move would be reciprocated. This, however, would not involve the UN.[93] Sík's measure was radical by

Eastern European standards; similar restrictions applied to Americans all over the Soviet bloc. As with any decision made by the Political Committee, the Soviet ambassador, Vladimir I. Ustinov, was consulted. He gave his blessing to Sík's initiative, as did the Hungarian minister of the interior, Biszku, and thus the diplomatic note announcing the removal of travel restrictions was handed to the U.S. legation.[94] Although this move was not insignificant, it paled in comparison with the freedoms Romania was seeking at that time. Gheorghiu-Dej had threatened Moscow that Romania would leave the Comecon, and Khrushchev had rescinded his plan for Comecon unification rather than work at cross-purposes with Romania's economic policy.[95]

If the Hungarians thought they could offer Mindszenty in exchange for a UN mandate, they were in for a disappointment. On April 5, 1961, the State Department official in charge of Eastern Europe, Harold Vedeler, told Zádor there would be no normal relations until the Hungarian question had reached a "satisfactory" resolution.[96] Given the ongoing reprisals in Hungary, this was of crucial importance, both to the Hungarians and for America's prestige as the champion of victims of communism. By then, the affair had become a battle of nerves. The president of the UN General Assembly, Frederick Boland, thought the United States should refrain from raising the issue because the "Asian-African" group that usually supported Western initiatives considered Hungary a "Cold War" matter.[97] The Soviets were throwing everything they had at jeopardizing the work of the UN's Special Committee on Hungary. Witnesses were intimidated, and the spiritus rector behind the investigation, the Danish diplomat Bang Jensen, was found dead in Central Park, the victim of what some thought was a KGB murder.

The U.S. ambassador to the UN, Adlai Stevenson, thought that the Hungarians might have been ready for a troop withdrawal – Kádár had referred to it in a speech – or for a political amnesty, but that it would not recognize UN authority. On August 3, Richard H. Davis, deputy assistant secretary of state, read a note to the interim Hungarian chargé, Károly Hackler, in which he expressed his "wish" that Hungary would release all political prisoners as part of a general amnesty during Boland's planned trip to Hungary. Davis intimated that a positive response would result in the Americans' dropping the Hungarian question.[98] Secretary of state Dean Rusk wanted the Hungarians to know that they would be expected to take drastic measures to improve their situation and resolve the Hungarian question. Amnesty for those imprisoned for their roles in 1956 would contribute significantly.[99] They worded their note in a way that did not suggest a setting of conditions, but rather "sincere realistic proposals." If Boland's trip was successful, Washington would drop the Hungarian question, accept the mandate, and begin bilateral talks.[100] This time, it was the Americans who were mistaken in thinking that the Hungarian government's dire predicament would induce it to seize opportunity to get out of its strangling international isolation.

In his report to the Foreign Ministry, Hackler qualified the American proposal as an effort to interfere. He reported the precise conditions without mentioning the wording of the "sincere proposal." Then a Hungarian News Agency reporter, Dénes Polgár, told an American journalist of Hungarian descent, André Marton, that the "opportunistic and incompetent" Hackler would not faithfully report what the Americans said and that Budapest would be able to cite interference in its domestic affairs. Marton reported these comments to the State Department,[101] and the following day the U.S. chargé, Horace G. Torbert, who displayed a genuine interest in mending fences between the two countries, repeated Rusk's message to Sík. Regarding a Soviet troop withdrawal, Sík referred to the Warsaw Pact and claimed that the party leader would construe any proposal for amnesty as an attempt to interfere in Hungary's affairs.[102] Boland's visit was called off. The Hungarians claimed it was because the Americans had made "unacceptable demands" concerning eventual Soviet troop withdrawal, liberalization of Hungarian travel abroad, and amnesty for 1956-ers.[103]

Developments in world politics did not help. The standoff in Berlin and the subsequent construction of the Berlin Wall, along with Kennedy's fiasco at the Bay of Pigs, sharpened tensions between the two blocs. Washington put the Hungarians on the spot with renewed energy, using it as a proxy to put pressure on Moscow. When János Radványi, a former officer of the Hungarian political police and the new Hungarian chargé, tried to convince presidential advisor Chester Bowles that the general amnesty was Hungary's own business, he was told that "1956 was not an internal problem."[104] Assistant secretary of state George Ball called the Hungarian problem a "special affair" that involved the "basic principles of the U.N." and warned that it would return to its place on the UN agenda.[105] Rusk again affirmed that there would be no normalization of relations between the United States and Hungary without a satisfactory resolution of the Hungarian question, which above all meant amnesty for the 1956-ers. Only then would the United States begin talks about an exchange of ministers or the eventual elevation of diplomatic representation to the embassy level.[106] And still there was no sign of an accord. Deputy foreign minister Károly Szarka complained of U.S. intervention and efforts to overthrow his government. When János Péter, an ordained bishop of the Reformed Church, replaced Sík as the new foreign minister, the U.S. legation in Budapest noted that this did nothing to help relations between the two countries.[107] At that point, however, Kádár signaled that his country was interested in making progress. He declared that Hungary's desire to settle bilateral relations was motivated by the hope that it could catch up with the West.

At one diplomatic reception, Kádár approached an American diplomat for the first time in his life. In this, as in many other respects, he would go through a remarkable change. After showing genuine hostility to the United States, seemingly in the Leninist belief that it represented the highest and most dangerous phase of capitalist development – imperialism – by the middle of the 1970s, he was eager to visit it. For now, he would strike a conciliatory note, explaining that conflicts in the world were between states, not people. He preferred not to use the word "enemy," generally referring to the United States as an "opponent." To ease tensions, he would joke that from a certain perspective, he would not like to dissuade the Americans from their armament programs because if they were to devote their strength solely to economic expansion, Hungary would find it even harder to catch up. His aims, the party leader explained, were to overcome the inflexibility of his political system and to reach parity with Austria – a more realistic objective than Khrushchev's plan to overtake the United States. He also explained his rationale for peaceful coexistence: though he complained that the United States would overthrow his system in thirty minutes if it could, he admitted he would do the same to America's. It had to be recognized that neither eventuality was on the horizon. Torbert interjected that the United States had different notions of building interstate relations. Americans were interested in the independence and prosperity of others; poverty and misery anywhere were a disadvantage to all. Kádár revealed his motives in replying that the poor were a problem, a reason progress needed to be made in Hungarian-U.S. relations. They parted with an almost cordial handshake.[108] Kádár appeared cold and reticent, convinced that he occupied a top spot on the list of America's enemies,[109] but Hungary's Achilles heel had been revealed: its economy.

The revolution of 1956 had emerged as a symbol of the struggle for freedom and against oppression. As the State Department's communiqué on the fifth anniversary put it, Hungarian patriots had fought courageously against uneven odds for their freedom and independence, and the free world would not forget their sacrifices. The communiqué emphasized virtues such as self-sacrifice and courage and ideals such as freedom and independence. To help promote its own internal cohesion, 1956 was portrayed as a struggle to be emulated by Americans. The president and the vice president, though, both rejected invitations to an event organized by the Hungarian Freedom Fighters' Association to commemorate the uprising.[110] There was no need to irk the Soviets, and revolution had since been replaced by evolution as the ideal method for transforming Eastern Europe.

Kádár's conversation with Torbert occasioned a shift in the attitudes of Hungarian functionaries, many of whom were accustomed to changing their masks as situations or party interests demanded. Szarka was behaving congenially and broached the opening of a commercial office in New York. Although the legation in Budapest would not reject the idea altogether, the State Department would have none of it. Chester Bowles, assistant secretary of state, instructed Budapest not to enter into any "initiative" with the Hungarians, however minor. He would allow them to discuss proposals to abolish the staff cap, travel restrictions, family unification, and work permits for the legation's Hungarian employees,[111] all of which fell under the jurisdiction of the Interior Ministry. Szarka also mentioned the negotiation of a cultural agreement, something that the United States and Romania were already discussing. Later, Washington would exert considerable pressure to conclude such an agreement, but at this point the State Department would reject Szarka's offer. They claimed that the United States did not usually sign formal cultural agreements with foreign states and would negotiate cultural exchanges only after relations were normalized.¹¹² Peaceful engagement did not yet include Hungary; the old policy of quarantine still seemed the preferable option.

The legation in Budapest tried to get things moving by suggesting that the regime was attempting to forge a better international image of itself and improve relations, even if it was not yet ready to pay the price. Domestically, the government's record was mixed. The leadership was seen to be countering popular anti-Soviet and anticommunist hostilities with a campaign against contrarianism, indifference, and apathy. At the same time, an antileftist trend and even an anti-Catholic campaign seemed to have appeared in the party hierarchy. The government had consolidated its stability and self-confidence, and though physical and psychological inculcation had not increased loyalties in the army, resistance to the regime was weak and sporadic.¹¹³

As a small sign of opening to the West, the Foreign Ministry appointed a new desk officer responsible for the United States, who was thought to be more knowledgeable and urbane, as well as intellectually faster, than his predecessor. János Bartha also had personal experience of the United States and spoke better English, which created expectations that he would improve the dialogue with the United States. The appointment of a new chargé d'affaires to Washington was also interpreted as a sign of progress. János Radványi had served as the chief of the protocol section of the Foreign Ministry and was thought to be enthusiastic and discreet. The legation in Budapest understood that Radványi regarded his mission as a great personal opportunity and entertained certain illusions about what he would be able to achieve.¹¹⁴ Later, Radványi sought to discredit his predecessor as a hard-liner, although he was told by State Department officials that despite the tensions between the two countries, Zádor had shown a correct and friendly attitude.¹¹⁵ Radványi would eventually create a scandal by becoming the first Iron Curtain ambassador to defect, and he would then make a scholarly impact in debunking disingenuous Hungarian efforts to mediate in the Vietnam War.

Even before the new chargé's arrival, the State Department made known that a favorable resolution of the Hungarian question at the UN could be expected only if domestic changes were to convince lawmakers and the U.S. public that such a concession could be justified. As an "effective argument," the State Department proposed an announcement that there was no one still in prison as a result of the 1956 revolution.[116] Since a partial amnesty had already been announced in 1960, this was not an impossible condition. There is no doubt that this condition, which was later called a "recommendation," would have infringed on Hungarian sovereignty if the country had been a sovereign state, but that was not the case. At the UN, deputy foreign minister Péter Mód accused Washington of linking normalization with amnesty. The State Department claimed that Hackler misunderstood what he was told. Amnesty was not meant to be a precondition; that *would* have amounted to interference in Hungary's domestic affairs. In an effort to find an acceptable wording, Turner Shelton indicated that some kind of a theatrical gesture would be required lest he dare utter the word amnesty. Radványi, who allegedly received personal instructions from Kádár to repair U.S.-Hungarian relations,[117] thought that this formulation was acceptable and told Shelton that his government would consider any serious advice,[118] but the Ministry of Foreign Affairs rejected Shelton's formula.[119] As a result, Radványi backpedaled and adopted a hard-line stance. He sought Foreign Minister Péter's "professional advice" in interpreting communications with the Americans. On April 26, 1962, he asked the State Department for new "suggestions" on ways to jump-start bilateral relations, as this was his mission in Washington. He was told that the Hungarian government would be expected to make a gesture clearly demonstrating that the events of 1956 were permanently closed. It was added that amnesty for the participants of the uprising was not a precondition, merely a suggestion.[120] Radványi reported this exchange to his superiors in Budapest, and to avoid any misunderstandings, he left the word "suggestion" in the original English. Still smarting from the upbraiding he had received from the foreign minister, he reversed his earlier stance and said that there was nothing new in the American formula, which "amounted to an intervention in our domestic affairs."

Radványi also volunteered his own appraisal of American politics. In the 1950s, Hungarians could not report on the United States without including an expression of moral outrage, and Radványi now took up this tradition in asserting that Washington was a "captive of its own propaganda." "They permeate their own public through and through with the poison of hatred and lies" and were hence "unable to break out of the circle they created even out of self-interest." At the same time, he warned Budapest that the administration would not pick a fight with Congress or with public opinion, and thus it could be years before the Hungarian question could be settled. He opined that even "within the Kennedy administration's subversive activities an American effort towards normalization can be discerned."[121] The Hungarians were still waiting to make a move,[122] so the State Department took the initiative. In a conversation with Dénes Polgár, a journalist with connections to the state security services, Vedeler reiterated that American diplomats had no desire to set conditions, but he also stressed that only an amnesty would reassure Congress and the public. If the government decided to exculpate participants in the events of 1956 at its own initiative, the Hungarian question would be resolved and concerns like trade, cultural relations, and Mindszenty could be addressed to their "mutual satisfaction." Vedeler warned that normalization talks would begin only if the Hungarian question was settled at the initiative of the United States, not if it sank into oblivion, or in any other way. The next step would have to be made by the Hungarians.[123]

A few days later, in what the U.S. chargé described as a generously executed gesture, Kádár indicated that he was ready to make progress, though he failed to mention any concrete steps. The Foreign Ministry signaled that Hungary would be ready to explore any domestic measures that might improve the country's position at the UN and thereby satisfy American conditions for improved relations. It was also added that "psychologically Hungary could not afford to sacrifice its pride and self-esteem by [giving] in to pressure." Zádor added that the Americans were mistaken if they thought that the Soviets were still exerting a decisive influence on the politics of its allies." Hence, he suggested, the decision on amnesty was in Hungarian hands. In contrast, Torbert thought that Hungarian independence from the Soviets was nominal at best. In an astute appraisal of the many sources of Hungarian conduct, he argued that Kádár's freedom of action was insignificant given Hungarian nationalism, Stalinism, Soviet interests, the pragmatism of progress, internal liberalization, and the memory of the role the liberal intelligentsia had played in the 1956 rebellion. Kádár was a successful tightrope walker; he made cosmetic changes, but held himself firmly in place.[124]

Budapest was eager to offer Mindszenty as part of the price of a general settlement, but this intention did not mesh with the cardinal's wishes. When the Hungarian deputy prime minister, Gyula Kállai, announced at a press conference that his government was ready to discuss the archbishop's future, Mindszenty sent a message to secretary of state Dean Rusk asking him to forward a letter to the Holy See in which Mindszenty expressed his desire to stay at the legation, even if he were allowed resume his ecclesiastical functions. His position was shared by the papal nuncio in Washington, who had been assured that Mindszenty could stay in the American mission since there was no realistic chance of an agreement.[125] The Holy See agreed on the grounds that Mindszenty was the Hungarian nation's spiritual leader. His presence in Hungary was desirable; his departure could have a depressive effect on the people.[126] In spite of all this, the Vatican was not looking for a way out and did not oppose the cardinal's departure. In fact, the papal state requested Hungarian government permission for Mindszenty to attend the Holy Synod in October 1962, where it hoped he would stay and allow himself to be sidelined. The United States also made overtures in support of this solution.[127] Budapest concluded from all this that the Americans were trying to rid themselves of the affair, and thus that the Hungarians were winning the diplomatic game that had been dragging on for years. The Political Committee's appraisal was that the Americans were trying to dump the cardinal and that their demands were therefore diminishing. Thus the "package" they put together was utterly disconnected from reality. It included a new condition for the Catholic primate's departure: the return of the Crown of Saint Stephen. This "political concession for normalization" would further require that Mindszenty stay in the Vatican and be stripped of his ecclesiastical functions. Communist leaders thought they might even be doing the Americans a favor, since the United States "would be able to get rid of both Mindszenty and the Hungarian Question."

In addition to a compromise on Mindszenty, the Political Committee was also ready for a settlement "of the matters relating to 1956 [for the] foreseeable future." Their price, however, would be unrealistic: the resolution of the Hungarian question, an exchange of ministers, and the return of the Holy Crown.[128] It was true that Mindszenty's refuge was causing problems. A Swedish publisher somehow found out that the aged prelate was working on his memoirs and asked for them to be smuggled out to Stockholm in an American diplomatic pouch. The Americans rejected the idea, partly on the grounds that a diplomatic pouch could not be used for such purposes and because the "unusual and sensitive" nature of Mindszenty's position would not allow him to use the building for ecclesiastical or political purposes.[129] This does not mean that they were ready to throw him out. Torbert appreciated "this gentleman's freshness and spirit" and his interest in current affairs, even though he was obstinate and spent most of his time reminding people how far he was from being senile. After his inauguration, America's first Catholic president, John F. Kennedy, made a point of greeting Mindszenty, assuring him of his "full sympathy," and making known that the U.S. government would grant him refuge as long as his personal security and freedom required it.[130] Thus the Hungarians misread the situation.

Nevertheless, the Hungarian chargé launched exploratory discussions after consulting with the Soviet ambassador, Anatoly Dobrynin. Relations between the Soviet Embassy and the Eastern European diplomatic missions in Washington were close and extended to Soviet briefings on world affairs and intelligence activities. Dobrynin agreed with both "the principle and the implementation."[131] Hungarian émigrés had already protested in the belief that the administration had decided to drop the Hungarian question. The British also let it be known that they were eager to discard the whole affair.[132] In September, Hungary proposed discussing the Mindszenty question in return for a preliminary American guarantee regarding the Hungarian question and the amnesty, so as to avoid any semblance of domestic interference.[133] Since it was becoming increasingly difficult to inscribe the issue on the UN agenda, Bruno Kreisky sought to convince Rusk that the Hungarians were more likely to take steps if there was no great external pressure on them.[134] UN envoy Stevenson fretted over the possibility of a Soviet diplomatic victory and recommended other measures to avoid a loss of prestige.[135]

Radványi was told that if the Hungarian government were to carry out the amnesty as a public policy, the Americans' first step would be to take care of the Hungarian question. As opposed to the Hungarian position, which tied the regulation of all outstanding issues to the amnesty,

Radványi indicated that trade, cultural exchange programs, and the exchange of chiefs of mission could be negotiated after the amnesty was declared. He made no mention of the Holy Crown. Shortly thereafter, deputy assistant secretary of state Richard H. Davis presented a "written document" – emphatically not a diplomatic note – which spelled out the American terms. In order to avoid the charge of domestic interference, the word "amnesty" was replaced with a formula expressing U.S. hopes that the Hungarian government, at its own initiative, would publicly release any persons still imprisoned for their roles in the revolution of 1956. If these hopes were satisfied, Washington would see to it that Sir Leslie Munro's Committee of Five, the group in charge of the Hungarian question, would be terminated, that no more resolutions critical of Hungary would be passed, and that Hungary's UN mandate would at last be recognized. The United States would issue a declaration calling attention to the new circumstances in Hungary and would affirm that the Hungarian question no longer served the cause of progress. Thereafter, negotiations would begin on the restoration of normal relations. These would include lifting the travel restrictions imposed on official personnel, as well as financial claims, family unification, cultural exchanges, and Mindszenty. Davis presented the text of the official declaration to Radványi for his personal use. At his government's instruction, the Hungarian chargé showed the document to Dobrynin, who voiced his "personal view" that if the Hungarians had already decided on certain domestic policies, the Soviet Union "can only concur."[136] The whole issue was uncomfortable for Moscow, and it is evident that Budapest was procrastinating rather than making a move against the wishes of the Soviet leadership.

In the meantime, the Cuban missile crisis erupted. U.S.-Soviet relations had been troubled for some time, partly as a result of Khrushchev's brinksmanship. First, he had set out to alter the four-power status of West Berlin, threatening to sign a separate peace with the German Democratic Republic (GDR) if his demands were not met. Then, succumbing to pressure from East German leaders, he moved to construct the Berlin Wall, which would become the metaphor for Europe's Cold War division. He thereby stabilized the GDR – and the situation in central Europe.[137] But when the German crisis had subsided, Khrushchev's efforts to alter the balance of power and preserve Fidel Castro's revolutionary regime led the

Soviets to deploy nuclear missiles in Cuba, and it was only the political prudence of President Kennedy that saved the world from a nuclear catastrophe. The Cuban fiasco may have played an important role in Khrushchev's subsequent removal. Kádár later claimed at a meeting with Averell Harriman in Budapest that Khrushchev, with whom he was on excellent personal terms, had confided to him his plan to deploy missiles in Cuba. He claimed to have tried to dissuade Khrushchev from carrying out the scheme, but to no avail. It is hard to say whether his story is true or not. It definitely reveals that the Hungarian leader wanted to be seen as a realist who understood international power. Normally, the Soviet allies in Eastern Europe would not have been formally consulted or even told about Soviet intentions; most were given limited information about the missile crisis, and only after the United States had broken the news.

This diplomatic tug-of-war around the general amnesty made it clear that the satellite states could defy the power that controlled them in matters relating to a third power as long as that third power was an opponent of their hegemon. Even though Dobrynin gave Budapest a green light for putting an end to the reprisals and accepting Washington's conditions for a settlement, the Hungarians kept dragging their feet. Radványi advised the Foreign Ministry that the amnesty would be equal to surrendering all "our principles," though he was obviously saying what he expected his superiors wanted to hear. Then Khrushchev told his counterpart in Hungary that there was nothing wrong with accepting the American conditions.[138] Shortly thereafter, the Eighth Congress of the HSWP announced that 95 percent of the people who had been "condemned for counter-revolutionary crimes" as a result of the events of 1956 had been released.

In late November, Harold Vedeler was negotiating with Foreign Ministry officials in Budapest when his hosts explained that it was hard for a small country like Hungary to be seen as bending to external pressure. Vedeler, who was satisfied with the Hungarian attitude, was reminded of Kádár's statement that the Presidential Council would review the cases of the last 5 percent who were still incarcerated.[139] Deputy Foreign Minister Mód also hinted that his government was considering an amnesty,[140] which was finally announced in April 1963. Washington was still dissatisfied with the steps the Hungarians took to implement Davis's conditions and chose to employ a new strategy. Washington announced the termination of Sir Leslie Munro's mission, which had been taking a lot of criticism. His assignment was taken over by the secretary-general of the UN, though the United States continued to advocate the suspension of Hungary's mandate. This recommendation hardly made it through the relevant committee; the Greek representative disregarded the instructions of his government and voted against the Hungarian mandate. The Hungarian mandate was eventually accepted at a special session of the UN in May 1963. By then, the Hungarian question was no longer on the agenda.

The Hungarian amnesty was the first American diplomatic success behind the Iron Curtain since the satellite regimes had established. The UN turned out to be an effective tool for putting strong pressure on Moscow and its client state, the bloody, tyrannical regime of János Kádár. As the Hungarian foreign minister would acknowledge, Hungary ended its campaign of reprisals as a result of American pressure. There were important lessons to be learned. The diplomacy of the client states was becoming more autonomous, making it possible for them to defy Moscow's will in questions of smaller importance. Hungarians did so, asserting what they perceived to be their sovereignty. U.S. diplomacy was thus forced to reckon with national self-esteem, even though communists were not believed to have such feelings.

6

The Dilemmas of External Transformation

American observers noticed that the communist regimes in Eastern Europe were becoming increasingly autonomous. They were beginning to assert that their national interests were not always identical with the Soviets'. Signs that they were heading toward more independence from Moscow made the European status quo acceptable to the United States, if not necessarily desirable. Some went as far as to argue that the Soviet occupation had produced an unprecedented stability in a former cockpit of continental hostilities. Soviet hegemony thus seemed preferable to an unchecked flow of unbridled nationalism. And while nationalism might have been part of the antidote to unrestricted Soviet control, it had to be handled with care.

The planned intensification of American trade and cultural contacts with Eastern Europe proved difficult to implement. In the Johnson years, it was propaganda rather than reality. As an exasperated Nicolae Ceaușescu aptly put it, not a single pillar of the bridge had been put in place. American analysts and policymakers could not agree whether to offer expanded cultural and commercial contacts as rewards for better behavior, or whether the establishment of trade and cultural exchanges would hasten a political liberalization. There were also security considerations. The battle lines in Eastern Europe were still drawn as if it were the 1950s. The State and Commerce Departments insisted on bridge building as a way of transforming the lands behind the Iron Curtain and diminishing European tensions. Eastern Europe also offered new markets to the

U.S. economy. The Pentagon and the Joint Chiefs of Staff, however, were still concerned about possible American contributions to Soviet military might and did their utmost to impede the implementation of the administration's new trade doctrine. Although these dilemmas would remain unresolved, the socialist states' desire for American trade, loans, and technical know-how was increasing. But due to a combination of interagency rivalries, congressional resistance, domestic interest group pressures, and sterile debate about the merits of interaction with the communist world, the United States missed a historical opportunity to transform the Eastern European landscape and save it decades of further devastation under dysfunctional dictators.

On the other hand, dealing with economically backward dictatorships was not a simple matter. Anxious to preserve their power with minimal concessions, these regimes used the increasing American willingness to negotiate as a means of extracting favors. By and large, they remained ideologically hostile to the United States, which they suspected of trying to subvert them. There was also the Kremlin to worry about, although the Soviets did not seem to resent Eastern Europeans' closer ties with the Americans, as long as it suited their interests. Both sides wanted scientific and academic exchanges, but with opposite purposes. The Hungarian communist government wished to bolster itself by bringing modern technology and scientific skill back to Hungary from the United States, while minimizing potentially subversive exchanges in the humanities. Washington, on the other hand, hoped to use precisely this sort of cultural exchange as an element in its policy of external transformation. Trade expansion was equally difficult. Eastern Europeans were unable to pay for the U.S. goods they hoped to purchase and had little with which to barter. Hungary hoped American credit would fund a modernization of its economy, allowing it to produce goods worthy of global marketing. The backwardness of the Hungarian economy made loans for badly needed machinery risky, and trade restrictions like CoCom made things even worse. Thus the policy of bridge building was fraught with contradictions.

American officials also had to contend with the mood swings in Moscow over the Americans' intentions. The Soviets were concerned about American intervention in various parts of the globe, but perhaps their greatest concern was a NATO proposal to pool nuclear weapons, which suggested to the Soviets that such devices would be shared with the Germans. "What if another Hitler arose?" Prime Minister Kosygin asked.[1] Averting such scenarios was the primary focus of Soviet diplomacy. And insofar as the Vietnam conflict hampered Soviet-American relations, it in turn impeded Hungarian efforts to mend fences with Washington.

TOWARD A MODUS VIVENDI

A reorientation of U.S. policy was necessitated by the fact that the French, the Germans, and the British were reappraising their relationships with the communist bloc and trying to make them more constructive. British military leaders had concluded that Soviet leaders were unlikely to risk the consequences of a third global conflict.[2] In question was the degree of independence with which the nations of Eastern Europe could conduct themselves. Security remained the chief concern and U.S. officials continued to see Soviet hegemony in Eastern Europe as a potential threat. Eastern European "vulnerability" could still be exploited, bearing in mind the "realities of power," namely Soviet preponderance in the region. At the same time, Western influence behind the Iron Curtain needed to be increased, and not by circumventing the local communist regimes, but rather with their consent. In 1964, secretary of state Dean Rusk argued for policies of peaceful engagement, particularly in the cases of Poland and Romania, and even for Hungary, which was commended for having moved toward a more liberal policy of "national reconciliation." President Johnson used the term "bridge building" to signify commercial, intellectual, and humanitarian exchanges with Eastern Europe, including tourism.[3] The earlier policy of "quarantining" Eastern Europe was labeled "passive, sterile, and defeatist."[4] The State Department supported Johnson and encouraged an intensification of trade relations in the hope that Romania and Hungary would be willing to go as far as Poland.

The practical implementation of bridge building would take a long time to catch up with the rhetoric. Romania began making strenuous efforts to purchase U.S. equipment for its oil refineries and synthetic rubber factories in the final year of the Kennedy administration, and though the project enjoyed the unqualified backing of the U.S. ambassador in Bucharest and (apparently) the president, the purchase never went through.

The Department of Commerce made it clear that there would be no rapid expansion of trade relations with Romania because of CoCom regulations and because the American business community was not ready. Despite congressional resistance, Kennedy permitted the sale of U.S. wheat to Eastern Europe, but the AFL-CIO was able to insert a proviso requiring that at least half the shipments sail under the U.S. flag, effectively sabotaging Kennedy's concession. Congressional opposition was at least partly a response to pressure from Eastern European immigrants, many of whom considered opening the American market to communists equivalent to a betrayal of the fatherland.

After his inauguration, Johnson decided that Romania would be the test case for the new approach to Eastern European trade. Up to that point, only Yugoslavia and Poland had been allowed to sell to the United States as most favored nations. The U.S. Chamber of Commerce was eager to follow up on the Johnson administration's pledge to intensify American economic interaction with the Soviet bloc. East-West trade had been impeded by denials of most-favored-nation (MFN) status and by the fact that the Export-Import Bank had refused to extend commodity credit to countries under communist leadership. U.S. firms also faced difficulties in acquiring licenses to market their products behind the Iron Curtain. These procedures were relaxed only for Romania and Poland. Bucharest made a particular effort to get its purchases licensed; it managed to secure permits for eleven plants' worth of equipment out of the fifteen for which it applied.

The importance of breaking into the untapped Eastern European market was underscored when Firestone announced the construction of a tire factory in Romania and its competitor, Goodyear, immediately launched a countercampaign. The Johnson administration was divided on the issue. Secretary of State Rusk and Secretary of Defense McNamara supported an unconditional intensification of trade relations in the belief that commerce was important enough to the communist regimes to force them into political concessions. Rusk and McNamara approved of the sale of any commodity without direct military significance. In contrast, the Departments of Commerce and Agriculture would restrict sales to items that could be "drunk or eaten," and only on a quid pro quo basis.[5] In April 1965, the Miller committee, set up by the president to investigate the question of trade with the Soviet bloc, presented its findings. Its report stated that U.S. trade policy should promote autonomy in Eastern Europe and that the Soviet bloc should adopt the trade practices of the rest of the world. The committee recommended relaxing U.S. licensing procedures on a country-by-country basis and for the president to be vested with the authority to extend a country's MFN status for a limited period. Because of the Vietnam War, however, the committee's recommendations were never implemented, and bridge building remained an empty doctrine. As Romanian party leader Nicolae Ceaușescu complained to Johnson, "not a single pillar" of this East-West bridge had been built.[6]

By 1964, the question was how far the United States wanted the satellites to go. That year, the CIA's Special National Intelligence Estimate asserted that Moscow and the client states had established a new and less rigid relationship. This was partly due to political changes and partly the result of the communist regimes' realization that they could devote more attention to their own national interests.[7] This statement suggests a misunderstanding of communist ideology common in U.S. appraisals. For most leaders of the communist persuasion, Soviet and national interests were two sides of the same coin, inseparable. The CIA also asserted that Eastern Europe was facing a significant transformation the central components of which would be internal liberalization and economic reform. These problems would be closely tied to the questions of autonomy and relations with the Western world. It was assumed that the Soviet bloc would become more diverse and that some countries would move toward political liberalization and more efficient economic principles. Leaders would approach these issues from the perspectives of national interests and local political conditions. And if the satellites were more independent from Moscow and closer to the West, Soviet intervention was thought to be less likely, a possibility only if "vital Soviet interests" were threatened. U.S. officials expected Moscow, absent challenges to its client-state arrangements or defections from the Warsaw Pact, would be willing to tolerate a variety of political systems and possibly even consent to manifestations of increased autonomy in foreign affairs.[8] Secretary of State Rusk instructed U.S. missions in Eastern Europe to refrain from the use of the term "satellite" in diplomatic correspondence; in his view the term was no longer adequate to describe these countries' relations to the Soviet Union.[9] Hence a new image of the Soviet zone was being *constructed* to fit the new administration's more activist doctrine. Yet this new image was also calibrated to accommodate the continued existence of an East-West divide.

Despite improvements, conditions behind the Iron Curtain were still far from perfect. Communist economies remained inefficient and therefore produced mass dissatisfaction, manifestations of which were expected.[10] Declining living standards in Poland and Czechoslovakia led the State Department to predict that instability there would grow. On the other hand, Romania, which the *New York Times* had called the most dynamically growing communist economy, and Hungary, where Washington perceived continued improvement, seemed to be stable. The best response to the threat of instability due to sluggish growth was an intensification of economic relations.[11] There were also security risks inherent in the Soviet-dominated area. The communist governments were involved in a subversive campaign to promote the worldwide victory of communism. Their activities included military and financial aid to the communists of the "free world," clandestine shipments of arms, and training subversives in guerrilla action, intelligence, propaganda, political oratory, and the indoctrination of youth. Czechoslovakia and the German Democratic Republic (GDR) were considered the most active in these areas, followed by Bulgaria. Poland, Romania, and Hungary seemed to limit their activities to intelligence, clandestine broadcasts, and student training, which was "modest" in comparison with the former countries. U.S. intelligence assumed that Hungary was collecting information on missile-launching sites and that there was close cooperation between Soviet, Czechoslovakian, and Hungarian intelligence agents.[12] This was still a traditional estimate in the sense that it appraised the Soviet bloc according to the threats it posed to the West.

American officials also took a new approach in appraising the dangers of increasing autonomy in Eastern Europe. This line of thought questioned the desirability of eliminating Soviet hegemony. The CIA's Special National Intelligence Estimate for 1964 assumed that hostilities between Eastern European countries and between Eastern Europe and the Soviet Union would come to the fore again soon. Frictions between Hungary and Romania could already be detected.[13] The Political Planning Council deemed the division of Europe unacceptable because it put the United

States in greater danger of a nuclear war. Yet there were also dangers inherent in the restoration of independence: "Unbridled nationalism in Eastern Europe might lead to possible renewal of the patterns of conflict that made the area such a cockpit prior to pax communista. This potential is evident in complex of latent and potentially dangerous territorial and minority issues in the area." This suggested that American goals in the countries then under Soviet domination would have to be less ambitious: "Continuing development of Western unity in close association with the US to a further loosening (*but not severing*) of abnormally tight bonds between the USSR and Eastern Europe, *reduction* in divisions between East and West" (emphasis mine). In this formulation, American goals fell significantly short of a restoration of European unity. The juxtaposition of Western unity with a recognition of the Soviets' role further amplified the message that Europe's division was no longer seen as unnatural. Thus "reassociation" would not mean "political union or military alliance." The policy of bridge building would serve to increase U.S. influence and diminish the unnaturally high level of Soviet influence, thus enhancing European security.[14] At this stage, no unanimous opinion had crystallized around a long-term goal; statements to this effect were contradictory.

Publicly, Secretary of State Rusk defined the long-term American goal in Eastern Europe as "evolution" toward the re-establishment of "national independence." His immediate goals, though, were incremental: work toward independence, decrease the danger of war, and slow the spread of communism.[15] In contrast, a State Department memorandum prepared for the National Security Council would go all the way: "We seek in Eastern Europe the establishment of conditions under which the people of each country may determine its own society; and where each country may enjoy national independence, security and normal relationship[s] with all other countries. This will mean the final dismantling of the Iron Curtain and the free association of Eastern Europe and the West." Thus the re-evaluation of American goals was still in a state of flux. The State Department's ambitious program would link the solution of the German question to the resolution of the status of Eastern Europe and work toward the construction of a "lasting" relationship with the Soviet Union. It recommended practical steps to break out of the diplomatic deadlock, including the settlement of outstanding claims with Hungary and Czechoslovakia, compromises on consular issues, and the lifting of travel restrictions on diplomatic personnel. These latter two countries would also be singled out for bilateral talks modeled on negotiations then underway with Romania and the Soviet Union. The elimination of discriminatory tariffs was expected to shift the economic focus of Eastern Europe toward the West, thus reducing its dependence on the USSR. Intellectual bridges would be constructed through the dissemination of American scholarships, library collections, scientific publications, cultural bulletins, and films. American officials would encourage English-language instruction and the establishment of chairs of American studies. Poland, Czechoslovakia, Hungary, and Romania were identified as suitable countries for cultural exchanges because they acknowledged the importance of American scientific and technological aid for the development of their economies. One official recommended a public relations drive to convince people in the Soviet bloc of America's peaceful intentions. This was especially important in light of ongoing NATO discussions of its plan to share nuclear arms with West Germany,[16] an idea Soviet propagandists exploited, describing it as malicious U.S. support for German "revisionism."

Washington was struggling to maintain the cohesion of the West at a time when the Soviet threat seemed to be receding. In those circumstances, putting an end to Europe's division was no longer an unquestioned dogma of American foreign policy. In fact, this ideal was gradually being left behind. "Promotion of Western cohesion is the primary objective. [...] Ending the partition of Europe is not necessarily the same thing as achieving a stable European settlement. The end of division could come about through the fragmentation of both alliances, could contribute to new conflicts and tensions, the end result could be the restoration of a futile past, not shaping a constructive future."[17] Washington's chief ally in NATO, Great Britain, was also re-evaluating its stance toward the Soviet Union and its client states. In 1964, the British Foreign Office concluded that the communist regimes were relying less on terror and coercion and more on improvements in living conditions. For these trends to continue, Eastern Europeans would need to modernize their economies with Western capital and technology. Britain could back reforms and détente by developing closer commercial, cultural, and scientific contacts. Any weakening of the Soviet hold over Eastern Europe would now come about through evolution rather than revolution. In the long run, trade and cultural exchanges would help Eastern Europeans gain greater autonomy from the USSR. The British economy would also profit from this trade with the Soviet bloc.[18]

Crucially, Hungarian émigré leaders supported the new American strategy. Former prime minister Ferenc Nagy and the former speaker of Parliament Béla Varga, both influential in émigré circles, claimed that their former countrymen preferred a policy of peaceful liberalization to one of liberation.[19] Their support mattered: the organization of East European émigrés, the Assembly of Captive Nations in Europe, had condemned the policy of bridge building, branding trade with the communists "immoral" because it meant importing goods produced by "slave labor."[20] Talks aimed at putting this new doctrine into practice occasionally degenerated into hostile exchanges. Americans and their communist counterparts were not always rowing in the same direction. One legacy of the 1950s was that Congress exerted a strong influence on policies toward Eastern Europe, often opposing ties with communist regimes or insisting on strict preconditions. Finally, there was no meeting of minds within the successive American administrations about the implementation of this new line. Hungary's case was special in the sense that there were numerous unsolved issues that did not burden relations with other communist states. Hungarian leaders were open to an expansion of ties, but set a hefty price in insisting on the return of the Crown of Saint Stephen. Progress remained painfully slow, even though the situation in Hungary was improving and the regime had managed to stabilize itself.[21]

The CIA concluded that Kádár had consolidated his power over the party while "silently" pushing his country down a path of gradual change and pragmatic improvements in the political and economic climate. He even managed to turn Hungarian nationalism to his advantage and, at least according to CIA analysts, had lost the stigma of a Soviet puppet. This relatively liberal line was expected to continue.[22] In 1963, the U.S. chargé in Budapest suggested that that year had been the best for the average Hungarian since the communists had seized power.[23] The historian János M. Rainer has observed that in Eastern Europe, connotations associated with the 1960s "remain to this day decidedly positive." It tends to be remembered as a decade of thaw, of breathing more freely, of hopes and chances and greater liberties than the previous decade had afforded. Despite political constraints, even the decade's cultural revolution managed to creep behind the Iron Curtain. Campaigns of forced collectivization and industrialization, brutal reprisals and discrimination against "class enemies" and "remnants of the old ruling classes," and protracted attacks on political opposition, lasted until roughly 1963. But then, the profound economic reforms introduced from 1963 to 1967 led to a measure of intellectual and cultural openness. Discrimination against social groups allegedly hostile to socialism abated. Kádár was not a reformer by instinct. Caught between Moscow and his own population, he ushered in reforms. These brought modest prosperity, the beginnings of a new social stratification in a fragmented and leveled society, some freedom of artistic self-expression, and more openness toward the capitalist world than anywhere else in the Soviet bloc. The youth protested mainstream socialist norms of behavior and tuned in to Radio Free Europe to follow American trends. Wearing outrageous clothing and hairstyles, they attended rock concerts where they tolerated cover versions of British and American originals. The fact that the police could bring these youths in for parading around in smuggled, illegally purchased apparel demonstrates the limits of Kádár's little freedoms.[24]

Now that the Hungarians' political amnesty had removed one of the chief hurdles to the normalization of their relations with the West, they introduced an economic reform. It was clear that these reforms could not work without "opening" to the West, thus their most important precondition was to bring ties with the United States to a normal footing. Given the Johnson administration's decision to engage with the communist regimes, the stage seemed to be set for rapid progress toward the desired intensification of the American presence in Hungary. In February 1964, Budapest proposed bilateral talks for the mutually acceptable resolution of outstanding issues.[25] As expected, the main goals were the settlement of economic disputes and the elimination of trade discrimination. The American legation supported the initiative, having heard rumors that Khrushchev was about to announce the withdrawal of Soviet troops. This hope, along with the positive outlook on Budapest's talks with the Vatican, gave rise to optimism that progress could be made with Washington. The legation proposed that the two parties focus on Archbishop

Mindszenty, financial claims, and lifting the Hungarians' restrictions on cultural activities and diplomatic personnel. American officials thought the Hungarian government would try to link outstanding financial claims to the country's most-favored-nation status and would work for a cultural agreement in order to enhance Hungary's prestige.[26] The Pentagon was optimistic that Soviet occupation forces would be pulled out because they thought – for reasons left unexplained – that the Red Army's position on the central front would be enhanced if the four divisions stationed in Hungary were pulled back to Soviet territory.[27] It was also assumed that Romania's overtures to the United States would stimulate Budapest to accelerate its normalization process.[28] None of these assumptions seem to have been correct.

National security advisor McGeorge Bundy recommended accepting the Hungarian offer on the grounds that an increased U.S. presence in Budapest promised substantial advantages. Hungary had gone further than any other satellite in de-Stalinizing its communist system, and this trend was continuing. Bundy expected the American owners of nationalized property to be compensated, a consular agreement to be signed, family unifications to be allowed, and commercial and cultural ties to be broadened.[29] In sum, talks would be opened because Hungary had declared an amnesty and the Kádár regime was thought to be pursuing policies of national appeasement, independence, and liberalization.[30]

BILATERAL RELATIONS IN THE MID-1960S

Theoretically, the conditions were ripe for a rapprochement. Both sides were motivated, but their positions were still far apart. The Hungarians were willing to negotiate on Mindszenty and a consular agreement, but they shunned a cultural accord. As with all deals, the devil was in the details. Budapest was ready to settle financial claims, but only *after* being granted most-favored-nation status, and had no desire to lift its restrictions on diplomatic personnel or its ban on U.S. information activities.[31] The settlement of financial claims proved to be another stumbling block. Washington insisted on payments as a condition of further progress. Hungary's trade balance with the United States was negative and included long- and short-term debt, compensation for nationalized property, the surplus-property loan, and compensation owed for American property damaged in the war. Hungary had only $6 million worth of property frozen in the United States. Most of the Hungarian property that had been taken into the American zone during World War II, estimated at $100 million, was thought to be impossible to collect. This included obligations to Jewish owners of valuables stolen from the "gold train," some of which ended up in the hands of American army personnel and some of which was auctioned off in New York.[32] The United States pointed out that the settlement of these claims would help Hungary borrow on international financial markets, which was Kádár's main motivation.[33] Western loans were an indispensable ingredient in the country's modernization and reform program. There was, however, no breakthrough, even though Hungarians understood that without normalizing relations with America, they would not get the loans they needed. A chief factor in stalling these negotiations may have been the Vietnam War, which froze relations for almost a decade.

Even though comprehensive talks started in Budapest in May 1964, no agreement was reached on any of the most problematic questions. Secretary of State Rusk offered to meet his counterpart, János Péter, to break the deadlock. The Political Committee authorized the foreign minister to tell Rusk that Mindszenty could be released and taken out of the country if his "silence" was guaranteed. On the other hand, the party leadership still insisted that the country's most-favored-nation status be the prerequisite for any settlement of financial claims.[34] Rusk was not completely opposed to MFN status, but it soon turned out that the differences could not be bridged.[35]

Mindszenty was still intractable. Saddled with the cardinal's upkeep, Washington was ready to accept the condition of "silencing" him politically. The problem was the Budapest-Vatican-Mindszenty triangle. Agostini Casaroli, the Vatican's state secretary for foreign affairs, indicated that Mindszenty wanted to retain his title as the Archbishop of Esztergom, the head of the Catholic Church in Hungary, and acknowledged that it would be hard to keep Mindszenty from making statements related to the Cold War. Mindszenty himself was reluctant to give up his refuge.[36] His personal beliefs had become intertwined with high politics. Mindszenty was convinced that his departure would constitute "negligence" toward the loyal priests he had appointed.[37] The communist leadership, evidently for the sake of some positive publicity, wanted the cardinal to sue for clemency, for that clemency to be granted by the Presidential Council (the country's highest legislative organ), and for the settlement to be published in the Hungarian press, as Kádár put it, "even on page 11 in the sports section." More importantly, they would not hear of Mindszenty's retaining his ecclesiastical functions, a condition that would freeze the situation for years to come.[38]

Considering that Budapest wanted to resolve its political issues before settling financial claims – precisely the reverse of American hopes – no positive outcome was in sight. The Hungarians referred to the settlement of financial claims as a burden on the country even though, as in the Romanian and Polish settlements, only a small fraction of its outstanding debt was to be paid; it was obvious that the political will for such a step was missing. Washington would not make progress in other areas until there was a deal on financial claims, but the stakes for Hungary were far higher. The economy had been struggling with a balance-of-payments deficit for some time, and by 1964, the year when the U.S.-Hungarian talks started, the proportion of short-term debt among Hungary's obligations was worse than it had been even in the 1930s. Half of the debt to the capitalist world was made up of loans that were due in less than three months. Thus from the mid-1960s, Hungarian leaders were forced to borrow medium-term loans in order to purchase capital goods from the West. The idea that the United States could serve as a source of financing for investments was raised during the second and third five-year plans. American financial markets were appealing because they offered dollars at less expensive rates than the European markets. The option to issue bonds would not be available to the Hungarian government until it settled its financial claims with the United States; membership in the World Bank and the IMF would also require American support.[39] On paper, at least, an agreement was in the interests of both sides: Hungary was in the process of discarding its inhibitions and using "capitalist" resources to finance its economy, while Washington was interested in stabilizing Eastern Europe and exerting more influence there.

Talks were held up by unforeseen events such as the illness of the leader of the U.S. delegation and the accidental forwarding of the necessary documentation from Washington to Bucharest. Again, though, the escalating conflict in Vietnam destabilized the commercial pillar of the bridge the diplomats were building. Americans feared that commodities they sold to Eastern Europe might be forwarded to North Vietnam. In January 1966, President Johnson asked for congressional authorization to use his presidential powers to sign trade agreements with Eastern Europe in the name of bridge building, but the bill did not make it through the legislature. Instead, the Fino amendment barred the Export-Import Bank from lending to countries that furnished economic or military aid to enemies of the United States, including the Soviet Union and every other communist country except Yugoslavia.[40] For the time being, at least, Budapest would not be able to get what it wanted, and the idea of talks began to lose their significance, even to the Hungarians. The softening of the Hungarian system was shown by the fact that Budapest made an overture regarding the IMF as early as 1966. The vice president of the Hungarian National Bank, János Fekete, approached the organization through Yugoslav mediation about the possible reception of Hungarian membership. Hungary expected to raise a long-term loan of $150–200 million "from capitalist states" to hike the standard of living to get popular support for the planned economic reform.[41]

"THE SWINISHNESS OF IMPERIALISM": SOFT POWER

Penetration into Hungary was not an impossible task. The United States Information Agency (USIA) felt that Hungary was fertile ground for American cultural initiatives. By the mid-1960s, Hungarian leaders were ready to loosen cultural controls in exchange for Western economic assistance. Their calculus was relatively simple. Political stabilization would require some degree of popular contentment, and this sense of satisfaction could be purchased with a hike in the standard of living. This, in turn, would require the inflow of Western capital, "capitalist" consumer goods, machinery, technology, and know-how. Thus, a normalization of relations with the United States was indispensable, and if normalization were to require concessions such as allowing Radio Free Europe to be freely received, Hungary would be penetrated with American popular culture. This threatened the ideological integrity of the state, but because of the previously outlined political and economic pressures facing the regime, it was left with little choice. Washington realized that gradual cultural penetration might encourage a step-by-step liberalization, from domestic reforms to an eventual opening up to the outside world.[42] There is no doubt that the members of the Political Committee also understood this dynamic.

Poland was the main target for American cultural initiatives. Positive developments in Poland led the USIA to an ambitious plan for a library and cultural center in Warsaw. In 1959, Poland signed an agreement for an academic exchange involving a thousand applicants, while Czechoslovakia sent one hundred and Hungary only nineteen. Private foundations also helped build East-West contacts. The Ford Foundation cooperated with the State Department in establishing cultural ties with the countries of Eastern Europe, especially their intellectual elites.[43] The Ford Foundation and the Kulturális Kapcsolatok Intézete (Institute of Cultural Relations), the agency responsible for external cultural contacts and also a clandestine subsidiary of the security apparatus, established an exchange program in 1964 whereby Hungarian artists, scholars, and scientists would be able to visit the United States.

The selection procedure for this program illustrates some of the complexities of creating ties with ideological regimes. The candidates on the list were carefully selected and vetted on the basis of professional and "political" criteria, meaning they were screened for reliability by the Institute of Cultural Relations and its close affiliates at the Ministry of Interior. The Ford Foundation was then allowed to invite a short list of twenty-five people, plus five "outstanding cultural and scientific personalities," on an annual basis. No more than half of those selected were to be representatives of the social sciences. In theory, at least, the Ford Foundation could also nominate its own candidates, but these nominees would not appear on the list of applicants without the prior approval of the Institute of Cultural Relations. Ford's short list was then forwarded to an organ called the Tudományos és Felsőoktatási Tanács (Council of Science and Higher Education), which vetted the names from the perspective of the "interest of the people's economy." And this was only the beginning of the convoluted process. Once approved by the council, the list was then sent to the Ministry of the Interior and the Scientific and Cultural Department of the Central Committee of the Hungarian Socialist Party for further winnowing. Finally, the presidium of the Institute of Cultural Relations, with the participation of deputy portfolio ministers and representatives of the party leadership, drew up a final list. It was only then that the Ford Foundation received the final list of candidates.[44]

Washington pushed hard to open American libraries in Iron Curtain capitals and entertained high hopes for the transformative effects thereof. But these calculations disregarded the fact that Hungarian state security agents (as well as those of other bloc countries) would monitor visitors to U.S. libraries, registering each individual in a file at the Ministry of Interior. Visitors could then be blackmailed into rendering services for state security organs. It is highly likely that the Hungarian librarian of the USIA facility in Budapest was recruited by state security agents. Even as late as 1981, freshmen majoring in English were warned that using the American library entailed personal risks.

The Hungarians did make a momentous concession soon after the Hungarian question was resolved: they stopped jamming Radio Free Europe. The regime ostensibly did so to induce the station to alter its radical stances, but the more fundamental cause was probably the expectation that it would lead to U.S. concessions on trade issues. Accidents do play a role in shaping history, however. The party authorized a decision to stop jamming on a provisional basis, but in a fateful misunderstanding, the Foreign Ministry announced it as a permanent measure. Although the Politburo was furious, the decision could not be repealed without risking a loss of face and was thus grudgingly left in place. The Political Committee also made a highly debated decision to allow the United States to participate in Budapest's 1965 International Trade Fair. This was an important breakthrough for American champions of external transformation, who sought to instill American values in the communist states and to effect the gradual democratization of closed political systems by sending goods and intellectual products behind the Iron Curtain. Participation in the Budapest International Trade Fair was an important beachhead for this economic and cultural penetration.[45]

Budapest was not unaware of American successes in this field, and party leaders were alarmed by the popular appeal of U.S. "propaganda." In 1965, the Political Committee devoted several sessions to the evergreen topic of imperialist subversion. Prime minister Jenő Fock, a leading economic reformer, contradicted those who said "imperialist propaganda in Hungary is unable to undermine the masses' confidence in the socialist system and diminish the attraction of socialist ideas." This he said was "not true, it is capable of doing so and is diminishing it."[46] The party's leadership thought that the United States and the Federal Republic of Germany were "trying to pit the socialist countries against the Soviet Union and each other, to subvert the socialist system, to nurture dissatisfaction towards the party and the government, ultimately against the social order and thus to prepare the restoration of capitalism in the socialist countries. They are trying to achieve all this with the wide-range use of foreign policy, economic, cultural, and personal contacts, as well as powerful anticommunist propaganda." They asserted that "subversive attempts mainly manifested themselves in the differentiated treatment of socialist countries," namely that some states got better treatment than others. Hostile intent was attributed to scientific and cultural contacts, which party leaders warned would "open the door for bourgeois ideology and its products under the pretext of peaceful coexistence." All this had alarming consequences for the future of socialism: "subversive propaganda plays a role in the sense that in the ranks of the public and particularly in certain circles of the youth and the intelligentsia there is an intensification of love of the West and of nationalism which is coupled with the downplaying of the results of socialism."[47]

What could be done in such a situation? Kádár was not in a position to go back to the isolation of the Stalinist years; the policy of opening up to the West was slowly gaining momentum. The only antidote seemed to be competition with this Western penetration. Gyula Kállai conceded that "the youth is not interested in or asking for the full exposition of Marxism but the satisfaction of their needs and adequate propaganda work in the meantime." He insisted that Hungarian propaganda continue to point out "the swinishness of imperialism," but this would obviously not be enough. Politburo member Lajos Méhes called attention to two strategies, one of which was surprising given the communists' officially antinational stance. He wanted the party's "agitation and propaganda to do an even better job of referring to our national sentiments and national self-esteem." Méhes also wanted to improve the quality of Hungarian popular music programming to offset the attraction of American musical broadcasts like *Teenager Party*. This was precisely what Washington wanted: the national idea and Westernizing popular culture, both produced by the communist governments themselves. The only thing better than Iron Curtain youths' listening to *Top of the Pops* on Radio Free Europe would be their tuning into domestic programming for the same sounds. At that time, Soviet programming still followed Voice of America's popular show *Music USA*, which had been aired for Soviet audiences since 1955.[48]

One Hungarian refugee recounted that he and a fellow student had listened to music on Radio Free Europe in their university club every night. Indeed, rock music, including the Hungarians' domestic version of it, may have played a critical role in the formation of a quasi-autonomous public sphere. In optimistic accounts, it helped dismantle the party-state's legitimacy.[49] There is little doubt that Hungarian youth used popular musical forms as a first line of resistance to communist indoctrination. In addition, music enhanced the appeal of the United States at a time when communist propagandists were trying to destroy America's image with accusations of murderous imperialism. The appeal of popular music put pressure on the authorities, who were no longer able to cut off the ample supply of Western radio programming. Moreover, as Anna Szemere has written, rock music emerged as a lucrative business and "as such, highlighted and exacerbated the tensions between socialist values and policies and the profit-orientation of the state-run entertainment industry."[50]

Everyday life had overtaken the decision makers. Kállai complained that if the party's youth magazine, *Magyar Ifjúság*, was still "a communist journal, I do not understand what communism means." He noted bitterly that the paper was "popularizing Western lifestyle without [any] critique [of] the West. . . . We do not find a single socialist hero in it except the Beatles."[51] In fact, this publication's cover regularly featured young girls in bikinis exhorting the youth to sign up for the communists' summer work camps under the slogan "Proletarians of the World, Unite."[52]

Károly Kiss, the hard-liner who served as deputy president of the Presidential Council, a select organ of the communist parliament, was openly pushing for an exchange of ministers with the United States, which the Americans interpreted as a sign of important change.[53] In 1965, Kádár declared that he was "willing to travel anytime and anywhere" to mend fences. Although he was hoping to limit his anti-imperialist protests to the area of ideology, the Vietnam conflict was assuming the dimensions of an East-West conflict and was impeding progress in bilateral relations. In suspending the normalization process, the Political Committee pointed out that its "main reason" for doing so was "the American aggression in Vietnam and its effect on the international situation."[54] The Foreign Ministry pointed out that "because of the situation created by the Vietnamese policy of the United States[,] we must forgo the restoration of normal relations for a while."[55] Thus a geographically unrelated crisis in a remote corner of the globe would alter the course of the Cold War in Europe. Had Kádár been able to achieve this opening to the West in the early 1960s rather than a decade later, the collapse of Hungarian communism would likely have come sooner, possibly pulling the entire Soviet bloc into crisis.

The U.S. legation mistakenly believed that the Hungarians were using the Vietnam conflict as an excuse and had actually canceled the normalization talks as a way of finding out how much the United States would be willing to "pay" for an agreement.[56] At the same time, the legation informed the State Department that Budapest made the war in Vietnam a key factor in their bilateral relations, pointing out that the tone and magnitude of the communists' propaganda could hardly be reconciled with Hungary's stated intention to normalize relations.[57] The Political Committee discussed the possibility of Hungarian government ministers' avoiding the American exhibition at the Budapest International Trade Fair and using the fair's opening statement to "condemn the aggression[s] in Vietnam and the Dominican Republic."[58]

While some party conservatives might have thought that the time had come to nip the Western initiative in the bud, reformers tried to block a reversion to isolationism. A key figure behind the drive to liberalize, Jenő Fock, thought that financial talks should be pursued based on economic criteria. Interestingly, another reform-oriented functionary, Rezső Nyers, wanted to suspend the talks. Kádár came out in support of resuming the talks while simultaneously making "political attacks" on the Americans. He also disagreed with the idea of recalling Hungarians from scholarship programs in the United States and with the motion that prominent recipients of new awards, like the ethnographer Gyula Ortutay, cancel their invitations. Kádár also rejected the idea that the world-renowned composer and musical pedagogue Zoltán Kodály use his upcoming visit to the United States to lodge protests. Although he had no formal training in foreign policy matters, Kádár's views were pronounced, and he usually prevailed. He held that in spite of the Vietnam War, relations with the United States should be settled. He added that in order to do so, the allies (meaning the USSR) would have to be consulted.[59] Kádár saw no reason to discriminate against American exhibitors or use the fair as a forum for anti-American propaganda. "Who should go and when to the American exhibit?" he asked rhetorically. "I have been working for years to take out the strong politics [from such matters] because it doesn't help us. The Hungarian soul likes the pen knife and goulash but doesn't like cutting rations."[60]

American participation in the fair was a double-edged sword for party propagandists. On the one hand, it trumpeted the regime's newfangled policy of tolerance. On the other hand, it underscored the popularity of the United States. Internal surveys conducted a few years later revealed that one million people (10 percent of Hungary's population) visited the American exhibition each year. The luxury items exhibited there fed the perception that "America is the home of unlimited possibilities where one can make a quick fortune."[61] The American legation in Budapest understood the regime's dilemma: the great success of the exhibition was proven by the "enthusiastic reaction" of the people, which suggested that their government had failed to persuade them to condemn the United States. As it basked in the glory of a successful fair, the government seemed likely to enhance its own popularity by opening its gates even wider to American cultural influences.[62]

There were many signs of the appeal of American soft power. "American machines and know-how made a positive impact," and two hundred "enthusiastic students" had shown up at a movie screening organized by the American legation.[63] American literature, theater, music, architecture, and technological and scientific feats were all well-received. According to American reports, Hungarians read, watched, and listened to a wide variety of American novels and plays with unusual enthusiasm. American performers played in front of full houses, making it almost impossible to get tickets to see them. Sometimes these guest performances went sour: the Hungarians were fully in charge of invitations, thus many times "unknown" performers would represent American culture very poorly.[64]

VIETNAM AND CHINESE GRANDFATHERS

Budapest continued to send mixed signals. Although the party chief made overtures for a settlement in February 1965, the Ministry of the Interior organized a demonstration in front of legation premises, and demonstrators broke into the building and caused material damage. The deputy foreign minister, Béla Szilágyi, tried to make things right by offering to investigate the affair,[65] but the State Department blamed the Hungarian authorities[66] and presented a strongly worded démarche.[67] Since there had been a similar outbreak of violence in Moscow, it is likely that the idea for it originated there. The chargé in Washington claimed that the demonstration had been exploited by pro-Chinese elements for their own purposes and declared that the Hungarian government would not tolerate any more violence directed toward foreign representatives. Radványi claimed that the socialist countries were putting great pressure on Hungary to restrict its relations with the United States, but that Hungary was resisting.[68] This explanation seems lame given that the other socialist states tended to be on far better terms with Washington than was Budapest. In fact, the U.S. legation now saw that the Hungarian party's viciously anti-American condemnation of the war in Vietnam was only a pretext; the Hungarians' real problem was the fear that normalization would increase American influence.[69] Kádár was thought to be interested in mending fences to gain prestige and trade advantages for Hungary, but only at the cost of minimal concessions.[70] Kádár may well have failed to recognize that anti-American propaganda was ruining his overtures to the Americans. It is also possible that the state security apparatus simply upstaged the party leader. Finally, the authorities may have acted under Soviet pressure. Although there is no direct evidence, the Hungarians ambiguity may have been caused by an upsurge of hawkish attitudes in the Kremlin. Marshal Andrei Grechko depicted the U.S. intervention in the Dominican Republic and the bombing of Hanoi as provocations against Moscow and urged active measures, including the mobilization of armed forces in Hungary and Germany for a demonstration effect. If Cuba were to be hit, Moscow would have to be ready to hit West Berlin.[71]

In responding to the American intervention in Vietnam, the Soviets faced a choice between their desire to build better relations with the United States and the fulfillment of their internationalist duty to the Vietnamese communists. The Kremlin knew that closer contacts with the United States were important to the Soviet economy, and Vietnam took on an increased significance because China was challenging the USSR's leading role in the international communist movement. Pragmatism impelled the Kremlin to turn a blind eye to the conflict in Indochina, but international solidarity with Hanoi was decisive in Soviet thinking. It would influence Moscow's stance toward Washington in ways that were detrimental to Soviet national interests.[72] Moscow put the blame on the Americans even though they were aware – just like Hungary's leaders – that the United States was not solely responsible for the crisis in Vietnam. A rapid and peaceful solution to the problem was not in China's interest, therefore Beijing put pressure on Hanoi not to negotiate. The leadership in Hanoi was divided on this point, although they remained confident in their eventual victory. Vietnamese communists wanted talks with the Americans for the sake of military victory and not to end the conflict politically. Hanoi wanted to improve its international image by pretending to negotiate in good faith, thereby weakening the position of the prowar faction in Washington and causing tensions between Saigon and Washington.[73]

Budapest shared the Soviets' dilemma but had no choice but to line up behind Moscow. The riot at the U.S. mission suggested that opening up to the Americans did not suit the Ministry of the Interior's ideas on foreign policy. The gap between public and private statements was wide. In December 1965, using the mediation of a businessman, Hungarian diplomats indicated to the State Department that Vietnam had no real significance in their negotiations with Washington and expressed hope that the United States would "restrain itself" in reaction to Hungarian propaganda.[74]

After some deliberation, Budapest accepted a proposal to resume talks in April 1966. Rezső Nyers wanted to focus on financial claims and trade relations while neglecting cultural exchanges on the grounds that such contacts "favored the Americans."[75] Hungarian authorities did their best to obstruct even the few cultural exchanges that were already under way.

They refused to authorize an American citizen to research the history of Hungarian-German relations in the Hungarian archives. The Institute of Cultural Relations acknowledged that the Vietnam conflict had made Budapest's position on cultural contacts more rigid than that of other socialist states. A high-level functionary of the institute, Gábor Vígh, complained to a U.S. legation official that Vietnam had prevented him from accepting a Ford Foundation scholarship to visit the United States, adding that things had descended to a nadir. Claiming that his office in Budapest was bugged, Vígh asked the American diplomat not to come to lunch.[76] More and more American visitors of Hungarian descent indicated that they had been treated rudely by communist authorities. Anti-American propaganda intensified; one billboard depicted a U.S. bomber unloading on Vietnamese women and children from a dark sky. Printed on the plane in red ink was the word "murderers."[77]

The death of the U.S. chargé in Budapest occasioned an offer by foreign minister János Péter to elevate diplomatic missions to the embassy level. Radványi, the head of mission in Washington, indicated that Hungary was not free to determine its foreign policy and would have to do what its "client" – meaning the Soviet Union – asked it to.[78] He reassured the State Department that in spite of appearances in Budapest, Hungary was interested in normalizing bilateral relations. In this spirit, Foreign Minister Péter told Rusk that Mindszenty's silence would not be a prerequisite for an exchange of ministers and requested American mediation between Budapest and the papal state. Although Rusk replied that Mindszenty might be an impediment, the State Department indicated on November 11 that the United States was ready to raise diplomatic relations to the embassy level.[79] Another unexpected event, however, delayed this move.

Washington had already requested an agreement on the new American ambassador to Hungary when Radványi, the designated Hungarian ambassador, asked for political asylum. This came only a few days after Ernő Bernáth, officially the cultural attaché in Washington but also the Hungarian intelligence services' resident agent, had announced his request for political asylum. Radványi was the only Soviet-bloc ambassador ever to defect. He claimed that his life was in danger because he knew too much about Péter's "false" peace talks between Washington and Hanoi, which Hungary had offered to mediate in 1965 and again in 1966, possibly with

Soviet consent. Radványi also cited his spouse's poor health and claimed that his work had been undermined by the "primitive interior ministry people" in the Hungarian legation. Finally, the diplomat suggested that his spouse's doctor was working for French intelligence, which was in "close contact" with the Soviets.[80] He compared himself to the former Hungarian prime minister Pál Teleki, who committed suicide in 1941 because he considered his country to be on the "wrong path."[81] Not surprisingly, Budapest condemned his defection as treason[82] and Radványi was sentenced to death in absentia. Kádár ordered a full-fledged investigation by the security establishment, which concluded that Radványi had been ensnared by the CIA.

In yet another round of bickering between the two countries, the Hungarians delayed the *agrément*, hence the new American ambassador, Martin J. Hillenbrand, would arrive a year after he was originally scheduled to. Péter warned him that international politics would influence their relationship but affirmed that outstanding issues would be solved on a pragmatic basis.[83] Progress would not be speedy, but neither would Budapest return to the policy of isolation. The foreign minister pointed out that the majority of his people wished for more contact with America and that Hungarian leaders would have to take that fact into account. The limits of bridge building were also made clear. Péter cited his country's interest in peaceful coexistence but made no secret of the fact that pragmatism served ideological ends and the preservation of the status quo; mutual recognition of the two political systems would be the cornerstone of peaceful coexistence.[84] Again, this sudden refreeze may have been motivated by external causes more significant than diplomatic defections. In the fall of 1966, the Arab-Israeli conflict escalated again. Moscow suspected the involvement of the Chinese and, so as not to lose ground, decided on a policy of strengthening the "forces of national liberation."[85]

A few months after the American ambassador's arrival, Hungarian demonstrators again gathered in front of the embassy to protest an intensification of the U.S. bombing campaign in Vietnam. They did not break into the building this time, but hurled stones and ink bottles, causing material damage and some light injuries. Eventually, police broke up the demonstration, which the embassy staff noted with satisfaction. Even so, the Americans thought the government had consciously allowed foreign students who were displeased with American conduct to gather and vent their anger. It was also noted that this demonstration was not necessarily in line with the wishes of the Foreign Ministry. The embassy also indicated that they had received numerous phone calls from "locals" warning them of what was about to happen.[86] This seemed to confirm the notion that the population did not share the anti-American sentiments the authorities had hoped to whip up.

Despite the rampant anti-American propaganda that permeated the Hungarian media, U.S. officials hoped that the exchange of ambassadors would usher in a new era in which old disputes would be settled and economic and cultural ties expanded. This optimistic outlook was justified by the view that Hungary was being led by a "pragmatic" communist regime that was trying to edge closer to the West out of geographical and economic necessity.[87] Immediate U.S. aims were modest even by regional standards. They included lifting the prohibition on information activities, the liberation of a U.S. citizen imprisoned in Hungary, and the protection of the embassy's premises by U.S. Marines, which had been allowed everywhere else in the Soviet bloc.[88] Hungary would be required to service a surplus property loan dating back to the aftermath of the war, and at a higher forint/dollar exchange rate,[89] a difficult problem for a state that was manipulating its currency to boost exports. Washington also hoped to open a cultural center in Budapest, which the Hungarians rejected outright because of the danger of increasing U.S. influence. On the other hand, Budapest wanted to see its U.S. consulates reopened for the "intensification of work in the circles of the Hungarian emigration." The opaque wording concealed the regime's desire to split the Hungarian diaspora and garner the support of more moderate organizations in the émigré community. This was a bright idea given that such groups could lend support to the more conciliatory, bridge-building American line toward Hungary. The regime's priority, however, was to acquire American backing for its impending economic reforms, including the opening of a commercial office in New York. An architect of the much-celebrated New Economic Mechanism, Jenő Fock, told the U.S. ambassador that Hungary could learn a lot from the United States in the field of technology. Hillenbrand recorded that Fock bent over backwards to be polite and charming. He praised the prime minister's good sense of humor, keen intellect, and debating skills.[90] Hillenbrand observed that Fock and foreign trade minister József Bíró made only veiled references to Vietnam.[91]

The prospect of change was dampened by Szilágyi, the deputy foreign minister, who told the head of the State Department Office of East European Affairs, John Leddy, that as long as the United States was intervening in Vietnam, it was unlikely that visible progress would be made. He also expressed dissatisfaction about trade discrimination, U.S. government support for Radio Free Europe, and the Radványi affair.[92] The latter revealed an interesting instance of role playing at the Hungarian Foreign Ministry. The role of the hard-liner seems to have been played by Szilágyi, while the part of the moderate was taken by the former chargé in Washington, Tibor Zádor. Only a few days after the Radványi affair, Zádor indicated to the U.S. Embassy that the Hungarian government had forgotten about the defection, which they knew to be "sincere" and "originally" unrelated to the CIA.[93] Although 1967 started off on the right note, with the Hungarian press reporting sympathetically on the death of two U.S. astronauts and urging an improvement in relations, Hillenbrand did not arrive at the best moment. Anti-American agitation was reaching new heights. The U.S. exhibition in the Budapest International Trade Fair was temporarily closed when someone (or some group) hurled a stone at the image of President Johnson, scribbled over his message in red ink, and tried to replace the star-spangled banner with a North Vietnamese flag.[94] Other demonstrators threw stones at the embassy, although unidentified phone callers expressed the regrets "of the Hungarian people" who had nothing to do with these incidents.[95]

Both parties expected to move forward on a quid pro quo basis. Budapest wanted to reopen the consulates, inaugurate its new commercial office, and lift the cap on U.S. diplomatic personnel, while Washington wanted a consular agreement to precede the opening of the commercial office. The embassy in Washington recommended that Budapest accept the U.S. condition for the commercial office and handle the matter of consulates separately.[96] The Soviet ambassador in Washington, Anatoly Dobrynin, agreed with the Hungarian objectives and noted that it was advisable to take advantage of mutually beneficial options even without an improvement in political conditions. Evidently, the Soviets were actually encouraging their client state to take action. In an exchange with the

Hungarian ambassador, a counselor at the Soviet embassy in Washington approvingly cited a statement by Senator William Fulbright suggesting that stagnation in Soviet-American relations helped those who wanted to worsen relations and that the Soviets were arguably dodging every initiative.[97]

Even though the Americans dropped the condition of predicating the opening of consulates on a consular agreement, Budapest refused to make any concessions even after the Soviets' encouragement, and talks between the deputy foreign minister and the U.S. ambassador stalled.[98] Hungary was interested in commercial ties while the United States pressed for cultural contacts. Because of their "political content," Szilágyi refused to discuss cultural exchanges.[99] These talks were conducted in the shadow of the military escalation in Vietnam, but there was not necessarily Soviet pressure behind the Hungarians' intransigence. Moscow was extending economic and military aid to the Vietnamese communists in open support of Hanoi. The leadership in Budapest was fully aware that Moscow was doing so to enhance its prestige as the leader of the international communist movement, but the Kremlin also wanted Hanoi to strike a compromise with Washington.

In the Soviets' estimation, the Vietnamese communists stood no chance of victory. Defense minister Marshal Grechko had suggested as much in Budapest. Hungary shared Moscow's view that there was no chance for a northern victory and that Chinese ambitions stood behind the North Vietnamese' intransigence. Brezhnev complained to Kádár that China wanted to provoke a war between the Soviet Union and the United States. The Hungarians were also aware of the bitter rivalry between China and the Soviet Union and their competition in sending aid to Vietnam. It was already apparent that the Soviets were interested in détente and arms reduction, but the conflict in Indochina impeded their progress in that direction. There were some indications that Moscow hoped to profit from a North Vietnamese victory, which it hoped would enable the Soviet Union to strengthen its influence in Hanoi and provide a counterweight to the Chinese there.[100] Kádár was a strong advocate of peaceful coexistence and arms reduction, though pragmatism had not yet overcome ideology. If party leaders had really wanted it, they could have exploited this duality in the Soviet approach to make progress with the Americans in the self-interest of their regime. They missed this opportunity, however, and Kádár blamed this failure on the Hungarians' unsuccessful attempt to mediate between Washington and Beijing. After the fiasco of the first attempt, Kádár harangued the Political Committee. He had strong words for the American imperialists, but he thought that Washington was not the only party to be blamed. He added that next time "the Chinese should fool around with their own grandfather."

At a meeting designed to normalize bilateral relations, Deputy Foreign Minister Szilágyi lectured a high-level delegation from the State Department that the United States had lost Hungary's sympathy. He declared that "the people would not understand" if the government took steps to improve the state of affairs with America while the bombings continued. John Leddy, who was trying to convince him that the two issues were unrelated, was chastened with the fact that the Americans' chief allies in Europe were the Germans, only recently the most aggressive, militaristic state in Europe.[101] By that time, Hungary had decided to recognize West Germany, a state Kádár professed to dislike, and canceled its establishment of diplomatic relations only under Soviet pressure.[102] The usually sympathetic Zádor, who had a track record of promoting better relations, also blamed the lack of progress on aggression in Vietnam; nothing could happen till the bombing stopped. Expressing personal sentiments, the diplomat said, "we are all angry" and expressed his incomprehension that a great power like the United States could not allow itself to stop bombing Vietnam.[103]

Thus, as the last year of his tenure approached, not even the first pillar of President Johnson's bridge to Hungary had been set. Engaging the communist regimes in meaningful interaction was difficult, and not only because they were not yet ready to accept American terms. In December 1967, for instance, the State Department, as a small gesture to the Hungarian ambassador and his "entourage," suggested lifting the travel restrictions previously applied to them, but the Department of Justice blocked the measure, citing its detrimental security consequences.[104] Policies of engagement require the consent of both sides, and both sides' consent remained highly conditional wherever national security was concerned. Ideology and the protection of the regime's integrity still dominated Hungarian thought, despite some Americans' insistence that communist principles were losing their importance. Hungary's ruling elites had exposed a measure of real sympathy with the cause of North Vietnam; the suffering of civilians there had aroused some genuine anti-American sentiment.

Ambassador Hillenbrand believed that Hungary had no other option than to build bridges. The country needed closer economic ties to make its reforms succeed, thus the regime would have to be pragmatic in opening itself to contact with the Western world.[105] For the time being, though, the exchange of ambassadors would not lead to the expected breakthrough. The Hungarians claimed they had frozen relations because of Vietnam, but there was good reason to think that more intensive contacts with the United States would have led to cultural penetration and a disintegrating effect on the communist political system. The paradox facing the communist regime was that the preservation of communism both *required* and *forbade* the construction of an intense relationship with the Western world. For Kádár's economic experiment to succeed, Hungary would need access to U.S. capital markets, commodities, and technology. They would try to restrict normalization to a deepening of economic relations, but the Americans' policy of engagement would make this impossible. Later, as the country was getting caught up in the resultant debt spiral, it would become essential for the regime to settle with the Americans in order to get most-favored-nation treatment. At that point, Hungarian leaders would attempt to preserve the existing system by agreeing to previously inconceivable concessions, the unintended consequences of which would drive the country's economy and the communist political order into bankruptcy.

Toward the end of the decade, prior to the Soviet invasion of Czechoslovakia, Washington's relations with Hungary were worse than with any other socialist country. As Szilágyi explained to Hillenbrand, contacts reached a new nadir.[106] Looking back from 1975, the American ambassador in Budapest told Kádár that the two states had experienced the worst relationship of the Cold War.[107] Budapest readily acknowledged that of all "socialist countries Hungary had the most restrictive relationship with the United States."[108] Both sides' diplomatic missions were kept under constant surveillance. Hillenbrand reported that telephone lines had been tapped and eavesdropping devices planted in diplomats' residences and in parts of the embassy to which Hungarians had access. A microphone found in Mindszenty's residence at the embassy had been lowered through the chimney. Since the Americans considered the Ministry of Internal Affairs capable of electronically eavesdropping on the embassy building, they used a "safe room" to talk freely. Some diplomats never got used to the absence of privacy and had to be transferred before their terms expired.[109] Budapest was not the only site of such difficulties: diplomats serving in Prague, for instance, were harassed by the police.[110] American officials visiting Hungary were forced to wait an hour or more for passport and customs inspections at the airport.[111] A U.S. diplomat pointed out that relations with Hungary were worse than those with the Soviet Union, Czechoslovakia, Poland, or even Bulgaria.[112] Hungary was the only country to have capped the size of the U.S. diplomatic mission; diplomats there had to present their itineraries for Foreign Ministry approval and request exit visas. The embassy's information activities were seriously curtailed and State Department officials were received on a lower level there than in any other socialist states.[113]

The examples of Romania and Poland demonstrate that this estrangement was not produced by Soviet pressure alone. It was also true that no other bloc country had been burdened with such recent memories of invading Soviet tanks. Still, the main causes may be found in internal conditions. Some leaders, including Kádár, may have felt personal antipathy toward the United States and its foreign policy and may have been more rigidly loyal to the Soviet cause than were their comrades in Warsaw or Bucharest. At one dinner, Deputy Foreign Minister Szilágyi told his astounded American guests that "the more Americans die in Vietnam, the better."[114] The Romanians sought to increase their international autonomy by seeking favors from other powers, including the United States and China, while such options were ruled out in Budapest. Internationally, Romania had been the more successful state, while Hungary's recent past was marked by catastrophic failures. Kádár never questioned the Soviet Union's strategy. He was persuaded that "anti-Soviet communism did not exist and never will," and the maxim that "communist world politics can never lose sight of the goal of world revolution" was also part of his credo.[115] The United States was the standard-bearer of "international imperialism" and anti-Sovietism and was a "potential enemy." Even so, the party's first secretary usually took a relatively moderate stance toward the United States in the debates of the Political Committee. Peaceful coexistence and a firm belief in communist doctrine went hand-in-hand: "There are countries that we must regard as potential enemies – the United States and other similar forces – and although we struggle against them ... we still think it is possible (and even correct and necessary) to have normal state-to-state relations and peaceful coexistence.... The final victory of socialism does not require war."[116] Kádár thus reduced the historical combat between communism and capitalism to a clash of words and a struggle for international appeal.

Kádár was explicit that any improvement in relations with America would be geared to progress between Moscow and Washington. He told Brezhnev that he would "adjust" his financial talks according to the terms of Soviet-American negotiations. Foreign Minister Péter pointed out to the U.S. ambassador that in order for the two countries to normalize their relationship, a significant improvement needed to take place in Soviet-American relations.[117] Yet even when Moscow "signed off" on progress, the Hungarians did not necessarily follow suit. Ideological constraints were not the only issue. Government agencies often failed to see eye-to-eye, at which point the more restrictive positions of the Interior Ministry usually prevailed. The Political Committee worried about attempts to split the Soviet bloc. This "concern" was at least partly feigned; as the records of the Warsaw Pact Political Consultative Committee reveal, the unity of the Soviet bloc had long been a myth. Communist leaders were often at each other's throats as temporary alliances formed to hinder or promote the acceptance of a Soviet proposal.

Kádár listened with sympathy as Brezhnev deplored U.S. designs to "Romanianize" the policies of the socialist countries. Loyalty to Moscow superseded Hungarian self-interest. When in the aftermath of the Warsaw Pact invasion of Czechoslovakia ambassador Hillenbrand tried to show sympathy toward the Hungarians, his remark that their participation in the military operation must have been against Kádár's intention – to which there was some truth – was corrected by the U.S. desk officer at the Hungarian Foreign Ministry. Bartha, who was considered in Washington to be pro-American, asserted that there was no divergence between the positions taken by Moscow and by Budapest; Hungarian participation in the invasion was not due to Soviet pressure. Hillenbrand perceived a facial gesture indicating the Hungarian's displeasure at the intervention in Prague. Hungary's participation in the Soviets' attack on Czechoslovakia, the ambassador thought, had a sobering effect on the country's self-perception and prospects. In the short run, its hopes for an opening to the West would turn for the worse.[118]

THE CHANGING IMAGE OF COMMUNISM

Kádár could not and would not change the fundamentals of his system and accepted reform as a pragmatic necessity, elements of which could still be dumped. American observers of the communist scene portrayed Kádár, perhaps simplistically, as a crafty sea captain attempting to stabilize his ship on the tempestuous waves of a stormy sea. Hillenbrand expected to have to deal with ideological zealots, but he discovered that the Hungarian communists were pragmatic masters of the power struggle rather than fiery ideologues.[119] Jenő Fock, a leading reformer, was found to be calm and self-assured, and the people the ambassador had to deal with tended to be knowledgeable, if artificially polite. The minister of internal trade, Miklós Szurdi, was a well-educated individual favorably disposed toward the United States. The protestant minister turned communist functionary János Péter was seen as a "shrewd aristocrat" who had "sold his soul to the communists" but who still resembled a "European foreign minister." His underling, Szilágyi, loved English clothes and Italian art, while Frigyes Puja, the deputy foreign minister, was known for his staunch loyalty to the Soviet cause and his intelligence. A rising star of the new generation, the technocrat Péter Vályi, who was put in charge of technological modernization, pleasantly surprised the American ambassador with his agreeable personality.[120] Rezső Nyers, a key player in the economic reforms, was seen by his American interlocutor as a terrific personality with a good sense of humor and an ability to communicate.[121] Thus American officials were constructing a new narrative about the Hungarian communist leaders with whom they interacted. The previous image of ideologically driven, implacably hostile functionaries, which had been constructed as part of a confrontational policy of liberation, was softened, if not replaced. But they thoroughly misinterpreted Kádár. This was a man who framed all his memories and external impulses with ideological prejudices. He remembered a childhood scolding as his first test in the class struggle, and even a spell in Rákosi's prison had not shaken his belief in the absolute truth of communist doctrine. He ascribed his unjust punishment at the hands of his fellow communists to an ulterior motive he need not comprehend.

If the image of Hungarian communists was being retouched to fit more comfortably with détente, so was the country's role in the Cold War. Hillenbrand thought Hungary's leadership was basically weak and insecure,[122] but pragmatic, and that its geographical position and economic necessities would draw the country closer and closer to the West. Kádár wanted economic benefits from the United States, as well as the domestic and international prestige mending fences with Washington would bring.[123] This rosy picture was tainted by the fact that Hungary was still conspicuously dependent on the Soviet Union[124] and that the recent invasion of its northern neighbor again exposed its precarious status as a satellite.[125] It could still play an important role in American foreign policy because its "key geographical position" could allow it to connect the Soviet sphere to the West. Because of its cultural affinity for the United States and the large Hungarian émigré community there, close links with the Americans already existed.[126] Hungarian sympathies were made apparent when individuals assured embassy employees and their spouses of their feelings of sorrow over the tragic deaths of U.S. astronauts in 1969.[127] Even though the regime showed little enthusiasm for America, the United States was popular among "the simple people."[128] Otherwise, Hungarians seemed indifferent and skeptical. They seemed to be engaged in passive resistance to their regime.[129] Students showed little interest in international or domestic affairs and had lost all their illusions about a better future, or so it seemed to their American observers.[130]

It has been suggested that the number of people watching American movies or purchasing American goods may be a good indicator of a country's attitude toward the United States. American popularity is problematic; friendly and adverse sentiments may be harder to gauge than that.[131] Personal sentiments may be equally ambiguous and complicated. Hungarians were generally thought to have been friendly even during the war, when they were officially Hitler's allies. The newspaper *Magyar Nemzet*, which had followed a markedly anti-German, liberal line during the war, now represented a slightly more liberal line than the official organ of the communist party. *Magyar Nemzet*'s editor-in-chief, Tibor Pethő, whose father had edited the paper during the war, expressed skepticism about the Warren Report on President Kennedy's assassination, and when embassy officials asked him why, Pethő stated that Texas oil tycoons had right-wing politics of their own. His views had been reinforced by a movie starring Marlon Brando. In response, the embassy encouraged Pethő to apply for a Ford Foundation scholarship.[132] At the same time, the editor-in-chief was an advocate of expanding cultural relations and claimed that an American cultural event would not even need advertising, as people would know where it was being held. The question was not *whether* to pursue cultural exchanges and risk penetration, but how to go about it. The results could be ambiguous. In 1969, a demonstration very different from the previous ones took place in front of the American Embassy on Szabadság (Liberty) Square. Members of the Nagyfa gang had gathered to pay tribute to the tragically deceased British guitarist of the Rolling Stones, Brian Jones, whom they took to be a representative of the American hippie movement. On their way, they chanted the SS march *Erika*, which they had picked up from an American war movie. Some of the gang's members greeted each other with the Hitler salute and hoped that West Germany would soon defeat the Soviet Union, which would allow Hungary to become like America.[133]

Budapest faced an image problem in the United States. Officials of the "fraternal countries" complained that the *New York Times* was consistently publishing positive articles on Hungary.[134] This trend was started in 1964 by David Binder and Max Frenkel, who depicted Kádár's rise as a success story.[135] But American officials still held a less-than-favorable picture of the country. One high-level visitor admitted that prior to his arrival, he had thought of Hungary as "a backward agricultural" area where poverty and famine prevailed and the churches were closed.[136] Budapest was meant to be a shop-window city, but American visitors considered the Hungarian towns of Transylvania cleaner and better kept, their churches in a better state of repair than those in Hungary. A diplomat with long experience in Hungary, Francis Meehan, thought that ethnic Hungarians in Transylvania were at least as well dressed as Budapesters and were more upbeat than the people he observed in the capital.[137] Hillenbrand saw the locals' pessimism about their futures reflected in a general lack of vigor. Even if the Hungarians vested their system with local traits, all the classical characteristics of a Marxist-Leninist state were present, including a large force of secret police.[138]

As time went by, the Hungarian regime started to look like a model to be emulated by other socialist states. Hillenbrand's successor Alfred Puhan, who had studied with the Hungarian sociologist Oszkár Jászi at Oberlin College, was already opining in 1969 that Hungary and Romania were the only communist client states that President Nixon could visit. The "domestic situation was balanced, the economy was doing really well and the political atmosphere in the country was really excellent."[139]

7

"The Status Quo Is Not So Bad": Détente

It is hard to disagree with historian Geraint Hughes' assessment that "throughout the late 1960s, Britain and other Western powers were above all concerned that the status quo in Europe should be upheld."[1] The European status quo would be sanctioned by an unlikely candidate. Richard Nixon had been known for his uncompromising anticommunist stance, but as president he espoused an unabashed realism. He and Henry Kissinger formed a tandem that would redefine American Cold War politics and treat the division of Europe as if it were permanent. Stability was to prevail at the expense of the independence of old nation-states. Nixon and Kissinger re-established contacts with China and negotiated a far-reaching if flawed agreement on strategic nuclear arms with the Soviets, thereby enshrining the doctrine of mutually assured destruction. One historian has argued that the State Department was prepared to accept the status quo as a first step in the process of overcoming it.[2] Yet State Department officials never clearly defined what they wished to achieve in Eastern Europe. Their goals remained vague, and there is no indication that they ever envisioned multiparty democracy or anything resembling the restoration of independence and sovereignty in the Soviets' satellites. Moreover, under both Nixon and Carter, the White House, and not the State Department, formulated policy toward Eastern Europe. For both administrations, the primary goals were liberalization and greater autonomy, though the meanings of these terms were left unexplained. Not for the first time in the twentieth century, the people of Eastern Europe were abandoned.

Bridge building, or peaceful engagement with communist countries through trade and cultural exchange, had yet to emerge as a clear-cut strategy. Its implementation was impeded by sterile philosophical debates, interagency disagreements, rivalries with and in Congress, and above all by the fact that America had little to gain from it. Security considerations continued to hamper trade with the communist bloc; though the Nixon administration wanted to pursue change in Eastern Europe, these concerns impeded any rapid expansion of contacts. Had bridge building been more doctrine than public relations campaign, the transformation of Eastern Europe could have come much sooner and been more complete. The status of these countries, however, was no roadblock to détente. The invasion of Czechoslovakia in 1968 was virtually overlooked even though there were concerns that the conflict might spill over into an accidental clash between the Soviets and NATO troops. This time around, the United States made sure not to encourage the Czechs to fight, though there was a limit to the Americans' tolerance; they warned of "unpredictable consequences" if the Soviets tried to intervene in Romania. The Nixon administration emphasized the importance of gradual change that would not invite a military response from the Soviets. Nixon's officials would stress that any buildup of contacts between America and the socialist states could not come at the expense of relations with the Soviet Union. The existing balance was deemed "not so bad" for the United States, thus the only chance Eastern Europe still had for liberation was change within the Soviet Union itself. Nixon wanted personal oversight over Eastern Europe and wished to control even the most insignificant developments between the United States and the Soviet bloc. He and his national security advisor sought to marginalize the State Department but only partially succeeded, as the State Department frequently acted without consulting the White House.

In Moscow, détente meant consolidating and broadening Soviet positions in the world, weakening U.S. positions in Western Europe, and avoiding simultaneous conflicts with China and the United States. The Soviet economy was also under great pressure, and détente offered an opportunity to ease the burden imposed on it by the arms race.[3] Détente would also come to mean the acceptance and legalization of Soviet hegemony in Eastern Europe. Hungary's modest economic reforms subjected it to two kinds of intensifying pressure. Muscovite politicians regarded some of Hungary's reforms as a creeping reintroduction of capitalism. The other form of pressure was financial: as the modernization envisioned by the reformers was externally financed, more and more concessions had to be made to get the loans required to keep the country running. Hungary's main market for capital was the United States, and as a result, the penetration of American culture and propaganda accelerated even though political relations remained cool and commercial contacts modest. The Nixon administration's willingness to build bridges more aggressively than its predecessor, coupled with Eastern Europe's increasing economic reliance on the Western world, gave shape to a permanently divided Europe, one guided by the principle of peaceful coexistence, with less confrontation and more extensive contacts between East and West.

HUNGARY AND THE SOVIET INTERVENTION
IN CZECHOSLOVAKIA

After the Prague Spring was brought to an end, American observers expressed astonishment and disappointment, and Hungary's self-definition as a viable road between East and West seemed to lose its viability.[4] Shortly thereafter, the first secretary of the Communist Party of the Soviet Union (CPSU) announced the doctrine of limited sovereignty, which vested the Soviet Union with the right to restore order and discipline behind the Iron Curtain. As the Soviets "restored order" to a potentially explosive situation, the West did nothing, in accordance with the existing Western view that stability trumped independence in Eastern Europe. Washington and London canceled all cultural, scientific, and commercial visits with representatives of the Soviet Union and the other participants in the invasion – Romania was famously not invited to take part in the operations – but that was all. London still went on to conclude a trade agreement with the Soviets; the Labour government wished to liberalize East-West trade and, together with France, to export computers to the Eastern bloc, though these plans were vetoed by Washington.[5]

NATO had two alternatives with regard to Czechoslovakia. One was to issue a strong warning to Moscow about the consequences of an invasion and thereby avoid a recurrence of the 1956 invasion of Hungary or of the 1948 communist putsch in Czechoslovakia. Instead, the West opted not to take any action that might provoke the Kremlin to use force. Even though this approach had failed in 1956, it was in tune with the idea of détente, which together with common defense had formed the core of NATO's official policy since 1967.[6] The West Germans made efforts to improve relations with their eastern neighbors and abandoned the Hallstein doctrine. President Johnson hoped that the Soviets would not interfere with détente by attacking Prague,[7] but when it came to unchallenged control of its zone, Moscow had invariably chosen to break with the West ever since 1945. Thirty years earlier, Britain had given Hitler a free hand in Czechoslovakia not only out of indifference and impotence, but also because Chamberlain had hoped that the rectification of the injustices of the treaty of Paris and German control of central Europe would stabilize a region that had long been a source of tension and conflict. In 1968, Czechoslovakia's independence was not a high price to pay for Soviet cooperation. French prime minister Georges Pompidou feared that Germany's Ostpolitik could destabilize Eastern Europe and thereby the whole continent by inciting them to revolt. After the invasion, the head of the Quai d'Orsay, Michel Debré, famously remarked that the invasion was a "minor traffic accident" on the road to détente. British prime minister Harold Wilson even wished to send Christmas cards to Eastern Europe's atheist rulers. Although the Foreign Office had concluded that the effort to develop a working relationship with the Soviet leadership since 1964 had yielded few discernible results, Wilson informed the Kremlin of his regret that Anglo-Soviet relations had stalled because of Czechoslovakia and suggested a visit to Moscow to discuss matters of common interest.[8]

The question was not just the future of Soviet-American relations and the relaxation of tensions. Washington needed Moscow's help in Vietnam, either in the form of active intervention in Hanoi on behalf of an agreement, or at least for the Soviets to refrain from actions that would impede a peaceful arrangement. As in 1956, American diplomats failed to appreciate that a movement toward liberalization was taking place. Dubček's seizure of power was dismissed as a coup and like Nagy he was not taken seriously. This was because American diplomats lived in isolation; Prague had refused to improve relations with the United States and there were no overt signs of dissatisfaction in Czechoslovakia. As a result of 1956, Radio Free Europe (RFE) programs were closely monitored to avoid provocation. Broadcasts were restricted to objective narrations of events as determined by the State Department.[9] After the Warsaw Pact invasion, Dean Rusk warned the United States Information Agency (USIA) to avoid repeating the mistakes they had made in Hungary, where the United States had "unintentionally" encouraged the victims of aggression by telling them that the United States would come to their assistance. He directed the USIA to report credible news only.

In the end, the crushing of the uprising in Prague, which had sought radical but not transformative change in the Czechoslovakian political system and more autonomy from the USSR, brought little change in East-West relations. It has been argued that the invasion brought home to the United States that the European status quo was permanent and therefore to be accepted. The State Department, however, had argued for accepting the permanence of European division and Soviet hegemony even earlier. On the other hand, the invasion only underscored the importance the Soviets still attached to their buffer zone. Their decision to use force was made to preserve socialism in Czechoslovakia, which they thought to be endangered, particularly by the West Germans. This decision was to be carried out, Grechko said, "even if it leads to a third world war." It was made despite concerns regarding the nuclear nonproliferation treaty and strategic arms limitation talks. It could plausibly be argued that by forcing West Germany to accept the permanence of division and to launch Ostpolitik, the invasion contributed to European détente. Bonn and the West as a whole came to the conclusion that they had to come to terms in Europe and reach some kind of détente based on a recognition of the status quo.[10] Brezhnev indicated that the invasion initiated a new era of dialogue in Soviet-American relations, too. This, he believed, was due to the Americans' recognition that "The United States was incapable of altering the status quo and [had to] recognize the reality [of] the Soviet Union's potential and influence."[11]

The Foreign Office did not think that turmoil was in Great Britain's interest because it could destroy the idea of peaceful coexistence on which détente was founded. And nothing could be done to liberalize the region anyway. London was in an uncomfortable position: Moscow had to be condemned in the UN, but without hostility, lest détente be jeopardized.[12] Although Washington and Paris often disagreed over matters of foreign policy, their positions on Prague were almost identical. Undersecretary of state Nicholas Katzenbach declared that nothing could be done to deter the Soviets, while in the French view, the West could not interfere in the Soviet-Czechoslovak dispute without harming the Czechoslovak liberals.[13] To induce liberalization, Washington contemplated returning Czech gold and approving Czechoslovakia's membership in the International Monetary Fund (IMF) and most-favored-nation status. As in 1956, the question was why Washington did not put a price tag on such invasions, especially considering that broader political and economic contacts provided some leverage and that détente put more at stake for the Soviets. But there were few options from which to choose. One possibility would have been for Congress to reject the nuclear nonproliferation treaty. Another was to suspend strategic nuclear arms reduction talks. It was pointed out, however, that both of these initiatives were more in the interest of the United States than the Soviet Union; to pressure the Kremlin in this way was to risk a self-inflicted wound.

After the invasion of August 1968, there was some apprehension that Moscow might repeat such an action in Yugoslavia or Romania. As Geraint Hughes argues, however, this fear was milder in London and Washington, as both capitals may have known from signals intelligence intercepts that the Kremlin had not contemplated such a move. It was also apparent that this invasion had been a defensive rather than an offensive move and posed no immediate threat to NATO. Nevertheless, the State Department proposed that if the Soviets occupied Romania, the United States should prepare to render military assistance to Yugoslavia in case Tito were to request it.[14] In spite of Romania's occasionally anti-Soviet stance, the formally nonaligned and strategically better-placed Yugoslavia was higher on the list of American priorities. Austria was still the most important country in East Central Europe, as suggested in a memorandum prepared by then-ambassador to France Charles Bohlen, who was certain that a Soviet move against Austria would launch the "Third World War."[15]

No similar statement was made about any other country in the region. Nevertheless, when Rusk was informed of Soviet troop movements near the Romanian border, he warned Dobrynin that an occupation of that country would have "unpredictable consequences" for world politics. The secretary used strong language to make clear that the U.S. response would not be so mild. Rusk emphasized "the gravity of the situation" and Washington's "deep concern," declaring in the "strongest possible terms" Washington's "expectation" that the USSR would refrain from the use of force against any other Eastern European country. Finally, he indicated that in the president's view the operation against Czechoslovakia was a grave mistake on the part of the Soviet Union and that a repetition of it would be tragic. The American people were "pretty mad" because of the Czechoslovak affair.[16] America's response was left opaque, but Rusk issued his starkest warning to the Soviets in connection with Romania. American anxieties were reflected in the desire to remove all West German forces from the border with Czechoslovakia and to avoid any provocative act in the Federal Republic of Germany (FRG).[17]

In 1968, the president who had ushered in the reconstruction of contacts with the Soviet bloc announced that he would not run again for the presidency. Under Johnson this new doctrine had not been translated into action. Ironically, it was his outspokenly anticommunist successor, Richard Nixon, who would eventually make it a reality. Nixon needed Soviet help to conclude the war in Vietnam and in fact subordinated the policy of détente to the Soviet role in ending the crisis. In order to put pressure on the Soviets, he carried out a foreign policy coup in opening up to China. He and his advisor Henry Kissinger hoped this would cause further problems in the already tense relationship between Beijing and Moscow. China could balance Soviet power and the Kremlin would as a result be forced into more cooperation with Washington in world politics. As a foreign policy realist, the president was willing to disregard ideological issues in his approach to international affairs. Nixon wanted an agreement on arms reduction; therefore his priority in international politics was the Soviet Union.[18]

TOWARD A NEW EUROPEAN STRUCTURE

After the invasion of Czechoslovakia, William Griffith, formerly the president of Radio Free Europe and later a professor at MIT, prepared a memorandum on American policy on Eastern Europe. He claimed that

"Peaceful engagement was not directed toward removing Soviet influence from Eastern Europe and did not intend to substitute Western penetration for Russian control. Its purpose was to heal peacefully the division of Europe."[19] These ambiguous definitions of American objectives sounded like a recognition of the European status quo. Though Nixon was known for his strident anticommunist rhetoric – he was the only U.S. official who visited the Hungarian refugees in Austria and his presidential library is decorated with Ferenc Daday's large-scale painting commemorating this event[20] – he had no intention of challenging Soviet hegemony in Eastern Europe, an area he intended to use to pressure Moscow toward a more cooperative stance in world politics. Yet neither was he permissive toward the communist governments. In contrast with several members of his administration, he believed that economic and trade concessions could be granted only after his conditions for them were met. Nixon did not expect economic or cultural penetration to democratize these dictatorial systems. Secretary of state William Rogers and the State Department were relegated to the sidelines even on the relatively minor issue of Eastern Europe. As Kissinger put it, the president wished to have "personal control" over U.S. policy toward the communist states.[21] Boundless personal ambition and animosity toward the foreign policy apparatus – perhaps including the secretary of state himself – may be among the reasons. Nixon seems to have seen foreign policy as a huge jigsaw puzzle in which control of the parts was the prerequisite to understanding the whole.

The State Department was tasked with implementing the president's policies. Kissinger thought that in a modern state the secretary of state should not be in charge of foreign affairs but rather function as an administrator. The president picked Rogers because he had no previous experience in external matters, which made it easier for the White House to take charge of international affairs. Kissinger accepted the appointment because he thought Rogers to be loyal, discreet, hard-headed, and capable of keeping his subordinates under control. Nixon had little confidence in the "bureaucrats" of the State Department. The National Security Council (NSC) had been reformed to improve its coordination of defense and foreign policies. Kissinger regarded international politics as a worldwide game of chess and subordinated Eastern Europe to this global outlook.[22] Only a relatively high level of congressional involvement kept the president and his national security advisor from exercising unchallenged control over US policy in Eastern Europe.

Kissinger and the president agreed that only the balance of power determined the behavior of states in the international arena, which was uninfluenced by individual states' political systems, moral considerations, and principles. This point is amply illustrated by Nixon's benign relationship with Nicolae Ceaușescu, who ran one of the most intolerant dictatorships in Soviet-controlled Europe. Idealists like Jimmy Carter and Ronald Reagan would expect regime changes to shore up international peace and U.S. security. Realists like Nixon and Kissinger were loath to interfere in the domestic affairs of other countries, something State Department officials made clear to communist functionaries over and over again. They were interested in shifting the balance of power toward America and did not think it possible or desirable to change the Soviet system.[23] General Brent Scowcroft espoused these ideas as part of Nixon's foreign policy staff and later as national security advisor under George H. W. Bush. Foreign policy realism allowed Romania, internally dogmatic but internationally more autonomous, to top the internally more liberal but otherwise pro-Soviet Hungary in Washington's "pecking order." Bucharest's independent foreign policy earned it "special treatment" even though Romania was known to be run by "a tightly centralized repressive regime."[24]

To some extent, Nixon's policies were conducive to the Kremlin's aim to convene an all-European conference that would sanction the continental status quo. As the CIA put it, "the Soviets have always made it clear that their security and other aspirations to a world role rest in the first instance on their position in Europe."[25] As soon as the Nixon administration was sworn in, Soviet ambassador Anatoly Dobrynin, who was becoming a permanent fixture on the international diplomatic scene, attempted to sound out whether Washington would accept a European settlement based on the current situation. Dobrynin, who would later serve as the president's "back channel" to the Kremlin, indicated that Moscow was ready for a dialogue covering several areas: the Middle East, Vietnam, and even central Europe, which the Soviets had previously refused to discuss. Kissinger thought the Soviet proposal came close to a recognition of the existing situation in Europe. Dobrynin's memorandum failed to mention the Brezhnev doctrine on limited sovereignty, and Kissinger interpreted this omission as saying that the doctrine applied only to Eastern Europe, and hence that the Soviets had renounced further expansion into Europe. He was therefore eager to gauge what the Soviets wanted.[26] The same day, an interagency committee recommended that the United States not challenge the Soviet Union's "national interests" by threatening its position in Eastern Europe.[27] Kissinger's aide on Eastern Europe, Helmut Sonnenfeldt, considered the European balance far from perfect but "not at all bad" for the United States, though he did not think it desirable to sanction it with U.S.-Soviet talks. He added that the United States should be the last country to give the Soviets a free hand in Eastern Europe, particularly in light of the "special relationship" the United States was formulating with Romania.[28]

By themselves the Soviet client states posed no risk to U.S. safety; what mattered was their contribution to Soviet military power and the extent to which they were dominated by Moscow. While the United States was ready for "more constructive" relations with the Soviet sphere to reduce the dangers and costs of rivalry, a national security directive emphasized the need to obstruct the Soviet Union's economic and military consolidation of the region – even though the United States was also trying to consolidate the region economically – and the need to promote more open societies.[29] In a broader sense, Washington's policy toward Eastern Europe was connected to a more permanent European arrangement. Sonnenfeldt advocated a balance in which the FRG, the Western Europeans, the Soviet Union, and its allies would all receive security guarantees. In the new European context, the two Germanys would guarantee not only their own security, but the security of their neighbors – the Soviet Union, Poland, and Czechoslovakia – from them. This memorandum is thus at least implicitly based on an acceptance of the Warsaw Pact's role in the European balance.

Sonnenfeldt conceived three scenarios for the reinforcement of European security, none of which envisioned the reunification of the continent or the dissolution of the military alliances.[30] State Department officials did not advocate an explicit recognition of Soviet hegemony, but in order to reach a long-term settlement they envisioned "normal" relations with the client states, which normalization would require a "reduction" – but not the elimination – of Soviet control. The Brezhnev doctrine had thus clearly left its mark on State Department thinking. Moreover, since they were in the best position to gauge the limits of the Kremlin's toleration, the leaders of the Soviet satellites would be left to determine how far they were willing to go.[31] The main concern was reducing Moscow's ability to use its allies as springboards for aggression. This policy would require greater autonomy in the Soviet bloc, but the transformation would have to remain gradual so as not to destabilize the region and trigger Soviet intervention. There was also concern that another Soviet invasion would highlight "American impotence" or lead to a Soviet-American confrontation and thereby further jeopardize America's interests in Eastern Europe.[32] Perhaps paradoxically, the Soviets' grand design for Europe was not all that far from the Nixon administration's, even though this might not have been apparent at the time. After the crisis in Czechoslovakia, Soviet policymakers concentrated their efforts on convoking a conference on European security and cooperation. They wanted Western recognition of the political and military realities of postwar Europe and to extract a pledge that the Western powers would not use military force to alter the status quo.[33]

Although the wording of high-level documents on U.S. intentions behind the Iron Curtain was often opaque, political leaders and high-level functionaries sometimes expressed their views more openly in private conversations. President Nixon assured the new Hungarian ambassador that he understood how Hungary's relationship with its neighbors was "influenced by geography and history," indicating he understood the constraints of Hungarian foreign policy.[34]

In 1971, the U.S. ambassador to Budapest, Alfred Puhan, met with prominent representatives of the Hungarian community in the United States. When asked about the prospects of liberation, he openly admitted to his audience that Hungary's only hope was slow change in the Soviet leadership.[35] The message that Washington had given up the goal of rolling back communism was communicated to Eastern European leaders as well. USIA director James Keogh declared in Budapest that the United States "does not interfere in the domestic affairs of other countries. We are not working on provoking revolutions or uprisings."[36] Deputy assistant secretary of state Richard T. Davies made it clear that the United States had no desire to improve U.S.-Hungarian relations "at the expense of Hungary's relations with the Soviet Union," a recognition that Hungary was the Soviet Union's ally.[37] Puhan assured the Hungarian prime minister that Washington "respected the Hungarian economic and social system." Martin J. Hillenbrand, who left his post in Budapest to become assistant secretary for European affairs, assured the Hungarian ambassador that the United States had "no wish to lure Hungary away from its allies."[38] The State Department's Policy Planning Staff indicated that the status of Soviet-American relations would shape America's stance toward Hungary.[39]

The strident rhetoric Washington had formerly used to describe the government in Budapest also changed. The fifteenth anniversary of the 1956 revolution was observed, but the Nixon administration did not extend its condemnation to "the present Hungarian government," which "had come a long way."[40] Secretary of transportation John Volpe had already accepted an invitation from the Association of Hungarian Freedom Fighters to participate in their commemoration, but when the Hungarian government found out and lodged a formal diplomatic protest, the secretary of state took the unprecedented step of asking Volpe to cancel his participation, which he did.[41]

NIXON AND THE DILEMMAS OF ENGAGING EASTERN EUROPE

Economics remained the cornerstone of relations between America and Eastern Europe. Even the most conservative regimes, such as the one in Bulgaria, were interested in the liberalization of U.S. trade and loan policies. Washington expected the expansion of economic relations to promote liberalization while leaving strategic controls intact. As always, the implementation was problematic. Security concerns were at odds with foreign policy initiatives, and the Department of Defense was reluctant to relax controls. Moreover, it remained unclear whether economic concessions would be granted as "rewards" for enacting political measures required by the United States, or granted in advance as encouragement to change. West German chancellor Willy Brandt's Ostpolitik rested on the principle that trade should never be tied to political questions, as the latter alone would suffice to "mellow" the Soviet system.[42] Nixon and Kissinger disapproved of the FRG's policy, fearing that it would weaken NATO and reinforce Moscow's position in Eastern Europe.⁴³

Some members of the Nixon administration would attach no strings to economic liberalization, while the president and his closest advisors wanted political preconditions. The formulation of economic policy involving the communist world was also partly the outcome of personal clashes within the administration. Domestic politics also played a role, and not only in the traditional struggle between Congress and the executive branch for control over foreign policy. The business community and the unions were also invested in the outcome. Congress itself was divided over the issue, particularly regarding the argument that Eastern Europe could become a significant market for American products during a recession. Trading with the communists was potentially lucrative. Western European firms were selling $6.5 billion worth of goods to the Soviet bloc annually, and while U.S. exports were only a fraction of that figure ($195 million), it was thought that American sales could climb to $500 million or even $700 million by 1969.

Shortly after his inauguration the president ordered a revision of U.S. trade policy toward the communist world. All government agencies were required to contribute, including the White House and the NSC staff. In keeping with the centralized nature of his administration, Nixon made the ultimate decision alone. Factors to be examined in the reappraisal included the impact of most-favored-nation (MFN) status, strategic trade controls, bilateral issues, security, and Washington's desire to have constructive relations with communist states. Trade policies were still contradictory; they were supposed to refuse the Soviets any goods with military potential while simultaneously bringing economic benefit to the United States. Finally, a distinction was to be made between the militarily dangerous Soviet Union and its harmless allies.⁴⁴ All government agencies interested in foreign trade, including the Department of Agriculture, supported trade liberalization. They expected the administration's open support for trade with communist states, the extension of MFN status, and a reduction in the number of embargoed commodities that would bring it more in line with the positive list used by Western Europeans. This stance was likely motivated more by political considerations than economic since it was expected that even in favorable conditions the Soviet bloc's share in annual U.S. trade would not exceed 1 percent. The Department of Agriculture asked the president to support business interests, claiming that granting MFN status to Eastern Europe was in the "national interest" of the United States. The Department of Labor concurred, advocating liberalization on a reciprocal basis, though with the warning that the AFL-CIO would not support liberalized policies toward the communist states unless they brought economic benefits to the United States.[45]

Although limits on transfers of technologies such as computers were believed to cause the communists serious hardships, advocates of trade expansion argued that the communist economies had hardly been affected by the wide range of export controls. It was also unclear whether liberalization would affect the power position of communist governments. According to some scenarios, they could be weakened; others suggested trade controls would reinforce their hold on power.[46] The secretary of the treasury realistically argued that the communist states would not be able to pay for their purchases, thus the economic yield of liberalization would be small, and possibly damaging domestically if the administration's political opponents in Congress were able to portray such policies as trading with the enemy. The White House Office of Emergency Preparedness saw no inherent security risk in lifting trade barriers, suggesting that doing so would reduce the Eastern Europeans' dependence on the Soviet Union. The agency predicted that Congress would veto any change as long as the war in Vietnam continued.[47] The CIA and the State Department agreed that the embargo had retarded the development of sophisticated weapon systems in the USSR but had not impeded economic growth to any appreciable extent, except insofar as it caused problems of quality. All in all, the embargo contributed only "marginally" to the communists' technological backwardness. The State Department expected the CoCom list to produce tensions with American allies, and that trade liberalization would not affect Soviet conduct. Even so, the State Department supported liberalization without reserve, including the extension of most-favored-nation status and the administration's open support for developing economic contacts with the East.[48] This seemed to be a "good thing" for propaganda, a positive influence on the thinking of the Eastern Europeans, or so the USIA thought.[49]

The cause of trade liberalization, however, faced formidable opposition. Pentagon analysts challenged the notion that it would be economically beneficial and argued that if any relaxation of trade controls were announced before Soviet-American talks began, the U.S. government would lose flexibility in its negotiating position. They recommended that political progress be the precondition of any move toward increased trade. Thus the Department of Defense found revisions of existing legislation conceivable only on a reciprocal basis and advocated further internal evaluations of the advantages that might accrue to America from liberalization. The Atomic Energy Commission also opposed significant changes due to security concerns.[50]

Thus there was no consensus regarding the costs and benefits of changing existing economic policies toward the Soviet bloc. This was not surprising in light of the fact that analysts had been reduced to speculation about the economic consequences of the controls. The president ruled against liberalization, declining to support any new legislation in that direction. In essence, the Pentagon's proposal was accepted; the NSC ruled that more liberal policies would follow adequate progress in political relations with Eastern Europe. Government agencies were instructed not to bring up the question of trade liberalization.[51] Thus economic concessions would be granted not to encourage closer relations with the United States or internal reform, but would be used as a carrot, to be granted as a reward only after the desired outcome was reached.

Sonnenfeldt was highly disappointed with the president's decision, which he thought made it look as though Moscow was dictating American policy toward Eastern Europe – even though he had "never hoped" that trade or cultural policies would be able to influence the Soviets.[52] Business circles also deplored the decision, and the press subjected the Nixon administration to further criticism. But Nixon may have anticipated the congressional mood: had he decided for liberalization, the legislature would likely have disapproved on the grounds that an extension of MFN status would have flooded the American market with cheap communist products at the expense of American jobs,[53] however groundless this fear may have been.

The complicated interplay of national security and foreign policy concerns in trade calculations is illustrated by a Franco-Polish affair. French officials attached great political and economic significance to the sale of a silicon transistor production line to Poland. This required CoCom approval, and the United States wanted to stop the French from circumventing CoCom and selling their equipment to the East. It was understood that this decision would influence Franco-American relations, but the sale entailed potential risks to U.S. security. While the State Department argued that the danger was minimal, the Pentagon claimed that the transaction would undermine CoCom and allow the Warsaw Pact to produce integrated circuits for its military communication systems. Eventually Kissinger brokered an agreement between the two agencies. The Pentagon accepted the State Department's position that the transaction should not be blocked, not only in the interest of relations with Paris but because obstructing the deal would encourage others to circumvent CoCom and thereby undermine the system of international controls.[54] Similar concerns surfaced when Boeing announced a $45 million deal to sell three passenger aircraft to the Romanian airline Tarom. As parts of its compensation, Boeing wanted to produce spare parts in Romania, an operation it hoped would reach 10 percent of the value of the deal. The Departments of State and Commerce supported the transaction because of the volume of business it represented and the hope that it would open up the Eastern market for U.S. commercial aircraft. The Pentagon, however, was concerned that modern technologies would make their way into Romania's military aviation industry. In response to these concerns, Boeing removed several state-of-the-art aircraft from the list of equipment it offered to Bucharest. Even so, the Department of Defense wanted to torpedo the sale. The NSC did not share any concerns, though, and recommended that the president sign off on the transaction.[55]

In early 1970, Congress decided to reduce the list of commodities that could not be sold to the Soviet bloc. This was in line with the NSC's position that the CoCom and American lists should be harmonized. Secretary of State Rogers, one of the main supporters of trade expansion, hoped that the congressional decision would lead to significant progress. Nixon resisted and recommended removing only 216 nonstrategic items.[56] In the fall of 1970, as the U.S. trade deficit grew drastically, Rogers and secretary of commerce Maurice Stans renewed their offensive to change Nixon's policy. Stans indicated that Eastern Europeans imported more from Japan than from the United States and argued that U.S. trade policy served no political or economic interest. It was simple economic self-interest for the United States to supply a larger share of Eastern Europe's imports.

The Department of Commerce worked with the USIA to promote U.S. exports and exhibit American products in trade fairs, and the tremendous success of American-made items at the Budapest International Trade Fair suggested Stans was on the right track. The secretary warned that the business community did not like having to relinquish opportunities to its Western European and Japanese competitors and recommended the elimination of legal obstacles to trade. George Schultz, who then headed the White House Office of Management and Budget, also supported the liberalization initiative, as did the chairman of economic advisors. The latter weakened the argument somewhat by stating that there was no chance for a significant American breakthrough into the Eastern European market. Nixon's own economic advisor thought that any surplus in exports arising from an extension of MFN status would have to be financed by American taxpayers.[57]

Such political delays thwarted several opportunities in Eastern Europe and the Soviet Union, causing resentment and animosity in the business community.[58] Rogers supported Stans and supplemented his argument with political ones. The secretary conceived of trade as a political "weapon," although he understood that there was little to import from Eastern Europe in exchange for American exports.[59] Rogers wanted American businesses to enjoy the same privileges in the Eastern European marketplace as their Western European competitors had. Trade concessions would also signal that the agreement between Bonn and Moscow did not mean that the West accepted the Soviet sphere of interest. Rogers also argued that the United States should balance West Germany's influence in Eastern Europe.[60] The Pentagon was skeptical of the transformative effect of trade and of the notion that the construction of more intensive commercial contacts would alter the international behavior of hostile communist powers. A doubter of the liberal tenet that trade leads to harmony in international affairs, which was espoused by Rogers and Stans, secretary of defense Melvin Laird asserted that only domestic liberalization could have this effect. He believed that internal democratization would come about as domestic economic problems intensified, rather than through a relaxation of external pressures. He doubted whether the communist states could pay for their purchases, which would mean that their imports would be financed by the United States. Thus, Laird argued, America would be solving the communists' domestic problems and helping them close the technological gap between themselves and the West. The secretary of defense therefore set impossible standards for trade expansion: economic transformation, convertible currencies, and trade free of any discrimination.[61] Such a shift in policy, however, would have required nothing short of regime change. Nixon's economic advisor was interested only in political arguments, and particularly in U.S.-Romanian relations. But even for him it was important to keep at bay liberal democrats like Walter Mondale and Edmund Muskie, who were out to limit presidential power and expand trade with Eastern Europe.[62]

Kissinger disagreed with Laird. He believed that trade with the United States was important for the small communist countries and that they would be willing to give something up for the privilege. There was no progress with the Romanians because the United States was not complying with their wish for credits and MFN treatment. Kissinger thought that MFN status would have a large political and psychological impact in Eastern Europe, while export loans would have only economic ramifications. He therefore recommended that the administration seek congressional authorization to grant concessions to Iron Curtain states on an individual basis, which would allow the United States to extract significant political concessions in return. The only open question was whether the political concessions should be extracted *in advance* from all Eastern European states, or just from the Soviets.[63] Secretary Stans tried personally to convince the president of the need for liberalization, but he failed. Nixon decided not to take any initiative in the matter.[64] His position was clear: he wanted political concessions in return for economic favors because he believed that trade was "infinitely" more important for the other side than for America.[65] Security and economic arguments continued to clash, and Nixon refused to permit the changes necessary to implement bridge building. Although the rhetoric and principles of American policy had changed fundamentally since the 1950s, genuine economic interaction with the USSR began to accelerate only with the Soviet-American trade agreement of October 1972. The United States negotiated several industrial accords worth $1.1 billion and sold wheat to the Soviets for another billion. The Department of Commerce simultaneously reduced the positive list from 550 items to a mere 73.[66]

Along with export controls, the other traditional pillar of U.S. policy toward Eastern Europe was psychological warfare. Clandestine operations and propaganda were supposed to exploit tensions between the Soviet Union and its clients, not in order to encourage revolutions but to weaken the Soviets' sway over the satellites. Despite condemnations of its programs by communist authorities and an annual Soviet outlay of $150 million in a largely unsuccessful effort to jam the station's broadcasts, Radio Free Europe had more than thirty million listeners. Besides RFE, which no longer incited anticommunist resistance, the CIA was also involved in publishing manuscripts smuggled from behind the Iron Curtain and in disseminating books that for political reasons were not available in the Soviet bloc. In a memorandum prepared in 1970, the CIA proposed to lend more support to dissidents and to help train new leaders who could provide democratic alternatives to Soviet-supported mass organizations.[67] Psychological warfare was meant to pressure the Soviet leadership into making decisions favorable to the United States in important matters of world politics. These actions were supposed to be carried out both in the USSR and in areas of vital interest to the Soviets such as Eastern Europe. The CIA was also ready to intensify tensions between Moscow and its satellites by harnessing the growing nationalism that Soviet military interventions and economic exploitation had aroused in Eastern Europe.[68] Scientific and technological exchange programs were also part of the psychological warfare and as such enjoyed presidential support. American officials thought that Eastern Europeans wanted these programs for the sake of economic and industrial progress and to diminish their dependence on the USSR. From an American perspective, such programs were important tools for enhancing the autonomy of Eastern European states and for awakening their interest in the United States. Scientific and technological exchanges became forms of leverage with which the United States pushed for the cultural exchanges it preferred.[69]

"NEEDLING THE SOVIETS": HUNGARY AND
THE NIXON ADMINISTRATION

By the early 1970s, the Nixon administration had decided it would support Eastern European independence up to the point of autonomy within the existing European power structure. Their international behavior – internal conditions did not matter – would be steered by the old carrot-and-stick method. The administration ranked the communist regimes in Eastern Europe so as to reward them according to their merits and to punish them by withholding various inducements. Nonaligned Yugoslavia headed the list, mainly because of its independent foreign policy. Romania came in second, also due to its autonomous foreign policy as well as the services it performed for the United States such as mediating in the Vietnam War, the Arab-Israeli conflict, and the Sino-American rapprochement. Poland, historically the most important state in the region, was clearly third as a result of its strategic significance, though its loyal pro-Soviet line and domestic rigor caused it to decline in the rankings. By the early 1970s, Kádár's Hungary, which had introduced the most sweeping – although in absolute terms modest – economic reform in communist history, was placed immediately after Poland. Czechoslovakia, which since the backlash against the Prague Spring had been governed by one of the region's most oppressive regimes, came next; the GDR and Bulgaria rounded out the list.[70] In practice, however, aside from Yugoslavia, which was not a member of the Soviet bloc, Poland still topped the rankings. Romania might have been the temporary favorite, but its significance paled in comparison to Warsaw's already close economic and cultural ties to the United States, which included ten million Americans of Polish origin and representatives of Polish descent in Congress. No other group in the region carried such weight in domestic American politics. Romania and Poland's similar status is reflected in the fact that these were the two states in Eastern Europe that President Nixon visited.

Washington wanted to see a more independent Poland with closer ties to Western Europe. Poland was already America's most important trading partner in Eastern Europe, and the goal there was "significant" American economic penetration. The Gierek regime was more open to the development of cultural relations than was its predecessor. In 1971, seven hundred Poles visited the United States in cultural exchange programs, double the 1965 number, but still less than half the number of Czechoslovaks (fifteen hundred) who had come in 1968. Technical and scientific exchange programs strengthened American prestige and influence, thus the U.S. government was willing to accept Warsaw's request that these programs not be made visible to the outside world. In stark contrast to other Eastern

European ethnic minorities, Polish Americans supported Washington's "pragmatic" policies toward Warsaw, even pressuring Washington to introduce an aid program for the Polish people. Poland's significance was demonstrated by the fact that the American diplomatic mission there was the largest in the region; its yearly budget was $2.1 million, more than the missions in Prague and Budapest combined. Radio Free Europe spent one-quarter of its budget on Poland; scientific and technical exchange programs there cost an additional $2 million per annum.[71]

If we leave constant factors like domestic importance and strategic position aside, by all other metrics Romania emerged as Washington's most important partner in the Soviet bloc. Bucharest was regarded as an "independent factor" in international affairs, a regime that aimed at preserving its independence from the Soviet Union. The country's positive image was not significantly impacted by the cult of personality of its leader or its "rigid, orthodox" domestic politics; in fact, in the American estimation, every aspect of life there was under the control of the Communist Party.[72] Romania was almost an ally, as Ceaușescu helped Nixon achieve his most important foreign policy goals in Vietnam, China, and the Middle East. Close personal contacts emerged between American and Romanian leaders on several levels. Ambassador Corneliu Bogdan met regularly with Kissinger and the president. Nixon had already been to Romania as vice president and had received a tumultuous welcome. Ceaușescu made a good impression; Nixon considered him a strong and sincere personality.[73] Although Washington benefited from Ceaușescu's foreign policy ambitions and frequent standoffs with Moscow, its policies toward Romania remained cautious.

Washington portrayed its relations with Romania as a model for other satellites and continued to support Romania's "maverick" foreign policy. But it was feared that Romania's independence from the Soviet Union could turn against American and Romanian interests if it moved beyond "a certain point." Moscow had important security interests in Romania, and the United States did not want Bucharest's "independence" to trigger Soviet intervention. In addition, Romanian politics was not supposed to have a negative effect on Soviet-American relations. Romania's strategic significance was viewed within the southeast European region as a whole. Together with Albania and Yugoslavia, Romania helped preserve the strategic balance of the Balkans and obstructed the Soviet Union's dominance of the peninsula. The restoration of Soviet hegemony would have caused "serious harm" to American interests in Western Europe, the eastern Mediterranean, and the Middle East. At the same time, it was acknowledged that the USSR had legitimate security interests in the Balkans and the Black Sea. The United States therefore recognized the "special relationship" between Moscow and Bulgaria and did not seek strategic advantages in Eastern Europe or the Balkans at the expense of the Soviet Union nor to exploit its relationships with Eastern European communist regimes so as to undermine Soviet security. It was also in the American interest for Albania to be free of Soviet influence, as the restoration of Soviet hegemony there could have altered the balance of power unfavorably for NATO and thereby made the positions of Yugoslavia and Austria more precarious.[74] America's political courtship of Romania was not one-sided, however; Bucharest made it clear that the United States played a prominent role in its foreign affairs. Although the Romanian leadership justified this relationship on principle, they also made no secret of the fact that they expected economic concessions and the elimination of trade discrimination in particular.[75]

In 1969, Nixon paid a visit to Romania. Ceaușescu invited him knowing that Romania was close to the president's heart because of the huge crowds that had greeted him in 1967 when he first went there as the former vice president. Nixon initially disregarded the invitation. What he wanted most was Moscow's support for a settlement in Vietnam, so when Soviet prime minister Alexei Kosygin signaled Moscow's unwillingness to offer it, Nixon decided to "needle" the Kremlin by visiting Bucharest. The State Department opposed the trip on the grounds that it could jeopardize Soviet-American relations, but to no avail. Later, Ambassador Bogdan claimed that Nixon had "twisted the Russians' nose."[76] The president asserted that he had no desire to detach Romania, but rather to demonstrate that national interests could be safeguarded even on Moscow's doorstep. The visit was also meant to convey that the Soviets would pay a price in rockier relations with the United States if they were to turn against their weaker neighbors again. Finally, it indicated to other communist states that they would have the opportunity to develop their economic and cultural relations with Washington. Nixon was greatly pleased by the enthusiasm of the Romanians, who observed his presidential convoy from the sidewalk, and he spoke warmly of the Romanian people to Ceauşescu. The president described the Romanian leader as cunning and intelligent; Kissinger thought him an ambitious power broker who had managed to make his country into an international political crossroads.[77]

As expected, the visit caused an uproar in Moscow; the Soviet leadership postponed an upcoming trip to Bucharest. The Soviets were upset that Nixon was trying to drive a wedge between socialist countries, and they expected their allies to condemn the visit. But the presidential trip meant more than upsetting the Soviets. Nixon left the American ambassador in Bucharest out of his meetings so he could discuss the sensitive issue of Romanian participation in bringing an end to the Vietnam War. The president was there to use Romania as an intermediary between Washington and Beijing. Through them, he sent a message to the Chinese capital that the United States was ready to normalize relations and indicated that there would not be a Soviet-American understanding at China's expense. Romanian vice president Emil Bodnăraş, who had entertained his visitors with a negative appraisal of Brezhnev's intellectual and political abilities, declared that the visit marked an end to spheres-of-interest politics and reinforced his country's national independence.[78] This spectacular visit, though, brought few tangible results. Bucharest expected to receive most-favored-nation status, but Kissinger thought it best to dampen the Romanians' expectations; dramatic change was less likely than slow improvement.[79] This failure to receive the coveted trade concession was met with incomprehension and great frustration in the Romanian capital. They had no idea that Congress had been ready to extend most-favored-nation status to Eastern Europe and that Nixon had killed it as revenge for the Soviets' perceived unwillingness to help in Vietnam. The Romanians took their vengeance by delaying the implementation of a cultural agreement that Nixon signed in Bucharest, which envisioned an American cultural center in the Romanian capital and a Romanian one in New York.[80]

Romania's leader had far-reaching plans involving the United States, including the exploration and exploitation of Black Sea oil, the extraction and processing of Romania's copper deposits – then valued at $1 billion – and participation in other Romanian investments.[81] When Ceauşescu reciprocated and visited Nixon in October 1970, Nixon told him that the prospects for bilateral trade were bright. Ceaușescu indicated that Romania needed foreign loans for its economy to continue growing. He reprimanded Congress for failing to support trade expansion and thanked the president for advocating the removal of political obstacles. Nixon showed his duplicity by confirming that he was working on it.[82] In reality, he had rejected a proposal to expand trade with any Eastern European country, including his favorite, Romania. Behind the scenes he supported Congress in its refusal to abrogate discriminative trade legislation, although he tried to persuade the business community to pursue trade with Romania.

Things started to change in 1971 as the United States was accumulating the largest balance of payments deficits in its history. Nixon rescinded the dollar's convertibility to gold, which led to depreciation. He expected this move to improve the foreign trade balance, and in these circumstances Eastern Europe began to acquire economic significance. Nixon rescinded the Fino amendment that had prohibited trade with countries that supported North Vietnam, as well as the requirement that foreign trade be conducted using American commercial vessels.

More significant change came at the recommendation of administration officials. Nixon dropped his opposition to congressional authorization of most-favored-nation status for Romania on an individual basis. Bucharest indicated that American loans and trade would not cause problems in the Soviet-Romanian relationship, and the Romanian ambassador launched a well-planned diplomatic offensive on behalf of improved trade relations with his country. Secretaries Rogers and Stans offered their full support, but the deliberations proved to be too time consuming. Nixon also wanted a strategic arms reduction deal with the Soviets and was concerned that the broadening of contacts with Romania might sour relations with Moscow and undermine an arms agreement. Thus, despite the potential benefits of trade expansion with Romania, Nixon rejected its MFN status, continuing to subordinate bridge building to relations with the USSR.

There were other problems as well. Extending trade benefits to a communist country while the war was still being waged in Vietnam might have been an unpopular measure. Nixon could count on congressional opposition; even his staff in the White House was against the removal of trade controls.[83] Political considerations, personal rivalries, and the ups and downs of Soviet-American relations all continued to constrain policies toward Eastern Europe.

In the meantime, because of Ceaușescu's visit to Beijing, Romania's relationships with the USSR and its loyal satellites deteriorated. The Warsaw Pact staged war games near Odessa, close to the Romanian border. Nixon's surprise announcement of a visit to Beijing raised alarms in Moscow about a Washington-Beijing-Bucharest triangle. In early August 1971, Eastern European and Soviet leaders met in the Crimean without a Romanian representative. Bucharest announced a war exercise, which it eventually dropped.[84] The State Department warned that matters between Moscow and Bucharest might take a turn for the worse in the forthcoming weeks. They did not think a Soviet invasion likely, though they could not rule it out "categorically."[85] Ceaușescu penned a letter to Nixon, calling attention to the Soviets' press campaign against his country. Ambassador Bogdan saw Kissinger, who assured him the United States would inform Moscow that any attack on Romania would kill détente for decades and that the United States attached significant value to Romanian independence and autonomous policies. The national security advisor added that his country would do nothing to prompt a "great power" to deprive Romania of its independence, and, obviously referring to the troop movements Romania was preparing, warned Bucharest not to threaten its neighbor either. The Romanian ambassador replied that this was part of a policy of deterrence. Nevertheless, Bogdan was satisfied with Kissinger's statement,[86] the strongest ever offered by a U.S. official on behalf of a state in the Soviet sphere.

Czechoslovakia's significance was defined by its "key geographical position" and its reputation as the most Western-oriented state in the region. Even so, American objectives there were limited due to the country's rigid, immobile political system. Washington hoped to retain the strong "historical ties" that attached it to Czechoslovakia, but trade expansion would not be possible until outstanding financial claims had been settled. Czechoslovakia was believed to be open to Western ideas and culture, thus after the Soviet invasion of 1968, America remained cautious and left the leading role in Prague to Western Europe, declining a larger role rather than testing the Soviets' toleration.[87] In early 1969, however, tensions again mounted in Czechoslovakia, and Washington began to fear another Soviet invasion. The Nixon administration may have taken such threats more seriously than its predecessors, but its message displayed the usual ambivalence of American policy toward Eastern Europe and a tacit recognition of the permanence of Soviet domination. Dobrynin was told that it was up to the Soviets what they did with their allies, but if they were to intervene, it would spell the end of the all-European conference on security. Considering that the conference was one of Brezhnev's priorities, this constituted a serious warning. The Soviet response was predictable: this was none of America's business.[88] U.S.-Czechoslovak relations changed for the worse after Soviet intervention put conservatives back in power in Prague. While Nixon saw "a great opportunity" in the development of scientific and technical exchange programs with Eastern Europe, he instructed American functionaries traveling there for this purpose to visit Poland and Hungary and to avoid Czechoslovakia.[89] No agreement was reached about the return of eighteen tons of Czechoslovak gold taken by the Germans in World War II, nor was there any settlement of outstanding financial claims. Although Prague had been eligible for MFN treatment prior to the invasion, it was now at the bottom of the list. Almost a year to the day after the invasion, Nixon refused to receive the departing Czechoslovak ambassador on the grounds that he represented a regime that was quickly reverting to "Neostalinism." Moreover, Czechoslovak authorities had arrested several American citizens, some of whom had been badly beaten.[90]

In the meantime, Hungary was gradually advancing up the Eastern European rankings, soon to replace its northern neighbor in third place. Under Kádár, who had once been called the "butcher of Hungary," the country had come to be known as the "best example" of communist reform, where domestic and economic policies were heading in a direction the United States liked. The price of reform was Hungary's close alignment with the Soviets' foreign and security policies. The United States wanted reforms there to continue, with special emphasis on the "new economic mechanism," which was thought to be introducing Western conditions and principles into the economy. Hungary was seen as a central conduit for economic cooperation between East and West. It was the first communist country to issue government bonds on the international financial market, which thereby moved the Comecon toward multilateralism and international markets. It was a special bonus that the reforms were carried out without the danger of destabilization and without the Soviets raising an eyebrow. The State Department admitted that it had no interest in an acceleration of Hungarian reforms that would drive the Soviets to want to suppress them. U.S. interests lay in meticulously planned and implemented reforms that would produce long-term stability and make it possible for the Soviets to reduce their forces in Hungary. In light of all this, the United States could do little in support of these reforms. It had to exercise restraint in its policies, but since these reforms served American interests, Washington backed Hungary's integration into the international financial system while American radio stations discussed the successes of Hungarian reform. This was an opportunity to increase bilateral trade; by 1970, Hungary's exports to the United States had reached $30 million, roughly equal to the Czechoslovak figure of $34 million but way behind the Polish export total of $95 million. Washington supported transfers of management and marketing skills that might benefit the economic reform, as well as Hungarian participation in the Commission on Security and Cooperation in Europe (CSCE) process and the central European arms reduction talks. In order to increase American interest in Hungary, the Americans also sought to intensify cultural contacts, including the appointment of a Hungarian professor at an American university. Radio Free Europe would be used to mobilize opinion in favor of more reform and to break the Hungarian government's information monopoly.[91]

Stability was the key issue. In itself, Hungary was merely "the nickels and dimes of our international relations and some of the nickels are wooden at that."[92] U.S. interest in Hungary remained modest; there was no urgency to resolve outstanding issues. This wording – that Hungarian reforms served U.S. interests in promoting stability – revealed that the current status quo was not unacceptable to Washington. In spite of this, bilateral relations remained cold, almost hostile. Ambassador Martin Hillenbrand, who had gone to Budapest with high expectations, concluded after a year there that neither side was sufficiently motivated to improve its relations with the other. He did not think Budapest was solely responsible for this state of affairs. Hillenbrand cited U.S. senator Mike Mansfield, who as the chairman of the Senate Foreign Relations Committee had emphasized that the United States was unwilling to show the kind of understanding and generosity toward the difficult fate of the Eastern European countries that would have been worthy of the "greatness of this nation." Hillenbrand, who would soon take charge of the State Department's Bureau of European Affairs, advocated MFN status and the harmonization of the American positive list with the Europeans', and he thought that the Hungarian request to open a commercial office in New York was justified. He thought that U.S. culture was highly popular in Hungary, but the United States did not sponsor any specialized exhibits there, offered no language-training program, and sent no American lecturers to Hungarian universities.[93]

HUNGARIAN DILEMMAS

Even though Hungarian propaganda depicted the United States as the enfant terrible of international politics, the Hungarian government considered its national interests to include an improvement of bilateral relations with America. In May 1969, Rezső Nyers, a former social democrat who belonged to the reform wing of the Communist Party, emphasized that good relations with the United States were more important than ever, particularly to the economy.[94] János Fekete, Kádár's banker and the vice president of the Hungarian National Bank, asserted that "beside the oil producing Arab states we regard the United States as the main source of our loans in the future."[95] The idea behind the Hungarians' economic reform was export-oriented growth. This implied economic modernization financed with external loans, which would be repaid in turn with revenues derived from exports made possible by this upgrade. There was no ideology behind the reform, only the motivation of political considerations like stabilization and shoring up public support for the still oppressive regime.[96] The reformers understood that without a normalization of Hungarian-U.S. relations, the country could not access international money markets. Scientific and technical exchange programs would also be crucial means of acquiring the management skills and technological expertise required by economic modernization. Even so, the decision to mend fences with Washington would not be taken easily. The ultimate dilemma was whether throwing the window open to the capitalist world would strengthen or weaken the regime. Conservatives argued that external influences would undermine the integrity of the political system, while reformers thought that malicious influences could be kept at bay and that the economic gains to be derived from capitalist contacts were their only remaining means of preserving the political system.

Cultural interactions were obstructed because they were seen as a tool of imperialist "subversion," but the study of "some topics" in the United States, such as agrarian and technical sciences, were deemed to be "of extraordinary significance for the people's economy." Thus the government organ responsible for exchanges, the Institute of Cultural Relations, asserted that "it is crucial that certain scientific areas be studied in the United States . . . therefore we are compelled to preserve our scientific-cultural relations even if on a limited basis."[97] The State Department correctly predicted that cultural exchanges could be broadened if scientific and technical exchanges were used as a carrot.[98] This danger did not escape Soviet attention. As early as 1965, Brezhnev had emphasized to Eastern European leaders that "the imperialists intended to broaden relations with the socialist countries so that by exploiting their economic, technical and scientific possibilities they could influence the domestic lives of our countries into the direction of their preference and to loosen our unity. Therefore it is especially important to preclude and struggle against ideological infiltration and subversion."[99] At the same time, access to Western technology was at least as important to the Soviets as it was to their small clients. Prime Minister Kosygin supported détente in the belief that the economic, financial, and technological resources of the West would soon become accessible. Soviet minister of oil Nikolai Baibakov told the Political Committee of the CPSU that if the Soviet-American economic and trade treaty were rejected, the Soviet Union would not be able to exploit its Siberian oil fields for at least thirty years.[100]

Thus it was hoped that gains from a scientific relationship with the United States would outweigh the social risks involved. Ford scholars "acquired considerable knowledge" during their stays overseas, which could then be put to "direct use" in "Hungarian research and production." They were introduced to disciplines that either did not exist or were inadequately funded in Hungary. The Institute of Cultural Affairs admitted that Ford scholars contributed even to the social sciences. In addition, Hungarian researchers participated in international scientific life, introduced the United States to Hungarian scientific achievements, and gained international recognition. The only problem was the Americans' desire to increase the representation of social scientists in the exchanges. The Hungarians suspected that this was in the interest of "subversion." Social scientists, however – who as we have seen were selected for their ideological and political reliability by the state security apparatus – also seemed to be the most sensitive to "the serious contradictions of the American way of life" and could do the most to propagate "the socialist system" by lecturing in the United States. Their obligatory reports about their experiences and their accounts of them in private conversations may not have been entirely the same. The authorities also feared that the specialists who received American training in management would give the United States indirect influence over the management of the Hungarian economy.[101] Despite their ambivalences, Hungarian officials were sure that exchanges with the United States would serve their regime's interests. In order to broaden economic and scientific exchanges, the regime would have to resolve its outstanding bilateral issues. Even though it would have been highly *useful* for Budapest to normalize its relations with Washington, ideological and external shackles continued to impede the Hungarian leadership.

The first Hungarian ambassador – picked by default after the original designate, Radványi, defected – arrived at his post in the aftermath of the invasion of Czechoslovakia. János Nagy, a career diplomat known for his professionalism and language skills,[102] was described in the White House as "intelligent and knowledgeable,"[103] something that had not been the norm in an age of reserving diplomatic posts for reliable party cadres. He was educated at the famed Reformed Church gymnasium of Sárospatak, known for its high academic standards, and as a young cadre of poor peasant stock was selected for crash foreign service training after the communists seized power. Even though Nagy had already served as his country's ambassador to India and Indonesia, his appointment to what was becoming Hungary's second most important diplomatic post after Moscow was highly unexpected, as there were several more senior diplomats in line for the job. Nagy was pleasantly surprised by the presentation of his credentials to President Johnson, whose large frame towered over him, and he still remembers the president's courtesy fondly. His introductory call to the State Department did not go as well. John Leddy was still smarting from a nasty remark Szilágyi had made about American deaths in Vietnam, and he brought it up to the ambassador. Leddy indicated that because of the crackdown in Prague, normalization with Eastern Europe would be slowed down, and he told Nagy that the first issue he expected to resolve was the personnel cap at the embassy in Budapest. When Nagy replied that his government linked the elimination of the cap to the reopening of the consulates and the commercial office in New York, Leddy retorted that the Hungarians liked to ask for unjustified unilateral concessions and were incapable of taking an opportunity to improve bilateral relations. Leddy declared that the Hungarian demands would be met only after a settlement of financial claims,[104] which was the most complicated and thorny issue of the many that plagued Hungarian-American relations.

The financial settlement would not have been a significant burden even though Hungary's trade with the United States was smaller than those of the other socialist states. Without it, however, there was no prospect for most-favored-nation status, which was vital for Kádár's economic experiment. Although there was still no breakthrough, 1969 brought a kind of turn. The Hungarian government reached an agreement with Hilton and Intercontinental for each to build a hotel on either bank of the Danube. On the Pest side the war had destroyed a spectacular row of elegant hotels, leaving empty spaces overlooking the Danube. Now this eyesore would be rebuilt as part of the regime's public relations campaign targeting the West. On the other side, almost opposite, Intercontinental's rival Hilton would reconstruct another equally prestigious and spectacular building in the castle district overlooking a silver strip of the Danube. The two would dominate the Budapest skyline and represent the emerging American influence. Two decades before the Iron Curtain was dismantled, America was building edifices that would rise above anything communists had built in downtown Budapest.

In February 1969, Kádár went to Moscow to hear Brezhnev's briefing on international matters. Brezhnev indicated that a new era of dialogue had started in Soviet-American relations. This he attributed to the Americans' recognition that "The United States was incapable of altering the status quo and must recognize the reality, the Soviet Union's potential and influence."[105] Brezhnev's statement was remarkable for more than one reason. Most importantly, it revealed, more than five years before the Helsinki summit, that the Kremlin understood the strategic shift that had occurred in Washington's approach toward Eastern Europe and its recognition of the Soviet occupation there as an established fact. His statement also made clear that he had no objection to a Hungarian overture to Washington, as long as Kádár was mindful of Soviet interests. The Hungarians, though, did not pounce on the opportunity provided by the apparent green light. They continued to drag their feet for several more years, and clearly not in deference to Soviet objections. Part of the reason was the internal division in the Hungarian leadership over reform and involvement with the West. Of course, there were limits to what Moscow would take, and the veteran Hungarian party leader understood this well. It is not a coincidence that Hungarian propaganda parroted the official Soviet line on Nixon's visit to Bucharest, that Nixon's visit aimed to "harm" Soviet interests, to deepen the rift between Romania and the rest of the socialist world, and to "disturb" the international communist movement.[106]

Moscow continued to send mixed signals. As the introduction of the New Economic Mechanism approached, the Hungarian leadership, in its search for a long-term source of stable credit, authorized exploratory membership talks with the IMF and the World Bank. Moscow, as the historian Richard Gough has argued, was informed, but the Soviet position was in a state of flux. Their indecision over whether Hungary should be allowed to join the international financial organizations may have reflected domestic conflicts. The Soviets had expressed their reservations at the Soviet-Hungarian intergovernmental talks of June 1967, but Deputy Prime Minister Mikhail A. Lesechko was now telling the Hungarians that it was their decision. Then in November 1967, Hungarian prime minister Jenő Fock was told in Moscow that this was not so. Prime Minister Kosygin declared that Lesechko had been mistaken and it would "not be right for a socialist country to join." The membership application was shelved.[107]

The Hungarian Foreign Ministry was ready to move ahead with normalization, albeit in carefully calibrated steps. The first was to resume the talks on financial claims that had been broken off in 1965 by the Vietnam War, in the hope of opening a Hungarian commercial office in New York and achieving most-favored-nation status. Hungary was also ready to sign the consular agreement desired by Washington, but only if the Hungarian consulates in Cleveland and New York were reopened. The Hungarian government agreed to raise the number of diplomatic personnel at the U.S. Embassy and took steps to relax travel restrictions. Budapest rejected Washington's offer to eliminate the stricture on information activities and even refused a cultural agreement[108] even though the Soviet Union had just signed such an agreement with the United States. The Hungarians absurdly demanded that "the hostile Hungarian emigration" in the United States be curbed or eliminated and were told that this was not possible. These proposals were checked with Soviet deputy foreign minister Georgi Kornienko, who agreed with the Hungarians' positions, particularly with the rejection of the cultural agreement.[109]

Precisely when the White House was re-evaluating its strategy toward Eastern Europe, Ambassador Nagy paid an introductory visit to the secretary of state. He indicated that his goal was to settle problems such as the size of the embassy staff, closed consulates, the limitation on information activities, and the commercial offices desired by Budapest. Rogers asked the ambassador whether the Hungarian press had ever published a favorable article about the United States.[110] The communist leadership seemed not to have realized that their public lambasting of the "imperialists" was at cross-purposes with getting economic assistance from them. Budapest made no secret that it was interested solely in the improvement of economic relations. Deputy secretary of foreign affairs Béla Szilágyi told the American chargé, Francis Meehan, that each side's desires were precisely opposed and that therefore no common denominator could be found: "For us it is the economic questions that matter and it is a shame the U.S. does not understand."[111]

Szilágyi was in charge of the Hungarian side of the bilateral talks, Ambassador Puhan the other. Puhan had studied with the radical sociologist Oszkár Jászi at Oberlin College in Ohio, which may explain why he was more sensitive to the predicament and mindset of the Hungarians than were most of his colleagues. He played a key role in the normalization process; it is doubtful whether it would have happened without him. Budapest made certain gestures to facilitate the talks: they allowed an American theatrical company to enter the country for the first time, the prime minister appeared at a Hungarian-American business roundtable, and Hungary imposed a limit on its textile exports to the United States over American concerns about dumping.[112] The negotiations were based on the principle of linkage between politics and economics, which guaranteed their failure. Financial claims were the only issue discussed separately, and Szilágyi was authorized to conclude an agreement. The balance of financial claims favored the Americans and the question for Budapest was how far Hungary's debt obligations could be lowered.[113] On the other hand, Washington made it clear that Hungary would not be treated as a most favored nation until the claims were settled, and perhaps not even then.[114] This was the reverse of what the Hungarians were hoping for: they wanted MFN status to precede the conclusion of the treaty. This small episode reveals that bridge building was not a straightforward strategy. If it had been, external transformation would have come far more quickly. Other issues still to be resolved included the Hungarian trade office in New York, the conclusion of aviation and consular agreements, visiting officials' freedom of movement in both countries, and the transfer of American pensions to Hungary, which entailed altering the politically imposed forint-dollar exchange rate. Ending the ban on information activities – propaganda – was not discussed except for the dissemination of a few hundred copies of the journal *America*.[115]

The talks began on May 26, 1969. Washington offered a commercial office in New York in return for an adjustment of the exchange rate and the renewal of Hungarian lend-lease payments the United States. The Hungarians were anxious to get access to American loans and "cheap dollars," and an agreement was concluded on August 14 with an exchange of letters. The exchange rate was raised substantially, from eleven forints per dollar to thirty, and the United States agreed to the commercial office.[116] The new exchange rate improved the livelihood of thousands of Hungarians who were getting by on donations or pensions from the United States. Further gestures were made: the United States pledged to start transferring pensions it had previously withheld because of the artificially low exchange rate, embassy staffs were increased, Budapest agreed to a guard detail of Marines at the U.S. Embassy. Finally, Hungary unilaterally exempted the U.S. ambassador from travel restrictions.[117] Both sides made important concessions, the Hungarians in modifying their exchange rate, the United States by permitting the trade office. And though these were relatively small matters in an area outside the main focus of American international politics, the White House felt that the State Department had gone too far, demonstrating once again that centralization was an obsession for Nixon and Kissinger.

Kissinger's advisor on Eastern Europe in the NSC, Helmut Sonnenfeldt, asked for information on the State Department's activities on the grounds that the president was interested but uninformed in Eastern European affairs. Not a single instruction sent to Puhan in Budapest had ever reached the White House. Sonnenfeldt fumed that Kádár had not behaved well when Czechoslovakia was invaded and was unhelpful in Vietnam, where, unlike the Romanians, Hungarian foreign minister János Péter had attempted to engage in self-aggrandizement. Péter's judgment was obviously influenced by the defected Hungarian diplomat János Radványi. Puhan, Sonnenfeldt thought, had gone as far as possible. It was time to revise the policy toward Hungary in light of Eastern Europe as a whole. Kissinger reminded the acting secretary of state that the president wished to exercise close control of policies that involved the communist states. Thus the State Department would be obliged to forward all initiatives relating to Hungary, including favors and problems, for the chief executive's review. And the State Department's activity in Hungary was not the only issue that had elicited the presidential staff's ire. Only a few weeks earlier, the White House had concluded that the State Department was attempting to "circumvent" Nixon's refusal to grant MFN status to Eastern Europe.[118] Puhan's modest progress went beyond what the president and his staff wanted to allow, and this episode contradicts other evidence suggesting that Nixon and Kissinger planned to focus on Beijing and Moscow and did not wish to challenge the State Department's bridge-building bureaucracy.[119]

CARDINAL MINDSZENTY

One of the skeletons in the closet of U.S.-Hungarian relations was the continued presence of Cardinal Mindszenty in the U.S. chancery in Budapest. The Political Committee wanted the cardinal relieved of his ecclesiastical functions before they would allow him to leave the country, or at least to have him suspended from his diocese in favor of a newly appointed apostolic governor. The cardinal, however, refused to leave unless he could retain his position as the archbishop of Hungary. He also insisted on the liberation of priests imprisoned in Hungary and the reconstruction of the Regnum Marianum church that had been demolished at the height of Stalinist terror in 1951.[120] That the prelate would also need the Vatican's consent to leave his refuge further complicated the matter. Thus the solution to this seemingly intractable problem – the only Cold War issue tied to a single individual – was beyond the scope of bilateral negotiations. The Americans wanted a quick solution because the old man's presence was causing some tension on the embassy premises. When Hillenbrand arrived, Mindszenty threatened to leave the building and put himself at the mercy of local authorities, with potentially drastic consequences for Hungarian relations with the United States. The cardinal was loath to desert his flock; his views may have coincided with those of the archbishop of Vienna, Cardinal König, who told State Department officials that the position of the church in Hungary was worse than anywhere else in the satellite states. König asserted that one Hungarian bishop was merely a puppet of the authorities while another was wavering between the government and the church. He further asserted that the four newly appointed bishops were under the government's sway and that the State Ecclesiastical Office had completely infiltrated the ecclesiastical hierarchy.[121]

In the meantime, Mindszenty's health was faltering, which confronted embassy officials with the need to ask local authorities for medical treatment. Although Cardinal Mindszenty spoke English with a heavy accent and many mistakes, his sermons at the embassy were solemn and uplifting liturgical experiences. He led a simple life and had few wishes. His modest meals, eaten in the embassy cafeteria with a small glass of beer, caused no problems. Even at the age of eighty, he still demonstrated his belief and occasionally his passion.[122] Hillenbrand's successor, however, was less tolerant of the situation and wanted to put an end to the cardinal's stay. He saw in Mindszenty "a stubborn old man [with whom] nothing could be done," and he believed "he would die at the embassy."[123] Puhan laid out a strategy: first, impress upon the Hungarians that the high priest's departure was in their interest; second, convince Washington to deal with the matter; and finally, persuade the Vatican to pressure Mindszenty to leave the country.[124] In this spirit, he told Hungarian diplomats that the United States would not return Hungary's Holy Crown until Mindszenty was allowed to leave. At the same time, he admitted that the "stubborn

German" would not go to the Vatican unless instructed to do so by the pope, which "cannot be counted on."[125]

Soon the bilateral talks bogged down because of international politics. Guided by attitudes at the Kremlin, Kádár convinced himself that Soviet-American relations were not good enough. Moreover, the United States was expanding its bombing campaigns from Vietnam into Cambodia in hopes of forcing Hanoi to negotiate. Moscow's view of Nixon turned for the worse. Brezhnev characterized him to Kádár as "an even more cunning and dangerous anticommunist than Johnson."[126] Foreign Minister Puja gave a hard-line speech at the UN that led to the cancellation of his meeting with the secretary of state. The Political Committee also refused the offer of a visit from American astronauts, which offended Washington. Puhan told the Hungarians that the president was particularly angry over the exceptionally harsh language of their rejection of the "moon travelers," which affair would "slow down" the improvement of relations. The ambassador was convinced that errors had been made in the translation that gave the Hungarian words the worst possible tone in English. Puhan advised that the offer state that the astronauts would go to other Eastern European capitals, otherwise the Hungarians would not accept it.[127] He hardly suspected that a "slowing down" was precisely what Budapest wanted to achieve, but the party first secretary had just returned from Moscow, where he promised the Soviets that Hungarian negotiations with the Americans would be brought into line with Soviet-American talks. Kádár reported to the Political Committee that this was why "we rejected the visit of the 'moon travelers' to Hungary. We shall pursue our claims and other talks in this spirit."[128]

Nixon had had high hopes for such a visit. In May 1968, large Czechoslovak crowds had turned out to see the commander of Apollo 8, Frank Borman, and the president now thought the time had come "to needle our friends in Moscow. It's time that we cause *them* a little headache."[129] It was in that spirit that he decided to send the astronauts to Budapest. After the Hungarians issued their harshly worded, negative reply, the White House decided it would "cool our relations with Hungary."[130] The ambassador in Budapest was instructed to negotiate only issues that served American interests.[131] Thus U.S.-Hungarian relations were being discussed on the highest levels in Moscow, Budapest, and Washington. The Hungarian

Foreign Ministry tried to ameliorate the situation by claiming that the original note had been much softer than its English translation and expressed hope that the "time will come when such a visit can take place."[132] Puhan was told that the fallout would favor the hard-liners. The ambassador informed his superiors that the Hungarians were trying to please their "Soviet masters."[133] Eventually Nixon authorized the resumption of talks, but silently and on the basis of strict reciprocity.[134] Puhan wanted to see the president about it, but his request was turned down so as not to give the president's imprimatur to further talks with Budapest.[135]

Even though it was in Hungary's economic interest to conclude the negotiations successfully, accommodation of the Soviet line continued to prevail. It was not until February 1970 that the matter was declared closed and Washington exempted the Hungarian ambassador from travel restrictions. Even though relations had cooled, Puhan decided to broach the Hungarians' most important issue, the return of the Holy Crown, the symbol of Hungarian statehood that had been in American protective custody since 1945. This was a crucial matter for both sides. For Kádár, the return of the Crown of Saint Stephen would be both the culmination of his efforts to gain international and domestic legitimacy for his regime and the consolidation of his personal legacy as a respectable statesman. For the United States, returning the crown would raise serious domestic political questions, chiefly about Eastern Europe's place in the bipolar struggle with the Soviet Union. Sending this religious symbol of historic continuity back to Hungary's communist leaders could be interpreted as an open gesture of acceptance of the permanence of Soviet control.

Both sides had pretended for two decades that this issue did not exist, but with the growing self-confidence of the government in Budapest and the slow but steady normalization of bilateral relations, it was bound to come up. The first impetus was given during a conversation Hillenbrand had with Szilágyi, which was "one of the most useful and promising" since his arrival in the Hungarian capital. Szilágyi called Nixon's speech on foreign policy realistic and made no mention of Vietnam or the Middle East. He did mention the matter of the crown jewels as a precondition of normalization.[136] Even though Rogers indicated that the time had not yet come, the Hungarians raised the issue with Emory Swank, a high-level official at the State Department who visited Budapest in May 1970. Swank told his hosts that the crown would be returned only if relations continued to improve, that is, there were no specific conditions that the Hungarians could meet. For the first time in a quarter-century, however, a first step was taken toward the return of the crown. In June, Rogers held an unofficial meeting with Iván Boldizsár, the editor-in-chief of the Hungarian English-language journal *New Hungarian Quarterly*. Rogers brought up the question of the crown and for the first time ever disclosed that it was being held in Fort Knox. Even though the conversation was supposed to be kept fully confidential – as was almost everything that had to do with sensitive Hungarian issues – it did not remain secret for long. Somehow Mindszenty got wind of the discussion and dispatched an angry missive to the president citing the president's promise that the ancient artifact would not be returned to what Mindszenty called these "followers of Satan." It was a false alarm; for the time being, domestic politics and the poor state of U.S.-Hungarian relations ruled out the return of the Holy Crown.

Budapest was still unwilling to take decisive steps even though they were ready to settle financial claims against them. The Politburo cited external reasons and grave internal concerns, which reflected the strength of the anti-Western group within the leadership. Conservatives deplored "growing American aggressiveness" resulting in the deterioration of international relations and the fact that the Americans were not ready to settle matters of "larger significance." In addition, American propaganda "undermined public spirits," particularly "in the midst of the youth, the intelligentsia, and the petit bourgeoisie," in which "circles [U.S. efforts] incited nationalism, anti-Soviet sentiment, suspicion against the party's politics, and denigrated conditions in the country."[137] Therefore bilateral talks would be slowed down. Relations with the United States were only a small segment of the conservative resurgence, which was directed against an alleged creeping return of capitalism and cultural Westernization.

Puhan was mistaken in attributing the Hungarians' backpedaling to Soviet influence only. He thought that "there was a great desire" among Hungarians to improve relations with the West, to attract American investments and cultural expositions, and to do their best to bring U.S. businessmen to Hungary. This was undoubtedly true of the people Puhan was likely to encounter, but not of those in the state security establishment or in leading positions in the party, whom he would not see and who were inimical to these aims. The ambassador painted a rosy picture of the Hungarian leader and his entourage, suggesting that Kádár was assisted by "unusually competent" men including Biszku, Németh, Komócsin, Fehér, Fekete, and Nyers, all of whom were doing their utmost to improve the quality of life. They could hardly have painted a more flattering picture themselves. The list reveals a certain ignorance of the political spectrum, as Biszku was a staunch conservative and one of the driving forces behind the bloody postrevolutionary reprisals and had signed off on hundreds of death sentences. Németh was also a conservative, while Komócsin was the leader of the new left-wing party opposition. In an effort to justify a more liberal approach to Hungary, Puhan argued that life had gotten better for the average Hungarian, who had "a lot of" money to spend. Restaurants served fairly good food, women were relatively well dressed, and buildings were being reconstructed at an accelerated pace so that the "dirtiness" of the city was disappearing. It seemed that "people in Budapest and Debrecen" were happier than elsewhere in Eastern Europe. The ambassador had not heard complaints about the secret police, although the presence of many plainclothes policemen was "obvious" to him. The political system had become more liberal, though the church's sway over people had weakened. He perceived significant Western influence, including an American cultural presence. Nationalism had been curbed, "with good reason," although in their attitudes toward the Peace Treaty of Trianon, the ambassador could not see any difference between "communist functionaries and Mindszenty." Antisemitism, though traditionally strong, was not noticeable to him.[138] On the other hand, he did not think that the youth supported the political system and called the regime's pretense that it did so a self-delusion. Rather, he thought that the youth had sunk into political lethargy, which meant that the regime did not have to face the kind of rebelliousness that Western governments did.[139] This analysis did not coincide with the view of the Hungarian police, which was then waging a well-publicized war against "West loving" youth gangs.

Since Budapest was eager to make progress on economic issues, the secretary of state's invitation to his Hungarian colleague to meet at the UN General Assembly in New York was greeted as an opportunity to move bilateral relations out of the deadlock.[140] The following episode, however, demonstrates that the foreign minister's ideological zealotry overrode rational considerations of economic and political self-interest. Ambassador Puhan, who stood behind the invitation, warned Foreign Minister Péter not to make his speech too combative, otherwise his meeting with Rogers would be jeopardized.[141] Péter had been involved with the Soviet-sanctioned Hungarian efforts to mediate the Vietnam War in 1965 and 1966 and had met Rogers' predecessor Dean Rusk on several occasions, thus he was no novice in international politics. Nevertheless, he used the forum of the General Assembly to deliver a vicious verbal attack on American foreign policy. He charged the United States with violating the nuclear nonproliferation treaty, a claim not even the Soviets had made. The speech was wholly unexpected and stunned even Hungarian diplomats. János Nagy remembered Péter's allegation that the Americans were ready to sell the atomic secret to the Japanese, a particularly grave insult. It turned out that the foreign minister had gotten his information from the French satirical journal *Canard Enchainé*, and although he promised to substantiate his allegations, he was never able to offer any proof.[142]

The meeting with Rogers went badly and the speech again halted progress in the normalization process. Péter's action is hard to explain, though it is conceivable that the emergence of a leftist opposition within the party played a role in the new setback.[143] The leader of this opposition, Zoltán Komócsin, congratulated Péter after the speech. Later, in a conversation with Puhan, the foreign minister hinted that the Soviets may have had something to do with the speech. He claimed that "with our critique" of the Americans, "we wanted to improve our relationship to the Soviets by exposing the mistakes."[144] He did not specify what these were, but he may have been referring to the economic reforms and clandestine efforts to engage the IMF. There is no doubt that Hungary was paying Moscow for its economic and other domestic reforms with blind loyalty in foreign policy. Yet Péter did not try to find a middle ground between criticism and unnecessary provocation of the Americans, even though the latter's economic assistance was important to the success of the reforms.

This tradeoff between domestic reforms and pro-Soviet foreign policy was clear to the ambassador, yet his optimism regarding bilateral improvements remained unbroken. There was no sign that the Hungarians wanted to go down the Romanian road; they deemed impossible even the most innocuous goals, such as the opening of an American cultural and information center in Budapest. In light of the experiences of 1956 and 1968, Puhan understood that Budapest would not pick a quarrel with the Kremlin; unlike Bucharest, Budapest lacked the economic base for such independent initiatives.[145] In his continuing optimism about the future of bilateral relations, he advocated the conclusion of a consular agreement, the lifting of the ban on information activities, and the further participation of the United States at the Budapest Trade Fair. In the longer run, he thought Hungary would become eligible for most-favored-nation status and he was the first American diplomat to advocate returning the Crown of Saint Stephen. He thought that Hungarian reforms benefited the United States because they might inspire Poland and Czechoslovakia to follow suit, which could affect the entire Soviet sphere.[146]

For the New Economic Mechanism to succeed, Budapest had to integrate itself into the international financial system and thereby undo one of the chief consequences of Sovietization. Membership in the World Bank and IMF was discussed in 1967 but shelved as a result of the intervention in Czechoslovakia. In 1971, the leadership asked for an IMF delegation to be sent to Budapest, but without specifying its purpose. Although Hungary did not formally seek membership in the organization, Washington contemplated its position in case such a request was made. A memorandum prepared by the president's economic advisor reveals American thinking on the future course of Eastern Europe. Hungary and Yugoslavia had gone furthest in transforming their economies and were interested in expanding their relations with the Western world. Membership in the IMF would be important for the Soviets' allies because it would force them to disclose data, which would have a "dramatic impact" on their economies and societies, thus their membership was in the interest of the United States. The State Department and the Department of the Treasury argued that the newly admitted countries should undertake all obligations entailed by membership, but Kissinger's assistant for international economic affairs, Fred Bergsten, thought this would lead to unacceptable political countermeasures by the Soviets.[147] Eventually the Hungarians backed down again and the United States did not have to formulate a position, but it was apparent that more Eastern European economic autonomy from the Soviets could create problems of its own.

In Budapest, assistant secretary of state Richard T. Davies wanted to concentrate on smaller issues, while a high-level functionary at the Foreign Ministry told him that the large issues would have to be resolved first. The Hungarians brought up most-favored-nation status, as usual, but Puhan bluntly told them it was out of the question as long as they were sending arms to Vietnam.[148] Davies departed with the impression that the Hungarian position on bilateral issues had changed and now required political progress to solve even minor issues.[149] Ambassador János Nagy assured Davies that Kádár's position was more flexible than that of the deputy foreign minister, who wanted to stress the importance of economic issues for Hungary.[150] Nevertheless, Kádár canceled Puhan's scheduled visit[151] and grounded relations yet again. The Foreign Ministry blamed Nixon's "aggressive policies."[152]

Shortly after the Political Committee canceled Puhan's meeting with Kádár, Péter suggested that Budapest was interested in moving ahead despite all claims to the contrary. Two records of the conversation survive. In the Hungarian version, the foreign minister declared that he wanted to "open a new page" in the history of Hungarian-American relations. Contradicting the Soviet position on the issue, Péter added that he wished to "have consultations" with American representatives about the European security conference because the "United States was also interested in it." The American version recorded a far more pronounced Hungarian position on the CSCE process. The Hungarian foreign minister confided that he and his Eastern European colleagues had made "a big mistake" in trying to exclude Canada and the United States from the CSCE. It was in the Hungarians' interest to bring about an all-European security system that would allow the withdrawal of foreign troops from East and West alike. He added that this was also in America's interest because it would alleviate the associated budget deficits.[153] The English record is revealing on several counts. First, it suggests that Hungarian reports, which inevitably landed in the Soviet Foreign Ministry, contained only watered-down versions of what Hungarian diplomats and functionaries were telling Westerners. Second, contrary to many indications including public pronouncements, there was a marked gap developing between Soviet and Hungarian interests. Clearly Péter was expressing hope that a Soviet troop withdrawal from Hungary would be made possible by a new European security framework. The Soviet-Hungarian standoff on this issue became even more apparent as Budapest attempted to insert itself into a planned central European demilitarized zone. Finally, his statements as recorded in the American minutes of the talks reveal the great dichotomy between Hungarian propaganda and its foreign policy objectives, a damaging contradiction that Hungarian leaders failed to appreciate.

Péter also unexpectedly brought up the Mindszenty question and declared that he did not regard its solution as a stumbling block for improving relations with the United States. The Hungarian conditions for his liberation were that he should not spoil church-state relations and that he should not be exploited for "Cold War" purposes. Péter disclosed to the ambassador that in his recent meeting with the pope, he was told that Mindszenty was more ready to leave the country than before. Péter asked for the ambassador's mediation in Washington and at the Vatican in arranging for Mindszenty's departure, as the aged cardinal was causing problems "for Hungary, the United States and the Vatican."[154]

Finally, when Mindszenty's long saga was coming to an end, international politics interfered again. Following Kissinger's secret trip to Beijing in June, Washington dramatically announced the president's impending visit to China. This marked the beginning of Washington's triangular diplomacy, a parallel and coordinated approach to Moscow and Beijing.[155] Given the recent Sino-Soviet border clashes, the Soviet leadership took this as a slap in the face. Officially, Budapest deplored the move, but behind closed doors normalization talks were being conducted in the interest of the economic reform. Again talks were jeopardized by a simultaneous renewal of anti-American propaganda. Only a few days after the tentative steps were taken to settle the Mindszenty question, Puhan warned the foreign minister of the harm that could be caused by articles in the party daily, *Népszabadság*, and other media, which painted Nixon's visit to China as an anti-Soviet move. Puhan claimed that the Hungarian interpretations outdid even the commentaries in the Soviet press. The ambassador noted that such statements made it hard to take seriously the claim that Hungary wanted to improve its relations with the United States; the high-level contacts desired by Budapest would not be possible in these conditions. After this clarification, the foreign minister announced, as if nothing had happened, that deputy prime minister Péter Vályi – an important proponent of economic reform – would like to visit Washington. The ambassador recommended the invitation to promote Hungary's slight autonomy in the Soviet bloc.[156] Shortly thereafter, it was announced that the Hungarian minister of foreign trade wished to invite his American counterpart Maurice Stans, the Nixon administration's staunchest supporter of trade expansion.

In the meantime, Puhan continued to work behind the scenes to resolve the Mindszenty issue. Operating from the bottom of the hierarchy, Puhan played an instrumental role in getting Mindszenty released and thereby removing one of the largest roadblocks to Hungary's policy of openness to the United States. If bridge building met with any success in Hungary, the efforts of the ambassador played a large role in it. He urged his superiors at the State Department to change their assumption that the Mindszenty affair was between the Vatican and the Hungarians and pushed Washington to play an active role in the solution. The Vatican was traditionally divided between those who would accept the status quo and work with the communist regimes and those who rejected any contact, and this dichotomy was apparent in the papal state's approach to Mindszenty. Giovanni Cheli, the Vatican diplomat responsible for Eastern European affairs, felt that Mindszenty was harmful to the position of the Catholic Church in Hungary and proposed that a high-ranking Hungarian ecclesiastical leader convince the cardinal of the need to depart. The cardinal was to be told that he was no longer regarded as an embodiment of anticommunism and that his cherished memoirs would not be published if he were to die on the embassy premises. Puhan informed the archbishop of Vienna, Cardinal König, that if this mission to convince Mindszenty were to fail, there would not be another opportunity. Cheli declared that Mindszenty's departure was vital for the well-being of the church in Hungary,[157] and in his letter to Mindszenty, presented by Cheli and Monsignor József Zágon, Pope Paul VI expressed his desire for the cardinal's departure. At the same time, Paul VI also instructed his delegates not to exert any pressure on the cardinal, who suspected that the Vatican and Washington were conspiring at his expense. Mindszenty sought guidance from President Nixon[158] and seemed to backtrack several times before he finally made up his mind in mid-September.[159] His decision seems to have been influenced by Nixon's cautiously worded advice that the interest of the church should guide his actions, a diplomatic way of suggesting he leave. In addition, Mindszenty was assured that his manuscript would be taken out of the country and given to his confidante in Vienna. After fifteen years of confinement, the cardinal at the Chancery finally stepped off the U.S. embassy premises on September 28, 1971, a fortnight after the agreement was concluded between Budapest and the Vatican. One of the largest roadblocks to normalization was removed, raising the Hungarians' hopes that the Crown of Saint Stephen would be returned in exchange.[160] Foreign Minister Péter praised the U.S. ambassador when he met Rogers later that fall; Puhan's "tactful and helpful" cooperation had contributed to the success, and it was not the first time he had promoted the improvement of U.S.-Hungarian relations.[161]

8

Nixon, Carter, and the Kádár Regime

At last, the international constellation favored normalization. On August 5, 1971, Brezhnev received a personal letter from Nixon in which the president asked Brezhnev to cooperate in answering the "large questions." Brezhnev proposed a summit,[1] and this was the point at which American policy toward Eastern Europe turned decisively toward accepting the permanence of Soviet control. Nixon traveled to Warsaw, where he declared his understanding of the predicament of Poland's geopolitical environment. He also told the new Hungarian ambassador that he attributed Hungary's "relationship to its neighbors" to the country's "historical and geographical" attributes.[2] Károly Szabó was thrilled by Nixon's "friendly, cordial" attitude.

Foreign minister Péter held a discussion with William Rogers and agreed that the international climate was conducive for the secretary of state's visit to Budapest. This would take place during the Nixon visit to Beijing and Moscow.[3] At his "own initiative," Puhan broached the possibility of a visit by the president by claiming that Hungary was the only socialist country outside Romania and Yugoslavia – which Nixon had already visited – where a presidential trip would be a political possibility.[4] The Political Committee welcomed the idea and instructed the Foreign Ministry to "consult" the "necessary people." The Foreign Ministry's position on the visit reveals the thinking behind several arguments for the new Hungarian policy. First, outstanding issues could be discussed at the highest levels. Second, there would be a chance to expound the Hungarians' pro-Soviet positions on international relations and thereby to "offset" the Romanians' and Yugoslavs' views. Finally, it would also strike a blow at the "right wing" émigré groups in the United States. Ministry personnel also imagined potentially negative consequences. "Illusions" might arise in the public's understanding of relations between Hungary and the United States; the president might use his visit to promote "subversion" and his own political goals.[5] Thus the Hungarians' motivation to receive Nixon was exactly the opposite of the Romanians'. Whereas Bucharest was driven by the desire to demonstrate its autonomy from Moscow, Budapest hoped to portray itself as the Soviets' most loyal ally, an identity that was theoretically consistent with high-level contact with the Americans for the purposes of economic gain. This episode turned out to be much ado about nothing; Nixon had no intention of returning to Budapest. Presidential visits were meant to show that America differentiated among the countries of the Soviet bloc and that the friendliest countries could profit from their positions.[6]

Ambassador Szabó reported that the National Security Council had proposed a quiet repatriation of Hungary's Crown of Saint Stephen by Christmas of 1971 or Easter of 1972.[7] This contradicted a resolution passed by the Senate according to which the return would not even be negotiated until democracy and freedom had been restored to the Hungarian people.[8] As domestic politics made this a touchy issue, the White House asserted that the restoration of the Holy Crown was not under consideration. Still, the rumors about it seem not have been unfounded. In the midst of the presidential campaign, an ambiguously worded article suggested that the return of the Holy Crown was not being planned "at present." The White House, however, was forced to "kill the duck": one White House staffer noted in despair, "Please please tell me this is not so. Are we trying to blow the entire East European vote or just turn off the Catholics?"[9] Concerned about anticommunist voters of Eastern European descent, the White House worried that returning the Holy Crown to the Hungarian regime would be seen as an American blessing of the state of affairs in Europe.

Soviet-American consultations then treated strategic arms limitations and conventional force reductions in central Europe simultaneously. Budapest cautiously signaled its readiness to participate in the talks with the proviso that Hungary be noted as a "faithful member of the Warsaw Pact and the Comecon."¹⁰ The State Department accepted the Hungarians' request for separate "consultations" on European force reductions,¹¹ which they hoped might lead to a partial or even full withdrawal of Soviet forces.

Washington did in fact suggest that it was ready to accept the division of Europe. Brezhnev indicated that he understood that the Americans had accepted European realities. The American position was similar to Bonn's: the West Germans wanted to make it clear that any improvement of their relations with Eastern Europe was not intended to provoke Moscow. Deputy assistant secretary of state Richard T. Davies told the Hungarian ambassador that that the United States wanted to improve bilateral relations within the framework of "realities" and "not at the expense of Soviet-Hungarian relations."¹² State Department officials declared that the United States was aware that Hungarian foreign policy had to take Soviet interests into account, although they made it clear that they would ignore the Soviet factor, particularly its ideological aspect; at the same time, they did not wish to "harm" Budapest's relations with Moscow.¹³ Secretary of State Rogers visited both Prague and Budapest, and in both capitals he made it clear that improved relations should not threaten Soviet interests. In fact, the pace of change would be decided in Eastern Europe. Deputy secretary of state Alexis U. Johnson explained that his country did not want to "cause problems in the relationship between Hungary and its friends," which would become a permanent formula for American policy aims through 1989. At the same time, Johnson alluded to the "pleasant" relationship between Yugoslavia and the Soviet Union, to which the Hungarian ambassador took exception, declaring that this example was "unrealistic," as Hungary was a member of the Warsaw Pact and its "voluntary" obligations were the "founding principle" of its foreign policy.¹⁴ Budapest, however, was becoming more tolerant of the United States as American goals in Eastern Europe changed. The officer at the American desk in the Hungarian Foreign Ministry assured Puhan that "the Americans generally appraised the situation soberly and did not nurture vain hopes that the improvement of our relations could be achieved by loosening our ties to our friends."¹⁵

Years later, the Foreign Ministry cited Nixon's February 1970 statement that the United States had no desire to undermine the Soviet Union's legitimate security interests yet regarded the Eastern European countries as sovereign entities, not simply parts of a Soviet bloc. The president emphasized that he would not accept any doctrine that would limit the Hungarians' right to seek better relations with the United States or other states.[16] While Washington still wished to use psychological warfare to cause tensions between Moscow and its satellites, rollback was no longer a goal. When a group of Hungarian émigrés asked Puhan about Hungary's prospects for liberation, the ambassador replied unequivocally that the only hope was for change from within the USSR itself. The State Department established three basic principles for the Soviet bloc: each state would be treated as a sovereign entity; the United States would establish permanent economic relations with them; and, finally, they would be integrated into the political affairs of "Europe as a whole."[17] In a memorandum to the president, William Rogers insisted that the people of Eastern Europe had to be assured that the United States would never accept the existing situation and would never bargain exclusively with the Soviet Union on issues that related to the nations of Eastern Europe.[18] He supported the restoration of national independence, but in gradual steps, lest drastic moves trigger Soviet security fears. If Soviet anxieties were to lead to another destabilization like that of 1968, regional instabilities might lead to a confrontation with the Soviet Union or underscore American inability to act. Thus, the pitfall of any decisive advocacy of national independence could be detrimental to U.S. interests in Eastern Europe.[19]

THE ROGERS VISIT

1972 was a decisive year in the history of détente and the status quo in Europe. Nixon visited China, opening a new era in Sino-American relations, and also signed a historic strategic arms limitation agreement in Moscow. Only one of his chief foreign policy objectives remained – a conclusion to the war in Vietnam. In fact, the war in Indochina had started to escalate again and almost foiled the president's long-awaited trip to Moscow. Nixon suspected that Soviet hands were directing the new North Vietnamese offensive, and despite Kissinger's advice and Soviet ambassador Dobrynin's assurance that Moscow had advised Hanoi to continue the peace talks, he toyed with the idea of calling off the summit.[20] The renewed American bombing campaign made the Soviet leadership doubt the wisdom of receiving Nixon. The highly publicized visits to Beijing and Moscow gave rise to the idea that U.S. leaders should visit Eastern Europeans as well, lest they get the impression that Washington was selling them out to Moscow. Nixon reassured Romanian foreign minister Corneliu Mănescu that his trip to Moscow would not jeopardize the interests of other countries.[21] There was no question that the president would travel to Poland, a country of the highest symbolic value. Despite Sonnenfeldt's agreement with the ambassador to Warsaw that Nixon should not see the head of the Polish Catholic Church, the president took Kissinger's advice and met with Cardinal Wyszinski, a provocative step in light of the tension between the Polish ecclesiastical leadership and the Communist Party.[22]

Nixon's remarks in Warsaw were cautious. Party first secretary Edward Gierek started their meeting by reminding of him of Poland's obligations to the Warsaw Pact. The president reiterated that "he appreciated, as a realistic man, the position of Poland in a sensitive part of Europe.... Polish leaders had alliances which they expected to keep... [but] can become our friends without being anybody else's enemy. Poland had strong neighbors on both sides, it is essential that it maintained good relations with them. We seek cooperation with Poland without any effort to embarrass its leaders... We will make no arrangements at the expense of small countries; we heed the interests of small nations."[23] Nixon and Kissinger's foreign policy realism sanctioned a recognition of the two blocs in Europe, a message William Rogers conveyed to Budapest.

Washington had started to sound out the Hungarians about Nixon's visit in May. Puhan urged the visit, proposing several concessions including the return of the Crown of Saint Stephen, most-favored-nation (MFN) status for Hungary, and the opening of consulates. He made it clear that without help from Washington he would not be able to break the deadlock.[24] Puhan did his best to reassure the Hungarians that the United States had no desire to cause difficulties for Hungary or to do anything that might result in "Soviet pressure" on the country, adding that it was up to the Hungarians to decide the pace and timing of the normalization process.[25] The Hungarians, however, rejected this overture. The foreign minister's explanation contained a veiled critique of Soviet policy: "because of the bombing in Vietnam, it would be hard to explain to the Hungarian public why Kádár receives Rogers and Brezhnev Nixon."[26] In

May of 1972, deputy foreign minister Frigyes Puja traveled to Moscow for "consultation" and was told that Budapest had done the right thing in rejecting the idea of Rogers' visit. A few weeks later, though, Soviet deputy foreign minister N. N. Rodionov was informed that the American initiative for the secretary of state's visit had been accepted. To mollify the Soviets the Hungarians added that Kádár would not receive Rogers, that they would "criticize" Nixon's "power politics," and they would sound out the American position on the European Conference on Security and Cooperation. Rodionov's response demonstrates the extent to which the situation in Eastern Europe had changed: he stated that the presidential visit had initiated a new era, one in which the Americans would be "realists" who understood that they "could not exploit the Rogers visit to weaken the cohesion of the socialist bloc." The Soviets added that though the secretary of state was a "moderate politician" and close to Nixon, Rogers played second fiddle to Kissinger and "the more important decisions in foreign policy were not made on his level."[27]

The Americans' change of heart regarding the status of Eastern Europe was now apparent behind the Iron Curtain. It was clear that Soviet approval for the Rogers visit had been sought only *after* it had been cleared in Budapest, although it is also apparent that Kádár tried to anticipate the Soviet position. Receiving Rogers in Budapest must have been made harder by the fact that the secretary made stops in Belgrade and Budapest. This was reflected in an attempt to play down the visit by envisioning relatively low-level meetings, even though no U.S. secretary of state had ever been to Hungary before. As the day of arrival approached, the circle of functionaries scheduled to see him was expanded, but it still did not include the party secretary.

The State Department's guidelines for Rogers emphasized that his visit was not intended as agitation against any third country and recommended that the secretary assure his hosts that the United States had no intention of luring away Hungary from its allies. In his arrival speech Rogers emphasized the "Hungarian spirit" that had enabled it to preserve its "national identity for centuries" and stressed that all peoples of the world strive "for the right of national independence."[28] How national independence could be squared with continued membership in the Warsaw Pact and the Comecon was left open. In his talks in Budapest the secretary supported Hungarian participation in the conventional force reduction talks, as Hungary was both geographically and historically a part of central Europe. He also sought to remove Vietnam as an obstacle to progress in bilateral relations.

Kádár waited until the last moment to see him, having initially pled shortness of time. Puhan presented a letter from Nixon in which the president asked the party first secretary to see Rogers. The secretary of state authorized the ambassador to make any argument to convince Kádár to meet with him. Foreign Minister Péter cited an unfriendly State Department pronouncement on Hungarian-American relations, the fact that the Holy Crown's return had been linked to a formula as vague as "the solution of certain questions," and the bombing of Vietnam. Puhan countered by saying that Rogers was aware of the speech in which Péter had called Vietnam the "vilest war in history." Puhan's statement reflected the secretary's determination to move beyond rhetoric and fix the two countries' relationship, but the following events provide some insight into the centralized decision-making process of the communist state.

On July 6, Péter prepared a memorandum for Kádár and Central Committee secretary Zoltán Komócsin outlining the contents of Nixon's letter.[29] Theoretically, a formal Politburo resolution would be required for the party leader to open official negotiations with the secretary of state. Kádár made the decision himself and had the members of the Political Committee telephoned for their sanction after he had made up his mind.[30] A rare handwritten note reveals his mindset: "it looks like I can't avoid this," he scribbled. During what ought to have been a major political triumph, he vacillated till the last moment.

Even though Rogers' trip to Budapest had been sanctioned in Moscow, Kádár may have been apprehensive about the Soviets. In February, Brezhnev had instructed him to "review" Hungary's economic reforms, which prompted Kádár to halt them.[31] Brezhnev's harsh critique of the conditions in Hungary – one Soviet official suggested that even the mention of it was dangerous – could have led Kádár to tread cautiously in foreign affairs. Moscow toyed with the idea of canceling President Nixon's visit over the escalation of the war in the Far East, and even though the Soviets did not officially inform their allies, news of this Soviet dilemma may still have made it to Budapest. Yet as the strategic arms limitation treaty (SALT I) was signed in May – an event the Soviet propaganda machine hailed as historic – there was in Hungary hardly any danger of even a verbal Soviet reprisal. Kádár's reluctance to see Rogers may also have indicated personal doubts. The Hungarian leadership informed Hanoi's ambassador of the talks and offered assurances that they did not signify a "sellout." The North Vietnamese leadership was sensitive to this possibility in light of Nixon's trips to Beijing and Moscow, and Kádár's temporizing may have been meant to temper Moscow's double-dealing.

Both parties were conciliatory. Rogers recounted that he had grown up as a poor boy in a small town where half the inhabitants were of Hungarian descent. He made it clear that bilateral relations would be developed at a pace that was convenient for Hungary and that the United States would not interfere in other countries' domestic affairs. Kádár emphasized that despite the "enormous differences" between the two countries, he thought it would be possible to establish "normal" relations without "chasing fantasies and dreams." Hungary was "motivated by its position" and "would be mindful of American and other interests." Kádár was driven by "people's desire to live in peace and happiness."[32] Rogers wanted to sign a cultural agreement, but Budapest rejected the idea. Rogers made no promises regarding the Holy Crown and did not invite his Hungarian colleague to reciprocate his visit; in the light of the astronaut affair, the State Department wasn't even sure the secretary would be received in Budapest. The Hungarians again misunderstood and interpreted this slight as a sign that they were "not important enough for America."[33] Immediately after his departure from Budapest, Rogers sent a message to the president claiming that his visit had "opened a new chapter" in U.S.-Hungarian relations. The secretary noted that American flags were displayed in visible places; pro-American sentiments could be discerned from the fact that the proprietor of a small shop had displayed an autograph received from Nixon in 1963 in his shop window.[34]

THE TRAP OF THE ECONOMY

The great economic collapse that would bury the communist system started with an escalation of indebtedness in the early 1970s. When the decade was over, Hungary would still be a committed member of the Soviets' political and military alliances, as well as their trading bloc, but financially it would already be dependent on the Western world and the United States for its survival. In the early 1980s, when the country was almost bankrupt, the Manufacturers Hanover Trust held Hungary's "most critical and most difficult loan."[35] Hungary had launched an externally financed modernization campaign in hopes of consolidating its political system, but ended up bankrupt, economically and politically. Its normalization of relations with the United States allowed it to gain almost unlimited access to the international financial markets that would ultimately doom its regime. The train of events that had begun with Mindszenty's release culminated in a final push toward normalization during Rogers' visit in the summer of 1972. This in turn opened the door for the conclusion of a claims agreement that would make Hungary eligible for MFN status, for which the Soviets and their allies had been scrambling competitively since the late 1960s. Thus the economy became the driving force behind Hungary's overtures to put relations with the United States on a normal footing and to prepare for further liberalization. International events would no longer hinder the normalization process.

As a result of the Rogers visit, Hungary and the United States signed an aviation agreement that gave American commercial aircraft landing rights for the first time since the Second World War. On October 12 the claims agreement was initialed, a breakthrough no doubt facilitated by the fact that the Soviets had just agreed to make lend-lease payments. A Hungarian memorandum on the talks enthusiastically reported that "the American delegation was cooperative in every respect and showed a fair and constructive attitude all along."[36] This was a far cry from the times when reports on conversations with Americans recounted how the Hungarians had lectured them on the evils of imperialism. Further progress was made when Budapest ratified a consular agreement that made it safer for U.S. citizens to travel to Hungary.

Even so, the two countries had little contact. Hungary's exports to the United States did not even reach 1 percent of their total foreign sales. Classified appraisals of the United States were no longer influenced by ideological prejudices, thus the Academy's Council on the World Economy stated that the United States was the "most important source of new technologies in the world economy" and urged the expansion of industrial imports and technological cooperation. This strategy, however, was impeded by the

Americans' restrictions on the sale of modern technology to the Soviet world. Still, in the economic sphere, the Cold War between the United States and Hungary was coming to an end. The Soviet Union's economic and technological backwardness was forcing its ally to turn to the United States, and several Hungarian socialist companies were able to conclude agreements with American corporations. Most significant was an agreement on the production of maize, one of Hungary's most important export commodities. Coca-Cola, Pepsi, and Hilton also made inroads,[37] and these burgeoning economic contacts were not limited to agriculture and consumer goods. The most advanced Hungarian industrial companies reached out to American partners: Magyar Vagon és Gépgyár signed an agreement with Steiger to build construction machines from Hungarian parts for sale on the Hungarian market because "the Soviets were unable to satisfy the Hungarian demands." The showcase of Hungarian industry, Rába, signed a deal to purchase a U.S. license to manufacture tractors and another one with Steiger allowing them to ship $100 million worth of rear axles by 1980, which would be four times the total value of all Hungarian industrial items sold to the United States up to that point. Egyesült Izzó concluded an agreement with its former parent company, General Electric, to furnish GE with integrated circuits;[38] by the early 1970s, Hungary was one of the largest markets in the world for American breeding cattle.[39] Americans began to trickle slowly into Hungary – fifty-three thousand of them in 1972 – a third of whom came to visit family. There was still no cultural agreement, but IREX and an accord with the Hungarian Academy of Sciences permitted a modest program of scientific and cultural exchange.[40]

One of the major obstacles to trade expansion was a relic of the opening phase of the division between East and West: among other outstanding claims, Hungary had not compensated U.S. owners for nationalized property. The task of signing a claims settlement and removing this impediment was assigned to the representative of a new generation of technocrats in the communist leadership, deputy prime minister Péter Vályi, a chemical engineer by training. Prior to his trip to Washington, Vályi had gone to Moscow for consultations with the powerful Soviet minister of foreign trade, Nikolai Patolichev. Patolichev briefed him about the best way to link the claims agreement with MFN status, which both the Soviets and

Hungarians coveted. The Soviet-American trade agreement of 1972 would have allowed the Soviets to suspend their annual lend-lease payments if the United States were to renege on its commitment to extend MFN status to the USSR. An official of the Soviet Foreign Ministry warned Vályi that the U.S. Congress had the power to veto offers of most-favored-nation status.[41] In preparation for his momentous visit to the American capital, the Hungarian Political Committee charged Vályi with broaching the subject of the Holy Crown, which the Hungarians treated as the largest obstacle to normalization and the return of which would be a test case for American acceptance of the permanence of communist rule in Eastern Europe.[42]

Armed with the Soviets' advice, the deputy prime minister requested a clause in the claims agreement saying that Hungary would "honor its claims obligations in harmony with the extension of MFN [most favored nation] status."[43] This would not fly. Henry Kissinger instructed secretary of commerce Frederick Dent not to give the Hungarians any open or implicit guarantees regarding their treatment as a most favored nation.[44] His reasoning went beyond the scope of strictly bilateral relations: Hungary was not supposed to "jump over" Romania in its trade relations with the United States.[45]

Still, the Hungarians' expectations were not altogether unwarranted. There was confusion within the Nixon administration about extensions of trade benefits to Eastern European states. Secretary Dent was acting in the belief that he would be negotiating most-favored-nation status with his Hungarian partner on the basis of a National Security Council (NSC) document then under consideration, NSM 163, which suggested that negotiations be started with Romania and Hungary without delay.[46] This also was the recommendation made by the president's special committee on most-favored-nation status. The State Department also supported the idea, albeit with the proviso that the Hungarians make progress in expanding cultural relations. The NSC debate encapsulated U.S. policy on Eastern Europe: the aim was to reduce, not eliminate Soviet influence. The presidential committee wanted the United States to express an interest in the region and to let its people know that America did not regard their nations as mere spheres of influence where exclusively Soviet interpretations of sovereignty would prevail. The committee argued that extending most-favored-nation status to Hungary would serve U.S.

interests by reducing the Soviets' sway.[47] Even after Vályi's arrival, the State Department proposed that most-favored-nation status should be extended to Hungary on the conditions that Hungary play a satisfactory role on the Vietnamese Control Commission, make progress in the field of cultural relations, and allow Hungarian media to offer more objective accounts of the United States and its foreign policy.[48] No one expressed any objections based on principle to the elimination of trade discriminations against Hungary.

On the highest level of decision making, however, vanity and high principles trumped the possible benefits of luring a satellite away from the Soviets' alliance. The NSC, meanwhile, wished to accentuate Romania's favored position, and thus the final NSC document prioritized Romania, which enjoyed the status of a quasi-ally. For Kissinger, Romania's services in the international arena were more important than Hungary's domestic reforms. And even in matters of such significance, gestures played a role. Kissinger declared that Bucharest should stay ahead of Budapest in every respect, because while Romania had put its hands in the fire for the United States, the Hungarians had not even allowed American astronauts to visit in 1969.[49] His overriding concern seems to have been to demonstrate that Washington would reward good behavior. This "lesson" seems to have gone over the Hungarians' heads; there is no indication that the Hungarian leadership understood the motivation behind the Americans' negative decision. When Nixon's new concepts for trade policy appeared in May 1972, they reiterated as their central tenet this notion that economic favors would be granted to Eastern Europe in return for political concessions.[50]

Because the final version of the new directive on Eastern Europe was delayed, the Vályi visit was almost postponed. That it took place was due to Kissinger, who kept an eye on even the smallest matters.[51] Vályi was told that the Holy Crown would not be returned until financial and cultural relations were fully normalized, even though his visit had been touted as a new chapter in U.S.-Hungarian relations. The State Department recommended that Nixon receive the Hungarian functionary as a demonstration of American appreciation of his presence in the Hungarian leadership.[52] Vályi made a good impression on his hosts, visiting industrial and agricultural sites, walking around, visiting bookstores,[53] hardly the communist stereotype. His official host, the Department of Commerce, refused to pay for his activities outside Washington, even though – as Ambassador Puhan recalled – the Hungarians had covered the costs of the Rogers visit "without a word." Puhan recommended that the money be raised privately.[54]

According to the terms of the claims agreement, Hungary was to pay $18.9 million in annual installments of $945,000, a minor sum by any measure. Thus this matter, which had been negotiated on and off since 1964, was finally resolved. As a compromise measure, a letter was attached to the agreement in which the Nixon administration promised to seek congressional approval for extending MFN status to Hungary. The Hungarians also attached a letter in which they reserved the right to suspend payments if they were not treated as a most favored nation. The deputy premier also brought up the Holy Crown and was told that the matter was under consideration, though the pope did not support its return. Vályi was pleased with the visit and declared that for some products, the American market could become an alternative to the European Economic Community (EEC), even if it would not be Hungary's main capitalist market. American goods also had potential for the Hungarian market because of their low prices.[55] The real significance of the agreement, however, was that it opened up American financial markets;[56] American banks would become Hungary's most important creditors in the country's drive to finance its economic reform.[57]

The State Department hailed the agreement as path breaking and saw to it that it received prominent press coverage. The Hungarians demonstrated flexibility by agreeing to sign it without an automatic guarantee of most-favored-nation status. The agreement was the culmination of a lengthy process and opened up the possibility not only of most-favored-nation status, but even the return of the Crown of Saint Stephen.[58] Encouraged by this apparent success, the State Department moved to conclude similar agreements with other communist states.[59] Later, however, it turned out that the agreement was flawed. The Hungarians signed it in the belief that its terms would exempt them from the Johnson Act, which denied U.S.-government-backed loans and the right to issue bonds in America to countries which had reneged on American debts. The Americans accidentally omitted from the agreement Hungarian flour debts that dated back to the 1920s and thus the Johnson Act would continue to apply to Hungary.

While Romania preceded Hungary in the "pecking order," the latter was ahead of Czechoslovakia. Soon after the Vályi visit, Rogers went to Prague, and the White House reacted with outrage. Sonnenfeldt complained that the visit had not been cleared with the White House and did not fit into a coherent vision of foreign policy. It put Nixon in a difficult position since the Romanian leader's visit had been put on hold. Sonnenfeldt declared that Poland was immeasurably more important than Czechoslovakia and deplored the fact that Rogers was the first NATO foreign secretary to go to Prague since the invasion of 1968. Although the White House was unable to call off the visit, Rogers was barred from discussing the primary questions of bilateral relations such as frozen bank accounts, Czech gold, or a claims agreement.[60] This struggle between the national security staff and the State Department resulted in a fractured U.S. policy toward the Soviet bloc. Thus Rogers was not quite telling the truth in Prague when he claimed that his visit embodied the spirit of Nixon's policy, which was that the United States was ready to normalize relations with any country regardless of its political and social system. Rogers repeated the messages he had delivered in Budapest: that Washington had no desire to intervene in foreign affairs, that all states could improve their relations with the United States at their own pace, and that his country had no wish to influence any state regarding the direction in which it wanted to develop.[61]

That the Nixon administration had accepted the Soviets' sphere of influence in East Central Europe is illustrated by its position on conventional arms at the Mutual and Balanced Force Reduction talks (MBFR), which were seen as the true pillar of European security. Willy Brandt, chancellor of the Federal Republic of Germany, saw in it the core of a new European security system aimed at bringing about change in the Soviet sphere and allowing German reunification. Nixon and Kissinger understood troop reductions as synonymous with strong Soviet influence in Europe but were forced to use them as a means of preventing unilateral U.S. troop reductions. For Brezhnev, they were a means of preserving the status quo.[62] In November 1972, several NATO member states proposed that negotiations on mutual arms and force reductions in East Central Europe begin in January 1973.[63] Following the Vietnam War, there was strong domestic pressure in the United States to reduce foreign commitments, including the stationing of troops abroad. Moscow eventually accepted the proposal on one condition: that the talks not extend to Hungarian territory, the linchpin between the Soviets' northeastern and Balkan spheres of occupation. American records indicate that Budapest wanted to participate in the negotiations in the hopes of achieving a Soviet troop withdrawal – or at least a reduction – and thereby easing the military burden on the Hungarian budget. From Brussels, the State Department was informed that the decision to exclude the Hungarians from the talks had been made above their heads.[64] Sonnenfeldt understood the Hungarians to have been outraged by the Soviets' position.[65] Hungarian sources reveal that Budapest was ready to negotiate on the condition that Italy be included in the talks, which was a bone of contention for Washington. America's allies in NATO supported Hungary's inclusion, without which an agreement would have been pointless, as the Soviets could have stationed in Hungary whatever troops they were willing to pull out elsewhere. American records indicate, however, that the Americans "privately agreed" to the Soviets' exclusion of Hungary from the talks.[66] If this is so, it is the clearest indication that Washington had accepted the permanence of Soviet power in East Central Europe. The negotiations therefore began under the premise that they would not include Hungarian forces or Soviet forces stationed in Hungary. In the view of the American NATO mission, this was cause for concern since the Soviets would able to reinforce their position in Eastern Europe by increasing the size of their force in Hungary, thereby exerting political and military pressure as far west as Yugoslavia.[67]

Despite Vályi's success, Hungary's relations with the United States turned for the worse again, which suggests that the possibilities for improvement in relations between East and West were limited; even during the heyday of détente the logic of the Cold War made such harmonization of interests impossible. Hungary was a member of the international committee that oversaw the implementation of the Paris treaty on Vietnam. On May 31, 1975, assistant secretary of state Kenneth Rush summoned the Hungarian ambassador and accused Hungary of partiality toward the North Vietnamese and of subverting the committee's mission. Only a day earlier, a démarche had been presented to another Soviet bloc member of the committee, Poland, with the same charge. The visit to Poland of two U.S. secretaries was postponed, though it was "clear" to the Americans that the Poles were under Soviet pressure to act the way they did.[68] Rush declared that the Control Committee was unable to fulfill its functions and that the Polish and Hungarian missions, which devoted their efforts to protecting the Vietnamese Democratic Republic and South Vietnamese Revolutionary Government, were responsible for this. Rush claimed that the Hungarians had "sabotaged" the committee and added that this activity would have an impact on bilateral relations with the United States. In Budapest, the Foreign Ministry categorically rejected the accusation. Due to its significance, the matter was discussed at the highest echelons of the U.S. government.[69]

These charges may have been well founded. The Political Committee's resolution revealed that "in line with the coordinated socialist position," the activities of the Hungarian mission had to "take into account the best interests" of the Vietnamese communists by "constant consultations with our South Vietnamese comrades and our allies."[70] Foreign Ministry functionaries made no secret of the fact that higher interests governed their behavior. The officer at the American desk told ambassador Puhan that the Hungarian government had obligations to its allies that had to be fulfilled even if they were unpleasant.[71] The matter was not left at that. Puhan presented a new démarche claiming that the Hungarians had disregarded the interests of peace in supporting the communist side, to the inevitable detriment of bilateral relations.[72] The White House instructed the State Department that all further steps toward Poland and Hungary would have to be predicated on their behavior on the Vietnamese Control Commission.[73] Deputy secretary of state George Springsteen told the Hungarian ambassador that the United States was holding back on bilateral relations, which would hinge on Hungary's impartiality on the commission.[74] As it turned out, the Vietnamese issue retarded the return of the Crown of Saint Stephen, Kádár's dearest objective in his dealings with the United States. The party leader told the departing American ambassador, whom he lavishly praised for his role in the progress made between the two states, that further improvement would depend on "the way international relations developed."[75]

In spite of this setback, the Nixon administration was ready to move on with the policy of economic rewards for good behavior. The secretary of state asked the Hungarian leadership to receive a delegation of American lawmakers for a high-level meeting, which he hoped would be productive. As a result, the senators were met by two leading figures of the reform wing of the Hungarian party, Rezső Nyers and Prime Minister Jenő Fock. Senator Frank Moss was highly pleased with the visit,[76] and later that year secretary of commerce Frederick Dent visited Budapest to reassure his anxious hosts that MFN status was on the right track. He also indicated that the United States expected to sign a cultural agreement with Hungary, a highly contentious issue for the leaders of the Hungarian communist party.[77]

CULTURAL PENETRATION

The Communist Party saw cultural exchanges as threats to national security and thus insisted on limiting them to the fields of science and technology. The party suspected that the motive of ideological subversion lay behind American intentions to promote exchanges in the humanities: "It often happens that Americans wish to enter to investigate seemingly innocent scholarly topics or invite Hungarians to the United States and only after careful scrutiny does it turn out that the scientific garb conceals hostile intentions." Hungarian American scholars were thought to be particularly dangerous from the perspective of subversive intent.[78] Without the approval of the state security apparatus, represented by a cover agency called the Institute of Cultural Affairs, an invitation to the United States could not be accepted. An associate of the Hungarian National Museum, for instance, was barred from speaking at New York University because the event was hosted by Béla Király, who had served as the commander of the National Guard in 1956.[79]

Nevertheless, the Hungarian authorities were forced to let their scholars and social scientists visit the United States and to let Americans come to Hungary. The Political Committee saw cause to step up the "struggle" against "imperialist penetration" because cultural exchanges were playing an increasing role in the Americans' subversive propaganda. And as the party's resolution ominously added, the effects of this policy "could not be left unnoticed."[80] The leadership incurred the risks of cultural exchange because they expected to send and receive scholars whose expertise was essential to the national economy. Cultural relations were viewed as a double-edged sword. Exchanges were "basically useful" and served the country's "interests," but also allowed Western powers to pursue "subversive activities" and to disseminate "false values and politically harmful commodities" in Hungary under "the guise of cooperation." In addition, it was suspected that the Americans were trying to "subjugate" Hungarian science.[81] Political reliability was thus essential to getting a scholarship to the United States, though this may actually have helped American propaganda efforts as many reliable party members were confronted with the falsehoods of communist propaganda. Party historian György Borsányi found Americans to be open and helpful, and his report on his field trip to the United States was full of praise.

The toleration of cultural programs was a tug-of-war between the state security services and the Foreign Ministry, between party hard-liners and "liberals." The former were apprehensive about opening up while the latter hoped that the intellectual and economic gains would outweigh the undeniable dangers of subversion. The case of Columbia professor István Deák illustrates the dilemmas that confronted the Hungarians and Americans charged with constructing cultural contacts. The acclaimed professor of history, who had been staying in Hungary on an IREX grant, an international exchange program sponsored by the U.S. government, was suddenly expelled from the country in November 1973. The incident suggests that the relative "liberalism" of the political system was only an illusion. The immediate reasons for his expulsion were unclear, but evidence suggests it was part of the power struggle between state security and the Foreign Ministry, as well as their respective party patrons. The Hungarians explained Deák's expulsion by accusing him of involvement in spying. The state security services kept a file on him because of his previous job at Radio Free Europe, which suggests that the real question is how he got admitted to the country in the first place. The Americans suspected that he might have resisted an attempt by Hungarian security services to recruit him. Revealingly, the Institute of Cultural Affairs hoped that the expulsion would reduce the number of American scholars of Hungarian descent who visited, which would be "in our interest." The matter caused an uproar in American academic circles, and IREX suspended its program with Hungary. While Deputy Foreign Minister Nagy claimed that this was an isolated case, Deák himself petitioned the cultural czar of Hungary, György Aczél, to investigate the affair.[82]

In Washington, opinions differed on how to deal with the issue. Deputy secretary of state Kenneth Rush opined that in other Eastern European states, state security activities had not been directed against American citizens.[83] Sonnenfeldt, on the other hand, accepted the Hungarians' explanation that the measures against Deák were aimed at him alone and were not characteristic of Hungarian politics in general.[84] He therefore opposed the reprisals urged by Zbigniew Brzezinski, himself a professor at Columbia University at the time. The State Department concluded that everything should be done to keep channels open, while Brzezinski asserted that in the view of the academic community the State Department was too defensive on the matter.[85] Differences of opinion also arose between the U.S. Embassy in Budapest and the IREX leadership. Stephen Dachy, the cultural attaché of Hungarian descent who spoke fluent Hungarian and was well informed about political conditions in Hungary, was ready to turn the page and put an end to American actions that might thwart the exchange programs. He distanced himself from the measures taken by what he called IREX's "stupid leadership."[86] In the meantime, IREX agreed with Columbia University that unless Budapest produced a satisfactory reply, they would call on every institution that collaborated with IREX to suspend their exchange programs with Hungary. The State Department, however, refused to deliver the message to Budapest because it wanted to avoid giving the impression that it was ganging up with IREX or engaging in reprisals.[87]

National security advisor Henry Kissinger asked IREX to adopt a conciliatory attitude, though he also wanted to let the Hungarian government know that "police politics" could result in the cancellation of mutually useful exchanges.[88] Puhan agreed with the secretary of state, fearing that IREX pressure could "destroy" cultural relations with Hungary. On the basis of what he was told by government officials, he thought that the expulsion was an isolated incident and that the Hungarians were not about to change their policy. He therefore recommended the "isolation" of the incident and the further expansion of cultural exchanges.[89] Shortly thereafter, IREX director Alan Kassof arrived in Budapest and threatened to close the program unless the authorities would allow the professor to return under the pretext of a family visit.[90] IREX insisted on a hard line despite the State Department's advice and was ready for a partial shutdown of the program until Deák received his visa.[91] The threats worked. Deák got the visa at the personal intervention of György Aczél,[92] which suggests that the Hungarian government dealt with the issue at the highest level. The professor's ordeal was not over, though. Even though he was readmitted to the country, the state security services got their revenge by tailing him with thugs who followed him everywhere, conspicuously watching his every move. Deák complained to IREX, which sent Kassof into a fit of rage. He threatened that the IREX leadership would not be prevented from expelling every Hungarian left in the United States. Cultural attaché Stephen Dachy, on the other hand, considered this response exaggerated and did not see why it was not understood that Deák had received his visa after lengthy diplomatic bargaining on humanitarian grounds. He opined that an overreaction would hurt only those who had helped Deák get his visa and would help only the "the dark forces" interested in disrupting relations with the United States.[93]

"THE BENEFITS OF SOVIET OCCUPATION": THE FUTURE OF EASTERN EUROPE

The United States was ready to tailor the pace and depth of advancing relations to the individual needs of the Soviet satellites. In contrast with the beginning of the Cold War, its aims were modest. "The primary U.S. interests in this region are the evolution of the individual states ... into more independent entities ... and the enhancement of the existing identification of the peoples of the area with the West. Such developments would reduce Soviet influence and weaken the security of the Soviet Union's military posture in Central Europe. [Hungarian reform] policies have good prospects of leading not only to evolutionary processes in Hungary, but possibly elsewhere as well. Such developments would help reduce tensions, lead to more cooperative relations." Changes were supposed to happen gradually so that the Soviets would not see the need to intervene.

Soviet military intervention would not only put an end to these "positive" developments but would also expose Washington's inability to do anything about it.

America was thought to be popular in Czechoslovakia and Poland and even in Hungary, which had stood on the other side in the war. The peoples of Eastern Europe were "still Europeans" and fundamentally "pro-American and anti-Soviet," with a "tremendous reservoir of goodwill" toward the United States. By the standards of the region, the Hungarian system was deemed to be humane and liberal, and the "conservative" backlash was not expected to change that. There was a chance that the Hungarian economic reforms, which were considered to be in the interest of the United States, would lead to the appearance of a "bourgeois mentality" and could even spill over into the neighboring states, thereby catalyzing a transformation and reducing political tensions between East and West. As American support of Hungarian reforms was to be low-key and not provocative to the Soviets, it seemed prudent to intensify commercial, cultural, and humanitarian contacts carefully lest conservative forces in Hungary become suspicious and use them as arguments against reform. American criticism of the recent conservative backlash was therefore cautious; the State Department urged Radio Free Europe to praise Budapest's increasing contact with the West and to stress positive developments in Hungarian-American relations rather than criticizing negative ones. To minimize tensions between Moscow and Budapest, the State Department wanted to keep relations with the Hungarians one step behind those with the Soviets, though this approach would change. The whole tone of American communication with the peoples behind the Iron Curtain was changing. The State Department urged high-level contacts with Hungarian leaders even though it was appalled by their record in international politics.

One important aim was to make the Hungarians less critical of American foreign policy than the Soviets were. Hungary's international policies were deemed to be inimical to the interests of the United States, and the State Department correctly pointed out that Budapest followed the Soviet line not only as a tradeoff for internal reforms but also "enthusiastically" and out of "conviction." Washington had leverage: Hungary's desire for most-favored-nation status and modern technology. In other areas, though, Hungarian developments were highly encouraging.

Robert C. Mudd, the first secretary of the embassy in Budapest, thought there were personal reasons behind the stagnation of bilateral relations. He claimed that Ambassador Richard Pedersen, who had been appointed in 1973, was "a weak and untalented man who knew nothing about Hungary and caused a great deal of harm to bilateral relations." Mudd also blamed the Hungarian ambassador, whom he described as subverting efforts to move ahead and as being responsible for the poor organization of the visits paid by Vályi and foreign trade minister József Bíró. Mudd also thought that the policies of the Hungarian Consulate in New York had hurt Hungary's cause. The diplomat's ill feelings toward his Hungarian counterparts did not stem from anticommunist prejudice. He praised foreign minister Frigyes Puja, who, despite his "orthodox" views and his stature as a pillar of the Communist Party, was sincere, ambitious, and rational. Mudd reassured the Hungarians that Pedersen's successor, Eugene McAuliffe, was a well-educated, experienced man.[94] Ultimately, this battle to create a bilateral relationship based on mutual advantage and at least some degree of trust was fought on the ground level by the diplomats and functionaries who were entrusted with implementing their governments' policies.

Budapest blamed the Americans, while the United States held a lack of Hungarian interest responsible for the stagnation between the two states. Ambassador Pedersen complained that "Brezhnev had been more positive on relations with the U.S." than Kádár had been at a recent party congress. He understood that the Hungarians had to take a variety of considerations into account, but warned that in Washington they were being compared to Poland.[95] The ambassador asserted that the Poles had made more strenuous efforts to improve relations with the United States than had Hungary and claimed that the major impediment to progress was the Hungarians' role in Vietnam and the anti-American rhetoric of the Hungarian press.[96] He thought that Radio Free Europe broadcasts were another part of the problem. On one hand, Radio Free Europe was forcing the government to report domestic and international news with "less distortion" than it otherwise might have, but on the other hand, the station was making too much fuss about negative phenomena, which reduced its popularity. He thought that objective reporting of positive developments would be more consistent with the spirit of détente than the currently strident tone.⁹⁷

Hungarian policy toward the United States was contradictory. While companies were signing agreements of cooperation with overseas partners and Americans were building luxury hotels in Budapest, the press continued to be highly hostile to the United States.⁹⁸ In the larger framework of the Cold War, however, the direction of Hungarian developments suited American interests. Kissinger's approach was pragmatic: there were no conflicting interests between the two states and "until Hungary attacked its neighbors" he saw a chance for further rapprochement.⁹⁹ In his philosophy, domestic reforms and the relative liberality of the regime did not matter too much. What counted more was independence in foreign policy, an attitude that was was emphasized by President Gerald Ford's visits to Romania and Yugoslavia.

On the surface, the Helsinki Agreement was a triumph for Soviet diplomacy. The postwar order and the Soviet sphere of interest finally gained international recognition. The only glimmers of hope were the provisions regarding human rights, which allowed for Western interference in Soviet and Eastern European internal matters. In Hungary, Kádár got the message and, in contrast to Brezhnev, referred to this issue in his domestic presentation of the Helsinki Agreement.¹⁰⁰ But these clauses would prove illusory, as American administrations tended to disregard them when it suited their interests. The Carter administration, which generally embraced human rights, opted to favor the Romanian regime despite its known disregard for them. KGB chairman Yuri Andropov saw the treaty as a defeat for the KGB. One historian claimed that Helsinki "blasted a breach in the security wall that Andropov had cemented across the communist bloc in Europe."¹⁰¹ Yet the Eastern Europe experience showed that this was closer to a tiny hole, the significance of which was minimal in comparison to international recognition of Moscow's permanent, hegemonic control, with little or no mechanism to force the Soviets or the local communist regimes to change their ways.

The treaty gave a final boost to the normalization of relations between the United States and Hungary. Foreign Minister Puja expressed interest in visiting the United States. Robert Ingersoll, Kissinger's deputy who visited Hungary after the Helsinki talks, predicted further unspectacular developments between "two sovereign states" on the basis of "mutual advantages."[102] This was a clear indication of America's recognition of both the Hungarian system and the permanence of the state of affairs in Eastern Europe. The cultural attaché in the American embassy interpreted Ingersoll's visit as an indication that a decision to normalize relations had been reached "on the highest level," meaning that the final obstacle, the return of the Holy Crown, would soon be negotiated.[103] Ingersoll's visit was low-key enough not to arouse Soviet suspicions about the Hungarians, whose alleged flirtations with capitalism had already gotten them into trouble with Brezhnev. Ingersoll met with the country's most influential party leaders. Deputy prime minister József Marjai indicated his country's interest in intensifying commercial ties and joint industrial programs, while the deputy secretary of state told the party leader responsible for international affairs that only a few family unification and emigration cases would need to be resolved before a deal on MFN status could be approved. Puja declared that his country was ready to satisfy the stipulations of the Helsinki Agreement regarding emigration and family unification.[104] The carrot of MFN status was beginning to work on Budapest, which indicated its willingness to satisfy the conditions set by the Jackson-Vanik amendment. As a gesture of good will, Budapest indicated that it was ready to settle a debt that had originated back in the 1920s.

The new U.S. ambassador to Hungary, Eugene McAuliffe, was a defense expert with good White House connections – he would be appointed deputy defense secretary the following year – and had served as the deputy head of the American NATO mission before his arrival in Budapest. His selection may have been a signal of the administration's increased interest in one of the communist bloc's more innovative states. McAuliffe offered to convey the Hungarian leader's messages directly to the White House and requested an opportunity to relay messages from the administration to the party leadership. He was instructed to reiterate to his hosts that his mission was to achieve normalization without "causing problems between Hungary and its allies." Kádár was in a generous mood. Acknowledging that the Hungarian media seldom published anything positive about the United States, he praised the Americans' role at the conference in Helsinki, which reinforced the division of Europe on the communist leader's mental map.

Kádár's statements provide a valuable insight into the thinking of a communist true believer. Referring to his fear of war, he stated that Hungary could be done in by just a few of the "atomic bombs that would accidentally fall from the traffic." The dramatic and politically driven transformation of the party leader's image is demonstrated by the ambassador's calling him a "person of historical importance." Kádár, who had put his comrade Imre Nagy to death, blurted out that "he had not wanted to be called a historical personality; he had never had such ambitions. The ambassador, if he knows roughly what 1956 meant for Hungary, will understand this." That he treated an American diplomat to such a rare display of his innermost thoughts suggests that he might have considered détente more than a calculation. It was an entirely new mindset. He then claimed that the post-1956 Hungarian regime had been "able to restore order relatively quickly with an amnesty," neglecting to mention that he had presided over more than two hundred executions and that the amnesty had been declared under strong American pressure. Referring to the relaxation of travel controls, he claimed that the Hungarians had lost their illusions about the capitalist world and that fewer people were defecting than in the times when the borders had been closed. Thus Hungary "was not afraid of" the human rights clauses of the Helsinki Agreement. He admitted that in most questions Hungarian foreign policy went hand-in-hand with the Soviets', but he believed that this served the interests of the people. He thereby indicated that the country's relative openness to the West was compatible with a pro-Soviet line. He even revealed that there were tensions within the Soviet alliance: "I don't envy the superpowers, which oftentimes find it easier to agree with one another than with their allies. They just issue a slogan and move full-speed ahead, then look back and wonder where their team is." The party leader indicated that he expected to advance bilateral relations for economic reasons. He spoke of two goals: most-favored-nation status and the return of the Holy Crown. McAuliffe probed Kádár about the possibility that a closer relationship with the United States might strain the Hungarians' alliance with the Soviet Union, asking whether it was causing Kádár any problems that so many high-ranking officials had lately visited Washington. Kádár's witty reply suggested that the scope of the relationship would remain limited: "No, but I wouldn't want them to hold a meeting of the Council of Ministers in Washington, either."[105]

The American position on the status of Eastern Europe was highly favorable for the Hungarian approach, which would consist of increasingly strong economic and financial ties to the West while remaining an unswerving political ally of the Soviet Union. In the midst of the presidential primaries for the 1976 election, the *Washington Post* leaked a presentation Helmut Sonnenfeldt, Kissinger's assistant on Eastern Europe, had delivered at a closed meeting of American ambassadors in London in December 1975. Sonnenfeldt stated that the United States should work to avoid a third world war by striving "for an evolution that makes the relationship between the Eastern Europeans and the Soviet Union an organic one." This claim came in handy for Republican candidate Ronald Reagan, who was then attacking the incumbent president for his policy toward the communist world. Reports of Sonnenfeldt's statements spread behind the Iron Curtain as well, and were given diverse interpretations. Kissinger biographer Jussi Hanhimäki has argued that Sonnenfeldt was expressing his own opinion, that the United States should aim to stabilize Eastern Europe so that the balance there would not be based solely on the Soviet military presence. If so, his remarks were easy to misinterpret. *New York Times* columnist C. L. Sulzberger shivered at the thought that an American official could be that cynical. But as Hanhimäki asserts, this was a misunderstanding. Sonnenfeldt was not trying to say what, for example, the Romanians had attributed to him: that the United States was encouraging the Soviets to annex Eastern Europe.[106] Hungarian diplomats got hold of a version of the text that contained the term "organic" – the usage of which Sonnenfeldt tried to deny – and this in itself suggests that Sonnenfeldt was sending a message to Eastern Europe. Sonnenfeldt's statement, which has finally become accessible, reveals that he did talk about an American encouragement of "organic relations" between the Soviet Union and the satellite states as a means to avert war. American policy, Sonnenfeldt argued, should aim at the "Finlandization" of the region, a process he imagined was "inevitable" and would take place within the next "century." These ideas were not encouraging to proponents of national independence in Eastern Europe. The NSC assistant argued that Americans should react to the aspirations of Eastern Europeans to become *more autonomous* within a strong Soviet geopolitical space. As examples, he mentioned the Soviet-Polish modus vivendi and Hungary, where Kádár had found a path that was acceptable to the Soviet Union but was still in accordance with the natural aspirations of the people to sprout "Hungarian roots." Paradoxically, although not quite illogically, Sonnenfeldt attributed this state of affairs to the fact that four Soviet divisions were stationed in Hungary, which meant that Hungarian reforms could not cause too much concern in Moscow. Finally, he acknowledged arguments that the United States was helping the Soviets maintain their control of Eastern Europe and repeated that the best America could do was to influence the way Moscow exercised its power.[107] Sonnenfeldt described the benefits of Soviet occupation to Hungarian officials, disingenuously calling it "a Soviet subsidy" of Hungary.[108] Aside from the fact the some of the comments revealed some ignorance from the part of the Ford administration's senior advisor on Eastern Europe, they betray Washington's acceptance of a divided Europe on a permanent basis. An American diplomat working in Budapest thought Sonnenfeldt had summarized the essence of U.S. policy precisely. Perhaps it was not a coincidence that the diplomat in question expressed this view to the Soviet Embassy in Budapest.[109] Given that Sonnenfeldt's statement became widely known, it is possible that Washington intended to circulate it as a way of reassuring Moscow about its intentions in Eastern Europe.

Be that as it may, Sonnenfeldt and Kissinger were forced to defend themselves. Sonnenfeldt attempted to deny that he or the United States accepted Soviet control of Eastern Europe. At a congressional hearing, he ambiguously stated that Washington supported "independence, national sovereignty, and autonomy" behind the Iron Curtain. Kissinger was similarly enigmatic. In a letter to Senator James Buckley, he repudiated the senator's charge that the administration had "sold" Eastern Europe to Moscow, claiming that the United States supported East European "autonomy and independence." The senator caught the contradiction and accused the secretary of "acknowledg[ing] and accept[ing] the Soviet Union's sphere of influence in Eastern Europe."[110] In fact, the United States now stayed away from any policy or statement that might have been construed as advocacy of a change in the status quo. The State Department instructed Radio Free Europe to avoid belligerent rhetoric, as the United States could not support any policy that might force the Soviets to intervene and halt the current "evolutionary process."[111] An interagency committee described the restoration of national independence in Eastern Europe as a goal, but it imagined only an "expansion" of East-West contacts, rather than continental reunification. Whether the Soviets would allow the restoration of national independence in their sphere of domination was not addressed.

Hungary received Sonnenfeldt's remarks with great sympathy. He was, after all, saying what they had wanted to hear in Budapest for a long time: that Washington was not seeking to weaken Hungary's ties to the Soviets. U.S. diplomats had been reassuring their Hungarian counterparts of this for some time, but this was the first time such reassurance had come from such a high level. On the other hand, Sonnenfeldt and Kissinger took heat from the Romanians. Ceaușescu's foreign policy advisor Mircea Malița complained that Sonnenfeldt's words could be interpreted as an expression of American uninterest in Eastern Europe. He also took exception to Sonnenfeldt's characterization of Romania as the "last Stalinist system in Eastern Europe," as well as to the implication that Bucharest would have more freedom to maneuver if it were occupied by the Soviets. Sonnenfeldt categorically rejected the accusations and declared that the United States did not support Soviet domination or even preponderance in Eastern Europe. He asserted that the United States would "support [the] national independence and sovereignty of all states" and that the "U.S. hopes to see relations between the USSR and Eastern Europe become more normal." Sonnenfeldt also added, though, the qualification that "Countries have areas of national interest.... One cannot change geography... the USSR cannot help but have an interest in you."[112] It is not surprising that his words failed to calm the Romanians' anxieties about American intentions. When Romania's ambassador saw Kissinger a few weeks later and asked for an explanation, Kissinger disingenuously declared that the United States did not accept spheres of influence and pledged that Washington would do everything it could to strengthen Romania's international position.[113] The Ford administration's controversial statements about Eastern Europe did not end there. In a televised presidential debate against candidate Jimmy Carter, Ford claimed that Eastern Europe was not subject to

Soviet domination, a gaffe that may have contributed to his loss that fall. Carter criticized Ford's remark on the campaign trail, though as president he would express a similar opinion in his private diary. In an entry from January 1979, Carter noted that the United States "pre-empted" Soviet influence in "Egypt, Indonesia, China, Yugoslavia, Romania, Scandinavia, Somalia, Angola, Hungary, North Korea, and the Mideast, where the Soviets have been rooted out altogether."[114] Aside from its insensitivity, the statement suggests that the president's knowledge of foreign affairs may have been limited.

THE CROWN OF SAINT STEPHEN

The Hungarian Holy Crown was captured by the U.S. Army in the final days of the Second World War, and its return was postponed by the onset of the Cold War. The history of the return of this symbol of Hungarian statehood and independence reflects the changing attitudes in both East and West regarding the European political status quo and sheds light on the importance of symbols in foreign relations. The internal debates over the return of the Holy Crown also reveal American attitudes toward the nations behind the Iron Curtain. The act of returning the Holy Crown was meant to show support for autonomy within the Soviet bloc and possibly to buttress János Kádár's position in the Hungarian leadership, as he was seen as the architect of reform and the defender of autonomy against internal and external dangers. Perhaps most importantly, the return of the Holy Crown was a gesture of recognition of the Soviet sphere of influence. Even though the Holy Crown was returned to Budapest in recognition of Hungary's internal liberalization, the Hungarian political process surrounding the return revealed that its system remained dictatorial, and in ways that were not always easily visible from outside.

The U.S. Embassy in Budapest, which was usually ahead of Washington in pioneering advances in bilateral relations, broached the possibility of a Nixon visit. The chargé d'affaires, Robert C. Mudd, added that the Crown of Saint Stephen could be returned right before the visit, or perhaps the president himself could bring it to Budapest. Mudd emphasized the "private" nature of his interest.[115] Later the embassy tried to deny that it had ever brought up a Nixon visit and claimed that a Hungarian diplomat had misunderstood what Mudd had told him.[116] Yet the Hungarian Embassy in Washington also learned that Nixon would be going to Budapest after his visit to Moscow and would be taking the crown jewels with him.[117] To be on the safe side, the Political Committee passed a resolution in favor of welcoming Nixon should he offer to visit.[118] This apprehension surrounding a possible presidential visit cannot be attributed simply to an eagerness to contribute to détente. It also reflected Hungary's growing dependence on U.S. assistance and increasing pragmatism in foreign policy. It is ironic that a president known for his virulent anticommunism was so eagerly awaited in a communist capital. When Ambassador Pedersen expressed his desire for a meeting with Hungarian bishops, they thought it was a sign that the United States was ready to return the Holy Crown. The State Ecclesiastical Office made a "recommendation" to the Foreign Ministry regarding the bishops the ambassador would be allowed to visit. These were then told to "broach" the subject of the Holy Crown with the ambassador.[119] On May 31, 1974, deputy secretary of state Arthur Hartman told the Hungarian ambassador that the Holy Crown would be returned "shortly" and that the "correctness" of the Hungarian side would contribute to the final decision.[120] Given that "the Czechs" were also preparing to invite Nixon to Prague, foreign minister Frigyes Puja recommended that the Political Committee also invite the president to Budapest. Ironically, the members of the communists' highest decision-making organ thought that the Republican president offered "the best hope that the U.S. would continue down the road of advancing relations with the Soviet Union and the socialist states."[121] Nixon's image was so positive behind the Iron Curtain that when the Watergate investigations were launched, communist leaders suspected that the malicious intentions of anti-Soviet forces were behind them.

It soon turned out that hopes regarding the Holy Crown were groundless; Nixon had no intention of going to Budapest. The State Department claimed that the embassy in Budapest had discussed the presidential visit without higher authorization and that there was no such plan.[122] In September, in the presence of a highly placed official of the State Department, U.S. senator Vance Hartke asserted to the Hungarian ambassador that the United States would return the Holy Crown if the government were to display it in a museum. Hartke claimed he had cleared his proposal – which he had formulated after a meeting with Cardinal Mindszenty – with the State Department.[123]

As it had so many times before, the Cold War intervened. The Hungarians were withdrawing their observers from strategic points in Vietnam, but the United States expected them to return.[124] Washington also complained that Budapest had rejected the visa applications of reporters from Voice of America and that there were family unification problems.[125] This was particularly irritating to the Nixon administration because congressional hearings were just then probing the question of the socialist states' eligibility for MFN status.[126] Ambassador Pedersen complained that Budapest cared less about its relations with the United States than did other socialist states. Budapest was also warned that foot dragging on a family unification issue would hurt Hungary's chances of achieving MFN status and could lead to the renegotiation of the claims agreement.[127]

The decision to "slow down" relations with the United States was a conscious one. Kádár sought out the American ambassador at the annual "liberation day" reception and declared that bilateral relations would advance "slowly," repeating the word twice for emphasis. Pedersen's interpreter, deputy foreign minister János Nagy, clarified the party leader's words and asserted that they had to be taken very seriously.[128] The reason may have been a conservative turn in home politics; at the instigation of the Soviet Union, reformers were dropped from the highest echelons of power.[129] The U.S. Embassy noticed that when Kádár returned from Moscow after his visit in October 1974, Hungarian propaganda about the Soviets was even more adulatory than usual. These repeated expressions of loyalty to Marxist dogma were occasioned by the need to preserve autonomy and reform in the face of Soviet leaders who were aware of the anticommunist sentiments of most Hungarians.[130] Soviet Embassy counselor Nikolai Mardoniev had reportedly warned that the Hungarians were disregarding the principles of Marxism-Leninism and that the situation there resembled the "bourgeois West."[131]

While the Soviets were desperately trying to reverse the reforms, the Hungarian leadership was equally desperate for MFN status and the access to international money markets that came with it. President Ford was ready to move ahead. American diplomats in Budapest wanted the State Department to inform Kádár that most-favored-nation treatment would be extended. They wanted to show American support for the party leader; the ambassador thought he was far superior to his colleagues in Eastern Europe and enjoyed the support of most Hungarians, who understood that Kádár was the "best" they could get.[132] In April, Frank Zarb, the deputy head of the White House Office of Management and Budget, led a delegation to Budapest, where talks exceeded "all expectations."[133] János Nagy was told that after negotiations with the Soviet Union and Romania, further talks with Hungary could begin.[134]

Most-favored-nation status was one of the chief questions during the era of détente, although its significance is rarely appreciated. The prospect of becoming a most favored nation was one of the driving forces behind Brezhnev's more conciliatory approach to Soviet-American relations. Negotiating an extension of MFN status to Moscow was a key component of Nixon and Kissinger's foreign policy. In 1973, Nixon submitted to Congress a Trade Reform Act that would have allowed the administration to eliminate the trade discriminations that then applied to Eastern Europe. At this point, the neoconservative senator Henry "Scoop" Jackson introduced an amendment to the bill that linked it to Soviet Jews' freedom to emigrate, an action motivated only in part by political conviction; Jackson also hoped to garner support for his re-election campaign. In response, the Soviets eased the emigration quota and supplied data about Jewish emigrants. Kissinger, who failed to appraise the real situation, told a concerned Brezhnev that the amendment was "peripheral." The Kremlin understood that Watergate was gradually undermining the administration's power. Thus in 1974, the Congress passed the Ford administration's trade bill, including the Jackson-Vanik amendment. Most-favored-nation status was to be linked to emigration and subject to an annual review. In response, however, the Soviets rescinded the 1972 Soviet-American trade agreement and rejected the trade bill as American intervention in Soviet affairs.[135]

In Budapest, the news landed like a bombshell. Many years of diplomatic efforts seemed to have come to naught. It was clear that the prospect of advancing U.S.-Hungarian trade relations had suffered a grave setback and that the lack of most-favored-nation status would be highly detrimental to Hungary's external economic relations and hence to the success of the reform. The first secretary of the American Embassy in Budapest wrote just after the event, "I cannot tell you how disappointed we were" when the Soviets rejected the trade bill. "Everything we have done here" since Vályi was in Washington in 1973 was with the aim of achieving MFN status for Hungary and "now we have no idea what to do."[136] A group of American lawmakers visiting Budapest were told that the stipulations of the bill were unacceptable and amounted to interference in Hungary's domestic affairs.[137] Representative Charles Wilson asserted that the law was directed against the Soviet Union and would allow Romania and Hungary to get most-favored-nation status in return for a written declaration. Not surprisingly, Budapest rejected this option.[138] Since President Ford required the amendment of the bill or that the countries in question fulfill the American terms, most-favored-nation status continued to be out of reach for most states in Eastern Europe.[139] Further progress was made contingent on the individual Eastern European state's positions on the international questions that mattered most to the United States, as well as on their efforts to resolve bilateral issues.[140] This formula favored the Romanians, who had backed the Americans in enough important international matters that the Soviets considered them insufficiently reliable to participate in the invasion of Czechoslovakia in 1968. Bulgaria was also eager to conclude a most-favored-nation agreement, but according to the White House "pecking order," still stood behind Hungary. Kissinger resented that the State Department had started talks with Bulgaria before Hungary and gave instructions to determine the order in which most-favored-nation status would be negotiated with the Eastern Europeans, lest states that did not diverge from the Soviet line at all be rewarded.[141]

The cover letter attached to the claims agreement would have allowed Hungary to suspend payments, but the Hungarian National Bank strongly advised against this measure, citing economic interests. American banks had been playing an important role in financing imports and the United States was already a significant source for Hungarian loans.[142] Nonpayment would rescind Hungary's most-favored-nation status[143] and thereby deny it access to the American market, which Hungarians hoped would complement the EEC as an outlet for Hungarian exports. János Nagy asserted that Hungary had lagged behind the other socialist states in normalizing its relations with the United States, but added that "there was not a single field where we are dependent on the U.S. or where they can cause us harm." Foreign minister Frigyes Puja scribbled on the margin, "This is not true."[144] By the mid-1970s, Hungary was becoming as economically dependent on the West as on the East.

Although Hungary's reforms, which merged market elements with central planning and liberalized cultural and travel policies, made the Hungarian regime one of Washington's communist favorites, the relationship between the two countries was still governed by the Cold War. Officials and businessmen from the United States were often denied visas; the ambassador complained that he was forced to wait ninety minutes to place a phone call from his residence.[145] Still, even as U.S.-Soviet relations began to deteriorate – due to the Soviets' buildup of strategic nuclear missiles and interventions in the Third World, as well as Washington's policy of balancing the Soviets with China – American relations with Hungary entered the homestretch toward full normalization. Thus despite the communist rhetoric, Soviet and Hungarian interests diverged.

The process began with a visit to Washington by deputy prime minister Gyula Szekér, who invited the president to come to Hungary. President Ford, who was still under fire for the Sonnenfeldt incident, decided to receive the deputy premier as a show of support for Eastern Europe and as evidence that the United States did not countenance exclusive spheres of influence. While Szekér emphasized the expansion of industrial and agricultural cooperation, arguing that most-favored-nation status would bring a two- to threefold increase in trade, Ford stressed the importance of an agreement on cultural exchanges. The deputy premier was accompanied by the country's most successful industrialist, the general manager of the heavy industrial concern Rába Művek, Ede Horváth, whose presence suggested a pragmatic approach to economic relations. Thus the tug-of-war over priorities in bilateral exchanges continued. After years of wrangling, Budapest signed an agreement on cultural, educational, scientific, and technical exchanges. The fact that all these disciplines were included in the same agreement, especially the inclusion of arts and humanities, represents a significant concession on the part of the Hungarians. The long-term negative consequences were to be reduced by a variety of measures. The celebration of the two hundredth anniversary of the United States was downplayed on radio and television programs, as well as through the publication of a book that "exposed" the manipulations of American intelligence services, including articles they had planted in the Hungarian American émigré press.[146]

The Hungarians did not let go of the bone of MFN status. Szekér asked secretary of commerce Elliot Richardson for the conditions of MFN treatment.[147] By November 1976, the Hungarians reversed their position and were willing to meet the terms set by the United States in harmony with the "coordinated foreign policy of the socialist countries." This would mean a circumvention of the Jackson-Vanik amendment by way of a unilateral declaration that Hungary accepted the terms of the Helsinki Agreement, as well as the U.S. legislation regarding emigration and family unification. In his conversation with the secretary of commerce, Szekér alluded to the need for the United States to take into account Hungary's "alliance system."[148] Several members of the Ford administration supported the extension of most-favored-nation status to Hungary. The economic significance of the Soviet bloc was increasing, particularly in the agricultural sector. Secretary of agriculture Earl Butz argued the importance of increasing exports, particularly of grain, and deputy secretary of state Robert Ingersoll emphasized that in addition to economic gains, East-West trade would make the atmosphere conducive to the settlement of political issues.[149] It was argued that the socialist bloc formed the most rapidly growing market in the world, with the potential to buy $175 billion worth of goods from the Western world over the coming five years. The United States was then selling 16 percent of all the commodities purchased around the world, but only 4 percent of those goods were purchased by the Soviet bloc. Both sides were looking for opportunities, but the economic significance of this agreement was disproportionately greater for Hungary and the rest of the Soviet bloc than for the United States. Washington expected that the elimination of economic restrictions would lead to less turbulent relations with the other side.

In "close accord" with their allies, the Hungarians decided to "to reinforce the American willingness to grant MFN unilaterally."[150] Szekér asserted that this possibility "was of great significance."[151] In December 1976, Foreign Minister Puja announced in Parliament that emigration and family unification were not causing problems in Hungary, which he claimed was clearly demonstrated by recent political practice. He then made a public offer to accept the principles of the Commission on Security and Cooperation in Europe (CSCE) in a joint declaration with the United States.[152] Hungary had paid back its flour debt, outstanding since the 1920s, and was consequently exempted from the Johnson Act. This conciliatory attitude was motivated by economics: Kádár's regime was struggling with a balance-of-trade deficit, a shortage of convertible currency, and a slowdown in economic growth.[153] Even so, mutual grievances surrounding the settlement of financial claims persisted. The Hungarians complained that America was deliberately obstructing an agreement so as not to have to return the Holy Crown. The Americans, on the other hand, claimed that Hungarians disliked and were suspicious of simple, clean solutions and that this "national trait" had to be taken into consideration when dealing with them.[154] Sonnenfeldt acknowledged that the Ford administration was eager to change the trade act, but suggested that doing so was impossible because of the communists' involvement in Angola.[155]

The Carter administration, which promised to renew American foreign policy, did not make significant changes in U.S. policy toward Eastern Europe. The new president stressed human rights and eschewed the "immoral" power politics of his predecessor. Carter embraced the tradition of Wilsonian idealism and internationalism even though he had earlier espoused the balance-of-power principle. Carter withdrew U.S. support from the dictatorial regimes of Nicaragua and Iran, seemingly oblivious to the fact that anti-American regimes could come to power there. Carter's foreign policy record was mixed: he normalized relations with China, brokered a peace agreement between two ancient foes, Egypt and Israel, and returned the Panama Canal; he also stood by helplessly as Iran revolted and the Soviet Union invaded Afghanistan, both of which undermined U.S. positions in the Near East. And despite the efforts of the president and his secretary of state, Cyrus Vance, the Soviet-American détente collapsed. A new agreement on strategic arms limitations, SALT II, was not ratified and a new confrontation over intermediate-range nuclear missiles in Europe was ushering in a new phase of Cold War hostilities.[156] One historian has characterized Carter's stance on human rights as hypocritical; American leaders knew that China's human rights record could not withstand close scrutiny but decided to mute their concerns and treat China as though it was an ally in foreign policy. Such cynicism was consistent with the Realpolitik practiced proudly by Nixon and Kissinger. It was merely hypocrisy when Jimmy Carter, who proclaimed human rights as the centerpiece of his foreign policy, chose to ignore Chinese practices.[157]

Carter's attitude toward Romania was almost identical. By the late 1970s, Romania's nationality policies, which had been moderate by Soviet bloc standards, were giving way to drastic measures directed against its Hungarian and German minorities. The State Department offered to put pressure on Romania in order to improve the lot of the Hungarian minority in Transylvania,[158] but, predictably, Budapest rejected the overture on the grounds that it was motivated by "clear American political intentions" rather than by "good intentions."[159] New York mayor Edward Koch advocated raising the issue directly with the Romanian leadership on the occasion of Ceaușecu's visit, but Carter refused. Although the president asserted that there was "great interest here in this subject," he disingenuously claimed that there was "already considerable dialogue on this issue within Romania." Carter indicated that this was "a centuries old problem, and it raises sensitive territorial questions." He must have known that Hungary had renounced its territorial ambitions in two separate international agreements it had signed since 1945, and that the current leadership shunned even the mention of the fact that such disputes had ever existed between the two states. Carter suggested that a "cooperative approach offers the best prospect for progress," a clear indication that he would not alter the U.S. stance toward Romania.[160]

The overall thrust of the administration's Eastern European policy did not change. Secretary of state Cyrus Vance affirmed that the administration's policies, such as the return of the Crown of Saint Stephen, were meant to support the "long-range goal of encouraging greater autonomy, national identity, and Western orientation in Eastern Europe." Vance suggested that "we cannot expect the emergence of a non-communist government in the foreseeable future."[161] The secretary hoped to encourage closer relations between West and East, to improve humanitarian conditions behind the Iron Curtain, and to forestall the Soviets' use of this territory for hostile purposes.[162] Members of Carter's foreign policy and security policy staffs did not see eye to eye on the philosophy of supporting communist regimes. While national security advisor Zbigniew Brzezinski prioritized independence from Moscow and hence supported Romania, Vance put a premium on internal reforms and favored Poland

and Hungary. The tension between the two men was reminiscent of the relationship between Kissinger and Rogers, and Vance would eventually resign when Brzezinski decided to liberate the American hostages in Teheran without his knowledge. Their approaches to the Soviet bloc, however, were similar. Brzezinski's staff encouraged him to emphasize the "consistency" of the administration's policies toward the Soviets in his dealings with the Eastern Europeans.[163] The policy directive the president signed for Eastern Europe was a compromise: Washington would reward both those states that were independent of Moscow in foreign policy and those that liberalized themselves internally. Carter proceeded to visit Poland even though experts warned him the Soviets could interpret such a trip as a provocation. Though the State Department advised against it, Carter and his spouse met with the head of the Polish Catholic Church, Cardinal Wyszinski.[164] The president said he had a "delightful visit" and observed "a remarkable degree of religious freedom." He advised Edward Gierek to become "a Christian believer" like himself and Cardinal Wyszinski.[165]

On one occasion, the president explained that the fear of communism had made the United States embrace any dictator who was on its side, and he pledged to change this approach.[166] Still, like the Nixon and Ford administrations, Carter's foreign policy team continued to support the "orthodox, rigid and nationalistic" Romanian leadership more than it did the less illiberal Hungarian. Carter invited Ceauşescu to Washington even though it was clear that "all aspects of economic, political, and social life were under the party's control" in Romania.[167] Carter lauded Ceauşescu's mediation in the Middle East crisis of 1973 and declared that Romania was capable of resolving its own human rights problems, though there was scant evidence for this claim. Bucharest thus profited from its tense relationship with Moscow, which helped attract American support.[168] The Americans' relationship with Yugoslavia worked according to the same logic: the further Belgrade drifted from Moscow, the closer it got to Washington, and vice versa. Carter's public advocacy of human rights in international relations and his continuing support for a regime with one of the poorest human rights records behind the Iron Curtain suggest that the Cold War was motivated more by traditional power politics and security concerns than by a clash of ideologies.

In 1977, the process of extending most-favored-nation status to Hungary reached its final stage. The Hungarians accepted a solution whereby the United States would sign the trade agreement unilaterally without affecting Hungary's status in the General Agreement on Tariffs and Trade (GATT), but they were unwilling to issue a declaration on emigration and family unification, lest it be "used against the other socialist states."[169] Because of the economic interests involved, the Foreign Ministry was authorized to negotiate as long as the Americans were to take this "acceptable" unilateral step.[170] Under pressure to resuscitate the economy, the party retreated on most-favored-nation status while trying to save face with a formula that would minimize damage to its relationship with Moscow. On April 8, the chargé in Budapest revealed his "private view" that the United States would find the Hungarian solution acceptable and would extend most-favored-nation status, renewable on an annual basis. He was told that Budapest was "flexible," and since Hungarian policy on emigration and family unification was "identical with the American," there was no obstacle to an agreement. On the other hand, Hungary was not yet ready to adopt the "Romanian" solution of guaranteeing in writing emigration rights and family unification.[171] Although the author of the trade amendment, Senator Charles Vanik, openly advocated most-favored-nation status for Hungary, Washington still procrastinated. The White House had not yet come up with appropriate political guidelines, and the fact that the Soviet Union was not eligible also caused problems. In addition, administration officials wanted to respect the sensibilities of the Romanians, who had gone through a "painful process" to earn most-favored-nation status.[172] In an ironic reversal of roles, Vanik, whose constituents included ethnic Hungarians, thought that Congress would approve most-favored-nation status for Hungary, and that Puja's statement in the Hungarian parliament would enable the president to ask Congress to exempt Hungary from the amendment. The Department of Treasury, on the other hand, opined that Puja's speech was not enough to satisfy the conditions of the amendment. The State Department insisted on a declaration addressing paragraph 402 of the Jackson-Vanik amendment,[173] and Vance told Puja that Congress would not change the legislation.[174] The new U.S. ambassador to Hungary, Philip Kaiser, told the prime minister that the majority of Congress supported the bill for Hungary because of its government's allegedly sympathetic approach to human rights and its creation of a relatively liberal domestic atmosphere.[175]

The breakthrough, the return of the Holy Crown, the symbol of Hungarian nationhood, came in 1977.[176] Hungary's system had achieved a reputation as the most liberal, economically soundest, and most innovative in Eastern Europe. As Secretary of State Vance put it, "Hungary has developed into the most internally liberal country in the Warsaw Pact."[177] Kádár, who had once been called "the butcher of Budapest," outshone all his competitors behind the Iron Curtain. It was even suggested that he was the only communist who could win a free election – a hypothesis that unfortunately could not be tested. Hungary was thought to be "the most open society in Eastern Europe," and "much of the credit" was attributed to "Kadar's skillful policy of gradualism."[178] Carter eventually accepted the domestic political costs of returning the Holy Crown in order to bolster relations with the Soviets and to demonstrate the benefits of having good relations with the United States. Budapest complied with the Helsinki Agreement on emigration and family unification. Thomas Gerth, the Hungarian desk officer at the State Department and the "guardian of the Crown" – he held the keys to the chest – considered relations between the two states unproblematic.[179] Robert C. Mudd declared that the Hungarian people had "accepted socialism" and supported the government's policies. Moreover, Hungary was pursuing a more independent, more Hungarian-oriented foreign policy "in several areas."[180] Other American officials also praised the Hungarian regime's relationship to its people.[181] In confidential diplomatic correspondence, Ambassador Kaiser deplored the "denigrating" use of the term "regime" to denote Kádár's political system, claiming that even those Hungarians who lived abroad and disliked their home country's political system would acknowledge in private conversations that the people of Hungary lived much better than their neighbors in Eastern Europe. Kaiser was particularly disturbed by the use of the term "regime" in light of the fact that communist and other dictators were constructing cults of personality while the Hungarian leader avoided the limelight.[182] The Hungarians' political system compared favorably to those of their communist brethren. In addition, the most appalling aspects of the dictatorship, such as its constant surveillance of its citizens, its omnipresent undercover informants, and its institutional infrastructure of coercion, remained hidden from casual foreign observers. American and other foreign officials tended to meet with the regime's more Western-oriented functionaries, who would tell them what they wanted to hear. More often than not, these officials failed to make in-depth inquiries about the real nature of the regime.

The Holy Crown's return was the final symbolic confirmation of Washington's acceptance of Soviet control in Eastern Europe. In 1945, the Crown Guards had taken it to the future American zone of Austria to keep it from being captured by the Soviets. It was subsequently seized by the U.S. military, and in August 1946, when the United States proposed to return the artifact to Budapest, Prime Minister Ferenc Nagy preferred that it remain in American custody rather than risk the approval of a Czechoslovakian plan to place the Holy Crown in a "UN museum." Nagy was apprehensive about the Soviets' intentions, too.[183] After the communists' seizure of power in 1947, the Hungarian Foreign Ministry issued an official appeal for the return of the Holy Crown, but by then the American position had changed and Budapest was told that the relic would not be sent back. Cardinal Mindszenty argued that since the Holy Crown was a religious object and had come to Hungary as a papal gift, it should be turned over to the Vatican. The Vatican's state secretary for foreign affairs, Cardinal Montini, the future Pope Paul VI, agreed, but the State Department's response encapsulated the position that the United States would maintain for the next thirty years.[184] U.S. officials were aware of the historical, religious, and symbolic significance of the coronation regalia and considered them to be the property of the Hungarian people. But any change in the status of the artifact would inevitably entail negative political consequences, therefore the time would never be ripe for a decision on the transfer or final placement of the crown jewels.[185]

U.S. authorities elaborated a legal justification for withholding the regalia, asserting that the crown jewels had not been removed from Hungary forcefully and had been handed over to the American authorities for safekeeping. They were therefore not eligible for restitution, but would instead be regarded as an object with "special status."[186] The Crown of Saint

Stephen, not for the first time in its history, had fallen captive to international politics. The Hungarians made one more effort to retrieve it in 1952 before the controversy lapsed for over a decade until normalization talks began in 1964. Hungary claimed that the Holy Crown had been removed from the country by retreating Germans, which, though untrue, served to undermine the American position that it was not eligible for restitution. Deputy foreign minister Béla Szilágyi claimed that the Americans were taking impeccable care of the Holy Crown, though it is hard to know how he arrived at this conclusion since the United States refused to disclose its location. State Department officials indicated that the Holy Crown would be returned after "positive change" took place in bilateral relations, though they failed to name any specific criteria.[187] The conditions under which the restitution would take place were deliberately left vague.

By the mid-1970s, this reticence had more to do with domestic politics than with the Cold War. Not just Hungarian Americans, but other communities of Eastern European émigrés opposed the return of the Holy Crown on the grounds that it would legitimize what they regarded as an illegitimate system. David Bender wrote an article for the April 14, 1970, issue of the *New York Times* in which he claimed that the day was drawing closer when Washington would find an occasion to return Hungary's national treasures. The article caused an uproar and the State Department was forced to refute the assertion. Emory Swank reassured Béla Varga, the former speaker of the Hungarian parliament and an eminent member of the Hungarian diaspora in the United States, that the move was not under consideration.[188] After his release from captivity in Hungary, Cardinal Mindszenty sent a letter to Nixon in which he expressed his concerns about the possible return of the Holy Crown to Budapest and reiterated his long-standing view that it should instead be transferred to the Vatican. Although Nixon's reply – that this step was not being considered – reassured the cardinal, he was also told that as the "property of the Hungarian nation," the Holy Crown would eventually have to go back to Hungary.[189] Sonnenfeldt was already fed up with the issue and demanded to know what had prompted Kissinger to broach the subject in the first place.[190] This issue seemed particularly sensitive during the 1972 election campaign, as Eastern European voters could easily have interpreted the return of the Holy Crown as a betrayal.

There is no doubt that the matter received unusually intense political attention in the United States given that it was technically a Hungarian matter. This was partly because the return of the Holy Crown would be an unusually powerful gesture toward a communist government, and partly because such a move would have domestic political ramifications. The Holy Crown was high on the agenda of the Hungarian leadership too. Deputy foreign minister Péter Várkonyi told his American counterpart that relations between the two countries could not be regarded as normalized until it was returned. Rogers' answer reveals that the State Department discussed the possibility of transferring it to the Vatican in the wake of Mindszenty's letter, but that the pope did not like the idea. Thus its fate continued to be under review.[191]

The Hungarians had hoped to get the artifact back after they agreed to sign the claims agreement of 1973 and asserted that it was hard to understand what further grounds the United States had for withholding it. They were told that further proof of good will would be needed – beyond the desire to acquire high technology from the United States – particularly in light of Deák's expulsion, which had caused a lot of damage.[192] Nevertheless, the genie was out of the bottle. A State Department communiqué dated March 1973 acknowledged that the Holy Crown was the property of the Hungarian nation and suggested that its return was contingent on the general improvement of bilateral relations.[193] Sooner or later, a decision would have to be made. In 1975, the Helsinki Agreement sanctioned Europe's boundaries, which seemed to countenance the division of the continent and Soviet hegemony over its eastern part for good. All that was left was to work for greater domestic liberty and a larger degree of external autonomy so as to make sure that the Eastern Europeans would not always act as the pliable puppets of their hegemon.

As had happened so many times before, the final push came from below. American diplomats in Budapest saw that the time was ripe for putting an end to the long dispute. They were keenly aware of the domestic changes that were taking place in Hungary and had a better sense of the appropriate responses than did their superiors in Washington. Some more recent heads of mission felt a distinct sympathy toward the country where they were stationed, and even a measure of understanding of the predicament in which its communist leaders found themselves, or at least of the problems faced by the reformers. These Americans tended to point out that the memory of the Cold War (as it had been known in the 1950s and 1960s) was fading and that the fiasco surrounding the Holy Crown was becoming an anachronism. By the mid-1970s, a quarter of Hungarians had been born after 1956, and some American officials claimed – erroneously – that most of the Stalinists there had either already died or been dismissed. East-West relations had gone through a transformation, and, as the embassy pointed out, so had the American domestic scene. A younger generation of lawmakers would be able to reach a positive resolution for Budapest, just as they had done in helping the Romanians achieve most-favored-nation status. This did not escape the Hungarians' attention, thus they tried to make the best of it. Since the United States was running out of reasons to hold it back, the embassy recommended a re-evaluation of its policy regarding the Holy Crown.[194]

At the same time, American diplomats tried to convince the Hungarians not to launch a publicity campaign because the United States would likely refuse any deal that made them appear to bow to pressure applied by a "small Communist country." But as Kádár was still pushing the issue, the Hungarian Embassy in Washington continued to raise the question, making it harder and harder to believe that "silent diplomacy" could work. The embassy was told that a member of the House Foreign Relations Committee, Charles Hackett, had been asked by an unidentified member of President Carter's staff to prepare a memorandum recommending that the Holy Crown be returned.[195] Thus Hungarian pressure forced the president to deal with an internally sensitive and potentially harmful question, and ultimately to make the most important symbolic gesture toward Soviet-dominated Europe in the history of the Cold War to that point.

The Carter administration began to give serious thought to putting an end to the matter in accordance with the wishes of the leadership in Budapest. Returning the Holy Crown could underpin the administration's policies of constructing long-term relations between the West and Eastern Europe and of improving the lot of the population there. The administration also wanted to impede the Soviet Union's ability to exploit the region for hostile purposes.[196] The issue divided Congress, but supporters of returning the Holy Crown were numerically superior to and more influential than those who opposed it. Among the proponents was the author of the trade bill that had famously wrecked Nixon's policy of détente with the Soviets, Charles Vanik. In 1976, Vanik had promised deputy prime minister Gyula Szekér that he would ask the national security advisor to support the return of the Crown of Saint Stephen to the people of Hungary, but Brzezinski would not commit himself. He referred to the "extremely sensitive and controversial" nature of the topic and said only that he was ready to continue the dialogue.[197] His response was surely influenced by the view of the NSC staff, which held that the Holy Crown was the ultimate sign of legitimacy. In his memoirs, Brzezinski asserted that the restitution of the Holy Crown symbolized Carter's new policy toward Eastern Europe, but without specifying what that new policy might have been. Brzezinski recalled that he and Vance were ready to move ahead on this question, and although he was initially apprehensive about the potentially negative effects on voters of Eastern European descent, he soon gave in.[198] In reality, Brzezinski had delayed the return of the Holy Crown for as long as possible.

The State Department was committed to the idea by 1977. William Luers, the official responsible for European affairs, saw no point in withholding it. If there was nothing the Americans could do for Hungary, he opined, the least they could do was to give back its Holy Crown. This story points to a defect inherent in the use of sanctions: once introduced, they are hard to rescind.[199] The Holy Crown, Vance argued, should be returned in order to encourage "greater autonomy, national identity, and Western orientation in Eastern Europe." But it was also a reward. Vance praised Hungary's record: "The Communist regime in Hungary is a far cry from being democratic but over the past few years Hungary has developed into the most internally liberal country in the Warsaw Pact." There was a good deal of wishful thinking in the secretary's views on Hungary; he claimed that the Hungarian state was "tolerant" of dissidents, that church-state relations were "good," and that there was "an openness to Western information." Vance's claim that Kádár had successfully defended these liberal positions against Warsaw Pact hard-liners perpetuated the myth – carefully nurtured by the Hungarian leadership – that Kádár was the only leader who stood between Hungary and a restoration of Stalinism.[200]

This rosy picture may have stemmed from a convenient ignorance of the realities of the Hungarian political system, which made it easier to justify the course of action the State Department wanted to take.

The Carter administration referred to the Holy Crown as a "symbol of independence and Christian traditions," which implied that its return could be taken as an anti-Soviet measure. The administration, however, also suggested the opposite, "that this action recognizes the legitimacy of the Communist regime in Hungary."[201] Administration officials were also aware of this other interpretation of the Holy Crown's symbolic significance, one that underlined its status as "the ultimate symbol of power and legality." William Hyland of the NSC asserted that the Holy Crown was the "ultimate sign of legitimacy,"[202] lending credence to the opinion of many of his contemporaries who thought that Washington wished to legitimate communist rule in Hungary. The president noted in his diary that he had returned the Holy Crown "as a symbol of Hungary's sovereignty and an inspiration to those who cherished freedom."[203]

Importantly, former prime minister Ferenc Nagy, an influential figure among moderate Hungarian Americans, supported the return. As prime minister, he had rejected its return in 1946 but was now ready to send it home. Nagy had been supportive of the policy of peaceful engagement that had replaced the doctrine of liberation. He argued that no communist system could derive legitimacy from the Holy Crown since it had ceased to have any constitutional significance when the republic was proclaimed in 1946. Moreover, its return would not change the Hungarian people's misgivings toward their government.[204] News of the administration's deliberations soon leaked out, and in April 1977 Ohio congresswoman Mary Oakar and six Hungarians met with NSC staffers, who falsely indicated that they knew of "no intention to give back the Crown." William Hyland was concerned about the political damage the Holy Crown could do and asserted that it would gain the United States nothing with the Hungarians. The national security advisor retorted that there was no point in "timeless, negative commitments."[205]

The State Department found moral and political reasons to support a favorable outcome for Hungary. Bilateral relations had improved and Budapest had cooperated in the implementation of CSCE resolutions. In fact, American officials feared that the United States would be in a difficult situation at the forthcoming CSCE conference in Belgrade if they did not return the Holy Crown. The State Department also underestimated congressional and popular opposition to the measure.[206] Mudd gave the first indication to the Hungarians that the return of the coronation regalia was imminent, falsely claiming that the president had made up his mind and that only technicalities were left to work out.[207] In March, however, the Hungarian-American press carried an article by a high-level official at the State Department who claimed that the administration would not consider the return of the Holy Crown until bilateral relations improved. Hungarian diplomats immediately asked the State Department for an explanation[208] and Mudd retracted his earlier statement, claiming that the president's final decision would be made shortly.[209] Deputy secretary of state Arthur Hartman sought to alleviate the Hungarians' anxieties by suggesting that the American position had not changed for the worse, inaccurately asserting that the only outstanding issue was the modality of the transfer. Hartman's visit was intended as a survey of the conditions in Hungary and was completed to the satisfaction of the State Department.[210] On that same day, at Brzezinski's behest, the president's Policy Review Committee postponed the decision pending approval of new guidelines for Eastern Europe.[211] All this reveals a measure of confusion in the decision-making process. As they had been under Nixon and Kissinger, the State Department and the president's national security staff were pitted against each other. Yet this confusion also demonstrates that the matter involved more than just a transaction between Washington and an insignificant communist country. The possible ramifications of the return of the Holy Crown were thus deliberated at the highest levels of power.

Vanik appealed to Carter to make a positive decision,[212] while the U.S. diplomats in Budapest acted almost as advocates for the Hungarian Political Committee. They advised the leadership in Budapest that most émigré Hungarians opposed the transfer of the crown jewels, which would make it necessary for the administration to obtain the approval of the Hungarian churches.[213] Again, there was a significant disconnect between the State Department and the National Security Council. While the latter was still undecided about what to do, State Department officials went as far as pressuring the Hungarian government to take the steps they thought would lead to a quick resolution and the return of the Holy Crown. Not only did the U.S. Embassy in Budapest talk the Hungarian Foreign Ministry into pressuring Hungarian ecclesiastical leaders to write supportive letters to their American counterparts, an embassy official even approached the State Ecclesiastical Office to offer his opinion about the reasons the archbishop of Hungary might be reluctant to pen the requested letter.[214] The chief mover seems to have been Stephen Dachy, the American cultural attaché of Hungarian descent. The Hungarians described him as one of the most knowledgeable diplomats on the Hungarian domestic scene, and thus he must have known that the bishops were merely pawns, forced to do the bidding of the State Ecclesiastical Office, which was itself little more than a subsidiary of the powerful security establishment. Later, Ambassador Kaiser reported a "moving meeting" with Mindszenty's newly appointed successor as archbishop of Esztergom, László Lékai, who expressed his "whole-hearted support" for the president's decision to return the Holy Crown.[215] There was little else he could do, as the clergy was under the control of the authorities, who determined what precisely they could do and say.[216] Thus if Kaiser hoped to affirm that the State Department's course was the correct one, his "proof" was a sham.

As more and more individuals and organizations began to protest the decision, the State Department strongly recommended to the Hungarian leadership that Archbishop Lékai should communicate to the Council of American Churches that the return of the regalia would be "in the interest of the Hungarian people." Budapest suspected that the Americans' advice concealed an intention to return the Holy Crown to the Catholic Church,[217] so the State Ecclesiastical Office took the necessary steps to allow the archbishop to issue a statement. Hungarian desk officer Thomas Gerth now claimed that the return would take place pending presidential decision only. Although he downplayed the influence of the protesters, he admitted in Budapest that the Carter administration was not in a position to disregard them completely. Washington therefore required that the Holy Crown be made accessible to all who wished to see it and insisted that it was being returned to the "representatives of the Hungarian nation."[218]

While the secretary of state was arguing that Washington had no right to retain the Holy Crown, the NSC saw the dangers inherent in returning it. The decision was influenced partly by domestic affairs, as it remained to be seen whether the president would "take the heat on something that would infuriate some members of the Hungarian-American community." The issue would also have an impact on the way U.S. policy toward Eastern Europe was perceived. The return of the Holy Crown, the NSC argued, would be viewed as "something new," but it remains unclear what "new" was supposed to mean. Many "anti-communists would conclude" that the United States was "putting a seal of legitimacy on Kádár," and it was questionable whether doing so would encourage autonomy, as Vance had hoped. The NSC staff wanted to see the matter discussed within the framework of an overarching strategy toward Eastern Europe, deliberations they hoped would delay the decision.[219] Brzezinski accepted the argument: "since there is consideration about extending MFN to Hungary also returning the Crown would be a strong sign of our interest that could be seen as a shift of our overall East European policy." Carter accepted his position and told him "don't heat up now."[220] On June 15, 1977, the national security advisor informed Vance of the president's intention to delay the final decision pending a reconsideration of Eastern European strategy. He indicated that this delay was motivated by domestic considerations.[221]

A month later, on July 15, Carter convened a meeting of his key advisors at which the secretary of state's position prevailed. Carter gave the go-ahead for the return and the news soon leaked out to the Hungarians. The Hungarian Foreign Ministry learned through West German sources that Carter had informed Chancellor Helmut Schmidt that the crown jewels would be returned despite the domestic difficulties of doing so. Carter disclosed that his decision had been influenced by Kádár's advocacy of détente and that he was considering inviting the Hungarian party chief to Washington.[222] On July 26, Gerth returned to Budapest, where he disclosed that the Holy Crown problem was close to being resolved, though he could not say when it would happen. He also mentioned that Carter was considering inviting Kádár to visit the United States, a gesture Carter intended to reciprocate by traveling to Budapest.[223] Ambassador Ferenc Esztergályos, who was highly active in convincing lawmakers of the wisdom of returning the Holy Crown, learned that the visit to Washington was being planned for 1979.[224]

Vance wanted to complete the transaction before the opening of the CSCE conference in Belgrade in mid-September. The recently appointed ambassador to Budapest, Philip Kaiser, broke the good news to his hosts when the NSC launched a new counterattack. Starting with a jibe against their rivals, the NSC expressed doubts about whether the president had actually agreed to return the Holy Crown, suggesting that this notion was merely a "State impression." They reiterated that the return of the Holy Crown would be seen as a "major signal," not just a reward to the Hungarians. Brzezinski agreed with his staff that the move would be seen as a "much larger signal" than a simple favor to Hungary. He suggested that the move be "deliberate and well-timed," at which point Carter reversed himself and instructed his advisor to make "no commitment" on the Holy Crown. He now wished to query Budapest about its plans for displaying the artifact "if it is returned."[225]

The problem was that nobody told the new ambassador to Budapest that the pledge to return the Holy Crown had been taken back. Kaiser, a wealthy supporter of the Democratic Party, had been told to break the good news when he presented his credentials to the head of state, Pál Losonczi.[226] Losonczi, obviously eager to move ahead as fast as possible, actually received Kaiser earlier than planned, on precisely the same day Vance was informed of the negative turn of events. Although Kaiser repeatedly urged the president to approve the transfer, he got no answer,[227] and it was only well after the event that Kaiser was told about the president's decision to delay it. Kaiser was tasked with a sensitive mission: sound out the Hungarians about their plans for displaying the Holy Crown were they to get it back. He was not allowed to assume any responsibility for making this happen,[228] but Kaiser disingenuously told Deputy Foreign Minister Nagy that the decision-making process had "reached the final stages." He added that the reception of the regalia – at that stage still fictitious – would need to reflect the notion that it was being returned "by the American people to the Hungarian people."[229] This language, rooted in American political traditions, concealed the fact that the United States was lending legitimacy to the country's communist rulers, and by extension to its domination by the Soviet Union. Kaiser also told Nagy that domestic politics forced the United States to insist that the artifacts be exhibited publicly. In this conversation, Kaiser referred to opponents of the return of the Holy Crown as "neofascists."[230] Whether he meant what he said cannot be known, but this was the type of language his hosts understood.

By some accounts, the final decision was made on September 13 in the framework of presidential directive NSC-21, which prescribed that the historic artifact should be publicly displayed.[231] The return of the Holy Crown and the extension of MFN status were now closely linked, as this directive instructed the State Department to open commercial talks following a ceremonial transfer. Most-favored-nation status could be granted on the condition that Hungary declare its intention to abide by the terms of the Jackson-Vanik amendment regarding emigration. The news was broken to Foreign Minister Puja on October 1. The only issues left to be settled were the date and location of the transfer ceremony, but Vance asked Puja not to make the news public.[232]

On November 4, the anniversary of the Soviet invasion of 1956, the Carter administration officially announced its decision to return the crown jewels. The announcement had to be made on that sad date because congresswoman Mary Oakar, who had a large ethnic Hungarian constituency, got wind of the plan and chose to protest it that day in an open letter to the president.[233] The White House was flooded with letters. The American-Hungarian Federation unanimously passed a resolution that the Holy Crown "must not be returned to Hungary's present rulers," and the Polish-American Congress expressed similar sentiments. On the other hand, the Hungarian Baptist Union saw the Hungarian government's willingness to accept it as an indication of its independence and an acknowledgment of Christian tradition. The William Penn Fraternal Society also expressed its support.[234] Congressional hearings were held, but the talks on the particulars were already under way between Kaiser and Nagy.[235] President Carter's diary reveals that the final, irrevocable decision was made only on November 11: Carter "was the strongest to go ahead"; Vance and Brzezinski "nervously" agreed.[236]

On December 16, the two governments issued a joint communiqué. It did not contain the date of the ceremony, which the Hungarian government did not wish to disclose, presumably as a precaution to keep large, spontaneous crowds from showing up. The Americans insisted that the reception committee needed to reflect the fact that the "Hungarian people" were receiving the Holy Crown. This meant that anyone who wished to attend would have to be allowed to. The Political Committee therefore made sure that "an organized crowd" of two hundred people – all hand-selected party loyalists, including representatives of the major religious denominations – would attend the reception. Kádár showed diplomatic tact by not insisting on attending after Washington intimated that his presence was not desirable. It would have been an affront to American conservatives of Eastern European descent to hand this sacred artifact over to a communist ruler. On another level, though, Kádár's absence was absurd; the Holy Crown's return was a recognition of his political record. Moreover, the legitimacy of the Hungarian Communist Party rested on the assertion that it was the only legitimate representative of the people. Thus the absence of the party leader reveals a kind of schizophrenia in the American attitude toward the communist regimes of Eastern Europe. The Hungarians suggested that the party leader would be open to a meeting with Secretary Vance, but this offer was also quietly rejected.

The lack of trust between the two parties is suggested by the fact that the Americans continued to come up with new demands virtually up to the moment of the transfer. Ambassador Kaiser was embarrassed to have to convey to the Hungarians that they would need to offer assurances that the Holy Crown would not be transferred to Moscow.[237] This final wish demonstrates how Eastern European mindsets and power relationships were misconceived in Washington. Not even the most ardently Stalinist Hungarian would ever have voluntarily transferred such a historical symbol to Moscow, and if Moscow had wanted such an artifact – which they did not – they had the power to acquire it whether their Hungarian clients liked it or not.[238]

Ambassador Nagy protested, citing Hungarian self-esteem and telling the American ambassador that he would agree to a wording that asserted the Holy Crown would never be removed from the country. Although the two sides agreed that the media would be allowed to report freely on the event, correspondents working for RFE and for Hungarian émigré papers were not admitted into Hungary, the Politburo calling the latter "fascists." The Hungarian media received precise instructions for covering the event, which revealed that domestic liberalization had been limited in scope and that press freedoms were still subordinate to political concerns. The media was not allowed to lambaste the United States for the tardy return of the crown jewels, but it was not supposed to "exaggerate" its significance either. The Political Committee even prescribed the size of the space each daily paper would be allowed to devote to its coverage of the event.

Carter claimed to have returned the Holy Crown because of its "religious and national significance," and the ceremony seems to have vindicated his optimism that it would encourage national feeling, as the Hungarians present sang the *Szózat*, a nineteenth-century patriotic piece exhorting Hungarians to remain faithful to their homeland in life and death. In substance, little if anything would change, but Brzezinski, who had delayed the transfer, was gratified with its results. In Budapest, he observed that Hungarians still "showed respect for the revered symbol" and that the "average Hungarian seem[ed] to be pleased with the decision." Brzezinski, whom Hungarian propaganda portrayed as a ruthless enemy of détente and the Soviet Union, revealed that he accepted the communist system in Hungary on a permanent basis. He believed that returning the Holy Crown would have beneficial effects on bilateral relations and wanted to invite the Hungarian party leader to Washington.[239] Carter made this political gesture in the hope that "the presence of this treasured symbol will serve to strengthen the attachment of the Hungarian people to their Christian origins, to their cultural and historical heritage and above all, their national independence."[240] He seemed to have had no reservations, but rather to have acted "with a genuine sense of pride" in the hope that the decision would enhance "relations between our two governments" and thereby "contribute" to "peace and prosperity."[241] The reference here to the two governments, rather than to the two nations, is noteworthy. The two were now seen as one and the same, and thus Kádár's continued rule no longer necessarily precluded national independence.

Vance and his Hungarian counterpart, Puja, discussed the possible beneficial effects of the deal on bilateral relations. Puja emphasized détente and peaceful coexistence, terms that were already going out of style but that reflected Kádár's preferences. They could also be interpreted as a message to Washington from the Soviets, who were distressed at having to take a back seat to the Sino-American relationship, which was improving spectacularly. Puja made the unprecedented gesture of inviting Vance to Budapest for an official visit in the midst of rapidly deteriorating Soviet-American relations, suggesting that the linkage between Soviet-American and Hungarian-American relations was no longer automatic.

The return of the Holy Crown, as noted by the national security advisor, was regarded as a "major gesture" by Eastern Europeans and by the Soviets. It was a clear signal that despite other major differences in world politics and disarmament, Washington regarded the communist regime in Hungary as relatively legitimate and, by implication, the Soviet sphere of influence as acceptable. Still, the conditions Hungary accepted, including the obligation to let any Hungarian view the crown jewels, helped erode the foundations of its closed political system. The United States no longer prioritized the elimination of communism: Carter and his administration wanted to see Eastern Europeans enjoy less repressive political systems and longer leashes from Moscow, but this did not mean full democracy and a rollback of Soviet power.

The Holy Crown, the ancient symbol of legitimacy and power in Hungarian history, was returned as a reward for the policies of a man who had helped the Soviets put down the 1956 revolution, which held out the possibility that the Eastern European status quo was changing. Kádár was portrayed as a political asset who had "gained a large degree of acceptance among the political elite and the public, and Hungarians credit the government with having achieved substantial improvements in living standards, a relaxed cultural atmosphere, and political and economic stability over the years since 1956."[242] Stability and order had become the key issues in the wake of the havoc wrought by the revolution. It did not seem to matter that his government was undemocratic and that his limited economic reforms[243] were financed by Western credits, which were not only harder and harder to come by, but which were often squandered on ill-conceived investments, consumption, and support for "fraternal" political movements.

The implicit message conveyed by the return of the Holy Crown was amplified by the extension of most-favored-nation status, which took place after months of diplomatic and linguistic wrangling over the stipulations of the Jackson-Vanik amendment regarding emigration from Hungary. Before the congressional debate over Hungary's most-favored-nation status, the Carter administration pressured Budapest to settle six family unification cases, but the Interior Ministry decided to resolve only two of them. This did not influence the decision. Carter may have emphasized the role of human rights in foreign policy, but in 1977 Vance gave human rights a new definition that placed the protection of citizenship and political rights at the bottom of the list.[244]

Hungary's most-favored-nation status was to be reviewed and renewed each year, a formula meant to ensure compliance with American principles regarding emigration and human rights. Again, as Eisenhower had imagined it, trade became a weapon in the positive sense. The Hungarians wanted to make sure they did not lose their MFN status, but the human rights criteria for MFN status were not applied equally to each Eastern European state. Romania was abusing human rights in every way: in emigration, in its monitoring of its citizens, in its treatment of its national minorities, and in its practice of state-sponsored terror. And yet, as Romania was a quasi-ally and a thorn in the Soviet Union's side, the American administration and Congress were willing to turn a blind eye. In fact, Romania was deprived of its MFN status only after it lost favor in Washington in the late 1980s.

Prudently, the Carter administration made it clear that its contacts with the communist states of Eastern Europe, which would be dealt with on an individual basis, would not be held hostage by the state of U.S.-Soviet relations. As it turned out, primarily because of its financial dependence on the "capitalist world," Hungary would also decouple its relations with "capitalist states" from the relationship between Moscow and Washington. Washington expressed its desire to work with the communist states as sovereign entities while also honoring the realities of power within the region. Moreover, the State Department made it clear that the United States would not pursue "reckless, destabilizing policies" in order to change the European status quo. Instead, the United States would take into consideration European security concerns and the limits of American influence. It would, however, work to broaden its commercial and humanitarian contacts and to improve the flow of information. The practical implementation of this policy included extensions of most-favored-nation status to deserving countries including Poland, Romania, and Hungary.[245] Some people went overboard in supporting the Hungarian candidacy; congressman William Frenzel returned from Hungary in the belief that the country's leadership was committed to human rights.[246]

Washington's open recognition of the permanence of the Soviet sphere of influence did not change the fact that détente was breaking down. Although when he came to power Carter was unwilling to "ass-lick" the Chinese like Nixon before him, by 1978 Brzezinski had prevailed on the president to extend diplomatic recognition to China and improve relations.[247] Moscow claimed this was done to jeopardize détente. Washington, meanwhile, accused the Soviets of exploiting loopholes in the SALT I agreement in order to achieve superiority in the field of intercontinental ballistic missiles.

In July 1978, Averell Harriman, a veteran diplomat serving as Carter's special envoy for disarmament, arrived in Budapest to ask Kádár to mediate the arrangement of a Carter-Brezhnev summit. Harriman and Kádár had already had an impromptu meeting at the Luzhniki stadium in Moscow, and the Hungarian leader later openly recounted that he was pleasantly surprised to feel an affinity for the American diplomat, who could not have been more different from himself. Harriman was a well-educated tycoon, while Kádár came from proletarian stock, having grown up in great poverty and experiencing life from early childhood as a struggle between the working class and its exploiters. In 1963, their meeting had broken the ice between the two states, whose relations were then extraordinarily strained. Now this doyen of American diplomacy was asking Kádár to intervene in the crisis of confidence between Washington and Moscow. The State Department prepared a biography of the party leader for Harriman's visit, constructing a convenient image of Kádár as an admirable proponent of East-West coexistence and a liberal reformer who presided over a country where political and economic stability prevailed. No mention was made of his role in the 1956 revolution or the bloody reprisals he orchestrated afterward. Uncomfortable facts were also omitted from the portrait the State Department prepared of Harriman's other destination, Ceaușescu's Romania. This particular State Department briefing descended to the depths of disinformation in its praise for Romania's nationality policies. Harriman celebrated his host's leadership and standing in the world as a respectable statesman, as well as Hungary's stance as "a loyal ally" of the USSR that had managed to maintain good contacts with the Western world. In language reminiscent of nineteenth-century formulations about "national death" (*nemzethalál*), Kádár reiterated the dangers of nuclear war and expressed his frustration with the narrow-mindedness of the Soviet leadership. And although the Hungarian leader rejected a "mediating role," he immediately forwarded Harriman's message to Moscow.[248]

Although in the aftermath of 1956, few European states and few European leaders were more anti-American than Hungary and Kádár, the situation had changed dramatically by the late 1970s. Driven by economic necessity and possibly even a changed perception of America's role in the world – and perhaps envious of the international prestige Romania had achieved – the Hungarian leader was eager to visit America. Puja broached the subject of Kádár's visit with Vance when they met in Budapest, and Brzezinski was receptive to the idea. Ambassador Kaiser considered Kádár a suitable candidate for mediating between Washington and Moscow and intimated to the party leadership that Kádár would be invited to the United States.[249] The question was in fact being discussed. When Senator Abraham Ribicoff visited Budapest, he was "very impressed" with the Hungarian first secretary and wondered why he had not been invited to Washington. Domestic political considerations were among the causes, as Kádár, despite his "policy of skillful gradualism," was still a divisive figure in the Hungarian American community. Because of this and the "turmoil caused by the return of the Crown," it was decided to "delay the visit" until after the election of 1980.[250] Thus an upper-level functionary of the Hungarian Socialist Workers Party (HSWP), János Berecz, was told in Washington that bilateral relations would be improved step by step and that high-level visits would have to wait.[251]

In the Foreign Ministry's triumphalist appraisal, Hungarian-American relations were "normalized" in 1978 and all that was left to do was to raise contacts to a "higher level," an obvious reference to the party leader's expected visit to Washington. But there were also ominous signs. The ministry's annual report indicated that although the Carter administration's aims had not changed, Soviet-American relations were deteriorating.[252] The United States made it clear that the "difficulties" in America's relations with the Soviets would not affect Washington's position toward the socialist states. On the other hand, the Soviet leadership was well aware that their allies were beginning to open independent lines of communication with the United States. Brezhnev sent a message to Budapest that was hard to misunderstand. He told Kádár that Washington was in the business of "Romanianizing" the socialist countries. He also claimed that NATO had "accepted long-term plans to undermine the socialist countries," though he did not reveal the source of this information. Referring to Hungary's attempts to join the International Monetary Fund (IMF), Brezhnev, who realized that Budapest was making political concessions for economic gains, issued a warning: "Nowadays there is a lot of talk about the IMF and the World Bank. American policies prevail in these organizations." Brezhnev declared, "The question of our unity is not a question of a *pud* of iron but a serious political task."[253] Although East-West relations were relapsing into the Cold War, this process did not devastate Hungary's relations with the Western world as it might have earlier. This fact, however, had little to do with political or ideological preferences. Hungary's financial survival now depended on Western loans, thus Budapest could boost exports to the capitalist world, irrespective of geographical distances.[254] Hungary had emerged as one of Washington's most important regional partners and was fast becoming the showcase of Eastern Europe, a role Moscow had previously given to Czechoslovakia.[255] And despite Hungary's disagreements with Romania, the two now shared at least one common trait: the onset of a new Cold War would jeopardize the relative autonomy they had achieved.

9

"Love Toward Kádár":
Reagan and the Myth of Liberation

Even though the United States had finally accepted the division of the continent on a permanent basis – and was not particularly secretive about having done so – the years of détente were coming to an end. Each side was accusing the other of violating the terms of the SALT I treaty. The Soviet Union may have been exploiting loopholes in the agreement to build superiority in the field of strategic nuclear missiles.[1] In fact, confidence between the two superpowers or indeed the two military alliances had never really taken hold. Security, as Churchill once put it, remained the "sturdy child of terror." While Moscow deplored American forward-based systems and wanted to get rid of them, NATO regarded them as essential to security in the light of the Soviets' conventional superiority in central Europe. In addition, the U.S. Senate failed to ratify the second SALT agreement. Rivalry in Africa intensified as the Soviets saw opportunities to draw a number of African countries into their ideological and political orbit. Moscow stepped up military aid to the continent, sending more than $40 billion there between 1978 and 1984.[2] Following the Cubans' lead, the Soviets perceived a revolutionary situation in Central America and began to support rebels in Nicaragua. The final blow to the dying détente was Brezhnev's decision to invade Afghanistan, which may have been due in part to a decision by NATO in December 1979 to deploy intermediate-range nuclear missiles in Europe.[3] As the historian Melvyn Leffler has argued, "When they made their decision to intervene in Afghanistan, Soviet leaders saw threat, not opportunity. The US and its NATO allies had just resolved to deploy new nuclear forces in Europe. This decision, in the Kremlin's view, jeopardized the principle of equal security on which détente was premised. . . . Feeling vulnerable, Brezhnev and his colleagues decided to take no chances in Afghanistan."[4] The NATO decision, however, was not consciously made to destroy détente. In fact, the decision emerged from "a complex multilayered negotiation process in which domestic, bureaucratic, institutional, and alliance politics intersected with increasingly adversarial Cold War circumstances." In fact, a "rather unenthusiastic U.S. administration had to be urged by the Europeans to respond firmly to Soviet nuclear politics."[5] The Soviet leadership initially rejected direct military intervention in Afghanistan, where a communist coup had driven a wedge between Iran and Pakistan. It was feared that Afghanistan could become the Soviets' Vietnam, which seems to be precisely what Washington wanted. Due at least in part to misinformation from U.S. sources that the Afghan ruler Hafizullah Amin was ready to reorient his policies toward the United States, the Soviet Political Committee decided to send troops in December 1979. By some accounts, Carter's national security advisor was jubilant.[6] Carter nevertheless condemned the Soviet intervention and warned them, "Unless you draw back from your present course of action, this will inevitably jeopardize the course of US-Soviet relations throughout the world."[7] Both sides were exaggerating the danger the other posed in world politics.

The fateful NATO and Soviet decisions to deploy a new generation of intermediate-range nuclear missiles in Europe raised the specter of limited atomic war there. The Soviets' decision, which stemmed from a perception of their own weakness, was made in complete secrecy; not even Soviet intelligence was informed. This was due to the influence of the Soviet military-industrial complex and their allies in the Foreign Ministry, including Andrei Gromyko; Brezhnev's influence on decision making had fatally weakened. The Soviet general staff had begun to contemplate the possibility of a limited war in 1979, and although Brezhnev was open to the idea of limiting the deployment to the number of older-generation missiles they replaced, he was unable to persuade Gromyko.[8] It was only in 1979 that Washington began to take these measures seriously and decided to deploy Pershing II and cruise missiles to Europe.

Brzezinski's pro-China line prevailed over Vance's preference for détente with the Soviets. Carter was being criticized from the right, so his reaction to the invasion of Afghanistan was firm: any attack on a nation in the Persian Gulf region would be treated as an attack on the United States itself. He increased the U.S. military budget and approved the construction of a new, mobile intercontinental missile system. This wasn't enough for his opposition, which accused the president of underestimating the communist threat and pursuing policies that encouraged Soviet aggression.[9]

Thus the policy of relaxing tensions and limiting competition to the sphere of ideology reached a dead end. Perhaps it was an illusion to think that the war of words dubbed an "ideological struggle" could have replaced intensive competition in the harder components of power. Words and ideology did reflect ambitions in the real sphere. Communist ideology predicted the triumph of socialism, and thus the communist propaganda war for the hearts and minds of men would have been meaningless without the victory of socialism as a political system. Peaceful coexistence and the thaw between the two world orders rested on their mutual consent to a sacrosanct postwar order in Europe. Change in the status of the states overrun by the Soviet Union in 1944–45 would happen in the distant future, if ever. More importantly, East Central Europe no longer made a difference in relations between the Soviet Union and the West. Western rhetoric supported the cause of freedom and national self-determination in the Soviet world, but détente required that behind closed doors the West underwrite the permanence of Europe's immoral divide.

While Moscow was undertaking commitments to support Soviet-type socialism outside the Soviet zone, its empire in Eastern Europe came under threat in Poland. Nationwide strikes on August 28, 1980, prompted the Soviet Ministry of Defense to contemplate military intervention, but the political leadership stopped short and organized only a show of force. Eventually the Polish leadership, which sought Moscow's military help in vain, took the Soviets' counsel and declared martial law in December.[10] President Reagan's reaction was telling: he saw the chance of a lifetime in the Polish revolution against "this damned force."

The new president got rid of his predecessor's punitive economic measures, which he deemed inimical to America's interests. Nevertheless,

East-West relations relapsed into a new era of hostility. Recent research has shown that Reagan's rhetoric was harsher than his real intentions toward the Soviet Union. Publicly, he called the Soviet Union an "evil empire," but in his second term he sought nuclear disarmament and a modus vivendi with the Soviets based on "realism, strength and dialogue."[11] On January 17, 1983, Reagan signed National Security Defense Directive 75, which committed the United States to checking and even reversing Soviet expansionism. Yet Reagan's policy toward the Soviet bloc remained cautious. In fact, nothing transformative was expected in the short term.[12] Although Reagan abhorred the communist system, he was more than ready to reach out to Soviet leaders behind the scenes in the hope of reaching an agreement that might avert a nuclear war, which Reagan was aware no one could win. When interviewed by the author in 2008, Reagan's confidant and advisor on Eastern Europe, deputy secretary of state John Whitehead, claimed that the president had harbored absolutely no intention of detaching the states of Eastern Europe from the Soviet Union.[13] President Reagan was more concerned with arms control discussions with Gorbachev than with substantive proposals to reshape central and Eastern Europe. As for the German question, Reagan's assistant secretary of state for European and Canadian affairs, Rozanne Ridgway, summed up the administration's position by arguing that the existing situation was stable and a source of peace and that renewed debate over the unification of Germany would be premature and unwise.[14] The Reagan administration preserved unchanged American policies on European balance that had been in place since the 1970s.

In 1982, the administration affirmed that Soviet bloc states could count on U.S. support for internal liberalization and more autonomous foreign policy. In 1983, Reagan's vice president, George H. W. Bush, toured Yugoslavia, Romania, and Hungary, the countries that had strayed furthest from the Soviet Union in one form or another. In Budapest, he reassured his hosts that the Reagan administration had no intention of disrupting the Soviet bloc, and in a highly publicized speech after the tour, Bush declared that Washington would support movement toward humanitarian or democratic ideals without hoping to destabilize any other country. To the consternation of the Hungarian leadership, Bush announced a policy of differentiation in the same speech. Closer political, economic, and cultural relations would be nurtured with countries like Hungary and Romania, which had demonstrated a higher level of openness and independence. The increasingly terroristic Romanian regime remained at the top of Washington's Eastern European pecking order, particularly in light of the fact that Poland had lost its most-favored-nation (MFN) status when Wojciech Jaruzelski declared a state of emergency. Even though Congress was increasingly skeptical about Romania's most-favored-nation status, given Bucharest's poor human rights record, Reagan extended it even as late as 1987. The State Department explained that the Jackson-Vanik amendment referred to emigration – which obligations Bucharest had fulfilled – and not to the freedom of religion, minority rights, or any other aspect of human rights. It was also argued that MFN status was the United States's only leverage on Romanian policy.[15] In fact, they had none.

A NEW CHAPTER IN HUNGARIAN-AMERICAN RELATIONS

The freeze in relations between the superpowers did not lead to the usual pattern of renewed Hungarian hostility toward the United States. Budapest hoped to weather the storm and retain its ties to Washington despite Soviet disapproval. Kádár understood that the Soviets were not beyond reproach. In Moscow, hopes of spreading Soviet-style socialism apparently did not disappear. Boris Ponomarev and Yuri Andropov may have thought that some states, such as Italy, were ripe for a socialist revolution.[16] This was not an illusion shared by Kádár, who was interested in the preservation of the status quo between capitalism and socialism, and in precluding a nuclear war, which he thought would destroy civilization. It was not that he was less of a communist than his colleagues in Moscow, only that he was more realistic than most of them. In 1981, he counseled the Polish leadership that there could be no clemency against class enemies: "The laws of humanitarianism are suspended against them."[17] At the same time, the aging party leader also feared Moscow's reaction. Hungary was struggling with a debt crisis and the lifeline for the government's policy of reconciliation was an uninterrupted flow of Western credit. If the regime wanted to survive, relations with the Western world had to be preserved whether the Soviets liked it or not. In fact, Western loans were helping sustain the stability of the Soviet Union's sphere of influence in East Central

Europe. By 1978, Hungary's net debt was twice the size of its exports in convertible currency. This growing debt was threatening Hungary with a dramatic reduction of imports, which would in turn lead to a marked decline in its standard of living. The government, whose power depended largely on constant improvement in the standard of living (whether the economy was growing or not), could not afford an economic setback. Although in 1984 the leadership adopted a program of austerity, this policy was soon discarded. If the standard of living was to be sustained in spite of sluggish growth, the only political option was to take more loans and thereby further increase the regime's dependence on the West. As the Political Committee put it, "If for whatever reason we do not get loans the economy will be a grave situation."[18] In the working-class district of Csepel someone placed a tiny coffin at the foot of Lenin's statue with the inscription "here lies socialism." The government was forced to implement the steepest price hike since the 1950s, thus violating the holy principle of socialism: price stability. Kádár's regime was in dire economic straits.

As a result, Budapest was prepared to strengthen its economic ties with the "capitalist" world even though some reformers continued to delude themselves by claiming that this would not lead to political dependence. The Soviet prime minister, Alexei Kosygin, thought otherwise and warned his Hungarian counterpart that the International Monetary Fund (IMF) was a political institution controlled by the Americans and exerted political control on those that it grasped in its "claws."[19] By 1978 Hungary was among the most indebted Soviet bloc states after Bulgaria and Poland, and the country's dependence on "capitalist loans" had reached a critical level. In 1979, the Hungarian leadership conducted talks for membership in the World Bank and the IMF even though joining would require a level of economic transparency the secretive communist states were reluctant to assume. The alternative was to reduce the standard of living, which left the Politburo no other choice. Eventually the talks were halted because of a Soviet veto. As Brezhnev put it critically, the Hungarians were consuming more than they produced. Apart from a brief period in 1979–1980, the situation worsened, and by 1982 the country was on the verge of bankruptcy. This prompted the party leadership to plunge into the abyss and join the IMF, apparently without explicit Soviet approval. The financial crisis had to be avoided, because "Hungary would then hand itself over to the West." Brezhnev offered a long-term credit of one billion rubles, but the pledge remained unfulfilled.[20] In response to this financial crisis, the party discussed a liberalization of private initiative in the service sector in 1980, as well as the introduction of austerity measures. The debt crisis, which was exacerbated by the second "oil shock" and a series of negative events in world politics, was clearly eroding the political system. In the new environment it was harder and harder to borrow at a time when foreign loans were the country's lifeline to survival. In September 1981, the Political Committee saw no other possibility for averting a collapse than to seek membership in the IMF, even if the Soviets disapproved. The application was announced on November 4, twenty-five years to the day after the Soviet invasion of 1956. Prime minister György Lázár informed his Soviet counterpart Nikolai Tikhonov only two days in advance. Since the Soviets effectively refused any support for the ailing economies of Eastern Europe, there was nowhere else to go. Hungarian hopes for a closer relationship with the European Economic Community (EEC), which they had raised in Bonn, had been dashed by the West German chancellor.

Hungary's move toward membership in the IMF while the Soviet Union was locked in political combat with the United States was motivated by the imperative to survive. President Carter's economic sanctions had exacerbated tensions within the Soviet bloc. In 1980, Eastern European leaders told their counterparts in Moscow that they could not afford to sever economic relations with the West.[21] Hungary's concerns were augmented by the crisis in Poland. Kádár was angry at the Polish leadership and baffled by the rise of the Solidarity movement. Nevertheless, he tried to convince Brezhnev not to intervene there.[22]

The Soviet world was changing fundamentally. The deputy head of the Central Committee's Department of International Affairs, Gyula Horn, explained Hungary's predicament in Washington in January 1980. State Department officials reaffirmed that Hungary's MFN status depended on its stance toward the United States.[23] At this point the Soviet leadership, which was surprised by the vehement reaction to its deployment of SS-20 missiles, instructed Hungary, Czechoslovakia, and the German Democratic Republic (GDR) to cancel impending high-level meetings with Western leaders. For Hungary this involved the cancellation of Foreign Minister Puja's visit to Bonn and that of a group of Hungarian MPs to Washington.[24] In a dramatic meeting of the Political Committee in which Kádár conjured the threat of a Soviet invasion, the Soviet ultimatum was accepted. The party first secretary was nevertheless able to convince the Kremlin not to force Hungary to freeze its relations with the West.[25] Bilateral relations suffered only a temporary setback. Secretary of State George Schultz was expected in Budapest, but at Kádár's recommendation his trip was canceled, even though the party leader had originally supported it. In these changing political circumstances he could not take the risk. What would happen, he asked, if Schultz were to "launch into a tirade against the Soviet Union here in Budapest and lambast its 'hegemonistic policies' or whatever the heck they call it?" He argued, "There is no way we can put a muzzle on the mouth of somebody like this."[26] Nevertheless, Kádár supported normalized relations; a return to open hostility was inconceivable.

Reflecting in 1984 on the experiences of the previous few years, the Hungarian Foreign Ministry noted that "our relations with the United States have shown an opposite movement in comparison with East-West relations: even though this relationship has still not reached the level some socialist states have already achieved with the Americans." The ambassador in Washington, Vencel Házi, noted that despite the deterioration of the "international atmosphere," "we were able to preserve the gains achieved in our bilateral relations." This language was wholly different from the way Hungarian officials had spoken about Americans before. This did not of course mean a turning away from the Soviet bloc. The basis of the good relationship, according to the Hungarians, was that the United States had accepted "our political order and system of alliance."[27] The Hungarian-American commercial treaty had increased the country's "maneuvering space on capitalist money markets and with multinational companies."[28] More openness consolidated the political system, or so it seemed. When in 1983 Bush mentioned preferential treatment in Vienna, Kádár reminded him of the political realities in Budapest. The "God-damned" Americans talked about differentiation, he fumed, which concealed their anti-Soviet intentions. Hungary, he declared, was a member of the Warsaw Pact and "the Soviet Union's ally and this will not change."[29] Occasionally the Soviets had to remind the Hungarians of this as well. In October of 1983, a high-level party functionary responsible for foreign affairs delivered a speech which prompted the ailing Andropov to express his "incomprehension and distress" to Kádár.[30] As the sole "respectable" Eastern European leader during the frosty period in which Soviet-American hostilities were renewed, Kádár received a host of Western leaders in the first half of 1984: Bettino Craxi, Helmut Kohl, and Margaret Thatcher.

Kádár was concerned about the deterioration of Soviet-American relations, and Budapest was inclined to mediate between Washington and Moscow. The ambassador in Washington reported that the State Department regarded Hungary as "the most suitable medium" through which they could send messages to the Soviets, and the Hungarians' positions were read as if they could be attributed to the Soviets.[31] There is no way of knowing what the basis for this information was. When Deputy Foreign Minister Nagy visited Washington in 1984 as talks on intermediate-range missiles were being resuscitated, he was told that such visits were of great importance to East-West relations and that similar channels needed to be left open.[32] It is true that the Hungarian party leader knew Andropov from the former KGB chief's days as ambassador in Budapest; Kádár regarded Andropov as his friend and even considered him a "conservative reformer like himself."[33] Perhaps it was because of the leaders' personal relationship that State Department officials regarded a visit to Washington by a high-level Hungarian functionary as being "of outstanding significance regarding East-West relations."[34] During his visit to Budapest as head of the U.S. delegation that negotiated with the Soviets on nuclear arms in Geneva, Max Kampelman told his Hungarian interlocutors that Hungary could play a unique role in the normalization of U.S.-Soviet relations, helping to bridge the communication gap between the two countries whose relations were "at a low point" that precluded the possibility of bridging the gap directly. Hence Hungary could make a large contribution to "peace and security."[35] Even so, Kádár would not become a second Ceaușescu. Budapest boycotted the Los Angeles Olympics. Hungarian television was allowed one hour a day to report on the event, but the public was not supposed to get overexcited. An illustrated book authored by a journalist who attended the Olympics was meant to fill in the information gaps left by these brief summaries of events, but the Political Committee banned the book and ordered the already printed copies to be destroyed, even though the projected sales suggested that it would be a lucrative enterprise.

"DISTASTEFUL, ANTI-SEMITIC, AND RACIST":
AMERICAN CULTURAL PENETRATION

In spite of the disappointment of 1956, the United States enjoyed a positive image in Hungary. The Political Committee noted that "the majority of the population treated the U.S. with naïveté and idealized the American way of life."[36] Despite anti-American propaganda, even some of Hungary's leaders began to form a more positive picture. After his visit overseas, the agricultural minister Pál Romány thought Hungary should adopt many aspects of American agricultural production. He was impressed by the high level of agricultural technology and the farmers' attitude toward work: "Children – the future farmers – are consciously raised for work and the love of agriculture," which enjoyed high social standing and high productivity.[37] The Hungarians were now interested in gaining unbiased, firsthand knowledge regarding relevant political and social issues. Already in 1970, IREX had arranged for the visit of four experts who were interested in issues such as the sociological effects of technological development in agriculture, the changing lives of farmers, and the effects of urban migration.[38]

The country's leadership wanted to steer clear of a spectacular American presence. At the same time, the United States lacked a clear commitment to and strategy for cultural penetration. The Hungarians refused to open an American cultural center even though the Soviets had accepted a "large and ostentatious" center. An American library was opened in Bucharest in 1972 and had had four thousand visitors in its first year. The U.S. Information Center, on the other hand, was reported to be poorly located, unfriendly, and overcrowded. The American ambassador to Hungary suggested that the American presence in Budapest reach the level of at least the French or the Italian. He wanted to invest in books on American Studies, English-language instruction, movie screenings, and scientific programs to be held in a new building.[39] Since potential visitors to the American library knew they would be recorded and monitored by the state security services, it is unlikely that even better facilities would have attracted larger numbers of people.

Even in the 1980s, when the regime was seeking economic favors, the West and the United States continued to be the enemy world in Hungarian propaganda. The state trading company responsible for toys "mistakenly" distributed toys with the inscription "US Army," and when party headquarters found out the company was instructed to withdraw the toys without delay.[40] The party also prescribed rules for cultural policy. The invitation of American jazz bands was not prohibited but not encouraged either. Crime fiction was a popular genre, but French and Scandinavian authors were given preference over British and Americans.

American literature still made an impact. According to literary historian István Bart, two collections of American short stories inspired two generations of Hungarian writers. The first, published in 1967, gave shape to "the rebellious sentiments of Hungarian youth." The second, which saw light in 1982, was "the first appearance of post-modern literature." In 1977, Hungarian authorities allowed the publication of Bernard Malamud's *The Tenants* even though the book's reviewer claimed that the novel "was exceedingly, brutal, uncouth, its language dirty, in places bordering on the distasteful . . . individual sentences could add up to a collection of anti-Semitic and racist texts."[41] Nevertheless, in 1978, thirty-eight American authors were published in print runs that reached almost 1.8 million copies.[42] In 1976, translations from English amounted to 70 to 80 percent of those from the Russian language. The year after that was a turning point: for the first time, more translations were made from English than from Russian. In 1984, Hungarians published twice as many British and American works as Soviet or Russian, and by 1990 the latter amounted to only 17 percent of the former. Up to that point, more English authors were translated than American, but in the year of the first free elections, twice as many American writings were made available to readers as were English.[43] The Czechoslovak public read Steinbeck, Faulkner, Arthur Miller, Tennessee Williams, and Carson McCullers, even Kerouac and Ginsberg.[44] The Hungarian selection was similar.

György Aczél, the country's cultural czar, did not think there was any cause for concern when it came to expanding contacts of a political nature or in the social sciences, as Hungarian experts could help "subvert" the United States.[45] The potential of the two countries, however, was not equal. In 1978, Hungarian movie theaters screened nineteen American pictures, while only two Hungarian films were shown in the United States. The Liszt Ferenc Chamber Music Ensemble toured the United States, as did the Hungarian Ensemble and the Hungarian Radio Orchestra, along with ten Hungarian music instructors, who were sent to teach the Kodály method, hardly the sorts who might subvert the American political system. In order for these exchanges to work, the Hungarians were forced to accept American visitors. The dilemmas and the bureaucratic tangles associated with cultural exchanges in communist states are well illustrated by the following example.

In 1970, the dance and music department of the Ministry of Culture proposed inviting the Count Basie jazz ensemble to Hungary. Soon, however, Basie's visit was engulfed by communist politics and bureaucratic struggles. The Travel Committee of the Ministry of Culture approved the proposal and sent it along to the Institute of Cultural Affairs, which also approved. Basie's visit was already being advertised as the greatest event of the year in Hungarian popular music when the proposal was forwarded to the Ministry of Foreign Affairs, which had some concerns. The American desk officer, János Bartha, asserted that according to "the appropriate resolution made at a higher level, we do not find it expedient to invite larger American orchestras and we oppose pop groups. From the foreign policy perspective, we have nothing against the visit of the Count Basie ensemble. Since, however, the mentioned higher organs usually oppose the invitation and propagation of large American groups, before we make the final decision we deem it essential to ask for the approval of comrade Aczél."[46]

America played a prominent role in Hungary's cultural and scientific exchanges with the Western world. In terms of the number of people involved, it was the second most important partner; it was also the destination where Hungarians spent the greatest amount of time abroad. In the mid-1980s, as many as forty American books were published a year in print runs totaling 2.1 to 3.4 million copies, in a nation of less than eleven million people. Cinemas showed twenty-five to thirty American movies per year and television enthusiasts were able to enjoy an average of one hundred programs from the United States each year, including *The Flintstones*.

The imbalance was enormous, as only a handful of Hungarian authors were published for the American audience, usually selling two or three thousand copies, while an average of only two movies a year were sold to the United States. The Foreign Ministry complained that the Americans refused to take the principle of mutuality into account. The flow of human traffic, however, was more balanced, with a hundred thousand Americans visiting Hungary each year and seven thousand Hungarians embarking on the trip to the United States.[47]

These visits did not always increase the two countries' popularity. One American who was visiting his family complained about the arduous procedure of registering with the authorities. His complaint was overheard by a police officer, who remarked, "You needn't come home." Leftover forints could not be changed back into dollars, and visitors were often forced to wait for hours before being allowed to cross the border, which they often blamed on the country's political system. One visitor complained that his bus was forced to wait at the border for thirteen hours.[48]

Sometimes firsthand experience of the United States could have an adverse effect on the Americans' image. The Hungarian Ministry of Agriculture signed an agreement with a U.S. foundation to send students to study agricultural technology. The purpose of the agreement was to "contribute to a mutual cultural understanding and friendship between Hungarians and Americans ... to get to know each other's culture, customs, economy and politics, history and traditions."[49] The actual experience, though, had little to do with these noble objectives. Graduates of the agricultural university were sent to remote, "second-rate" American farms, "far removed from cultural life," and were made to perform hard physical labor. Some of the grantees claimed that the conditions were "humiliating."[50] Their negative experiences of this exchange program were brought up even in the Political Committee.

Still, trade and economic relations continued to intensify. In 1978, Hungary's exports to the United States increased by 43 percent over the previous year. Its deficit was still high: Hungarian exports accounted for just $83 million out of the $237 million worth of commodities exchanged between the two states. Minister of Foreign Trade József Bíró noted, "I wish we had enough goods to sell."[51] As a result of the MFN treaty, bilateral trade doubled between 1977 and 1980. By 1980, eighty-two Hungarian-American economic agreements had come into force, half of them in the field of machine industry. The three U.S.-Hungarian joint venture companies included a cooperative enterprise involving Tungsram and its precommunist parent company, General Electric. There were also three independent Hungarian companies in the United States and four American ventures operating in Hungary, including one belonging to the pharmaceutical giant Eli Lilly. The United States was seen as a potential alternative to the more protectionist EEC.[52]

While the new Cold War was escalating between East and West, a momentous breakthrough in the penetration of the Iron Curtain occurred in 1983, largely unnoticed at the time. George Soros, the Hungarian-born financier and philanthropist, approached the Hungarian Embassy with an offer to establish a cultural exchange program. Soros wanted to establish a foundation "that could coexist with the Communists, while undermining their system."[53] He offered a significant amount of money for the development of the Hungarian economy, society, and sciences, including support for the purchase of books and equipment and financing for scholarships and study abroad programs. Soros's offer was welcomed from the outset even though it was regarded as a security challenge. The positive response was no doubt motivated by the lack of funds that had forced the country to open up to the West in the first place. The Ministry of Foreign Affairs consulted the head of the counterintelligence services, János Bogye, who saw an opportunity in Soros's offer. He hoped to use Soros's funds for propaganda activities in the Western world, including the dissemination of Hungarian films. An apparatus, he wrote, "which is capable of converting Hungarian film and video materials into the NTSC system costs 130,000 dollars. Perhaps we could also buy a video camera."[54] As far as the money was concerned, the Hungarians' expectations were met. Soros's funds provided financing for "areas of cultural and scientific life which in the current financial situation would not otherwise have received hard currency or even forints."[55]

Soros traveled to Budapest to discuss his plans in October 1983. He did not conceal the fact that he wanted to contribute to the creation of a Hungary "which he would not want to emigrate from." Soros offered $1 million per annum with the requirement that the Hungarians match his offer and the proviso that he reserved the right to reduce the amount. Soros, who at the age of ten had offered all his pocket money to help the Finns in their defense against Soviet aggression, now insisted on conditions that challenged the centralized, party-controlled political system. He wanted the two foundations in Budapest and New York to be established with an organizational structure in which foreigners and independent Hungarians would play a role in awarding support and scholarships.[56] The Hungarians accepted Soros's program, even though they refused to officially sanction the Fulbright exchange program that same year even though several Hungarian intellectuals were able to visit the United States with Fulbright support in the 1980s.[57]

In 1985, Soros's program spent $1.5 million on purchases including books, medical instruments, and printing presses, as well as on funding archaeological research in Egypt. Not all of its activities were innocent. The Hungarian-born American billionaire was allegedly "supporting programs in the United States which aimed explicitly at supporting opposition circles in Hungary." In the view of the Hungarian Embassy in Washington, the Soros-financed Open Society Fund "invited to the United States exclusively personalities who are involved in oppositional-hostile activities or who were in close contact with such circles."[58] The American Embassy in Budapest intervened with the Hungarian authorities to expedite the exit visas. Soros's bold program was pushing the limits of the political system, and although the government could have terminated it, the "soft" dictatorship took the risk in the hope that it could keep the outcome under control. Soros's activities were tolerated even though it was understood that his aim in Hungary was "to develop western-style liberal thinking and to relax the 'closedness' of the system," which was "obviously not in line" with Hungary's "aspirations." The Political Committee's worst fears were confirmed by the fact that members of a homegrown opposition – which began to appear in an organized form in 1985 – were receiving support. Nonetheless, the cooperation was deemed worthwhile because Soros's funds help sustain scientific and cultural life.[59]

Washington showed understanding regarding Hungarian difficulties. In 1981, deputy secretary of state Lawrence Eagleburger told his hosts in Budapest that the United States sympathized with Hungarian efforts. Eagleburger publicly advocated his government's differentiating between countries such as Yugoslavia and Hungary, which had liberalized their economies, and the hard-liners of the Soviet bloc. He declared that differential treatment would make itself felt in the U.S. disposition toward trade relations with Hungary, which would be treated as "liberally as possible" in the field of export controls. This message was particularly important for a Hungarian economy that was struggling with outdated technology. Eagleburger reassured his hosts that the "U.S. had no desire to change the perspectives of Hungarian foreign policy." As his "private view," he told the head of the Central Committee's Foreign Relations Department, János Berecz, that alongside NATO he regarded the "Warsaw Pact as a pillar of European stability." Eagleburger also delivered a letter from secretary of state Alexander Haig to foreign minister Frigyes Puja, a Soviet loyalist. Haig was one of President Reagan's chief advisors on foreign policy; along with secretary of defense Caspar Weinberger and CIA director William Casey, he was considered a hard-line hawk who shared the president's desire to establish U.S. military superiority. The tone of his letter, however, was accommodating and suggested, like Eagleburger's statements, that the Reagan administration had no desire to change the status quo in Europe. Haig praised the Hungarians' position on Poland, which was that Poland's problems were to be solved by the Polish people. And in what could be interpreted as a message to Moscow, Haig asserted that the U.S. position rested on the principle of nonintervention in Poland's domestic affairs. The secretary expressed his satisfaction with bilateral relations and expressed his hope that these would continue to develop.[60] In his response, Puja asserted that Hungary ascribed great significance to Soviet-American relations. Puja also signaled that in spite of its insignificance in world politics and its loyalty to the alliance system of which it was a member, Hungary was prepared to "contribute positively" to international cooperation.

THE MYTH OF LIBERATION

Before Ronald Reagan became president, he asserted that his policy toward the Soviet Union was simple: "We win and they lose." National Security Defense Directive 32 committed the United States to exert what pressure it could to weaken the Soviet Union's economy and to ally itself with the dissident forces of the Soviet bloc.[61] Yet victory would not mean rolling the Soviets back from their sphere of influence in Eastern Europe. Reagan regarded the state of emergency in Poland as a personal affront and forced his allies to embargo the Urengoy–Western Europe pipeline, an essential source of Soviet oil revenues. Casey and Weinberger launched clandestine operations on the Soviet border to put Moscow under pressure.[62]

In June 1982, Reagan replaced Haig with George Schultz, who would in time show more flexibility and pragmatism in dealing with the Soviet Union. In February, Schultz arranged for a meeting between Reagan and Soviet ambassador Anatoly Dobrynin. The president emphasized his desire to be constructive, but not long after, on March 8, Reagan publicly called the Soviet Union an "evil empire," thereby inspiring anti-American hysteria behind the Iron Curtain. He then announced the Strategic Defense Initiative, a measure that reflected his belief that the doctrine of mutual assured destruction was absurd and his conviction that a nuclear war could not be won. He pushed for the deployment of the new intermediate-range missiles and approved a military exercise called Able Archer, which simulated a nuclear war in Europe. Simultaneously, throughout 1982 and 1983 Reagan insisted that he wanted to talk with the Soviet leaders, declaring that he was not trying to force the Soviet Union to abandon its standing as a great power or its legitimate national interests.[63]

Though Reagan was targeted by hostile Hungarian propaganda, he still received József Marjai, the deputy prime minister responsible for economic matters. Marjai was there to negotiate membership in the IMF, which may explain why the president found time to see him. Reagan told him he would continue to support the cause of U.S.-Hungarian relations,[64] and with U.S. support Hungary became a member of the IMF. Deputy secretary of state Kenneth Dam declared that this was the practical consequence of the policy of differentiation,[65] and this time the president was fully behind the State Department. Reagan was known for his strident anticommunist rhetoric, but he decided to start a dialogue with Eastern Europe, even with the conservative communist regimes like Czechoslovakia's. The idea of revitalizing relations with Eastern Europe came from an investment banker, John Whitehead, who was close to the president and wanted to shake up U.S. policy toward the forgotten states of East Central Europe. Reagan liked the idea and made Whitehead his special envoy to the region, appointing him to the rank of deputy secretary of state.[66]

The highest-level U.S.-Hungarian meeting ever took place when Soviet-American relations were reaching a new low. The ailing Andropov called Reagan unpredictable. Then the Soviets shot down a South Korean airliner and Andropov, in the belief that the Americans did not know the truth, publicly denied the incident.[67] Moscow rejected the American "zero solution" for the "Euromissiles" and the Soviet delegation walked out of the talks in Geneva. These were the conditions under which Vice President Bush went to Budapest as part of a European tour in September 1983.

Bush's visit revealed that the Reagan administration's goals in Eastern Europe were limited and had remained essentially the same since the 1960s: domestic liberalization and some measure of autonomy from the Soviets, although the two did not necessarily have to go together. Bush was impressed with Kádár. Years later, he called the conversation he had with the communist leader "one of the most memorable" he had ever had with a statesman. At the time, President Reagan was publicly saying that communist regimes did not dare face free elections: "From Stettin on the Baltic to Varna on the Black Sea the regimes planted by totalitarianism have had more than 30 years to establish their legitimacy. But none – not one regime – has yet been able to risk free elections. Regimes planted by bayonets do not take root."[68] His vice president, however, suggested otherwise. As in the earlier phases of the Cold War, public statements made by members of the U.S. administration differed greatly from the sentiments they expressed in private. Bush asserted that "the love and esteem of the Hungarian people towards Kádár was such that if elections with any rules were held in Hungary he would be reelected the country's leader by a large majority."[69] As president in 1989, Bush would reaffirm his appreciation for Kádár. And Bush wasn't the only member of the Reagan administration who was enthralled by the man who had orchestrated the mass reprisals in Hungary after 1956. After meeting Kádár in Budapest in 1985, Secretary of State Schultz – whom Reagan considered to be carrying out presidential policy[70] – called the Hungarian leader "one of the outstanding politicians of the day," saying that he had "profited and learned a great deal" from meeting with him.[71] Kádár, on the other hand, still harbored ambiguous sentiments toward the Americans, who he thought were playing a double game. On the one hand, he claimed they were conducting high-level relations, but on the other, "the CIA and all the attached parts, Radio Free Europe and so forth are cooperating with the opposition with the consent of the [U.S.] government."[72]

The Hungarians' aim in meeting with the vice president was twofold. They wanted "to assert the national interest," meaning receive more flexible treatment in export licensing and extended MFN terms without annual reviews. At the same time, they wanted to help keep the East-West dialogue afloat in the arctic cold of renewed confrontation between the superpowers, to "break with the policy of cold war" in line with a "foreign policy coordinated with the allies." The Foreign Ministry intended to inform Bush of "the sincerity of the Soviet Union's desire for peace and of its willingness to reach an agreement." The Hungarians hoped to be able to influence Bush's thinking to the extent possible considering the "modest" means available to them.[73] At his press conference in Budapest, Bush claimed that the deployment of U.S. missiles in Europe would facilitate the disarmament process and specifically help to reach an agreement in Geneva on intermediate-range missiles.

In his conversation with the vice president, the party first secretary emphasized the importance of "preserving contacts and of a dialogue." Kádár praised the Americans' role in maintaining the dialogue, which revealed that he no longer saw world politics solely from the Soviet Union's perspective. Bush asked questions about the Soviet Union and the downing of the South Korean aircraft, then reiterated that in spite of the pretenses, Reagan took disarmament seriously. Bush also met the prime minister, György Lázár, and praised Hungary's – visibly failing – economic reforms and emigration policy. He told Lázár that trade policies were not independent of world politics and that Hungary's MFN status could therefore not be extended for more than a year. He stressed the need for Hungary to make an effort to convince doubters and the supporters of the policy of differentiation that Hungary was different from the other socialist states.[74]

Soon after the Bush visit, Secretary of State Schultz told the Hungarian ambassador in Washington that the vice president's stay was considered a success. In the aftermath of the crisis caused by the destruction of the South Korean airliner, the secretary of state made it clear that Washington was open to a dialogue with the Kremlin. Schultz explained that in bilateral relations the United States would refrain from spectacular moves and would follow a policy of small steps. He added that the United States was ready to reach agreements with the Soviet Union on every important issue, although he admitted that the Soviets' attitude toward the South Korean airliner had caused disenchantment in the American leadership. Schultz then asked the ambassador about the personality and character of Andropov. The secretary of state sent a reassuring message to Budapest and Moscow by stressing that in the development of American-Hungarian relations, the United States had no desire to do anything that would disrupt Hungary's membership in the Warsaw Pact. Thus he reiterated the traditional American position that the United States did not mean to challenge the Soviet Union's security interests in Eastern Europe. The secretary's statements underscored the Reagan administration's multifaceted approach to dealing with the Soviets, which mixed public pressure and harsh anti-Soviet propaganda with behind-the-scenes conciliation.

Schultz's reassurances regarding American intentions in the Soviet sphere were important in light of the remarks Bush made in Vienna right after his stop in Budapest. In a manner typical of the discrepancy between Bush's public and private rhetoric about Eastern Europe, Bush drew distinctions between Soviet client states and criticized the wall separating East and West. The address caused great consternation in Budapest. Hungarian diplomats protested, claiming that it was in stark contrast with the sober atmosphere that had prevailed in the meeting in Budapest. Under the pretext of responding to the Bush speech, Soviet deputy foreign minister Viktor Komplektov criticized Hungarian foreign policy. He declared that the Soviets had to be careful "that our opponents should not to be able to draw the conclusion from our behavior that in certain questions we disagree." He stressed the importance of "acting in unison and condemning the American leadership." Although Komplektov's remarks worried the Hungarian leadership, their effects were short-lived. Sándor Rajnai, a high-level officer of the Hungarian state security services who was serving as the ambassador to Moscow, soon reported that "the small anxiety produced by our western relations has subsided."[75]

The Soviets had larger concerns than a satellite that was experimenting with more intensive Western relations while remaining loyal in matters that were essential to the Soviets. Soon after Bush's trip to East Central Europe, the Soviets' missile-warning system falsely detected an American nuclear strike. In October, U.S. Marines landed in Grenada and overthrew Maurice Bishop's Marxist government. East German military intelligence misinterpreted the NATO military exercise code-named Able Archer and warned the Soviets that NATO was preparing to launch an attack. The world was on edge. Hungarian media revealed that the subway line under Budapest was an atomic shelter and publicized procedures for reaching it in case of emergency. On December 1, the Soviet leadership informed the Warsaw Pact member states that unless countermeasures were taken, the Americans would be able to launch an unexpected attack on the socialist countries; as the war in Grenada suggested, the Americans' class interests had motivated them to prepare for a full-scale war.[76] In these circumstances, the Soviets may have seen the ongoing U.S.-Hungarian dialogue as a useful alternative to the policy of confrontation. Moreover, it was clear to Moscow that the Hungarians were in a critical financial position – Budapest was hours away from bankruptcy at one point in 1982 – and thus had no choice if they wanted their political system to survive.

Shortly after his speech in Vienna, Bush received the Hungarian ambassador. In an unprecedented gesture, the vice president requested that the ambassador relay to the leadership in Budapest his "regret" if his statement in Vienna had been unclear. Bush also suggested that the United States was not interested in changing the European order. The policy of differentiation was not one of division since Washington accepted that "the socialist states belong to one system of alliance on the basis of ideology" while being different in their national characteristics, aspirations, and attitudes.[77] Obviously for the ears of the highest leadership, Bush explained that President Reagan was resolved to move forward on disarmament but could not allow the Soviet Union to enjoy permanent military superiority. Házi also broke with a long-standing tradition and did not criticize Bush's statement that the Soviet Union was responsible for the deterioration of relations. He stated that "unilateral, sometimes exaggerated accusations are not useful from either side." Otherwise, the Hungarians now "welcomed the policy of differentiation if it takes into account objective historical, economic, ethical, and socio-political differences."[78] It was a different matter that it ought not be announced.

In spite of such progress, the Cold War still imposed strict limits on bilateral relations. The communist regime in Hungary sought progress in order to acquire capital, know-how, and above all, technology with which to modernize its economy. The United States, however, continued to impose the strictures on technology transfers that had been in effect since 1948. To some extent, these restrictions, motivated by security, were at odds with liberal economic principles and America's self-interest. U.S. companies were deprived of business opportunities and the U.S. economy lost a potentially significant export market. After the Soviet invasion of Afghanistan, economic warfare came to the forefront once again. The Pentagon's position prevailed over the Departments of State and Commerce. Ernő Kemenes, chairman of the Hungarian National Planning Office, was well aware of the significance: the technological gap between East and West was widening, and technology was playing an increasingly important role in the economy.[79]

Hence for instance in 1985 secretary of defense Caspar Weinberger opposed the sale of Hughes commercial helicopters to Hungary on the grounds that they could be used for military purposes. In 1984, the Hungarians decided to modernize their telephone system and purchase the necessary technology from either AT&T or IT&T. IT&T approached the Hungarian Embassy to get the deal for itself, and the U.S. ambassador in Budapest, Nicholas Salgo, a successful businessman of Hungarian descent, intervened with secretary of commerce Malcolm Baldrige to expedite an export license. This was not enough, however, as the Pentagon feared that Hungary might use the technology for military communications. There was also a chance they would transfer the technology to the Soviet Union, where it would be installed in the "noses of spacecraft."[80]

This ban on technology transfers was not unwarranted. U.S. officials charged Hungary with violations of the trade controls and with making significant efforts to transfer technology to the Soviet Union. When Gyula Horn, the party functionary overseeing foreign affairs, visited Washington, he was confronted with the accusation that Budapest "was handing over too many high-tech commodities to the Soviet Union."[81] Deputy secretary of state John Whitehead complained that "Hungary's intelligence services had participated in the illegal acquisition of technology."[82] Back in 1981 and 1982, the Hungarians, in collusion with Japanese businessmen, had smuggled American laser equipment into Hungary. Just before George Schultz's trip to Budapest in 1985, the State Department threatened to curb Hungarian officials' freedom of movement because Hungarian intelligence had got hold of U.S. high technology. Later, in 1987, American authorities managed to foil an illegal attempt to acquire computers and microelectronic devices of significant military value. The Hungarians participated by establishing a phony foreign trading company in Singapore and ordering a Japanese device with sensitive American components.

The growth of trade relations was also impeded by the Hungarians' failure to conduct market research to determine which commodities could be sold in the United States.[83] The most important reason for this oversight, of course, was that they had little to sell on the American market.[84] Even so, bilateral trade, dominated by industrial products, grew from $188 million in 1978 to $450 million a decade later. At the same time, American banks were less and less active in helping the Hungarians collect the loans they desired. The reason for this, as the Hungarian Foreign Ministry observed in 1988, was that "they were eyeing the growth of our debts and our unrealized plans with more and more suspicion."[85] Eastern European states, even the ones at the top of Washington's preference list, were under close scrutiny. Most-favored-nation status was not granted indefinitely, and the fact that this status had to be reviewed and extended every year impeded the growth of trade. In order to remedy the situation, Ferenc Havasi, the party leader responsible for economic affairs, asked for an exemption under the Generalized System of Preferences when he went to Washington in 1985.

Hungarian diplomats made strenuous efforts to extend their most-favored-nation treatment for more than a year, but to no avail. The reason was that although Congress found Hungarian emigration law acceptable, it thought that the law was still too stringent.[86] Even Romania was forced to go through the annual review process. Another new focus of Hungary's diplomatic offensive in the United States was the opening of a general consulate in California. The State Department repeatedly rejected this request because they suspected that the Hungarians would exploit it for espionage purposes on behalf of the Soviet Union. Hungarian officials justified their request by claiming that the role of the West Coast had grown in the American economy, but given Hungary's export potential and geographical position, this explanation was hardly convincing.

The real reason may have been the proximity of California's high-tech hub, Silicon Valley. Hungarian intelligence may have wanted to get close to it after U.S. authorities changed the location of the Soviet consulate, removing the Soviets from this center of computer technology.[87] Mark Palmer, the U.S. ambassador to Budapest who had previously served as deputy assistant secretary of state for Soviet and East European affairs, told deputy minister of foreign affairs László Kovács that he opposed the opening of the consulate on the grounds that Hungarian intelligence was "aggressively" attempting to acquire American technology all around the world.[88] Palmer had already protested such activities in his capacity as a high-level official at the State Department. The U.S. Embassy made known that it had information about the Hungarians' illegal importation of items on the CoCom list, including microelectronics. The embassy feared that if this information reached Secretary of Defense Weinberger or his deputy Richard Perle, it would become "a serious matter with harmful consequences."[89]

As a reminder that the Cold War was very much alive even between the United States and the Soviets' satellites, U.S. officials alleged that Hungary and other socialist states were involved in supporting and even training terrorists. In 1984, the State Department delivered a "nonpaper" – an unofficial document – about terrorism and the illegal acquisition of technology by the Soviet allies, threatening them with reprisals including limits on personnel and movement. Washington claimed that the internationally known terrorist Carlos the Jackal had "recently" paid a visit to Budapest. Because of the seriousness of the matter, the Soviet general staff wanted the socialist countries to deliver a "coordinated" reply. The Hungarian Foreign Ministry "categorically" rejected the American accusation, which it attributed to the "aspirations of extremist forces" within the Pentagon.[90] In reality, as the reform communist and would-be prime minister Gyula Horn admitted, Carlos regularly spent time Hungary until he was eventually expelled. American diplomats also complained that when Hungarian Americans repatriated, their passports were taken and not returned. Such action was clearly not approved by the Foreign Ministry; as a high-level official noted in a memorandum, "what we are doing with the passports is uncivilized."[91]

Despite these conflicts, Hungary continued to be one of Washington's favored Soviet client states, its status preserved by its strategic position and political importance.[92] Hungary's privileged position alongside Romania and Poland was demonstrated by its relatively high-level contacts, though these simultaneously caused some tension with Moscow. Gorbachev's advisor Oleg Bogomolov once remarked that "it is a mortal threat to mention Hungary as they will put the stamp of revisionism on you."[93] Washington paid less attention to Hungary than to either Romania or Poland. Internationally, Hungary did not cause problems and there was no influential Hungarian émigré politician who could bring it into focus.[94]

Being unproblematic was enough to earn the support of the Reagan administration. Ferenc Havasi, the party leader responsible for economic affairs, paid an official visit to Washington in 1984 and was received by Schultz, Bush, and even Reagan himself. His meeting with Reagan was due to the influence of the ambassador to Budapest, Nicholas Salgo, who was personally acquainted with the president. Czechoslovakia's deputy foreign minister was in Washington at the same time as Havasi but was not invited to the State Department in any official capacity. It wasn't one's communism that mattered, but one's orientation. Reagan told Havasi that his visit reflected the "normalized," "good" relationship between the two countries and that Hungary had taken the initiative to maintain the dialogue between the two blocs and to improve their relationship. The president told Havasi that the United States was interested in solving the "Euromissiles" problem in a way that would not cause the Soviets to lose prestige.[95]

Despite the ideological and political chasm that separated them, some members of the Reagan administration developed respect for Hungary's leadership. George Schultz traveled to Budapest in December 1985 at a time of renewed controversy over thefts of U.S. technology. At the same time, the Soviet leadership was putting pressure on party leaders in Eastern Europe to intensify their struggle against imperialist subversion. Immediately before Secretary Schultz's arrival in Budapest, the State Department delivered a nonpaper threatening to impose travel restrictions on Hungarian embassy officials if they conducted espionage in the

United States. The U.S. Embassy's counselor, Kenneth Smith, explained that the threat was issued because Hungarian intelligence had got hold of some valuable pieces of American high technology.[96] Shortly before his trip to the Hungarian capital, the secretary of state participated in talks in Moscow, where he declared that the United States was interested in encouraging a more open atmosphere in the countries adjacent to the Soviet Union. The communist daily paper, *Pravda*, condemned the remark as an attempt to interfere in the internal affairs of the socialist states and declared that such efforts to weaken and divide the socialist states were doomed to failure. Only recently had the newly appointed first secretary of the Communist Party of the Soviet Union (CPSU), Mikhail Gorbachev, disclosed to the Communist Party leaders of Eastern Europe that he expected an "intensification of ideological vigilance" and "much tighter cohesion in all spheres of the communist commonwealth." In April, Warsaw Pact leaders gathered in Moscow to extend their treaty for another thirty years. Gorbachev praised "the unity of action" that "thwarted the attempts by imperialism to subvert or destroy the socialist order in any of the fraternal countries." The Soviet client states were coming under pressure from both the Soviets and the United States.[97] Thus in Bucharest, Schultz warned that Romania could lose its most-favored-nation status unless it improved its human rights record, a statement that marked the beginning of a slow change in Washington's policy toward Romania, even though the State Department would continue to turn a blind eye to human rights violations. Citing the country's foreign policy, emigration policy, and business opportunities, it supported an extension of Romania's most-favored-nation status even in 1987.

In Budapest, Schultz negotiated with prime minister György Lázár, who stressed that Hungary welcomed "the investments of foreign capital." This time there was no need to pressure Kádár to meet the American secretary. Kádár and Schultz discussed a variety of topics. The wily old party leader brought up the execution of Imre Nagy, claiming that the Soviets had pledged not to execute him. None of this was true; he had insisted on killing Nagy himself. Nevertheless, he left a positive imprint. Schultz reported to Reagan that Kádár "provides the sense of duration and the steady hand in politics."[98] Clearly, one of the most influential members of the president's foreign policy team preferred the stability of the status quo to the changes heralded by the emergence of a democratic opposition in Hungary. As the prime minister's comments showed, times had changed since the early 1970s. From the Hungarian angle, long gone were the days of communist optimism when catching up to and surpassing the West were the order of the day. In 1985, the question was a matter of bare survival. The Hungarians wanted to extract concessions on transfers of technology, most-favored-nation status, and preferential customs treatment, but Schultz did not make any commitments. The time was ripe to push for change in Hungary, as the Americans' leverage was strong.

The secretary of state discussed two other areas: human rights and the policy of differentiation. Referring to the situation of the Hungarian minority in Transylvania, which had long been causing tensions between Hungary and Romania, Schultz declared that the United States's ethnic and religious diversity made it more sensitive than the average nation to human rights issues, wherever in the world these issues came up. Regarding the policy of differentiation, Schultz stressed geographical, ethnic, and historical diversity, and the wording satisfied Hungarian expectations.[99] After the visit, John Whitehead told Hungarian diplomats that the United States was ready to expand economic and political relations.[100]

Hungarian propaganda, however, remained hostile to the United States, and American diplomats complained that the Hungarian media's portrayals of U.S. policy in Libya instilled hatred toward American citizens who visited Hungary. There were other problems as well. For instance, the authorities discouraged people from visiting the American library. The U.S. Embassy's security official had not received a phone line to his Budapest residence for a year.[101] The United States criticized the firing of the oppositionist intellectual Sándor Lezsák on the grounds that he had been sacked only for organizing events that provided chances for free expression "in the spirit of Helsinki." Congress was critical of Hungary's human rights policies even though they were better than those of other socialist states. Washington deplored the harassment of opposition figures and the use of police against demonstrators.

On the other hand, the Hungarians charged that Radio Free Europe was interfering in domestic affairs, inciting both acts of subversion and the organization of an opposition.[102] From the 1960s, Radio Free Europe had used soft power to promote a gradual system change and simultaneously sought to influence the behavior of the communist regimes themselves in a more liberal and national direction. Former Hungarian propaganda chief János Berecz "became convinced that Western broadcasts were among the accepted sources of information among the youth." It is not surprising that Radio Free Europe was seen as a major irritant and that the Soviet bloc launched a campaign to discredit Radio Free Europe, Radio Liberty, and other "subversive" Western information programs.[103] President Reagan's assistant national security advisor responsible for communication and information affairs did not reject the accusations and told the Hungarian ambassador that there had been problems with Radio Free Europe director George Urban before. He told Ambassador Bányász that Radio Free Europe "is following an interventionist line lately and this is out of tune with the position of the U.S. government." None of these issues caused a real setback. When Gyula Horn was in Washington in early 1986, the Americans broached the idea of a Reagan-Kádár meeting in Washington.[104] Thus the staunchly anticommunist president went further in recognizing Hungary's long-standing communist ruler than had any chief executive before him. And the fact that the Hungarian leader – who had once proclaimed that the United States was the most dangerous of all imperialists – was eager to go to Washington speaks volumes about the change that occurred in bilateral relations.

In November 1986, a congressional delegation headed by Steny Hoyer of Maryland went to Budapest to appraise the human rights situation there and evaluate Hungary's candidacy for permanent most-favored-nation status. In Budapest, Hoyer criticized the Romanian leadership's human rights record.[105] Reagan's personally appointed advisor on Eastern Europe, John Whitehead, also visited Budapest in November 1986. He praised the Hungarian leadership "for the full guarantee of the rights of freedom" and for the implementation of "market principles in economic policy," which could "serve as a model for the Soviet leadership." The deputy secretary of state declared that among the socialist states, Hungary was "closest to the United States," although he was critical of the country's foreign policy, which lacked independence. Whitehead complained to Foreign Minister Péter Várkonyi, an expert on the history of U.S.-Hungarian relations, that when the UN passed resolutions to condemn the United States, Hungary invariably toed the Soviet line. He urged his hosts to review the tone and content of such resolutions and to signal their independence by occasionally voting against or abstaining. He recommended the recognition of Israel and, startlingly, for the Hungarians to exit from the Warsaw Pact.[106] Whitehead promised that he would inform his hosts of any progress in U.S.-Soviet talks, claiming that the information the Soviets' provided to their allies was not always precise. The Hungarians stressed that they were ready to develop relations in every area and requested concessions in the field of technology transfers. Whitehead promised to intervene on behalf of the Hungarians in their attempt to acquire a high-capacity computer.[107] After returning to Washington, Whitehead started consultations on the question of technology transfers to Hungary.[108] At the same time, Ambassador Salgo warned against broaching the matter of the Hungarian consulate on the West Coast, which he deemed hopeless because of the spying scandals that had recently been revealed in the United States. He mentioned that several Soviet diplomats had been expelled as spies in 1986 and that officials in Washington thought that Hungary wanted a West Coast consulate for the purposes of intelligence gathering.[109] The matter must have been urgent; when the high-level party functionary Mátyás Szűrös went to Washington, this was one of the topics he raised in meetings with Schultz, Whitehead, Bush, and other top level officials. Szűrös was anxious to intensify bilateral trade and invited American "working capital" into Hungary. He sued for "second- or even third-generation technology, some of which had already found its way into the Soviet Union, such as IT&T's telephone center to upgrade [Hungary's] obsolete phone system," or two Siemens computers that were needed because Hungary was preparing to introduce a new tax system. Thus Hungary, though still communist, was presented as an opportunity for capitalist investment.[110] In this vein, Szűrös met with the management of McDonnell Douglas to negotiate the purchase of airliners. American officials were fundamentally pleased with Hungary's record, but they were also critical of some aspects of the country's policies.

Vice President Bush urged closer cooperation in the struggles against drug trafficking and terrorism, which could send "a positive signal to the American business world." The fact that the United States was suggesting cooperation in international politics to an adversary showed that the Cold War paradigm was slowly being transcended. Secretary of State Schultz praised Hungary's political and economic liberalization but urged further changes to promote American investment: more transparency to reveal economic development strategy and more independence for firms. In sum, the secretary was proposing the gradual dismantling of the centrally planned economy. Cold War politics still applied to export controls. There was no chance of eliminating the annual mandatory review of Hungary's MFN status, although there was some chance for small improvements in the area of technology transfers: a review of certain items on the CoCom list, such as supercomputers, and a more expedient licensing process. Whitehead repeated that the critical issue for the United States was the Hungarians' voting record at the UN, where they invariably followed the Soviets, even in matters of no significance. His position was to some extent countered by the secretary of state, who told Szűrös that his conversation with Kádár helped him understand Hungary's predicament. Szűrös also met with former secretary of state Kissinger, who had earlier also criticized the servility of Hungarian foreign policy. He had apparently changed his mind, as he told his interlocutor that Hungarian foreign policy was "rational and no one expected Hungary to go against its system of alliance, and Hungarian politics does not needlessly irritate the Soviets." Assistant secretary of state for European and Canadian affairs Rozanne Ridgway reminded Szűrös that bilateral relations were a function of the Soviet-American relationship, although she acknowledged that the fundaments of the relationship with Hungary were sturdy enough to withstand some ups and downs. Kissinger and Nixon had tacitly recognized the prevailing European order in the hope that this would make it possible for a process of liberalization and democratization to take place within the communist regimes. The Reagan administration may have seen an opportunity to speed up this process.

Most lawmakers expressed a positive view of Hungarian politics. The chairman of the House Foreign Affairs Committee, Dante Fascell of Florida, claimed there was strong congressional support for relations with Hungary, which "reacted well to international challenges relating [to] human rights issues." Senator Christopher Dodd of Connecticut averred that Congress was the key to the development of relations and therefore recommended that as many senators as possible be invited to Hungary so as to get acquainted with the situation there. Dodd assured Szőrös that the United States would support the protection of the Hungarian minority in Transylvania, a significant statement in the midst of the Romanian leadership's drive to liquidate village communities there. Steny Hoyer, who had recently visited Hungary, claimed that Hungary had the best human rights record in the socialist bloc. Hoyer thought that the Hungarian model was the direction in which Gorbachev was trying to go. On the other hand, the cochair of the Congressional Commission on Security and Cooperation in Europe complained that there were more and more instances of human rights violations in Hungary. Yet another representative praised the measures Hungary had taken on behalf of its Jewish community.[111] Szűrös found that although there was general agreement in Washington that Hungary was the most liberalized satellite, further liberalization and a more independent foreign policy would be required in order to receive economic rewards. Soon after the Szűrös visit, Whitehead, who apparently took seriously his pledge to revitalize Washington's relations with Eastern Europe, again traveled to Budapest, where he met the whole Hungarian leadership including Kádár and the new prime minister, Károly Grósz. The hosts continued to push for the liberalization of technology transfer policy, most-favored-nation status, and a Hungarian consulate on the West Coast.[112] Whitehead declared that Hungary was now Washington's most important partner in Eastern Europe, ahead of its previous favorite, Romania, which was losing its privileged position in U.S. foreign policy due to its domestic tyranny.

Whitehead declared that the United States would support economic reforms but was also critical of Hungarian practices. He accused his hosts of illegal acquisitions of American technology. Whitehead also complained that Hungary was running a trade surplus with the United States, a situation he wanted rectified. Whitehead asserted that the development of Hungarian-American relations would be greatly accelerated if "the Hungarian government, when purchasing the airplanes, would accept the offer made by McDonnell Douglas." He added that the financial conditions offered by the giant U.S. firm were "much better than any other offer." Competition for the untapped East European markets was thus on its way. When Hungary decided to purchase John Deere tractors from the United States, the president of the Bundesverband der Deutschen Industrie warned that if the deal was "concluded as planned, it would have a negative impact on West German investment in Hungary." Whitehead also discussed with the Hungarian foreign minister the question of arms shipments to Iran, requesting that Hungary halt its sales of military trucks to Teheran.[113] Although Várkonyi claimed to have no knowledge of such transactions, which was plausible given the secrecy of the regime, he did promise to "look into it."[114] The deputy secretary of state also raised the question of international terrorism.[115] A memorandum prepared for the head of the Hungarian Socialist Workers Party (HSWP) CC International Affairs Department, Gyula Horn, reveals that Hungary provided Whitehead with a detailed report about the suspects in an attack on a South Korean airliner.[116]

U.S. policy toward Eastern Europe began to change toward the end of the 1980s for a number of reasons. First of all, Reagan was an idealist who really believed that the United States should promote the cause of democracy around the world. Secondly, Gorbachev's reforms gave a green light to change behind the Iron Curtain for the first time since 1953, when Stalin's death and the breakdown of Stalinist systems forced Moscow, however briefly, to allow "national communism" and limited reforms. Finally, reform communists in Poland and Hungary responded to the critical financial and political situation by introducing democratic elements into their political systems and liberalizing their centralized command economies. In fact, the satellite region was entering a phase of great political, social, and economic disarray. The regimes in Poland and Hungary were struggling with the mounting burden of unmanageable financial crises, augmented by precipitous drops in their standards of living and the rise of viable political oppositions. Whereas the loosening of party control nourished the popular thirst for change in Poland and Hungary, as predicted by Alexis de Tocqueville, the Romanian regime ushered in a reign of terror and an unprecedented degree of economic shortage. In different ways, all three countries were exhibiting symptoms of a final crisis in their political systems, even though this state of affairs remained obscure to most foreign observers. In Hungary, members of the political opposition and representatives of the reform wing of the ruling party met for the first time in 1987 to hammer out a consensus for dealing with the country's acute and profound political, economic, and moral crises. Although the liberals and the populists did not see eye-to-eye on relations with the ruling party, and the populists were willing to accommodate the reform communists to gain legitimacy, it was clear that a new chapter in Hungarian politics was beginning.[117] Despite Gorbachev's reforms, Soviet policy toward Eastern Europe had still not changed. Gorbachev had not yet granted the kind of latitude to agents of domestic change that would come in 1988. In July 1986, Gorbachev told Polish leaders that "socialist gains are irreversible" and emphasized the importance of "socialist internationalism." Defense minister Sergey Sokolov told Warsaw Pact defense ministers in May 1987 that the alliance would have to maintain combat readiness for the indefinite future and called on the member states to contribute more to joint defense efforts. In Czechoslovakia, Gorbachev insisted that the Soviet Union "came to the right conclusion in 1968."[118]

An Interagency Intelligence Memorandum prepared in June 1987 forecast an increase in Eastern European unrest, although it did not predict that such disturbances would spiral out of control. The authors of the memorandum likewise failed to consider dissident activists to be a serious challenge to the regimes, nor did they think that Washington would be able to exert any influence on events behind the Iron Curtain. The memorandum did suggest that the communist regimes would seek closer economic ties with the United States.[119] Curiously, the memorandum's writers did not appreciate that the opposition in Hungary was becoming more organized and was actually picking up strength. Thus the potential for radical change there was underestimated. Despite their limited opportunities for action, U.S. officials did begin to view themselves as active participants rather than just observers of the Soviet sphere. For the first time since the Geneva summit in 1995, a National Security Study Directive (NSSD) proposed that the president broach the question of the satellites at a summit with a Soviet leader. NSSD No. 305, accepted in the spring of 1988, made several recommendations for the Reagan-Gorbachev meeting in Moscow. Reagan was supposed to make it clear to Gorbachev and the Western Europeans that the best guarantee for stability and the long-term improvement of East-West relations would be to move beyond the postwar continental division.[120] The recommendation was ambiguous in suggesting that moving beyond the East-West division was a prerequisite of improving East-West relations. In fact, American goals regarding the future status of Eastern Europe would remain as equivocal as this through 1989. Reagan eventually decided not to broach the question of Eastern Europe with Gorbachev.

An analyst at the Hungarian Embassy may have been close to the truth about the Reagan administration's line when he opined that "the weakening of the socialist states [and] the economic-social reforms call for caution and the inclination to avoid undertaking concrete obligations."[121] Reagan was inclined to move beyond the established Cold War paradigms. His Strategic Defense Initiative indicated that he was unwilling to accept the absurd logic of mutual assured destruction. In 1982, he talked about a "crusade for freedom" and insisted that Marxism-Leninism would be sent to the ash heap of history. He publicly challenged Gorbachev to "tear down" the Berlin wall. But some of these statements reflected his ultimate vision more than his immediate goals.[122] The strident rhetoric concealed more realistic aims. In fact, while the president foresaw more democracy in Eastern Europe, he was not thinking of tearing them away from the Soviet Union.[123] The United States understood that Eastern Europe was going through a crisis, but it was not interested in an explosion. As the Hungarians were preparing to participate at the Sofia meeting of the Warsaw Pact Political Consultative Committee, they appraised American intentions toward the region. According to the Hungarians' analysis, the Americans were driven by a desire to maintain stability, and although they advocated radical institutional changes and political pluralism in Eastern Europe, they would not go beyond "certain limits."[124] U.S. diplomats made no secret of their desire to see profound change. Whitehead indicated there was a unique opportunity for political and economic liberalization of the region in that the countries of Eastern Europe had turned to the West for help in resolving their real problems, which in turn would allow Western leaders to extract basic reforms in a peaceful way.[125]

When it came to economic regime change, the United States was knocking on an open door. The Hungarian regime was rapidly decentralizing its economy, even though some pillars of the system – such as full employment, soft budget constraints for preferred enterprises, and the state's monopoly on trade and finances – were still sacrosanct. Deputy Prime Minister Marjai advocated Hungary's integration into the world economy and a common Hungarian-U.S. front against the protectionism of the EEC. Marjai also began to advocate the transformation of the dysfunctional Comecon. The Hungarians' recommendation was to make the financial unit of the organization, the transferable ruble, partially convertible. The proposal was made out of desperation, as the Soviet Union, the economy of which was faltering under Gorbachev's failed reforms, had piled up a debt of $1 billion in its clearing account with Hungary.

The American stance on economic transformation was ambiguous. U.S. officials embraced efforts to establish a "socialist market economy," but already in early 1988 secretary of commerce William Verity warned Marjai that the United States would not be ready to support the Eastern European systems with loans and aid. Instead, he said, the United States would support transformation through the transfer of management skills and know-how and the development of economic relations.[126] Even though many Hungarians were dreaming of a new Marshall Plan, this time it was clear at an early stage of the events that led up to the regime change that assistance of such magnitude would not be supplied to the eastern part of the continent.

A REFORM COMMUNIST IN AMERICA

In the midst of political turmoil and the rapid deterioration of the country's financial situation, the sclerotic and increasingly conservative Kádár was replaced by a moderate reformer, Károly Grósz. While the old leader was out of touch with reality, many (though not all) thought his successor would be able to deal with the country's mounting problems. Seeing an opportunity to shape events, Washington reacted rapidly and invited the new first secretary of the party for a visit in June 1988. Reagan had invited Gorbachev to America to convince him of his peaceful intentions and to show him that democracy was an example to follow.[127] His intentions with Grósz were similar. He saw Kádár's successor as a member of the "new generation" in Eastern Europe; Grósz was not known to be a "liberal," but was nevertheless assumed to be someone who could be molded. His hosts hoped his introduction to the Western world would convince him that democracy and market economics were the future, and indeed, when Grósz visited relatives living in California, he was deeply impressed by their lifestyle.[128] American officials were struck by the starkly pessimistic mood of the Hungarians they negotiated with,[129] and Grósz was in a dejected mood. The economic situation in Hungary was dramatic, and Grósz was afraid that if things got out of hand, the chaos of 1956 might repeat itself, an eventuality he dreaded. Driven to desperation by the dire economic situation, which he could not hope to handle, he soon relinquished the role of prime minister to Miklós Németh, a much younger and bolder reformer. Before Grósz's arrival, State Department officials made known that they were displeased with the brutality police had displayed at a demonstration in Budapest on June 16, the anniversary of the execution of Imre Nagy. In addition, they indicated that on the occasion of the party first secretary's visit, the United States would broach the topics of the identification of the martyred prime minister's grave, his reburial, and the revision of Hungary's restrictive emigration law.[130] Before the visit, the Hungarian Foreign Office prepared a stark appraisal of Hungary's place in U.S. foreign policy, which stated that Hungary's importance had diminished, meaning that the United States "would not expend political capital in the Hungarian interest."[131]

Although it was not considered an official visit, Grósz was offered the opportunity to lay a wreath on the Tomb of the Unknown Soldier. President Reagan praised certain aspects of U.S.-Hungarian cooperation such as the struggle against international terrorism and drug trafficking. Reagan asserted that he was satisfied with the human rights situation in Hungary, which provided sufficient grounds to further intensify relations. Reagan also indicated that he wanted to see the growth of U.S. exports to Hungary and stressed the importance of the purchase of U.S. aircraft. Reagan's veiled criticism of the Hungarians' trade surplus with the United States was not unexpected, as John Whitehead had already warned Hungarian officials that the United States expected the situation to be remedied. Secretary of commerce William Verity announced that the administration had recommended the authorization of the sale of the aircraft and added that McDonnell Douglas would "come up with a better offer than ever." Vice President Bush underscored the prominence of Eastern Europe by announcing that the United States would improve relations with Hungary independently of the state of U.S.-Soviet relations. The United States also held out a major concession: the secretary of commerce announced that Hungary would be allowed to open a commercial office without diplomatic status in California. This economic concession, however, required political ones in return. For more than a year, the precondition for an extension of MFN status had been the modification of Hungary's emigration law. On the other hand, when the Hungarians broached the issue of debt relief, secretary of the treasury James Baker made it known that this was out of the question. No relief was in sight in the field of technology transfer either. Federal Reserve chairman Alan Greenspan urged more transparency so as to encourage American investment. Grósz announced that Hungary wanted to intensify relations "on the basis of mutual gains." The party first secretary then took the first cautious steps toward an economic regime change that in the space of two years would turn Hungary's foreign trade back toward the west again. By the time of his arrival in America, the first fast-food chain behind the Iron Curtain had opened its doors in the shopping district of downtown Budapest, and talks were underway to open fifty more around the country with the participation of a Hungarian agricultural company. Grósz signed a $100 million deal for the construction of a joint-stock glass-production company, the first such arrangement with the West since the war. Interest in doing business in Hungary was picking up: the Hyatt negotiated the construction of hotels around Hungary's largest vacation area, Lake Balaton; General Motors explored the sale of automobiles; and McDonnell Douglas negotiated deals to sell aircraft and helicopters. The establishment of a $200 million investment fund was also discussed.[132] The economic Iron Curtain was coming apart precisely at the moment when the government was mulling over dismantling the physical barrier along the Austro-Hungarian border. Still, the Americans' only offer of economic assistance was to send a retired expert from the private sphere to help resolve economic management issues for a monthly salary of $6,000. In addition, an IBM expert was sent to the U.S. Embassy in Budapest to promote investment.

In October, Reagan's advisor on Eastern Europe, John Whitehead, returned to Budapest. His arrival received great media publicity. He was informed by Grósz that Hungary was preparing to establish diplomatic ties with Israel and South Korea. The deputy secretary, however, was in a critical mood. He reiterated his criticism of his hosts' voting record at the UN. Moreover, Whitehead asserted that Hungarian imports from the United States had plummeted by 27 percent and warned that unless this trade imbalance was rectified, "our bilateral trade relations will have to be re-evaluated." This push was at odds with the Hungarians' policy of trying to even their balance of payments and to use the income derived from foreign trade to stay afloat in their sea of debts. In 1988, Ceausescu's dictatorial repression reached a new peak as his policy of "systematization" led to the destruction of villages in Transylvania. The Hungarian minority in Transylvania was targeted by these policies and the increasingly liberalized Hungarian media provided continual media coverage. The party leadership could no longer afford to remain silent. When the issue was broached in the Hungarian leadership's meeting with Whitehead, the deputy secretary disingenuously claimed that there was nothing the United States could do to influence Romania's domestic politics. Perhaps surprisingly, he then brought up the sensitive question of Hungary's withdrawal from the Warsaw Pact. He made it clear that Soviet troop withdrawals could not be tied to the pulling out of American forces from Western Europe.[133] Whitehead's stunning proposal may have been connected to a revelation that Grósz had brought up Soviet troop withdrawals during his visit to Moscow and received a positive response from Gorbachev.[134]

Unexpectedly, however, a spying scandal caused another setback in bilateral relations. U.S. counterintelligence agents apprehended Clyde Lee Conrad, who had served as a sergeant first class in the Eighth American Army stationed in the Federal Republic of Germany. Conrad was recruited by his superior, a Hungarian emigrant by the name of Zoltan Szabo, a colonel in the Hungarian military intelligence service, for which he had been gathering information since 1974. Conrad and his group stole several thousand pages of Cosmic Top Secret NATO documents and passed them on to the Hungarian and Czechoslovak military intelligence services. The documents contained sensitive information on NATO defenses in Germany as well as strategic and operational plans involving conventional and nuclear weapons. In accordance with a secret agreement signed by Hungary and the Soviet Union in 1949, the intelligence services of both states were obligated to cooperate in intelligence gathering against foreign powers and to share all the information at their disposal. Hence the representative of the Soviet military intelligence directorate, the GRU, shared office space with the Hungarian intelligence officers in Budapest. All raw intelligence received in Budapest was immediately passed on to that officer, who then forwarded it to Moscow. Hungarian officers took no exception to this arrangement, as they regarded spying for the Soviet Union as a matter of internationalist duty. The ring was busted only when Conrad's Hungarian liaison officer, the former Hungarian military attaché in London, István Belovai, betrayed the operation to the CIA. Belovai was not privy to the identity of Clyde Lee Conrad, which took the CIA some time to figure out. The Soviet mole in the CIA, Aldrich Ames, did find out that it was Belovai who had alerted the CIA to the security breach and gave him up to the GRU. Belovai was apprehended in 1984, well before Conrad was caught, and even though the prosecutor sought the death penalty for Belovai, he got away with being sentenced to military prison.[135] Although Belovai was released after the regime change, he was never rehabilitated. This was one of the many bitter ironies of the ambiguous way the new democratic systems dealt with their communist pasts.

Whitehead indicated that the Conrad case had caused great consternation in Washington and would adversely affect bilateral relations. He wanted to see "unpublicized" guarantees that similar problems would not recur. Whitehead acknowledged that intelligence gathering belonged to the "realities" of international politics, but suggested that the United States took exception to the Conrad case "because it involved vital Western security interests" and because Hungary was spying on behalf of the Soviet Union. He asserted that the Hungarians' interests in the United States could suffer and exhorted his hosts to consider their national interests.[136] It is unclear whether Whitehead understood the mechanisms of Soviet control and that Hungary was a Soviet client state required to perform services. Even though Whitehead accepted the party leader's claim that he had had no knowledge of the affair, Secretary of Commerce Verity announced that the United States would not implement the agreements Grósz had signed in Washington. President Reagan's pledge to allow a West Coast consulate was rescinded, a big setback given that Hungary had been striving for years for such a consulate. The State Department did accept a pledge from Grósz that such an incident would not happen again. Secretary of Commerce Verity indicated that relations could return to normal in the following presidential cycle as long as "the Hungarian leadership pursued not only consistent economic and political reforms, but was also strengthening its national independence." Whitehead went as far as to claim that despite the spying scandal, relations between the two states were "better than ever."[137]

The U.S. ambassador in Budapest, Mark Palmer, was less satisfied with the local conditions. In a reversal of roles, it was now the lower ranks of American diplomats who were pushing for more liberalization than the administration in Washington. In 1989, Palmer would consistently defy his administration's policy and push for full democratization until he was finally recalled at the end of that year. Palmer publicly advocated putting internal liberalization into practice. On October 24, 1988, in front of a large audience at the opening ceremony of the annual meeting of the American Society of Travel Agents, held in Budapest that year, Palmer declared that, "sadly," Hungarian authorities had prohibited a commemoration of the 1956 revolution the day before, which showed that Hungary still had a "long way" to go. Palmer was not officially summoned to the Foreign Ministry, but at the opening ceremony of the International Management Center, deputy foreign minister László Kovács indicated that Károly Grósz was displeased with Palmer's statements, not so much because of their content but because the ambassador had publicly criticized a government decision. Palmer responded by saying that the credibility of his speech would have suffered had he not brought up the banning of the 1956 commemoration and the blatant presence of police and the Workers' Guard.[138] Palmer met the commander of the Workers' Guard, Sándor Borbély, and advocated transforming it into a military organization more along the lines of the American National Guard.

During his talks in Budapest, the State Department official responsible for human rights, Robert Schifter, stressed the importance of establishing the rule of law in Hungary. Schifter suggested that the jurisdictions of the police and the judiciary be properly circumscribed and stressed the need to protect the autonomy of private citizens. While acknowledging that progress had been made in this direction, he indicated that there was still a need for an open society. He urged the Hungarians to take steps toward a constitutional state, though he did not criticize any particular human rights violations. In fact, Schifter promised that as a result of the "liberalization" of the political system, Hungary's MFN status would be extended indefinitely, although this would require further legislation guaranteeing Hungarians' freedom of movement.[139] At the same time, Schifter supported the extension of even Romania's MFN status. In Congress, he was accused of not having read even his own reports on the human rights situation in Romania. Thus while the State Department advocated further liberalization, it was not a prerequisite for normal contacts. The push for democratic transformation would come from domestic sources.

10

1989:
"Together We Liberated Eastern Europe"

The day the Soviet Union collapsed, George H. W. Bush penned a personal note to his friend Mikhail Gorbachev in which he immodestly declared, "Together we liberated Eastern Europe and unified Germany."[1] Did this bold claim do justice to the complicated history of the transition from the Cold War to the reunification of Europe, the restoration of multiparty democracy, and national independence in Eastern Europe? The answer to this question is not only a matter of historical truth. The clarification of the process of transition will shed light on the dynamics of systemic change in international politics at the end of the Cold War. The British historian Ian Kershaw has averred that history would not have taken the same course without Adolf Hitler, and it is likely that the events of 1989 could not have happened without Mikhail Gorbachev. But Gorbachev did not cause the cataclysm of 1989. No single individual or entity can be credited with ending the Cold War, which was not ended by design. Gorbachev's new course provided the environment in which internal developments in the countries of Eastern Europe – Poland and Hungary in particular – changed the prevailing international order.

The president's claim of liberation highlighted the chasm that separated his private and public statements throughout 1989. Speaking to a wider audience on the same occasion, Bush made more modest assertions about his and the Soviet leader's roles in what transpired that year: "Together we worked to liberate Eastern Europe and to achieve German unification." Although the public statement allowed others to claim responsibility for "liberation," it is still misleading in that it suggests that the transformation was little more than an "arrangement" among the former adversaries of the Cold War. The president's national security advisor, Brent Scowcroft, also felt in retrospect that Bush had ended the Cold War: "It happened under President Bush, and it happened the way it did in considerable part because of his great skill at diplomacy about eliciting cooperation from people.... He did not create change. But what he did is manage it in a way that these really cataclysmic changes in the world structure took place without a shot being fired."[2] The historical record suggests otherwise. In fact, the Bush administration feared a "major conflict in Europe between East and West,"[3] therefore it was "important for the U.S. to keep its moves moderate in Eastern Europe so as to avoid stimulating an explosion."[4] The rearrangement that occurred in the international system may have been generated by piecemeal change in the former Soviet satellites. Marc Trachtenberg has pointed out that the Cold War did not start in Eastern Europe. Aside from a brief period under President Eisenhower, it was seldom the focus of international politics. But in 1989 this all-but-forgotten part of Europe took center stage. It was here that the Cold War – which I understand to include the artificial separation of Eastern Europe from the rest of the world – was ended, and the first decisive steps toward the reunification of Europe were taken.

In this final chapter, I will attempt to clarify the part Hungary and the great powers played in the liberation of Eastern Europe, with a focus on the American role. This in turn will help highlight the process of change in international politics in 1989. Sequences of events matter because they may explain causality. The largely peaceful collapse of Eastern European communism in 1989 was due as much to the fundamental reorientation of Soviet foreign policy under Mikhail Gorbachev as to the courage and restraint of protesters in Eastern Europe.[5] But it was the profound and protracted domestic change in Eastern Europe that broke the camel's back and pushed the process of transformation beyond anything Gorbachev or Bush had envisioned. In an emblematic image of the breaching of the Cold War continental divide, Austrian foreign minister Alois Mock and his Hungarian counterpart Gyula Horn are seen cutting the barbed wire that separated their states. They were not, however, caught performing a spontaneous act. They were posing for the camera that recorded this "historic deed." Images often conceal more about an event then they reveal. When the picture was taken, the barbed wire had already been removed and had to be partially restored for the photo opportunity. Initially, Austria was highly concerned about the removal of the border barrier, fearing refugees, political destabilization, and a possible adverse reaction on the part of the Soviets. Horn, too, was initially skeptical about the wisdom of the move. More importantly, the removal of the barrier was not due to a single decision made at the highest level. Instead, it resulted from a random sequence of decisions made at several echelons of power in Hungary. Finally, it must be noted that the removal of the barbed wire was not meant to open the border for human traffic. Border controls remained in effect and were in fact briefly tightened in the summer of 1989 to impede the flight of East Germans to Austria. The removal of the physical Iron Curtain was just one – albeit significant – step toward releasing the Germans in September 1989. The opening of the border was the unintended and unforeseen consequence of a series of moves at the top as well as at the grassroots level within the context of the devolution of the ruling party's power. Opening the border benefited East Germans who were eager to flee their homeland and had the effect of destabilizing the German Democratic Republic (GDR) by pulling its plug. This in turn released the genie of German reunification. This story encapsulates the whole history of 1989: a combination of actions led to much larger consequences than anyone intended at the outset.

Some scholars of international relations argue that redistributions of power cause transformations in the international system.[6] In 1950, China's involvement in the Korean War stimulated a series of political and social transformations that would otherwise have been inconceivable in Mao's new republic.[7] Could not the reverse have happened in 1989? Domestic transformation behind the Iron Curtain, particularly in Poland and Hungary, triggered structural changes in the international system that led to the end of the bipolar world order. This radical transformation of the existing international system contributed to the decline of the Soviet Union as a world power by depriving it of its forward position in Europe.

The "credit" for ending the Cold War tends to be assigned to Gorbachev and to the political reorientation of the superpowers. A leading authority on the Cold War, Melvyn Leffler, has argued that "No one was more responsible for ending the Cold War than Gorbachev. Reagan was critically important, but Gorbachev was the indispensable agent of change."[8] Similarly, John Lewis Gaddis has written that "Gorbachev had made it clear, to the peoples and the governments of Eastern Europe, that the door was now open."[9] Another historian of the end of the Cold War has asserted that Gorbachev "did not intend to end the division of Europe; he was more interested in internal change. Changes in foreign policy were merely designed to help perestroika succeed." He hoped to give socialism a "second wind." Bush's diplomacy, on the other hand, allowed the division of Europe to be resolved and helped bring the Cold War to an end "with a whimper not a bang."[10] Svetlana Savranskaya took another view, concluding that "the Cold War ended in Eastern Europe, swept away by the rise of popular movements.... East Europeans took the initiative and were able to use the Bush administration's pause and the confusion on both sides of the Atlantic to their own advantage."[11] The historian Robin Okey has suggested that "all that was needed, arguably, to set the revolutions of 1989 in train were ... Solidarity's electoral victory and the opening of the Hungarian western border."[12] In fact, as Mary Sarotte has written, events on the ground in Europe mattered more than superpower action.[13] Two main points should be made here. First, the relationship between Gorbachev's circle and the satellites was not unidirectional. In fact, the Soviet leadership acted and modulated its policies under the influence of – and even pressure from – Eastern Europe. Secondly, Gorbachev's political reorientation was a necessary but not sufficient prerequisite for the transformation of the former satellites and the reunification of the continent. For all his good will, Gorbachev wanted to preserve the European system formulated in Moscow in 1944 and Yalta in 1945. There is no indication that Gorbachev realized at any point in 1989 that the Soviet empire in Eastern Europe could come to an end. When the Hungarian prime minister broached the subject of dismantling the Iron Curtain on the Austrian border, Gorbachev showed no sign of comprehending the significance of what was being proposed. In fact, he was never confronted with such a stark choice, as change was piecemeal. At no point did the Kremlin have to decide whether to save the empire. What happened in 1989 was the reverse of the process of Soviet colonization and political Stalinization in Hungary in 1945. No political leader was ever confronted with a clear-cut decision about the country's political future. Small decisions were made that eventually culminated in the establishment of Stalinism and client status. Gorbachev wished to preserve socialism right through 1989. He did want profound change. He wanted the two halves of Europe to live side by side in harmony, much the way men like George F. Kennan or James Byrnes or Walter Lippmann thought possible in 1946: a division of the continent on an amicable basis with many contacts between the halves, perhaps with common purposes. He also wanted a thorough transformation of the communist systems in Eastern Europe, the institutional, social, and economic systems of which were still essentially Stalinist, even in reform Hungary. But he never indicated that he would accept the collapse of communism and the institutions of Soviet control, Comecon and the Warsaw Pact. None of the Western powers envisioned the transition into full democracy and the reconnection of Eastern Europe to Western Europe. The initiative to get rid of this system came from the former satellites, where a combination of domestic factors caused the ruling parties to lose control. The new order came about spontaneously. As Paul Ricoeur has pointed out, history is not a record to be played. Many different outcomes were possible in 1989. Full parliamentary democracies with open and free societies in Eastern Europe and the full elimination of the East-West division was not an inevitable outcome. The fact that change went this far can be attributed to the role of the weak states in the Soviet zone. In this sense, as Mary Buckley put it, Gorbachev was "an essential enabler of revolutions in Eastern Europe ... facilitator, trigger approver, persuader and loser.... Gorbachev ignited motors that would then run without him controlling the gears."[14] Yet as one looks at the history of change leading up to the free elections, it is clear that their origin was indigenous.

There was more to the Soviets' control of Eastern Europe than met the eye. Military occupation was just the most visible among many formal and informal modes of control. In fact, military presence was not even necessary; prior to 1968 there were no troops in Czechoslovakia, and there were none in Romania after 1958. Thus when Gorbachev accepted troop reduction in some countries, he was not giving up all control. It is easy to forget that few leaders are in a position to make decisions alone, and Gorbachev was not one of them. Moreover, Mark Kramer has made the important point that events in Eastern Europe played a crucial role in the transformation of the Soviet Union itself through the spillover effect. This international demonstration effect transformed the context in which Soviet leaders operated, undercut the ideological raison d'être of the Soviet regime, and laid bare the illegitimacy of the communist systems, all of which exerted a powerful effect on Soviet elites.[15] The role of glasnost has been explained by Hungarian historian Zoltán Ripp, who averred that along with the economic crisis, it was the political turnaround in the Soviet Union that rocked the foundations of Kádárism in Hungary, as attempts to defer radical reform could no longer be justified by external circumstances.[16]

Through 1989, there was agreement between Moscow and the West that the Yalta structure of Europe would survive, albeit on a cooperative basis. As NATO's assistant secretary general for political affairs Henning Wegener put it in November 1989, the "Warsaw Pact... could well perform useful functions and enhance stability if reformed on the basis of strict equality."[17] In the fall of 1989, undersecretary of state Lawrence Eagleburger expressed nostalgia for "the remarkably stable and predictable atmosphere of the Cold War."[18] But the programs of all the opposition movements in Hungary contained the restoration of national independence and sovereignty, which involved neutrality and hence a full Soviet withdrawal. From early 1989, Hungarian officials pushed for a radical transformation of the Warsaw Pact's decision-making process. Opposition movements and parties began to question the country's membership in the organization early in the year, and top-level Hungarian officials raised the issue of neutrality with high-level American officials in September. Added to the far-reaching domestic transformation that had taken place, it was clear by the end of the year that the transformation could not be contained within the framework envisioned by the great powers.

HUNGARY AS A PACESETTER FOR
CHANGE IN EASTERN EUROPE

By the second half of the 1970s, János Kádár's Hungary was hailed as the most liberalized regime behind the Iron Curtain. Hungarian economic reforms seemed to suggest that Soviet-style socialism and the Western system of capitalism would one day converge. Kádár's image had changed from the "butcher of Budapest" to a statesman of European repute. The grand old man of U.S. diplomacy, Averell Harriman, asked for Kádár's mediation between Brezhnev and Carter in 1978,[19] and German chancellor Helmut Schmidt stated that Kádár, by virtue of his personal and international prestige, could play a key role in improving East-West relations.[20]

In spite of its initial success, the much-vaunted economic reform of 1968 soon ran into trouble and by 1982 Hungary was on the brink of bankruptcy. The economy was dependent on Western loans and trade for survival. Therefore, in spite of Soviet instructions to the contrary, Western contacts were intensified, particularly with West Germany and the United States. Since the regime's legitimacy rested on the growth of the citizens' economic well-being, Kádár was not politically strong enough to sustain the protracted austerity measures that would have been required to deal with the external imbalance, and thus by 1989 Hungary's foreign debt was among the highest in Europe. Ironically, the measures of economic austerity that were introduced in 1982 meant that the regime had reneged on its commitment to keep the standard of living high, but since there was no political will to sustain them, the measures eventually proved inadequate to solve Hungary's financial problems. Thus the much praised economic reform led not only to an intolerable level of external debt, it also subverted the regime's political legitimacy. By 1983, the government was at a crossroads. The leadership had to launch structural changes to increase the competitive edge of the economy, a step for which the country's top economic experts had been preparing since 1982. The austerity measures and the resulting loan from the International Monetary Fund (IMF) had reined in the financial crisis, but IMF experts and reformers inside and outside the party were warning the leadership that short of a new round of liberalization, the bankruptcy crisis would soon recur. Party conservatives, however, were afraid that the drastic steps proposed by experts such as János Kornai – who, in a book published in 1980, showed that chronic shortage was an inherent flaw of planned economies and hence could not be set right within the confines of that system – would lead to capitalism. Instead of a more radical program, the party accepted a watered-down version. In 1985, concerned that the effort to stabilize the balance of payments and the resulting rapid decline in standards of living could undermine the country's political stability, Kádár adopted a policy of "acceleration" to be financed by loans. "Believe me," the Old Man, as Kádár was fondly called in comradely circles, told the Politburo, with "0.5 percent growth we cannot exist, we cannot win over the masses." Ferenc Havasi, the party secretary responsible for economic matters, made no secret of the political connotations either: "1985 is the year of the Thirteenth Party Congress, the elections, and the 40th anniversary of the Liberation. It is the role of honor of the economy to assist the success of these important political programs." The result of the new twist in economic policy was catastrophic; by 1987 the country was back to square one, again on the verge of bankruptcy.[21]

State security controls were lowered in 1983 when the Hungarian-born financier George Soros, who actively pushed for open societies to replace the immobile, sclerotic, and secretive systems that existed in Eastern Europe, was allowed to establish a cultural foundation in Budapest. Despite Soros's subversive intent, the party approved his plan because of the funds Soros brought with him. In an effort to improve economic performance, private enterprise was gradually reintroduced, and trade and joint ventures with the capitalist world became a priority. In 1988, Reagan's special envoy to Eastern Europe was pushing the Hungarian Socialist Workers' Party (HSWP) to purchase American-made commodities of high value in return for economic help, and a year later the Federal Republic of Germany (FRG) and the United States were competing for the Hungarian market. One of the world's largest companies, General Electric, returned to Hungary with an investment of $150 million. Even though it was evident in Moscow that the regime in Budapest was rapidly unraveling, the Soviet leadership refused to salvage it with loans. In 1985, independent candidates were allowed to participate in the national elections, and although these were rigged by the security apparatus, it was clear that the party's stranglehold on politics was weakening. A meeting of intellectuals of various persuasions in Monor in the year Gorbachev came to power launched the slow process that would lead to the multiparty system adopted in 1989.

In 1987, reform intellectuals published two important documents. One envisioned a radical transformation of the economy to go hand in hand with political change.[22] The other outlined a profound overhaul of the single-party system and the role of the Communist Party in the country's political structure. As his system was gradually unraveling, Kádár sought to hold on to the levers of power by assigning reform to a set of new leaders who would safeguard the single-party system. Simultaneously, an internally divided opposition began to take shape with a meeting that took place in 1985. In the view of the ruling party, the emerging opposition was divided into "bourgeois radicals" who "rejected all forms of socialism" and "national radicals" interested in the "fate" of the nation. Because of its dependence on Western economic contacts, the regime was compelled to refrain from serious reprisals.

Eventually, party leaders started to establish links with nationalist opposition figures and movements. Henceforth the activities of the party focused on driving a wedge between the various factions of the opposition and thus forestalling the emergence of a unified front. The party's grip on the levers of power, however, was weakening. By 1986, the Writers' Association, an influential and formerly communist-dominated group, had come under the sway of populist writers. Still, in 1987 the Politburo continued to define politics as a means to assert "class rule" and rejected any notion of sharing power. While announcing a move to reconstruct the economy by fusing central planning, market mechanisms, and mixed ownership, the party declared war on "antisocialist" ideology in order to preserve the "dictatorship of the proletariat." Simultaneously, the liberal samizdat *Beszélő* advocated a "social compromise" between party and society in which the ruling elites would concede human rights and the rule of law in return for holding on to power. Given the circumstances, this was a radical program, and it was rejected by the nationalists. The latter had no desire to provoke a confrontation with the regime, as attaining legal status was in the forefront of their efforts. They proceeded by engaging party reformers such as Imre Pozsgay, who sympathized with at least some of the causes and grievances of the nationalist opposition but who could not be seen alongside radicals of the democratic opposition.

Tensions among opposition groups occasioned a policy of *divida et impera*. State security sought to make the most of this division by "planting agents into all opposition groups of any significance." The consequences of this move are unfathomable and to date no effort has been made to appraise its potentially destructive effects on Hungarian democracy. In early 1988, the Hungarian Democratic Forum, itself a hodgepodge of ideological currents ranging from national liberal through conservative to national radical, established itself as a formal organization. It was emphatically not a party, and it was soon followed by a loose grouping called the Network of Free Initiatives, a precursor of the Alliance of Free Democrats. The Democratic Forum defined itself as neither a government nor an opposition organization and announced that the establishment of a multiparty system was inexorable. Hungary would become a democracy of popular representation founded on local governments, autonomous civil groups, and parliamentarianism. Foreshadowing the bitter ideological struggle that would pit liberals against populists after 1989, the forum rejected all forms of exploitation, whether in the form of a "totalitarian state or private capital." This message resonated well with the legacy of 1956, which was a democratic, not a procapitalist, movement.

The formation of noncommunist political groups was coupled with a startling reawakening of civil initiatives, a form of social activity the communists had destroyed in 1946. This was exemplified by a mass movement for the protection of the Danube, which in May mobilized a crowd of two thousand people to demonstrate against the construction of a hydroelectric power plant. A far larger crowd turned out in September after the government decided to go ahead with the project, which was widely regarded as a selling out of the national interest and a symbol of the incompetence of the planned economy. The struggle over the Danube would significantly erode popular support for the government. History – or rather the interpretation of it – had an even larger impact on the future than did politicized environmental protection. The interpretation of the 1956 uprising as a counterrevolution had served as one of the legitimizing pillars of the established political system. A newly established organization, the Committee of Historical Rectification, challenged the political order by calling for a public commemoration of the execution of Imre Nagy. It was disbanded by the police, but the genie was already out of the bottle. The reinterpretation of recent history, the debunking of historical lies, and the filling in of blank spots would directly affect the outcome of the political struggle. The 1956 revolution, itself inspired by the rebellious tradition of 1848, would rally the average citizen against the regime. Although the commemoration of the revolution in October was foiled by the threats of a political leadership keenly aware of its delegitimizing effect, the national question could no longer be suppressed. This was the issue over which party reformers could and would give in to the nationalist opposition in the hope of luring it away from the liberals. A demonstration on June 27 against the Ceaușescu regime's repressive measures in Transylvania attracted something close to one hundred thousand protesters. The national cause championed by the opposition led to the opening of the border to refugees from Transylvania, the first step toward the opening of the Austrian border to East Germans fleeing to West Germany.

Discussion groups organized by the Hungarian Democratic Forum advocated the elaboration of a new constitution and parliamentary reform, but not regime change. Although Kádár branded all alternative groups including the Democratic Forum as "antisystem" organizations, reformers distinguished between the formations that were outright hostile and the Democratic Forum, with which they thought it would be possible to engage in dialogue. New prime minister Károly Grósz would hear of no cooperation with any political group. His rigid stance revealed a fissure in the top leadership of the ruling party that would eventually lead to its self-destruction. By late spring, the aged Kádár, whose grip on political reality was increasingly fragile, became a burden. Two days after receiving KGB chairman Vladimir Kriuchkov, who urged him to step down, this sturdy pillar of communist stability who had reigned in his country for a quarter-century resigned. He was succeeded by Grósz, who as a moderate was acceptable to all the factions of his party, as well as the Soviets and the West. His modest reforms, however, would soon be out of tune with the realities of his country's politics.

In November 1988, the Network of Free Initiatives transformed itself into the Alliance of Free Democrats. Their program included national sovereignty and European unity. Simultaneously with the formation of the Alliance of Free Democrats, the "historical parties" emerged from deep hibernation, first and foremost the Independent Smallholder Party on November 18, followed by the Social Democratic Party at the end of the same month. Although the HSWP was unable to forestall these developments, the security services planted agents in the ranks of these groups to exacerbate already existing internal tensions and to influence their political platforms. Thus the historical parties were split between moderates who would collaborate with the ruling party and those who supported a more pronounced oppositionist line. Grósz's brief reign, dubbed *grósznoszt* in Budapest slang, attempted to accommodate change without having to relinquish power or to alter the basic principles of the political system. While the new party chief urged profound economic transformation, his public utterances revealed him to be a political hard-liner. In the midst of this tsunami of new parties, the ruling party insisted on the formula of "socialist pluralism" and a single-party system even though a de facto multiparty system already existed. Grósz attempted to rally his party with a speech on November 29, declaring that Hungary was facing "class struggle" and summoning his party to confront "hostile counter-revolutionary forces." Otherwise, he threatened, "anarchy and chaos... white terror would prevail." Although his rhetoric was obsolete and out of place, it did strike a chord with many in the West who feared that the devolution of communist power in Eastern Europe would mean a resurgence of unbridled nationalism and ethnic hatred. In a narrow circle, the party leader discussed the possibility of declaring a state of emergency. Grósz's bellicose speech prompted the leaders of eight independent organizations to sign a letter proposing a national Round Table.

Grósz was faced with a double whammy. Alongside the difficult political environment, the economy had reached a critical phase that made structural change inevitable. By the middle of 1987, the country was facing bankruptcy; IMF director John Whittome made known that austerity measures and structural reforms needed to be implemented without delay. These problems resulted from the ill-conceived policy of growth acceleration, the declining value of the dollar against currencies in which Hungarian loans were floated, and large-scale investments at home and abroad that turned out to be financially catastrophic. After Kádár was ousted, Hungary committed itself to a string of measures that would lead to an economic regime change. In return for an agreement with the IMF, the government pledged to narrow the range of subsidized commodities, to reduce funding for unprofitable companies, and to allow companies to set wages and conduct foreign trade. Private individuals would be allowed to form limited liability companies and state firms would be transformed into joint-stock companies. This would come in addition to other measures of creeping capitalism such as the introduction of sales and income taxes.[23]

At the turn of 1988 and the "miracle year," 1989, the West confronted a dilemma. Hungary required fundamental political and economic changes in order to avoid massive unrest, but if these changes were to spiral out of control, the country could be thrown into disarray, with unforeseeable consequences for regional stability. Thus Western leaders supported transformation along a tightrope: going far enough to satisfy the domestic appetite for democracy and to stave off economic collapse, but stopping short of upsetting the status quo and possibly the peace and equilibrium of Europe. In July 1989, the deputy head of the HSWP Central Committee's foreign relations department, Imre Szokai, summed up the Hungarian perception of the Western attitude: "It is the firm view of our western European partners that to preserve European stability and the historically evolved status quo there should be no regime change in Hungary [and] Hungarian politics should not impinge upon the USSR's security, military and political interests. They consider even mention of Hungary's exit from the Warsaw Pact as dangerous fiction.... The activities of [U.S.] ambassador Mark Palmer are in stark contrast to this."[24] Palmer's activity did not necessarily reflect the views of his government. He later admitted to having had "differences of opinion with some members of the Bush administration about how aggressively an ambassador could support the opposition."[25] Although Washington's grand strategy was allegedly "to end the Cold War and the division of Europe through the peaceful, democratic transformation of the eastern half," in its practical implementation U.S. policy was cautious and not at all different from the European approach to the communist world, where, as presidential advisor Robert Hutchings put it, reforms had outpaced even the boldest objectives.[26] For example, the Bush administration envisaged a transition period of a few years to full democracy. This calendar would soon be overtaken by events.

SOVIET RESPONSES

Soviet reactions to the rapid disintegration of the satellite zone were hard to predict. Soviet civilian and military leaders at the time continued to see the region – which provided the Soviet Union with the strategic presence in Europe necessary to its status as a world power – as an economic and military asset. Little if anything in Soviet policy toward Eastern Europe had changed after Gorbachev came to power. The new leader insisted on strengthening the Warsaw Pact, which in 1985 was extended for another thirty years. In May 1987, defense minister Marshal Sokolov called on the Eastern European governments to contribute more to the alliance's defense efforts, and when Gorbachev visited Czechoslovakia that year, he publicly condoned the intervention of 1968. Gorbachev's rhetoric began to change in 1988 when he pledged unconditional respect for the principles of equality and noninterference and to allow the socialist countries to define for themselves the path of their development. In July 1989, the Soviet Politburo decided not to use force against Eastern Europe, but the decision was not disclosed so as not to weaken the communist regimes.[27] The historian Csaba Békés aptly called this policy "the floating of the Brezhnev doctrine."[28] In any case, it is doubtful whether the Soviet Union was in a position to use force against more than one of its allies. In 1956, when the Soviet Union was closer to the peak of its strength than in 1989, the Kremlin would not consider using force against both Poland and Hungary. Even then, the first Soviet intervention that took place on October 24 failed to reach its objective of suppressing resistance in the streets of Budapest. It is unlikely that the Soviets could have intervened in more than one satellite with the hope of winning without unacceptable losses. Finally, the use of force would have deprived Gorbachev's reforms of any legitimacy and would have tarnished his reputation beyond repair. Moreover, some elements in the Soviet elite were known to deplore the "loss" of Eastern Europe.[29]

The assumption that Gorbachev no longer regarded Eastern Europe as a priority for Soviet foreign policy is often used as an explanation for his policies in 1989.[30] This explanation suggests that Gorbachev let the former satellites loose, but it does not hold water. In 1988–89, Gorbachev saw Hungarian leaders at least as often as any Soviet leader before him had; First Secretary Grósz, Prime Minister Németh, and Party President Nyers were all received in Moscow in 1988–89. KGB chairman Vladimir Kriuchkov also appeared in Budapest to persuade Kádár to resign. In addition to bilateral meetings, the Soviet leader met his East European counterparts at meetings of the Warsaw Pact. Soviet ambassador Boris Stukalin pursued a hands-on diplomacy in Budapest. Deputy foreign minister Ivan Aboimov visited in September 1989 and met not only government and party leaders, but also the chairman of the Hungarian Democratic Forum. None of this suggests that the Soviets' allies were not important to them anymore. Let us not forget that Khrushchev did not bother to travel to Budapest during the Hungarian crisis of 1956, yet nobody would argue that Eastern Europe had not mattered to him. In any case, Eastern Europe had never belonged to the realm of *foreign* policy for the Kremlin. Satellite affairs tended to be treated as matters of domestic as much as external politics. Closely related to the former claim is the notion that it cost the Soviets a lot of money to keep Eastern Europe. Were this true, it would explain the Soviet motive for letting Eastern Europe go. Only Soviet memoirs make this claim, however, and there is no credible research to support it. Soviet leaders have always liked to pretend that they poured money into Eastern Europe, while we know that the opposite was true. Hungarian documents from the late 1980s suggest that the net transfer of wealth went from Hungary back toward the imperial center. But even if we accept that the truth was in the middle – at least one Soviet organ, the Central Committee, said that Eastern Europe was an economic asset – later Soviet claims should be treated with skepticism. Because of the artificial nature of the Comecon's currency, the transferable ruble, the fact that pricing was the result of political bargaining, and the highly complicated and often hidden nature of export subsidies to the Soviet Union, the question of who supported whom must be left open. The fact remains that at the end of 1989 the Soviet Union was no longer paying for products imported from Hungary and had a deficit of $1 billion on the bilateral clearing account. Gorbachev hoped that Budapest would "solve its problems by better utilizing the possibilities of socialism."[31] In July 1989, he told the attendees of the Warsaw Pact Political Consultative Committee that reforms were intended to "demonstrate the superiority of socialism."[32] As one historian put it, Gorbachev's decision to push far-reaching changes in Eastern Europe was based on the expectation that reform-minded communist leaders would emerge and join him in the pursuit of socialism. Gorbachev began moving away from Marxist-Leninist principles after the transformation of Eastern Europe in 1989.[33] When the Hungarian premier paid Gorbachev a visit in March 1989, he reflected on a speech Gorbachev had recently given in Kiev. Gorbachev said all the right things: the diversity of socialism, noninterference, full equality. His speech contained one proviso, namely that the socialist states had one common objective. Németh took this to mean that each country would construct "democratic socialism." Gorbachev told him that he would prefer plurality within one party, otherwise "do as you please." He deplored Pozsgay's speech on the reinterpretation of 1956, which he said contained "extremities." This was a clear indication of the limits of change Gorbachev wanted to see. Yet the Soviet leader also made it clear that he would not use military force. The prime minister then broached a topic that had shocked him after he was sworn in: the deployment of nuclear missiles at an ultra-secret location. Németh wanted the Soviets to take them out. Gorbachev would not commit himself, but in December Németh received a letter from Prime Minister Nikolai Rizhkov that the warheads had been removed. The warheads left as they had come: nobody in Hungary was informed or had even noticed.

That Gorbachev wanted to reform socialism – whatever that may have meant – was apparent to external observers. In late November 1989, Senator Richard Lugar of Indiana warned Bush that "in public statements Gorbachev continues to defend socialism and argue that economic reform and not economic revolution is under way in Eastern Europe. His analysis is wrong."[34] The Soviets seemingly failed to realize that the ancien régime could be discarded altogether. In July 1989, when the multiparty system had already been recognized, Anatoly Dobrynin, head of the International Department of the Communist Party of the Soviet Union (CPSU), confided that the Soviet leadership had not even considered the possibility of a coalition government in Hungary.[35] There is evidence that the leaders in Moscow did not grasp the possible ramifications of the changes that were transpiring in their sphere of interest. When Prime Minister Németh told Gorbachev in March that he was having the border barrier dismantled and that doing so might have consequences for other socialist countries, Gorbachev did not seem to understand what he was driving at. Many months after the Hungarian Political Committee abolished the one-party system in the midst of the East German refugee crisis, Deputy Foreign Minister Vladimir Petrovsky, a specialist of Western Europe and the United States, took his wife on vacation at the shore of balmy Lake Balaton. He used the occasion to confer with leading functionaries of the Foreign Ministry, including the minister himself, and was briefed on the political situation by the Soviet special services. Nevertheless, after the visit, Petrovsky asserted that "the Soviet Union, Poland, and Hungary would be the pathbreakers of the renewal of socialism."[36] Apparently, ideological blinders still impeded an objective appraisal of the situation.

Was Eastern Europe still an asset? CPSU analysts thought that trade with Eastern Europe "greatly favored" the Soviet Union. Moreover, Hungary suffered from the Soviets' large and growing trade deficit in transferable rubles. But converting the system to U.S. dollars, as proposed by some Hungarian experts, could have produced a crippling Hungarian deficit of $1.2 billion within a year. Hungary depended on Soviet energy, but the Soviet Union was no longer able to pay for its imports from Hungary; as a result, Hungary had a trade surplus of a billion dollars, which it could not afford. "From the outset [the socialist states] formed a security zone, which provided strategic defense for the center of socialism. Today . . . the role of Eastern Europe remains essentially the same," CPSU analysts argued in early 1989.[37]

In 1988, Gorbachev had announced unilateral troop reductions in East Central Europe and the western military districts of the USSR. This was followed by Hungary's budget-dictated decision in March 1989 to reduce its own forces. On May 16, 1989, the Political Committee of the HSWP passed a resolution to push for a Soviet troop withdrawal. But Gorbachev protested that the proposed reduction was hasty and should be tied to the Vienna arms reduction talks. The same applied to Soviet troop reductions. In Vienna, Hungary pushed for both cuts in the Hungarian forces and a Soviet withdrawal. Although initially Hungarian negotiators gained the impression that the Soviet military "no longer regarded the stationing of troops in adjacent states a prerequisite of security," Moscow's position shifted frustratingly slowly.[38] It soon turned out that little had changed in the Soviet attitude toward military matters. Although on May 16 the Political Committee passed a resolution that called for negotiations on the withdrawal of Soviet troops stationed in Hungary, there was little to suggest that the Soviet Union would agree to anything more than a partial pullout. In the Treaty on Conventional Forces in Europe (CFE) talks in Vienna, things were conducted in the old way. The Soviet delegation confronted the allies with accomplished facts and "sought to degrade coordination [of policy positions] to the level of supporting the Soviet stance." According to a Hungarian account of the proceedings, "the Soviet delegation was ill-prepared" and unwilling to compromise. The thinking of the Soviet military remained unchanged: "They are preparing to preserve their East European presence in an unchanged form ... they expect an unconditional recognition of Soviet security needs."[39] Moscow was sending mixed messages about the future of Soviet military occupation. When Nyers visited Moscow, Gorbachev agreed to a declaration that Soviet troop reductions could lead to full withdrawal. But high-ranking Soviet officials continued to emphasize that the Warsaw Pact must remain the "bedrock of our collective security." In September, Soviet military journals published an article by army general Piotr N. Lashchenko praising the 1956 invasion of Hungary. Clearly, as Mark Kramer has noted, the article was meant to ensure that the political changes in Budapest would not alter the rationale for deploying troops in Hungary.[40]

In March, Gorbachev explicitly rejected the dissolution of the Warsaw Pact, which he sought to retain on a democratized basis.[41] Soviet deputy foreign minister Ivan Aboimov called "the presence of Soviet troops in Hungary an important guarantee of European security" and was worried by statements demanding their full withdrawal.[42] Soviet Defense Minister Dmitri Yazov asserted that the Warsaw Pact was the only guarantee of European stability and would "remain strong irrespective of developments in Eastern Europe."[43] Yazov also declared that his "whole life was being betrayed as he watched the communist regimes collapse."[44]

Gorbachev's concept of a "common European home" did not necessarily include European reunification as it ultimately unfolded. In April 1989, high-ranking Soviet foreign ministry officials explained that Gorbachev's vision was built on "the respect for European political and territorial realities, [and] the maintenance of the alliances" founded on cooperation. The German question would be solved on the basis of a common German identity, but two German states. In fact, the Soviet Foreign Ministry revealed that the idea of the "common European home" may have been conceived to offset the process of Western integration. As a high-ranking official in the Soviet Foreign Ministry explained, "West European aspirations for political and military integration are at odds with positive European processes, the idea of 'common European home.'... Political methods, the reduction of... armed forces, doctrinal change, and the improvement of East-West relations can balance the negative effect of West European political-military integration, which may be influenced in a direction that is favorable for us."[45] In briefing the Warsaw Pact allies on the outcome of the Malta summit with Bush, the Soviet leader declared that although there was an "objective need for efforts to overcome the division of Europe, [it was] unacceptable to realize unity based on the liquidation of socialism and exclusively on the basis of western values, [and] the replacement of the Brezhnev doctrine with a sort of Bush doctrine."[46] Canadian prime minister Brian Mulroney and his Swedish counterpart had an unofficial conversation with the general secretary a few days prior to the Malta summit. When asked about the possibility of Polish and Hungarian withdrawal from the Warsaw Pact, Gorbachev affirmed that there should be no changes in the alliance because it "would be seriously destabilizing."[47] Soviet military commanders vigorously opposed the dissolution of the Warsaw Pact. Lt. Gen. Ivan Mikhalin summed up the view of many of his peers in claiming that "the West is isolating us on the periphery of the European continent." The commander of the Pacific Fleet added that the USSR had "returned to the situation in 1939."[48] Facing fierce opposition to any reconsideration of the Soviet role in Europe, not only in military circles but also in the party, the reformers around Gorbachev could likely not have renounced the instruments of Soviet presence in East Central Europe without the major upheavals in the adjacent states, even if they had really wanted to. Thus the initiative for liberation had to come from outside the Soviet Union.

AUSTRIAN AND ITALIAN RESPONSES

Neutral Austria, which had built a close relationship with Kádár's Hungary, was sensitive to challenges to Soviet control because of its precarious geographical position, the proximity of Soviet forces, and its vulnerability to a potential flood of refugees. Only two days after the HSWP Central Committee (recognizing a fait accompli) made the historic decision on February 11, 1989, to accept a multiparty system – albeit with the proviso that the party would retain its preponderant position in politics and society – and a re-evaluation of the 1956 revolution that undermined the ruling party's legitimacy, Prime Minister Németh explained to Chancellor Franz Vranitzky that Hungary would introduce democracy and a "socialist market system." Vranitzky responded that "the danger of domestic changes in Hungary spiraling out of control causes great anxiety in the Austrian leadership."[49] Hungarian diplomats learned that the Austrian Socialist Party was baffled and deeply troubled by the discussion of neutrality and the question of 1956 under way in Hungary and was skeptical about the possibility of "real elections."[50] A Freedom Party politician, Friedhelm Frischenschläger, stated that "European stability rested on the status quo."[51] Furthermore, the Austrians emphasized Gorbachev's precarious position and the dire consequences of his potential removal.

Aside from Wiener Allianz president Ernst Baumgartner, who advocated Hungary's return to the principles of Leninism, Austrians recommended slow and predictable democratization.[52] The general secretary of the Austrian Foreign Ministry, Thomas Klestil, queried Gyula Horn, Hungary's foreign minister, about the limits of transformation and wondered when these would lead to tensions with the USSR. Austrians feared the ramifications of change for themselves. Foreign minister Alois Mock was concerned that the Hungarian decision in February to remove the electronic border defense system would increase the number of Eastern European refugees arriving in Austria. Growing financial burdens could lead Austria to alter its refugee policy.[53] By midsummer, Austrian socialists expressed anxiety that the HSWP might fall to pieces and anarchy would set in, a danger just as real as the reversal of reforms. Their message, as reported by the Hungarian Embassy in Vienna, was that "Hungary should not cause a headache for Europe again."[54] Austrian views remained unchanged throughout 1989. The spokesman for the center-right Austrian People's Party reiterated that the USSR and the stationing of Soviet troops abroad were important factors in stabilizing Eastern Europe, a statement likely prompted by rumors of an impending Romanian attack on Hungary.[55]

Austria was part of Italy's Quadragonale initiative, launched in Budapest in November 1989, which aimed at promoting regional cooperation between Italy, Yugoslavia, Austria, and Hungary in the fields of industry, science, transportation, and environmental protection. Italian Foreign

Minister Gianni De Michelis saw the initiative, which received Soviet and American blessings, as Italy's way of helping the region to find its place in the "common European home," but the project was not entirely altruistic. Harking back to the old rivalry between Rome and Berlin, an Italian official explained in mid-October that it was "more advantageous for Hungary to use Italy's mediation toward the EC than Germany's." One must take into account, he argued, the problems with the balance of power that might arise "once Germany is unified."[56] The Hungarians were receptive, but problems arose with Yugoslavia and Austria at an early stage. In 1990, the Quadragonale was broadened into a Pentagonale including Czechoslovakia, but the initiative petered out.

THE WEST GERMAN RESPONSE

By the late 1980s, the FRG emerged as Hungary's most important political and economic partner.[57] This was due to Bonn's efforts to democratize and liberalize Eastern Europe by promoting *Wandel durch Annäherung* (change through rapprochement), but from the Hungarian perspective, the main consideration was the need for economic reform. Indeed, according to some accounts, Kádár's crucial removal from power in 1988 was encouraged by the prospect of West German financial aid.[58] Throughout its history, Hungary had been part of the Germanic political, cultural, and economic space; the interwar period saw the gradual growth of German economic and political influence at the expense of Italy's. In the late 1980s, it was assumed that Germany would regain the influence it once wielded there.

In the crucial year of 1989, politicians in the FRG on both the right and left wings of the political spectrum, like their counterparts elsewhere in Western Europe and the United States, encouraged reforms in Poland and Hungary but were highly concerned about their pace and scope. Chancellor Helmut Kohl expressed a positive view of several Eastern European regimes. When Gorbachev complained about the clan-like nature of the Bulgarian government, Kohl retorted that he "liked the Bulgarians." He commended the progress made by Bulgaria and claimed that Bulgarian representatives visiting the FRG "think and operate with very modern concepts and they vividly absorb our economic experience." Kohl added that he "really liked" Bulgarian leader Todor Zhivkov, whom he considered a "very flexible politician." Kohl expressed similarly warm feelings toward the Hungarians. In a particularly twisted reading of history, he wrote to Bush that for "over a thousand years there had been no armed conflict between Germany and Hungary," neglecting to mention that the Wehrmacht had invaded Hungary in 1944. He praised Hungarian foreign policy and urged the president to provide economic support.[59] At their meeting in February 1989, Kohl told British prime minister Margaret Thatcher that if events spiraled out of control in Hungary, it could upset the balance in Europe. He also expressed concern about the country's ability to service its debt. Foreign minister Hans-Dietrich Genscher spoke disparagingly of the Hungarian opposition, claiming that it existed only on paper and, unlike in Poland, had no charismatic leadership.[60] Genscher believed that more arms control in Europe would reduce the likelihood of Soviet military or even political intervention in Eastern Europe. He felt that the Soviets wanted stability, which he thought would rest on the consent of the public in the region and on these countries' remaining in the Warsaw Pact. Therefore Genscher urged the West to "stress" that it would not profit from the problems Eastern European reforms might cause for Moscow.[61] Only a few days before the first pluralistic election in Poland, Chancellor Kohl suggested to President Bush that "the U.S. and the FRG should help Wojciech Jaruzelski."[62] Regarding a proposed World Bank loan to Poland designed to keep its faltering economy afloat, the Germans equivocated. Robert Blackwill speculated that Bonn would keep open the loan until the "Poles agreed to Bonn's desiderata with respect to the treatment of ethnic Germans in Poland."[63] Speaking to Gorbachev a day after the Hungarian Round Table talks got under way on June 13, Kohl reassured Gorbachev that his advice to the Hungarians was that they "should not accelerate too much, because you might lose control over the levers of control and the mechanism will start to destroy itself" (*Mozhno poteriat' richagami upravlenia i mekhanism nachniet rabotat' vraznos*).[64] In conversations with Hungarian party leaders, the West Germans urged self-restraint. The chairman of the Free Democrats, Wolfgang Mischnick, warned that a break with the Warsaw Pact would be tantamount to giving up the chance to implement the reforms.[65] Baden-Württemberg's premier, Lothar Späth, cautioned against the immediate introduction of a market economy and expressed admiration for the reforms. Regarding the opposition, he added that "unrealistic viewpoints were threatening the country's stability." Foreign Minister Horn reassured Späth that Hungary would not leave the Warsaw Pact and, sensing the West German mood, he denigrated the democratic opposition by claiming that they "operated with Stalinist methods and may cause problems in foreign policy." Horn falsely claimed that "radicals" were receiving support from the United States.[66] The Federal Republic's apprehension was affirmed in a conversation between President Richard von Weizsäcker and Bush shortly before the latter's landmark visit to Warsaw and Budapest. Obviously alarmed by the outcome of the Polish election, Weizsäcker declared that "the reform process in the East must go ahead under control and not become too turbulent." He claimed that Poland and Hungary wanted to come closer to the West but stay in the Warsaw Pact. Weizsäcker suggested the timehonored method of regulating the international status of Eastern Europe in negotiations among the great powers. He suggested that Bush "have quiet talks with Moscow about the future of Eastern Europe." The German president also disclaimed any ulterior motive: Germany "does not want another option to the East."[67] Simultaneously, Kohl also reassured Gorbachev that he was aware of the realities of European politics: "I am not a coward... but I... know history and geography very well."

By then a narrative of transformation in Hungary was taking root in Bonn, according to which the reform wing of the Hungarian Socialist Workers' Party was solely responsible for the changes while the opposition was only jeopardizing them by being reckless. In this spirit, Volker Rühe, general secretary of the Christian Democratic Union (CDU), told HSWP president Rezső Nyers, who was complaining about the prospect of a "right-wing danger," that "no fundamental reform in Hungary could have happened without the reform forces of the HSWP and no other parties could have come into existence without it." Rühe was concerned that the opposition would use "demagogic, nationalistic slogans to mobilize the masses in order to oust the HSWP from power."[68] But leaders of the opposition Hungarian Democratic Forum reassured Rühe that the communists would be involved in the new government and that the forum would respect the country's foreign alliances.[69] Upon hearing Nyers' warning about the danger of destabilization and the imminent split in the HSWP,

Social Democratic Party (SPD) president Hans-Jochen Vogel stated that in normal circumstances he would not welcome the establishment of a communist party, but "in Hungary this would be particularly welcome." He expressed an interest in deep-seated change "short of chaos," shorthand for complete regime change. Vogel's thinking was informed in part by concern for Soviet politics: he told Nyers that "Gorbachev's fall would be tragic."[70]

In June 1989, Kohl reassured Gorbachev that the FRG would refrain from interference in the internal developments of other states, including Poland and Hungary, "so as not to plunge Europe back to a time of tension and mistrust."[71] When the chancellor met Németh in Gymnich on the 5th of August, the prime minister appeared ambivalent about Hungary's role in the Warsaw Pact, claiming that neutrality was not part of his party's plans, but that any foreign intervention would force him to rethink that position. He also asserted that developments in Poland were causing problems for Gorbachev and revealed that the Soviet leader was putting pressure on the Polish party to stay in power. Németh then complained about a comment made by Senator Alan Cranston of California, who had opined in an interview that the precondition of U.S. aid to Hungary was a coalition government. Kohl declared that Bush did not think that way and intimated that he would ask the president to support Hungary. He also affirmed that "reforms should not be precipitate." This was also the German message for Poland: Kohl disclosed that the minister of labor was on his way to Warsaw with instructions to tell Lech Wałęsa, the leader of the Solidarity movement, to "keep their [Polish] actions within bounds so as not to endanger reforms."[72]

After October 1989, Kohl hoped for an arrangement that would allow the ruling party, now renamed the Hungarian Socialist Party following a schism in the HSWP, to continue to be a part of the government. He told Bush that the "present government was taking an enormous risk: the changes have their origins in the reform movement in the Communist Party, but it is not at all certain that the reformers will be able to get credit in the course of the election... there might be a coalition."[73] Bonn's preference for the reform communists was made known to Budapest. In the chancellor's view, as communicated by his political adviser, Friedberg Pflüger, stability and predictability were the precondition of helping Hungary. "The guarantee for all this would be a Socialist–Democratic Forum coalition resulting from elections to be held as soon as possible."[74] This was a clear attempt to interfere in Hungarian domestic affairs and to move them in a direction that by that point was against the will of most voters. But the regime change would not be scripted in Bonn, or in Moscow for that matter. As late as February 1990, the foreign ministry in Bonn "recommended" that Hungary stay in the Warsaw Pact and Comecon because its leaving would "harm" the FRG's talks with the USSR.[75]

THE FRENCH RESPONSE

Robert Hutchings has observed that "Eastern Europe had little place in the [French] strategic vision except as part of the distant goal of a Europe free of the superpowers."[76] French historian Thomas Schreiber has written that some French political circles were not enthusiastic after the Polish elections of June 1989 and the opening of Hungarian borders to East Germans in September; President Mitterrand himself remained cautious.[77] Mitterrand's main concern was to preserve stability, and this consideration came before the restoration of independence. The French president made no secret of this. He spoke with Bush shortly after the latter concluded his visit to Budapest. Mitterrand declared that "it was important not push the East European states to withdraw from the Warsaw Pact, which might have to exist to the end of the century for stability. . . . It is simply too soon to talk about dissolving the Warsaw Pact."[78] Despite Gorbachev's rhetoric about turning over a new leaf in European history, many in Western Europe as well as the Bush administration remained concerned about Soviet intentions. Shortly after the Austro-Hungarian border was opened and the first noncommunist prime minister of postwar Poland was sworn in, Mitterrand expressed his concern for the future of NATO: he told Bush that "the USSR could come into France in a few days."[79]

Only briefly had Eastern Europe ever played a pivotal role in French policies. Starting in 1920, Paris had supported the Little Entente to safeguard France's eastern security against Germany and Russia, but had failed to provide explicit security guarantees for its protégés.[80] In the

"Together We Liberated Eastern Europe"   389

mid-1930s, the French backed away from the system they had created in Eastern Europe. Although the 1960s saw a renewed French interest in the region, Paris was not about to take responsibility for it, and French economic activity was far smaller than that of West Germany. Mitterrand turned down Kohl's offer of a common policy toward the East, even though France was wary of German designs in the communist part of the continent. Paris may have found it too risky to support changes that threatened to upset stability behind the Iron Curtain. Domestic changes had to satisfy the criteria of stability and predictability.

Initially, Mitterrand was forward-looking. In November 1988, he talked to HSWP first secretary Károly Grósz about the need to transcend Yalta and for Europeans to decide on their own fates. Mitterrand stressed the need for cooperation "against American cultural expansionism on the wings of Japanese technology."[81] This was perhaps a subtle hint that it was more important to rid France of the United States than to rid the East of the Soviets. In early 1989, French business began to take an active interest in Hungary. Although in Hungary's estimation France recognized that Germany was making economic inroads, not even a symbolic measure was taken to facilitate Hungarian exports to France.[82] The French response to the abolition of the single-party system was cautious. It was reported that because of the anxiety exhibited by political circles regarding the pace of reform, the French company Matra canceled its plans to create a joint venture in Hungary.[83] On February 15, Mitterrand's advisor Loic Hennekine told a Hungarian diplomat, László Vass, that Paris supported Hungary's reforms but did not want these to destabilize the continent or to lead to political and economic crisis.[84] A Hungarian summary of French views emphasized that they deplored "demagogic" demands such as Hungary's exit from the Warsaw Pact. Paris did not understand why, in contrast to Poland, the Hungarian government had backed down against the opposition. A more gradual, predictable reform process was required.[85] Although one French official reckoned that in ten years' time Hungary might become a member of the European Community, on February 28, 1989, French planning minister Lionel Stoléru told the president of the Hungarian National Planning Office, Ernő Kemenes, that the EC wanted to become a bastion in the economic struggle against the United

States and Japan and that therefore transition in the East should not impede the strong union of the twelve. A rapid acceleration of the reforms in Eastern Europe, Stoléru thought, would end in catastrophe.[86]

In October, the HSWP was dissolved, ending the party-state system that had existed in Hungary since 1948. The communists' rapid demise alarmed the French Socialist Party, which opined that the victory of the right wing was not in the interest of Western Europe or Hungary.[87] On November 17th, Elysée secretary-general Jean-Louis Bianco explained that Western assistance to Hungary should not interfere with Hungarian-Soviet relations. The USSR had clarified the limits of change, which were the continued existence of the alliances and the inviolability of boundaries, conditions that the United States and Western Europe accepted.[88] Quai d'Orsay director Jacques Blot described the dangers of an exclusive German orientation to a Hungarian diplomat, arguing that France could provide the right political, cultural, and economic counterbalance.[89] In early December, former president Valéry Giscard D'Estaing met state minister Imre Pozsgay, who had recently traveled to Washington to sound out whether the Bush administration would strike a deal with the Soviets behind the Hungarians' backs. Giscard claimed to agree with Mitterrand that the transition period in Hungary would be lengthy. But membership in the EC required compatible economies and membership in NATO, which in Giscard's view ruled out even Austria's entry.[90]

It was apparent to the Hungarians that France wanted slow and limited change. According to a briefing on Mitterrand's talks in the GDR, which the Hungarians received from the French Embassy in East Berlin, the president regarded unification as a German matter, but preferred to maintain the GDR's international status. Unification should not lead to destabilization in Europe or to border changes.[91] As Budapest humorists put it, the French president loved Germany so much, he wanted to see two of them. Mitterrand went to Budapest in January 1990. His hosts stressed the importance of French support for the transition. Mitterrand declared that he had come to give an impetus to bilateral relations and to discuss the future of Europe. Earlier, he argued, Europe had been under the "tutelage" of great powers, but the Bush-Gorbachev meeting in Malta had offered the opportunity to transcend this state of affairs. Since 1945

"Together We Liberated Eastern Europe"   391

there had been no stable continental balance, and this would have to be rectified through negotiation. German unification was unavoidable, but it should not be hastened. It would take at least ten years to build a European confederation. Political and legal arrangements would have to be made between the two halves of Europe to guarantee security and economic cooperation.[92] Thus the Soviet bloc would survive at least temporarily. In this respect there had been no change in Mitterrand's position since 1988. The president thought that "the Warsaw Pact might have to exist to the end of the century for stability."[93]

THE BRITISH RESPONSE

As Geraint Hughes has shown, "traditional British policy towards Eastern Europe ... emphasized stability rather than self-determination ... [as] violent uprisings ... could have a dangerous impact on European security."[94] In 1989, London perceived similar threats if the reforms went too far. Robert Hutchings, who saw events as an insider, argues that "British thinking ... saw few prospects for meaningful change and many dangers for the cohesion of the West."[95] Foreign secretary Geoffrey Howe admitted that the changes in Eastern Europe raised a number of strategic issues, primarily in Western policies toward the Soviet Union.[96] London initially suggested that Hungarian reforms might improve Gorbachev's chances. Margaret Thatcher, who had been skeptical of Kádár's reforms,[97] told foreign minister Péter Várkonyi in mid-March 1989 that the success of Hungarian perestroika could influence Gorbachev's choices and serve as a model for the USSR. The British leader claimed to have told Gorbachev that Hungary was a showcase for socialist transformation.[98] The phrase "socialist transformation," a term used by the conservative wing of the reform communists in Hungary, suggested that Thatcher was mindful of Soviet concerns. A few days earlier, the British ambassador in Budapest had asked opposition leaders to be more patient with the Hungarian leadership and not to cause unnecessary complications.[99] In September, Thatcher assured Gorbachev of her sympathy with the Soviet position according to which reform in Eastern Europe should not question the Warsaw Pact.[100] As one historian of 1989 has concluded, "the British memory of the first half of the 20th century was a painful one; the second half looked much better in comparison, so she [Thatcher] was understandably loath to make any changes."[101]

Foreign Office officials explained that the future of Eastern Europe depended on the progress of the USSR, which was the most dangerous state in Eastern Europe and hence needed – for the good of all – to feel secure. The dissolution of the Warsaw Pact would increase the Soviets' sense of insecurity, which would have unpredictable outcomes. Therefore Britain attributed great significance to regional stability and advised the reform states to be wary; too many things should not be changed at once. London did hope to provide economic assistance to Poland and Hungary; the question was how this could be done without jeopardizing mutual security. The British finally declared that they hoped for the presence of reform communists – Pozsgay, Németh, Horn – in the coalition government after the election, which would be able to count on London's support just like Solidarity had in Poland.[102]

EC RESPONSES

Just like the member states, the European Community (EC) groped for an appropriate response to the Eastern challenge and was more concerned with the Soviet threat perception than with anything else. In January, Jacques Delors, the EC president, talked about the advantages of a single European market, but concerning the "common European home," the head of the EC secretariat for political cooperation, Giovanni Januzzi, told the Hungarian ambassador in Brussels that the EC had no intention of "surrendering its own building."[103] The EC sent mixed signals. At the G7 summit in July, it was decided that the EC would coordinate the aid the G24 had offered to Poland and Hungary. Januzzi simultaneously outlined EC expectations for Hungary, welcoming its rapprochement with the EC without expecting it to "eschew socialism" or to adopt "wild capitalism." In other words, Hungary would end up with a communist-led government. Moreover, Januzzi indicated that for the sake of European stability, it was Hungary's "obligation" to remain in the Warsaw Pact, just as France was in NATO.[104] NATO secretary general Manfred Woerner set his sights on a "Europe of self-determination and freedom and free of the Berlin Wall and the Brezhnev doctrine."[105] But he did not think it was realistic to convince Gorbachev that it was better to have "friendly neighbors" than a military alliance. The Russians, Woerner asserted, "see the Warsaw Pact as the great achievement of the war," which "contributes to a feeling of security" and was "a condition of their world power position."[106]

AMERICAN RESPONSES

Historical works and memoirs reconstructing the events of 1989 give the impression that the Bush administration's policies were highly concerned with the dramatic and quickly unfolding transition behind the Iron Curtain. As far as one of the pacesetters of the transition, Hungary, was concerned, in the first months of 1989, little if anything changed in the normal flow of bilateral relations; the Bush administration paid little heed to the developments unfolding there. This was still essentially a Cold War relationship. In May 1989, Robert Hutchings, President Bush's special assistant for Eastern Europe, asserted that "Hungarian intelligence was among the countries that were the most hostile regarding American interests."[107] Deputy secretary of defense Paul Wolfowitz acknowledged that this activity was related to Soviet policies directed at the acquisition of prohibited items and demanded guarantees that Hungarian intelligence would not transfer illegally acquired technology to the Soviets.[108] Because of the Conrad affair and the illegal acquisition of computer parts, U.S. officials suspected that Hungary might also have played a role in a terrorist attack against a South Korean aircraft. In a conversation with interior minister István Horváth in January 1989, Ambassador Palmer said U.S. intelligence knew that "internationally known terrorists regularly spend time in Hungary." Palmer added that the two perpetrators of the attack on the South Korean aircraft had also visited Hungary. Palmer warned the minister that "certain people" in Washington thought that Hungary had had something to do with the terror attack.[109]

Even though important political changes were occurring in Budapest, there was little Miklós Németh and his reform administration could do about their economic woes. The Hungarians were in a difficult predicament. Kádár's social contract offered prosperity in return for a silent acceptance of the political state of affairs. The Soviet Union was no longer in a position to bail out its allies; in fact, Moscow was no longer paying for Hungarian exports to the USSR. The Comecon, which had always been a political organization masking the Soviets' economic domination, had collapsed, and the Soviet Union had accumulated a $1 billion deficit with Hungary. International organizations, the World Bank, and the IMF urged stringent and immediate austerity measures, which would have been politically suicidal for the incumbent regime. The Hungarians had nowhere to go for help. Minister of Foreign Affairs Gyula Horn informed the prime minister that he expected "substantial American support" for the "consolidation of our economic and financial situation and our reform program." Horn told Senator Cranston that the "East" would not help and that the United States could play a "key role."[110] The Hungarians were told that a relaxation of CoCom controls had been ruled out because of their intelligence activities and their illegal acquisitions of technology.[111] Automatic exemption from the Jackson-Vanik amendment would require a change in Hungarian legislation regarding emigration, as well as the abolition of a category in the penal code that criminalized shirking work.[112] In addition, State Department officials protested that Hungary was running a trade surplus of $100 million with the United States and demanded the rectification of this situation, even though Hungary was on the verge of financial collapse.[113] Even though there were widespread expectations of large-scale U.S. aid, the State Department made it clear that no Marshall Plan was forthcoming. Even though Poland and Hungary were treated separately from the rest of Eastern Europe, "they could not count on significant financial support from the [U.S.] administration even if the political situation warranted it."[114] The fact that Hungarian diplomats returned to the question of financial aid despite this information shows how drastic the country's economic predicament was.[115]

As early as 1988, John Whitehead asserted in Budapest that Eastern Europe would need to become more prominent in U.S. foreign policy "in the near future," as the emerging social changes provided an opportunity to realize American goals. Whitehead urged the states of Eastern Europe to exploit this "unique" and "ephemeral" opportunity to turn to the West for assistance in order to solve their problems and thereby implement lasting political and economic change peacefully.[116] Budapest was eager to take advantage of the apparent opportunity. In early January 1989, Prime

Minister Németh told Senator Arlen Specter of Pennsylvania that he was aiming at a profound transformation of the political and economic system in Hungary. This change would lead to "a democratic pluralistic constitutional state," a "market economy," and "national cooperation." The prime minister must have suspected that the rapid changes aroused concerns in Washington. He therefore made it clear that the transformation would take place in agreement "with the prospective coalition partners," with an eye to maintaining "economic and political stability." Thus the Hungarian leadership was committed to profound but peaceful change that would not disturb international stability.[117]

On January 31, 1989, Grósz convened a meeting of the Political Committee. The forum's deliberations led to a volte-face in the ruling party's policies. A senior member of the plenum, the former social democrat and economic reformer Rezső Nyers, averred that events had left the party behind. There was no other way but a multiparty system, although Nyers hoped that this could be contained within the notion of "socialist pluralism." A week later, the Politburo decided to propose a multiparty system to the Central Committee. This momentous step did not result from the growing self-confidence, influence, and popular support of the opposition alone. In January, due to the country's deteriorating financial position, the IMF had demanded drastic austerity measures, including a cut of $8 billion from expenditures and a 10 percent devaluation of the forint. Then, without the approval of the party leadership, Imre Pozsgay announced that the 1956 uprising had been a popular revolt, thereby destroying his party's historical legitimacy. Although Pozsgay was subsequently reprimanded for his "putsch like" action, his statement was not retracted. On February 7, the Political Committee accepted the multiparty system, although the party's first secretary declared that an immediate regime change would result in a civil war. It was not made clear how long it would take to implement the new system, and the HSWP wanted to make sure that the party would remain a dominant force. This was to be achieved in a two-stage transition. In stage one, the communists would receive guarantees and find a coalition partner, which would allow them to form a majority without a total overhaul of the political system. Only in the second phase would there be fully free competition for voters. This arrangement would be similar to Poland's. Although the communist party relinquished its monopoly on power, the Central Committee maintained that the party would continue to play a decisive role and wanted constitutional guarantees to assure its hegemonic role. Advocates of reform thought the party would gain the majority of votes in the 1990 election, thus the communists were eager to codify a new constitution and pass it in parliament in order to define the fundaments of the new political system.[118]

In the meantime, the incoming Bush administration was preoccupied with its re-evaluation of U.S. foreign policy, including an appraisal of Gorbachev's intentions. Henry Kissinger traveled to Moscow with the knowledge and tacit blessing of Bush's deputies. In the vein of Churchill's diplomacy some forty-five years earlier, Kissinger proposed a "political dialogue" with the Soviet leadership that would help to promote an orderly "political evolution" in Eastern Europe and eliminate the "potential for instability." The aim would be to defuse the "dangerously volatile conditions" in the region and to avert any "political explosions." Kissinger claimed that he had "discussed this matter in detail with Bush's entourage," and that the new administration would be ready to discuss these questions in "a confidential format" while "taking into account the USSR's legitimate security interests." Although Gorbachev welcomed the proposal, he was concerned it would give the impression of Soviet-American collusion at the expense of Europe.[119] A memorandum written by the president's special assistant for national security affairs, Peter Rodman, who had worked extensively with Kissinger, sheds light on the former secretary's thinking. According to Rodman, Kissinger may have believed that "we were in a pre-1914 situation," deplored the West's inability to articulate its political program for Europe, and criticized Acheson's policy of postponing negotiation to a vague future. Rodman himself was concerned that "inability to formulate what we really want forfeits the initiative to Gorbachev," which he conceived as "perverse and dangerous." He suggested that the West put forward "a vision of self-determination" for an assurance that "it had no military design in the region." Rodman's concern was of a dual nature. A comprehensive strategy was needed for "an era of enormous fluidity" and also as a "competitive strategy" to offset Gorbachev's peace offensives.[120] In a column published in the *New York Times*, secretary of state James Baker suggested that the administration condoned the Kissinger plan. The Polish-American Congress expressed concern that Kissinger's idea raised the apparition of a "second Yalta." National Security Council staffer Condoleezza Rice thought that the émigré community had argued with "some justification" that "it would be unwise to set the limits of East European autonomy at a time of dynamic change in the region through discussions with Moscow."[121] Nevertheless, Rice and fellow NSC staffer Robert Blackwill agreed that a "more refined version of the Kissinger ideas" should receive consideration.[122] Kissinger's initiative revealed the continuity in Washington's thinking on Eastern Europe, namely the overriding importance of Soviet security at the expense of national self-determination. Concern for stability was not confined to Kissinger. Already in the fall of 1989, undersecretary of state Lawrence Eagleburger was expressing nostalgia for the "remarkably stable and predictable atmosphere of the Cold War."[123] On the other hand, a high-level official at the State Department during the Reagan administration, Thomas Simons, claimed that Soviet hegemony behind the Iron Curtain was viewed as essentially unstable.[124] The timing of the Kissinger proposal was propitious for the Hungarian communists who wanted to share the responsibility for economic chaos and political disarray with opposition groups while attempting to preserve their overwhelming influence in politics and society.

In their recollection of these events, the president and his national security advisor asserted that the changes in Poland convinced them that the Cold War had to end where it began: in Eastern Europe. The Bush administration, they claimed, broke with the doctrine of containment, allowing the restoration of independence in the Soviet Bloc and the reunification of the continent to become the primary concerns of American foreign policy. Relations with the Soviet Union and arms reduction talks were allegedly subordinated to these goals. All this had to be done so as not to provoke a repetition of the tragic Soviet intervention of 1956. Bush's assistant for Eastern Europe, Robert Hutchings, affirmed that the Bush administration had radical goals that were coupled with cautious implementation. The president and his advisors elevated Eastern Europe to prominence in world politics, and Hutchings claimed that this was in part motivated by the desire to avoid restoring Germany to a dominant position in *Mitteleuropa*. The American role was important because France would not play a prominent role in the region. The former advisor confirmed that the president and Scowcroft were afraid of a Soviet crackdown; he recalled receiving intelligence indicating that a provocation was being prepared in the GDR to trigger a Soviet intervention.[125] Mark Palmer, the U.S. ambassador in Budapest and a close and sympathetic witness of the dramatic days of 1989, held a contrary view. Palmer claimed that the Bush administration prioritized keeping Gorbachev over the liberation of Eastern Europe and that Secretary of State Baker was concerned with the volatility of Gorbachev's position. He thought that Reagan was more radical than Bush or Scowcroft, both of whom emphasized stability.[126] Historians James M. Goldgeier and Michael McFaul have argued that Bush and his associates were not regime changers: they believed in the doctrine of balance of powers and would not do anything that could undermine Gorbachev's power.[127]

Bush had no desire to topple every regime in Eastern Europe; he repeatedly expressed appreciation for Jaruzelski and Kádár, as well as the Hungarian government. Following their meeting in 1983, Bush described Kádár as a man of enormous capacity and leadership capability. Revealing considerable callousness – or ignorance – Bush praised "Hungary's human rights record and effort to foster tolerance" and averred that there was "no discord between the two countries on human rights and fundamental freedoms." Further, Bush asserted that he was "impressed by Hungary's innovative policies giving opportunities for enterprising and creative citizens."[128] In 1989, when Kádár had already been sidelined and arrangements for the reburial of his famous victim, Imre Nagy, were already being made, the president confided to Austrian chancellor Franz Vranitzky that "the view of Kádár in the U.S. was based on his role in 1956, but his own view was more tolerant, as was that of the Hungarian people."[129] Bush expressed his appreciation of Jaruzelski in a warm personal letter to the general in which he credited Jaruzelski for the role he had played "in support of Poland's democratic transformation" and for "advancing the cause of democracy in Poland."[130]

Brent Scowcroft acknowledged that the Bush administration could be criticized for being overcautious and fearing that Gorbachev would be overthrown, which he was in 1991. He admitted that the administration did not want chaos, just gradual and sustainable change. The dissolution of the Warsaw Pact was not a primary concern; "we were very wary of the

Soviet Union." Scowcroft, who had served in the Nixon administration, also highlighted the fact that détente had not fulfilled expectations and the administration wanted to make sure it would not get carried away. Germany was the real geopolitical issue for the United States. Looking back on 1989 with twenty years' hindsight, the general confessed, "Perhaps I was a little too cautious."[131]

What were, after all, the U.S. position and role in the transformations of 1989 and the subsequent reunification of the continent? And what does this reveal about the dynamic of change in international politics? Looking back on 1989, the outcome seems almost a foregone conclusion, but this was not so for contemporary observers. Shortly after these events, the historian Arthur Schlesinger admitted that he had not thought that the events of 1989 would ever happen.[132] Even though the Soviet client states were in difficult economic and political situations, they had weathered such hardships before. If, as Stephen Cohen convincingly suggests, the Soviet Union was not ready to collapse in 1991, then neither were its allies.[133] It was evident, of course, that profound changes would happen. But the noted Kremlinologist Charles Gati, who envisioned the slow devolution of Soviet power in peaceful circumstances, warned in *Foreign Affairs* that the Soviet Union would not just go home and its allies would not sink without a fight.[134]

Only a few days after Hungarian guards began to remove the barbed wire on the Austrian border on May 2nd, Helmut Sonnenfeldt, Kissinger's former aide on Eastern Europe, had a conversation with a Hungarian diplomat. Sonnenfeldt explained that in the longer run he could see "Eastern Europe, and mainly Poland and Hungary, being transformed along the Finnish or the Austrian model, but only if the relaxation of international tension with the progress of troop and arms reduction created a situation in which both the Warsaw Pact and NATO were dissolved and the member states became independent." Henry Kissinger did not think it would be realistic for the Soviet bloc or the Warsaw Pact to dissolve, nor for any of the member states to defect. In a speech delivered in May, one-time hardliner Zbigniew Brzezinski emphasized the need to observe the Soviets' "legitimate security interests." He asserted that the United States was interested in the transformation – but not the disintegration – of the Warsaw Pact so that it might become a real political alliance.[135] Gati envisioned an internationally guaranteed zone of peace in Eastern Europe made up of states friendly to the Soviet Union. They would be willing to observe the Soviet Union's legitimate security interests and eventually become entities like Finland or Austria, or perhaps independent states within the Warsaw Pact, although to Gati this idea was fast becoming irrelevant. All this shows that the thinking about the future of Eastern Europe had not changed since the first scenarios for a negotiated settlement on Eastern Europe were put to paper after the death of Stalin. These statements reveal that thinkers of different persuasions agreed that the Soviet Union's "legitimate security interests" held primacy over national independence.

Statements emanating from the Bush administration confirmed that Washington expected important changes, but the Americans did not speak with one voice regarding the existing European system. Secretary of state James Baker addressed the Berlin Press Club only a few days after the historic meeting between Bush and Gorbachev in Malta. Although the title, "A New Europe, a New Atlanticism: Architecture of the New Era," suggested a radical departure from the old European system, Baker's vision remained cautious. He acknowledged that the political and economic "reforms" of the East would enhance European stability and Soviet security, yet he added that "the new architecture must have a place for old foundations and structures that remain valuable – like NATO." While the secretary emphasized the need to overcome the division of Germany, he did not foresee the unification of Eastern and Western Europe. Instead, he predicted that "the Conference on Security and Cooperation in Europe [CSCE] process could become the most important forum of East-West cooperation."[136] The president's pronouncements were much bolder. In a statement after his meeting with Gorbachev, Bush proclaimed that "our hopes for a historic transformation of Europe from a divided continent into a continent whole and free are coming true.... Our governments committed themselves... to seek an end to the painful division of Europe. We have never accepted this division." Bush also discussed the CSCE as a "bridge," however, lending some ambiguity to his statement.

Referring to the tragic experience of 1956, the president did not want to "exacerbate problems" in Poland or Hungary.[137] In a memorandum on his forthcoming visit to Europe, national security advisor Brent Scowcroft declared that "the Cold War must end where it began, with an end to the division of Europe." In a surge of liberal emotion, he asserted that "the only durable basis for the reconciliation between East and West will be the true sharing of common values, self-determination, individual rights, and pluralistic societies."[138] Scowcroft, however, was essentially a foreign policy realist and set no timetable for the momentous changes he envisioned. Nevertheless, before Bush departed for his historic trip to Europe, which involved a crucial meeting in Brussels to discuss the future of the North Atlantic alliance, an opportunity seemed to present itself "to redraw the whole postwar military and political map of Europe."[139] Presidential assistant Robert Gates, on the other hand, was not even sure that the Soviet Union was becoming "less of a threat," because, as he put it, "we cannot be sure what the outcome of glasnost and perestroika will be, nor can we be certain that a more modern Soviet economy means a less threatening Soviet military." The USSR, Gates claimed, continued to increase its military spending and still adhered to the Brezhnev doctrine. He therefore advocated an "increase of the strains under which Soviet policy must operate, to force on the Kremlin a far greater degree of moderation and circumspection." Gates did not anticipate significant change in Europe. He expected the Soviets to want the Eastern Europeans to stay in the Warsaw Pact and the Comecon.[140] Bush called the changes behind the Iron Curtain encouraging, but asserted that NATO "should not disperse out of euphoria."[141] The State Department also maintained a cautious stance; when the Hungarians apparently broached the possibility of Hungarian neutrality, State Department officials responded that a neutral, pro-Western Hungary was conceivable only in the long run.[142]

Spurred by the rapid disintegration of the single-party systems in Poland and Hungary, the removal of the network of fences on the Hungarian-Austrian border, and Gorbachev's publicity tour in Western Europe, the White House announced that President Bush would include Budapest and Warsaw on his forthcoming European tour. The president confided that "as Gorbachev cruised around Western Europe, it was appropriate for him to show his support for changes in Eastern Europe."[143] Bush noted that "the West should show proper support and avoid the dangers that might come from rhetorical overstatement." The United States wanted to see "progress there continue but must pursue a balanced policy."[144] The idea of the presidential visit to Eastern Europe did not, however, originate within the Bush administration, a fact that highlights the new administration's detachment from the events unfolding behind the Iron Curtain. The idea was first broached by Reagan's former special advisor on Eastern Europe, John Whitehead, who had visited the region in March. Whitehead thought a presidential visit would differentiate Poland and Hungary from their more conservative neighbors. Although he sent his letter in mid-March, it was more than three weeks before it was forwarded to Scowcroft.[145]

Budapest understood that Washington expected peaceful change. Deputy Secretary of State Lawrence Eagleburger praised Hungarian boldness in opening the Austrian border and expressed sympathy for its reforms.[146] American diplomatic sources nevertheless suggested that Washington anticipated that changes would remain under control. The limits of Moscow's tolerance were hard to predict.[147] Ambassador Palmer gave a speech in Moscow in which he stressed that the United States had no desire to detach Hungary from the Soviet Union and that Washington was interested in predictable, peaceful, and gradual change.[148]

Soviet reactions to the news of the presidential visit were mixed. Foreign minister Eduard Shevardnadze welcomed the announcement and declared that Moscow would respect nations' rights to choose their own paths.[149] An article published on May 12th in the Soviet army periodical *Krasnaya Zvezda* accused the United States of "driving a wedge between the socialist countries," of "trying to alter the balance of power on the continent," and of "casting doubt on European realities."[150] Similar outbursts from Soviet army officers were not uncharacteristic and would multiply after 1989. In a private message dated July 4th, an apprehensive Gorbachev asked Bush to be "more considerate if he wants to help."[151] Baker understood that the Soviet position on Eastern Europe required a reserved American posture: "They do not want us aggressively fomenting change. They will allow change so long as the East European states stay in the Warsaw Pact."[152] In the estimation of the National Security Council, the president's initiatives for Poland and Hungary were "small," and the council expected that their political and economical impact would be "slight." NSC staffers opined that the future of democratic reforms rested on finding a solution to the short-term economic problems in Poland and, to a lesser extent, Hungary. They therefore recommended that the president offer private enterprise grants of $100 million and $25 million respectively, as well as the rescheduling of Poland's debts.[153] In retrospect this was still a modest offer and well below the expectations of the recipients. The United States was *"concerned"* about the events unfolding in Eastern Europe and advocated a "concerted Western approach."[154] Condoleezza Rice worried that the "desperate regimes" and populations were "looking to us for more than we can deliver."[155]

A senior national security staffer, Eric Melby, warned that the most important foreign policy interest of the United States was "the prevention of major conflict in Europe between East and West." Melby reminded everyone that the "last World War and the Cold War that followed began in Poland." On the other hand, Soviet ability to engage war in Europe depended on Soviet domination of Poland, and there was a "historical opportunity to help bring about a democratic ... transformation in this flashpoint of European security." The situation was complicated by the fact that the outcome could turn sour. If the democratic experiment in Poland and Hungary failed or "exploded into prolonged civil strife and Soviet intervention the fate of reform in the Soviet Union will be jeopardized, perhaps doomed." The stakes were high: "Who knows what would happen to Mr. Gorbachev in such circumstances?" Possibilities for "major progress" in East-West relations during the Bush administration would "end." Hence the stakes were high; "the future of Poland," which was going through "destabilizing political change," would affect "vital U.S. national interest." Therefore "to the extent to which" it was in the power of the United States, it was crucial for the United States "to insure the democratic experiment in Poland succeeds."[156] From the perspective of the United States, the rapid collapse of communism was highly dangerous and promising at the same time, but the most important thing was to avert a war. Thus the Bush administration tried to play it safe by seeking to limit the pace of change. These alarmist views were shared at the highest level of the Bush administration. National security advisor Brent Scowcroft explained to Yugoslavia's foreign minister, Budomir Lončar, that it was "important for the U.S. to keep its moves moderate in Eastern Europe so as to avoid stimulating an explosion."[157]

Shortly before setting out for his destinations in Eastern Europe, Bush promised "a peaceful transition to a democratic future" and proclaimed that "ending the division of Europe is no longer an idle hope . . . it is our goal."¹⁵⁸ Thus Bush's rhetoric had grown bolder since the meeting with German chancellor Helmut Kohl at which he had spoken in a toast about the "easing" of European division. On arrival, the president toned his rhetoric down significantly. In his state dinner toast in Poland, Bush cited John Quincy Adams, soberly asserting that America "goes not abroad in search of monsters to destroy. She is the well-wisher to the freedom and independence of all."

There is no doubt that one of the goals of the presidential visit to Warsaw was to bolster Jaruzelski. The Round Table talks in Poland had produced a compromise on semifree elections based on power sharing between the opposition and the ruling party. U.S. ambassador John R. Davis Jr. feared that the opposition's "total victory or something close to it" would lead to a "hardline crackdown." Jaruzelski's election as president was jeopardized by a resounding opposition victory at the polls, and U.S. diplomats were concerned that the failure to elect Jaruzelski would destabilize the situation. In an effort to secure the general's victory, Davis offered tactical advice to Solidarity deputies on methods for electing Jaruzelski without actually voting for him. Shortly before Bush's arrival, Davis warned that the "tremors" of the impasse "continued to build intensity."¹⁵⁹

But there was more to it than fear of domestic turmoil. Bush suggested to Thatcher that since the general had a "terrible image in America," and to boost Jaruzelski's international reputation, he wanted to give Jaruzelski "some exposure in the U.S. to help him," as he had become "a symbol of repression. General Jaruzelski's visit to the UK would be helpful in America. . . . Though it was a cosmetic matter, General Jaruzelski should change his glasses."¹⁶⁰ The president made no secret of his controversial view in the Polish capital. He indicated to Prime Minister Mieczisław Rakowski that Jaruzelski was "a controversial but widely respected figure in the United States" who was "trying to lead Poland to a new era." The historian Gregory Domber has observed that throughout the visit, the Americans treated Jaruzelski as a head of state and Wałęsa like a private citizen, "an awkward and degrading designation that the Communists assigned to Wałęsa ever since he was released from prison in 1982." Bush's warmth in private meetings with Jaruzelski contrasted with his awkward personal interaction with Wałęsa.¹⁶¹ When the president had to choose between the communists and the opposition, he opted for the former. Nothing made the Bush administration's support for Jaruzelski more apparent than his invitation to Washington.

Bush had set out for Warsaw with some unease. When Nixon went, there had been mass demonstrations, which Bush had wanted to avoid, fearing that they could provoke clashes with the police and give the Soviets a pretext to intervene. "We wanted to avoid a Soviet crackdown," Scowcroft remembered. Surprisingly, Bush sought to convince President Jaruzelski – who had declared a state of emergency in Poland in 1981 and had become a pariah of international politics as his counterpart Kádár had in 1956 – to stay. Robert Hutchings explained this by noting Bush's desire to ensure that the accords of the Polish Round Table would be honored. Thomas Simons thought that the president wished to keep the general in power for the sake of stability.[162]

In private, Bush made no mention of ending the Cold War or of his notion of a Europe whole and free. He began by reassuring Jaruzelski that "he would do nothing to complicate the difficult and delicate job that Poland and Jaruzelski face." Bush indicated that "he had not come to Poland to place strains on the Soviet alliance." The United States, he declared, would "contribute positively to the reforms while stopping short of interference." In turn, Jaruzelski affirmed his commitment to bloc politics. He recounted to Bush Gorbachev's statement that "during his visits to Germany and France he had been careful not to imperil U.S. interests" and expressed approval that both leaders were "responsive to the needs of East-West cooperation and of reform in the Soviet bloc." Jaruzelski recalled that Gorbachev had been "quite concerned" by Bush's earlier statement that he wanted to see Soviet troops out of Poland, to which the president replied that he was not trying to be "contentious, only to look to the future." Their conversation convinced Jaruzelski that the United States saw the benefits of stability, and he said he would communicate this to Gorbachev.[163] Bush's decision to invite Jaruzelski to Washington drew the "vigorous protest" of an organization called "Solidarity in Exile," which requested that the invitation be rescinded.[164] Jaruzelski's invitation haunted the Bush administration well into 1990. By then the policy of keeping the communists in power had become obsolete. Prior to the Polish presidential election of 1990, what seemed like a good idea in 1989 – Bush and the communist general posing together in front of the White House – was no longer considered desirable. Although a number of high-level officials in the State Department thought that the visit, scheduled for October 1990, should go ahead, others felt that in light of the developments, it would be highly embarrassing. Presidential advisor Robert Hutchings put it aptly: "at a time we are trying to project our support for the new Eastern Europe, receiving a symbol of the old regime with highest protocol honors could send a confusing signal to the Poles and others." For Hutchings the rescinding of a long-standing invitation was still preferable to the "image of Jaruzelski with the President on the South Lawn."[165] The Bush administration did not withdraw the invitation, but eventually Jaruzelski canceled the trip in a private note he wrote to Bush on September 24th.[166]

In Hungary, while the communists were trying to insert themselves into the main political current by participating in a national commemoration of 1848 on March 15, some of the more radical opposition organizations were ratcheting up their demands. These included the establishment of parliamentary democracy and constitutionalism, as well as – more ominously for the status quo – the restoration of sovereignty, neutrality, and the full withdrawal of Soviet troops. Such demands would lead to the reunification of the continent and national self-determination for the peoples of Eastern Europe, which went further than either Gorbachev or Bush wanted. Fidesz leader Viktor Orbán put it succinctly: "We cannot speak of national independence while there are Russian troops in Hungary." Yet there was no consensus within the opposition about the future they envisioned. While the Democratic Forum searched for a Hungarian third way, the liberals wanted to adopt Western models, which some nationalists feared could lead to a new type of subjugation. It would be left to the Opposition Round Table, which commenced on March 22, 1989, to find common ground among the opposition factions and to determine a strategy for engaging with the ruling party. The basic principle that unified the participants was that none of them would share in a monopoly of power with the ruling party. Since the unity of the opposition stood on shaky grounds, communist efforts to sow dissent were not doomed to failure.

The HSWP was interested in holding the new national election while they still had a realistic chance of winning. The Németh government suspended the construction of the Nagymaros-Gabcikovo power plant, exacerbating Hungary's already tenuous relations with the rigid Czechoslovak regime but countering the speedy erosion of the Hungarian government's public support. Still, the communists were rapidly losing ground. When Grósz met Reagan in 1988, he made a pledge that would eventually help undermine communist power: to rebury Imre Nagy. The communists were held to this promise by the opposition. In a last-ditch effort, with the help of Soviet comrades, Grósz tried to discredit Nagy in the eyes of the public. He alleged that Nagy had been an agent of the Soviet secret service, Cheka, and its successor, the NKVD, and even that he had taken part in the infamous execution of the Tsar and his family. The "evidence" to support this story was supplied by the KGB. Hungarian state security agents launched a clandestine campaign to tarnish Nagy's planned reburial among Western diplomats so as to avert alleged radical actions that would threaten stability. In the meantime, István Csurka demanded on behalf of the Democratic Forum that the representatives of "young Hungary" be given a voice at the funeral. Party conservatives were not ready to lose this battle for power. In an interview granted to the *New York Times*, the party's first secretary asserted that the HSWP would not surrender control. An unnamed associate added that this part of Europe belonged to the socialist world and that free elections would not be held until 1994. Nevertheless, on June 9, the ruling party and the Opposition Round Table, the precarious unity of which was preserved in spite of party efforts to divide it, signed an agreement on the basic principles that would govern the National Round Table. This stipulated the need to hold free elections and that the transition had to remain peaceful.

A week later and only a few days after the massacre at Tiananmen Square, the ceremonial reburial of Imre Nagy and five other martyrs of the Nagy trial took place. The commemoration symbolically turned a page in Hungarian history by breaking with the current regime. Imre Mécs called for national solidarity, and in a powerful oration, Viktor Orbán implored the nation to split with the communist dictatorship and elect a government that would negotiate the withdrawal of the Soviet occupying forces. He drew a sharp line between the opposition and the enemy, the ruling party. It was the unfolding of the scenario that Bush did not want to see and had sought to block by spectacularly throwing his support behind the reform communists in Budapest. Orbán's open call for full Soviet troop withdrawal was a challenge to the world order, which rested on the survival of both military blocs. By then, however, all Hungarian opposition organizations were demanding neutrality and a gradual secession from the Warsaw Pact. Foreign Minister Horn was concerned about possible Soviet reactions to the fall of the HSWP and a regime change. A political analysis prepared for the Central Committee warned that in case of a political turnaround in the Soviet Union, military action could not be ruled out for the "protection of socialism." Horn therefore emphasized that Hungary would remain faithful to a reformed Warsaw Pact and Comecon.[167] While the HSWP was eliminating some of the more visible manifestations of party-state control, it was also preparing for the world after the election. On June 26, the State Ecclesiastical Office was abolished. In the meantime, leading party functionaries dubbed "parachutists" were transferred into top positions elsewhere. In early June, the state security services were instructed to assist with the peaceful transition to the multi-party system but in such a way that the HSWP could preserve its positions and maintain control over the transition. In addition, opposition parties were to be subverted and discredited, although not all of them in equal measure. The party's central committee revamped the party leadership. Although Grósz, who had lost credibility due to his political ineptitude, was not forced to resign, his powers were constrained by a four-member presidium headed by Nyers.

Presidential advisor Robert Hutchings later remembered that the Americans were bolder in Budapest than in Warsaw in their attempts to accelerate reforms. Scowcroft thinks of his short stay in the Hungarian capital as one of the most memorable events of his life. For many Hungarians, too, Bush's visit remains an event to remember. As Bush spoke freely in the storm in front of the Parliament, where the revolution of 1956 had begun, he seemed to lend America's unlimited power to the nation's aspirations. Visiting Karl Marx University in Budapest was one of the public highlights of the president's journey behind the Iron Curtain. Speaking in front of dignitaries, faculty students, and a bust of the bearded revolutionary, Bush proclaimed that "the Iron Curtain has begun to part. And Hungary is leading the way." He added, "We can work together to move beyond containment, beyond the Cold War."

Behind closed doors, the president was more reserved. Although he may not have been aware of it when he landed in Budapest, the communist leadership had accepted the main principles of a new law regulating assembly and association in the hope that they could introduce a measure of pluralism while avoiding a multiparty system. Politburo member György Fejti asserted that the party could "not let groups that are against our constitutional order use elections for their political gain." The new system, they hoped, would rest on the principle of "socialist pluralism."[168] Bush told the reformist prime minister, Miklós Németh, that the United States had no intention of forcing its values on Hungary and would like to avoid even the semblance of intervening. According to the Hungarian records, Bush, in language similar to other Western leaders', declared that he "did not mean *to cause problems for Gorbachev* or the Hungarian leadership and has no intention of interfering in the relations between Hungary and its allies"[169] [emphasis mine]. In Hutchings' version, Bush added, "the better we get along with the Soviets, the better it is for you."[170] In Warsaw, the president delivered a similar message: "He had not come to Poland to place strain on the Soviet alliance.... The United States would contribute positively to the reforms while stopping short of interference."[171] This was essentially the same idea American diplomats had been conveying to the Eastern Europeans since the early 1970s. Németh countered by claiming that the "Brezhnev doctrine is dead," adding that Hungarian reforms could strengthen Gorbachev's hand. The newly installed party president, the veteran Rezső Nyers, asserted that Hungary had not enjoyed such international latitude since 1947. Immediately after Bush left, Nyers visited Gorbachev, with whom he shared his disappointment. Referring to Bush's modest offer of $25 million in financial aid, he told Gorbachev that Bush had left no illusions regarding significant economic assistance to Hungary. He reassured his host, however, that Bush would not interfere in domestic affairs, which as Nyers put it, was the "basis" of US-Hungarian relations.[172]

On the surface, the presidential visit was successful. Bush announced that he would extend the Hungarians' MFN status indefinitely once the

Hungarian parliament passed the new law of emigration. Bush also promised to extend Generalized System of Preferences (GSP) tariff status and the overseas investment guarantee (OPIC) that Budapest had been seeking since at least the middle of the 1980s. The latter concessions were made contingent on the abolishment of a passage in the Hungarian penal code that criminalized unemployment, although this measure was already before the Parliament. Foreign Minister Horn and Secretary of State Baker agreed to launch talks on the liberalization of CoCom restrictions for Hungary even though, as they diplomatically put it, the legal conditions for the liberalization of export controls were not yet in place in Hungary.[173] Ever since the post-Kádár Hungarian leadership had broached the issue of a large American loan to alleviate its economic and financial crisis, it was clear that no new Marshall Plan would be considered for Eastern Europe. Even so, the Hungarians were disappointed in the $25 million Bush had announced, particularly since their ambassador in Washington was lobbying for $2 billion. In real value, it was not more than the Truman administration had offered in 1946 when Hungary had been slipping into the Soviet zone. Hungarian diplomats were interested in finding out why Washington was being so tight-fisted. According to information gathered in Washington, they surmised that in comparison to the economy of Poland, a country that was strategically more important to the United States than was Hungary, the state of the Hungarian economy was not considered to be critical. In addition, they found that Washington wanted to wait out the free elections in order to avoid being seen as propping up the existing regime.[174] The only way to make sense of it is to assume that it was an integral part of the long-standing American semicommitment to the Iron Curtain states. This symbolic handout suggested that the United States had not deserted Eastern Europe, but at the same time did not challenge Soviet supremacy either. It was made plain to the Hungarians that there was no easy way out of their economic predicament. Even though Horn had warned that the IMF recipe for economic salvation was unacceptable, the State Department insisted that Hungarian authorities accept the IMF's conditions.[175]

Although Poland received a larger chunk of American money, the amount was nowhere near the magnitude Solidarity expected. In 1981, President Reagan hinted at the possibility of a new Marshall Plan for Poland, and at the end of the 1980s, not just Poles but Hungarians were also entertaining hopes of a large-scale Western bailout. Solidarity leaders discussed a mini-Marshall Plan in 1989 and suggested a figure of $10 billion. The prevailing atmosphere in Washington was that the bankrupt states would not be eligible for significant Western sums. An NSC draft reiterated "that we will not repeat the mistakes of the 1970's by throwing money at a problem ... even as Poland takes steps of political reform, it is still a member of the Warsaw Pact, and we will take no steps that compromise our security."[176] Even though it was apparent that Poland's success depended on whether the new government could handle the economic crisis, a high-level meeting with the president immediately before his trip to Warsaw "broke down whenever the question of spending USD came up." As NSC staffer Robert Blackwill noted, "Expectations in Warsaw and Budapest were ignored and strategic considerations did not come up. Harry Truman would have been appalled by the comments of everyone except the president and Gates."[177] While visiting Poland in July 1989, Bush's chief of staff John Sununu condescendingly indicated that he "did not want to pump too much money into Poland because Poles would be like kids and would not know when to stop."[178] A statement by British premier John Major may have summed up a general Western feeling of uncertainty, but also conveyed a measure of disdain: "The West should not smother them [Poland] with so much help that they do not take the necessary steps. The British government also wonders what Gorbachev's real goals are in Eastern Europe." Bush had no intention of smothering Eastern Europe with money. Using callous rhetoric, he told Mitterrand that although many congressmen were urging more money for Poland, "he did not want the money to go down the drain."[179] Horn bitterly remarked to Bush that "we do need help, although we have to rely on ourselves."[180]

After his official talks, Bush met the representatives of the Hungarian opposition. This was a motley crew of people representing almost every point along the Hungarian political spectrum, including future prime minister Viktor Orbán. Bush and Scowcroft disclosed in their memoir that the representatives of the reform wing of the ruling party made the best impression.[181] Bush's comment to Mark Palmer immediately after the event was more scathing: "Your friends will never rule this country."[182] Brent Scowcroft shared the president's jaundiced judgment. The people he met at the American Embassy struck him as "men of the past"; the energy was "in the young Turks" of the party. Curiously, Bush and the first freely elected prime minister, József Antall, eventually developed a cordial, even close relationship, although Antall may not have been present at the meeting in July 1989.

Bush hoped that the Communist Party would remain an important force in Hungarian politics. He praised Nyers' role in furthering political and economic reforms and praised the moderate stance of the Hungarian opposition. Nevertheless, he believed that with its new leaders, the reformed Hungarian Socialist Workers Party had every chance to remain the largest party after the free elections.[183] Only a few days prior to his conversation with the president, Nyers asserted at the Bucharest meeting of the Warsaw Pact Consultative Committee that the Western states were "hoping to force the socialist states to their knees economically. We must view their aspirations precisely, without illusions."[184]

After the trip, the president met Soviet chief of staff Sergei Akhromeiev and asked him to convey to Gorbachev that his visits to Budapest and Warsaw were "in no way conjured up to complicate life in the Soviet Union."[185] Moscow appreciated Bush's restraint. The U.S. Embassy in Budapest reported that Dobrynin had discussed the Bush visit with the Hungarian leadership, who pointed out to him how careful the president had been to state that he was not trying to create instability or problems between Hungary and the USSR. The embassy reported that "the Soviets themselves have noted this and appreciated the President's efforts to pursue a moderate line." Soviet contacts were pleased that the financial aid Bush had offered to Poland was less than anticipated.[186] Other Soviet reactions were mixed. Tass released a statement claiming that the United States wanted to encourage Poland and Hungary to move away from socialism, while *Krasnaya Zvezda*, which had been harshly critical of the visit beforehand, claimed that Bush had contributed to the general improvement of East-West relations. The Soviet Foreign Ministry concurred, saying that the president had helped to build a "common European home."

Bush felt the need to reassure his own allies that he would not meddle in Eastern European affairs. He reassured Dutch prime minister Ruud Lubbers that in Hungary and Poland he had "stressed that the U.S. offers no threat to Gorbachev."[187] The president offered a symbolic sum to suggest that the United States had an interest in Eastern Europe, but at the same time would not interfere in the Soviet sphere, which he regarded as sacrosanct. In late September, President Szűrös broached the question of neutrality to national security advisor Brent Scowcroft, who reiterated that the United States "wanted to appear helpful but not provocative."[188] Almost simultaneously with this meeting, President Bush reassured Shevardnadze that that while the United States wanted to support changes toward democracy in Eastern Europe, it "did not want to be reckless or silly about it."[189] The American accommodation of Soviet interests involved an effort to keep the communists in power. Bush decided to bring Jaruzelski to the United States to bolster his image. The idea of "helping" Jaruzelski had been proposed by Chancellor Kohl.[190] Despite his bold rhetoric on ending the division of Europe, privately the president used every opportunity to reassure the Soviets that he was mindful of their interests. Shortly after the agreement to introduce a multiparty system was reached in Hungary, the president asked Thatcher to inform Gorbachev that "Western support for reform in Eastern Europe is not intended to threaten Soviet security interests."[191] NATO allies were concerned with the Soviets' response to the president's tour behind the Iron Curtain. Dutch foreign minister Henri van der Broek wanted to know whether the Kremlin was "worried about Western activities in Eastern Europe." Baker told him that the Soviets "did not want us to aggressively foment change. They will allow change so long as the East European states stay in the Warsaw Pact."[192]

Shevardnadze was concerned that the rapid changes in Eastern Europe would lead to general destabilization with catastrophic consequences. He called on the United States not to exploit the situation to its own advantage. Baker confirmed that Washington supported changes that did not endanger Soviet interests, but warned that any attempt to terminate them would negatively affect Soviet-American relations. Although the United States pledged in private conversation to support peaceful change, the American line was identical to the European: the Eastern Europeans were asked to exercise restraint.

The Bush visit occasioned a public showdown between hard-liners and reformers in Hungarian foreign policy. Foreign policy had been one of the communist state's most ideological and most secretive domains. Now the public was informed of the expectations regarding the United States with unprecedented openness. Former foreign minister Frigyes Puja published a scathing critique of the allegedly pro-Western orientation of the Németh cabinet, which deputy foreign minister László Kovács refuted with great vigor. The Kovács article announced the return of national interest to Hungarian foreign policy. He reassured the public that the United States "had no interest in the destabilization of Hungary" nor any desire "to test the limits of the Soviet Union's tolerance," and he emphasized that "East-West relations were conducive to such visits." Kovács reacted to Puja's accusations of "selling out" to the West: "Such former leaders criticize Hungarian foreign policy who took part in making decisions that led to indebtedness . . . and have undertaken international obligations that exceeded Hungary's capabilities. . . . I find it strange that such people worry about the fate of the nation who previously denied even the sheer existence of national interest, the representation and assertion of which they deemed to be the task of internationalism."[193]

This newly found independence became apparent when, on September 11, the government opened the borders to the large number of East German citizens who had been vying to cross into Austria since May.[194] The breaching of the Austro-Hungarian border, which threw the door open to German unification, would not have been possible except as the unforeseen and unintended outcome of a prior set of events. Few of the developments of 1989 signified more spectacularly the often spontaneous, often accidental nature of historical change. The border opening would not have been possible without government players, civil initiatives, and the fortuitous interaction between states and political movements within Hungary. Closed borders were essential for the survival of communist regimes; some, like the GDR, went to extreme lengths to keep their citizens locked up. Hungary got rid of the minefield on its western perimeter only in 1970. The idea of getting rid of the obsolete system of barbed-wires fences cropped up in 1981 and was broached again at a Border Guard Conference in 1987. The goal at that time was not to get rid of border controls, but to guard borders more efficiently.

Border guards responded to four thousand false alarms annually, and the costs of maintaining the obsolete electronic system became increasingly burdensome in a time of stringent financial austerity imposed by

Hungary's spiraling external debt. The issue gained momentum under the newly installed government of Miklós Németh in 1988. Németh was intent on freeing his government from party tutelage and took the initiative in the matter. He was supported by an increasingly popular reformer, Imre Pozsgay, who declared publicly that the border system was obsolete and ready to be dismantled. Party leader Grósz initially opposed the move but surrendered at the February 28 meeting of the Political Committee. The decision was not motivated solely by finances and the complaints of the border guard service. In 1987, the government had introduced a "world passport," which allowed citizens to travel to destinations of their choice for the first time since the communists had seized power. This move made the retention of the physical barriers pointless. Although the world passport was designed to placate a restless public that was increasingly dissatisfied with the political situation, it eventually backfired, as people took their savings abroad to purchase washing machines and refrigerators. Tourism, which had added $370 million to state coffers in 1987, now produced a deficit of $420 million, another exacerbating factor in the unsustainable economic situation that faced the reigning political elite. The liberalization of tourism also further eroded the argument for keeping up the border guard system.

When the removal was announced in March 1989, Romanian and East German leaders immediately grasped the potential danger. East Berlin threatened to treat Hungary as a Western state for travel purposes. For decades, Lake Balaton had been a favored meeting spot for relatives from the two parts of Germany, whose vacations were watched over by omnipresent Stasi agents. In 1989, the number of GDR citizens visiting the sunny shores of the lake was augmented by travelers who had misinterpreted the removal of the "Iron Curtain" and thought that the road to Austria was open. By then, there were already tens of thousands of refugees from Romania, mostly – although not exclusively – ethnic Hungarians from Transylvania. At a time when the growing opposition was applying heavy pressure to do something about the plight of the Hungarian minorities abroad, particularly in Romania, where they suffered day-to-day persecution, the government could not afford to stand idly by if they wanted to stay in power. Already in June 1988, the administration had been compelled to authorize a mass demonstration organized by alternative groups on behalf of Transylvania. The deputy interior minister had announced that "it was the duty of Hungarian authorities to assist those who are fleeing from Romania."[195] Ever since 1988, the onset of Ceaușescu's village-destruction program, Hungary had provided some refuge to these desperate illegal arrivals, even though according to a bilateral agreement they should all have been returned to Romania. Budapest needed a legal basis for not returning the refugees to Romania and the only option was to sign the Geneva Convention on Refugees, which entered into force on June 12. Rapid political reform in Hungary eroded border controls on the Romanian-Hungarian border, allowing those enticed by the reforms to flood into Hungary and escape the terror at home. In 1989, fourteen thousand such people were given temporary residence. Membership in the Geneva Convention, which was motivated by the growing influx of refugees from Romania, increased the likelihood that East German citizens would find a route to West Germany through Hungary.[196]

When the tearing down of the Iron Curtain finally got under way on May 2, East German Politburo member Günter Schabowski, who would soon unwittingly help open the Berlin Wall, felt that a new phase of his life had started. Schabowski understood that this might be the beginning of the end of the East German state, as the Soviets no longer guaranteed its existence. The situation was precarious: in 1988, 1.6 million East Germans, 10 percent of the country's population, passed through Hungary. Nevertheless, the government assured East Berlin that the border would remain under tight control and that transgressors would be handed over to the Stasi and returned to the GDR as before. On June 9, the FRG's foreign minister, Hans Dietrich Genscher, demanded that the Hungarian authorities stop the practice of returning refugees to the GDR and of putting a stamp in the passports of those who had been expelled from Hungary for trying to cross the border. Although after June 12 Hungary officially gave up the practice of handing over border violators to the GDR, the border remained closed, even after Foreign Minister Horn and his Austrian colleague Alois Mock symbolically cut the wire. Their picture, which traveled around the globe, encouraged even more East Germans to proceed to Hungary in the hope of liberation, but they soon found that border guards were still stopping them. In fact, the interior minister told the West German ambassador that Hungary would not become a "springboard" for German immigration.

Bonn's response to the refugee crisis, which involved a growing number of GDR citizens camping on the grounds of the FRG's embassy in Budapest, was ambivalent. Ambassador Arnot told the minister of internal affairs that Hungary's actions were at odds with its public statements on human rights and suggested that the refugees be accommodated in private homes. Arnot simultaneously made known to deputy foreign minister Ferenc Somogyi that "a massive flight of people from the GDR to the FRG was not in their [West Germany's] interest."[197] State secretary Walter Priesnitz told the German press that people should stay where they were so that the reunification did not occur in the FRG. Similar statements were made by SPD president Hans-Jochen Vogel and a member of the Kohl cabinet, Hans Klein. The West German Embassy in Budapest asked the Foreign Ministry to take action to dissuade East Germans from trying to flee to the West through Hungary.[198] Bonn was sending mixed messages: state secretary Jürgen Sudhoff arrived in Budapest on August 16 with the message that Budapest should turn a blind eye and open its borders. In the meantime, around eight hundred people crossed the border illegally in the month of August alone; on the eighth, a group of a hundred reached Frankfurt through Hungary.

The way out of the impasse was provided by an event that encapsulated the semispontaneous, semiplanned, and definitely unpredictable nature of change. At a dinner with Otto Habsburg on June 20, Ferenc Mészáros, a member of the Debrecen branch of the Hungarian Democratic Forum, broached the idea of an event that would later be called the Paneuropean Picnic, which was to take place near Sopron on the Austro-Hungarian border. Otto, the grand old man of European politics, immediately supported the idea and assumed responsibility for the event. In an unusual show of unity, preparations for the event were undertaken by civilians and many of the new parties: the Hungarian Democratic Forum, the Smallholders, the Alliance of Free Democrats, and the Alliance of Young Democrats. In the meantime, representatives of the Stasi were negotiating in Budapest on a settlement. In order to forestall an outcome favorable to East Berlin and to test Soviet reaction, Imre Pozsgay acted as the other patron of the event, with the explicit support of the prime minister. News that the border would be open for a few hours quickly reached East Germans through flyers advertising the picnic, in all likelihood disseminated by West German intelligence. Although Pozsgay and Németh assumed that groups of people would exploit this opportunity to cross into Austria, the border guards received no clear instructions to give East Germans free passage during the picnic.

On August 19, the day of the event, border guards were still under orders to prevent illegal crossings. Suddenly, a group of 100 to 150 people rushed the makeshift border crossing. Disregarding his orders, the commander in charge, Lt. Col. Bella, let them go; in the next few days, several hundred people escaped in a similar manner. Only a few days earlier, a man who had tried to flee across the border with his family was shot in a scuffle with the guard who tried to stop them. The model for the resolution of the crisis was ready. Horn still feared that the Russians would be "on our backs again." Still, on August 25, he and the prime minister met Kohl in Gymnich and promised to open the border. The Hungarians were under some pressure from Palmer, who at his own initiative indicated that unless they released the Germans, Hungary would not get a cent of American money. As it turned out, they got only a pittance anyway. After the meeting in Gymnich, Horn traveled to East Berlin, where at a series of icy meetings he informed the GDR's leaders that Hungary would "suspend" the relevant clauses of the 1969 bilateral agreements and "temporarily" open its border with Austria.

The GDR was running out of options and rapidly losing its viability. Even the Stasi rejected the idea of imposing travel restrictions, so East German diplomats launched an effort to lure back their citizens by pledging that they would not be punished and that any application for immigration would be treated favorably. All efforts failed dismally. In a last-ditch attempt, East German diplomats mobilized Soviet support, again with little result: the Soviet ambassador in Bonn told Genscher that a violation of the GDR's sovereignty would have serious repercussions for stability and Soviet–West German relations.[199] For domestic political reasons, SPD politician Karsten Voigt leaked the date of the planned release of East German citizens to the press, which forced the prime minister to postpone the operation while East Germany continued to put pressure on the Soviet Union and Hungary. Voigt thereby risked its success for partisan political gain.

The Hungarian government finally opened the border at midnight on September 11. All in all, fifty thousand people would leave the GDR through Hungarian territory. Although Kohl exploited the timing of the release to overcome his political opponents in the CDU, he and West German diplomats contributed little to the positive outcome. A historian of German unification has asserted, "The Berlin Wall really began to come down when the Austro-Hungarian border was opened. This was the beginning of the end of the GDR."[200] German party leader Erich Honecker responded by restricting travel to Hungary, but the problem re-emerged in Prague. The West Germans negotiated a one-time release agreement between Czechoslovakia and the East Germans. Honecker insisted that the "freedom trains" pass through GDR territory before reaching the FRG. This only hastened his regime's downfall, as thousands of would-be emigrants crowded platforms along the route, hoping they could jump aboard. "The refugees from Czechoslovakia thus emboldened their fellow citizens in the GDR to contemplate leaving forever."[201]

While the HSWP was widely credited internationally with releasing the Germans, its domestic standing deteriorated. Early elections would have been beneficial for them, and a part of the opposition supported it. This would have allowed the party to remain in a strong position, whereas any procrastination diminished their chances. In addition, the HSWP wanted a new constitution by September to cement the communists into their positions of power. Finally, the communists wanted to elect a president with relatively wide-ranging powers by direct popular vote. Imre Pozsgay, the highly popular and prominent reformer, would be their candidate, as he was also acceptable to the populist elements in the opposition. There would thus be a bargain struck between the ruling party and the moderate opposition, similar to the power-sharing arrangement in Poland. At a meeting of the Opposition Roundtable on September 15, however, the more radical elements rejected a compromise with the ruling party. The Democratic Forum thought it was necessary to strike a bargain for the sake of a peaceful transition, and eventually an agreement was signed between the opposition and the HSWP, with two organizations abstaining. Four important issues remained unresolved: party organizations in the workplace, the Workers' Guard, the election of the president, and the ruling party's assets. The liberals then decided to hold a referendum so voters could decide whether the president would be elected directly or by a newly elected parliament. The latter would ruin Pozsgay's chances. As the HSWP was losing ground at an accelerated pace, the Fourteenth Congress convened on October 6 and announced its demise. On October 7, a "new" Socialist Party was formed by the majority that had seceded from the old, but this move came too late to stem the anticommunist tide that was sweeping the country. Although the Socialist Party distanced themselves from the communist past and its crimes, they still defined themselves as a Marxist party with the goal of establishing a democratic socialist state – an aim that toward the end of 1989 was increasingly out of tune with the general sentiment. Even so, at that point the chairman of the Democratic Forum, József Antall, declared that a stable coalition was inconceivable without the socialists.[202]

The administration's hands-off policy in Eastern Europe started to change in September as events in central Europe were beginning to overtake the Bush administration's conservative stance. In July, General Jaruzelski, citing the danger caused by the state of the Polish economy, sought a $1 billion food aid package, a $2 billion IMF loan, and an $800 million World Bank loan, as well as the rescheduling of Poland's debt. At the time this was considered "well beyond anything" the United States could support.[203] It was becoming apparent that the United States was not doing enough and was "losing leadership" in the middle of the continent. The time had come for visionaries to replace accountants and for a modern version of the Marshall Plan, a Bush Plan, to emerge. Congress and the public needed a more strategic vision as America was losing credibility in Poland and among her Allies.[204] The economist Geoffrey Sachs weighed in, advocating urgent Western support for stabilization in Poland, which was in the midst of "despair and paralysis" that threatened to cause political paralysis.[205] In response, the Bush administration agreed to contribute $200 million for a stabilization fund requested by the Poles and to encourage the most developed industrial states to make up the rest. The president also pushed for the rescheduling of Poland's debt. Prime Minister Margaret Thatcher supported the stabilization program, although she preferred not to set a precise figure. In view of the fact that Poland and Hungary were developing into "pluralistic societies," Chancellor Kohl offered $200 million dollars for the stabilization fund and three billion German marks for a guarantee framework for loans to Poland.

In the wake of the momentous decision to open the Austrian border, which set in motion a train of events that ended the postwar division of Germany, a member of the Politburo who acted as the speaker of the Hungarian parliament, Mátyás Szűrös, proceeded to Washington. Szűrös reassured his hosts of the peaceful nature of the transition and the need for stability, and that the political transformation would be coupled with a transition to a market economy based on both public and private ownership. He asserted that Hungary's problems were so grave that they could not be resolved "without external help." Szűrös declared that financial and economic assistance could be expected from Western quarters, albeit not in the form of aid, but trade and financial concessions. Turning to foreign policy, the speaker, who would soon be sworn in as the new Hungarian republic's interim president, also announced that "in the longer run the objective was to achieve Finnish or Austrian type neutrality." This was a return to the program first announced in 1956. Szűrös thought that the timeline for this transition could be around ten years and emphasized that "taking into account realities at present [Hungary] was not preparing to leave the Warsaw Pact." Scowcroft's response dampened all expectations. He reiterated that the United States was interested in peaceful and gradual transformation, but only at a pace that would not cause problems for either Hungary or the Soviet Union. "We want to help without appearing to be provocative." Scowcroft did not respond either to the question of neutrality or the plea for economic assistance, making it clear to the Hungarian leadership and the opposition that Hungary could not count on external help in their difficult predicament. Eagleburger added that the United States was not seeking to "destabilize" the region.[206] Deputy Foreign Minister Ferenc Somogyi broached the question of neutrality again when he went to Washington in October, but the president's special assistant for national security affairs, Robert Blackwill, who also served as senior director for European and Soviet affairs, affirmed that he did not think this was a timely issue.[207] Despite Bush's claim to the contrary, the relationship with Gorbachev remained the priority. The United States reassured the Soviets that although the United States fully supported the process of political and economic reform in Eastern Europe, the United States "did not want the changes to threaten" the Soviet Union. A quid pro quo emerged: the Soviets indicated to the United States that they would not use force to block reform in Eastern Europe and Washington did not urge Poland and Hungary to leave the Warsaw Pact.[208]

The first small steps toward severing the ties to Moscow were already taking place. The Hungarian security apparatus was still very closely linked to the Soviets'.[209] Robert Blackwill demanded further information on the "Conrad" affair, as well as a declaration that the Hungarian services would loosen their ties to the Soviets and would no longer work under the direction of or in close cooperation with the KGB.[210] At this point, deputy foreign minister László Kovács was sent to Washington. He presented a memorandum stating that the sixteen Soviet advisors working for the security services had left the country.[211] The *rezidentura* in Washington noted that in reality the Soviets left only the Ministry of the Interior *building*. Because of U.S. pressure, the head of the foreign intelligence service, János Bogye, instructed the *rezidentura* to be more careful and "organize contacts with the fraternal countries on a clandestine basis."[212]

In the meantime, Bush's propaganda continued to emphasize the American commitment to European change. In a message to the newly proclaimed republic in Hungary, the president reaffirmed his commitment "to build a common future of freedom and prosperity . . . a Europe whole and free." There was thus a marked contrast between the administration's public statements and its reserved stance behind closed doors. A theme paper drafted by the State Department suggested that the idea behind Bush's slogan "Europe whole and free" was not dissimilar to Gorbachev's "common European home."[213] It may have been less bold than it sounded. In fact, if that was true, Bush's "vision" was not one of continental reunification, but rather one that resembled notions already put forward in the 1960s about close and amicable contacts between East and West that fell short of the restoration of European unity.

Deputy secretary of state Lawrence Eagleburger had never made any secret of the fact that he was not displeased with the current equilibrium in Europe. In September, he expressed grave concern about the possible negative consequences of changes behind the Iron Curtain. Eagleburger thought reforms and the weakening of Soviet control in Eastern Europe might bring to the surface long-suppressed ethnic hostilities and national rivalries and put the German question back on the international political agenda. Eagleburger suggested that the United States would not be a key player in the changes and that "it is ultimately the Europeans themselves who have the principal stake in making the transition to a new and undivided Europe a peaceful and orderly one."[214] Soon, developments in Germany began to cast doubts on the viability of the postwar European structure. Mass demonstrations took place in Leipzig on October 9, and with Gorbachev's approval, Erich Honecker was ousted. The new leader, Egon Krenz, traveled to Moscow at the end of the month. Gorbachev and Krenz agreed that reforms were needed so that unification would not become a real option. On November 6, East Berlin announced that a new travel law was in the making; one hundred thousand people had left since the Hungarian border had been opened in September.[215] Travel liberalization, which had been designed to bolster the Hungarian government's waning popularity, only hastened its downfall, and it worked even more quickly on the East German regime. On November 9, after a botched press conference by the government spokesman, the East German population got the impression that the Berlin Wall had been opened. Since the border guards had received oral orders not to shoot, 69,000 people crossed the border from East to West Berlin on foot, while another 9,700 drove. The dramatic events on the ground caught the European political elite off guard. Chancellor Kohl was on a state visit to Poland when he heard the news. Hurrying back to Berlin, Kohl asserted German national unity. Mitterrand was shocked by the events. Thatcher was most horrified by the prospect of reunification, which had now become a distinct possibility. She expressed fear that "any attempt to raise the question of reunification would undermine Gorbachev's position and open a Pandora's Box of border claims right through Central Europe."[216]

A State Department theme paper, drafted precisely a week after the opening of the Berlin Wall, asserted that gradual and controlled change "may be in doubt with prospect of instability arising not only in the GDR, but in Bulgaria and Czechoslovakia as well." Gorbachev had expressed concern over the potentially "chaotic situation with unforeseeable consequences" that could arise from the rallies in Berlin and urged Bush to give the appropriate instructions to the U.S. Embassy in West Berlin.

He warned Kohl to prevent any destabilization and not to undermine "postwar realities," that is, the "existence of two Germanys."[217] The State Department therefore suggested the president reassure the Soviets that the United States would "encourage peaceful *reform* and the *reduction* of tensions and structural barriers dividing the continent." German unification was a "long-term goal" and the United States would "not encourage countries to withdraw from the Warsaw Pact."[218]

Mass demonstrations took place in Prague on November 20 and in Bratislava on November 23. In the midst of the turmoil, on November 24, the U.S. representative at the Vienna conventional force reduction talks, Lynn Hansen, informed Hungarian diplomats that the American government would remain cautious regarding changes in Eastern Europe. Stability, which was guaranteed by the two military alliances, would remain the chief concern.[219] After receiving an indication that the Soviet Union was willing to consider a confederated structure for Germany, Kohl introduced his Ten-Point Program on November 28, in which he envisioned a confederation of the two German states with an ultimate view to union. The announcement of the program, which did not contain any clear statement about Germany's lack of interest in restoring its prewar borders, caused an uproar in Moscow on the eve of the Malta summit. Shevardnadze remarked that "even Hitler did not allow himself something like that."[220]

Concerns about stability in Eastern Europe were not altogether unfounded, although at this stage they had less to do with historical inevitability than with the nature of the Romanian dictatorship. Hungarian-Romanian relations plummeted, and on June 19 the Hungarian Ministry of Interior warned the party leadership of Romanian preparations for military action against Hungary, allegedly planned for the fall.[221] In light of this intelligence, Hungarian leaders, including future prime minister József Antall, reaffirmed Hungary's commitment to the Warsaw Pact.[222] Antall told Soviet deputy foreign minister Ivan Aboimov that Hungary wanted "guarantees" from the alliance "against potential attack from the neighborhood . . . we cannot exclude the danger of [Romanian] attack." But Aboimov may have been aware that Hungary was already exploring other possibilities, warning his interlocutor that "any breach of European stability would create a very dangerous situation."[223]

The Poles were also forthcoming regarding the Soviets' concerns for their positions in Europe. Prime Minister Tadeusz Mazowiecki and Foreign Minister Krzysztof Skubiszewski reassured Shevardnadze that since the Soviet Union was the main guarantor of Polish security, Poland would continue to stay in the Warsaw Pact and to fulfill its duties in the alliance. Warsaw would take into account the Soviet Union's interests and needs and would expect Moscow to respect Polish sovereignty, including the freedom to choose its own political system. Jaruzelski proclaimed that the nurturing of friendly relations and cooperation was in the best interest of both parties. Shevardnadze asserted that the Soviet Union was ready to work together with the new Polish government.[224]

The Western allies agreed that at least for the time being the Warsaw Pact would have to stay. Mitterrand emphasized the Warsaw Pact's role in European stability. Margaret Thatcher insisted, "It is very important for the future, for defense, peace and the negotiation of arms reductions, to retain the two alliances." Thatcher argued that the European order should "stay the same until after 10 to 15 years of genuine democracy." In a conversation with Bush, Spanish prime minister Felipe Gonzales expressed concern that "all of the policy problems, defense agreements, and border problems can go backward if the alliances are not maintained." When Gonzales recommended that the Eastern Europeans needed to be kept in the Soviet alliance for four or five more years, Bush concurred because he thought "it would make it easier for Gorbachev to move forward."[225]

MALTA

The approaching summit caused anxiety about the possibility of a new Yalta. On behalf of the Hungarian Organizations in North America, István Gereben exhorted the president "not to ignore the lessons of Yalta."[226] The Hungarian government was eager to sound out both Moscow and Washington on the prevailing attitude regarding the great flux in the Soviet Bloc. News from Moscow was reassuring in the sense that the Soviets pledged noninterference and not to provide "recipes and advice regarding the political and economic processes there." The states of Eastern Europe would be allowed to choose "the type of social system best suited for the interests of the people." On the other hand, the Kremlin expected noninterference from the West as well: the Soviet Union "rejects any political or other pressure on the countries of Eastern Europe, any intervention in their domestic affairs, and the setting of any economic or political preconditions for economic or other relations." Moscow also made it clear that the West should not exploit the situation in Eastern Europe to "destabilize the situation or to change the borders or other realities of post-1945 Europe. The existing political and economic structures ensure European stability."

The Soviet position regarding Europe had not changed through 1989: "postwar European borders and structures must not be threatened." Moscow officials asserted that there was an agreement between the Soviets and Western Europe regarding this point and that the United States would not challenge the status quo either.[227] This position was retrospectively reaffirmed by chief of staff Sergei Akhromeiev, who admitted that he and his colleagues in the military regarded the Warsaw Pact and the presence of Soviet forces in Eastern Europe "as the bedrock of Soviet security." Ominously, Col. Pyotr Skorodenko called on Eastern European governments to "use revolutionary violence ... against all counterrevolutionary organizers."[228]

It still remained unclear what kind of Europe the United States wanted to see. The Bush administration encouraged democratic change while keeping the postwar European structure intact. Nobody seemed to have thought through whether it was even possible to reconcile these two aims. State minister Imre Pozsgay traveled to Washington to sound out the president's position on Eastern Europe prior to the forthcoming summit. National security advisor Brent Scowcroft wanted it made clear to Pozsgay that Washington still insisted on the strategic status quo in Europe: "the U.S. is not looking to gain strategic advantage or make life difficult for Gorbachev." On the other hand, Hungary's "evolution to democracy" was "vital to stability and security in Europe," including Soviet security.[229] Bush reiterated that the United States would not interfere in Hungary's domestic affairs and that he would "not join Gorbachev to influence others." Pozsgay considered Bush's "word as guarantee that no agreement will emerge from this summit, and there will be no compromise on our interests." Pozsgay asked the president to convince Gorbachev to let Hungary go its "own way."[230] This road would be very different from the road envisioned by Pozsgay. On November 26, a referendum was held that confirmed that the country's president would be elected by the parliament, effectively destroying Pozsgay's chances at the presidency. The Democratic Forum, which implored its supporters to boycott the vote, suffered a significant loss of prestige and was forced to backtrack and join the strident anticommunist campaign championed by the Alliance of Free Democrats and the Young Democrats. As Pozsgay's popularity rapidly diminished, the former communists' chances of power sharing were coming to naught.

The president did not go to Malta to liberate Eastern Europe or to force Gorbachev to renounce Soviet geopolitical positions in Europe. The region was one of many pressing world political issues discussed, including Soviet intervention in Central America. Eastern Europe may not even have been the primary topic, which would not be surprising given that neither leader was preparing to change the status quo in Europe or the bilateral structure of world politics. Although public expectations were high, behind the scenes it was made clear that there would be limited change. As always, the American position was contradictory: honoring Moscow's security interests while advocating the freedom of Eastern Europeans to choose their own forms of government. The contradiction was always apparent, as Soviet interests would impose a limit on the choices any new government in Eastern Europe could make. Thus the old paradigm prevailed: stability over national independence. A high-level functionary of the State Department, Curt Kamman, told a Soviet diplomat that Malta would not be a second Yalta and that the two leaders would not decide the fate of Eastern Europe.[231] The president's disarmament advisor, Edward Rowny, insisted that Malta should not become an agenda-setting summit.[232] Scowcroft did not want the president to discuss the future of Europe. He wanted Gorbachev to know that the United States had no desire to take advantage of the Soviet Union's difficulties in its sphere of influence, but that the peoples of the region must be given the opportunity to determine their own political and economic futures.[233] Eventually the summit had no particular agenda.[234]

Both leaders made it clear that although they supported national self-determination, change in Eastern Europe should not threaten stability and thus would be confined to the limits of the existing European structure. Bush conceded that his policies were designed so as not "complicate" Gorbachev's life: "That's why I have not jumped up and down on the Berlin Wall." He indicated that the Soviet Union was "closer" to Eastern Europe than was the United States, thereby implying his recognition of Soviet primacy there. Asserting that he was "well aware of the Helsinki language about borders," the president asked the Soviet leader what "he saw beyond the status quo."[235] Gorbachev agreed that changes should be kept within the "Helsinki" framework, arguing for "the need to improve stability and to limit the damage" by preserving the "instruments that have maintained the balance," including the military alliances and the Comecon. Gorbachev took exception to the alleged U.S. intention to overcome the European division on the basis of "Western values," in which case, he asserted, the situation could become "quite messy." In response, Bush claimed that the United States endorsed self-determination; this did not mean "the imposition of our system on Czechoslovakia, the GDR, or Romania." With that, the conversation turned to the Middle East.

Right after the meeting, Gorbachev gave the Warsaw Pact allies his own interpretation of the summit, making it plain that the Soviet Union still considered Eastern Europe its exclusive economic and security sphere. He described Bush as a pragmatist who, unlike Reagan, "did not want to educate" him. Gorbachev claimed to have told the president that the "application of Cold War methods could lead to very serious consequences." Gorbachev acknowledged that the "need for changes and the elimination of the current division of Europe is an objective." He added, though, that it was "unacceptable to achieve unity on the basis of the elimination of socialism and exclusively on the basis of Western values, or the replacement of the Brezhnev doctrine with a sort of Bush doctrine. The right of people for independent development must be respected everywhere." According to Gorbachev's account, Bush affirmed the stabilizing role of the alliances and recognized the need for their transformation on a more cooperative basis. Gorbachev added that both sides had agreed that no precipitate action should be taken to eliminate the alliances or withdraw troops.[236]

A briefing for the member states of NATO also stressed Gorbachev's insistence on preserving "the instruments of stability," that is, the military alliances.[237] State Department officials also asserted that the military alliances would remain the pillars of stability.[238] The commander of the

USSR's Southern Group of forces in Hungary, Col.-Gen. Matvei Burlakov, was adamant that the retention of Soviet forces in Hungary was still justified for strategic reasons and that the reduction of troops could be realized only in strict reciprocity with NATO. In a similar vein, Gen. M. Yasyukov added that the continued presence of troops in the GDR was essential so long as NATO "still poses a threat." Igor Sergeev, commander-in-chief of the Soviet Strategic Missile Forces, opined that "if we lose our expanse [in Eastern Europe] we will be closer to danger."[239] The summit in Malta was not a game changer. Its effect on the outcome of the cataclysm of 1989 was negligible.

Transition from a relatively stable and predictable world to an unpredictable and possibly unstable one was risky. Despite statements in memoirs to the contrary, American relations with Eastern Europe were still subordinated to policies toward the USSR. Western leaders unanimously repeated that their policies in Hungary were not meant to "cause problems for Gorbachev." Fears of German hegemony (amplified by the prospect of unification) and the threats of regional chaos and conflict made continued Soviet hegemony in a democratized and cooperative form an appealing solution. The West, while seeking "gradual and peaceful" transitions to democracy, put stability and peace before full self-determination in Eastern Europe. In the new structure, the two cooperative parts of Europe would be bound together by a network of political, economic, and security arrangements, but the division would remain. The Soviet military presence in Eastern Europe would be reduced or even eliminated, but the Warsaw Pact would endure. In a broader context, this insistence on the Warsaw Pact was tied to American security concerns as well. If the Warsaw Pact were dissolved, the rationale behind NATO could also be questioned. The dissolution of NATO, however, was inconceivable for Western European countries that were concerned with the Soviet and possibly German challenges to their security. Revealingly, Mitterrand confided to Bush his fear that "the USSR could come into France in a few days."[240]

Moscow gave repeated assurances that the Brezhnev doctrine was dead and that it tolerated democratization wherever it led. But the Soviets made it clear that they preferred it to stay within the confines of socialism. The West was also willing to see democratic governments under reformed communist leadership. Gorbachev hoped to preserve the Soviet bloc in a more democratic form: the Soviet leadership regarded the Warsaw Pact as a pillar of stability and peace. Full troop withdrawal was a long-term prospect. As strange as it may sound, in 1989, for the first time since 1945, there was a meeting of Soviet and Western minds about an important aspect of the European structure. But in the course of that year, events in Hungary and Eastern Europe moved beyond this scenario, and Moscow refrained from trying to halt the process. The West, in face of the irreversible transformation of the Eastern European scene and German unification, would accept the eventual restoration of self-determination and the withering of communist power in the region. Still, continental reunification would be a long and painful process for the nations once hidden behind the Iron Curtain.

As early as 1989, a narrative began to take shape in which Western leaders were assigned leading roles in the transformation of the Soviet zone. Bush's press secretary claimed that "from the very start of the Administration, President Bush has taken the lead in supporting reform in Poland and Hungary." At the Lord Mayor's Banquet that November, Margaret Thatcher claimed that the "US, Britain, and the Western European countries put freedom once more on the offensive."[241] Although it is conceivable that the U.S. nonpolicy reassured the Soviets and did not impede change, it was hardly a catalyst. Nevertheless, even with the United States removed from the equation, the result would have been the same. And had Eastern Europeans heeded Washington's advice, we might still be living in a world divided into East and West. Put another way, if the Bush administration's position had been the yardstick by which the opposition in Eastern Europe measured its actions, pluralism in Eastern Europe might have been curtailed and the continental reunification might not have happened the way it did. The Bush administration's policy was not born out of fear alone. Rather it fit well into a long tradition of American and Western European policies that placed the interests of stability ahead of national independence in Eastern Europe. Bush and his administration remained within the paradigm worked out in the 1960s, one that was not comfortable with the bipolar order but found it workable. Indeed, the transition in Eastern Europe threatened to upset this balance and usher back the long-gone days of chaos in the lands between Russia and the West. Although this position was not altogether unrealistic, it also stemmed from remnants of old prejudices Western elites shared about Eastern Europeans.

Bush suggested that Jaruzelski wear new glasses to help his image in the United States. Thereby he revealed that all he wanted was that communists don a new mask. Appearances mattered and not essence. Washington feared that the dissolution of the Warsaw Pact would question the raison d'être of NATO, which was the very pillar of the transatlantic alliance, which a generation of Western politicians had worked so hard to construct. Thus, paradoxically, the collapse of communism seemed to threaten the security of the West.

All this is not to say that the United States did not contribute to the regime change in 1989. Most importantly perhaps, without America's adverse relationship with the Soviet Union, there would have been no Gorbachev, perestroika, or glasnost. After the consolidation of the Soviet bloc, the United States began to challenge the postwar order. Psychological and economic warfare may not have overthrown the communist regimes, but it did impede the economic and political consolidation of the Stalinist order and provided a lifeline of information from the Western world. After the late 1950s, the United States no longer wanted to undermine Eastern Europe. More modest political goals were set that required stability rather than unrest. New policies were gradually implemented that were designed to increase the distance between Moscow and its allies and to mellow the communist regimes. Eventually, these policies helped open Hungary to the West and to liberalize its humanitarian and cultural policies. Most importantly, economic penetration thrust Hungary – and Poland – into a debt trap and a financial crisis that played a crucial role in undermining the power of the Communist Party and thereby facilitated the transition to genuine pluralism.

Although the Bush administration supported reform in Eastern Europe and proclaimed a Europe "whole and free" through 1989, the United States was wedded to the strategic status quo in Europe to avoid war and to keep Gorbachev in power. But as the communists were voted out of power in East Central Europe, German unification was becoming reality and the contours of a new European structure were beginning to emerge, which forced the U.S. establishment to rethink America's role in Eastern Europe. The thinking started in the National Security Council. Robert Hutchings predicted that a power vacuum would emerge in Eastern Europe and that "we may soon be faced with a situation in which the only outside influences in the region are Germany and the Soviet Union." This was not the framework "of a stable European security order," as it invited a "return to the cyclical pattern of Russian-German conflict." Hutchings' historically grounded main message was that the United States "needs to stand between Russia and Germany." He was not thinking in military terms, but enhanced political, cultural, and economic presence. In view of America's limited resources, Hutchings presented a clear set of preferences: Poland, Czechoslovakia, and Hungary, in that order. The "cost of leaving it to the Europeans (meaning the Germans)," he warned, "will be high."[242] The argument was burdened with a self-contradiction, namely, that the author envisioned that the Americans would shift their foreign policy to engage Eastern Europe, but would have limited resources. The contradiction was not lost on Brent Scowcroft, who wondered how the United States would fit in between the USSR and Germany. He was in agreement that in an environment where the Federal Republic of Germany was filling in the power vacuum left by the collapse of communism, Eastern Europe was "a key in strengthening" America's "future position in Europe."[243] Not only was there the concern that Eastern Europe could become the object of the ambitions of German economic power and the Soviet Union, but he also pointed out that the "resurgence of national animosities" were already "threatening the revolutions of 1989." Therefore, the United States needed to be engaged in the region more than ever.[244] Germany's role and relapse into bad old habits was also a concern for Deputy Secretary of State Lawrence Eagleburger. He feared the "possibility" that a unified Germany could push everyone into seeking spheres of influences, "the UK and France aligned and the smaller European states searching for larger partners." The thrust of American policy therefore had to be the extension of U.S. influence "throughout the European continent."[245] Washington's policy remained sensitive to Soviet security concerns and avoided being seen as rushing into the void left by the Soviet Union.[246] By the end of 1990, after the Gulf War, the administration saw the need to put the spotlight back to central Europe. When the new Hungarian prime minister, József Antall, proposed a Central European Defense Union, the United States declared its support.[247] Although Antall was told it would take time for Hungary to join European political and security structures, the dissolution of the Warsaw Pact was clearly not a taboo anymore. For the first time in history, the conversation that led to NATO expansion and American security guarantees for the lands between Germany and Russia had begun.

Conclusion

What is striking about U.S. policy toward Hungary – and more broadly speaking, toward East Central Europe – is that at certain junctures it exerted a profound influence on events and sometimes none at all. The ability of American foreign policy to leave its mark on the region depended to a large extent on the willingness of the countries there to engage themselves with the United States.

Washington faced hard choices in East Central Europe. In World War II an opportunity presented itself to exploit the satellites' eagerness to break with Hitler in order to help the Allied war effort. Decision makers were well aware that defection from the Axis by Hungary (and Romania and Bulgaria) might lead to their occupation by the Wehrmacht. It was also no secret that the Germans were physically exterminating the Jewish populations of the territories they occupied,[1] and that the vast majority of Hungary's Jewry had survived deportation under the current regime despite political persecution and legal discrimination. There was also a sizeable Jewish community left in Romania. Nevertheless, in agreement with the British – and most likely with Moscow – the United States decided to force the defection of both countries even if that move led to their German invasion. It looked as though the choice was between Scylla and Charybdis: on one hand the harsh effect of German occupation of enemy states, and on the other the reduction of German military presence at the site of the invasion to win the war. It is another matter that by the time the Allies set foot in France, most of the German troops diverted to occupy

Hungary had already left. The decision to bomb Budapest in the wake of the German occupation can also be questioned. The city's contribution to the German war effort was minimal and the assumption that bombarding civilians would break the enemy's morale was not being born out elsewhere in Europe. The many civilian casualties in the working-class districts of the Hungarian capital fueled Hungarian Nazi propaganda that the Jews were behind the bombing, which justified their ghettoization and punitive measures against them.[2]

Despite claims to the contrary, American policies had no impact on Soviet actions in Eastern Europe after 1945 and were not responsible, as some historians have claimed, for its Stalinization. By the time the Marshall Plan was announced, the Soviet Union had constructed an economic empire, established its military sphere, and constructed regimes where all the elements for the construction of Stalinist states were put in place. When the Truman administration decided in 1948 that the extension of Soviet power into the heart of Europe was inimical to the security of the United States, policies were devised to roll back Soviet power and undermine, and if possible overthrow, the communist regimes in Eastern Europe. Perhaps the most important element of this strategy was economic warfare, which promised to undermine communist power and reduce Soviet military potential. This policy, however, turned out to be highly problematic. First of all, the State Department and other agencies did not see eye-to-eye on what items to hold back from the communist bloc. There was concern that the embargo would tarnish America's image as a liberal power and hinder U.S. efforts to promote free trade. Secondly, the cooperation of the European allies was needed for the embargo to reach its aims, and such cooperation was difficult because their economies relied far more on trading with the eastern bloc than did the U.S. economy. For this reason, many European allies were willing to circumvent the embargo. The trade dispute with Washington strained the alliance and caused political friction. While the economic controls did cause problems for the communist bloc, they did not cause its downfall. In Hungary, cutting trade with the West hurt heavy industry, exacerbated the shortage of consumer goods, and added to the country's technological backwardness.

Some of the policies Washington pursued in the 1950s to dislodge the Soviets from Eastern Europe were highly contentious. Rolling back the

Soviets became a national security priority when the communists seized Prague. Psychological warfare sought to convince Eastern Europeans to resist their communist masters even though it was understood that there was only a thin dividing line between passive and active resistance. State Department officials thought that an armed uprising behind the Iron Curtain could lead to disastrous consequences for the people involved. In 1953, Eisenhower showed great restraint during the East Berlin uprising, declaring that the time to roll back the Soviets had not arrived. His administration's response to the crisis in Hungary was initially prudent: in view of the danger a confrontation would have caused to the population in Europe, and to the Hungarians themselves, armed intervention was ruled out from the start. A political solution was favored in the form of a negotiated settlement for the status of Eastern Europe in return for a vaguely defined security guarantee for the Soviets. By contrast, U.S. propaganda recklessly urged the Hungarians to liberate themselves even though there was no possibility of helping them.

In 1945 the Soviets enjoyed local superiority. A decade later, the situation had not changed. During the revolution of 1956, Soviet policymakers did not discuss the U.S. reaction when they decided to invade. The Kremlin firmly believed that the Soviet Union's (inferior) nuclear arsenal would deter an armed response. The crisis in Hungary is one of the few *hard* proofs we have from the Cold War that nuclear deterrence works.

Politics is a learning process and to the great credit of the next administrations, the lessons of 1956 were learned. In 1968 policy and propaganda were brought into line. After establishing that intervention in Czechoslovakia was neither possible nor expedient, propaganda outlets were instructed not to incite the population to fight. Former U.S. ambassador to Hungary Mark Palmer told the author that the one lesson from 1956 that Americans would not forget was not to incite people they cannot help to rise up. A window of opportunity for the United States to shape the fate of the region occurred precisely after the hope of "liberation" faded. The framers of American foreign policy gradually dropped the dream of throwing back the Soviets behind their borders of 1939. Instead the communist regimes would be transformed into more autonomous and more democratic entities through an evolutionary process.

The intensification of cultural, scientific, and humanitarian contacts countered the regime's monopoly of information and helped offset communist indoctrination; the gradual expansion of trade and economic relations created financial problems for the communist regime in Hungary and elsewhere, which precipitated a fatal political crisis.

Yet the construction of closer ties had major difficulties. As both sides found out, it was easier to atrophy relations than to reconstruct them; in some cases it was not until the early 1970s that relations were normalized. For the United States, dealing with communist systems – and for the communist governments to deal with the United States – created problems. Each was highly alien culturally to the other and therefore it was hard for each to gauge the other's intentions. This meant that policy initiatives were sometimes misconstrued. The fact that the Soviet Union had an inordinately powerful influence over the foreign policies of most of its client states made the situation even more difficult. Both sides miscalculated. In 1948, the Hungarians imprisoned an American businessman, Robert Vogeler. Party leader Mátyás Rákosi continuously ratcheted up their demands for his release as they overestimated the American commitment to liberate him. They had no idea that the Truman administration was willing to do almost nothing to liberate him. As a result they kept raising the stakes and eventually ended getting less than they started out with. Talks over Cardinal Mindszenty lasted fifteen years because the Political Committee underestimated the U.S. commitment to protect him and therefore the price they charged for letting the cardinal go – the Crown of Saint Stephen – was too steep. Misunderstandings sprang from the fact that neither side really understood the political system of the other very well. When President Nixon imposed a stricture on the development of U.S.-Hungarian relations in retaliation for Budapest's rude rejection of his offer to send astronauts on a good will visit to Budapest, he did not know that this was precisely the reaction the Hungarian leader wanted. Kádár was under pressure from the Soviets to cut back on his country's expanding contacts with capitalist states. The double irony of the situation was that the American ambassador in Budapest, who was eager to make progress, claimed that the Hungarian note Nixon cited as rudely worded was mistranslated, and the original version of the note that elicited the president's ire was couched in softer language. Thus it was a comedy of errors: a mistranslated diplomatic document, a misinterpretation of Hungarian intentions, and a misguided reprisal.

The Hungarians were highly offended by the bad press they got in the United States even though the State Department was working for the normalization of bilateral relations. They did not want to understand that the State Department had little control over American media. The same was too for U.S. officials, who had no idea that the party and state apparatus was fully integrated with the state security services and that the people with whom they interacted were usually not quite who they purported to be. The narrative of a reform-minded, liberal Hungary, which was only constrained by the Soviets, was fed to foreign diplomats and journalists by the security services. It is interesting that the story line that was concocted in the Ministry of the Interior survives in Western historical literature on Hungary to this day.

Economic incentives were given for good behavior. Romania received them for an autonomous foreign policy, the unfortunate result of which was that the regime in Bucharest got away with a highly oppressive domestic politics at home. Washington ended up propping up that tyrannical dictatorship with economic favors until the late 1980s. While in Hungary the normalization of contacts and the construction of closer economic, cultural, scientific and humanitarian ties helped soften the communist system, in Romania it had the opposite effect.

Although the erosion of dictatorships was a professed aim of the intensification of contacts with the communist regimes, their collapse was an unintended outcome of these policies. In 1989 the Bush administration's cautious stance regarding the changes occurring in Poland and Hungary led it to try and uphold their political systems rather than give way to the most ambitious goals of the opposition. Such a stance may actually have been helpful. It relieved Gorbachev's concerns that the United States would take advantage of the situation at the Soviet Union's expense. Here, too, the lessons of 1956 are apparent. It is a different matter that the Bush administration may have shown too much preference to the "reform communists" of Hungary and Poland. Thus although Washington contributed to the failure of the one-party systems, it cannot be credited with the democratic transitions in 1989. The United States may not have been able to have its way most of the time in Eastern Europe, but its force of attraction was great even when its influence was small.

In World War II, Hitler's satellites from Finland to Bulgaria, with the exception of the most rabidly pro-German elements, rapidly became disenchanted with the Axis. From as early as 1942, they sent out secret peace feelers to negotiate with the British and the Americans even while they were contributing to the German war effort. Although it was more likely that the Red Army would occupy them, they all clung to the irrational hope that the British and the Americans would arrive ahead of the Russians. It was an irony of history that some of Hitler's allies were oriented to the United States and Great Britain, while Czechoslovakia, an ally, was pro-Soviet.

An American army survey concluded that the majority of Hungarians were pro-British and favorably disposed to the Americans. Even though the Romanians eventually brought themselves to surrender to the Soviets, the Hungarians waited until it was too late to sue for peace from Moscow. Aside from the communists and some fellow travelers in the democratic parties, all Hungarian democratic political forces hoped to see the country in the American sphere of influence. The country's largest postwar party, the Independent Smallholder Party, requested American assistance to counter the Soviet-sponsored communist onslaught. Even the Communist Party supported participation in the Marshall Plan before the Kremlin implied that it should be rejected.

From 1948 on, the increasingly dictatorial government became openly hostile to the United States. American property was nationalized without compensation and bourgeois sabotage trials presented America as irredeemably hostile to the newly established people's democracy. In spite of the intensive anti-American propaganda and the absence of contact between the two states, even the communist government was aware of the high popularity enjoyed by America. Evidence suggests that Hungarians expected the United States to prevail in a military clash with the USSR and, listening to Radio Free Europe and the Voice of America, expected liberation to come. Many insurgents fought against Soviet regular troops in 1956 in the hope that the United States, or an American-led coalition, would come to their aid. Not even the letdown felt by many Hungarians in 1956 ultimately changed America's image for the worse. America's popularity had many components: soft and hard power, economic and military might, coupled with the attractions of popular culture. Even though the measurements of the United States's appeal may have been crude, there were enough signals to legitimize a pro-American approach. During the war, the presence of a vocal pro-German political force and electorate, as well as the threat of German occupation and the proximity of the Soviet Union, did not allow for an open pro-American orientation. The conservatives that remained in power until March 1944 were convinced that America would have a deciding voice at the peace table. Therefore, the government used whatever tiny room for maneuver it thought it had and passed on military intelligence to the Western powers. Horthy's regime was in dire straits. Surrender to the Allies was necessary to avoid another disastrous peace. A precipitate move could lead to an invasion by Hitler's forces. There was no way of knowing that for military reasons this was what the Allies wanted.

What was the meaning of all this in terms of international politics? For Hungary, Romania, Bulgaria, and Poland the room for maneuver in international politics was reduced to a singular point. With the possible exception of Czechoslovakia, no other outcome was possible except integration into the Soviet Union's sphere of influence. The Soviet Union was unmoved by Western warnings against unilateral action. Curiously, however, all this did not spell the end of the possibility of an autonomous foreign policy for the satellites, at least after the thaw that followed Stalin's death. The German Democratic Republic was able to manipulate Soviet leader Nikita S. Khrushchev to construct the Berlin Wall to save the communist regime; Romania exploited the Sino-Soviet-U.S. triangle to eke out more autonomy in the Warsaw Pact and economic support that would sustain the regime. Bucharest did not take part in the military integration of the WTO. In the 1970s, Henry Kissinger declared that Romania's independence was a concern for the United States. Hungary introduced reform at the price of remaining loyal to every twist and turn of Soviet foreign policy through 1989.

Despite these small freedoms, all satellites were bound to the Soviet Union and had no possibility of leaving Moscow's orbit. Gorbachev's reforms, the fatal weakening of the communist regimes due to the rise of political opposition, and serious economic problems opened a window of opportunity for these states that allowed them to change their status. Domestic changes in the Soviet Bloc spilled over into international politics and led to the demise of the international system that had held sway since the end of the Second World War.

NOTES

INTRODUCTION

1. See e.g., the former German Democratic Republic, Romania, or Austria. Hope Harrison, *Driving the Soviets Up the Wall: Soviet–East German Relations 1953–1961* (Princeton, N.J.: Princeton University Press, 2003); Joseph F. Harrington and Bruce J. Courtney, *Tweaking the Nose of the Russians: Fifty Years of American-Romanian Relations, 1940–1990* (Boulder, Colo.: East European Monographs, 1991); and Günter Bischof, *Austria in the First Cold War, 1945–55: The Leverage of the Weak* (London: MacMillan, 1999).

2. In Czechoslovakia the policies of the democratic parties actually played a strong invitational role for the Soviet Union. Vít Smetana, "Concessions or Conviction? Czechoslovakia's Road to the Cold War and the Soviet Bloc," in *Imposing, Maintaining and Tearing Open the Iron Curtain: The Cold War and East-Central Europe, 1945–1989*, ed. Mark Kramer and Vít Smetana (Lanham, Md.: Lexington Books, 2014), 55–86. For the pro-Soviet intellectual climate, see Vladimir Papoušek, "Panslavism in the Work of Czech Writers in Wartime Exile," in *The Phoney Peace: Power, and Culture in Central Europe, 1945–1949*, ed. Robert B. Pynsent (London: School of Slavonic and East European Studies, University College, 2000). Recent and earlier works discussing the Sovietization of Eastern Europe based on archival evidence from the former Soviet bloc include Anne Applebaum, *Iron Curtain: The Crushing of Eastern Europe 1944–1956* (New York: Doubleday, 2012); Robert Gellately, *Stalin's Curse: Battling for Communism in War and Cold War* (New York: Knopf, 2013); Mark Kramer, "Stalin, Soviet Policy and the Consolidation of a Communist Bloc in Eastern Europe, 1944–1953," in *Stalinism Revisited: The Establishment of Communist Regimes in East Central Europe*, ed. Vladimir Tismaneanu (Budapest: Central European University Press, 2009); Igor Lukes, *On the Edge of the Cold War: American Diplomats and Spies in Postwar Prague* (Oxford: Oxford University Press, 2012); Walter M. Iber and Peter Ruggenthaler, eds., *Stalins Wirtschaftspolitik an der sowjetischen Peripherie: Ein Überblick auf der Basis osteuropäischer Quellen* (Innsbruck-Wien-Bozen: StudienVerlag, 2011). For the Soviet economic exploitation of East Germany, see Norman Naimark, *The Russians in Germany: A History of the*

Soviet Zone of Occupation 1945–1949 (Cambridge, Mass.: Belknap Press of Harvard University Press, 1995). For Hungary, see László Borhi, *Hungary in the Cold War 1945–1956: Between the United States and the Soviet Union* (Budapest: Central European University Press, 2004). Works emphasizing that U.S. foreign policy forced the Soviets to Bolshevize Eastern Europe include Peter Kenez, *Hungary from the Nazis to the Soviets: The Establishment of the Communist Regime in Hungary 1944–1988* (Cambridge: Cambridge University Press, 2009) and Vladislav Zubok and Constantine Pleshakov, *Inside the Kremlin's Cold War from Stalin to Khrushchev* (Cambridge, Mass.: Harvard University Press, 1997).

3. Bischof, *Austria in the First Cold War*.

1. PEACE OVERTURES, THE ALLIES, AND THE HOLOCAUST, 1942–1945

1. Frazer Harbutt, *Yalta 1945: Europe and America at the Crossroads* (New York: Cambridge University Press, 2010), 85.

2. Pell's Telegram to the State Department, National Archives and Records Administration (NARA), Washington, D.C., Record Group (RG) 226, Office of Strategic Services (OSS), entry 170, box 593.

3. John Flourney Montgomery, *The Unwilling Satellite* (New York: Devin-Adair Company, 1947).

4. Telegram by Dulles, July 14, 1943, in Neil H. Petersen, ed., *From Hitler's Doorstep: The Wartime Intelligence Reports of Allen Dulles, 1942–1945* (University Park: Pennsylvania State University Press, 1996), 82.

5. OSS Interagency Memorandum, Alan H. Rado to Reginald Foster Regarding Memorandum on Hungary by William Donovan, March 1944; "Information on Hungary," comments by Ensign Putzell on R&A and SI Memorandum, March 24, 1944, NARA, RG 226, OSS, entry 190, box 593.

6. "Implementation Study for Overall Special Programs for Strategic Services in the Balkans as they Pertain to Hungary," OSS Planning Group, December 31, 1943, NARA, RG 226, OSS, entry 144, box 30.

7. See Tibor Frank, "Diplomatic Images of Admiral Horthy: The American Perspectives of Interwar Hungary," in *Ethnicity, Propaganda, Mythmaking: Studies in Hungarian Connections to Britain and America, 1848–1945*, ed. Tibor Frank (Budapest: Akadémiai Kiadó, 1999).

8. See Thomas Sakmyster: *Hungary's Admiral on Horseback: Miklós Horthy, 1918–1944* (Boulder, Colo.: East European Monographs, 1994), 150.

9. Memorandum by Dulles on the Hungarian Situation, December 17, 1943, in Petersen, *From Hitler's Doorstep*, 180–81.

10. Aladár Szegedy-Maszák and László Csorba, *Az ember ősszel visszanéz ... Egy volt magyar diplomata emlékiratából* (Budapest: Európa-História, 1996), 189–91.

11. Memorandum sent by Tibor Eckhardt to the Hungarian government, February 1943, NARA, RG 226, OSS, entry 190, box 593.

12. Cited in Stephen D. Kertesz, *Between Russia and the West: Hungary and the Illusions of Peacemaking* (Notre Dame, Ind.: Notre Dame University Press, 1984), 177.

13. Cited in Szegedy-Maszák, *Az ember ősszel visszanéz*, 181.

14. Nicholas Kállay, *Hungarian Premier: A Personal Account of a Nation's Struggle in the Second World War* (New York: Columbia University Press, 1954), 182.

15. Antal Czettler, *A mi kis élet-halál kérdéseink: a magyar külpolitika a hadba lépéstől a német megszállásig* (Budapest: Magvető, 2000).

16. Petersen, *From Hitler's Doorstep*, 45.

17. Keith Sainsbury, *Churchill and Roosevelt at War: The War They Fought and the Peace They Hoped to Make* (New York: New York University Press, 1994), 143–44.

18. Ibid., 48.

19. Telegram, Kelley to the State Department, December 2, 1942, NARA, RG 59, General Records of the State Department, decimal files 1940–1944, box 2955.
20. Elizabeth Hazard: *Cold War Crucible: United States Foreign Policy and the Conflict in Romania 1945–1953* (Boulder, Colo.: East European Monographs, 1996), 20.
21. Draft letter to General V. Strang, deputy chief of staff, Military Intelligence Division War Department, March 17, 1943, NARA, RG 59, General Records of the State Department, decimal files 1940–1944, box 2955.
22. The information originated from an Abwehr agent operating in Zurich, Hans Bernd Gisevius. Telegram by Dulles to Donovan, June 12, 1943, in Petersen, *From Hitler's Doorstep*.
23. Memorandum from the assistant secretary (Berle) to Sumner Welles, March 1943, Draft Letter to General V. Strang, NARA, RG 59, General Records of the Department of State, decimal files 1940–1944, box 2955.
24. Beatrice Bishop Berle and Travis Beal Jacobs, eds., *Navigating the Rapids 1918–1971: From the Papers of Adolph Berle* (New York: Harcourt Brace Jovanovich, 1973), 429–31; Memorandum, December 17, 1942. NARA, RG 226, OSS, entry 210, box 593.
25. State Department aide-memoire to the British government, April 28, 1943, NARA, RG 59, General Records of the Department of State, decimal files 1940–1944, box 2955. Gyula Juhász, *Magyar-brit titkos tárgyalások 1943-ban* (Budapest: Kossuth Könyvkiadó, 1978), documents 22/a/b.; Péter Sipos and István Vida, "The Policy of the United States towards Hungary during the Second World War," *Acta Historica Academiae Scientiarum Hungaricae* 29, no. 1 (1983): 86; Czettler, *A mi kis élet-halál*, 322.
26. McClintock to the State Department, May 6, 1943, NARA, RG 59, General Records of the Department of State, decimal files 1940–1944, box 2955.
27. Aide-memoire by the British Embassy in Washington, April 2, 1943; aide-memoire by Campbell to Dunn, April 20, 1943. NARA, RG 59, General Records of the Department of State, decimal files 1940–1944, box 2955. Foreign Secretary Eden stated that Hungary preserved her independence to a larger extent than any other southeast European satellite.
28. Joint Chiefs of Staff (JCS) Redefined Terms for Hungary, August 5, 1944, NARA, RG 218, JCS, geographical files 1942–45, box 91.
29. András Joó, *Kállay Miklós külpolitikája: Magyarország és a háborús diplomácia 1942–1944* (Budapest: Napvilág, 2008), 192; Czettler, *A mi kis élet-halál kérdéseink*, 350.
30. Kállay, *Hungarian Premier*, 350.
31. Telegram by Dulles, July 8, 1943, in Petersen, *From Hitler's Doorstep*, 79–80.
32. Telegram by Dulles, July 14, 1943, in ibid., 82.
33. Memorandum from Adolph Berle to the secretary of state regarding the Quebec trip and foreign policy toward Hungary, August 18, 1943, NARA, RG 59, General Records of the Department of State, decimal files 1940–1944, box 1956.
34. Telegram by Dulles to the director (Donovan), OSS, the secretary of state (Hull), September 21, 1943, NARA, RG 226, OSS, entry 210, box 462.
35. Barcza jelentése a külügyminiszternek, May 21, 1943 [Barcza to the foreign minister], August 5, 1943, Bodleian Library, Oxford, Macartney Papers, box 5.
36. See Juhász, *Magyar-brit titkos tárgyalások*, 63–65.
37. The memorandum is cited by a memorandum by W. Harrison, December 1943, Public Record Office Foreign Office, 371–39251. I thank Péter Sipos for this document.

38. Churchill is cited in Czettler, *A mi kis élet-halál kérdéseink*, 312.
39. Memorandum by Roger A. Pfaff, acting chief X-2 Branch for General Donovan, July 24, 1944, NARA, RG 226 OSS, entry 211, box 5.
40. István G. Vass, "Bakách-Bessenyey György tárgyalásai az Egyesült Államok megbízottaival Bernben 1943. augusztus 28. és 1944 március 19. között." *Levéltári Közlemények* (1995), 65, document 1, 161–64.
41. Ibid., document 2, 164–65.
42. Szegedy-Maszák, *Az ember ősszel visszanéz*, 345–47.
43. Czettler, *A mi kis élet-halál*, 386.
44. Memorandum for Brigadier General Hayes E. Kramer, chief, MIS Pentagon, September 14, 1943, NARA, General Records of the Department of State, central files 1940–1944, European War, box 2956.
45. Telegram by Dulles to the director of the OSS, the secretary of state, September 21, 1943, NARA, RG 226 OSS, entry 210, box 462.
46. Memorandum of the Division of European Affairs of the State Department to General Strand and George F. Kennan, Lisbon, October 5, 1943, NARA, RG 59, General Records of the State Department, central files, 1940–1944, box 2956.
47. Aide-memoire, British Embassy, Washington, D.C., October 13, 1943, telegram by the British ambassador at Ankara, October 2, 1943, NARA, RG 59, General Records of the Department of State, central files 1940–1944, box 2956.
48. Memorandum by the Division of European Affairs of the State Department, October 16, 1943, Memorandum from Acting Secretary Stettinius to William Leahy, chief of staff to the commander-in-chief of the U.S. Army and Navy, October 23, 1943, NARA, RG 59, General Records of the Department of State, central files 1940–1944, box 2956.
49. Bakách-Bessenyey követ Ghyczy Jenő külügyminiszterhez [Minister Bakách-Bessenyey to Foreign Minister Jenő Ghyczy], October 14, 1943, in Vass, "Bakách-Bessenyey György tárgyalásai," document 9, 177; András Joó, *Kállay Miklós külpolitikája: Magyarország és a háborús diplomácia 1942–1944* (Budapest: Napvilág, 2008), 205.
50. Bakách-Bessenyey követ Ghyczy külügyminiszterhez [Minister Bakách-Bessenyey to the foreign minister], October 28, 1943, in G. Vass, "Bakách-Bessenyey György tárgyalásai," document 9, 177.
51. Wodianer Andor lisszaboni követ jelentése a külügyminiszternek [Report by the minister in Lisbon, to the foreign minister], Magyar Nemzeti Levéltár Országos Levéltára (MNL OL), Külügyminisztérium (Küm), 192, Pol.
52. Vörnle János jelentése a külügyminiszternek [Report by Vörnle to the foreign minister], MNL OL, Küm, 179, Pol.
53. Cited in Robert Murphy's telegram to secretary of state, July 21, 1944, in Sipos and Vida, *The Policy of the United States towards Hungary during the Second World War*, 82.
54. Oleg Rzheshevsky, ed., *War and Diplomacy: The Making of the Grand Alliance. Documents from Stalin's Archives, Edited With a Commentary* (Amsterdam: Harwood Academic Publishers, 1996), Documents 6, 26.
55. Ralph B. Levering, Vladimir Pechatnov, Verena Botzenhart-Viehe, and Earl C. Edmondson, *Debating the Origins of the Cold War: American and Russian Perspectives* (Lanham, Md.: Rowman & Littlefield, 2002), 90.
56. Orme Sargent is cited in Hazard, *Cold War Crucible*, 14.
57. John Lamberton Harper, *American Visions of Europe: Franklin D. Roosevelt, George F. Kennan and Dean D. Acheson* (Cambridge: Cambridge University Press, 1994), 93–96.
58. Churchill to Roosevelt, October 7, 1943, in Warren F. Kimball, ed., *Churchill*

and Roosevelt: *The Complete Correspondence*, 3 vols. (Princeton, N.J.: Princeton University Press, 1992), 2: 498–99.
59. Sainsbury, *Churchill and Roosevelt at War*, 39.
60. First plenary meeting, November 28, 1943, Bohlen minutes, in U.S. Department of State, *Foreign Relations of the United States: Diplomatic Papers (FRUS)*, (Washington, D.C.: Government Printing Office, 1961), 493.
61. Eden to Churchill, October 21, 1943, cited in Martin Gilbert, *Road to Victory: Winston S. Churchill 1941–1945* (London: Heinemann, 1986), 536–37.
62. The first plenary session, Bohlen minutes, in U.S. Department of State, *FRUS: The Conferences at Cairo and Tehran, 1943*, 494–95.
63. David Hunt, "British Military Planning and Aims in 1944," in *British Political and Military Strategy in Central, Eastern and South-eastern Europe in 1944*, ed. F. W. Deakin, Elisabeth Barker, and Jonathan Chadwick (London: MacMillan, 1988), 30.
64. For the controversy over the campaign in Italy, see Robin Edmonds, *The Big Three: Churchill, Roosevelt, and Stalin in War and Peace* (London: Hamish Hamilton, 1991).
65. Hunt, "British Military Planning and Aims in 1944."
66. Memorandum, Dewitt C. Poole to James Grafton Rogers, February 15, 1943, NARA, RG 226 OSS, entry 210, box 344.
67. See Gábor Bátonyi, *Britain and Central Europe, 1918–1933* (Oxford: Clarendon Press, 1999).
68. On British policies toward Eastern Europe in the interwar period see ibid.; for the war see Elisabeth Barker, *British Policy in South-East Europe in the Second World War* (London: Macmillan, 1976); Harbutt, *Yalta*, 24–25 on British prejudices, and 40–169 for the unfolding of the British territorial deal with the Soviets.
69. Harbutt, *Yalta*, 86.

70. Ibid., 153.
71. Memorandum by the U.S. Delegation at the last discussion in Moscow, October 30, 1943, in U.S. Department of State, *FRUS: The Conferences at Cairo and Tehran*, 130–31.
72. Harbutt, *Yalta*, 167.
73. Ibid., 153.
74. Churchill's letter to Roosevelt, May 31, 1944; Kimball, *Churchill and Roosevelt*, 3:153–54.
75. Roosevelt's letter to Churchill, June 10, 1944, in ibid., 177.
76. Churchill's letter to Roosevelt, June 11, 1944, in ibid., 178–79.
77. Cited in Sainsbury, *Churchill and Roosevelt at War*, 43.
78. Cited in Harbutt, *Yalta*, 169.
79. Elisabeth Barker: "Problems of Alliance: Misconceptions and Misunderstanding," in *British Political and Military Strategy in Central, Eastern, and Southern Europe in 1944*, ed. William Deakin, Elisabeth Barker, and Jonathan Chadwick (London: Macmillan, 1988).
80. Gilbert, *Road to Victory*, 991–92.
81. Telegram by Harriman to the president, October 10, 1944, Library of Congress, Washington, D.C., Manuscript Division, Papers of Averell Harriman, box 174.
82. In September 1944 Eden wrote to Churchill that if Britain abandoned Bulgaria it would lose all its credibility in the Balkans.
83. Churchill's letter to Attlee, December 3, 1944, in Gilbert, *Road to Victory*, 1028.
84. Telegram by Harriman to the president, October 11, 1944, Library of Congress, Manuscript Division, Papers of Averell Harriman, box 174.
85. Memorandum by the Joint Planning Staff Committee, August 22, 1943, Public Record Office, Cabinet (PRO, CAB) 121/441. I owe knowledge of this document to Éva Figder.

86. The deputy chief to the chief of staff, August 23, 1943, in Juhász, *Magyar-brit titkos tárgyalások*, 219–20.
87. Churchill's letter to Roosevelt, October 7, 1943, in Kimball, *Churchill and Roosevelt: The Complete Correspondence*, 2:498–99.
88. Memorandum of conversation by A. W. G. Randell with Professor Namier, October 14, 1943, in Juhász, *Magyar-brit titkos tárgyalások*, 271.
89. Richard Breitman, *Official Secrets: What the Nazis Planned, What the British and Americans Knew* (New York: Hill & Wang, 1999), 144–45.
90. Memorandum from William Donovan to the State Department, October 23, 1943, NARA, RG 218, JCS, geographical files 1942–1945, box 191. The document was forwarded to the JCS on December 9.
91. "Proposal by the Hungarian Minister in Sweden," report by the Joint Staff planners, undated [December 1943], NARA, RG 218, JCS, geographical files 1942–1945, box 191.
92. The secretary of state to the legation in Stockholm, January 19, 1944, NARA, RG 218, JCS, geographical files 1942–1945, box 191.
93. Telegram by the secretary of state to the minister in Stockholm, January 13, 1944, NARA, RG 59, General Records of the Department of State, central files 1940–1944, box 2956.
94. Jackson, memorandum to Dulles, December 18, 1943, Seeley Mudd Library, Princeton, N.J., Papers of Allen Dulles.
95. Leahy's memorandum is cited in memorandum from Cordell Hull to Admiral William Leahy, March 16, 1944, NARA, RG 218, JCS, geographical files 1942–1945, box 191.
96. Memorandum for Allen Dulles, November 3, 1943, Seeley Mudd Library, Princeton, N.J., Papers of Allen Dulles, PDF file 1943021100003537.

97. Memorandum from Hull to Madrid, sent to Stockholm, London, Berne, and Ankara, November 18, 1943, NARA, RG 59, General Records of the Department of State, central files 1940–1944, box 2956.
98. Memorandum by Adolph Berle, December 1943, NARA, RG 59, General Records of the Department of State, central files 1940–1944, box 2956.
99. Overall Deception Policy for War with Germany, undated [December 1943], Library of Congress, Manuscript Division, Papers of Averell Harriman, box 171.
100. Telegram by Harriman, "Article by Gavrilov," Library of Congress, Manuscript Division, Papers of Averell Harriman, Box 537.
101. Telegram for Donovan and Macgruder, cited in Shlomo Aronson, *Hitler, the Allies, and the Jews* (Cambridge: Cambridge University Press, 2004), 220.
102. Anthony Cave Brown, *Bodyguard of Lies* (New York: Harper and Row, 1975), 1: 479–508.
103. Gyula Juhász, "A magyar-német viszony néhány kérdése a második világháború alatt," *Történelmi Szemle* 27, no. 2 (1984).
104. Brown, *Bodyguard of Lies*, 504.
105. Similar views were expressed the head of the Central Department of the Foreign Office, F. K. Roberts, on November 16: the Hungarian volte-face had to be postponed until it was the most advantageous from the perspective of the war effort. Memoranda by the Foreign Office on talks with Hungary, November 13–22, 1943, in Juhász, *Magyar-brit titkos tárgyalások*, 285.
106. Memorandum by W. Harrison, December 11, 1943, in ibid., 294, document 95/c.
107. See a memorandum by F. K. Roberts, in ibid., 284–86, document 91.
108. Memorandum by Harriman, Library of Congress, Manuscript Division, Papers of Averell Harriman, box 175.

109. Czettler, *A mi kis élet-halál kérdéseink*, 387, 392. Szegedy-Maszák, *Az ember ősszel visszanéz*, 302–3.
110. Memorandum by Dulles, November 22, 1943. Seeley Mudd Library, Princeton, N.J., Papers of Allen Dulles.
111. Memorandum by Dulles, November 24, 1943, Dulles on the Hungarian situation, December 17, 1943, in Petersen, *From Hitler's Doorstep*, 180.
112. Memorandum from the OSS (Hugh Wilson) to Adolph Berle, undated [December 1943], NARA, RG 59, General Records of the Department of State, central files 1940–1944, box 2956.
113. OSS Planning Group, "Implementation Study for Overall Special Programs for Strategic Services in the Balkans as They Pertain to Hungary," December 31, 1944, NARA, RG 226, OSS, entry 144, box 30.
114. Memoranda by Foreign Office officials, December 11–14, 1943, D. Allen, F. K. Roberts, C. Harvey, and A. Cadogan, in Juhász, *Magyar-brit titkos tárgyalások*, 295–96, document 95/c.
115. The SOE's reply to the message by the Hungarian government, December 8, 1943, in ibid., 292–93, document 95/b.
116. OSS Planning Group, "Implementation Study for Overall Strategic Programs for Strategic Services in the Balkans as They Pertain to Hungary," December 31, 1943, NARA, RG 226, OSS, entry 144, box 30.
117. JCS Memorandum for William Donovan, proposal by Hungarian staff officer, November 1943, NARA, RG 226, OSS, entry 190, box 654.
118. András Joó, "Világháborús intrikák: a magyar béketapogatózások és az isztanbuli színtér fontos mozzanatai," *Századok* 142, no. 6 (2008): 1450–56.
119. Hungarian special plan, undated, NARA, RG 226, OSS, entry 190, box 593.
120. Memorandum from William Donovan to the JCS, November 20, 1943, NARA, RG 226, OSS, entry 190, box 654.
121. Interoffice memorandum, William H. Shepardson to William Donovan, February 25, 1944, NARA, RG 226, OSS, entry 190, box 593.
122. "Proposal by Hungarian General Staff Officer," report by the Joint Planners to the Joint Chiefs of Staff, December 2, 1943, NARA, RG 218, JCS geographical files, box 191.
123. "Note on Collaboration with Hungary," November 11, 1943, NARA, RG 226, OSS, entry 210, box 447.
124. Report on Draft Agreement, December 23, 1943, NARA, RG 226, OSS, entry 210, box 226.
125. Joó, "Világháborús intrikák," 1455–56.
126. Telegram from Bern, January 2, 1944. NARA, RG 226, OSS, Entry 211, Box 5. Hatz's role in leaking this information remains to be clarified. Historian András Joó claims that Hatz informed the Germans in order to clear himself since Hungarian intelligence knew that the Germans had already found out about the talks. Joó, "Világháborús intrikák."
127. Memorandum from General Donovan for Roger A. Pfaff, acting chief, X-2 Branch, July 24, 1944, NARA, RG 226, OSS, entry 211, box 5.
128. Hungarian scheme, undated [January 1944], NARA, RG 226, OSS, entry 210, box 447.
129. Joó, "Világháborús intrikák," 1456–58.
130. Telegram by Dulles, January 26, 1944, in Petersen, *From Hitler's Doorstep*, 222–23.
131. "Provisions for Imposition Upon Hungary at the Time of Surrender Approved by JCS for Communication to EAC," February 1944, NARA, RG 218, JCS, geographical files, 1942–1945, box 191. Acting secretary of state (Stettinius) to Admiral Leahy, February 28, 1944, NARA, RG 218, JCS, geographical files 1942–1945, box 191.

132. "Soviet Armistice Draft, Romania," April 11, 1944, Library of Congress, Manuscript Division, Papers of Averell Harriman, box 172.

133. President Beneš's letter to Foreign Minister Gafencu," telegram by Dulles, March 16, 1944, in Petersen, *From Hitler's Doorstep*, 242.

134. "Answer to Hungarian Interim Reply," February 9, 1944, NARA, RG 226 OSS, entry 11, box 447.

135. "Final Hungarian Reply," February 14, 1944, NARA, RG 226 OSS, entry 11, box 447.

136. See Czettler, *A mi kis élet-halál kérdéseink*, 439.

137. Cable by Dulles, October 2, 1943, telegram 205 to Algiers, in Petersen, *From Hitler's Doorstep*, 137–39, 193–94.

138. Telegram by Dulles to Algiers, December 22, 1943, NARA, RG 226, OSS, entry 210, box 462.

139. Telegram by Dulles to Washington and Algiers, January 6, 1944, ibid.

140. Telegram from Bern, February 24, 1944, NARA, RG 226, OSS, entry 210, box 462.

141. Donovan to Algiers, 24 March 24, 1944, NARA, RG 226, OSS, entry 210, box 462; Gamele, Beale and Brewster to Glavin and 154, March 21, 1944, NARA, RG 226, OSS, entry 210, box 462.

142. The OSS got hold of the message sent by the German Embassy in Budapest to Wilhelmstrasse. "Kamay Message on Sparrow," telegram from Bern, May 15, 1944, NARA, RG 226, entry 211, box 5.

143. Zoltán András Kovács, "A Janus arcú tábornok: Adalékok Ujszászy István vezérőrnagynak, a VKF 2 osztály és az Államvédelmi Központ vezetőjének az ÁVH fogságában írott feljegyzéseihez," in *Vallomások a holtak házából*, ed. György Haraszti (Budapest: Corvina K., 2007), 98.

144. "The party will be instructed specifically to avoid any political implications." Memorandum from the Allied commander in chief to general commander in chief Middle East Forces, March 2, 1944, NARA, RG 226, OSS, entry 210, box 462.

145. A brief memorandum was prepared of the conversation that took place on July 28, 1965, Seeley Mudd Library, Princeton, N.J., Papers of Allen Dulles.

146. Telegram from Sweden regarding Hungarian attitude regarding U.S., JCS memorandum, March 15, 1944, NARA, RG 218, JCS, geographical files 1942–1945, box 191.

147. Guy to Goldberg, March 11, 1944, NARA, RG 226, OSS, entry 210, box 654; outgoing telegram to Brindisi, March 13, 1944, NARA, RG 226, OSS, entry 190, box 593; Colonel Glavin to Donovan, March 27, 1944, NARA, RG 226, OSS, entry 210, box 464.

148. Telegram by McFarland to Donovan, March 19, 1944, NARA, RG 226, OSS, entry 190, box 593.

149. Dr. Wilhelm Höttl, interview, February 19, 1966, to Dick Slurman for Roy Alexander from Franz Spelman, Munich Stringer, Seely Mudd Library, Princeton, N.J., Papers of Allen Dulles.

150. Dulles, cited in Aronson, *Hitler, the Allies, and the Jews*, 221.

151. Sainsbury, *Churchill and Roosevelt at War*, 38.

152. Barcza a külügyminiszternek, May 21, 1943; Barcza a külügyminiszternek, August 5, 1943, Bodleian Library, Oxford, Macartney Papers, box 5.

153. Szegedy-Maszák, *Az ember ősszel visszanéz*, 330.

154. Károly Urbán and István Vida, "Budapest 1941. Május-1944. március. Részlet Barcza György Diplomataemlékeim című emlékiratának második kötetéből," *Századok* 121, no. 23 (1987): 397–98.

155. Memorandum by Szegedy-Maszák, Bodleian Library, Oxford, Macartney Papers, box 5.

156. Memorandum by Barcza György, May 21, 1943, Bodleian Library, Oxford, Macartney Papers, box 5.

157. Bakách-Bessenyey's memorandum to Foreign Minister Ghyczy, January 27, 1944, in G. Vass, Bakách-Bessenyey's talks in 1943–1944, 198, document 22.

158. For a discussion of the role of inducements in international relations, see Robert Jervis, *American Foreign Policy in a New Era* (New York and London: Routledge, 2005).

159. See for example the former GDR, Romania, or Austria. Hope Harrison, *Driving the Soviets Up the Wall: Soviet-East German Relations 1953–1961* (Princeton, N.J.: Princeton University Press, 2003); Joseph F. Harrington and Bruce J. Courtney, *Tweaking the Nose of the Russians: Fifty Years of American-Romanian Relations, 1940–1990* (New York: East European Monographs, 1991); Günter Bischof, *Austria in the First Cold War, 1945–55: The Leverage of the Weak* (London: MacMillan, 1999).

2. CUIUS REGIO, EIUS RELIGIO

1. For Stalin's policy during and after the war, see Gerhard Wettig, *Stalin and the Cold War in Europe: The Emergence and Development of the East-West Conflict, 1939–1953* (Lanham, Md.: Rowman & Littlefield, 2008); Norman Naimark and Leonid Gibianski, eds., *Establishment of Communist Regimes in Eastern Europe, 1944–1949* (Boulder, Colo.: Westview Press, 1996); Eduard Mark, *Revolution by Degrees: Stalin's National Front Strategy for Europe, 1941–1947*, Cold War International History Paper no. 31 (Washington, D.C.: Woodrow Wilson Center, 2001).

2. Nicholas Nyárádi, *My Ringside Seat in Moscow* (New York: Thomas E. Crowell, 1952), 54.

3. On American prejudices regarding Eastern Europeans and the debates on Soviet intentions there, see Hugh DeSantis, *The Diplomacy of Silence: The American Foreign Service, The Soviet Union and the Cold War* (Chicago: University of Chicago Press, 1980).

4. Record of conversation, participants: Edvard Beneš and Averrell Harriman, December 1943, Library of Congress, Washington, D.C., Manuscript Division, box 174.

5. Kennan to the secretary of state, October 13, 1944, in U.S. Department of State, *Foreign Relations of the United States Diplomatic Papers (FRUS), 1944, Europe*, vol. 4 (Washington, D.C.: Government Printing Office, 1944).

6. See Igor Lukes, *On the Edge of the Cold War: American Diplomats and Spies in Postwar Prague* (Oxford: Oxford University Press, 2012), 8–9.

7. Cited in Justine Faure, *L'Ami Américain: La Tschéchoslovaquie enjeu de la diplomatie Américaine* (Paris: Tallandier, 2001), 45.

8. Truman to Churchill, October 17, 1947, in G. W. Sand, ed., *Defending the West: The Truman-Churchill Correspondence, 1945–1960* (Westport, Conn.: Praeger, 2004), 165.

9. Harriman to Hopkins, September 18, 1944, Hull to Harriman, September 18, 1944, Harriman to the secretary of state, September 20, 1944, Library of Congress, Manuscript Division, Papers of Averell Harriman, box 174.

10. Kennan to Harriman, September 18, 1944, Library of Congress, Manuscript Division, Papers of Averell Harriman, box 174.

11. Letter by Admiral Leahy, May 16, 1944, in U.S. Department of State, *FRUS, the Conferences at Malta and Yalta, 1945* (Washington, D.C.: Government Printing Office, 1945), 107–8. The JCS are cited by Stanley M. Max, *The Anglo-American Response to the Sovietization of Hungary* (Ann Arbor, Mich.: East European Monographs, 1985), 177.

12. Faure, *L'Ami Américain*, 66.

13. Geir Lundestad, *The American Non-Policy towards Eastern Europe, 1943–1947: Universalism in an Area Not of Essential Interest to the United States* (Tromsö: Universitatsforlaget, 1978). On America's open spheres, see Eduard Mark, "American Policy Toward Eastern-Europe and the Origins of the Cold War 1941–1946: An Alternative Interpretation," 313–36, *Journal of American History* 68, no. 2 (September 1981).

14. Günter Bischof, *Austria in the First Cold War, 1945–55: The Leverage of the Weak* (London: MacMillan, 1999).

15. On the various aspects of the Soviet-German struggle for Hungary, see Krisztián Ungváry, *The Siege of Budapest: 100 Days in World War II* (New Haven, Conn.: Yale University Press, 2005).

16. Bischof, *Austria in the First Cold War*, 94.

17. Lukes, *On the Edge of the Cold War*, 10–11.

18. Department of State, Interim Research and Intelligence, December 31, 1945, National Archives and Records Administration (NARA), Washington, D.C., Microfilm Division, Department of State Interim Research and Intelligence Service, microfilm 3467.

19. Office of Strategic Services (OSS), October 23, 1944, NARA, Microfilm Division, OSS Research and Analysis Branch, reel no. 2417.

20. Memorandum from the U.S. Mission to the secretary of state, September 15, 1945, in U.S. Department of State, *Foreign Relations of the United States (FRUS): Diplomatic Papers, 1945: Europe*, vol. 4 (Washington, D.C.: Government Printing Office, 1945), 869–73.

21. The representative in Hungary (Schoenfeld) to the secretary of state, August 21, 1945, U.S. Department of State, *FRUS, 1945: Europe*, 4:852–53.

22. DeSantis, *Diplomacy of Silence*.

23. The acting secretary of state to the legation in Hungary, October 6, 1947, in U.S. Department of State, *Foreign Relations of the United States (FRUS), 1947: Eastern Europe; the Soviet Union*, vol. 4 (Washington, D.C.: Government Printing Office, 1947), 393–94.

24. Telegram by Schoenfeld to the secretary of state, April 30, 1946, in U.S. Department of State, *Foreign Relations of the United States (FRUS), 1946: Eastern Europe, the Soviet Union*, vol. 6 (Washington, D.C.: Government Printing Office, 1946), 290–91.

25. The minister in Hungary to the secretary of state, May 2, 1946, in U.S. Department of State, *FRUS, 1946: Eastern Europe, the Soviet Union*, 6:293–94.

26. To Saint, Washington, Administrative Report, August 16, 1946, NARA, Record Group (RG) 226, OSS, entry 211, box 35.

27. Faure, *L'Ami Américain*, 92–95.

28. For Soviet-German rivalry in Romania see Gabriel Gorodetsky, *The Grand Delusion: Stalin and the German Invasion of Russia* (New Haven, Conn.: Yale University Press, 1999).

29. Bischof, *Austria in the First Cold War*.

30. The chargé in the Soviet Union (Kennan) to the people's commissar for foreign affairs of the Soviet Union (Molotov), March 2, 1946, in U.S. Department of State, *FRUS, 1946: Eastern Europe, the Soviet Union*, 6:265–67.

31. The secretary of state to the minister in Hungary, June 4, 1946, in U.S. Department of State, *Foreign Relations of the United States (FRUS), 1946: Paris Peace Conference: Documents*, vol. 4 (Washington, D.C.: Government Printing Office, 1946), 300–301.

32. Rákosi Sztálinhoz továbbított levele, July 2, 1946, [Rákosi's letter to Stalin], in Lajos Izsák and Miklós Kun, eds., *Moszkvának jelentjük: Titkos dokumentumok* (Budapest: Századvég, 1994), 95–97.

33. The secretary of state to the legation in Hungary, February 22, 1947, in U.S.

Department of State, *FRUS, 1947: Eastern Europe; the Soviet Union*, 4:269–71; on U.S. reactions to Kovács's arrest see Lundestad, *The American Non-Policy towards Eastern Europe*, 137–40.

34. Magyar Nemzeti Levéltár Országos Levéltára (MNL OL), Budapest, Külügyminisztérium (Küm), USA admin., XIX-J-1-K, 25 c, 55. doboz, 40.934/47.

35. The deputy director of the Office of East European Affairs to the secretary of state, March 1, 1947, NARA, RG 59, the General Records of the Department of State, decimal files 864.00/3–147; the secretary of state to the legation in Hungary, March 3, 1947, U.S. Department of State, *FRUS, 1947: Eastern Europe; the Soviet Union*, 4:272–75. Both telegrams were sent on the same day.

36. The acting chairman of the Allied Control Commission (ACC) to the chief of the United States representation on the ACC, March 8, 1947, *FRUS, 1947*, 4:277.

37. Schoenfeld to the secretary of state, March 21, 1947, in ibid., 288–89.

38. Memorandum from Hickerson to Acting Secretary of State Acheson, March 12, 1947, NARA, RG 59, General Records of the Department of State, decimal files, 864.00/3–1247; the minister in Hungary to the secretary of state, March 21, 1947, in U.S. Department of State, *FRUS, 1947: Eastern Europe; the Soviet Union*, 4:288–89; *New York Times*, March 8, 1947.

39. Memorandum of conversation by Barbour, U.S. Department of State, *FRUS, 1947: Eastern Europe; the Soviet Union*, 4:292.

40. The ambassador in the Soviet Union to the acting secretary of state, March 5, 1947, in ibid., 276.

41. The minister in Hungary to the secretary of state, January 27, 1947, in ibid., 264–65.

42. Ibid., 50.

43. In the Soviet view the peace treaty restored sovereignty. See Reshenie Politburo TsK VKP(b) ob utverzhdenii proekta o mirnom dogovore s Vengriei na soveschanii zamestyitelei v SMID v Londone, March 21, 1946; T. V. Volokitina et al. eds., *Transilvanskii Vopros vengero-ruminskii territorialnii spor i SSSR, 1940–1946 Dokumenti* (Moskva: Rosspen, 2000), doc. 102, 371.

44. Mátyás Rákosi, *Visszaemlékezések 1940–1956*, ed. István Feitl et al., 2 vols. (Budapest: Napvilág Kiadó), 2:377.

45. NARA, RG 263, Records of the CIA, Grombach Organization, correspondence with sources, P, entry 13, box 1.

46. *New York Times*, May 31, 1947.

47. Record of conversation between Szegedy-Maszák and Walwourth Barbour, June 2, 1947, NARA, RG 59, General Records of the Department of State, decimal files 864.00/6–247; Mclintock to Rusk, June 2, 1947, in ibid. The acting director of the Office of Eastern European Affairs to the secretary of state, June 3, 1947, in U.S. Department of State, *FRUS, 1947: Eastern Europe; the Soviet Union*, 4:317–19.

48. Walter Laqueur, *Europe in Our Time: A History 1945–1992* (New York: Penguin Books, 1993), 36–38.

49. Cited in Miklós Lojkó, "Conservative Realignment in British Policy on Central Europe and the Balkans during the Early Interwar Years," in *Európa, nemzet, külpolitika: Tanulmányok Ádám Magda 85.születésnapjára*, ed. László Borhi and Attila Pók (Budapest: Aura, 2010), 153–70.

50. See John Kent, "British Postwar Planning for Europe 1942–45," in *The Failure of Peace in Europe, 1943–1948*, ed. Antonio Varsori and Elena Calandri (New York: Palgrave Macmillan, 2001), 44–46.

51. Ignác Romsics, "A brit külpolitikai és a 'magyarkérdés', 1914–1946," *Századok* 130, no. 2 (1996), 273–339; the second secretary of the British Embassy to the acting head of Division of European Affairs, June 9, 1947, in U.S. Department of State, *FRUS, 1947: Eastern Europe; the Soviet Union*, 4:315–16; Max, *The Anglo-American Response*, 28.

52. The secretary of state to the legation in Budapest, June 10, 1947, in U.S. Department of State, *FRUS, 1947: Eastern Europe; the Soviet Union*, 4:317–19.

53. Marek Kamiński, *Wobliczu sowieckego ekspansjonizmu: Polytika Stanów Zjednocznych Wielkiej Britanii Wobec Polskii i Czechosłowacji, 1945–1948* (Warsaw: Instytut Historii PAN, 2005), 348–51.

54. Memorandum by the director of the Office of Eastern European Affairs, July 1, 1947, in U.S. Department of State, *FRUS, 1947: Eastern Europe; the Soviet Union*, 4:317–19.

55. László Borhi, *Magyarország a hidegháborúban, 1945–1956: A Szovjetunió és az Egyesült Államok között* (Budapest: Corvina, 2005), 128.

56. The secretary of state to the legation in Hungary, June 6, 1947, in U.S. Department of State, *FRUS, 1947: Eastern Europe; the Soviet Union*, 4:314. Marshall to the legation in Prague, June 6, 1947, NARA, RG 59, General Records of the Department of State, decimal files 864.00/6-397.

57. Szegedy-Maszák's letter to Freeman Matthews, June 6, 1947, NARA, RG 59, General Records of the Department of State, decimal files 864.00/6-647.

58. The minister in Hungary (Chapin) to the secretary of state, July 22, 1947, in U.S. Department of State, *FRUS, 1947: Eastern Europe; the Soviet Union*, 4:340–48.

59. Faure, *L'Ami Américain*, 128–29.

60. Lukes, *On the Edge of the Cold War*, 4.

61. The minister in Hungary (Chapin) to the secretary of state, July 29, 1947, in U.S. Department of State, *FRUS, 1947: Eastern Europe; the Soviet Union*, 4:351–52.

62. The minister in Hungary (Chapin) to the secretary of state, October 2, 1947, in ibid., 384–92; the acting secretary of state to the legation in Hungary, October 6, 1947, in ibid., 393–94.

63. Nicholas Spulber, "Problems of East-West Trade and Economic Trends in the European Satellites of Soviet Russia," in *The Fate of East Central Europe*, ed. Stephen D. Kertesz (Notre Dame, Ind.: Notre Dame University Press, 1956), 399–401.

64. For the documents on U.S. companies in Hungary see MNL OL, Küm, XIX-J-1-j, USA admin, 9. doboz and 55. doboz.

65. MNL OL, KS, 276. f., 67. cs., 155. őe.

66. Robert Vogeler, *I Was Stalin's Prisoner* (New York: Harcourt, Brace, 1951), 144.

67. István Pál, "A Vogeler-ügy," in *Gyarmatokból impérium: Magyar kutatók tanulmányai az amerikai történelemről*, ed. Tibor Frank (Budapest: Gondolat, 2007), 217–35.

68. MNL OL, Küm, XIX-J-1-j, USA tük, 1945–1964, 9. doboz, 26. tétel.

69. Memorandum from Dean Acheson to the president, February 2, 1949, in U.S. Department of State, *Foreign Relations of the United States (FRUS), 1949: Eastern Europe; the Soviet Union*, vol. 5 (Washington, D.C.: Government Printing Office, 1949), 460–61.

70. Lundestad, *The American Non-Policy towards Eastern Europe*, 80.

71. Peter Kenez, *Hungary from the Nazis to the Soviets: The Establishment of the Communist Regime in Hungary, 1944–1988* (Cambridge: Cambridge University Press, 2009). Kenez argues that Sovietization was only a fallback option for the Soviets when efforts to cooperate with Washington failed.

72. Rákosi Mátyás beszéde [presentation by Mátyás Rákosi], May 17, 1946, Politikatörténeti Intézet Levéltára, 274. f. 2. cs. 34. őe.

73. Kamiński, *Wobliczu sowieckego ekspanjonizmu*, 358.

3. ROLLBACK

1. Fraser J. Harbutt, *Yalta, 1945: Europe and America at the Crossroads* (New York: Cambridge University Press, 2010).

2. Mark Kramer, "Stalin, Soviet Policy and the Consolidation of a Communist Bloc in Eastern Europe, 1944–1953," in *Stalinism Revisited: The Establishment of Communist Regimes in East-Central Europe*,

ed. Vladimir Tismaneanu (Budapest: Central European University Press, 2009), 89.

3. Ibid., 164–65.

4. Tor Egil Førland defined economic warfare as a policy designed to undermine the pillars of the opponent's economic power. See Tor Egil Førland, "Cold Economic Warfare: The Creation and Prime of CoCom, 1948–1954" (Ph.D. diss., University of Oslo, 1991), 22.

5. John Lewis Gaddis, *The Long Peace: Inquiries into the History of the Cold War* (New York and Oxford: Oxford University Press, 1987), 159.

6. Letter submitted by Averell Harriman to the National Security Council, in U.S. Department of State, *Foreign Relations of the United States (FRUS), 1948: Eastern Europe; the Soviet Union*, vol. 4 (Washington, D.C.: Government Printing Office, 1948), 506–7.

7. Førland, "Cold Economic Warfare," 45.

8. Alan Dobson, *US Economic Statecraft for Survival 1933–1991: Of Sanctions, Embargoes and Economic Warfare* (New York: Routledge, 2002), 90.

9. Report by the Joint Chiefs of Staff to the Secretary of Defense, June 26, 1950, in U.S. Department of State, *Foreign Relations of the United States (FRUS), 1950: Central and Eastern Europe; the Soviet Union*, vol. 4 (Washington, D.C.: Government Printing Office, 1950), 152–53.

10. Report by the secretary of the National Security Council (NSC), August 1950, in ibid., 163.

11. Førland, "Cold Economic Warfare," 124.

12. On the effect of the Korean War on export controls see Joseph F. Harrington and Bruce J. Courtney, *Tweaking the Nose of the Russians: Fifty Years of American-Romanian Relations, 1940–1990*, East European Monographs no. 296 (Boulder, Colo.: East European Monographs, 1991), 124–38.

13. March 1954, National Archives and Records Administration (NARA), Washington, D.C., Record Group (RG) 263, Central Intelligence Agency (CIA) National Intelligence Estimate (NIE) 100-3-54, box 2.

14. Harrington and Courtney, *Tweaking the Nose of the Russians*, 157–58.

15. On the economic policies of "New Look" see Tor Egil Førland, "Cold Economic Warfare"; "Selling Firearms to the Indians: Eisenhower's Export Control Policy, 1953–54," *Diplomatic History* 15, no. 2 (April 1991): 231–32; Robert Spalding Jr., "'A Graduate and Moderate Relaxation': Eisenhower and the Revision of American Export Control Policy, 1953–1955," *Diplomatic History* 17, no. 2 (1993): 223–50.

16. Memorandum from the Joint Logistical Committee to the Joint Chiefs of Staff (JCS) on the Revision of the Relaxation of the Export of Strategic Commodities to the Soviet Bloc, December 9, 1949, NARA, RG 218, 1951–53, 091; memorandum to the secretary of defense on the Export Control of the United States, ibid., 1954–56, September 28, 1954, CCS, 091.31, section 26.

17. "Trends in National Security Programs and the Fiscal and Budgetary Outlook through Fiscal Year 1959," January 27, 1956, NARA, RG 273, NSC, 5609/2.

18. A külügyminiszter a washingtoni magyar követnek [The foreign minister to the minister in Washington], January 20, 1954, Magyar Országos Levéltár Nemzeti Levéltára (MNL OL), Budapest, Külügyminisztérium (Küm), USA admin, XIX-J-1-k, 25/c, 55. doboz, 01134 titk. I. 1954.

19. Olt Károly feljegyzése a keményvaluta helyzetről 1955-ben és 1956 elején [Memorandum by finance minister Olt on the hard currency situation], April 15, 1956, MOL OL, KS, 276. f., 66. cs., 71. őe.

20. Károly Urbán, "Sztálin halálától a forradalom kitöréséig: a magyar-szovjet kapcsolatok története (1953–1956)," unpublished manuscript (Budapest, 1996), 25–39.

21. Memorandum from the deputy assistant secretary of state for economic affairs (Kalijarvi) to the secretary of state, July 18, 1956, NARA, RG 59, General Records of the Department of State, lot file 76D232.

22. A külkereskedelmi miniszter (Háy László) feljegyzése Magyarország külkereskedelmi helyzetéről [Memorandum by minister of foreign trade Hay on Hungary's foreign trade], October 13, 1956, MNL OL, KS, 276. f., 67. cs., 178. őe.

23. Hungarian Interest in US Wheat and Cotton, Amleg Budapest to the State Department, April 2, 1955, NARA, RG 59, General Records of the Department of State, central files, 411, 6441/4-2255. See also Hungarian Interest in United States Trade, Amleg Budapest to the State Department, June 24, 1955, August 9, 1955, ibid. 411, 6441/6-2455 és 411, 6441-8-955.

24. Progress Report Submitted by the Operations Coordinating Board to the NSC, Progress Report on NSC 174, United States Policy toward the Satellites of Eastern Europe, February 29, 1956, in U.S. Department of State, *Foreign Relations of the United States (FRUS), 1955–1957: Eastern Europe*, ed. John P. Glennon, vol. 25 (Washington, D.C.: Government Printing Office, 1955–57), 121–28. In 1950 the PPS predicted that neither the embargo nor Western economic aid would be enough to cause a schism between the USSR and the satellites.

25. The information was derived from an émigré whose job had been to procure technical equipment. The American Embassy in Vienna to the State Department, October 20, 1953. NARA, RG 59, General Records of the Department of State, decimal files 864.00/20–2056.

26. I have found no concrete evidence on the existence of such a company, but a memorandum penned by Rákosi foresaw the establishment of trade companies like this in Belgium, Holland, Sweden, or Tangiers. See Rákosi feljegyzése operatív külkereskedelmi vállalatokról [Rákosi on the establishment of operative foreign trading companies], April 21, 1949, MNL OL, KS, 276. f., 65 cs., 281. őe.

27. Mátyás Rákosi, *Visszaemlékezések, 1940–1956*, ed. István Feitl et al., vols. 1–2 (Budapest: Napvilág Kiadó), 2:847.

28. The American legation in Vienna to the State Department, July 25, 1952, NARA, RG 59, General Records of the Department of State, decimal files 864.00/10–25552.

29. The agreement was meant to be used for the purchase of spare parts for French-made automobiles, but Hungary used it to get hold of spare parts for British- and American-made cars. Étude sur la Hongrie, June 1952, Archive du Ministère des affaires étrangères, Serie Europe 1944–1960, Hongrie vol. 40.

30. Harrington and Courtney, *Tweaking the Nose of the Russians*, 149.

31. Meeting of the Political Committee of the Hungarian Workers Party (HWP) on May 19, 1956, MNL OL, KS, 276 f., 53 cs., 101. őe.

32. Soprovoditelnoie pismo L. Beria G. Malenkovu [Cover letter by Beria to Malenkov], June 1–2, 1953, Galina P. Murashko, ed., *Vostochnaia Evropa v Dokumentakh Rossiskikh Arkhivov* (Novosibirsk: Sibirskii Khronograf, 1998), 2:918.

33. See the reports by the U.S. Embassy in Vienna above. See also Rákosi, *Visszaemlékezések*, 846, 863.

34. The Soviet ambassador in Budapest informed Molotov on May 30, 1953, that Hungarian foreign debt to countries such as the Federal Republic of Germany was the highest within the "lager" and that half of the gold reserve had been tied down as collateral for the loan. Kiselev k Molotovu [Kiselev to Molotov], May 30, 1953, Arkhiv Vneshnei Politiki Rossiskii Federatsii, Moscow, fond 077, opis 33, papka 166, delo 240.

35. Kenneth Osgood, *Total Cold War: Eisenhower's Secret Propaganda Battle at Home and Abroad* (Lawrence: University Press of Kansas, 2006), 34–35.
36. Ibid., 16, 35.
37. Justine Faure, *L'Ami Américain: La Tschéchoslovaquie enjeu de la diplomatie Américaine* (Paris: Tallandier, 2001), 192.
38. Ibid., 196.
39. Osgood, *Total Cold War*, 41.
40. Ibid., 44.
41. Cited by Christopher Tudda, *The Truth Is Our Weapon: The Rhetorical Diplomacy of Dwight D. Eisenhower and John Foster Dulles* (Baton Rouge: Louisiana State University Press, 2006), 26.
42. The U.S. legation to the State Department, February 2, 1953, NARA, RG 59, General Records of the Department of State, decimal files 764.00/10–654.
43. National Operations Plan: USSR, East European Satellites, OCB-16, November 13, 1953, NARA, RG 59, General Records of the Department of State, Records Relating to the Participation of the State Department in the OCB and the National Security Council (NSC) 1947–53, lot file 62D430, box 31.
44. The American legation to the State Department, Pattern of Democratic Action under a Totalitarian Regime, February 2, 1956, NARA, RG 59, General Records of the Department of State, decimal files 764.00/2–656.
45. The U.S. legation in Budapest to the State Department, October 6, 1954, NARA, RG 59, General Records of the Department of State, decimal files 764.00/10–654.
46. Kiss Károly jelentése Rákosi Mátyásnak [Report by Kiss to Rákosi], April 5, 1955, MNL OL, KS, 276. f., 65. cs., 283. őe.
47. Szigeti Károly, az angol-amerikai osztály vezetőjének feljegyzése Barnes fogadásáról, [Memorandum by the head of the Anglo-American Divison on Barnes' reception] October 13, 1956. MNL OL, Küm, XIX-J-1-j, USA tük, 1947–1964, 140t, 26. doboz, sz. n.
48. See also Osgood, *Total Cold War*, 41.
49. Radio Free Europe Handbook, November 30, 1951, National Security Archives, Washington, D.C. (NSAWDC), Soviet Flashpoints Collection (SFC), record no. 66367.
50. Columbia University Bureau of Applied Research on Listening to Voice of America (VOA) and other Foreign Stations in Hungary, November 1953. NSAWDC, SFC, record no. 64444.
51. Amcongen Frankfurt to the State Department, July 16, 1956, NARA, RG 59, General Records of the Department of State, decimal files 764.00/7–1956.
52. AmEmbassy Tel Aviv to the State Department, interview with recent arrival from Hungary, May 12, 1955, NARA, RG 59, General Records of the Department of State, decimal files 764.00/5–1255.
53. Flossmann győző és társai, Magyar Függetlenségi Front, 1952 undated [Győző Flossman and associates, Hungarian Independence Front], Állambiztonsági Szolgálatok Történeti Levéltára [Historical Archives of the National Security Services] (ÁBTL), Budapest, 10–50986 V-73203.
54. Ibid.
55. Faddi Ottmár és társai, az ÁVH jelentése a Belügyminisztériumnak [Ottmár Faddi and associates, Report by the State Security Authority to the Ministry of Interior], June 19, 1954. ÁBTL, 10–5114, V-127372.
56. The Counter Intelligence Corps was originally established in 1917 as Counter Intelligence Police; after 1945 it was tasked with finding war criminals. It was able to identify a large number, some of which they recruited for U.S. intelligence. Following 1947 it was assigned new duties including intelligence against the Soviet bloc. The Gehlen organization, which cooperated with the CIA, also recruited war criminals. See Douglas Botting and Ian Sayer,

America's Secret Army: The Untold Story of the Counter Intelligence Corps (New York: Franklin Watts, 1989), 319–21, 341.

57. Horváth Kálmán és társai, kihallgatási jegyzőkönyv [Kálmán Horváth and associates, record of interrogation], 1954, ÁBTL, 10-5114-54, V-111 790. The alleged conspiracy was uncovered in Kecskemét, where the country's most important military air base was located. In a similar case in 1951 a certain István Dudás was recruited by his sibling to organize a partisan group to support the U.S. Army in case of war. He claimed that the arms would be parachuted near the location of a hamlet. Since Dudás did not receive specific instructions to launch the conspiracy, he did nothing. In spite of this he was executed along with his brother. Dudás István és társai [István Dudás and associates], 1951, ÁBTL, 5575–51, V-81327-2.

58. Ráth Gedeon és társai kihallgatási jegyzőkönyv [Gedeon Ráth and associates, record of interrogation], 1952, ÁBTL, 37-5079/1952, V-112 524/1.

59. Flossmann Győző és társai, Magyar Függetlenségi Front [Győző Flossman and associates, Hungarian Independence Front], 1952, ÁBTL, 10-50986, V-73203.

60. American legation Budapest to the State Department, February 2, 1956, NARA, RG 59, General Records of the Department of State, decimal files 764.00/3–256.

61. The U.S. Embassy in Vienna to the State Department, May 11, 1956, NARA, RG 59, General Records of the Department of State, 764.00/5–1156; interrogation of Hungarian defector, Frankfurt, Germany, May 31, 1956, NARA, RG 59, General Records of the Department of State, decimal files 764.00/5–3156.

62. American Consulate general (Amcongen) Frankfurt to the State Department, July 19, 1956, NARA, RG 59, 764.00/11–1456.

63. Interview with recently escaped man, Amcongen Munich to Francis M. Stevens, director of East European Affairs, State Department, August 23, 1956, NARA, RG 59, General Records of the Department of State, decimal files 764.00/-2356.

64. American legation Budapest to the State Department, February 11, 1953, NARA, RG 59, General Records of the Department of State, decimal files 764.00/2–1156.

65. Walter Hixson, *Parting the Iron Curtain: Propaganda, Culture and the Cold War, 1945–1961* (London: MacMillan, 1997), 65–66; and James Marchio, "Rhetoric and Reality: The Eisenhower Administration and Unrest in Eastern Europe 1953–1956" (Ph.D. dissertation, American University, 1990).

66. Amcongen Frankfurt to the State Department, March 4, 1956, NARA, General Records of the Department of State, RG 59, 764.00/3–1456; Amembassy Vienna to the State Department, October 3, 1956, ibid. 764.00/10–356.

67. Amcongen Frankfurt to the State Department, March 14, 1956, NARA, RG 59, General Records of the Department of State, decimal files 764.00/3–1456.

68. Amcongen Frankfurt to the State Department, July 16, 1956, NARA, RG 59, General Records of the Department of State, decimal files 764.00/7–1656. According to a Hungarian report dated September 12, 1956, the balloons were usually sited near the border but they also appeared in the vicinity of Budapest twenty-two times.

69. Amcongen Frankfurt to the State Department, July 16, 1956, NARA, RG 59, General Records of the Department of State, decimal files 764.00/7–1656.

70. The American Embassy in Vienna to the Department of State, Comments of Escapees concerning Balloons and Leaflets sent to Hungary, March 24, 1955, MNL OL, XXXII-17, 1. doboz.

71. Határozat a Belügyminisztériumnak a belső reakció ellen kifejtett munkájáról [Resolution on the Ministry of Interior's

Struggle against Internal Reaction], May 11, 1956, MNL OL, KS, 276. f., 53. cs., 286. őe.

72. The American Embassy in Vienna on Balloon Action in Hungary, January 7, 1955, MNL OL, XXXII-17, 1. doboz.

73. Dispatch 1086, Balloons to Hungary, March 24, 1955, in Csaba Békés, Malcolm Byrne, and János M. Rainer, eds., *The 1956 Hungarian Revolution: A History in Documents* (Budapest: Central European University Press, 2002), 66–68.

74. The American Embassy in Vienna on Balloon Action in Hungary, January 7, 1955, MNL OL, XXXII-17, 1. doboz.

75. A Külügyminisztérium jegyzéke a budapesti amerikai követségnek [The Foreign Ministry's note to the U.S. legation in Budapest], February 9, 1956, MNL OL, Küm, USA tük, XIX-J-1-j, 4/fh, 6. doboz, 002118/56.

76. A Külügyminisztérium jegyzéke a budapesti amerikai követségnek [The Foreign Ministry's note to the U.S. legation in Budapest], July 28, 1956, MNL OL, Küm, USA tük, XIX-J-1-j, 6. doboz, 112 118/2.

77. Jelentés Rákosi Mátyásnak [Report to Rákosi], February 23, 1952, MNL OL, KS, 276. f., 65. cs., 95. őe.

78. Az MDP Politikai Bizottságának határozata a Belügyminisztérium belső reakció ellen kifejtett munkájáról [Resolution by the Political Committee of the HWP on the Actions of the Ministry of Interior against Domestic Reactionaries], MNL OL, KS, 276. f., 65. cs. 26. őe.

79. Gaddis, *The Long Peace*, 174. On Office of Policy Coordination (OPC) see Peter Grose, *Operation Rollback: America's Secret War behind the Iron Curtain* (Boston: Houghton Mifflin, 2000); Gregory Mitrovich, *Undermining the Kremlin: America's Strategy to Subvert the Soviet Bloc, 1947–1956* (Ithaca, N.Y.: Cornell University Press, 2000).

80. Vojtech Mastny, *The Cold War and Soviet Insecurity: The Stalin Years* (Oxford: Oxford University Press, 1998), 118.

81. Peter Grose, *Gentleman Spy: The Life of Allen Dulles* (Boston: Houghton Mifflin, 1994), 322.

82. Harrington and Courtney, *Tweaking the Nose of the Russians*, 149.

83. National Security Directive, December 28, 1955, NSAWDC, SFC, record no. 62351.

84. Rákosi feljegyzése az MDP PB számára [Memorandum by Rákosi to the Political Committee of the HWP], MNL OL, KS, 276. f., 65. cs., 26. őe.

85. Határozat a Belügyminisztérium állambiztonsági szerveinek a belső reakció ellen kifejtett tevékenységéről [Resolution on the Actions Taken by the Ministry of Interior Against Domestic Reaction], MNL OL, KS, 276. f., 53. cs., 26. őe.

86. Grose, *Operation Rollback*, 167–73.

87. Faure, *L'Ami Américain*, 384.

88. Weissengruber János és társai [János Weissengruber and Associates], December 1952, ÁBTL, 10–50910/52, V-89 932. András Lada was allegedly sent by the CIA to destroy targets in Sztálinváros. See Lada András és társai [András Lada and associates], 1954, ÁBTL, 10–514 75 954, V-1116 808–2.

89. Harrington and Courtney, *Tweaking the Nose of the Russians*, 168–71.

90. American legation Budapest to the State Department, July 7, 1956, NARA, RG 59, General Records of the Department of State, central files 611.64/7–1356. The Hungarians claimed that Ravndal proposed the talks. The Ministry of Foreign Trade opined that the currency shortage made it desirable to raise Hungarian exports to the United States but warned that the U.S. proposal had political implications. See A Külkereskedelmi Minisztérium feljegyzése Rákosi Mátyásnak [Memorandum by the Ministry of Foreign Trade to Rákosi], June 20, 1955, MOL OL, KS, 276. f., 65. cs., 283. őe.

91. Meeting with Sík, American legation Budapest to the secretary of state, July 22, 1956, NARA, RG 59, General Records

of the Department of State, central files 411.6441/8–955; American legation Budapest to the State Department, August 29, 1955, ibid.

92. Feljegyzés Christian Ravndal látogatásáról [Memorandum on a visit by Ravndal], May 8, 1956, MNL OL, Küm, USA tük, XIX.-J-1-j, 4/a, 4. doboz, 004782/1.

93. Ravndal to the secretary of state, May 5, 1956, in U.S. Department of State, FRUS, 1955–1957: Eastern Europe, 25:162.

94. Megbeszélés McKissonnnal [Conversations with McKisson], July 24, 1956, MNL OL, Küm, USA tük, XIX-J-1-j, 5/e, 15. doboz, 00594/1. In 1955 the Hungarian authorities arrested two Hungarian employees of the U.S. legation and sentenced them for espionage on behalf of a foreign power. Seven other legation workers who did not have diplomatic status had already been arrested, and nothing could be found out about their fate or whereabouts. Two American journalists, Endre Marton and his spouse, were also arrested that year.

95. Kollégiumi előterjesztés a magyaramerikai kapcsolatok megjavításának lehetőségeiről [Memorandum by the College of the Foreign Ministry on the improvement of Hungarian-American relations], June 4, 1956, MNL OL, Küm, USA tük, XIX-J-1-j, 26/a, 1948–1958, 6. doboz, sz. n.

96. Jegyzőkönyv a Külügyminisztérium Kollégiumának üléséről [Record of meeting by the College of the Foreign Ministry], June 11, 1956, MNL OL, Küm, XIX-J-1-j, USA tük, 26/a, 1948–1958, 6. doboz, sz. n.

97. Feljegyzés Kefauver amerikai demokrata párti szenátor látogatásáról Rákosi és Hegedűs elvtársaknál [Record of conversation with the participation of Rákosi, Hegedűs, Senator Kefauver], September 20, 1956, in ibid.

98. Szigeti Károly feljegyzése Ravndal követ látogatásáról [Memorandum by Szigeti on visit by Minister Ravndal], June 15, 1956, MNL OL, Küm, USA tük, XIX-J-1-j, 1947–1964, 140t, 26. doboz, sz. n.

99. Report by Vice Consul Ernest Nagy to the State Department on conversation with Mihály Székely, July 8, 1955, MNL OL, XXXII-17, 1. doboz.

100. Az utazási korlátozásokról szóló bejelentés [Announcement of travel restrictions], MNL OL, Küm, USA tük, XIX-J-1-j, 15, doboz, 007151/1956 and memorandum of conversation, participants: Hoover, Leverich, and Kós, September 4, 1956, NARA, RG 59, General Records of the Department of State, central files 611.6411/9–456.

101. Tudda, *The Truth Is Our Weapon*, 1–10.

102. Ibid., 26–78.

103. Cited in Gaddis, *The Long Peace*, 174.

104. Robert Bowie and Richard H. Immerman, *Waging Peace: How Eisenhower Shaped an Enduring Cold War Strategy* (Oxford: Oxford University Press, 2000), 158–77; Richard H. Immerman, *John Foster Dulles: Piety, Pragmatism and Power in U. S. Foreign Policy* (Wilmington, Del.: Scholarly Resources, 1999), 39–50, 60–85; Gaddis, *The Long Peace*, 149–89.

105. Christian Osterman, ed., *Uprising in East Germany, 1953: The Cold War, the German Question and the First Major Upheaval Behind the Iron Curtain* (Budapest: Central European University Press, 2001), 176–77, 327.

106. Mark Kramer, "The Early Post-Stalin Succession Struggle and the Upheavals in East-Central Europe: Internal-External Linkages in Soviet Decision-Making," pt. 3, *Journal of Cold War Studies* 1, no. 3 (Winter 1999): 19–20; Marchio, *Rhetoric and Reality*, 210–11. In June and July two hundred thousand people received food packages and 5.5 million packages were handed out altogether. East German authorities had to accept that a significant part of the population was won over by the Americans. The food program mixed humanitarian goals with psychological and political ones. As

expected in Washington, the program increased domestic tension in the German Democratic Republic and impeded the consolidation of the East German Communist party's power. Hungry Germans were fed and the German Democratic Republic's food shortage was highlighted. Ostermann, *Uprising in East Germany*, 322–25.

107. See Timothy Snyder, *Bloodlands: Europe between Hitler and Stalin* (New York: Basic Books, 2010).

108. Kramer, "The Early Post-Stalin Succession Struggle," 26–27.

109. National Operations Plan USSR, East European Satellites, OCB 16, November 13, 1953, NARA, RG 59, General Records of the State Department, Records Relating to State Department Participation in the OCB and NSC, 1947–53, lot file 62D430, box 31.

110. Interim U.S. Psychological Strategy Plan for Exploitation of Unrest in Satellite Europe, Psychological Strategy Board D-45, June 22, 1953, NARA, CIA declassification program.

111. Memorandum for the OCB by Elmer Staats, executive officer, September 7, 1954, NARA, RG 59, General Records of the Department of State, Records Relating to State Department Participation in the OCB and NSC 1947–53, lot file 62D430, box 31.

112. Additional Actions to Implement, NSC 174, OCB, August 24, 1954, ibid.

113. Tudda, *The Truth Is Our Weapon*, 87.

114. Statement of Policy by the National Security Council on United States policy toward the Soviet satellites in Eastern Europe, NSC-174, December 11, 1953, in U.S. Department of State, *Foreign Relations of the United States (FRUS), 1952–1954: Eastern Europe; Soviet Union; Eastern Mediterranean*, ed. William Z. Slany, vol. 8 (Washington, D.C.: Government Printing Office, 1952–54), 82.

115. Ronald W. Preussen, "John Foster Dulles and the Predicaments of Power," in *John Foster Dulles and the Diplomacy of the Cold War*, ed. Richard H. Immerman (Princeton, N.J.: Princeton University Press, 1990), 35.

116. Memorandum of conversation, subject: The liberation of Eastern Europe, Participants: Rowmund Pilsudski, Jerzy Lerski, and Allan Vedeler, March 20, 1953, NSAWDC, SFC, record no. 66171.

117. Memorandum from Fuller to Stelle, December 3, 1956, NARA, RG 59, PPS 1956, lot file 66D487, box 78.

118. Memorandum from William Crawford to Walwourth Barbour, September 28, 1955, NARA, RG 59, General Records of the Department of State, decimal files, 764.00/-2855.

119. Memorandum by Robert McKisson, July 1, 1955, NARA, RG 59, General Records of the Department of State, decimal files 764.00/7-155. The standard reply said that the State Department looked forward to the day when the peoples of the region regained their freedom and independence.

120. Report by the National Security Council on Interim Objectives and Actions to Exploit Unrest in the Satellite States, June 28, 1953, NSAWDC, SFC, Record no. 62113.

121. Immerman, *John Foster Dulles*, 77–79.

122. Memorandum from Louis Halle to Robert Bowie and Jacob Beam, July 27, 1953, NARA, RG 59, PPS, lot file 1947–53, members chronological files, Louis Halle Jr., box 47.

123. Telegram from Charles Bohlen to the secretary of state, December 10, 1956, NARA, RG 59, PPS, lot file 66D487, 1956, box 76 (Soviet Union).

124. Memorandum by L. W. Fuller, July 21, 1953, NARA, RG 59, PPS 1947–53, lot file 64D563, box 29 (Europe).

125. Ibid.

126. A Dialectical Approach to the Possibilities of Accommodation by Negotiation between the Free World and the Soviet

Bloc," 1953, NARA, RG 59, PPS, 1947–53, lot file 64D563, box 47.

127. "United States Policy Respecting Eastern Europe," March 5, 1954, NARA, RG 59, PPS, lot file 65D101, box 88.

128. On January 5, 1955, the OCB pointed out that save for negotiations there seemed to be no possibility of detaching a satellite from the USSR without significantly increasing the risk of war. See U.S. Department of State, *FRUS, 1955–1957: Eastern Europe*, 25:9.

129. Memorandum by the Policy Planning Staff, 1955, NARA, RG 59, PPS, 1955, lot file 66D, box 64. PPS member John C. Campbell recommended that if the Soviet Union accepted German unification, pulled out from Czechoslovakia and Poland, and allowed the countries of Eastern Europe to choose their military alliances, the United States would pull out all its forces from Europe except those in Great Britain. Ibid.

130. "Basic U. S. Policy in Relation to the Four-Power Negotiations," July 11, 1956, in U.S. Department of State, *FRUS, 1955–1957: Eastern Europe*, 25:46–47.

131. Mark Trachtenberg, *Constructed Peace: The Making of the European Settlement, 1945–1963* (Princeton, N.J.: Princeton University Press, 1999), 136–45.

132. Marchio, *Rhetoric and Reality*, 247.

133. Vladislav Zubok, "Soviet Policy Aims at the Geneva Conference of 1955," in *Cold War Respite: The Geneva Summit of 1955*, ed. Günter Bischof and Saki Dockrill (Baton Rouge: Louisiana State University Press, 2001), 55–74.

4. 1956

1. Gábor Gyáni, "Socio-Psychological Roots of Discontent: Paradoxes of 1956," *Hungarian Studies* 20, no. 1 (June 2006): 65–74.

2. See Charles Gati, *Failed Illusions: Moscow, Washington, Budapest and the 1956 Hungarian Revolt* (Stanford, Calif.: Stanford University Press, 2006).

3. On the Soviet response see János M. Rainer, "Döntés a Kremlben: Kísérlet a feljegyzések értelmezésére," in *Döntés a Kremlben: A szovjet pártelnökség vitái Magyarországról* (Budapest: 1956-os Intézet, 1996), 111–55. On the relationship between Poland and Hungary in Soviet decision making, see Mark Kramer, "New Evidence on Soviet Decision-Making and the 1956 Polish and Hungarian Crises," *Cold War International History Project Bulletin* 8–9 (Winter 1996–97): 358–84.

4. For a typical appraisal of the significance of Eastern Europe, see the PPS paper "U.S. Policy toward Soviet Satellite States in Eastern Europe," in U.S. Department of State, *Foreign Relations of the United States, 1949: Eastern Europe; the Soviet Union*, vol. 5 (Washington, D.C.: Government Printing Office, 1949) 21–26. In the view of the PPS, "These states are in themselves of secondary importance on the European scene . . . but in the current two-world struggle they have meaning primarily because they are in varying degrees politico-military adjuncts of Soviet power and extend that power into the heart of Europe. . . . It is assumed that there is general agreement that, so long as the USSR represents the only major threat to our security and to world stability, our objectives with respect to the USSR's European satellites must be the elimination of Soviet control from those countries and the reduction of Soviet influence to something like normal dimension."

5. Eisenhower to Tito, National Security Archives, Washington, D.C. (NSAWDC), Soviet Flashpoints Collection (SFC), record no. 66140.

6. Cited by Gregory Mitrovich, *Undermining the Kremlin: America's Strategy to Subvert the Soviet Bloc, 1947–1956* (Ithaca, N.Y.: Cornell University Press, 2000), 39–40.

7. National Security Staff Study, Annex to National Security Council (NSC) 5608, July 8, 1956, U.S. Policy towards the Satel-

lites of Eastern Europe, in U.S. Department of State, *Foreign Relations of the United States, 1955–1957: Eastern Europe*, ed. John P. Glennon, vol. 25 (Washington, D.C.: Government Printing Office, 1955–57), 199.

8. Memorandum of Discussion of the 301st Meeting of the National Security Council, October 26, 1956, in U.S. Department of State, *FRUS, 1955–1957: Eastern Europe*, 25:296.

9. David Holloway and David McFarland, "The Hungarian Revolution of 1956 in the Context of the Cold War Military Confrontation," *Hungarian Studies* 20, no. 1 (June 2006): 31–39.

10. Officials of the State Department concluded in 1953 that any armed uprising on territory controlled by Moscow was doomed to failure and might result in the "biological annihilation" of the people involved. See Memorandum of conversation with Polish émigrés, March 20, 1953, NSAWDC, SFC, record no. 66171. In 1955 the United States Information Agency (USIA) affirmed that "U.S. policy may not adopt a course of action which would precipitate hostilities, because the premature uprising and consequent annihilation of dissident elements on the basis of exhortations or promises we are not able to support." See Memorandum from Robert E. Delaney of the Office of Policy and Programs, Soviet Orbit Division, United States Information Agency, to Frances B. Stevens of the Office of East European Affairs, January 24, 1955, in U.S. Department of State, *FRUS, 1955–1957: Eastern Europe*, 25:10–11.

11. Dulles to the American Embassy in Belgrade, October 25, 1956, National Archives and Records Administration (NARA), Washington, D.C., Record Group (RG), General Records of the Department of State, decimal files 764.00/10–2556. As early as 1950 Dulles had stated that since people were unarmed, violent uprising was hopeless and even worse than hopeless because it would lead to massacre. See Ronald W. Preussen, "Walking a Tightrope in the Twilight: John Foster Dulles and Eastern Europe in 1953," unpublished paper prepared for the Europe and the Cold War conference, November 1998, at the Sorbonne, Paris.

12. Dwight D. Eisenhower, *The White House Years: Waging Peace, 1956–1961*, vols 1–2 (Garden City, N.Y.: Doubleday, 1965), 2:63.

13. Ibid., 2:65–66.

14. Cited in Bennett Kovrig, *Of Walls and Bridges: The United States and Eastern Europe* (New York: New York University Press, 1991), 89.

15. Ibid., 95.

16. Csaba Békés, "The 1956 Hungarian Revolution and World Politics," Cold War International History Project, Working Paper no. 16 (Washington, D.C.: Woodrow Wilson International Center for Scholars, 1996), 15.

17. Ibid., 15.

18. Policy Planning Staff Position Paper, October 29, 1956, NARA, RG 59, PPS, lot file 66D487 1956, box 80.

19. Harold Stassen, interview on John Foster Dulles, NSAWDC, SFC, record no. 64, 493.

20. Memorandum by the special assistant to the president, NSAWDC, SFC, record no. 64, 493.

21. Csaba Békés, *Az 1956-os forradalom a világpolitikában: tanulmány és válogatott dokumentumok* (Budapest: 1956-os Intézet, 1996).

22. For the speech see U.S. Department of State, *FRUS, 1955–1957: Eastern Europe*, 25:318.

23. The Soviet Presidium did not concern itself with the United States at all.

24. Eisenhower, *The White House Years*, 2:80; Kovrig, *Of Walls and Bridges*, 95.

25. October 30, Archives de Quai d'Orsay, Europe 1944–60, Hongrie, vol. 62, folios 207–16.

26. Bohlen to the secretary of state, October 30, 1956, NSAWDC, SFC, record no. 65 692. The French chargé reported the same terminology: "écraser comme les mouches." Ministère des Affaires Étrangères, in Commission des Publications des Documents Français, *Documents Diplomatiques Français, 1956, Tome III (24 octobre–31 dècecembre)* (Paris: Imprimerie nationale, 1990), 82–83.

27. The Embassy in the Soviet Union to the State Department, October 30, 1956, 22 p.m., in U.S. Department of State, *FRUS, 1955–1957: Eastern Europe*, 25: 346–47.

28. The information was derived from the Indian ambassador in Moscow, Krishna Menon. See the American legation in Budapest to the Department of State, January 8, 1957, NARA, RG 59, General Records of the Department of State, central files 611.64/1–857.

29. "L'URSS parait disposée, dans la déclaration de 30 Octobre á renoncer á l'empire économique et, sous certaines conditions, á l'empire militaire qu'elle exerçait sur les états satellites depuis la fin de la guerre," Telegram to the Quai d'Orsay, November 2 1956, Archives de Quai d'Orsay, Europe, 1944–1960, vol. 116, fol. 39.

30. Cited in Csaba Békés, "Az Egyesült Államok és a magyar semlegesség 1956-ban," in *Az 1956-os Magyar Forradalom Történetének Dokumentációs és Kutatóintézete: Évkönyv: 1994*, ed. János M. Bak, B. András Hegedűs, and György Litván (Budapest: 1956-os Intézet, 1994), 165–78.

31. State Department memorandum, October 31, 1956, NSAWDC, SFC, record No. 65 283.

32. Bohlen to the secretary of state, November 2, 1956, NARA, RG 59, 764.00/11–256. On November 1 the British ambassador in Budapest concluded that the Soviets had changed their minds and were cracking down on the country with the force of arms. Fry to the Foreign Office, in Éva Haraszti-Taylor, ed., *The Hungarian Revolution of 1956: A Collection of Documents from the British Foreign Office* (Nottingham: Astra Press, 1995), 155–56.

33. Peter L. Hahn, *The United States, Great Britain and Egypt, 1945–1956, Strategy and Diplomacy in the Early Cold War* (Chapel Hill: University of North Carolina Press, 1991), 231.

34. Draft Statement of the Planning Board of the National Security Council: U.S. Policy on the Developments in Poland and Hungary, NSC 5616/1, October 31, 1956, in U.S. Department of State, *FRUS, 1955–1957: Eastern Europe*, 25: 354–59.

35. The acting secretary's staff meeting, November 2, 1956, in U.S. Department of State, *FRUS, 1955–1957: Eastern Europe*, 25: 364.

36. See Susan L. Carruthers, *Cold War Captives: Imprisonment, Escape, Brainwashing* (Berkeley: University of California Press, 2009), 70.

37. Kovrig, *Of Walls and Bridges*, 79, 92.

38. On Otto Habsburg's behalf, Hungary's wartime ambassador to Madrid, Ferenc Marosy, asked Franco to send military aid to the Hungarian freedom fighters on November 4. Franco convened his cabinet the same night, where it was decided to send an army of volunteers to Hungary. See Gyula Borbándi, *Magyarok az Angol kertben: A Szabad Európa Rádió története* (Budapest: Európa, 1996), 225.

39. Ibid.

40. Lodge's talk with the Spanish foreign minister, November 6, 1956, NARA, RG 59, General Records of the Department of State, decimal files 764.00/11–656; Fischer Howe to the acting secretary of state (Hoover), November 8, 1957, ibid., 764.00/11–856; acting secretary of state to the U.S. Embassy in Madrid, November 8, 1956, ibid., 764.00/11–856.

41. NSC 5616/1, in U.S. Department of State, *FRUS, 1955–1957: Eastern Europe*, 25: 354–59.

42. Draft to the UK delegation in New York by the Foreign Office, November 2, 1956, in Haraszti-Taylor, *The Hungarian Revolution of 1956*, 161.

43. Commission des Publications des Documents Français, *Documents Diplomatiques Français, 1956, Tome III*, 159. The French draft resolution called on the leadership in Moscow to pull out its troops from Hungary, to recognize and respect Hungarian neutrality. The U.S. Mission in New York to the secretary of state, November 2, 1956, NARA, RG 59, General Records of the Department of State, decimal files 764.00/11-256.

44. Dulles to United States Mission to United Nations (USUN) New York, November 2, 1956, NARA, RG 59, General Records of the Department of State, decimal files 764.00/11-256. See also Caroline Pruden, *Conditional Partners: Eisenhower, the United Nations, and the Search for a Permanent Peace* (Baton Rouge: Louisiana State University Press, 1998), 243. Pruden argued that Eisenhower and Dulles were worried that the British-French draft would distract attention from Suez.

45. In a conversation with Stassen, Dulles doubted whether an Austrian type of neutrality should be offered to Eastern Europeans. See memorandum of conversation between Dulles and the director of foreign operations, October 26, 1956, in U.S. Department of State, *FRUS, 1955–1957: Eastern Europe*, 25:305.

46. Burke C. Elbrick of the State Department told the Italian ambassador, Manlio Brosio, that neutrality was a sensitive issue since it inevitably raised the question of the German Democratic Republic and German unification. Yet the United States had no intention of surrounding the Soviet Union with a cordon sanitaire and did not expect the satellites to turn against the Soviets if their position changed. See December 27, 1956, NARA, RG 59, General Records of the Department of State, decimal file 764.00/12-2756.

47. Günter Bischof and Stephen E. Ambrose, eds., *Eisenhower: A Centenary Assessment* (Baton Rouge: Louisiana State University Press, 1995), 11.

48. The acting secretary's meeting, November 2, 1956, in U.S. Department of State, *FRUS, 1955–1957: Eastern Europe*, 25: 364.

49. Ibid.

50. NSAWDC, SF, record no. 62 596. The French Foreign Ministry's view was that "At present it cannot be known whether the Hungarian people will be dedicated enough . . . to show similar courage as the workers of Poznan." Archives Diplomatiques de Quai d'Orsay, Europe, Hongrie 1944–1960, vol. 88.

51. It is a common view that the Suez crisis overshadowed the Hungarian, and the November 1 meeting of the NSC is often used to prove this point. Allen Dulles gave a report on the situation in Budapest after which the meeting went on to discuss the events in the Middle East without discussion. It is clear that the fact that there was no discussion because of the relative importance of these events. In the report Dulles stated that the situation in Hungary was settling down and the Soviets were seemingly retreating. In light of this, Suez may have seemed more urgent.

52. Secretary's Staff Meeting, October 31, 1956, U.S. Department of State, *FRUS, 1955–1957: Eastern Europe*, 25:402, note 8.

53. Richard Nixon, interview concerning John Foster Dulles, NSAWDC, SFC, record no. 65106.

54. Report on the satellites, June 4, 1956, NARA, RG 59, General Records of the Department of State, PPS, lot file 66D487, box 78; the American legation in Budapest to the State Department, "Briefing Memorandum on the Current Situation in Hungary, Prepared in Anticipation of Mr. William Crawford, Deputy Director, Office of East European Affairs," January 7, 1955, NARA,

RG 59, General Records of the Department of State, decimal file 764.00/1–755. See also W. Park Armstrong's report to Dulles: The New Course failed to solve the problems of industry and agriculture, life conditions did not change in 1954. See memorandum on National Intelligence Estimates (NIE) 12.5.55, "Current Situation and Probable Developments in Hungary," July 4, 1956. NA, RG 59, General Records of the Department of State, decimal file 764.00/4–755.

55. Telephone call from Mr. Shanley to J. F. Dulles, October 29, 1956, cited in Kovrig, *Of Walls and Bridges*, 92.

56. Memorandum for the chairman of the Joint Chiefs of Staff (JCS), October 25, 1956, NARA, RG 218, Records of the Joint Chiefs of Staff (RJCS), 1953–57, 091 Poland, box 15. The JCS thought that Gomułka was probably anti-Russian and *unlike* Nagy did not spend a long time in the Soviet Union.

57. Telegram from the Embassy in Austria to the Department of State, October 31, 1956, in U.S. Department of State, *FRUS, 1955–1957: Eastern Europe*, 25:353.

58. Hoover to the legation in Budapest, October 31, 1956, NARA, RG 59, General Records of the Department of State, decimal files 764.00/10–3156.

59. Telegram from the Department of State to the legation in Budapest, November 3, 1956, in U.S. Department of State, *FRUS, 1955–1957: Eastern Europe*, 25:373. Wailes was supposed to say that the U.S. administration was deeply moved by the suffering and sacrifice of the Hungarian people and would take urgent measures to embrace the cause of Hungarian freedom and independence in the UN.

60. "NSC 5616/2 Interim US Policy on Developments in Poland and Hungary," November 19, 1956. The full document is published in Csaba Békés, Malcolm Byrne, and M. János Rainer, *The 1956 Hungarian Revolution: A History in Documents* (Budapest: Central European University Press, 2002), 439.

61. Memorandum from Arthur Radford to the secretary of defense on the Polish policy of the U.S., November 30, 1956. NSAWDC, SFC, record no. 75515.

62. Ibid.

63. Memorandum from the chief of staff of the U.S. Air Force to the JCS on the Polish policy of the U.S., November 30, 1956, NSAWDC, SFC, Record No. 71527.

64. JCS Draft Statement, May 6, 1957, NARA, RG 218, Records of the Joint Chiefs of Staff, 1957 062 (5–26–45), box 3.

65. Transcript of a teletype conversation between the legation in Hungary and the Department of State, October 25, 1956, in U.S. Department of State, *FRUS, 1955–1957: Eastern Europe*, 25:284–85.

66. On the president's views regarding escalation, see Marc Trachtenberg, *Constructed Peace: The Making of the European Settlement, 1945–1963* (Princeton, N.J.: Princeton University Press, 1999).

67. Walter L. Hixson, *Parting the Iron Curtain: Propaganda, Culture, and the Cold War, 1945–1961* (London: MacMillan, 1997), 80.

68. PPS staff meeting, October 30, 1956, NSAWDC, SF, record no. 66148.

69. Hoover to the American Embassy in Madrid, November 8, 1956, NARA, RG 59, General Records of the Department of State, decimal files 764.00/11–856.

70. Memorandum of conversation, participants: Carlton, Senator Ralph Flander's assistant; Jacob Beam, EU, Reports of Proposed Spanish Intervention in Hungary, April 12, 1957, NARA, RG 59, General Records of the Department of State, decimal files 764.00/4–1257.

71. Memorandum to the secretary of state, call of the Austrian ambassador regarding the handling of Hungarian refugees, October 29, 1956, in U.S. Department of State, *FRUS, 1955–1957: Eastern Europe*, 25:327.

72. Telegram from the Embassy in the Federal Republic of Germany to the

Department of State, November 5, 1956, in U.S. Department of State, *FRUS, 1955–1957: Eastern Europe*, 25:400.

73. Robert Murphy, interview regarding John Foster Dulles, NSAWDC, SFC, record no. 65105.

74. See Geraint Hughes, "British Policy Towards Eastern Europe and the Impact of the 'Prague Spring,' 1964–68," *Cold War History* 4, no. 2 (January 2004): 116.

75. Trachtenberg, *Constructed Peace*, 161. Trachtenberg argued that Eisenhower would not have hesitated to use tactical nuclear weapons if the Soviets had attacked and might even have been prepared to deliver a "preemptive" nuclear strike if it had been "obvious" that the Soviets were preparing for war.

76. See István Hargittai, *Judging Edward Teller: A Closer Look at One of the Most Influential Scientists of the Twentieth Century* (Amherst, N.Y.: Prometheus Books, 2010).

77. Memorandum of discussion at the 301st meeting of the National Security Council, October 26, 1956, in U.S. Department of State, *FRUS, 1955–1957: Eastern Europe*, 25:299.

78. The British Embassy in Washington to the Foreign Office, November 1, 1956, in Haraszti-Taylor, *The Hungarian Revolution of 1956*, 152–53.

79. Gati, *Failed Illusions*.

80. Henry Kissinger, *Diplomacy* (New York: Simon & Schuster, 1994), 562–63.

81. H. W. Brands, *The Devil We Knew: Americans and the Cold War* (New York: Oxford University Press, 1993).

82. Michael Walzer, *Just and Unjust Wars: A Moral Argument with Historical Illustrations*, 3rd ed. (New York: Basic Books, 2000), 86–95.

83. John Lewis Gaddis, *We Now Know: Rethinking Cold War History* (Oxford: Clarendon Press, 1997), 235.

84. Peter Grose, *Gentleman Spy: The Life of Allen Dulles* (Boston: Houghton Mifflin, 1994), 437.

85. Ronald W. Preussen, "John Foster Dulles és Kelet Európa," 228–37, and Raymond Garthoff, "A magyar forradalom és Washington," 214–27, both in *Évkönyv V, 1996–1997*, ed. Hegedűs B. András et al. (Budapest: 1956-os Intézet, 1997).

86. The CIA report is cited in Hixson, *Parting the Iron Curtain*, 85.

87. Notes on the 39th meeting of the Special Committee on Soviet and Related Problems, October 26, 1956, in U.S. Department of State, *FRUS, 1955–1957: Eastern Europe*, 25:301–2.

88. Cited in Irén Simándi, "A magyar forradalom a Szabad Európa Rádió hullámhosszán," I. rész [part I], *Társadalmi Szemle* no. 11 (2002): 36–61.

89. Transcript of Radio Free Europe (RFE) programs, "Armed Forces Special no. B-1," October 28, 1956, in Békés et al., *The 1956 Hungarian Revolution*, 286–88.

90. George Urban, *Radio Free Europe and the Pursuit of Democracy: My War within the Cold War* (New Haven, Conn.: Yale University Press, 1997), 218–19; Borbándi, *Magyarok az Angol Kertben*, 239.

91. Amcongen Frankfurt to the State Department, comments by Hungarian defector, February 4, 1957, NARA, RG 59, General Records of the Department of State, decimal files 764.00/2–457.

92. Western radio listening in Hungary before and after the uprising: Comments by a Hungarian national, January 3, 1957, NARA, RG 59, General Records of the Department of State, decimal files 764.00/1–357.

93. Report on Hungarian refugee opinion, RFE Radio Analysis Section, Munich, Special Report no. 6.

94. Amcongen Frankfurt to the State Department, comments by Hungarian defector, February 4, 1957, NARA, RG 59, General Records of the Department of State, decimal files 764.00/1–357. Gallicus worked for RFE; his real name was Imre

Mikes. See Borbándi, *Magyarok az Angol Kertben*, 228–29.

95. Amcongen Frankfurt to the State Department, Hungarian uprising, comment by Hungarian national, February 4, 1957, NARA, RG 59, General Records of the Department of State, decimal files 764.00/2-457.

96. Christopher Tudda, *The Truth Is Our Weapon: The Rhetorical Diplomacy of Dwight D. Eisenhower and John Foster Dulles* (Baton Rouge: Louisiana State University Press, 2006), 95.

97. Mark Kramer, "The Early Post-Stalin Succession Struggle and the Upheavals in East-Central Europe: Internal-External Linkages in Soviet Decision-Making, part 3," *Journal of Cold War Studies* 1, no. 3 (Winter 1999): 25, 28.

98. At an interagency meeting it was proposed that until the Soviet army was reported to be moving out, the rebels should be told "not to lay down their arms." This was rejected, but no one suggested that the Hungarians be told the truth about their chances of winning. See notes on the 40th meeting of the Special Committee on Soviet and Related Problems, October 29, 1956, in U.S. Department of State, *FRUS, 1955–1957: Eastern Europe*, 25:324–25.

99. Telegram from the Embassy in the United Kingdom to the Department of State, October 26, 1956, in ibid., 303.

100. Ibid., 26–27.

101. "Plausible denial" was an element of psychological warfare.

102. Brian McCauley, "Hungary and the Suez, 1956: The Limits of Soviet and American Power," *Journal of Contemporary History* 16, no. 4 (1981): 794–95.

103. Békés, "The 1956 Hungarian Revolution and World Politics."

104. Elsewhere Békés has written that the United States had no leverage to force the Soviets to relinquish Hungary and a direct intervention would likely have led to a world war. See Csaba Békés, "Hideg-

háború, enyhülés és az 1956-os forradalom," in *Évkönyv V, 1996–1997*, ed. Hegedűs B. András et al (Budapest: 1956-os Intézet, 1997), 201–13.

105. Kovrig, *Of Walls and Bridges*, 102.

5. REPRISALS AND BRIDGE BUILDING

1. Cited by István Vida, "Az MSZMP Politikai Bizottságának 1958. január 15-i határozata Külügyminisztérium munkájáról," in *Magyarország (Nagy) hatalmak erőterében. Tanulmányok Ormos Mária 70. születésnapjára*, ed. Ferenc Fischer, István Majoros, Mária Ormos, and József Vonyó (Pécs: University Press, 2000), 631.

2. Cited by Andrew Felkay, *Hungary and the USSR, 1956–1968: Kadar's Political Leadership* (New York: Greenwood Press, 1989), 184.

3. See György Földes, "Kötélhúzás felsőfokon: Kádár és Brezsnyev," in *Ki volt Kádár? Harag és részrehajlás nélkül a Kádár-életútról*, ed. Árpád Rácz (Budapest: Rubin-Aquila-Könyvek, 2001), 106.

4. Csaba Békés, "A Kádári külpolitika 1956–1968: Látványos sikerek – 'láthatatlan konfliktusok,'" in *Európából Európába: Magyarország konfliktusok kereszttüzében, 1945–1990*, ed. Csaba Békés (Budapest: Gondolat, 2004), 238.

5. On the descending hierarchy of international control see Hedley Bull, *The Anarchical Society: The Study of Order in World Politics* (New York: Columbia University Press, 1977).

6. A Külügyminisztérium feljegyzése az USA-val való kapcsolatok normalizálásáról [Memorandum by the Foreign Ministry on the normalization of relations with the U.S.], October 30, 1958, Magyar Nemzeti Levéltár Országos Levéltára (MNL OL), Budapest, Külügyminisztérium (Küm), XIX-J-1-k, USA admin. 11. doboz, 4/b sz.n.

7. Telegram from the embassy in Hungary to the Department of State, October 3, 1967, in U.S. Department of State, *Foreign Relations of the United States, 1964–1968:*

Eastern Europe, vol. 17 (Washington, D.C.: Government Printing Office, 1996), 313–14.

8. Telegram from the embassy in Hungary to the Department of State, conversation with Kádár, introductory call, November 30, 1967, in ibid., 318–320.

9. Vladislav Zubok, *A Failed Empire: The Soviet Union in the Cold War from Stalin to Gorbachev* (Chapel Hill: University of North Carolina Press, 2007), 202–3, 221.

10. Az MSZMP KB Politikai Bizottságának ülése, Kádár János hozzászólása [Meeting of the HSWP Political Committee, contribution by János Kádár], May 11, 1965, MNL OL, M-KS 288. f., 5. cs., 365. őe.

11. Instruction from the Department of State to the legation in Hungary, October 21, 1960, in U.S. Department of State, *Foreign Relations of the United States, 1958–1960: Eastern Europe Region, Soviet Union, Cyprus*, vol. 10, pt. 1 (Washington, D.C.: Government Printing Office, 1993), 126–30. Mikoyan is cited by Anatoly Dobrynin, *In Confidence: Moscow's Ambassador to America's Six Cold War Presidents (1962–1986)* (New York: Times Books, 1995), 92.

12. Zubok, *A Failed Empire*, 218–20.

13. A washingtoni magyar követség elemzése a magyar-amerikai viszonyról, [The legation in Washington on Hungarian-U.S. relations] [1959], MNL OL, Küm, USA tük, XIX-J-1-j, 9. doboz, 5/a, 0020461.

14. Borhi László, "Iratok a magyar-amerikai kapcsolatok történetéhez," *Történelmi Szemle*, no. 3–4 (1998): 341.

15. Joseph F. Harrington and Bruce J. Courtney, *Tweaking the Nose of the Russians: Fifty Years of American-Romanian Relations, 1940–1990*, East European Monographs no. 296 (Boulder, Colo.: East European Monographs, 1991), 187–90.

16. Memorandum of discussion, 366th meeting of the National Security Council, May 22, 1958, in U.S. Department of State, *FRUS, 1958–1960: Eastern Europe Region, Soviet Union, Cyprus*, 10, pt. 1:12–18.

17. Draft paper prepared by N. Spencer Barnes of the Policy Planning Staff, "Long Term Trend in the Soviet European Satellites," June 27, 1958, in ibid., 40–44. The PPS was divided; not everyone shared the view that the communist regimes would become widely accepted and thus consolidate their position permanently.

18. Department of State Guidelines for Policy and Operations, "The Bloc Countries in Eastern Europe," February 1963, National Archives and Records Administration (NARA), Washington, D.C., Record Group (RG) 59, Policy Planning Council (PPC) 1963–64, lot 70, D199, box 260.

19. Memorandum of discussion, 366th meeting of the National Security Council, May 22, 1958, in U.S. Department of State, *FRUS, 1958–1960: Eastern Europe Region, Soviet Union, Cyprus*, 10, pt. 1:12–14; National Security Council Report, "Statement of United States Policy toward the Soviet Dominated Nations in Eastern Europe, in ibid., 18–31; memorandum of discussion of the 369th meeting of the National Security Council, June 19, 1958, in ibid., 34–40. The Operations Coordinating Board (OCB) came out in support of evolution. In a striking break with its earlier position, the agency thought that under conditions of relative military balance between the two blocs, the use of voluntary force (including inciting rebellion) was not envisioned. Therefore efforts to realize U.S. aims would rest on slow development and not the principle of revolution. See Operations Coordinating Board Report, "Report on Soviet-Dominated Nations in Eastern Europe" (NSC 58/11), July 15, 1959, in ibid., 95–98.

20. Suggested reply to Francis Chorin [1960], NARA, RG 59, Records of the Department of State, Internal Affairs of Hungary 1960–1963, 611.64, microfilm roll 93.

21. The Department of State to the American legation in Budapest, November 1, 1960, NARA, RG 59, General Records of

the Department of State, decimal file 764, 1960–63, microfilm roll 1.

22. Bennett Kovrig, *Of Walls and Bridges: The United States and Eastern Europe* (New York: New York University Press, 1991), 107–8.

23. Ibid.

24. Treasury comment on Poland guideline paper, March 16, 1962, NARA, RG 59, General Records of the Department of State, Executive Secretariat Policy Guidelines 1962–66, lot file 67D396, box 5.

25. Charles Vanik to the secretary of state, March 31, 1960, NARA, RG 59, General Records of the Department of State, central file 1960–1963, 611.64, microfilm roll 93.

26. Justine Faure, *L'Ami Américain: La Tchécoslovaquie, enjeu de la diplomatie Américaine, 1943–1968* (Paris: Tallandier, 2004), 341–42.

27. Guidelines for Policy and Operations, Poland, May 1962, NARA, RG 59, General Records of the Department of State, Executive Secretariat, lot file 67D396, box 5, Poland.

28. Harrington and Courtney, *Tweaking the Nose of the Russians*, 210–15.

29. Department of State Guidelines for Policy Operations, "The Bloc Countries in Eastern Europe," February 1963, NARA, Washington, D.C., Record Group (RG) 59, PPC, 1963–64, lot file 70D199, box 260.

30. Statement by Harriman, undersecretary of state for political affairs, to the Subcommittee on Europe of the House Committee on Foreign Affairs, March 10, 1964, NARA, RG 59, PPC 1963–64, lot file 70D199, box 260.

31. Guidelines for Foreign Policy and Operations, Poland, May 1962, NARA, RG 59, General Records of the Department of State, Executive Secretariat, lot file 67D396, box 5, Poland.

32. János Radványi, *Hungary and the Superpowers: The 1956 Revolution and Realpolitik* (Stanford, Calif.: Hoover Institution Press, Stanford University, 1972), 31.

33. A Magyar Népköztársaság jegyzéke az Egyesült Államok budapesti követségének [Note by the People's Republic of Hungary to the U.S. legation in Budapest], May 1957, MNL OL, Küm, XIX-J-1-j, USA tük, 4. doboz, 4/a, 002418/1.

34. A Magyar Népköztársaság jegyzéke az Egyesült Államok budapesti követségének [Note by the People's Republic of Hungary to the U.S. legation in Budapest], MNL OL, Küm, XIX-J-1-j, USA tük, 4. doboz, 4/bd, sz.n.

35. Instruction by the State Department to American diplomatic missions, December 5, 1957, NARA, RG 59, General Records of the Department of State, 864.181/12–557.

36. The chargé in Hungary (Ackerson) to the State Department, October 29, 1959, NARA, RG 59, General Records of the Department of State, 61164/10–2757; U.S. Department of State, *Foreign Relations of the United States, 1955–1957: Eastern Europe*, ed. John P. Glennon, vol. 25 (Washington, D.C.: Government Printing Office, 1955–57), 679–84.

37. The chargé in Hungary (Ackerson) to the Department of State, November 14, 1957, NARA, RG 59, General Records of the Department of State, 61164/11–1457.

38. Melinda Kalmár, *Ennivaló és hozomány: A kora kádárizmus ideológiája* (Budapest: Magvető, 1998).

39. Memorandum from the Deputy Director of the Office of East European Affairs to the Assistant Secretary of European Affairs, November 8 1957, U.S. Department of State, *FRUS, 1955–1957: Eastern Europe*, 25: 685–90.

40. Radványi, *Hungary and the Superpowers*, 32–33.

41. Zádor Tibor ideiglenes ügyvivő Horváth Imre külügyminiszternek. Tárgy: a magyar-amerikai kereskedelmet gátló tényezők [Report by Zádor to the minister of foreign affairs, factors impeding U.S.-

Hungarian trade], December 31, 1957, MNL OL, Küm, USA tük, XIX-J-1-j, 1. doboz, 005851.

42. Zádor jelentése Horváthnak, látogatás Malone szenátornál [Zádor to Horváth, visit by Senator Malone], MNL OL, Küm, USA tük, XIX-J-1-j, 12. doboz, 5/c, 0028/1958.

43. Zádor Tibor jelentése a Külügyminisztériumnak, filmbemutató tartásáról [Zádor on film screening], February 28, 1958, MNL OL, Küm, USA tük, XIX-J-1-j, 1947–1964, 140t., 26. doboz, 002065; Bartha János ideiglenes ügyvivő jelentése Sík külügyminiszternek filmbemutató tartásáról [Bartha to Sík on film screening], ibid., 104/2, 1958.

44. Irányelvek a magyar-amerikai kapcsolatok alakításához, Amerikai Referatúra [Principles on U.S.-Hungarian relations], January 16, 1958, MNL OL, Küm, XIX-J-1-j, USA tük, 11. doboz, 4/b, ikt. sz. n.

45. Harrington and Courtney, *Tweaking the Nose of the Russians*, 194–201.

46. The chargé in Hungary to the Department of State, May 5, 1958, NARA, RG 59, General Records of the Department of State, 611.64/5-958. See also Tamás Magyarics, "Az Egyesült Államok és Magyarország, 1957–1967" *Századok*, no. 3 (1996): 573.

47. Magdolna Baráth and István Feitl, "Két összefoglaló a magyar-szovjet tárgyalásokról," *Múltunk*, no. 4 (1993): 82–185.

48. Magyarics, "Az Egyesült Államok és Magyarország," 576.

49. Memorandum by the Department of State Policy Planning Staff, July 11, 1958, NARA, RG 59, General Records of the Department of State, lot file 60D216, box 2, Wilcox.

50. Radványi, *Hungary and the Superpowers*, 42–43. At the September 2 meeting of the Political Committee, Ferenc Münnich declared, "If anybody is interested in having an American diplomatic mission here working in large numbers it is the international enemy, the government of the U.S. We do not need to tread carefully here. Their mission here is an important spy center for them and they will not liquidate it. We are a sovereign state they should keep their noses out of here. We have no interest in having them. Let's not court them if they want let them go home." MNL OL, M-KS 288. f. 5. cs. 93. őe.

51. MOL, Küm, USA tük, XIX-J-1-j, 3. doboz, 4/a, 00941/5.

52. Ibid. The United States published the reply.

53. Radványi, *Hungary and the Superpowers*, 49.

54. Memorandum from Wilcox and Elbrick to Murphy, October 7, 1958, NARA, RG 59, Records of the Department of State, lot file 60D216, box 1, Wilcox.

55. Despatch from the legation in Hungary to the Department of State, October 10, 1958, NARA, RG 59, Records of the Department of State, decimal file 864.413/10–2358.

56. A Magyar Népköztársaság válasza az 1958. október 18-i USA jegyzékre [Hungarian reply to the United States], October 21, 1958, MNL OL, Küm, XIX-J-1-k, USA admin, 11. doboz, 4/b, sz.n.

57. Despatch from the legation in Hungary to the Department of State on the future of Mindszenty, November 20, 1958, in U.S. Department of State, *FRUS, 1958–1960: Eastern Europe Region, Soviet Union, Cyprus*, vol. 10, pt. 1:54–59.

58. Feljegyzés az USA-val való kapcsolatok normalizálásáról [Memorandum on normalization], October 30, 1958, MNL OL, Küm, USA admin, XIX-J-1-k, 11. doboz, 4/b, sz.n.

59. Deputy foreign minister Géza Kardos asserted that the U.S. claim amounted to $US81 million against the Hungarian claim of $US17 million. Kardos Géza feljegyzése a magyar-amerikai pénzügyi problémákról [Kardos's memorandum on financial issues], January 21, 1960, MNL

OL, Küm, USA tük, XIX-J-1-j, 6. doboz, 4/b, 001479.

60. Magyarics, "Az Egyesült Államok és Magyarország," 583.

61. CIA National Intelligence Estimate, "Political Stability in European Satellites," NIE 12–59, 11 August 1959, in U.S. Department of State, *FRUS, 1958–1960: Eastern Europe Region, Soviet Union, Cyprus*, vol. 10, pt. 1:100–102.

62. Letter by Charles Vanik to the secretary of state, March 31, 1960, NARA, RG 59, General Records of the Department of State, central file 1960–1963, 611.64, microfilm roll 93.

63. Theodore Papendorp, second secretary to the Department of State, "Visiting Hungary," March 19, 1961, NARA, RG 59, General Records of the Department of State, central file 1960–1963, 611.64, microfilm roll 93.

64. For Bailey's view, see the American legation in Hungary to the Department of State, August 10, 1960, NARA, General Records of the Department of State Internal Affairs of Hungary 1960–1963, decimal file, microfilm roll 5; Francis Short is cited in American legation in Budapest to the Department of State, June 13, 1961, in ibid.; for Charles Wiley's view see American legation to the Department of State, July 11, 1961, in ibid.; Nicholas Feld's memorandum is cited in American legation in Hungary to the Department of State, "Trip to Tihany," August 3, 1961, in ibid.; U.S. visitors' views are in American legation to the Department of State, November 23, 1961, in ibid.; for the *Christian Science Monitor* correspondent see American legation in Hungary to the Department of State, June 28, 1962, in ibid.; Halász is cited by American legation in Budapest to the Department of State, June 14, 1965, in ibid.; the *Wall Street Journal* is cited in Harrington and Courtney, *Tweaking the Nose of the Russians*, 217.

65. Faure, *L'Ami Américain*, 372–73.

66. Ibid., 369.

67. American legation in Budapest to the Department of State, "The Hungarian Economy in 1959," January 27, 1960, NARA, RG 59, General Records of the Department of State, Internal Affairs of Hungary, decimal file 1960–63, microfilm roll 3; American legation in Hungary to the Department of State, "The Hungarian Economy in 1961," January 27, 1962, ibid.; American legation in Budapest to the Department of State, August 3, 1961, in ibid.; American legation in Hungary to the Department of State, March 15, 1962, in ibid.

68. American legation to the Department of State, November 30, 1962, NARA, RG 59, General Records of the Department of State, Internal Affairs of Hungary, decimal file 764, microfilm roll 5.

69. Faure, *L'Ami Américain*, 350.

70. Joseph S. Nye Jr., *Soft Power: The Means to Success in World Politics* (New York: Public Affairs, 2004), 12–13.

71. American legation to the Department of State for the United States Information Agency (USIA), March 29, 1962; State Department to the legation in Hungary, September 7, 1961, in ibid.; American legation to the secretary of state, June 22, 1960, in ibid.; secretary of state (Herter) to the legation in Hungary, July 13, 1960, in ibid.

72. Policy Planning Council, "Bridge-building in Eastern Europe," July 31, 1964, NARA, RG 59, Records of the Department of State, Lindley files, lot file 71D273, box 4: "The US in Eastern Europe can draw upon considerable assets of goodwill [...] This fund of resources is perhaps unique throughout the region and unmatched by any Western country." In 1966 the Policy Planning Council declared that "The US has the most prestige of any Western nation in Eastern Europe." See highlight of secretary's Policy Planning Meeting, July 27, 1966, in ibid., box 5.

73. American legation to the secretary of state, August 24, 1961, NARA, RG 59,

General Records of the Department of State, Internal Affairs of Hungary, central file 1960–63, microfilm roll 93.

74. American legation to the Department of State, conversation with Hungarian intellectuals, April 12, 1961, NARA, RG 59, General Records of the Department of State, decimal file 764, microfilm roll 1.

75. Dispatch from the legation in Hungary to the Department of State, "Recommendations Regarding US Policy Toward Present Hungarian Regime, January 23, 1959, in U.S. Department of State, *FRUS, 1958–1960: Eastern Europe Region, Soviet Union, Cyprus,* 10:62–71.

76. Zádor Tibor jelentése Sík Endrének, látogatás Livingstone Merchantnél, az európai ügyek államtitkáránál [Zádor's report to Sík visit by Livingstone Merchant], February 17, 1959, MNL OL, Küm, XIX-J-1-j, USA tük, 15. doboz, 5/e, 001867.

77. According to a typical analysis of the Foreign Ministry, "After the War American Imperialism sidelined and replaced the traditional colonialists and demonstrated an unprecedented level of colonial exploitation.... For the sake of colonial exploitation and in order to preserve its leading position among the Western powers the U.S. announced a struggle against communism and the progressive forces of the world." At the same time "the consolidation of the socialist bloc, the Soviet Union's huge technological and scientific advances, the ineluctably growing freedom struggle of the colonial peoples has proven that the Dulles line is untenable." Az amerikai referatúra feljegyzése, "Az Egyesült Államok külpolitikája és a magyar-amerikai viszony" [The Foreign Ministry's memorandum, U.S. foreign policy and bilateral relations], November 30, 1959, MNL OL, Küm, XIX-J-1-j, USA admin., 11. doboz, 4/bd, sz.n.

78. Radványi, *Hungary and the Superpowers,* 84–85.

79. Bitta István feljegyzése Zádor Tibornak [Memorandum by Bitta], March 13, 1959, MNL OL, Küm, USA tük, XIX-J-1-j, 15. doboz, 5/e, sz.n; A III. sz. politikai osztály javaslata a magyar-amerikai kapcsolatok javítására [Recommendation for the improvement of bilateral relations], April 2, 1959, ibid., 001479.

80. In 1938 the United States banned meat imports from Hungary due to an epidemic of foot-and-mouth disease. After the war, efforts to sign a new animal health agreement failed because of political hostilities.

81. Az MSZMP KB Külügyi Osztályának előterjesztése az MSZMP KB Politikai Bizottságának (Sík Endre, Hollai Imre) [Recommendation by the Central Committee's Foreign Affairs Department], February 26, 1960, MNL OL, KS, 288. f., 5. cs., 172. őe.

82. In October 1959 probably at the behest of Bruno Kreisky, the Hungarian foreign minister declared that if Austria made a serious offer for the release of the archbishop, Hungary would consider it. The Americans told the Austrians that they would accept a solution that would guarantee Mindszenty's safe passage if this was acceptable to the Holy See and the cardinal. Kreisky forwarded the U.S. position to the Vatican. Memorandum from the deputy assistant secretary of state for European affairs (Kohler) to Secretary of State Herter, December 9, 1959, in U.S. Department of State, *FRUS, 1958–1960: Eastern Europe Region, Soviet Union, Cyprus,* 10:104–6.

83. Az MSZMP KB Külügyi Osztályának előterjesztése az MSZMP KB Politikai Bizottságához, Javaslatok a Mindszenty-kérdés rendezésével kapcsolatban (Péter János, Hollai Imre) [Recommendations for the Political Committee on Mindszenty], March 25, 1960, MNL OL, M-KS, 288. f., 5. cs., 176. őe.

84. Az MSZMP KB Külügyi Osztályának előterjesztése a Politikai Bizottságnak a magyar-amerikai viszony normalizálásáról [Recommendations on

normalization], May 12, 1960, MNL OL, M-KS 288. f., 5 cs, 183. őe.

85. Memorandum of conversation, April 27, 1960, participants: Joseph Mileger, Harold Vedeler, Robert McKisson, NARA, RG 59, Records of the Department of State, Internal Affairs of Hungary, central file, 1960–63, microfilm roll 93.

86. Dobrynin, *In Confidence*, 40–41.

87. The Foreign Ministry asserted that "before any major initiative is made we must take into account that since May Soviet-American relations have deteriorated." They also pointed out there was no prospect of change regarding trade controls. A Külügyminisztérium III. területi osztályának feljegyzése [The Foreign Ministry's memorandum], August 11, 1960, MNL OL, Küm, USA admin, XIX-J-1-k, 11. doboz, 4/bd, sz.n.

88. Instruction from the Department of State to the legation in Hungary, October 21, 1960, in U.S. Department of State, *FRUS, 1958–1960: Eastern Europe Region, Soviet Union, Cyprus,* 10:126–30.

89. Foy Kohler to the secretary of state regarding U.S.-Hungarian relations, January 26, 1961, NARA, RG 59, Records of the Department of State, central file 611.64, microfilm roll 93.

90. The American legation in Budapest to the Department of State, 1960, NARA, RG 59, Records of the Department of State, central file 611.64, microfilm roll 93.

91. Memorandum from Foy Kohler and Woodruff Wallner to the secretary of state (Herter), February 21, 1961, NARA, RG 59, Records of the Department of State, Internal Affairs of Hungary, 1960–1963, microfilm roll 1.

92. Sík Endre feljegyzése Biszku Bélának [Memorandum for Biszku], April 14, 1961, MNL OL, Küm, USA tük, XIX-J-1-j, 4. doboz 4/a, 001745/61.

93. Zádor Tibor jelentése Sík Endrének, Beszélgetés Vedelerrel, a State Department főosztályvezetőjével [Conversation with Vedeler], April 26, 1981, MNL OL, Küm, XIX-J-1-j, 15. doboz, 5/e, 003499/1.

94. Péter János feljegyzése Biszku Bélának [Memorandum for Biszku], MNL OL, Küm, USA tük, XIX-J-1-j, 4. doboz, 4/a, 001745/1961.

95. Harrington and Courtney, *Tweaking the Nose of the Russians*, 221–22.

96. Memorandum of conversation, U.S.-Hungarian Relations, April 5, 1961, NARA, RG 59, Records of the Department of State, Political Relations between the United States and Hungary, 1960–1963, microfilm roll 93.

97. Telegram from New York (Yost) to the secretary of state, June 5, 1961, NARA, RG 59, Records of the Department of State, Hungary 1960–1963, microfilm roll 1.

98. Telegram from New York to the secretary of state, May 25, 1961, ibid.

99. Radványi, *Hungary and the Superpowers*, 84–86; Magyarics, "Az Egyesült Államok és Magyarország," 583.

100. Rusk to the American legation in Hungary, August 2, 1961, NARA, RG 59, Records of the Department of State, Hungary 1960–1963, microfilm roll 1.

101. Memorandum of conversation, August 3, 1961, ibid.

102. Telegram from Budapest, August 4, 1961, ibid.

103. A IV. Területi főosztály Amerikai Referatúrájának feljegyzése Szőke György számára [Memorandum by the American desk], January 4, 1962, MNL OL, Küm, USA tük, XIX-J-1-j, 11. doboz, 4/bd, sz.n.

104. Memorandum of conversation, June 13, 1963, participants: Chester Bowles, Radványi János, NARA, RG 59, Records of the Department of State, Hungary 1960–1963, Political Relations between the United States and Hungary 1960–1963, microfilm roll 93.

105. Telegram by George Ball to New York, June 12, 1962, ibid., roll 2.

106. Telegram by Rusk to the legation in Hungary, August 1962, ibid.

107. The American legation to the Department of State, conversation with Szarka, September 12, 1961, NARA, RG 59, Records of the Department of State, Hungary 1960–1963, Political Relations Between the United States and Hungary 611.64, microfilm roll 93; American legation in Hungary to the Department of State, September 14, 1961, ibid.
108. The legation in Hungary to the secretary of state, conversation with Kádár, September 29, 1961, NARA, RG 59, Records of the Department of State, Hungary 1960–1963, decimal file 764, microfilm roll 3.
109. The American legation to the Department of State, October 2, 1961, ibid.
110. Roger Tubby, assistant secretary for public affairs, to Béla Király, Hungarian Freedom Fighters Federation, October 20, 1961, ibid. roll 1: "Hungarian patriots bravely struggled against tremendous odds to win national independence and freedoms to which all mankind and all nations are entitled [...] free men everywhere will pay tribute to the valor of the Hungarian people and reaffirm their respect for Hungary's struggle against Soviet imperialism. The free world will not forget the sacrifices of the Hungarian people."
111. The American legation to the secretary of state, October 19, 1961, NARA, RG 59, Records of the Department of State, Hungary 1960–1963, Political Relations Between the United States and Hungary 611.64, microfilm roll 93; acting secretary of state (Bowles) to the U.S. legation in Hungary, November 23, 1961, ibid.
112. State Department to the legation in Hungary, January 16, 1962, NARA, RG 59, Records of the Department of State, Hungary 1960–1963, Political Relations between the United States and Hungary 611.64, microfilm roll 93.
113. The American legation in Hungary to the secretary of state, February 1962, NARA, RG 59, Records of the Department of State, Hungary 1960–1963, microfilm roll 1.
114. The American legation to the Department of State, new U.S. desk officer in Hungary, November 2, 1961, NARA, RG 59, Records of the Department of State, Hungary 1960–1963, Political Relations Between the United States and Hungary, Microfilm, roll 93; American legation to the Department of State, Radványi transfer, February 15, 1962, ibid.
115. Memorandum of conversation, participants: Radványi, Zádor, Kohler, Davis, Trost, February 21, 1961, ibid.
116. Zádor Tibor jelentése Péter Jánosnak, Amerikai külügyi tisztviselők meghívása [Memorandum on the invitation of State Department officials], January 23, 1962, MNL OL, Küm, USA tük, XIX-J-1-j, 15. doboz, 5/e, 001234.
117. Radványi, Hungary and the Superpowers, 92–93.
118. Radványi János jelentése Péter Jánosnak [Radványi to Péter], March 24, 1962, MNL OL, Küm, USA tük, XIX-J-1-j 15. doboz, 001224/13.
119. A Külügyminisztérium feljegyzése [Memorandum by the Foreign Ministry], April 16, 1962, MNL OL, Küm, USA tük, XIX-J-1-j, 15. doboz, 01224/2.
120. Memorandum of conversation, April 26, 1962, participants: Radványi, McGhee, McKisson, NARA, RG 59, Records of the Department of State, Political Relations between Hungary and the United States, microfilm roll 93.
121. Radványi János jelentése Péter Jánosnak, McGhee államtitkárral folytatott megbeszélés [Memorandum of conversation with McGhee], April 29, 1962, MNL OL, Küm, USA tük, XIX-J-1-j, 15. doboz, 5/e, 05115.
122. Rácz Pál Radványi Jánosnak, Beszélgetés McGheevel [Conversation with McGhee], May 24, 1962, ibid., 005115.
123. Polgár Dénes feljegyzése [Memorandum by Polgár], May 21, 1962, Radványi

János jelentése [Report by Radványi], May 25, 1962, both in MNL OL, Küm, USA tük, XIX-J-1-j, 15. doboz, 5/e, 005413. U.S. diplomacy used Polgár as a backchannel straight to the Political Committee.

124. The American legation in Budapest to the secretary of state, May 31, 1962, NARA, RG 59, Records of the Department of State, Political Relations between Hungary and the United States, 611.64, 1960–63, microfilm roll 93.

125. Memorandum of conversation, February 13, 1962, participants: Edigio Vagnozzi, Harold C. Vedeler, August Velletri, in U.S. Department of State, *Foreign Relations of the United States, 1961–1963*, vol. 16 (Washington, D.C.: Government Printing Office, 1996), 14–16.

126. Memorandum of conversation, situation of Mindszenty, May 2, 1962, participants: Edigio Vagnozzi, Harold Vedeler, August Velletri, in ibid., 22–23.

127. Jegyzőkönyv az MSZMP KB Politikai Bizottságának üléséről, August 7, 1962, MNL OL, M-KS 288. f., 5. cs., 274. őe.

128. Előterjesztés az MSZMP KB Politikai Bizottságának, "Határozati javaslat a magyar-amerikai viszony normalizálásáról és a Midszenty-ügyről folytatandó tárgyalások kérdésében" [Draft resolution on normalization and the talks concerning Mindszenty], August 10, 1962, in ibid., 275. őe.

129. The American Embassy in Stockholm to the American legation in Budapest, January 21, 1961, NARA, RG 59, General Records of the Department of State, Political Relations Between the United States and Hungary, 1960–1963, microfilm roll 93; the Department of State to the embassy in Stockholm, January 29, 1960, ibid.

130. Torbert to the Department of State, March 14, 1961, ibid.; John F. Kennedy to Cardinal Mindszenty, February 2, 1961, ibid.

131. Radványi János összefoglalója Péter János külügyminiszternek [Radványi's memorandum for Péter], September 11, 1962, MNL OL, Küm, XIX-J-1-j, USA tük, 6. doboz, 001224/6.

132. Telegram from New York to the secretary of state, May 15, 1962, NARA, RG 59, Records of the Department of State, Internal Affairs of Hungary 1960–1963, microfilm roll 2.

133. Memorandum of conversation, September 1, 1962, participants: Radvanyi, Vedeler, Davis, NARA, RG 59, Records of the Department of State, Political Relations between Hungary and the United States, microfilm roll 93.

134. Memorandum of conversation, September 26, 1962, participants: Kreisky, Rusk, NARA, RG 59, Records of the Department of State, Internal Affairs of Hungary, 1960–1963, microfilm roll 2.

135. Telegram to the secretary of state, September 26, 1962, ibid.

136. Az amerikai Külügyminisztérium emlékeztetője a magyarkérdés és az amnesztia tárgyában [Memorandum by the State Department on the question of the amnesty], October 10, 1962, MNL OL, Küm, XIX-J-1-j, USA tük, 4/bd, 6. doboz; Radványi János ügyvivő jelentése az amerikai Külügyminisztérium emlékeztetője tárgyában [Memorandum by Radványi regarding the U.S. memorandum on amnesty], November 7, 1962, ibid., 001224/8/1962.

137. See Hope M. Harrison, *Driving the Soviets Up the Wall: Soviet-East German Relations, 1953–1961* (Princeton, N.J.: Princeton University Press, 2003).

138. Radványi, *Hungary and the Superpowers*, 140–41.

139. The American legation in Hungary to the secretary of state, November 24, 1962, NARA, RG 59, Records of the Department of State, Political Relations between Hungary and the United States, 611.64, 1960–63, microfilm reel 93.

140. Radványi jelentése Péter Jánosnak [Report by Radványi to Péter], December

21, 1962, MNL OL, Küm, XIX-J-1-j, USA tük, 6. doboz, 00598.

6. THE DILEMMAS OF EXTERNAL TRANSFORMATION

1. Jonathan Haslam, *Russia's Cold War: From the October Revolution to the Fall of the Wall* (New Haven, Conn., and London: Yale University Press, 2011), 229–30.

2. Geraint Hughes, *Harold Wilson's Cold War: The Labour Government and East-West Conflict, 1964–1970*, Royal Historical Society Studies in History, new series (Woodbridge, Suffolk, Rochester N.Y.: Boydell Press, 2009), 39.

3. Bennett Kovrig, *Of Walls and Bridges: The United States & Eastern Europe* (New York: New York University Press, 1991), 107–8.

4. "The Bloc Countries and Eastern-Europe," Department of State Guidelines for Policy and Operations, February 1963, National Archives and Records Administration (NARA), Washington, D.C., Record Group (RG), General Records of the Department of State, Executive Secretariat, 1961–1966, box 5.

5. Joseph F. Harrington and Bruce J. Courtney, *Tweaking the Nose of the Russians: Fifty Years of American-Romanian Relations, 1940–1990*, East European Monographs no. 296 (Boulder, Colo.: East European Monographs, 1991), 252.

6. Ibid., 268.

7. Special Report by the CIA, March 27, 1964, in U.S. Department of State, *Foreign Relations of the United States, 1964–1968: Eastern Europe*, vol. 17 (Washington, D.C.: Government Printing Office, 1996), 2–8.

8. "Changing Patterns in Eastern Europe," submitted by the director of CIA, National Intelligence Estimate 12-64, July 22, 1964, NARA, RG 59, Records of the Department of State, Policy Planning Council, lot file 70D199, 1963–64, box 260: "East European leaders are increasingly free to approach these questions in light of national aspirations and local political conditions."

9. NARA, RG 59, Records of the Department of State, Policy Planning Council (PPC), lot file 70D199, box 260.

10. "Changing Patterns in Eastern Europe," submitted by the director of CIA, National Intelligence Estimate 12-64, July 22, 1964, NARA, RG 59, Records of the Department of State, Policy Planning Council, lot file 70D199, 1963–64, box 260.

11. "The Situation in Eastern Europe," the director of research and intelligence of the Department of State to the acting secretary of state, April 16, 1964, NARA, RG 59, Records of the Department of State, PPC, lot file 70D199 1963–64, box 260.

12. "Eastern Europe's Involvement in Communist Conspiratorial Activities," director of research and intelligence of the Department of State, July 9, 1964, NARA, RG 59, Records of the Department of State, PPC, lot file 70D199 1963–64, box 260.

13. "Changing Patterns in Eastern Europe," submitted by the director of CIA, National Intelligence Estimate 12-64, July 22, 1964, NARA, RG 59, Records of the Department of State, Policy Planning Council, lot file 70D199, 1963–64, box 260.

14. "Policy Planning Council – Bridge-building in Eastern Europe," July 31, 1964, NARA, Records of the Department of State, RG 59, Policy Planning Council, lot 70 D199, box 260.

15. Harrington and Courtney, *Tweaking the Nose of the Russians*, 230.

16. National Security Action Memorandum (NSAM) 304, "Action Program for US Relations with Eastern Europe," August 4, 1964, NARA, RG 59, Records of the Department of State, PPC, lot file 70D199 1963–64, box 260.

17. "The US and East-West Relations in Europe," memorandum by the Department of State, August 3, 1963, NARA, RG 59, Records of the Department of State, Ernest

K. Lindley files 1961–1969, lot file 71D273, box 4.
18. Hughes, *Harold Wilson's Cold War*, 44–47.
19. Memorandum of conversation, "The Hungarian Situation and US-Hungarian Relations," September 10, 1964: The participants were Ferenc Nagy, Béla Varga, Richard H. Davis, Harold C. Vedeler, Robert B. Wright, Robert McKisson, and Christopher Squire, NARA, RG 59, Records of the Department of State, central files 64–66, box 2275.
20. Justine Faure, *L'Ami Américain: La Tchécoslovaquie, enjeu de la diplomatie Américaine, 1943–1968* (Paris: Tallandier, 2004), 336.
21. The Situation in Eastern Europe, the director of the Department of State Research and Analysis Branch to the acting secretary of state, April 16, 1964, NARA, RG 59, Records of the Department of State, PPC, lot file, 70D199 1963–1964, box 260.
22. "Changing Patterns in Eastern Europe," submitted by the director of CIA, National Intelligence Estimate 12–64, July 22, 1964, NARA, RG 59, Records of the Department of State, Policy Planning Council, lot file 70D199, 1963–64, box 260.
23. Owen T. Jones to the secretary of state, political assessment of Hungary 1964, NARA, RG 59, Hungary, central files, 1964–1966, box 2275.
24. János M. Rainer, "The Sixties in Hungary: Some Historical and Social Approaches," 4–26, and Sándor Horváth, "Hooligans, Spivs and Gangs: Youth Subcultures in the 1960s," 199–223, both in *Muddling Through the Long 1960s: Ideas and Every Day Life in High Politics and the Lower Classes of Communist Hungary*, ed. János M. Rainer and György Peteri, Trondheim Studies on East European Cultures and Societies 16 (Budapest: Institute for the History of the 1956 Hungarian Revolution, 2005).

25. A Magyar-Forradalmi Munkás-Paraszt Kormány 3062/1964 számú határozata [Resolution 3062/1964 by the Revolutionary Workers' Peasants' Government], February 19, 1964, Magyar Nemzeti Levéltár Országos Levéltára (MNL OL), Budapest, Külügyminisztérium (Küm), XIX-J-1-j, USA tük, 6.doboz, 4/b 002812; A Külügyminisztérium jegyzéke [Memorandum by the Foreign Ministry], February 24, 1964, ibid.
26. The American legation in Budapest to the secretary of state, February 26, 1964, NARA, RG 59, Records of the Department of State, Hungary, central files 1964–66, box 2277.
27. Memorandum of conversation, "Retention of Soviet Armed Forces in Hungary," January 21, 1964: participants, R. Heath Mason, counsellor of British Embassy, and Harold C. Vedeler, ibid.
28. Despatch by the legation in Hungary to the Department of State, July 18, 1964, ibid.
29. Memorandum from the president's special assistant for national security (Bundy) to President Johnson, April 14, 1964, in U.S. Department of State, *Foreign Relations of the United States, 1964–1968: Eastern Europe*, vol. 17 (Washington, D.C.: Government Printing Office, 1996), 301.
30. The American legation in Budapest to the secretary of state, December 8, 1964, NARA, RG 59, Records of the Department of State, Hungary, central files 1964–66, box 2278.
31. A Külügyminisztérium feljegyzése a magyar-amerikai tárgyalásokól [Hungarian-U.S. talks], February 18, 1964, MNL OL, M-KS 288. f., 5. cs., 327. őe; memorandum of conversation, claims settlement, November 30, 1964, NARA, RG 59, Records of the Department of State, Hungary, central files 1964–66, box 2278.
32. János Honvári, "Pénzügyi és vagyonjogi tárgyalások és egyezmények Magyarország és az Egyesült Államok között,

1945–1978," Századok 143, no. 1 (2009): 43–44, 47, 55.
33. Csaba Békés, "A Kádári külpolitika 1956–1968: Látványos sikerek – 'láthatatlan' konfliktusok," in Európából Európába: Magyarország konfliktusok kereszttüzében, 1945–1990, ed. Csaba Békés (Budapest: Gondolat, 2004), 245–46. Economics motivated Hungary's relations with the FRG as well.
34. Jegyzőkönyv az MSZMP KB Politikai Bizottságának üléséről. Előterjesztés az Egyesült Államok külügyminiszterével folytatandó tárgyalásokkal kapcsolatban [Recommendation regarding talks with the secretary of state], November 26, 1964, MNL OL, M-KS 288. f., 5. cs., 352. őe.
35. Péter-Rusk találkozó [Péter-Rusk meeting], December 4, 1964, MNL OL, Küm, XIX-J-1-j, USA tük, 6. doboz, 4/b, 116612/1964; memorandum of conversation, New York, secretary's delegation to the Nineteenth Session of the UNGA, participants: Secretary, Mr. Givan, Péter, Radványi, in U.S. Department of State, Foreign Relations of the United States, 1964–1968: Eastern Europe, vol. 17 (Washington, D.C.: Government Printing Office, 1996), 305–6.
36. Jegyzőkönyv az MSZMP PB Politikai Bizottságának üléséről [Record of Politburo meeting], October 29, 1963, MNL OL, M-KS 288. f., 5. cs., 318. őe.
37. Telegram from the legation in Hungary to the Department of State, March 11, 1964, in U.S. Department of State, Foreign Relations of the United States, 1964–1968: Eastern Europe, vol. 17 (Washington, D.C.: Government Printing Office, 1996), 299–300.
38. Jegyzőkönyv az MSZMP KB Politikai Bizottságának 1965. szeptember 14-én megtartott üléséről [Record of the September 14, 1965, meeting of the Political Committee], MNL OL, M-KS 288. f., 5. cs., 37. őe.; MSZMP KB Politikai Bizottságának ülése [Meeting of the Politburo], October 29, 1963, ibid., 318. őe.

39. Honvári, "Pénzügyi és vagyonjogi tárgyalások és egyezmények," 60–61.
40. Harrington and Courtney, Tweaking the Nose of the Russians, 270.
41. Attila Mong, Kádár hitele: A magyar államadósság története, 1956–1990 (Budapest: Libri Kiadó, 2012), 99–101.
42. Memorandum from the United States Information Agency (USIA) (Edward R. Murrow) to W. A. Harriman, September 16, 1963, Library of Congress Manuscript Division, Papers of Averell Harriman, box 470.
43. Faure, L'Ami Américain, 346–47.
44. Tervezet: Előterjesztés az Ügyvezető Elnökség részére a Ford Ösztöndíj tapasztalatairól [Draft Memorandum on the Ford Scholarship], September 30, 1967, MNL OL, Kulturális Kapcsolatok Intézete, XIX-A-33-a, USA-6022-1968, 217. doboz.
45. NSAM 304, "Action Program for US Relations with Eastern Europe," August 4, 1964, NARA, RG 59, Records of the Department of State, PPC, lot file 70D199 1963–64, box 260.
46. Az MSZMP KB Politikai Bizottságának ülése [Meeting of the Politburo], November 23, 1965, MNL OL, M-KS, 288. f., 5. cs., 380. őe.
47. Az MSZMP KB Politikai Bizottságának határozata [Politburo Resolution], April 26, 1966, MNL OL, M-KS, 288. f., 5 cs., 393. őe.
48. Walter L. Hixson, Parting the Iron Curtain: Propaganda, Culture, and the Cold War, 1945–1961 (London: MacMillan, 1997), 114–15.
49. See Anna Szemere, Up from the Underground: The Culture of Rock Music in Postsocialist Hungary (University Park: Pennsylvania State University Press, 2001).
50. Ibid., 11.
51. Az MSZMP KB Politikai Bizottságának ülése [Meeting of the Politburo], November 23, 1965, MNL OL, M-KS, 288. f., 5. cs., 380. őe.

52. Sándor Horváth, "Hooligans, Spivs and Gangs: Youth Subcultures in the 1960s," in *Muddling Through the Long 1960s: Ideas and Everyday Life in High Politics and the Lower Classes of Communist Hungary*, ed. M. János Rainer and György Péteri (Budapest: Institute for the History of the 1956 Hungarian Revolution, 2005).

53. The American legation in Hungary to the Department of State, discussion with Károly Kiss, March 16, 1964, NARA, General Records of the Department of State, Political Affairs and Relations, central policy file 1964–1966, box 2279.

54. Előterjesztés az MSZMP KB Politikai Bizottsága számára [Recommendation for the Political Committee], April 26, MNL OL, M-KS 288. f., 5. cs., 393. őe.

55. A Külügyminisztérium V. Területi Főosztályának előterjesztése [Recommendation by the Foreign Ministry], 1965, MNL OL, Küm, XIX-J-1-j, USA tük, 12. doboz, 5 b/t sz. n. 1965.

56. The American legation in Hungary, "US Policy Assessment," February 9, 1966, NARA, General Records of the Department of State, Political Affairs and Relations, central policy file 1964–1966, box 2278.

57. Airgram from the legation in Hungary to the Department of State, August 31, 1965, in U.S. Department of State, *Foreign Relations of the United States, 1964–1968: Eastern Europe*, vol. 17 (Washington, D.C.: Government Printing Office, 1996), 308–10.

58. Jegyzőkönyv az MSZMP KB Politikai Bizottságának 1965. május 11-én megtartott üléséről [Record of Politburo Meeting, May 11, 1965], MNL OL, M-KS 288. f., 5. cs., 365. őe.

59. Jegyzőkönyv az MSZMP KB Politikai Bizottságának 1965. szeptember 14.-én megtartott üléséről [Record of the September 14 meeting of the Political Committee], MNL OL, M-KS, 288. f., 5. cs, 37. őe. In Kádár's own words: "Why do the Americans want to normalize relations with Hungary? This fits into their own line, they have been saying for a year and a half that they believe in peaceful coexistence while they are bombing Vietnam, and they want to normalize with us. This somehow falls into our line although we must inform our allies."

60. Jegyzőkönyv az MSZMP KB Politikai Bizottságának 1965. május 11-én megtartott üléséről [Record of Politburo Meeting, May 11, 1965], MNL OL, M-KS 288. f., 5. cs., 365. őe.

61. Feljegyzés az amerikai gazdasági propagandáról [Memorandum on U.S. economic propaganda] (1972), MNL OL, M-KS, 288. f., 5. cs., 34. őe.

62. The American legation (Tims) in Hungary to the Department of State, August 5, 1965, NARA, RG 59, General Records of the Department of State, Political Affairs and Relations, central file, 1964–1966, box 2278.

63. Memorandum from the USIA to the president (Nixon), May 14, 1969, NARA, Nixon Presidential Materials, institutional H files 1969–1974, box H-133; the American Embassy to the secretary of state, December 20, 1969, NARA, RG 59, General Records of the Department of State, central file 1969–1969, box 2181.

64. The American Embassy in Hungary to the secretary of state, "US Policy Assessment: Hungary," January 10, 1969, NARA, RG 59, General Records of the Department of State, central file 1969–1969, box 2183.

65. Budapest to the secretary of state, February 18, 1964, NARA, RG 59, General Records of the Department of State, Political Affairs and Relations, central file, 1964–1966, box 2279.

66. The Department of State to the U.S. legation in Hungary, February 16, 1965, ibid.

67. The Department of State to the U.S. legation in Budapest, February 13, 1965, ibid.

68. Memorandum of conversation, March 10, 1965, participants: McKisson, Squire, Radványi, ibid., box 2278.
69. The American legation in Hungary (Tims) to the Department of State, August 5, 1965, ibid.
70. The American legation in Hungary to the Department of State, "US Policy Assessment of Hungary," February 9, 1966, ibid.
71. Haslam, *Russia's Cold War*, 225.
72. Anatoly Dobrynin, *In Confidence: Moscow's Ambassador to America's Six Cold War Presidents (1962–1986)* (New York: Times Books, 1995), 140.
73. Qiang Zhai, *China and the Vietnam Wars, 1950–1975* (Chapel Hill and London: University of North Carolina Press, 2000), 166–68.
74. Robert V. Rodsa, Bown Brothers Harriman Co., to George Ball, December 20, 1965, memorandum of conversation, participants: Rodsa, Radványi, NARA, RG 59, General Records of the Department of State, Political Affairs and Relations, central file, 1964–1966, box 2278.
75. Jegyzőkönyv, az MSZMP KB Politikai Bizottságának üléséről [Memorandum of Politburo meeting], April 26, 1966, MNL OL, M-KS 288. f., 5. cs., 393. őe.
76. The U.S. legation in Hungary (O'Shaughnessy, Tims) to the Department of State, "Increased Tension in Cultural Relations," June 23, 1966, NARA, RG 59, General Records of the Department of State, Political Affairs and Relations, central file, 1964–1966, box 2278.
77. The American legation to the Department of State, "Rude Treatment of American Visitors," June 6, 1966, ibid.; The American legation to the Department of State, June 6, 1966, ibid.
78. Memorandum of conversation, September 20, 1966, participants: Tihanyi, Radványi, ibid.
79. Jegyzőkönyv az MSZMP KB Politikai Bizottságának üléséről Javaslat a magyar-amerikai kapcsolatok szintjének emeléséről [Minutes of the Meeting of the Political Committee of the HWSP, Recommendation on U.S.-Hungarian relations] November 15, 1966, MNL OL, M-KS 288 f., 5. cs., 409. őe.; memorandum of conversation, October 6, 1966, participants: Péter, Rusk, in U.S. Department of State, *Foreign Relations of the United States, 1964–1968: Eastern Europe*, vol. 17 (Washington, D.C.: Government Printing Office, 1996), 311.
80. Memorandum of conversation, "Hungarian Chief of Mission Asks for Refuge in US," May 16, 1967, NARA, RG 59, Records of the Department of State, central files 1967–69, box 2182.
81. Memorandum of conversation, May 20, 1967, participants: Harriman, Kohler, Radványi, NARA, RG 59, Records of the Department of State, central files 1967–69, box 2180.
82. At the initiative of the U.S. Senate, Radványi's death sentence was taken up again in 1989 and the Hungarian Supreme Court ruled that the death sentence could not be carried out because of limitation.
83. Telegram from the embassy in Hungary to the State Department, November 20, 1967, in U.S. Department of State, *Foreign Relations of the United States, 1964–1968: Eastern Europe*, vol. 17 (Washington, D.C.: Government Printing Office, 1996), 315–17.
84. Telegram from the embassy in Hungary to the Department of State, October 30, 1967, in ibid., 318–320.
85. Haslam, *Russia's Cold War*, 233.
86. Telegram by the American Embassy in Hungary to the Department of State, "Demonstrations against Embassy," June 8, 1967, NARA, RG 59, Records of the Department of State, central files 1967–69, box 2182.
87. The American Embassy to the Department of State, "Policy Assessment of Hungary," August 6, 1967, in ibid.

88. The Department of State to the embassy in Hungary, October 18, 1967, ibid., box 2183.
89. A Külügyminisztérium amerikai referatúrájának feljegyzése [Memorandum by the American desk], May 17, 1968, MNL OL, Küm, XIX-J-1-j, USA tük, 8. doboz, 4-1-002337/1-1968; Bartha János feljegyzése [Memorandum by Bartha], November 27, 1968, ibid., 003744-1968.
90. The ambassador in Hungary to the secretary of state, "Conversation with Fock," November 17, 1967, NARA, RG 59, Records of the Department of State, central files 1967–69, box 2183.
91. The American ambassador to the secretary of state, November 26, 1967, ibid., box 2181.
92. The American Embassy in Hungary to the Department of State, Leddy-Szilágyi conversation, October 1, 1967, NARA, RG 59, Records of the Department of State, central files 1967–69, box 2181.
93. The American Embassy in Hungary to the Department of State, conversation with Zádor, October 11, 1967, ibid.
94. The American Embassy in Hungary to the Department of State, May 29, 1967, ibid., box 2182.
95. The American Embassy in Hungary to the Department of State, June 8, 1967, ibid.
96. Szilágyi Béla külügyminiszter-helyettes megbeszélése Meehan amerikai ügyvivővel [The deputy foreign minister's conversation with Meehan], March 7, 1969, MNL OL, Küm, XIX-J-1-j, USA tük, 10. doboz, 1-002337/2-1968; the American ambassador in Hungary to the Department of State, December 12, 1967 NARA, RG 59, Records of the Department of State, central files 1967–69, box 2183.
97. Józan Sándor ideiglenes ügyvivő jelentése Péter János külügyminiszternek [Report by Józan to Foreign Minister Péter], May 30, 1968, MNL OL, Küm, XIX-J-1-j, USA tük, 8. doboz, 4-1-001933/1-1968;

Nagy János nagykövet jelentése a Külügyminisztériumnak a baráti országok diplomatáinál tett bemutatkozó látogatásról [Nagy's report on introductory meeting with ambassadors of fraternal countries], May 19, 1968, ibid., 4-1-001933/1-1968.
98. Lásd Hillenbrand nagykövet látogatása Puja Frigyes külügyminiszter-helyettesnél [Hillenbrand's introductory meeting with Deputy Foreign Minister Puja], July 11, 1968, ibid., 7. doboz, 4-1-00361/20-1968; Scott első titkár bemutatkozása, August 17, 1968, ibid.
99. The American Embassy in Hungary to the Department of State, January 19, 1968, NARA, RG 59, Records of the Department of State, central files 1967–69, box 2183.
100. For this perspective see Haslam, *Russia's Cold War*, 230.
101. The American Embassy in Hungary to the Department of State, September 27, 1967, memorandum of conversation, participants: Szilágyi, Házi, Nagy, Kiss, Leddy, Tims, Toon, NARA, RG 59, Records of the Department of State, central files 1967–69, box 2183.
102. Radványi claimed that the negotiating delegation with the FRG had been selected when the Soviet Union said no. See János Radványi, *Hungary and the Superpowers: The 1956 Revolution and Realpolitik* (Stanford, Calif.: Hoover Institution Press, Stanford University, 1972).
103. The American Embassy in Budapest to the Department of State, October 11, 1967, conversation with Zádor, NARA, RG 59, Records of the Department of State, central files 1967–69, box 2183.
104. The deputy attorney general (Richard K. Kleindienst) to Elliot Richardson, December 30, 1967, NARA, RG 59, Records of the Department of State, central files 1967–69, box 2183.
105. The embassy in Hungary to the secretary of state, "Policy Assessment of Hungary," August 6, 1967, ibid.

106. The American Embassy to the Department of State, Leddy-Szilágyi conversation, October 1, 1967, ibid.
107. A Külügyminisztérium V. Területi Osztályának feljegyzése McAuliffe amerikai nagykövet bemutatkozó látogatásáról Kádár Jánosnál [Ambassador McAuliffe's introductory meeting with Kádár], December 9, 1975, MNL OL, Küm, XIX-J-1-j, USA tük, 27. doboz, 10-003036/7-1975.
108. Hillenbrand to the secretary of state, January 10, 1969, memorandum of conversation with Szilágyi, NARA, RG 59, General Records of the Department of State, central files 1967–1969, box 2182.
109. Martin J. Hillenbrand, *Fragments of Our Time: Memoirs of a Diplomat* (Athens: University of Georgia Press, 1998), 253.
110. Faure, *L'Ami Américaine*, 383.
111. Vacsora Puhannal [Dinner with Puhan], August 14, 1969, MNL OL, Küm, XIX-J-1-j, USA tük, 1-00361/31-1969.
112. Randé Jenő beszélgetése Philip Arnolddal, a State Department magyar referatúrájának kulturális előadójával [Conversation with the State Department Hungarian desk officer], January 16, 1969, MNL OL, Küm, USA tük, XIX-J-1-j, 10. doboz, 1-00361/1-1969.
113. A Külügyminisztérium feljegyzése, részvétel a Puhan által adott vacsorán [Participation at Puhan's dinner], April 2, 1971, MNL OL, Küm, XIX-J-1-j, USA tük, 17. doboz, 4-14/00399/2/1971.
114. The American Embassy in Hungary to the Department of State, September 27, 1967, memorandum of conversation, September 27, 1967, participants: Szilágyi, Házi, Nagy, Kiss, Leddy, Tims, Toon, NARA, RG 59, Records of the Department of State, central files 1967–69, box 2183.
115. Cited by György Földes, "Kötélhúzás felsőfokon: Kádár és Brezsnyev," in *Ki volt Kádár? Harag és részrehajlás nélkül a Kádár-életútról*, ed. Árpád Rácz (Budapest: Rubin-Aquila-Könyvek, 2001), 106.

116. Nagyköveti konferencia [Conference of ambassadors], 1967, MNL OL, M-KS 288. f., 32. cs., 22. őe.
117. A Külügyminisztérium V. Területi Főosztályának feljegyzése Pedersen amerikai nagykövet Péter Jánosnál tett látogatásáról [Memorandum of Ambassador Pedersen's meeting with the foreign minister], September 4, 1973, MNL OL, Küm, XIX-J-1-j-USA tük, 17. doboz, 116-002985/2-1973.
118. The American Embassy to the Department of State, August 27, 1968, NARA, RG 59, Records of the Department of State, subject numeric files, 1967–69, box 2180; the American Embassy to the Department of State, "The Hungarian Scene After the Czechoslovak Invasion," September 18, 1967, ibid.
119. The American Embassy in Hungary to the Department of State, January 8, 1968, NARA, RG 59, Records of the Department of State, central files 1967–69, box 2181.
120. The embassy in Budapest to the Department of State, August 17, 1970, NARA, RG 59, Records of the Department of State, central files 1970–73, box 2183; personal impressions, October 24, 1967, ibid., box 2182; conversation with Puja, July 19, 1968, ibid.; conversation with Vályi, April 19, 1968, ibid.
121. The American Embassy in Hungary to the Department of State (Meehan), conversation with Nyers, May 25, 1969, ibid., box 2183.
122. The American Embassy in Budapest to the Department of State, "Policy Assessment of Hungary," August 6, 1967, NARA, RG 59, General Records of the Department of State, central files 1967–69, box 2183.
123. The American Embassy to the Department of State, "Policy Assessment of Hungary," January 24, 1968, ibid.
124. The American Embassy to the Department of State, "Policy Assessment of Hungary," February 16, 1967, ibid.
125. The American ambassador to the secretary of state, August 27, 1968, ibid.

126. The American Embassy to the Department of State, "Policy Assessment of Hungary," January 24, 1968, ibid.
127. The American Embassy to the Department of State, February 5, 1967, ibid.
128. The American Embassy to the Department of State, November 25, 1969, NARA, RG 59, Records of the Department of State, subject numeric files 1967–69, box 2180.
129. The American Embassy to the Department of State, January 8, 1968, ibid.
130. The American Embassy to the Department of State, December 20, 1968, ibid., box 2181.
131. See Geir Lundestad, *The United States and Western Europe from 1945: From "Empire" by Invitation to Transatlantic Drift* (New York: Oxford University Press, 2003).
132. The American Embassy in Hungary to the Department of State, "Discussion with *Magyar Nemzet* Editor," January 2, 1967, NARA, RG 59, Records of the Department of State, subject numeric files, 1967–69, box 2180.
133. Horváth, "Hooligans, Spivs and Gangs," 217.
134. Rejtjeltávirat, Csatorday Károly jelentése a Külügyminisztériumnak [Csatorday's report to the Foreign Ministry], November 25, 1969, MNL OL, Küm, XIX-J-1-j, 10. doboz, sz. n.
135. Tibor Glant, *Emlékezzünk Magyarországra, 1956: Tanulmányok a magyar forradalom és szabadságharc amerikai emlékezetéről* (Budapest: Kiss József, 2008), 51.
136. Szalai János, a Vám- és Pénzügyőrség Országos Parancsnokának jelentése Faluvégi Lajos pénzügyminiszternek V. Acree-vel, az USA pénzügyigazgatójával folytatott megbeszéléséről [Meeting of the commander-in-chief of the Hungarian Duty and Customs Defense with V. Acree], September 30, 1976, MNL OL, Küm, XIX-J-1-j, USA tük, 20. doboz, 527-003843/1-1976.

137. The American Embassy in Hungary (Meehan) to the Department of State, May 14, 1969, NARA, RG 59, Records of the Department of State, subject numeric files 1967–69, box 2180.
138. The ambassador in Budapest to the secretary of state, October 28, 1968, ibid.
139. Alfred Puhan amerikai nagykövet beszélgetése Bartha János főosztályvezetővel [Puhan's conversation with Bartha], February 1, 1971, MNL OL, Küm, XIX-J-1-j, USA tük, 17. doboz, 14-14/00399/1971.

7. "THE STATUS QUO IS NOT SO BAD"

1. Geraint Hughes, *Harold Wilson's Cold War: The Labour Government and East-West Politics, 1964–1970*, Royal Historical Society Studies in History, new series (Woodbridge, Suffolk, Rochester, N.Y.: Boydell Press, 2009), 160–61.
2. Stephan Kieninger, "Transformation versus Status Quo: The Survival of the Transformation Strategy during the Nixon Years," in *Perforating the Iron Curtain: European Détente, Transatlantic Relations, and the Cold War, 1965–1985*, ed. Poul Villaume and Odd Arne Westad (Copenhagen: Museum Tusculanum Press, University of Copenhagen, 2010), 104.
3. Jonathan Haslam, *Russia's Cold War: From the October Revolution to the Fall of the Wall* (New Haven, Conn.: Yale University Press, 2011), 214–15, 240.
4. "The American Embassy to the Department of State, The Hungarian Scene after the Czechoslovak Invasion," September 18, 1968. National Archives and Records Administration (NARA), Record Group (RG) 59, Records of the Department of State, subject numeric files 1967–1969, box 2180.
5. Hughes, *Harold Wilson's Cold War*, 152.
6. Sipos Péter, "Az Egyesült Államok, a NATO és az 1968-as szovjet intervenció" *Történelmi Szemle* 50, no. 3: 383–406.

7. Justine Faure, *L'Ami Américain: La Tchécoslovaquie, enjeu de la diplomatie Américaine, 1943–1968* (Paris: Tallandier, 2004), 408.
8. Hughes, *Harold Wilson's Cold War,* 152–53, 157–58.
9. Faure, *L'Ami Américain,* 392–95, 401.
10. Haslam, *Russia's Cold War,* 248, 249–51.
11. Jegyzőkönyv az MSZMP KB Politikai Bizottságának üléséről, 1969. február 15, Magyar Országos Levéltár Nemzeti Levéltára (MNL OL), Budapest, M-KS, 288. f., 5. cs., 484. őe.
12. Geraint Hughes, "British Policy Towards Eastern Europe and the Impact of the 'Prague Spring,' 1964–68," *Cold War History* 4, no. 2 (2004): 124–35.
13. The secretary of state to CINCPAC, July 19, 1968, National Archives and Records Administration (NARA), Washington, D.C., Record Group (RG) 59, General Records of the Department of State, Records of Ambassador Charles Bohlen 1942–1971, box 37; memorandum from Bohlen to Undersecretary of State Rostow, meeting with the French ambassador, July 23, 1968, ibid.
14. The assistant secretary of state for European affairs (Leddy) to the secretary of state, August 24, 1968, ibid.
15. Memorandum from Bohlen to the secretary of state, "Possible Soviet Attack on Austria," September 23, 1968, ibid.
16. Memorandum of conversation, August 30, 1968, participants: Rusk, Thompson, Dobrinin, ibid.
17. Contingency telegram from the Department of State to the U.S. Embassy in Bonn, July 27, 1968; the executive secretary (Benjamin Read) to Walt Rostow, July 27, 1968, ibid.
18. Robert Dallek, *Nixon and Kissinger: Partners in Power* (New York: HarperCollins Publishers, 2007).
19. Memorandum from William Griffith to the National Security Advisor (Kissinger) (1969), NARA, Kissinger office files, Henry A. Kissinger administrative and staff files transition, box 1.
20. Tibor Glant, *Emlékezzünk Magyarországra, 1956: Tanulmányok a magyar forradalom és szabadságharc amerikai emlékezetéről* (Budapest: Kiss József, 2008), 171–72.
21. Memorandum from Kissinger to the acting secretary of state, "Presidential Control of Policy towards Eastern Europe" (August 1969), NARA, Nixon Presidential Materials, Staff, National Security Council (NSC) files, country files, Europe, box 693.
22. Dallek, *Nixon and Kissinger,* 71, 83–85.
23. See James M. Goldgeier and Michael McFaul, *Power and Purpose: U.S. Policy toward Russia after the Cold War* (Washington, D.C.: Brookings Institution Press, 2003), 5–7.
24. Memorandum for the president, "Improving Relations with Romania," July 15, 1969, NARA, Nixon Presidential Materials, Staff, country files, Europe, box 702.
25. National Intelligence estimates (NIE) 11–69, "Tendencies in Current Soviet Policy," February 27, 1969, in U.S. Department of State, *Foreign Relations of the United States, 1969–1970,* vol. 12 (Washington, D.C.: Government Printing Office).
26. Memorandum from the President's assistant for the National Security Council to Nixon, February 18, 1969, in ibid., 50–51.
27. Paper prepared for the NSC by the Interdepartmental Group, February 18, 1969, in ibid., 52–63.
28. Memorandum from Sonnenfeldt to Kissinger, "U.S.-Soviet Diplomacy on European Security," January 8, 1970, in ibid., 352–54.
29. National Security Study Memorandum (NSSM) 35, February 18, 1968, in ibid.; NARA, Nixon Presidential Materials Staff, NSSM 1969–74, institutional H files, box H-133.

30. Memorandum from Sonnenfeldt to Kissinger, "A Review of U.S. Policy toward Europe," January 14, 1970, NARA, Nixon Presidential Materials Staff, NSC files, country files, Europe, box 667.

31. John N. Irwin to Martin J. Hillenbrand, Willis C. Armstrong, "PARA Review on Eastern Europe" (1972), NARA, RG 59, General Records of the Department of State, Executive Secretariat Briefing Books 1958–1976, lot file 72D317, box 131.

32. PARA review, Eastern Europe, March 31, 1972, ibid.

33. Vojtech Mastny, "The Warsaw Pact as History," in *A Cardboard Castle? An Inside History of the Warsaw Pact*, ed. Vojtech Mastny and Malcolm Byrne (Budapest: Central European University Press, 2005), 40.

34. Introductory call, Szabó Károly and Nixon, NARA, RG 59, General Records of the Department of State, box 2353.

35. Memorandum of conversation, U.S.-Hungarian relations, participants: Alfred Puhan, András Pogány, Zoltán Béky, László Irinyi, István Gereben, Tibor Eckhardt, József Hám, József Kővágó, Nicholas Nyárády, John R. Vought, and Robert B. Morley, June 23, 1971, NARA, RG 59, General Records of the Department of State, central policy files, political and defense, box 2353.

36. A Külügyminisztérium feljegyzése James Keogh-al folytatott megbeszélésről [Memorandum of conversation with James Keogh], undated, MNL OL, Küm, XIX-J-1-j, USA tük, 16. doboz, 13-00361/4/1870.

37. Szabó Károly nagykövet számjeltávirata a Külügyminisztériumnak [Ambassador Szabó's telegram], December 9, 1971, MNL OL, Küm XIX-J-1-j, USA tük, sz. n.

38. Memorandum of conversation, Szabó, Hillenbrand, Wilgis, October 26, 1971, NARA, RG 59, General Records of the Department of State, central policy files, political and defense, box 2353.

39. J. Campbellnek, az Egyesült Államok Külügyi Tanácsa tagjának megbeszélése Bényi Józseffel [Conversation by Foreign Relations Council member Campbell with Bényi], January 30, 1976, MNL OL, Küm, XIX-J-1-j, USA tük, 17. doboz. 1–001118–1976.

40. Memorandum from Helmut Sonnenfeldt to General Haig, "Secretary Volpe and the Anniversary of the Hungarian Revolution," May 19, 1971, NARA, Nixon Presidential Materials, Staff, country files, Europe, box 667.

41. William Rogers to John Volpe, July 5, 1971, NARA, RG 59, General Records of the Department of State, central policy files, political and defense, box 2353.

42. Alan P. Dobson, *US Economic Statecraft for Survival 1933–1991: Of Sanctions, Embargoes, and Economic Warfare* (New York: Routledge, 2002), 186.

43. Dallek, *Nixon and Kissinger*, 215.

44. National Security Study Memorandum 35, "U.S. Trade toward Communist Countries," March 28, 1969, NARA, Nixon Presidential Materials, institutional H files 1969–1974, box H-133.

45. Memorandum for the president by acting secretary of commerce (Rocco Siciliano), May 14, 1969, ibid., box 142; memorandum for the president, Office of Special Trade Representative for Trade Negotiations, Executive Office, May 1969; memorandum for the president by the secretary of agriculture, May 15, 1969; memorandum from the secretary of labor to the president, May 15, 1969, ibid., box H-133.

46. NSSM 35, May 12, 1969, NSSM 35, "U.S. Trade toward Communist Countries," March 28, 1969, NARA, Nixon Presidential Materials, institutional H files 1969–1974, box H-133.

47. Memorandum from the secretary of treasury to the president, May 14, 1969, ibid.; memorandum for the president, Office of Emergency Preparedness, May 14, 1969, ibid.

48. Memorandum from the acting secretary of state to the president, May 14, 1969, ibid.

49. Memorandum from the United States Information Agency (USIA) to the president, May 14, 1969, ibid.

50. Memorandum from the secretary of defense (Laird) to the president, May 15, 1969, ibid; memorandum by the Atomic Energy Commission, May 15, 1969, ibid.

51. Action resulting from the NSC meeting on East-West Trade, May 21, 1969, NARA, Nixon Presidential Materials, Staff, National Security Council institutional files, policy papers, National Security Decision Memorandums (NSDMs) 1969–1974, box H-210; NSDM 15, May 28, 1969, ibid.

52. Memorandum from Sonnenfeldt to Kissinger, May 1969, in U.S. Department of State, *Foreign Relations of the United States, 1969–1970*, vol. 12 (Washington, D.C.: Government Printing Office, 2006), 160.

53. Memorandum from the secretary of commerce (Stans) to Kissinger, October 31, 1969, NARA, Nixon Presidential Materials, Staff, National Security Council institutional files, policy papers, NSDMs, box H-210; memorandum from William E. Timmons to Bergsten, 1970, ibid.

54. Memorandum from Kissinger to the deputy secretary of defense, October 20, 1969, NARA, Nixon Presidential Materials Staff, country files, Europe, box 693; memorandum from Kissinger to the president, October 1969, ibid.

55. Memorandum from the NSC (Phil Odeem, Sonnenfeldt) to Kissinger, January 5, 1972, ibid., box 702.

56. Memorandum from the secretary of state (Rogers) to the president, January 26, 1970, NARA, Nixon Presidential Materials, Staff, National Security Council institutional files, policy papers, NSDMs, box H-210; memorandum from Fred Bergsten to Kissinger, April 15, 1970, ibid.

57. Memorandum from the secretary of commerce to Nixon, September 26, 1970, ibid; memorandum from the secretary of commerce to the president, October 1970, ibid; memorandum from Schultz to Kissinger, October 14, 1970, ibid.; memorandum from the chairman, Economic Advisors (McCracken) to Bergsten, October 13, 1970, ibid; memorandum from Flanagan to Bergsten, October 18, 1970, ibid.

58. Memorandum from the Department of Commerce (Siciliano) to Kissinger, January 7, 1971, ibid.

59. Memorandum of conversation, participants: Nixon, Stans, Rogers, Haig, November 15, 1971, in U.S. Department of State, *Foreign Relations of the United States, 1971–1972*, vol. 14 (Washington, D.C.: Government Printing Office, 2006).

60. Memorandum from the secretary of state (Rogers) to the president, October 22, 1970, NARA, Nixon Presidential Materials, Staff, National Security Council institutional files, policy papers, NSDMs, box H-210.

61. Memorandum from the secretary of defense (Laird) to the president, November 26, 1970, ibid.: "By financing some of their needed exports we would help the present governments cope with pressing economic problems and close more quickly the technological gap with the US [...] Unlikely that short-term relief of internal economic problems will lead hostile communist powers to modify their international relations in our favor. On contrary, it seems that relaxation of East-West tensions depends on the liberalization of the political and economic orders of the hard-core communist powers. Such liberalization is more likely to come from the existence of internal economic pressures than from their elimination."

62. Memorandum from Bergsten to Kissinger, December 3, 1970, ibid.; memorandum from Bergsten to Kissinger, January 8, 1971, ibid.

63. Memorandum from Kissinger to the president, February 9, 1971, ibid.

64. NSDM 99, March 1, 1971, ibid.
65. Memorandum of conversation, Nixon, Stans, Rogers, Haig, November 15, 1971, ibid.
66. Dobson, *US Economic Statecraft for Survival 1933–1991*, 182.
67. Memorandum from Kissinger to the president (1970), "Exploitation of Tension in the Soviet Union and Eastern Europe" with attached CIA paper, in U.S. Department of State, *Foreign Relations of the United States, 1969–1970*, vol. 12 (Washington, D.C.: Government Printing Office, 2006), 455–60.
68. Memorandum from the director of the CIA (Helms) to the president, "Tensions within the Soviet Union and Eastern Europe: Challenge and Opportunity," May 13, 1970, ibid., 482.
69. Memorandum from Kissinger for the secretary of state, "Expansion of Scientific and Technological Exchanges with Eastern Europe," December 1969, memorandum from Rogers for the president, December 24, 1969, NARA, Nixon Presidential Materials, Staff, country files, Europe, box 667.
70. Memorandum from Flanagan to Kissinger, November 23, 1971, NARA, Nixon Presidential Materials, Staff, National Security Council institutional files, policy papers, NSDMs, box H-210; memorandum from Sonnenfeldt to Kissinger, meeting with Ambassador Stoessel, September 19, 1970, NARA, Nixon Presidential Materials, Staff, country files, Europe, box 693.
71. PARA review, Eastern Europe, March 31, 1972, NARA, RG 59, General Records of the Department of State, Executive Secretariat, briefing books 1958–1976, lot file 72D317, box 131.
72. State Department briefing paper, Romania (1972), NARA, RG 59, General Records of the Department of State, briefing books 1958–1976, lot files 72D317, box 131.
73. Memorandum from Sonnenfeldt to Kissinger regarding the President's conversation with Ambassador Bogdan, July 12, 1969, NARA, Nixon Presidential Materials, Staff, country files, Europe, box 702.
74. PARA review, Albania, Bulgaria, Romania, April 28, 1972, NARA, General Records of the Department of State, Executive Secretariat, briefing books 1958–1976, lot file 72D317, box 131.
75. Memorandum of conversation, Secretary of State Rogers, Ambassador Bogdan, February 20, 1969, NARA, Nixon Presidential Materials, Staff, country files, Europe, box 702.
76. Joseph F. Harrington and Bruce J. Courtney, *Tweaking the Nose of the Russians: Fifty Years of American-Romanian Relations, 1940–1990*, East European Monographs no. 296 (Boulder, Colo.: East European Monographs, 1991), 285–89.
77. Dallek, *Nixon and Kissinger*, 146.
78. Memorandum for Kissinger, Ambassador Meeker's conversation with Bodnaras, July 4, 1970, in Dallek, *Nixon and Kissinger*, 147; in Harrington and Courtney, *Tweaking the Nose of the Russians*, Emil Bodnaras stated, "Signifies an end to the spheres of influence approach by the US and the USSR which those powers had followed since Yalta. Signified a new status for Romania, a position of national independence for Romania as a country not under the influence of any power."
79. Memorandum from Kissinger to John P. Walsh, acting executive secretary, July 19, 1969, NARA, Nixon Presidential Materials, Staff, country files, Europe, box 702.
80. Memorandum from Frank Shakespeare to Kissinger, "Romanian Roadblock for Establishing US Cultural Center in Bucharest," March 13, 1970, ibid; memorandum from Theodore Eliot, executive secretary, to Kissinger, April 16, 1970, ibid.
81. "Message by Ceaususcu to Nixon as Read by Vasile Pungan" (1970), ibid.
82. Memorandum of conversation, Oval Office, October 26, 1970, participants: Nix-

on, Kissinger, Henry Barnes, Ceaușescu, Celac, and Popescu, ibid.

83. Harrington and Courtney, *Tweaking the Nose of the Russians*, 313–16; memorandum from Kissinger to Nixon, "Secretary Rogers' Conversation with Romania Foreign Minister Manescu," June 12, 1970, NARA, Nixon Presidential Materials, Staff, country files, Europe, box 702; memorandum from Kissinger to Nixon, July 7, 1970, ibid.; memorandum from Kissinger to Rogers, Stans, December 8, 1971, ibid.; memorandum from Sonnenfeldt and Hormats to Kissinger, November 30, 1971, ibid.

84. Harrington and Courtney, *Tweaking the Nose of the Russians*, 318–19.

85. Memorandum from Sonnenfeldt to Kissinger, August 4, 1971, NARA, Nixon Presidential Materials, Staff, country files, Europe, box 702.

86. Memorandum of conversation, August 31, 1971, participants: Kissinger, Bogdan, ibid.

87. PARA Review, Eastern Europe, March 31, 1972, ibid.

88. Memorandum from Sonnenfeldt to Nixon, January 21, 1969, ibid., box 667; memorandum from Kissinger to the president, March 1969, ibid.

89. Memorandum from Kissinger to DuBridge, June 22, 1970, ibid.

90. Memorandum from Kissinger to Nixon, August 7, 1967, ibid.; memorandum from Kissinger to the secretary of state, August 16, 1969; memorandum for Kissinger and Don Lesh, August 28, 1969, ibid.; memorandum from Kissinger to the president, September 6, 1969, ibid.

91. PARA Review, Eastern Europe, March 31, 1972, ibid.: "Hungary in pursuing its own interest is also serving US interest."

92. The American Embassy in Budapest to the secretary of state, "U.S.-Hungarian Relations in Light of Hungarian Party Congress," December 11, 1970, NARA, RG 59, General Records of the Department of State, subject numeric file 1970–1973, box 2352.

93. The American Embassy in Budapest to the secretary of state, "Policy Assessment: Hungary," January 10, 1969, NARA, RG 59, General Records of the Department of State, central file 1969–1969, box 2183.

94. The American Embassy in Hungary to the Department of State (Meehan), conversation with Nyers, May 25, 1969, NARA, RG 59, Records of the Department of State, central files 1970–73, box 2183.

95. Fekete János feljegyzése Nagy János külügyminiszter-helyettes számára, 1975. január 23. MNL OL, Küm, XIX-J-1-j, USA tük, 28. doboz. 528.00/081-1975.

96. János M. Rainer, "The Sixties in Hungary: Some Historical and Political Approaches," in *Muddling Through the Long 1960s: Ideas and Everyday Life in High Politics and the Lower Classes of Communist Hungary*, ed. M. János Rainer and György Peteri, Trondheim Studies on East European Cultures and Societies (Budapest: Institute for the History of the 1956 Hungarian Revolution, 2005), 16.

97. Kulturális Kapcsolatok Intézete, Belső terv [Institute of Cultural Relations, internal plan], USA (1968), MNL OL, Küm, XIX-J-1-j, USA tük, 10. doboz, 001149/3-1968.

98. Memorandum from Rogers to the president, "Expansion of Cultural Exchanges," December 24, 1969, NARA, Nixon Presidential Materials, Staff, country files, Europe, box 667: Science and technology exchanges "are useful tradeoff against cultural exchanges, in which we have a greater interest than the East Europeans."

99. Csaba Békés, "A Kádári külpolitika 1956–1968: Látványos sikerek – 'láthatatlan' konfliktusok," in *Európából Európába: Magyarország konfliktusok kereszttüzében, 1945–1990*, ed. Csaba Békés (Budapest: Gondolat, 2004), 247.

100. Vladislav Zubok, *A Failed Empire: The Soviet Union in the Cold War from Stalin*

to Gorbachev (Chapel Hill: University of North Carolina Press, 2007), 220.

101. Tervezet – Előterjesztés az Ügyvezető Elnökség részére a Ford-ösztöndíjprogram tapasztalatairól [Draft recommendation for the presidium on the Ford Scholarship], September 30, 1967, MNL OL, Kulturális Kapcsolatok Intézete (KKI), XIX-A-33-a-USA, 217. doboz, 6022-1968.

102. Memorandum of conversation, participants: Nagy, Lisle, October 15, 1968, NARA, RG 59, General Records of the Department of State, central file 1967–1969, box 2183: "Ambassador has superior command of English and handles himself as a professional."

103. Memorandum from Robert King to Zbigniew Brzezinski, June 22, 1978, Jimmy Carter Presidential Library, Carter Presidential Papers, Staff Officers National Security Council, Brzezinski material, country file, Hungary.

104. Memorandum of conversation, participants: Nagy, Leddy, October 17, 1968, NARA, RG 59, General Records of the Department of State, central file 1967–1969, box 2183. The Department of State to the American Embassy in Hungary, December 23, 1969: Hungarians "have a penchant for seeking unwarranted one-sided concessions from the US and persistent failure to grasp opportunities for taking concrete steps to improve atmosphere of bilateral relations." Ibid.

105. Jegyzőkönyv az MSZMP KB Politikai Bizottságának üléséről [Record of Politburo meeting], February 15, 1969, MNL OL, M-KS 288. f., 5. cs., 484. őe.

106. Értékelés Nixon budapesti látogatásáról [Evaluation of Nixon's visit], MNL OL, Küm, XIX-J-1-j, USA tük, 11. doboz, 4-13-001366/21-1969.

107. Richard Gough, *The Good Comrade: János Kádár, Communism and Hungary* (London: I. B. Tauris, 2006), 161.

108. Lásd Jegyzőkönyv a Politikai Bizottság 1969. április 9.-én tartott üléséről [Record of Politburo meeting], April 9, 1969, MNL OL, M-KS, 288. f., 5. cs., 487. őe; Előterjesztés az MSZMP KB Politikai Bizottságának [Recommendation for the Politburo], March 31, 1969, MNL OL, M-KS, 288. f., 32. cs., 1. őe; A Magyar Forradalmi Munkás-Paraszt Kormány Határozata a Magyar Népköztársaság és az Amerikai Egyesült Államok államközi kapcsolatairól [Government resolution on U.S.-Hungarian relations], April 24, 1969, MNL OL, Küm, XIX-J-1-j, USA tük, 4-1-0069/10-1969.

109. Józan Sándor konzultációja a Szovjetunió Külügyminisztériumában [Józan's Consultations in the Soviet Foreign Ministry], July 16–19, 1969, MNL OL, Küm, XIX-J-1-j, USA tük, 10. doboz, 00361/29-1969.

110. Memorandum of conversation, Nagy's introductory call, March 14, 1969, NARA, RG 59, General Records of the Department of State, central file 1967–1969, box 2183.

111. Szilágyi Béla megbeszélése Meehan ügyvivővel [Szilágyi's consultation with Meehan], March 7, 1969, MNL OL, Küm, XIX-J-1-j, USA tük, 10. doboz, 1-00361/9-1969.

112. The American Embassy in Hungary to the Department of State, April 11, 1969, NARA, RG 59, General Records of the Department of State, central file 1967–1969, box 2183.

113. Feljegyzés a magyar-amerikai vagyonjogi tárgyalások taktikai elgondolásairól, 1969. május 13, MNL OL, Küm, XIX-J-1-j, USA tük, 12. doboz, 4-52-002660-1969.

114. Alfred Puhan amerikai nagykövet bemutatkozó látogatása Szilágyi Béla külügyminiszter-helyettesnél [Introductory call by Puhan], June 26, 1969, ibid.

115. Javaslat az amerikai-magyar megbeszélésekhez [Recommendations for U.S.-Hungarian talks], July 9, 1969, ibid.

116. Bartha János feljegyzése Puhan nagykövettel folytatott beszélgetéséről [Re-

cord of conversation, Bartha, Puhan], July 26, 1969, ibid. 10. doboz, 1-00361/24-1969.

117. Feljegyzés a magyar-amerikai kapcsolatokról [Memorandum of U.S.-Hungarian talks], December 2, 1969, ibid.

118. Memorandum by Sonnenfeldt, August 1969, NARA, Nixon Presidential Materials, Staff, country files, box 667; memorandum from Kissinger to the acting secretary of state (August 1969), ibid., box 693; memorandum from Al Haig to Bergsten, July 4, 1969, ibid., box 667; memorandum from Bergsten to Kissinger, July 9, 1969, ibid.

119. Kieninger, "Transformation versus Status Quo," 111.

120. Margit Balogh, *Mindszenty József 1892–1975* (Budapest: Elektra Kiadóház, 2002), 311–12.

121. The American Embassy in Vienna to the Department of State, "Koenig on the Hungarian Church," July 8, 1969, NARA, RG 59, General Records of the Department of State, central file 1967–1969, box 2182.

122. Martin J. Hillenbrand, *Fragments of Our Time: Memoirs of a Diplomat* (Athens: University of Georgia Press, 1998), 256–58.

123. Feljegyzés a július 4.-i fogadásról [Memorandum on July 4 reception], July 7, 1969, MNL OL, Küm, XIX-J-1-j, USA tük, 10. doboz, 1-00361/20-1969.

124. Alfred Puhan, *The Cardinal in the Chancery and Other Recollections* (New York: Vantage Press, 1990), 191.

125. Nagy János washingtoni nagykövet beszélgetése Puhan amerikai nagykövettel [Nagy's conversation with Puhan], July 12, 1969, MNL OL, Küm, XIX-J-1-j, USA tük, 10. doboz, 1-00361/31.

126. Jegyzőkönyv az MSZMP KB Politikai Bizottságának üléséről [Record of Politburo meeting], September 1, 1969, MNL OL, KS 288. f., 5. cs., 498. őe.

127. Bartha megbeszélése Puhannal [Bartha's Conversation with Puhan], October 9, 1969, MNL OL, Küm, XIX-J-1-j, USA tük, 10. doboz, 1-00361/34-1969; Puhan, *The Cardinal in the Chancery*, 177–78.

128. Jelentés az MSZMP KB Politiki Bizottságának és a Kormánynak a Szovjetunióban tett külügyminiszteri látogatásról [Report on the foreign minister's visit to the USSR], December 12, 1969, MNL OL, M-KS 288. f., 5. cs., 18. őe.

129. Memorandum for Kissinger, June 2, 1969, NARA, Nixon Presidential Materials, Staff, country files, box 667.

130. Memorandum from Theodore C. Eliot, executive secretary, to Hillenbrand, September 13, 1969, NARA, RG 59, General Records of the Department of State, central policy files 1967–1969, political and defense, box 2183.

131. The secretary of state to the American Embassy, September 20, 1969, NARA, Nixon Presidential Materials, Staff, country files, box 667.

132. Telegram from Puhan to the Department of State, September 29, 1969, NARA, RG 59, General Records of the Department of State, central foreign policy files 1967–1969, political and defense, box 2183.

133. Telegram by Puhan to the acting secretary of state, September 23, 1969, NARA, Nixon Presidential Materials, Staff, country files, Europe, box 667.

134. NARA, RG 59, General Records of the Department of State, central policy files, 1970–1973, box 2353.

135. Memorandum from Sonnenfeldt to Kissinger, "Appointment with the President for Alfred Puhan," March 3, 1970, NARA, Nixon Presidential Materials, Staff, country files, box 667.

136. The American Embassy in Hungary to the secretary of state, March 6, 1970, NARA, RG 59, General Records of the Department of State, central policy files, 1970–1973, box 2353.

137. Jegyzőkönyv az MSZMP KB Titkárságának 1970. július 6-án megtartott üléséről [Record of the July 6 meeting of

the HSWP CC Secretariat], MNL OL, M-KS 288. f. 5. cs., 357. őe.

138. Puhan to the Department of State, "Hungary One Year After," July 21, 1970, NARA, RG 59, General Records of the Department of State, central foreign policy files 1967–1969, political and defense, box 2183.

139. The American Embassy in Budapest to the Department of State, "Impact of the Youth and US National Interest," February 9, 1971, NARA, RG 59, General Records of the Department of State, subject numeric file 1970–1973, box 2353.

140. Department of State Action Memorandum, Hillenbrand to the secretary of state, July 27, 1970, NARA, RG 59, General Records of the Department of State, central policy files, 1970–1973, box 2353; Puhan to Rogers, July 13, 1970, ibid.

141. Telegram from Rogers to Puhan, July 28, 1970, NARA, RG 59, General Records of the Department of State, central policy files, 1970–1973, box 2353.

142. János Nagy, interview with the author, 2009.

143. On the rise of the left within the party, see Tibor Huszár, *Kádár János politikai életrajza 1957. november–1989. június* (Budapest: Kossuth Kiadó, 2003), 233–56.

144. Péter János külügyminiszter megbeszélése az amerikai nagykövettel [Foreign minister Péter's discussion with the American ambassador], May 13, 1971, MNL OL, Küm, XIX-J-1-j, USA tük, 17. doboz, 4-14/00700/9-1971.

145. The American Embassy in Budapest to the secretary of state, "U.S.-Hungarian Relations in Light of Hungarian Party Congress," December 2, 1970, NARA, RG 59, General Records of the Department of State, central policy files, 1970–1973, box 2353.

146. The American Embassy in Hungary to the Department of State, "Policy Assessment of Hungary 1970," January 15, 1971, NARA, RG 59, General Records of the Department of State, central policy files 1970–1973, box 2353.

147. Memorandum from Bergsten to Kissinger, February 8, 1971, NARA, Nixon Presidential Materials, Staff, country files, box 667.

148. Feljegyzés Richard T. Davies külügyi államtitkár-helyettes magyarországi látogatásáról [Memorandum, visit by deputy assistant secretary of state Richard T. Davis], March 9, 1971, MNL OL, Küm, XIX-J-1-j, USA tük, 16. doboz, 4-13-001480/3-1971.

149. Nagy János számjeltávirata, April 6, 1971, MNL OL, Küm, XIX-J-1-j, szjt 3242.

150. Memorandum by Deputy Assistant Secretary Davies on meeting with Nagy, April 6, 1971, NARA, RG 59, General Records of the Department of State, central policy files 1970–1973, box 2353.

151. Jegyzőkönyv a Politikai Bizottság üléséről [Record of Politburo meeting], July 13, 1971, MNL OL, M-KS 288. f., 5. cs., 558. őe.

152. Davis's impressions were correct. The Foreign Ministry's memorandum revealed that because of the "aggressive turn" in Nixon's foreign policy "the difficult questions" were brought to the forefront.

153. Péter János külügyminiszter megbeszélése Puhan nagykövettel [Foreign Minister Péter's conversation with Puhan], May 13, 1971, MNL OL, Küm, XIX-J-1-j, USA tük, 17. doboz, 4-14/00700/9-1971; the American Embassy in Hungary to the secretary of state, meeting with Péter, May 14, 1971, NARA, RG 59, General Records of the Department of State, central policy files 1970–1973, box 2353. See also Puhan, *The Cardinal in the Chancery*, 198.

154. Ibid.

155. Zubok, *A Failed Empire*, 216.

156. The American Embassy in Hungary to the secretary of state, July 21, 1971, NARA, RG 59, General Records of the Department of State, central policy files 1970–73, box 2353.

157. For documents relating to Mindszenty's departure see NARA, Nixon Presidential Materials, Staff, country files, Europe, box 693. For documents relating to 1971 see Ádám Somorjai, ed., *Mindszenty bíboros az amerikai nagykövetségen* (Budapest: Magyar Egyháztörténeti Enciklopédia Munkaközössége [METEM], 2008), 5–368.

158. Mindszenty letter to Nixon, NARA, Nixon Presidential Materials, Staff, country files, Europe, box 693; Somorjai, *Mindszenty bíboros az amerikai nagykövetségen*.

159. On complications regarding the departure, see Puhan, *The Cardinal in the Chancery*, 205–15.

160. Jegyzőkönyv Fock Jenő és Nyers Rezső megbeszéléséről Cannon és Moss amerikai szenátorokkal [Record of conversation by Jenő Fock and Rezső Nyers with Senators Moss and Cannon], April 28, 1973, MNL OL, Küm, XIX-J-1-j, USA tük, 17. doboz, 134-002570/5-1973.

161. Memorandum of Conversation, October 14, 1971, participants: Péter, Szabó, Rogers, and Davies, NARA, RG 59, General Records of the Department of State, central policy files 1970–1973, box 2353.

8. NIXON, CARTER, AND THE KÁDÁR REGIME

1. Vladislav Zubok, *A Failed Empire: The Soviet Union in the Cold War from Stalin to Gorbachev* (Chapel Hill: University of North Carolina Press, 2007), 216.

2. Szabó Károly számjeltávirata a Külügyminisztériumnak [Szabó's telegram to the Foreign Ministry], October 22, 1971, Magyar Nemzeti Levéltár Országos Levéltára (MNL OL), Budapest, Külügyminisztérium (Küm), XIX-J-1-j, USA tük, szjt 8675; introductory call, Nixon-Szabó, National Archives and Records Administration (NARA), Washington, D.C., Record Group (RG) 59, General Records of the Department of State, box 2353.

3. A New York-i képviselet számjeltávirata a külügyminiszternek [The mission in New York to the Foreign Ministry], October 15, 1971, MNL OL, Budapest, Külügyminisztérium (Küm), XIX-J-1-j, USA tük, szjt 9462.

4. Az amerikai referatúra feljegyzése [Memorandum by the American desk], December 16, 1971, MNL OL, Küm XIX-J-1-j, USA tük, 17. doboz, 146-002766/3-1971.

5. Jegyzőkönyv a Politikai Bizottság 1971. december 28-án megtartott üléséről [Record of Politburo meeting, December 28, 1971], MNL OL, M-KS 288. f., 5. cs., 571. őe.

6. Memorandum from Sonnenfeldt to Kissinger, U.S.-Polish relations, September 19, 1970, NARA, Washington, D.C., Nixon Presidential Materials, Staff, country files, Europe, box 693.

7. Szabó Károly számjeltávirata a Külügyminisztériumnak [Szabó's telegram to the Foreign Ministry], December 2, 1971, MNL OL, Küm, XIX-J-1-j, USA tük, szjt 10044.

8. Szabó számjeltávirata a Külügyminisztériumnak [Szabó's telegram], November 17, 1971, ibid., szjt 10610.

9. Memorandum from Alexander Haig to Chuck Holson, January 25, 1972, NARA, Nixon Presidential Materials, Staff, country files, Europe, box 693; memorandum from Chuck Holson to Al Haig, January 12, 1972, ibid.

10. Memorandum of conversation, October 26, 1971, participants: Szabó, Hillenbrand, Wilgis, NARA, Record Group (RG) 59, General Records of the Department of State, central policy files 1970–1973, box 2353.

11. Szabó Károly számjeltávirata a Külügyminisztériumnak [Szabó's telegram to the Foreign Ministry], November 28, 1971, MNL OL, Küm, XIX-J-1-j, USA tük, szjt 9879.

12. Szabó Károly számjeltávirata a Külügyminisztériumnak [Szabó's telegram],

December 9, 1971, MNL OL, Küm, XIX-J-1-j, USA tük, szjt. 11369.

13. Memorandum of conversation, October 29, 1971, participants: Szabó Károly, Alexis U. Johnson, John A. Baker, NARA, RG 59, General Records of the Department of State, central policy files 1970–1973, box 2353.

14. Szabó Károly számjeltávirata a Külügyminisztériumnak [Szabó's telegram to the Foreign Ministry], November 1 1971, MNL OL, Küm, XIX-J-1-j, USA tük, szjt. 10019.

15. Bartha János távirata a washingtoni nagykövetségnek [Bartha to the embassy in Washington], January 8, 1972, MNL OL, Küm, XIX-J-1-j, USA tük, 17. doboz, 4-14/00700/261-1971.

16. The speech is cited in a Foreign Ministry memorandum, April 20, 1976, MNL OL, Küm, XIX-J-1-j, USA tük, 18. doboz, 1-2878/1976.

17. Kenneth Rush is cited by assistant secretary of state for European affairs William Luers at a hearing of the Congress Foreign Affairs Committee's Subcommittee for European and Middle East Affairs, "Eastern Europe, An Overview," September 7, 1978. The speech was forwarded to the Foreign Ministry in Budapest, MNL OL, Küm, XIX-J-1-j, USA tük, 23. doboz, 1-005139/1978.

18. Memorandum for the president by William Rogers, April 19, 1972, NARA, General Records of the Department of State, Executive Secretariat, lot file 74D416, box 164/A.

19. Briefing Book 1972, Eastern Europe, NARA, General Records of the Department of State, Executive Secretariat, lot files 72D303, box 98.

20. Robert Dallek, *Nixon and Kissinger: Partners in Power* (New York: HarperCollins Publishers, 2007), 371–73.

21. Memorandum of conversation, participants: Nixon, Manescu, March 21, 1972,
NARA, Nixon Presidential Materials, Staff, country files, Europe, box 702.

22. Memorandum from Sonnenfeldt to Nixon, April 19, 1972, NARA, Nixon Presidential Materials, Staff, country files, Europe, box 693; memorandum from Kissinger to Dwight Chapin, undated, ibid.

23. Memorandum of conversation, Nixon, Kissinger, Rogers, Jablonski, Olszowski, Trampynczki, Hillenbrand, Stoessel, Mosbacher, June 1, 1972, ibid; memorandum of conversation, participants: Nixon, Gierek, June 1, 1972, ibid.

24. The American Embassy in Budapest to the secretary of state, January 11, 1972, NARA, RG 59, General Records of the Department of State, central policy files 1970–1973, box 2353; the American Embassy in Budapest to the secretary of state, March 17, 1972, ibid.

25. Memorandum of conversation with Bartha, the American Embassy in Budapest to the secretary of state, NARA, RG 59, General Records of the Department of State, central policy files 1970–1973, box 2353.

26. MNL OL, Küm, XIX-J-1-j, USA tük, IV-135, 002680.

27. MNL OL, Küm, XIX-J-1-j, Szovjetunió tük, 144, 95. doboz, 002830/1972.

28. State Department briefing books, 1972, Hungary, NARA, General Records of the Department of State 1958–1976, lot files 72D317, box 131.

29. Jelentés a Minisztertanácsnak Rogers látogatásáról [Report to the Council of Ministers on the Rogers visit], July 12, 1972, MNL OL, Küm, XIX-J-1-j, USA tük, 12. doboz, 135-002680-1972.

30. Jelentés Kádár János és Komócsin Zoltán számára [Report for Kádár and Komócsin], July 5, 1972, MNL OL, M-KS 288. f., 5. cs., 585. őe; Aczél György feljegyzése Kádár Jánosnak [Memorandum from Aczél to Kádár], July 5, 1971, ibid.

31. Tibor Huszár, *Kádár János: Politikai életrajza volume 2 1957. november – 1989.*

június (Budapest: Szabad Tér, 2003), 238–43.

32. Feljegyzés Kádár és Rogers megbeszéléséről [Memorandum of conversation, Rogers, Kádár], July 7 1972, MNL OL, Küm, XIX-J-1-j, USA tük, 12. doboz, 135-002680/15-1972.

33. Feljegyzés Pedersen amerikai nagykövet búcsúlátogatásáról Puja Frigyes Külügyminiszternél [Ambassador Pedersen's farewell call with Foreign Minister Puja], May 27, 1975, MNL OL, Küm, XIX-J-1-j, USA tük, 25. doboz, 146-001196/1975.

34. Memorandum from Rogers to Nixon, NARA, RG 59, General Records of the Department of State, central policy files 1970–1973, box 2353.

35. Tájékoztató a magyar-amerikai bankkapcsolatokról [Information on Hungarian-American banking relations], May 30, 1988, MNL OL, Küm, XIX-J-1-j, USA tük, 16. doboz, 13-001955/5-1988.

36. A washingtoni magyar nagykövetség feljegyzése a magyar-amerikai vagyonjogi tárgyalásokról [Memorandum on U.S.-Hungarian claims talks], November 9, 1972, MNL OL, Küm, XIX-J-1-j, USA tük, 19. doboz, 528-001126/9-1972.

37. Feljegyzés a magyar-amerikai műszaki-tudományos együttműködésről [Memorandum, U.S.-Hungarian technological-scientific cooperation], June 14, 1974, MNL OL, Küm, XIX-J-1-j, USA tük, 18. doboz, 71-001897/7-1974.

38. A Gazdaságpolitikai osztály tájékoztatója a Politikai Bizottságnak a magyar-amerikai gépipari együttműködésről [Information for the Politburo, U.S.-Hungarian cooperation machine industry], July 9, 1975, MNL OL, KS, 288. f., 5. cs., 1975.

39. The American ambassador in Budapest to the secretary of state, April 23, 1974, NARA, PDF, 1974.

40. A washingtoni nagykövetség jelentése a magyar-amerikai kapcsolatokról [Information, U.S.-Hungarian relations], January 11, 1973, MNL OL, Küm, XIX-J-1-j, USA tük, 17. doboz, 4-14-00882/1-1973; a Nemzetközi Kapcsolatok Titkárságának előterjesztése a magyar-amerikai kapcsolatokról [Memorandum by the International Relations Secretariat], January 1973, ibid., 18. doboz, 511-001016-1973; A Világgazdasági Kutató Tanács tájékoztatója a Nemzetközi Gazdasági Kapcsolatok Bizottsága részére [Information by the World Economy Research Council], January 1973, ibid., 51-001817-1973.

41. Nagy János feljegyzése Vályi Péter moszkvai útjáról [Memorandum on Vályi's visit to Moscow], February 19, 1973, MNL OL, Küm, XIX-J-1-j, USA tük, 17. doboz, 4-130-00588/11-1973.

42. A Minisztertanács 3051/1973 számú határozata [Resolution 3051/1973, Council of Ministers], February 15, 1973, MNL OL, Küm, XIX-J-1-j, USA tük, 17. doboz, 130-00588/12-1973.

43. A Minisztertanács 3052/1973 számú határozata [Resolution 3052/1973, Council of Ministers], February 15, 1973, MNL OL, Küm, XIX-J-1-j, USA tük, 19. doboz, 528-00585/2-1973.

44. Memorandum from Kissinger to Dent, March 2, 1973, NARA, Nixon Presidential Materials, Staff, country files, Europe, box 667.

45. Memorandum from Sonnenfeldt to Kissinger, February 26, 1973, ibid.

46. Memorandum from Frederick B. Dent for Kissinger and Peter M. Flanigan, February 23, 1973, ibid.

47. Memorandum from Stoessel, acting chairman, Ad Hoc Group on Economic Policy toward Eastern Europe, for Kissinger and Flanigan, February 1, 1973, in U.S. Department of State, *Foreign Relations of the United States, 1973–1976*, vol. E-15, pt. 1, Documents on Eastern Europe (Washington, D.C.: Government Printing Office, 2008).

48. Memorandum from Eliot to Kissinger, March 14, 1973, ibid.

49. Senior Review Group Meeting, March 7, 1973, ibid.
50. National Security Decision Memorandum 212, May 2, 1973, ibid.
51. Memorandum from Sonnenfeldt to Kissinger, January 27, 1973, NARA, Nixon Presidential Materials, Staff, country files, Europe, box 667.
52. Memorandum for the president by Kenneth Rush, prepared meeting with the Hungarian deputy premier, March 2, 1973, NARA, RG 59, General Records of the Department of State, central policy files 1970–1973, box 2353.
53. The American ambassador in Budapest to the secretary of state, December 29, 1972, NARA, Nixon Presidential Materials, Staff, country files, Europe, box 693.
54. From the American embassy in Budapest to the secretary of state, February 11, 1973, NARA, RG 59, General Records of the Department of State, central policy files 1970–1973, box 2352.
55. Feljegyzés Vályi Péter miniszterelnök helyettes amerikai útjáról [Memorandum on Vályi's visit in the U.S.], March 22, 1973, MNL OL, Küm, XIX-J-1-j, USA tük, 17. doboz, 4-130, 00588/16/1973.
56. A Külügyminisztérium előterjesztése [Foreign Ministry memorandum], July 18, 1973, MNL OL, Küm, XIX-J-1-j, USA tük, 14-003875/9-1975.
57. Tájékoztató a magyar-amerikai bankkapcsolatokról [Memorandum on U.S.-Hungarian banking relations], MNL OL, Küm, XIX-J-1-j, USA tük, 14-003875/9-1975.
58. Memorandum from Walter J. Stoessel Jr. to the secretary, "Visit of Hungarian Deputy Premier Vályi," February 15, 1973, NARA, RG 59, General Records of the Department of State, central policy files 1970–1973, box 2352.
59. Memorandum from Kissinger to Nixon, October 14, 1972, NARA, Nixon Presidential Materials, Staff, country files, Europe, box 693; memorandum from Sonnenfeldt to Kissinger, October 13, 1972, ibid.; memorandum from acting secretary of state John N. Irwin, II to the president, September 29, 1972, NARA, RG 59, General Records of the Department of State, central policy files 1970–1973, box 2353.
60. Memorandum from Sonnenfeldt to Kissinger, July 7, 1973, NARA, Nixon Presidential Materials, Staff, country files, Europe, box 667: "This trip was never formally prepared or cleared by the White House. ... Rogers not authorized to discuss the precise scenario or substance of the U.S. position in these negotiations as these have to be cleared by the White House."
61. "Secretary Rogers' Meeting with the Czechoslovak Secretary General, Prime Minister," participants: Husak, Štrougal, Chnoupek, Rogers, Sherer, Stoessel, Bray, July 9, 1973, ibid.: "No desire to intervene in domestic affairs, each country had to decide its own tempo, no pressure from the U.S. for countries to move into a particular direction."
62. Stephan Kieninger, "Transformation versus Status Quo: The Survival of the Transformation Strategy during the Nixon Years," in *Perforating the Iron Curtain: European Détente, Transatlantic Relations, and the Cold War, 1965–1985*, ed. Poul Villaume and Odd Arne W. Westad (Copenhagen: Museum Tusculanum Press, University of Copenhagen, 2010), 108–9.
63. Előterjesztés a Minisztertanácsnak, Az európai fegyverzetcsökkentésre irányuló tárgyalások előkészítése [Preparing for force reduction talks], January 31, 1973, MNL OL, Küm, XIX-J-1-j, HCS 1973, 115. doboz.
64. The American ambassador in Brussels to the secretary of state, February 16, 1973, Nixon Presidential Materials, Staff, country files, Europe, box 67.
65. Memorandum from Sonnenfeldt to Kissinger, February 23, 1973, ibid.: "The Hungarians made it clear that they are out-

raged by the Soviet position and have even urged the West to be tough."

66. The Soviets complain "about our bad faith in not supporting the Soviet position as agreed privately," ibid; memorandum from Sonnenfeldt to Kissinger, January 17, 1973, ibid.; "The Soviets want us to agree... in private that the actual reductions areas exclude Hungary." See memorandum by Vorontsov handed to Brent Scowcroft, February 13, 1973, ibid. Moscow wanted either to exclude Hungary from the area of force reduction or to include it together with Italy.

67. The U.S. Mission NATO to the secretary of state, "UK Paper on Hungary," August 20, 1974, NARA, PDF, 1974.

68. Memorandum from executive secretary Thomas Pickering to Kissinger, "Secretary Weinberg's visit to Poland," April 11, 1973, NARA, Nixon Presidential Materials, Staff, country files, Europe, box 693.

69. Szabó Károly számjeltávirata a Külügyminisztériumnak Kenneth Rush külügyminiszter-helyettessel folytatott megbeszéléséről [Telegram by Szabó to the Foreign Ministry on conversation with Rush], March 31, 1973, MNL OL, Küm, XIX-J-1-j, USA tük, 1973 szjt 3418; Puhan to the secretary of state, "Ambassador Nagy on Rush Protest Regarding the Hungarian Role in the ICCS," NARA, Nixon Presidential Materials, Staff, country files, Europe, box 693.

70. A Külügyminisztérium jelentése az MSZMP KB Politikai Bizottságának és a Minisztertanácsnak a vietnami háború befejezéséről és ezzel kapcsolatos feladatainkról [Report on tasks related to the termination of hostilities in Vietnam], January 1973, MNL OL, M-KS, 288. f., 5. cs., 603. őe.

71. The American embassy in Budapest to the secretary of state (1974), NARA, PDF, 1974.

72. Puja Frigyes külügyminiszter feljegyzése Puhan amerikai nagykövet látogatásáról [Memorandum by Foreign Minister Puja on visit by Puhan], April 9, 1973, MNL OL, Küm, XIX-J-1-j, USA tük, 17. doboz, 116-003003-1973.

73. A washingtoni nagykövetség számjeltávirata a Külügyminisztériumnak [The embassy's report to the Foreign Ministry], April 20, 1973, MNL OL, Küm, XIX-J-1-j, USA tük, szjt. 4187.

74. A washingtoni nagykövet jelentése a magyar-amerikai viszonyról [Report on Hungarian-U.S. relations], July 5, 1973, MNL OL, Küm, XIX-J-1-j, USA tük, 17. doboz, 4-14-00882/3-1973.

75. A Külügyminisztérium V. Területi Osztályának feljegyzése Puhan nagykövet Fock Jenőnél tett látogatásáról [Memorandum, Puhan's visit with Fock], July 10, 1973, MNL OL, Küm, USA XIX-J-1-j, USA tük, 17. doboz, 116-003003/4-1973.

76. Jegyzőkönyv Fock Jenő és Nyers Rezső megbeszéléséről amerikai szenátorokkal [Memorandum, Fock, Nyers meeting with senators], May 5, 1973, MNL OL, Küm, XIX-J-1-j, USA tük, 17. doboz, 134-002570/5/1973.

77. A Kulturális Kapcsolatok Intézetének átirata [Memorandum, Institute of Cultural Relations], February 26, 1974, MNL OL, Küm, XIX-J-1-j, USA tük, 18. doboz, 71-001897/2-1974.

78. Kulturális és tudományos kapcsolataink az Egyesült Államokkal [Memorandum regarding our cultural relations with the United States], undated, MNL OL, Küm, XIX-J-1-j, USA tük, 18. doboz, 71-001897-1974.

79. Polgár Endrének, a Kulturális Kapcsolatok Intézete főosztályvezetőjének feljegyzése Bartha János külügyi főosztályvezetőnek [Memorandum from the Institute of Cultural Relations to the Foreign Ministry], May 6, 1977, MNL OL, KÜM, USA tük, XIX-J-1-j, 003048/-1977.

80. A Politikai Bizottság 1973. május 22-i határozata az imperialista propaganda ellen folytatott harc tapasztalatairól és erősítéséről [Politburo resolution on

anti-imperialist struggle], May 22, 1973, MNL OL, XIX-J-1-j, vegyes, 14. doboz, II-81-003395-1973.

81. A Kulturális Kapcsolatok Intézetének összefoglaló jelentése, "Beszámoló a tőkés országokkal folytatott kulturális és tudományos kapcsolatokról, valamint a fellazítási politika ezen a területen tapasztalt megnyilvánulásairól" [Report on cultural and scientific contacts with capitalist states and subversion in these areas], March 1973, ibid., 13. doboz, 002079/1-1973.

82. Feljegyzés Nagy János megbeszéléséről Puhan nagykövettel [Memorandum, Nagy's conversation with Puhan], January 19, 1974, MNL OL, Küm, XIX-J-1-j, USA tük, 17. doboz, 146-00464-1974; Deák's letter, ibid., 19. doboz, 72-001041/3-1974.

83. NARA, Nixon Presidential Materials Staff, country files, Europe, box 693.

84. Sonnenfeldt's letter to Zbigniew Brzezinski, October 4, 1974, NARA, RG 59, General Records of the Department of State, lot files 81D286, box 9.

85. Brzezinski's Letter to Sonnenfeldt, September 11, 1971, ibid.; Titus, Department of State East European Affairs, to Brzezinski, July 16, 1974, ibid.: "We should ... do all we can to keep the channels open."

86. Feljegyzés Dachy kulturális attasé látogatásáról [Dachy's visit], January 26, 1974, MNL OL, Küm, XIX-J-1-j, USA tük, 19. doboz, 72-001041/4-1974.

87. The secretary of state (Kissinger) to the American ambassador in Budapest, January 19, 1974, NARA, PDF, 1974.

88. The secretary of state to the American ambassador in Budapest, January 28, 1974, ibid.

89. The American ambassador in Budapest to the secretary of state, January 24, 1974, NARA, PDF, 1974.

90. A Kulturális Kapcsolatok Intézete elnökének átirata Nagy Jánosnak [Memorandum by the Institute of Cultural Affairs], February 8, 1974, MNL OL, Küm, XIX-J-1-j, USA tük, 19. doboz, 72-001041/5-1974.

91. The secretary of state to the American embassy in Budapest, 1974, NARA, PDF, 1974.

92. A Kulturális Kapcsolatok Intézetének átirata a Külügyminisztériumhoz [The Institute of Cultural Affairs to the Foreign Ministry], February 26, 1974, MNL OL, Küm, XIX-J-1-j, USA tük, 19. doboz, 001041/5-1974.

93. The American ambassador in Budapest to the Department of State, June 17, 1974, NARA, PDF, 1974.

94. A Nemzetközi Gazdasági Kapcsolatok titkárságának feljegyzése [Memorandum, Secretariat of International Economic Relations], January 31, 1975, MNL OL, Küm, XIX-J-1-j, USA tük, 25. doboz, 146-001196-1975.

95. Feljegyzés Pedersen búcsúlátogatásáról [Pedersen's farewell visit], March 24, 1975, ibid., 26. doboz, 146-002129/1-1975.

96. The American ambassador in Budapest to the Department of State, "Tour d'horizon, János Nagy," September 30, 1974, NARA, Department of State, PDF, 1974.

97. The American ambassador to the secretary of state, December 2, 1974, NARA, Department of State, PDF, 1974.

98. The American embassy in Budapest to the secretary of state, April 30, 1974, NARA, Department of State, PDF, 1974; the American embassy Budapest to the Department of State, "Annual US Policy Assessment, Hungary," August 8, 1974, NARA, RG 59, Department of State, P reel printouts 1974, box 85D.

99. Nagy János feljegyzése Puja Frigyes külügyminiszter-helyettes megbeszéléséről Henry Kissinger amerikai külügyminiszterrel [Memorandum of conversation with Kissinger], August 5, 1975, MNL OL, Küm, XIX-J-1-j, USA tük, 27. doboz, 144-004556-1975.

100. The American embassy in Budapest to the secretary of state, August 9, 1975, NARA, Department of State, PDF, 1975.

101. Jonathan Haslam, *Russia's Cold War: From the October Revolution to the Fall of the Wall* (New Haven, Conn.: Yale University Press, 2011), 269.

102. The American embassy in Budapest to the secretary of state, "Prepared Toast for Robert Ingersoll," August 26, 1975, NARA, Department of State, PDF, 1975.

103. A Kulturális Kapcsolatok Intézetének átirata a Külügyminisztériumnak [The Institute of Cultural Affairs to the Foreign Ministry], September 10, 1975, MNL OL, Küm, XIX-J-1-j, USA tük, 25. doboz, 146-001196/2-1975.

104. Feljegyzés Marjai József megbeszéléséről Ingersoll amerikai külügyminiszter-helyettessel [Conversation, Marjai and Ingersoll], September 17, 1975, MNL OL, Küm, XIX-J-1-j, USA tük, 27. doboz, 135-004651/11-1975; Feljegyzés Gyenes András megbeszéléséről Ingersollal [Conversation, Gyenes and Ingersoll], September 17, 1975, ibid.; Feljegyzés Puja Frigyes megbeszéléséről Ingersollal [Conversation, Puja and Ingersoll], September 18, 1975, ibid.

105. A Külügyminisztérium V. Területi Osztályának feljegyzése McAuliffe amerikai nagykövet bemutatkozó látogatásáról Kádár Jánosnál [McAuliffe's introductory visit, Kádár], December 9, 1975, MNL OL, Küm, XIX-J-1-j, USA tük, 27. doboz, 10-003036/7-1975; Puja Frigyes külügyminiszter feljegyzése McAuliffe amerikai nagykövet látogatásáról [McAuliffe introductory visit, Puja], March 15, 1976, MNL OL, Küm, XIX-J-1-j, USA tük, 27. doboz, 14-003875/11-1975.

106. Jussi Hanhimäki, *The Flawed Architect: Henry Kissinger and American Foreign Policy* (New York: Oxford University Press, 2004), 444.

107. For Sonnenfeldt's speech and the contributions, see U.S. Department of State, *Foreign Relations of the United States, 1973–1976*, vol. E-15, pt. 1, Documents on Eastern Europe (Washington, D.C.: Government Printing Office, 2008); A Külügyminisztérium V. Területi Osztályának feljegyzése a Sonnenfeldt doktrínáról [Memorandum by the Foreign Ministry on the Sonnenfeldt doctrine], April 20, 1976, MNL OL, Küm, XIX-J-1-j, USA tük, 18. doboz, 1-2878-1976.

108. Memorandum of conversation, "U.S.-Hungarian Relations," May 5, 1976, participants: Sonnenfeldt, Andrews, Gerth, and Nagy Esztergályos, NARA, RG 59, General Records of the Department of State, lot files 81D286, entry 5339, Records of the Counselor, 1955–1977, box 9.

109. A Külügyminisztérium Nemzetközi Politikai Kapcsolatok Főosztályának feljegyzése [Memorandum, international political relations of the Foreign Ministry], April 29, 1976, MNL OL, Küm, XIX-J-1-j, USA tük, 18. doboz, 1-002878/5-1976.

110. Sonnenfeldt's statement, April 12, 1976, Henry A. Kissinger to James Buckley, March 27, 1976, James Buckley to Brent Scowcroft, May 5, 1976, all in NARA, RG 59, General Records of the Department of State, lot file 81D286, box 9.

111. Memorandum from John A. Armitage to Sonnenfeldt, April 14, 1976, ibid.

112. Memorandum of conversation, April 16, 1976, participants: Mircea Malita, Corneliu Bogdan, Sonnenfeldt, James Montgomery, NARA, RG 59, General Records of the Department of State, lot files 81D286, entry 5339, Records of the Counselor, 1955–1977, box 10.

113. Memorandum of conversation, June 1, 1976, participants: Kissinger, Sonnenfeldt, Bogdan, Ionita, ibid.

114. Jimmy Carter, *White House Diary* (New York: Farrar, Straus and Giroux, 2010), 282.

115. Várkonyi József feljegyzése [Várkonyi's memorandum], January 31, 1974,

MNL OL, Küm, XIX-J-1-j, USA tük, 131-001644/2.

116. The American Embassy to the secretary of state, "Possible Presidential Visit to Hungary," June 10, 1974, NARA, Nixon Presidential Materials, Staff, country files, Europe, box 693.

117. A washingtoni nagykövetség számjeltávirata a Külügyminisztériumnak [Telegram to the Foreign Ministry], March 6, 1974, MNL OL, Küm, XIX-J-1-j, USA tük, szjt. 2616.

118. Jegyzőkönyv a Politikai Bizottság üléséről [Record of Politburo meeting], February 12, 1974, MNL OL, M-KS 288. f., 5. cs., 630. őe.

119. Az Állami Egyházügyi Hivatal átirata a Külügyminisztériumnak [The State Ecclesiastical Office to the Foreign Ministry], March 13, 1974, MNL OL, Küm, XIX-J-1-j, USA tük, 18. doboz, 28-002290-1974.

120. A washingtoni nagykövetség számjeltávirata a Külügyminisztériumnak [Telegram to the Foreign Ministry], May 21, 1974, ibid., szjt. 5946.

121. Puja Frigyes előterjesztése a Politikai Bizottságnak [Recommendation by Puja to the Foreign Ministry], May 15, 1974, ibid., 17. doboz, 14-00959/10-1974.

122. Szabó Károly nagykövet számjeltávirata a Külügyminisztériumnak [Telegram to the Foreign Ministry], May 29, 1974, ibid., MNL OL, Küm, XIX-J-1-j, USA tük, szjt. 5946.

123. A washingtoni nagykövetség számjeltávirata a Külügyminisztériumnak [Telegram to the Foreign Ministry], September 11, 1974, MNL OL, Küm, XIX-J-1-j, USA tük, szjt. 9818.

124. A Nemzetközi Gazdasági Kapcsolatok Titkárságának feljegyzése [Memorandum, Secretariat of Economic Relations], January 31, 1975, MNL OL, Küm, XIX-J-1-j, USA tük, 25. doboz, 146-001196-1975.

125. Esztergályos Ferenc beszélgetése Armitage külügyminiszter-helyettessel [Memorandum of Conversation, Esztergályos, Armitage], September 22, 1974, MNL OL, Küm, XIX-J-1-j, USA tük, szjt. 10522; A washingtoni nagykövetség számjeltávirata a Külügyminisztériumnak Kovács megbeszéléséről Andrews külügyi osztályvezetővel [Memorandum of conversation between Kovács and Andrews], September 20, 1974, ibid., szjt. 10279.

126. Nagy János megbeszélése Pedersen nagykövettel [Nagy's conversation with Pedersen], October 2, 1974, MNL OL, Küm, XIX-J-1-j, USA tük, 17. doboz, 146-00464/9-1974.

127. A washingtoni nagykövetség jelentése [Report by the embassy in Washington], October 8, 1974, MNL OL, Küm, XIX-J-1-j, USA tük, 17. doboz, 14-005323/1974.

128. The American ambassador in Budapest to the secretary of state, "Kádár's Views and U.S.-Hungarian relations," April 10, 1974, NARA, PDF, 1974.

129. Tibor Huszár, *Kádár: A hatalom évei, 1956–1989* (Budapest: Corvina, 2006), 202–45.

130. The American ambassador to the secretary of state, "Kádár Visit to USSR," October 4, 1974, NARA, Department of State, PDF, 1974.

131. The American Embassy in Budapest to the secretary of state, October 30, 1974, ibid.

132. The American ambassador in Budapest to the secretary of state, ibid.

133. The American ambassador in Budapest to the secretary of state, April 22, 1974, ibid.

134. The American ambassador to the secretary of state, February 11, 1974, ibid.

135. Hanhimäki, *The Flawed Architect*, 340–42; 379–80.

136. Robert C. Mudd to William A. Shepherd, Hungarian affairs officer, January 16, 1975, MNL OL, XXXII-17, 2. doboz.

137. A Külügyminisztérium V. Területi Osztályának jelentése kongresszusi képviselők látogatásáról [Report, visit by

congressmen], January 20, 1975, MNL OL, Küm, XIX-J-1-j, USA tük, 28. doboz, 2-00649-1975.

138. A washingtoni nagykövetség feljegyzése beszélgetésről a Magyarországon járt képviselőkkel [The Embassy's memorandum of conversation with congressmen back from Hungary], February 27, 1975, ibid., 2–00649/1–1975.

139. Presidential Guideline (1975), NARA, General Records of the Department of State, lot files 81D276, box 9.

140. Memorandum from George Springsteen to Brent Scowcroft, October 6, 1975, ibid.

141. Memorandum of conversation, May 12, 1976, participants: Kissinger, Sonnenfeldt, Hartman, Armitage, Andrews, ibid.

142. Fekete Jánosnak, az MNB alelnökének feljegyzése Nagy János külügyminiszter-helyettesnek [Memorandum by Hungarian National Bank vice president Fekete], January 23, 1975, MNL OL, Küm, XIX-J-1-j, USA tük, 28. doboz. 528-00/081-1975.

143. Szalai Béla külkereskedelmi miniszter feljegyzése Nagy János külügyminiszter-helyettesnek [Memorandum by deputy foreign trade minister Szalai], January 23, 1975, ibid.

144. Nagy János külügyminiszter-helyettes feljegyzése [Memorandum by deputy foreign minister János Nagy], February 17, 1975, ibid. 16. doboz, 131-001644/1-1974.

145. Puja Frigyes feljegyzése McAuliffe amerikai nagykövet látogatásáról [Puja's memorandum on visit by McAuliffe], March 15, 1976, MNL OL, Küm, XIX-J-1-j, USA tük, 27. doboz, 14-003875/11-1975; Nagy János feljegyzése McAuliffe látogatásáról [Nagy's memorandum on visit by McAuliffe], March 26, 1976, MNL OL, Küm, XIX-J-1-j, USA tük, 17. doboz, 1-001277/2-1976.

146. A Belügyminisztérium átirata Nagy Jánosnak [Memorandum by the Ministry of Interior], December 7, 1976, MNL OL, Küm, XIX-J-1-j, USA tük, 20. doboz, 7-0041/5-1976.

147. Szekér Gyula feljegyzése Richardson kereskedelmi miniszterrel folytatott megbeszéléséről [Szekér's memorandum on conversation with Commerce Secretary Richardson], November 30, 1976, MNL OL, Küm, XIX-J-1-j, USA tük, 571–004830/6–1976.

148. Nagy János jelentése Marjai Józsefnek [Nagy's report to Marjai], January 31, 1978, MNL OL, Küm, XIX-J-1-u-sz. n./N. J.-1978, 42. doboz.

149. For the records of the hearings, see MNL OL, Küm, XIX-J-1-j, USA tük, 19. doboz, 5-00456-1976.

150. Bartha János külügyminisztériumi főosztályvezető tájékoztatója Esztergályos Ferenc nagykövet számára [Memorandum by Bartha], February 10, 1977, MNL OL, Küm, XIX-J-1-j, USA tük, 5–00770/1–1977.

151. Szekér Gyula Puja Frigyesnek [Szekér's memorandum to Puja], February 16, 1977, MNL OL, Küm, XIX-J-1-j, USA tük, 21. doboz, 5-00770/2-1977.

152. Puja Frigyes külügyminiszter feljegyzése Szekér Gyula miniszterelnök-helyettesnek [Puja's memorandum to deputy prime minister Gyula Szekér], February 4, 1977, MNL OL, Küm, XIX-J-1-j, USA tük, 21. doboz, 5-00770/2-1977.

153. The American embassy in Budapest to the secretary of state, February 9, 1975, NARA, Records of the Department of State, PDF, 1975.

154. The American embassy in Budapest to the secretary of state, 1975, ibid.

155. Memorandum of conversation, "U.S.-Hungarian Relations," May 5, 1976, ibid.

156. On Carter's foreign policy see Campbell Craig and Frederik Logevall, *America's Cold War: The Politics of Insecurity* (Cambridge, Mass.: Belknap Press of Harvard University Press, 2009), 289–302.

157. Warren I. Cohen, *America's Response to China: A History of Sino-American Rela-*

tions (New York: Columbia University Press, 2010), 234.

158. Az MSZMP KB Külügyi Osztályának jelentése [Report by the Foreign Affairs Department of the Central Committee of the Hungarian Socialist Workers Party], June 5, 1978, MNL OL, Küm, XIX-J-1-j, USA tük, 22. doboz, 1-004038-1978.

159. A Külügyminisztérium V. Területi Osztályának feljegyzése Vas Zoltán telefonhívásáról [Memorandum of phone call by Vas], January 23, 1978, MNL OL, Küm, XIX-J-1-j, USA tük, 23. doboz, 195-00/621/9-1978.

160. Carter to Koch, May 3, 1978, Carter Presidential Library, Carter Presidential Papers, White House central file, confidential file, Hungary.

161. Memorandum from Cyrus Vance to President Carter, June 3, 1977, Carter Presidential Library, Carter Presidential Papers, Staff Offices, National Security Affairs, Brzezinski material, country file, Hungary.

162. Memorandum from Cyrus Vance to the President (1977), NARA, RG 59, Records of the Department of State, PS 40134–1856.

163. Memorandum from Robert King to Zbigniew Brzezinski, June 22, 1978, Carter Presidential Library, Carter Presidential Papers, Staff Offices, National Security Affairs, Brzezinski material, country file, Hungary.

164. Zbigniew Brzezinski, *Power and Principle. Memoirs of the National Security Advisor, 1977–1981* (New York: Farrar, Straus and Giroux, 1983), 296–98.

165. Carter, *White House Diary*, 155.

166. Craig and Logevall, *America's Cold War*, 289.

167. State Department Briefing Paper, Romania (1973), NARA, RG 59, General Records of the Department of State, lot files 81D286, entry 5339, Records of the Counselor, 1955–1977, box 131; The American Embassy to the secretary of state, December 24, 1975, NARA, Records of the Department of State, PDF, 1975.

168. Joseph F. Harrington and Bruce J. Courtney, *Tweaking the Nose of the Russians: Fifty Years of American-Romanian Relations, 1940–1990*, East European Monographs no. 296 (Boulder, Colo.: East European Monographs, 1991), 434, 440.

169. Puja Frigyes feljegyzése Szekér Gyulának [Puja's memorandum for Szekér], MNL OL, Küm, XIX-J-1-j, USA tük, 21. doboz, 5-00770/2-1977.

170. Ibid.

171. Feljegyzés Bartha János beszélgetéséről Mudd ügyvivővel [Memorandum of conversation with Mudd], April 8, 1977, ibid., 1-001002/2-1977.

172. A washingtoni nagykövetség feljegyzése, [Memorandum by the embassy in Washington], May 6, 1977, ibid., 5-007709-1977.

173. Nyerges János feljegyzése [Memorandum by Nyerges], June 28, 1977, ibid., 5-00770/13-1977.

174. Feljegyzés Puja Frigyes magyar és Cyrus Vance amerikai külügyminiszter megbeszéléséről [Memorandum of conversation, Puja, Vance], October 4, 1977, ibid., 20. doboz, 1-005285/1977.

175. Philip Kaiser amerikai nagykövet látogatása Lázár György miniszterelnöknél [Ambassador Kaiser's visit with Prime Minister Lázár], October 15, 1977, MNL OL, Küm, XIX-J-1-j, USA tük, 18. doboz, 1-004379/6-1977.

176. Tibor Glant, *A Szent Korona amerikai kalandja, 1945–1978* (Debrecen: Kossuth Egyetemi Kiadó, 1997), 66–112.

177. Letter to W. Obbagy, November 5, 1977, Carter Presidential Library, Carter Presidential Papers, White House central file, confidential file.

178. Memorandum from Stephen Larrabee to Madeleine Albright, NSC, January 23, 1979, Carter Presidential Library, Carter Presidential Papers, White House central file, confidential file.

179. Feljegyzés a State Department magyar referensének látogatásáról Barthа Jánosnál [The Hungarian desk officer's visit with Bartha], May 19, 1977, MNL OL, Küm, XIX-J-1-j, USA tük, 18. doboz, 1-00278/3-1977.
180. A Kulturális Kapcsolatok Intézetének feljegyzése [Memorandum by the Institute of Cultural Relations], June 27, 1977, MNL OL, Küm, XIX-J-1-j, USA tük, 20. doboz, 1-004077/1977.
181. Nyerges János feljegyzése [Nyerges's memorandum], MNL OL, Küm, XIX-J-1-j, USA tük, 21. doboz, 5-00770/2-1977.
182. The American ambassador to the secretary of state, December 24, 1975, NARA, Records of the Department of State, PDF, 1975.
183. Schoenfeld to the Department of State, August 21, 1946, MNL OL, XXXII-17, 3. doboz. In 1946 Prime Minister Nagy indicated that the relics should stay in U.S. custody until the stabilization of the political situation in Hungary. Memorandum, Legal Issues Concerning the Crown of St. Stephen, June 15, 1977, MNL OL, XXXII-17, 2. doboz.
184. Memorandum from Civil Affairs Division, Department of the Army to U.S. forces in Austria USFA, Office of Military Government in Germany, Berlin, September 3, 1948, MNL OL, XXXII-17, 3. doboz.
185. The Hungarian Holy Crown, memorandum drafted by A. C. Klay (1977), MNL OL, XXXII-17, 3. doboz.
186. Ibid.
187. Ibid.
188. Memorandum of conversation, March 21, 1970, participants: Varga Béla, Lady Malcolm Douglas-Hamilton, Emory C. Swank, Robert McKisson, John R. Vought, MNL OL, XXXII-17, 2. doboz.
189. Mindszenty József levele Richard Nixon amerikai elnöknek [Mindszenty's letter to Nixon], October 26, 1972, letter by acting assistant secretary of state for European affairs Russel Fessenden to Mindszenty, December 6, 1972, in MNL OL, XXXII-17, 2. doboz.
190. Memorandum from Sonnenfeldt to Haig, January 20, 1972, NARA, Nixon Presidential Materials Staff, country files, Europe, box 667.
191. Call of Hungarian Deputy Vályi on Secretary Rogers, March 6, 1973, MNL OL, XXXII-17, 2. doboz.
192. The U.S. Embassy (Pedersen) to the Department of State, November 8, 1974, MNL OL, XXXII-17, 2. doboz.
193. Glant, *A Szent Korona amerikai kalandja*, 67.
194. The American Embassy in Budapest to the secretary of state, September 1975, MNL OL, XXXII-17. 2. doboz.
195. A washingtoni nagykövetség feljegyzése [Memorandum by the embassy in Washington], September 13, 1976, MNL OL, Küm, XIX-J-1-j, USA tük, 19. doboz, 004800-1976.
196. Memorandum from secretary of state Cyrus Vance to the president on strengthening relations with Hungary (1977), MNL OL, XXXII-17, 2. doboz.
197. Charles Vanik's memorandum to Zbigniew Brzezinski, March 8, 1977, Carter Presidential Library, Carter Presidential Papers, central file, executive file, Hungary; memorandum from Brzezinski to Vanik, March 17, 1977, ibid.
198. Brzezinski, *Power and Principle*, 299.
199. Thomas Simons, statement to the author.
200. Memorandum from Vance to the president, June 3, 1977, MNL OL, XXXII-17, 2. doboz.
201. Letter to W. Obbagy, November 5, 1977: "Some allege that this action recognizes legitimacy of Communist regime in Hungary" which "overlooks fact that we have diplomatic contact on ambassadorial level." Carter Presidential Library, Carter Presidential Papers, White House confidential file, Hungary.

202. Synopsis of Patrick Kelleher, the Holy Crown of Hungary, Papers and Monographs of the American Academy in Rome, vol. XIII, Rome, 1951. The synopsis is among the Brzezinski papers and this part was marked on the margin. Carter Presidential Library, Carter Presidential Papers, Staff Offices, NSC Affairs, Brzezinski material, country file, Hungary; memorandum from William Hyland to Brzezinski, March 15, 1977, Carter Presidential Library, Carter Presidential Papers, White House central file, executive file, Hungary.

203. Carter, *White House Diary*, 132.

204. The secretary of state (Vance) to the American Embassy in Rome (Lodge), May 1977, Suggestions for conversation with Casaroli, MNL OL, XXXII-17, 2. doboz.

205. Memorandum for Brzezinski from William G. Hyland, April 29, 1977, Carter Presidential Library, Carter Presidential Papers, Staff Offices NSC Affairs, Brzezinski material, country file, Hungary.

206. Memorandum from George Vest to Tarnoff (July 1977), MNL OL, XXXII-17, 2. doboz.

207. Bartha János beszélgetése Mudd ügyvivővel [Bartha's conversation with Mudd], MNL OL, Küm, XIX-j-1-j, USA tük, 18. doboz, 1-00278-1977; Glant, *A Szent Korona amerikai kalandja*, 69.

208. A Külügyminisztérium V. Területi Osztályának feljegyzése [Memorandum by the Foreign Ministry], March 12, 1977, MNL OL, Küm, XIX-J-1-j, USA tük, 19. doboz, 10-001100/2–1977.

209. Bartha János feljegyzése beszélgetésről Mudd ügyvivővel [Bartha's memorandum of conversation with Mudd], April 8, 1977, MNL OL, Küm, XIX-J-1-j, USA tük, 19. doboz, 1-001002/2-1977.

210. Jelentés az amerikai külügyminiszter helyettessel folytatott beszélgetésről [Memorandum of conversation with deputy secretary of state], April 14, 1977, MNL OL, Küm, XIX-J-1-j, USA tük, 18. doboz, 1-00278/2-1977.

211. Glant, *A Szent Korona amerikai kalandja*, 79.

212. Feljegyzés Dachy kulturális attaséval folytatott megbeszélésről [Memorandum of conversation with Dachy], April 27, 1977, MNL OL, Küm, XIX-J-1-j, USA tük, 19. doboz, 10-001100/5-1977.

213. Miklós Imre, az Egyházügyi Hivatal Elnökének feljegyzése Mudd ügyvivővel folytatott megbeszéléséről [Memorandum of conversation, president of State Ecclesiastical Office Miklós, Mudd], February 15, 1977, MNL OL, Küm, XIX-J-1-j, USA tük, 10-001100/1-1972.

214. Memorandum by the Foreign Ministry regarding statements made by the U.S. cultural attache Stephen Dachy on the Holy Crown, April 27, 1977, MNL OL, Küm, XIX-J-1-j, USA tük, 19. doboz, 10-001100/5-1977.

215. Kaiser's telegram to Budapest, November 30, 1970, Carter Presidential Library, Carter Presidential Papers, Staff Offices, National Security Council (NSC) Affairs, Brzezinski material, country file, Hungary.

216. In 1974, when the then U.S. ambassador Richard Pedersen announced that he wished to see leaders of the Hungarian churches, the State Ecclesiastical Office briefed the bishops the ambassador was allowed to see and told them to express their desire to the ambassador that they wished the Holy Crown to be returned to Hungary. Even the formula they had to use was predetermined. The course of action was reviewed and approved by the Foreign Ministry. See memorandum from the State Office of Ecclesiastical Affairs to the Foreign Ministry, March 13, 1974, MNL OL, Küm, XIX-J-1-j, USA tük, 18. doboz, 28-002990-1974.

217. Feljegyzés Mudd látogatásáról Nagy Jánosnál [Memorandum on Mudd's visit with Nagy], April 29, 1977, MNL OL, Küm, XIX-J-1-j, USA tük, 19. doboz, 10-0011005-1977.

218. Feljegyzés Gerth látogatásáról [memorandum on Gerth's visit], May 19, 1977, MNL OL, Küm, XIX-J-1-j, USA tük, 18. doboz, 1-00278/3-1977.
219. Memorandum for Brzezinski from Robert Hunter and William G. Hyland, June 12, 1977, Carter Presidential Library, Carter Presidential Papers, Staff Offices, NSC Affairs, Brzezinski material, country file, Hungary.
220. Memorandum from Brzezinski to the president, June 14, 1977, ibid.
221. Memorandum from Brzezinski to Vance, June 15, 1977, ibid.
222. Jelentés Manfred Schülerrel, a kancellári hivatal államtitkárával folytatott megbeszélésről [Memorandum of conversation with Schüler], July 25, 1977, MNL OL, Küm, XIX-J-1-j, USA tük, 19. doboz, 10-001100/8-1977.
223. Beszélgetés Mudd ügyvivővel és Gerth magyar referenssel [Memorandum of conversation with Mudd and Gerth], July 26, 1977, MNL OL, Küm, XIX-j-1-j, USA tük, 18. doboz, 1-00278/5-1977.
224. A washingtoni nagykövetség jelentése a Külügyminisztériumnak [Report to the Foreign Ministry by the embassy in Washington], March 22, 1978, MNL OL, Küm, XIX-J-1-j, USA tük, 1–00381/1–1978.
225. Memorandum from Brzezinski to the president with Carter's handwritten note, August 3, 1977, Carter Presidential Library, Carter Presidential Papers, Staff Offices, NSC Affairs, Brzezinski material, country file, Hungary.
226. Memorandum from Vance to President Carter, July 27, 1977, MNL OL, XXXII-17, 2. doboz.
227. The State Department to the U.S. ambassador (August 3, 1977), MNL OL, XXXII-17, 2. doboz; the U.S. ambassador (Kaiser) to the secretary of state (Vance), August 3, 1977, ibid.
228. Telegram by Nimetz to the U.S. ambassador, August 17, 1977, MNL OL, XXXII-17, 2. doboz.

229. Feljegyzés Kaiser látogatásáról Nagy Jánosnál [Nagy's memorandum on Kaiser's visit], MNL OL, Küm, XIX-J-1-j, USA tük, 19. doboz, 10-001100/10-1977; Glant, *A Szent Korona amerikai kalandja*, 82.
230. Nagy János feljegyzése Kaiser látogatásáról [Nagy's memorandum on Kaiser's visit], August 26, 1977, MNL OL, Küm, XIX-J-1-j, USA tük, 19. doboz, 10-001100/11-1977; Glant, *A Szent Korona amerikai kalandja*, 83.
231. Memorandum from Vest to the deputy secretary of state through Nimetz, October 11, 1977, MNL OL, XXXII-17, 2. doboz; Glant, *A Szent Korona amerikai kalandja*, 75–76.
232. Puja és Vance találkozójáról [Vance, Puja meeting], October 4, 1977; Glant, *A Szent Korona amerikai kalandja*, 83.
233. Glant, *A Szent Korona amerikai kalandja*, 85.
234. For the letters see Carter Presidential Library, Carter Presidential Papers, Staff Offices, NSC Affairs, Brzezinski material, country file, Hungary.
235. Ibid., 105–7.
236. Carter, *White House Diary*, 153.
237. A Politikai Bizottság 1977. december 13-i jegyzőkönyve és a Külügyminiszter javaslata a Politikai Bizottságának [Record of the December 13 meeting of the Politburo; recommendation for the Politburo by the Foreign Ministry], December 9, 1977, MNL OL, 288. f., 5. cs., 733. őe.
238. János Nagy, statement to the author.
239. Memorandum by Brzezinski (January 1978), "Highlights and sidelights on the return of the Holy Crown of Saint Stephen," Carter Presidential Library, Carter Presidential Papers, Staff Offices, NSC Affairs, Brzezinski material, country file, Hungary.
240. Carter's letter to Justice Williams, January 6, 1978, Carter Presidential Library, Carter Presidential Papers, White House executive file, Hungary.

241. Carter's message to Losonczy, January 6, 1978, ibid.
242. Hungary, Political Overview, May 1980, Carter Presidential Library, Carter Presidential Papers, Staff Offices, NSC Affairs, Brzezinski material, country file, Hungary.
243. The most important aspects of the Stalinist economic model such as the soft budget constraint, the predominance of state ownership, and the centralization of finances and trade were left in place.
244. Bennett Kovrig, *Of Walls and Bridges: The United States & Eastern Europe* (New York: New York University Press, 1991), 176.
245. Nagy János jelentése a Washingtonban folytatott magyar-amerikai külügyminisztériumi konzultációról [Nagy's report on U.S.-Hungarian consultations], July 17, 1978, MNL OL, Küm, XIX-J-1-j, USA tük, 22. doboz, 1-003275/5-1978; statement by William H. Luers, deputy assistant secretary of state for European affairs, September 1978, ibid. The speech was made available to the Hungarian embassy in the United States.
246. Letter from Congressman Frenzel to Carter, September 16, 1977, Carter Presidential Library, Carter Presidential Papers, White House executive file, Hungary.
247. Cohen, *America's Response to China*.
248. Minutes of conversation between Harriman, Kádár, July 18, 1978, Library of Congress, Manuscript Division, Papers of Averell Harriman, box 598. The brief Hungarian memorandum of the meeting did not contain Kádár's negative remarks on the USSR. See MNL OL, M-KS, Kádár János titkársága, 35. cs., 1978.
249. Nemes Dezső feljegyzése Kádárnak [Memorandum for Kádár by Nemes], December 19, 1978, Kádár János titkársága, ibid.; Feljegyzés Kaiser és Rényi megbeszéléséről [Memorandum of conversation, Rényi Kaiser], December 19, 1979, ibid.

250. Memorandum from Stephen Larrabee to Madeleine Albright, "Visit of First Secretary Kadar," January 23, 1979, Carter Presidential Library, Carter Presidential Papers, White House central file, confidential file, Hungary.
251. Az MSZMP KB Külügyi Osztályának jelentése [Report by the Foreign Relations Department of the Central Committee], June 5, 1978, MNL OL, Küm, XIX-J-1-j, USA tük, 22. doboz, 1-004038-1978.
252. A Külügyminisztérium V. Területi Osztályának feljegyzése a magyar-amerikai kapcsolatokról [The Foreign Ministry's memorandum on U.S.-Hungarian relations], November 22, 1978, MNL OL, Küm, XIX-J-1-j, USA tük, 22. doboz, sz. n.
253. Jelentés a Politikai Bizottságnak Kádár János és Leonyid Iljics Bresznyev találkozójáról [Report to the Politburo, Kádár-Brezhnev meeting] July 31, 1978, MNL OL, KS, 288. f., 5. cs., 752. őe.
254. János Honvári, "Pénzügyi és vagyonjogi tárgyalások és egyezmények Magyarország és az Egyesült Államok között, 1945–1978," *Századok* 143, no. 1 (2009): 37–82, 68, 70.
255. Justine Faure, *L'Ami Américain: La Tchécoslovaquie, enjeu de la diplomatie Américaine, 1943–1968* (Paris: Tallandier, 2004), 364. This was successful due to the encouragement of visits from the West. In 1960 an American journal wrote that Czechoslovakia was the only country where the "West was right." See ibid., 372.

9. "LOVE TOWARD KÁDÁR"

1. On the collapse of détente see Raymond Garthoff, *Détente and Confrontation: American-Soviet Relations from Nixon to Reagan* (Washington D.C.: Brookings Institute Press, 1985).
2. Jonathan Haslam, *Russia's Cold War: From the October Revolution to the Fall of the Wall* (New Haven, Conn.: Yale University Press, 2011), 312–13.

3. Vladislav Zubok, *A Failed Empire: The Soviet Union in the Cold War from Stalin to Gorbachev* (Chapel Hill: University of North Carolina Press, 2007), 263.

4. Melvyn Leffler, *For the Soul of Mankind: The United States, the Soviet Union, and the Cold War* (New York: Hill and Wang, 2007), 332–33.

5. Kristina Spohr-Readman, "Conflict and Cooperation in Intra-Alliance Nuclear Politics," *Journal of Cold War Studies* 13, no. 2 (Spring 2011): 39–89.

6. Haslam, *Russia's Cold War*, 323–24.

7. Leffler, *For the Soul of Mankind*, 335.

8. Haslam, *Russia's Cold War*, 303–9.

9. Campbell Craig and Frederik Logevall, *America's Cold War: The Politics of Insecurity* (Cambridge, Mass.: Belknap Press of Harvard University Press, 2009), 302–8.

10. Haslam, *Russia's Cold War*, 335–37.

11. Jack F. Matlock, *Reagan and Gorbachev: How the Cold War Ended* (New York: Random House, 2005).

12. Leffler, *For the Soul of Mankind*, 352–53.

13. John Whitehead, interview with the author, May 2008.

14. Christopher Maynard, *Out of the Shadow: George H. W. Bush and the End of the Cold War* (College Station: Texas A&M University Press, 2008), 29.

15. On domestic debate regarding Romania's MFN status see Joseph F. Harrington and Bruce J. Courtney, *Tweaking the Nose of the Russians: Fifty Years of American-Romanian Relations, 1940–1990*, East European Monographs no. 296 (Boulder, Colo.: East European Monographs, 1991).

16. Haslam, *Russia's Cold War*, 296.

17. János Tischler, "The Hungarian Party Leadership and the Polish Crisis of 1980–1981," *Cold War International History Bulletin* 11 (Winter 1998).

18. György Földes, *Az eladósodás politikatörténete, 1957–1986* (Budapest: Maecenas, 1995), 144, 147.

19. Attila Mong, *Kádár hitele: A magyar államadósság története, 1956–1990* (Budapest: Libri Kiadó, 2012), 165.

20. Richard Gough, *A Good Comrade: János Kádár, Communism and Hungary* (London: I. B. Tauris, 2006), 207–8.

21. Zubok, *A Failed Empire*, 269.

22. János Tischler, "Kádár and the Polish Crisis of 1980–1981," *Cold War International History Bulletin* 11 (Winter 1988).

23. Csaba Békés, "Magyar külpolitika a szovjet szövetségi rendszerben, 1968–1989," in *Magyar Külpolitika a XX. Században: Tanulmányok*, ed. Ferenc Gazdag and J. László Kiss (Budapest: Zrínyi Kiadó, 2004), 157–58.

24. Ibid., 158–60.

25. Ibid., 160–63.

26. Kádár János elvtárs felszólalása a Politikai Bizottság 1981. június 23-i ülésén. Jelentés a Magyar Népköztársaság és az Amerikai Egyesült Államok kapcsolatairól [Comrade János Kádár's speech at the June 23, 1981, meeting of the Politburo], Magyar Nemzeti Levéltár Országos Levéltára (MNL OL), Budapest, M-KS, 288. f., 5. cs., 829. őe, 1981.

27. A külügyminisztérium felhjegyzése [Memorandum by the Foreign Ministry], MNL OL, Külügyminisztérium (Küm), XIX-J-1-j, USA tük, 133/1984 Szt.

28. A külügyminisztérium feljegyzése Havasi ferenc washingtoni útjához [Memorandum by the Foreign Ministry on Havasi's visit to Washington], undated, MNL OL M-KS 288. f. 32. cs. 4. őe.

29. Kádár János felszólalása a Politikai Bizottság 1983. április 19-i ülésén. Napirendi pont: Jelentés a magyar-amerikai kapcsolatokról szóló határozatok végrehajtásáról és az előttünk álló feladatokról [János Kádár's report on the implementation of resolutions on Hungarian-American relations], April 19, 1983, MNL OL, M-KS, 288. f., 5. cs., 880. őe., 1983.

30. Gough, *A Good Comrade*, 220.

31. Házi Vencel washingtoni nagykövet távirata Nagy János külügyi államtitkárnak [Report by Vencel Házi to the state secretary of foreign affairs], June 20, 1984, MNL OL, Küm, USA tük, XIX-J-j, 1984, 28. doboz, 00705/1.

32. Házi Vencel nagykövet távirata Nagy János külügyi államtitkárnak [Telegram by Ambassador Házi to Nagy], July 12, 1984, MNL OL, Küm, USA tük, XIX-J-1-j, 1984, 28. doboz, 003705/6.

33. Gough, *A Good Comrade*, 219.

34. Házi Vencel távirata a Külügyminisztériumnak [Telegram by Házi to Nagy], October 1, 1984, MNL OL, Küm, USA tük, XIX-J-1-j, 1984, 28. doboz, 004975.

35. Feljegyzés Max Kampelman budapesti látogatásáról [Memorandum on visit by Max Kampelman], September 11, 1985, MNL OL, Küm, USA tük, XIX-J-1-j, 29. doboz, 4-134, 004876. Two senators who visited Hungary in 1985 indicated that Hungary could act as a bridge between East and West.

36. Feljegyzés a Magyarországra irányuló amerikai propagandáról [Memorandum on American propaganda targeting Hungary], undated, MNL OL M-KS 288. f. 5. cs. 34. őe.

37. Jelentés a Minisztertanács számára a mezőgazdasági és élelmezésügyi miniszter látogatásáról az Egyesült Államokban [Memorandum on the visit of the minister of agriculture in the United States], October 19, 1976, MNL OL, Küm, USA tük, XIX-J-1-j, 20. doboz, 551-005358-1976.

38. Note to files: Hungarians, April 10, 1970, MNL OL, KKI, XIX-A-33-a-5405-1970, 221. doboz; A Kulturális Kapcsolatok Intézetének átirata a Külügyminisztériumnak [Transcript of the Institute of Cultural Affairs to the Foreign Ministry], April 16, 1970, ibid., 5279–1970.

39. The American ambassador in Budapest to the secretary of state, "Cultural Center in Budapest," October 12, 1975, National Archives and Records Administration (NARA), Records of the Department of State, PDF, 1975.

40. Az MSZMP KB gazdaságpolitikai osztályának feljegyzése Szurdi István belkereskedelmi miniszternek [Memorandum from the Department of Economic Policy of the Hungarian Socialist Workers Party Central Committee to the minister of internal trade], February 24, 1973, MNL OL, M-KS, 288. f., 22. cs., 4. őe, 1973.

41. István Bart, *Világirodalom és könyvkiadás a Kádár-korszakban* (Budapest: Scholastica, 2000), 39, 100–105.

42. A Kulturális Minisztérium feljegyzése [Memorandum by the Ministry of Culture], April 12, 1979, MNL OL, Küm, USA tük, XIX-J-1-j, 1–002562/8–1979.

43. Bart, *Világirodalom és könyvkiadás*, 112–13.

44. Justine Faure, *L'Ami Américain: La Tchécoslovaquie, enjeu de la diplomatie Américaine, 1943–1968* (Paris: Tallandier, 2004), 351.

45. Jegyzőkönyv a Politikai Bizottság 1979. január 9-én megtartott üléséről [Record of the January 9 meeting of the Political Committee], MOL, M-KS, 288. f., 5. cs., 763. őe, 1979.

46. A Zene- és Táncművészeti Főosztály javaslata a 'Count Basie' jazz-együttes magyarországi vendégszereplésére [Proposal by the Music and Dance Department for the Hungarian tour of the 'Count Basie' Jazz ensemble], February 12, 1970; A Művelődésügyi Minisztérium átirata Kulturális Kapcsolatok Intézetének [Memorandum from the Institute of Cultural Affairs to the Ministry of Foreign Affairs], February 26, 1970; A Kulturális Kapcsolatok Intézetének átirata a Külügyminisztériumnak [Memorandum from the Institute of Cultural Affairs to the Ministry of Foreign Affairs], March 5, 1970; A Külügyminisztérium átirata a Kulturális Kapcsolatok Intézetének [Memorandum from the Ministry of Foreign Affairs to the Institute of Cultural Affairs], March 17,

1970; A Kulturális Kapcsolatok Intézetének belső kézírásos feljegyzése [Handwritten internal memorandum by the Institute of Cultural Affairs], March 27, 1970, MNL OL, Kulturális Kapcsolatok Intézete (KKI), XIX-A-33-a-7028-1970, 221. doboz.

47. A Külügyminisztérium feljegyzése a magyar-amerikai kapcsolatokról [Memorandum by the Foreign Ministry on Hungarian-American relations], December 6, 1985, MNL OL, Küm, USA tük, XIX-J-1-j, 28. doboz, 14-002235/3-1985.

48. Esztergályos Ferenc nagykövet jelentése Puja Frigyes külügyminiszternek az 1977-es idegenforgalomról [Report by Ambassador Esztergályos to Foreign Minister Puja on tourism], undated, MNL OL, Küm, USA tük, XIX-J-1-j, 25. doboz, 5-001626/1978.

49. Megállapodás [Agreement], 1977, MNL OL, Küm, USA tük, XIX-J-1-j, 25. doboz, 5-001879/1/1978.

50. A washingtoni nagykövetség jelentése [Report by the embassy in Washington], March 8, 1978, MNL OL, Küm, USA tük, XIX-J-1-j, 25. doboz, 5-00384/1/1978.

51. Ibid.

52. Jelentés a Minisztertanácsnak a magyar-amerikai kapcsolatokról [Report to the Council of Ministers on Hungarian-American relations] (1981), MNL OL, Küm, USA tük, XIX-J-1-j, 21. doboz, 14-00388/11-1981.

53. Anna Porter, *Buying a Better World: George Soros and Billionaire Philanthropy* (Toronto: Tap Books, 2015), 86.

54. Bogye János rendőr vezérőrnagy, a Belügyminisztérium III/I. Csoportfőnöksége vezetőjének átirata Házi Vencel külügyminiszter-helyettesnek [Memorandum, head of the III/I Section of the Ministry of Interior, General Bogye to Deputy Foreign Minister Házi], July 18, 1983, MNL OL, Küm, XIX-J-1-j, USA tük, 25. doboz, 142-004038/1-1983.

55. Tájékoztató az Agitációs és Propaganda Bizottság részére a Soros Alapítvány működéséről, [Information on the Soros Fund to the Agitation and Propaganda Committee], January 9, 1986, MOL, M-KS, 288. f., 36. cs., 15. őe, 1886.

56. Bogye János vezérőrnagy belügyi főcsoportvezető-helyettes átirata Házi Vencel külügyminiszter-helyettesnek [Memorandum from deputy department head general of the interior János Bogye to Házi], July 18, 1983, MNL OL Küm, USA tük, XIX-J-1-j, 25 doboz, 142-004038/1-1983.

57. Házi Vencel távirata Várkonyi Péternek [Dispatch by Házi to Várkonyi], October 15, 1984, MNL OL, Küm, USA tük, XIX-J-1-j, 29. doboz, 71-005550-1984.

58. Tétényi Pál átirata Horn Gyulának [Tétényi to Horn], March 6, 1985, MNL OL, M-KS 288. f., 32. cs., 2. őe.

59. A Magyar Tudományos Akadémia tájékoztatója az Agitációs és Propaganda Bizottság részére [Memorandum from the Hungarian Academy of Sciences to the Agitation and Propaganda Committee], January 9, 1986, MNL OL, M-KS, 288. f., 36. cs., 15. őe.

60. Jelentés Eagleburger külügyminiszter-helyettes budapesti tárgyalásairól [Report on the talks of Undersecretary of State Eagleburger in Budapest], October 24, 1981, MNL OL, Küm, USA tük, XIX-J-1-j, 21. doboz, 13-005807/2-1981.

61. Sean Wilentz, *The Age of Reagan: A History, 1974–2008* (New York: Harper, 2008), 151–55.

62. Zubok, *A Failed Empire*, 272.

63. Leffler, *For the Soul of Mankind*, 355–56; Wilentz, *The Age of Reagan*, 165.

64. Esztergályos Ferenc számjeltávirata a Külügyminisztériumnak [Telegram by Esztergályos to the Foreign Ministry], May 2, 1982, MNL OL, Küm, USA tük, XIX-J-1-j, 21. doboz, 14-001154/9-1982.

65. Feljegyzés Kenneth Dam, az amerikai külügyminiszter első helyettesének látogatásáról [Visit by assistant secretary of state Kenneth Dam], March 28, 1983, MNL

OL, Küm, XIX-J-1-j, USA tük, 25. doboz, 135-002258/2-1983.
66. John Whitehead, interview with the author, May 2008.
67. Zubok, *A Failed Empire*, 24.
68. Leffler, *For the Soul of Mankind*, 340.
69. A washingtoni nagykövetség számjeltávirata a Külügyminisztériumnak [The embassy in Washington to the Foreign Ministry], September 15, 1986, MNL OL, Küm, XIX-J-1-j, USA tük, 27. doboz, 4–53, 004315/2.
70. Leffler, *For the Soul of Mankind*, 362.
71. A washingtoni nagykövetség számjeltávirata [The embassy in Washington to the Foreign Ministry], March 19, 1987, MNL OL, Küm, USA tük, XIX-J-1-j, 21. doboz, 4–13.
72. Kádár is cited in Tibor Huszár, *Kádár: A hatalom évei, 1956–1989* (Budapest: Corvina, 2006), 292.
73. Koncepcióterv George Bush magyarországi látogatásához [Draft concepts for the visit of Bush], September 5, 1983, MNL OL, Küm, USA tük, XIX-J-1-j, 24. doboz, 131-002059/7-1983.
74. Jelentés a Minisztertanácsnak Bush amerikai alelnök látogatásáról [Report to the Council of Ministers on Bush's visit], undated, MNL OL, XIX-J-1-j, USA tük, 14. doboz, 131-002059–1983.
75. Rajnai Sándor moszkvai nagykövet levele Szűrös Mátyásnak, továbbítva Várkonyi Péternek [Letter by the ambassador in Moscow to Szűrös forwarded to Várkonyi], November 14, 1983, MNL OL, Küm, XIX-J-1-u, Várkonyi Péter irathagyatéka, 80. doboz.
76. Zubok, *A Failed Empire*, 274–75.
77. A washingtoni nagykövetség jelentése Házi Vencel nagykövet látogatásáról Bush alelnöknél [Report by the embassy in Washington on Házi's Visit to Bush], November 30, 1983, MNL OL, Küm, XIX-J-1-j, USA tük, 24. doboz, 116-005517/3-1983.
78. Témavázlat Marjai Józsefnek Ermarth elnöki tanácsadóval folytatandó megbeszéléséhez, [Draft talking points for Marjai's talks with Ermarth] (1987), ibid.
79. The September 28 issue of *Washington Post* is cited in Bennett Kovrig, *Of Walls and Bridges: The United States and Eastern Europe* (New York: New York University Press, 1991), 233–41. See also Alan P. Dobson, *US Economic Statecraft for Survival 1933–1991: Of Sanctions, Embargoes, and Economic Warfare* (New York: Routledge, 2002).
80. A washingtoni nagykövetség rejtjeltávirata [Telegram by the embassy in Washington], October 30, 1984, MNL OL, Küm, USA tük, XIX-J-1-j, 29. doboz, 56005558-1984; A washingtoni nagykövetség rejtjeltávirata [Telegram by the embassy in Washington], November 23, 1984, ibid., 56–005558/1; Bényi József feljegyzése az amerikai ügyvivővel folytatott megbeszéléséről [Conversation, Bényi, U.S. chargé], November 8, 1984, ibid. 28. doboz, 14-003798/4-1984.
81. Feljegyzés Horn Gyula washingtoni megbeszéléseiről [Memorandum, Horn's talks in Washington], June 2, 1986, MNL OL, Küm, XIX-J-1-j, USA tük, 25. doboz, 4-116-003263/1986.
82. A Külügyminisztérium V. Területi Osztályának feljegyzése John Whitehead külügyminiszter-helyettes magyarországi látogatásáról [The Foreign Ministry on visit by deputy secretary of state John Whitehead], November 17, 1987, MNL OL, Küm, XIX-J-1-j, USA tük, 18. doboz, 4-135-002484/6/1987.
83. Feljegyzés az MSZMP KB számára Havasi Ferenc washingtoni útjáról [Memorandum for the Political Committee on Havasi's visit in Washington], February 11, 1985, MNL OL, Küm, USA tük, XIX-J-1-j, 28. doboz, 13-00125/7-1985.
84. Feljegyzés Horn Gyula washingtoni megbeszéléseiről [Horn's talks in Washington], June 2, 1986, MNL OL, Küm, USA tük, XIX-J-1-j, 4–116–003263/1986.

85. Tájékoztató a magyar-amerikai bankkapcsolatokról [Information on Hungarian-American bank relations], May 30, 1988, MNL OL, Küm, XIX-J-1-j, USA tük, 16. doboz, 13-001955/5-1988.
86. A washingtoni nagykövetség számjeltávirata Steny Hoyer, a Kongresszus EBEÉ bizottsága társelnökével folytatott megbeszélésről [Telegram by the embassy in Washington on talks with Steny Hoyer], June 20, 1986, MNL OL, Küm, XIX-J-1-j, USA tük, 25. doboz, 4-134-003549/1/1986.
87. The information on the Soviet consular district is from Thomas Simons, interview with the author, May 2008.
88. Kovács László feljegyzése [Memorandum by Kovács], May 18, 1988, MNL OL, Küm, XIX-J-1-j, USA tük, 16. doboz, 13-001955/5-1988.
89. Az V. Területi Osztály feljegyzése [Memorandum by the Vth Territorial Department], May 30, 1984, MNL OL, Küm, USA tük, XIX-J-1-j, 0034411/1984.
90. A washingtoni nagykövetség számjeltávirata [Telegram by the embassy in Washington], March 15, 1984; A washingtoni nagykövetség számjeltávirata [Telegram by the embassy in Washington], March 26, 1984; Az V. Területi Főosztály feljegyzése [Memorandum by the Vth Territorial Department], "Visit by Military and Air Attaché Zotov," March 23, 1984, MNL OL, Küm, USA tük XIX-J-1-j, 1984.
91. Az V. Területi Osztály feljegyzése K. Smith amerikai első beosztott látogatásáról [Visit by chargé, K. Smith], June 21, 1984, ibid.
92. Mark Palmer előadása a kelet-európai országokról. A magyar nagykövetség jelentése a külügyminiszternek [Presentation on the socialist countries by Mark Palmer], January 17, 1986, MNL OL, Küm, USA tük, XIX-J-1-j, 24. doboz, 10-00653.
93. Gyovai Gyula levele Szűrös Mátyásnak, továbbítva Várkonyi Péternek [Letter by Gyovai to Szűrös] (November 1985),

MNL OL, Küm, XIX-J-1-u, Várkonyi Péter irathagyatéka, 80. doboz.
94. Mark Palmer, interview with the author.
95. Feljegyés az MSZMP KB-nek Havasi Ferenc amerikai látogatásáról [Memorandum for the HSWP Central Committee on Havasi's visit to the United States], MNL OL, Küm, USA tük, XIX-J-1-j, 28 doboz, 13-00125/7-1985.
96. A magyar nagykövetség jelentése a Külügyminisztériumnak [Report to the Foreign Ministry], December 5, 1985, MNL OL, Küm, USA tük, XIX-J-1-j, 30. doboz, IV-135, 005640; Feljegyzés az amerikai nagykövetség tanácsosával folytatott megbeszélésről [Conversation with the counselor of the U.S. Embassy], December 13, 1985, ibid.
97. Mark Kramer, "The Demise of the Soviet Bloc," in *The End of the Beginning: The Revolutions of 1989 and the Resurgence of History*, ed. Vladimir Tismaneanu and Bogdan C. Iacob (Budapest: Central European University Press, 2012), 173, 177.
98. Cited in Gough, *A Good Comrade*, 222.
99. Házi Vencel nagykövet jelentése Várkonyi Péter külügyminiszternek Schultz látogatásának visszhangjáról [Report by Házi to Várkonyi on the repercussions of the visit by Schultz], January 21, 1986, MNL OL, Küm, USA tük, XIX-J-1-j, 25. doboz, 4-116, 00649/1986.
100. A washingtoni nagykövetség rejtjeltávirata a Külügyminisztériumnak [The embassy in Washington to the Foreign Ministry], October 10, 1986, MNL OL, Küm, USA tük, XIX-J-1-j, 25. doboz, 4-135-00482/1986.
101. A washingtoni nagykövetség rejtjeltávirata Kuchel külügyi főosztályvezető és Révész Miklós megbeszéléséről [Conversation between Kuchel and Révész], January 13, 1986, MNL OL, Küm, XIX-J-1-j, USA tük, 25. doboz, 4-14-001971/1986; A Külügyminisztérium V. Területi Osztályának

feljegyzése Smith amerikai tanácsos látogatásáról [Visit of U.S. Embassy counselor Smith], June 4, 1986, ibid. 24. doboz, 14-001233/1-1986.

102. Feljegyzés Bányász Rezső és Walter Raymond Jr. Megbeszéléséről [Conversation between Bányász and Walter Raymond], July 9, 1985, MNL OL, Küm, USA tük, XIX-J-1-j, 31. doboz, 21–42.

103. A. Ross Johnson, *Radio Free Europe and Radio Liberty: The CIA Years and Beyond* (Washington, D.C.: Woodrow Wilson Center Press, 2010), 135, 185, 192–93.

104. Feljegyzés Horn Gyula washingtoni megbeszéléséről [Horn's talks in Washington], June 2, 1986, MNL OL, Küm, USA tük, XIX-J-1-j, 4-116-003263/1986.

105. Feljegyzés Bányász Rezsőnek, a Tájékoztatási Hivatal elnökének [Memorandum for chairman of the Information Office Bányász], November 3, 1986, MNL OL, Küm, XIX-J-1-j, USA tük, 25. doboz, 4-116-003549/3/1986.

106. John Whitehead, interview with the author.

107. A Külügyminisztérium V. Területi Osztályának feljegyzése John Whitehead külügyminiszter-helyettes látogatásáról [Visit by John Whitehead], November 14, 1986, MNL OL, Küm, XIX-J-1-j, USA tük, 25. doboz, 4-116-005368/1986.

108. A washingtoni nagykövetség számjeltávirata [Telegram by the embassy in Washington], November 11, 1986, MNL OL, Küm, XIX-J-1-j, USA tük, 25. doboz, 4-135-005368/1/1986.

109. A Külügyminisztérium V. Területi Osztályának feljegyzése Salgó amerikai nagykövet búcsúlátogatásáról [Farewell visit, Ambassador Salgo], October 30, 1984, MNL OL, Küm, XIX-J-1-j, USA tük, 25. doboz, 4-116-005380/4/1986.

110. Témavázlat Marjai József találkozójához a State Department magyar ügyekben illetékes szakértőivel [Talking points, Marjai's meeting with State Department officials responsible for Hungarian affairs], November 3, 1987, MNL OL, Küm, XIX-J-1-j, USA tük, 18. doboz, 4–13–0050022/2/1987.

111. Jelentés a Politikai Bizottságnak Szűrös Mátyás amerikai útjáról [Szűrös's visit in Washington], MNL OL, Küm, USA tük, XIX-J-1-j, 21. doboz, 13-001102/2-1987.

112. Témavázlat Grósz Károlynak John Whitehead külügyminiszter-helyettessel folytatandó megbeszéléséhez [Talking points for Grósz's meeting with Whitehead] (1987), MNL OL, Küm, XIX-J-1-j, USA tük, 16. doboz, 00/182-1988.

113. Documents indicate that Hungary violated its neutrality by sending arms to Iraq.

114. A Kereskedelmi Minisztérium feljegyzése a Külügyminisztériumnak [Memorandum from the Ministry of Commerce to the Ministry of Foreign Affairs], January 31, 1990; A Külügyminisztérium Irattára, NSZK SZT [Archive of the Foreign Ministry, FRG Top Secret], 1990, 54. doboz, 109-5, 00464.

115. Feljegyzés Whitehead külügyminiszter-helyettes látogatásáról [Memorandum on John Whitehead's visit], November 19, 1987, MNL OL, Küm, USA tük, XIX-J-1-j, 25. doboz, 4-116005368/1986.

116. Tárgyalási tématerv Horn Gyulának [Talking points for Horn], June 2, 1988, MNL OL, Küm, XIX-J-1-j, USA tük, 00278/1988.

117. Zoltán Ripp, *Rendszerváltás Magyarországon 1987–1990* (Budapest: Napvilág, 2006).

118. Cited in Kramer, "The Demise of the Soviet Bloc," 181, 184.

119. Interagency Intelligence Memorandum, June 10, 1987. National Security Archives, Washington, D.C. (NSAWDC), End of the Cold War project, box 1.

120. National Security Decision Directive No. 305, Objectives of Moscow Summit, April 26, 1988, NSAWDC, End of the Cold War project, box 3.

121. Pataki István feljegyzése a Külügyminisztériumnak [Memorandum by Pataki for the Foreign Ministry], December 3, 1987, MNL OL, Küm, XIX-J-1-j, USA tük, 21. doboz, 103-002610/1-1987.
122. Thomas Simons, interview with the author.
123. Mark Palmer, interview with the author.
124. Témavázlat Kovács László szófiai Varsói Szerződés konzultációjához [Talking points for Kovács's consultations at the Sofia meeting of the Warsaw Pact], August 26, 1988, MNL OL, Küm, XIX-J-1-j, USA tük, 16. doboz, 13-sz. n.-1988.
125. A Külügyminisztérium V. Területi Osztályának feljegyzése az Egyesült Államok kelet-európai politikájáról [Memorandum by the Foreign Ministry on the Eastern European policy of the United States], January 28, 1988, MNL OL, XIX-J-1-k, USA admin 1988, 16. doboz, 1-1196-1988.
126. Marjai József miniszterelnök-helyettes, kereskedelmi miniszter jelentése William Verity amerikai kereskedelmi miniszterrel folytatott tárgyalásáról [Report by Deputy Prime Minister Marjai on talks with Secretary of Commerce Verity], June 24, 1988, MNL OL, XIX-J-1-k, USA admin 1988, 1-9333/T-1988.
127. Matlock, *Reagan and Gorbachev*, 125.
128. Mark Palmer, interview with the author.
129. Thomas Simons, interview with the author.
130. Feljegyzés Kovács László washingtoni konzultációjáról [Kovács's consultations in Washington], July 16, 1988, MNL OL, Küm, XIX-J-1-j, USA tük, 17. doboz, IV-135, 03500.
131. Bánlaki György főkonzul jelentése a Külügyminisztériumnak [Report by Consul General Bánlaki to the Foreign Ministry], May 20, 1988, MNL OL, Küm, XIX-J-1-j, USA tük, 16. doboz, 4–13, 001955/6.
132. Jelentés a Politikai Bizottságnak Grósz Károly amerikai látogatásáról [Report to the Political Committee on Grósz's visit in the United States], August 4, 1988, MNL OL, Küm, XIX-J-1-j, USA tük, 16. doboz, 00/182-1988.
133. Kovács László jelentése Whitehead külügyminiszter-helyettes látogatásáról [Report by Deputy Foreign Minister Kovács on visit by Whitehead], October 21, 1988, MNL OL, Küm, USA tük, XIX-J-1-j, 17. doboz, 4-135-002278/5-1988.
134. András Oplatka, *Egy döntés története: Magyar határnyitás 1989. Szeptember 11 nulla óra* (Budapest: Helikon, 2010), 60.
135. Belovai István Belovai, *Fedőneve – Scorpion* (Budapest: I. Belovai, 1998).
136. Kovács László jelentése Whitehead külügyminiszter-helyettes látogatásáról [Report by Deputy Foreign Minister Kovács on visit by Whitehead], October 21, 1988, MNL OL, Küm, USA tük, XIX-J-1-j, 17 doboz, 4-135-002278/5-1988.
137. A washingtoni nagykövetség rejtjeltávirata [Telegram by the embassy in Washington], October 10, 1988, MNL OL, Küm, USA tük, XIX-J-1-j, 17. doboz, 135-002278/6/1988; A washingtoni nagykövetség számjeltávirata [Telegram by the embassy in Washington], November 11, 1988, ibid. 002278/10/1988.
138. Kovács László feljegyzése [Memorandum by Kovács], November 2, 1988, MNL OL, Küm, XIX-J-1-k, USA admin 1988, 1-9382-1988; A Külügyminisztérium Területi Osztályának feljegyzése Palmer nagykövet megnyilvánulásáról [Memorandum by the Foreign Ministry on Palmer's statements], October 25, 1988, ibid.
139. A Külügyminisztérium Tervező és Elemző Osztályának feljegyzése Schifter külügyminiszter-helyettes budapesti tárgyalásairól [Memorandum by the Foreign Ministry on Deputy Secretary of State Schifter's talks in Budapest], December 31, 1988, MNL OL, Küm, XIX-J-1-k, USA admin. 1988, 18. doboz, 1-689-2-1988.

10. 1989

1. Bush's letter to Gorbachev, undated, George H. W. Bush Presidential Library (BPL), Nicholas Burns files, Subseries, chronological files, box 8.
2. Cited in Christopher Maynard, *Out of the Shadow: George H. W. Bush and the End of the Cold War* (College Station: Texas A&M University Press, 2008), 122, 128.
3. Memorandum from Eric Melby to Brent Scowcroft, July 5, 1989, BPL, Scowcroft files, USSR chronological files, Soviet power collapse in Eastern Europe files.
4. Memorandum of conversation, June 15, 1989, participants: Brent Scowcroft, Budomir Lončar, ibid., 5439.
5. Mark Kramer, "The Demise of the Soviet Bloc," in *The End of the Beginning: The Revolutions of 1989 and the Resurgence of History*, ed. Vladimir Tismaneanu and Bogdan C. Iacob (Budapest: Central European University Press, 2012), 172. On the role of protests in the transformation of the region see Padraic Kenney, *A Carnival of Revolution: Central Europe 1989* (Princeton, N.J.: Princeton University Press, 2002).
6. Kenneth Waltz, *Theory of International Politics* (Reading, Mass.: Addison-Wesley Publishers, 1979), 100–101.
7. Jian Chen, *Mao's China and the Cold War* (Chapel Hill: University of North Carolina Press, 2001), 60.
8. Melvyn Leffler, *For the Soul of Mankind: The United States, the Soviet Union, and the Cold War* (New York: Hill and Wang, 2007), 466.
9. John Lewis Gaddis, *The Cold War: A New History* (New York: Penguin Press, 2006), 236. For a reappraisal of the U.S. role in 1989 see Günter Bischof, *Running against the Clock': The Bush Administration and Its "Beyond Containment" Policy towards Eastern Europe* [forthcoming].
10. Maynard, *Out of the Shadow*, 128–29.
11. Svetlana Savranskaya, "The Logic of 1989: The Soviet Peaceful Withdrawal from Eastern Europe," in *Masterpieces of History: The Peaceful End of the Cold War in Europe, 1989*, ed. Svetlana Savranskaya, Thomas Blanton, and Vladislav Zubok (Budapest: Central European University Press, 2010), 47.
12. Robin Okey, "Echoes and Precedents: 1989 in Historical Perspective," in *The 1989 Revolutions in Central and Eastern Europe: From Communism to Pluralism*, ed. Kevin McDermott and Matthew Stibbe (Manchester: Manchester University Press, 2013), 37.
13. Mary Sarotte, *1989: The Struggle to Create Post-Cold War Europe* (Princeton, N.J.: Princeton University Press, 2009), 22.
14. Mary Buckley, "The Multifaceted External Soviet Role in Processes towards Unanticipated Revolutions," in *The 1989 Revolutions in Central and Eastern Europe: From Communism to Pluralism*, ed. Kevin McDermott and Matthew Stibbe (Manchester: Manchester University Press, 2013), 55, 69.
15. Mark Kramer, "The Collapse of East European Communism and the Repercussions within the Soviet Union, part 2," *Journal of Cold War Studies* 6, no. 4 (Fall 2004): 3–64.
16. Zoltán Ripp, *Rendszerváltás Magyarországon, 1987–1990* (Budapest: Napvilág, 2006), 22.
17. "NATO at Forty: New Vision of East-West Relations," November 20, 1989, Magyar Országos Levéltár Nemzeti Levéltára (MNL OL), Budapest, Külügyminisztérium (Küm), XIX-J-1-j, NATO 1989, 111. doboz, sz. n.
18. Cited in Kenneth Waltz, "The Emerging Structure of International Politics, 1993," in *Realism and International Politics*, ed. Kenneth Waltz (New York: Routledge, 2008), 166.
19. Library of Congress, Manuscript Division, Papers of Averell Harriman, box 598.
20. Jelentés Manfred Schülerrel, a kancellári hivatal államtitkárával folytatott

megbeszélésről [Record of conversation with Manfred Schüler], July 25, 1977, MNL OL, Küm, XIX-J-1-j, USA tük, 19. doboz, 10-001100/8-1977.

21. See Attila Mong, *Kádár hitele: A magyar államadósság története, 1956–1990* (Budapest: Libri Kiadó, 2012), 221–72.

22. The forthcoming paragraph is based on Ripp, *Rendszerváltás Magyarországon*, 13–144.

23. Mong, *Kádár hitele*, 268–70.

24. Javaslat a PIB részére [Recomendation for the Political Executive Committee], July 1989, MNL OL, M-KS 288. f., 5. cs, 1078. őe.

25. Cited in István Bodzabán, Antal Szalay, and Endre Aczél, eds., *A puha diktatúrától a kemény demokráciáig* (Budapest: Pelikán, 1994), 131.

26. Robert L. Hutchings, *American Diplomacy and the End of the Cold War. An Insider's Account of US Policy in Europe, 1989–1992* (Washington, D.C.; Woodrow Wilson Center Press, 1997), 46–47. See also Michael R. Beschloss and Strobe Talbott, *At the Highest Levels: The Inside Story of the End of the Cold War* (Boston: Little Brown and Company, 1993); and George Bush and Brent Scowcroft, *A World Transformed* (New York: Vintage Books, 1998).

27. For the appropriate quotes see Kramer, "The Demise of the Soviet Bloc," 172–90.

28. Csaba Békés, *Európából Európába: Magyarország konfliktusok kereszttüzében, 1945–1990* (Budapest: Gondolat, 2004).

29. Mark Kramer, "The Collapse of East European Communism and the Repercussions within the Soviet Union, part 3," *Journal of Cold War Studies* 7, no. 1 (Winter 2005): see in particular pages 1–24.

30. Gorbachev's alleged "neglect" of Eastern Europe was famously discussed in Jacques Lévesque, *The Enigma of 1989: The USSR and the Liberation of Eastern Europe* (Berkeley: University of California Press, 1997).

31. Cited in Magdolna Baráth and M. János Rainer, eds., *Gorbacsov tárgyalásai magyar vezetőkkel: dokumentumok az egykori SZKP és MSZMP archívumaiból 1985–1991* (Budapest: 1956-os Intézet, 2000), 178–85.

32. Gorbacsov beszéde a VSZ PTT bukaresti ülésén [Gorbachev's speech], July 8, 1989, MNL OL, Küm, XIX-J-1-j, VST 1989, 107. doboz, 001367/12.

33. Kramer, "The Collapse of East European Communism, part 2," 6, 10.

34. Richard Lugar to President Bush, November 21, 1989, BPL, Records of White House Office of Management, subject files, foreign affairs.

35. Barabás jelentése Palmer és Dobinyin kijelentéseiről [Report on statements by Palmer, Dobrynin], July 25, 1989, MNL OL, Küm, XIX-J-1-j, Szu tük 1989, 83. doboz, 001245/3.

36. András Oplatka, *Egy döntés története: Magyar határnyitás, 1989. Szeptember 11. nulla óra* (Budapest: Helikon, 2010), 189–90.

37. Cited in Baráth and Rainer, *Gorbacsov tárgyalásai*, 250–51.

38. Szovjet álláspont a HCS tárgyalásokon [Soviet position at the CFE talks], January 16, 1989, MNL OL, Küm, XIX-J-1-j, Európa 1989, 96. doboz, 00139/4.

39. Gyarmati István, Horváth Dezső jelentése a bécsi haderőcsökkentési tárgyalásokról [Report on the CFE talks in Vienna], July 17, 1989, MNL OL, Küm, Európa 1989 96. doboz, 00275/48.

40. Kramer, "The Collapse of East European Communism, part 3," 6.

41. Cited in Baráth and Rainer, *Gorbacsov tárgyalásai*, 156–68.

42. Jelentés Aboimov látogatásáról [Report on Aboimov's visit], October 20, 1989, MNL OL, Küm, XIX-J-1-j, Szu tük 1989, 84. doboz, 003982.

43. Jazov védelmi miniszter a VSZ-ről [Iazov on the WTO], November 23, 1989, MNL OL, Küm, XIX-J-1-j, Európa, 97. doboz, 00275/3.

44. Kramer, "The Collapse of East European Communism, part 3," 8.
45. Feljegyzés moszkvai konzultációról [Memorandum on consultations in Moscow], April 24, 1989, MNL OL, XIX-J-1-j, Moszkva tük 1989, 84. doboz, 002112.
46. Jelentés a Minisztertanácsnak a VSZ tagállamai vezetőinek tanácskozásáról [Report on the meeting of WTO leaders], December 4, 1989, MNL OL, Küm, XIX-J-1-r, 144/HGY, 94. doboz.
47. Bush's working dinner with Mulroney, November 29, 1989, BPL, http://bushlibrary.tamu.edu/research/memcons_telcons.php.
48. Kramer, "The Collapse of East European Communism, part 3," 30–32.
49. Jelentés a Minisztertanácsnak [Report to the Council of Ministers], February 15, 1989, MNL OL, Küm, XIX-J-1-j, Ausztria tük 1989, 19. doboz, 00342/2.
50. Osztrák vélemények az átalakulásról [Austrians on the transition], February 21, 1989, MNL OL, Küm, XIX-J-1-j, Ausztria tük 1989, 19. doboz, 001225.
51. Osztrák vélemény az átalakulásról [Austrian view on the transition], March 3, 1989, MNL OL, Küm, XIX-J-1-j, Ausztria tük 1989, 19. doboz, 001225/3.
52. Megbeszélés Prattnerrel [Conversation with Prattner], April 25, 1989; Beszélgetés Baumgartnerrel [Conversation with Baumgartner], April 18, 1989, MNL OL, Küm, XIX-J-1-j, Ausztria tük 1989, 19. doboz, 00225/10.
53. Jelentés Klestil látogatásáról [Klestil's visit], March 7, 1989, MNL OL, Küm, XIX-J-1-j, Ausztria tük 1989, 19. doboz, 00125.
54. Jelentés osztrák véleményről [Austrian views], July 6, 1989, MNL OL, Küm, XIX-J-1-j, Ausztria tük 1989, 19. doboz, 001225.
55. A bécsi nagykövetség számjeltávirata [Telegram by the embassy in Vienna], August 3, 1989, MNL OL, Küm, XIX-J-1-j, Ausztria tük 1989, 20. doboz, 003390.
56. A római nagykövetség jelentése [Report by the embassy in Rome], October 10, 1989, MNL OL, Küm, XIX-J-1-j, EK 1989, 110. doboz, 002988/6.
57. I wish to thank Andreas Schmidt-Schweitzer for the Hungarian state security documents relating to FRG policy toward Hungary.
58. See Victor Sebestyen, *Revolution 1989: The Fall of the Soviet Empire* (New York: Pantheon Books, 2009), 214.
59. Memorandum of conversation between Mikhail Gorbachev and Helmut Kohl, June 13, 1989, in *Masterpieces of History: The Peaceful End of the Cold War in Europe, 1989*, ed. Svetlana Savranskaya, Thomas Blanton, and Vladislav Zubok (Budapest: Central European University Press, 2010), 478; letter from Helmut Kohl to George Bush, June 28, 1989, 486.
60. Az állambiztonsági szolgálatok feljegyzése [Report by the Security Services], April 10, 1989, Állambiztonsági Történeti Levéltár (State Security Archives, ÁBTL), Budapest, Német Szövetségi Köztársaság (Federal Republic of Germany, NSZK), 1989, 6719–1058.
61. Memorandum of conversation with Hans-Dietrich Genscher, February 21, 1989, BPL, http://bushlibrary.tamu.edu/research/memcons_telcons.php.
62. Telephone conversation, President Bush and Chancellor Kohl, May 31, 1989, http://bushlibrary.tamu.edu/research/memcons_telcons.php. Kohl's next statement has been excised from the record.
63. Memorandum from Robert Blackwill to Brent Scowcroft, July 3, 1989, BPL, Scowcroft files, USSR chronological files, Soviet power collapse in Eastern Europe files.
64. Record of conversation between Mikhail Gorbachev and Helmut Kohl, June 14, 1989, National Security Archive, Washington, D.C. (NSAWDC), End of the Cold War Project, box 2. The translation provided in Savranskaya, Blanton, and Zubok,

Masterpieces of History (477), takes the edge off Kohl's blunt statement.

65. Feljegyzés Nyers Rezső látogatásáról az NSZK-ban [Nyers' visit in the FRG], June 24, 1989, MNL OL, M-KS 288. f. 32. cs, 44. őe.

66. Jelentés Lothar Späth, Baden-Württemberg miniszterelnökének látogatásáról [Report on visit by Lothar Späth], June 6, 1989, MNL OL, M-KS 288 f. 32. cs. 58. őe. NSZK/1989/A.

67. The president's meeting with Richard von Weizsäcker, June 6, 1989, http://bushlibrary.tamu.edu/research/memcons_telcons.php.

68. Rühe is cited by Imre Szokai in Recommendation for the Political Executive Committee, MNL OL, M-KS 288. f., 5. cs., 1078 őe.

69. Feljegyzés az MSZMP Nemzetközi kapcsolatok osztálya számára Volker Rühe látogatásáról [Memorandum on Volker Rühe's visit], August 24, 1989, MNL OL M-KS 288. f. 32. cs. 58. őe.

70. Feljegyzés az MSZMP-nek Hans-Jochen Vogel és Nyers Rezső megbeszéléséről [Memorandum of discussion, Vogel, Nyers], October 16, 1989, MNL OL M-KS 288. f. 32. cs. 58. őe. NSZK/1989/A.

71. Hanns Jürgen Küsters and Daniel Hofmann, eds., *Deutsche Einheit: Dokumente zur Deutschlandpolitik: Sonderedition aus den Akten des Bundeskanzleramtes 1989/90*, Digital Library 21 (Berlin: Directmedia, 2004), 278–87.

72. Memorandum by foreign minister Hans-Dietrich Genscher on Chancellor Kohl's discussion with Prime Minister Németh and Foreign Minister Horn, August 25, 1989, cited in Magdolna Baráth, Lajos Gecsényi, and Gábor Máthé, eds., *Sub Clausula 1989: Dokumentumok az 1989-es rendszerváltozás történetéhez*, A dokumentumokat válogatta és a jegyzeteket készítette Lajos Gecsényi and Gábor Máthé (Budapest: Magyar Közlöny, 2009), 630–633.

73. Telephone call from Chancellor Kohl to President Bush, October 23, 1989, http://bushlibrary.tamu.edu/research/memcons_telcons.php.

74. Magánbeszélgetés Friedberg Pflügerrel [Conversation with Pflüger], coded telegram, November 22, 1989, ÁBTL, NSZK 1989, 39/8714.

75. Feljegyzés Dr Martin Heckerrel folytatott megbeszélésről [Conversation with Hecker], February 12, 1990, ÁBTL, NSZK 1989, 39/1124.

76. Hutchings, *American Diplomacy*, 15–17.

77. Thomas Schreiber, *Les Actions de la France á L'Est ou les Absences de Marianne* (Paris: L'Harmattan, 2000), 198–200.

78. Memorandum of the president's conversation with French president Mitterrand, July 14, 1989, http://bushlibrary.tamu.edu/research/memcons_telcons.php.

79. Telephone conversation between Bush and Mitterrand, September 16, 1989, ibid.

80. Magda Ádám, *A Kisantant és Európa, 1920–1929* (Budapest: Akadémiai Kiadó, 1993); and Adam Adamthwaite, *Grandeur and Misery: France's Bid for Power in Europe, 1914–1940* (London: Arnold, 1990).

81. Tájékoztató Grósz franciaországi látogatásáról [Grósz's visit in France], undated, MNL OL, Küm, XIX-J-1-j, Franciaország tük 1989, 35. doboz, 00547.

82. A Külügyminisztérium feljegyzése [Memorandum by the Foreign Ministry] (January 1989), MNL OL, Küm, XIX-J-1-j, Franciaország tük 1989, 35. doboz, 00428.

83. A párizsi nagykövetség rejtjeltávirata [Telegram by the embassy in Paris], February 17, 1989, MNL OL, Küm, XIX-J-1-j, Franciaország tük, 1989, 35. doboz, 0070/1.

84. A párizsi nagykövetség rejtjeltávirata [Telegram by the embassy in Paris], February 15, 1989, MNL OL, Küm, XIX-J-1-j, Franciaország tük 1989, 35. doboz, 00104.

85. Francia nézetek az átalakulásról [French views on the transition], April 25, 1989, MNL OL, Küm, XIX-J-1-j, Franciaország tük 1989, 35. doboz, 001104/1.

86. A párizsi nagykövetség rejtjeltávirata [Telegram by the embassy in France], February 17, 1989, MNL OL, Küm, XIX-J-1-j, Franciaország 1989, 35. doboz, 001104/6; Jelentés Stoleru és Kemenes megbeszéléséről [Conversation between Kemenes and Stoleru], February 28, 1989, ibid., 001104/8.

87. Jelentés a francia szocialista párt véleményéről [Views of the French socialists], November 3, 1989, MNL OL, Küm, XIX-J-1-j, Franciaország tük 1989, 35. doboz, 001104/1.

88. Feljegyzés Bianco és Vass megbeszéléséről [Conversation between Bianco and Vass], November 17, 1989, MNL Ol, Küm, XIX-J-1-j, Franciaország tük 1989, 35. doboz, 00724/8.

89. Feljegyzés megbeszélésről Blot külügyi főigazgatóval [Conversation with Blot], November 22, 1989, MNL OL, Küm, XIX-J-1-j, Franciaország tük 1989, 00724/9.

90. Feljegyzés Pozsgay és Giscard D'Estaing megbeszéléséről [Conversation between Pozsgay and Giscard D'Estaing], December 6, 1989, MNL OL, Küm, XIX-J-1-j, Franciaország tük 1989, 35. doboz, 001104/9.

91. Jelentés Mitterrand NDK-beli látogatásáról [Report on Mitterrand's visit in the GDR], January 2, 1990, A Külügyminisztérium Irattára (Archive of the Foreign Ministry, KIT), German Democratic Republic, Top Secret, 1990, 51. doboz, 108–13.

92. Jelentés Mitterrand látogatásáról [Report on Mitterrand's visit], January 23, 1990, KIT, Franciaország SZT 1990, 26. doboz, 00160/6.

93. The president's meeting with French president François Mitterrand, July 13, 1989, http://bushlibrary.tamu.edu/research/memcons_telcons.php.

94. Geraint Hughes, "British Policy Towards Eastern Europe and the Impact of the 'Prague Spring', 1964–68," *Cold War History* 4, no. 2 (2004): 134.

95. Hutchings, *American Diplomacy*, 14.

96. Bodzabán, Szalay, and Aczél, *A puha diktatúrától*, 153.

97. Margaret Thatcher, *The Downing Street Years* (New York: HarperCollins, 1993), 455–57.

98. Jelentés Várkonyi londoni látogatásáról [Várkonyi's visit in London], March 17, 1989, MNL OL, Küm, XIX-J-1-j, Anglia tük 1989, 15. doboz, 00412/13.

99. Várkonyi feljegyzése Hornnak [Várkonyi's memorandum to Horn], March 11, 1989, MNL OL, Küm, XIX-J-1-j, Szu tük 1989, 83. doboz, 001245/1.

100. Cited in Csaba Békés and Malcolm Byrne, eds. *Political Transition in Hungary, 1989–1990: International Conference: A Compendium of Declassified Documents and Chronology of Events* (Budapest: 1956-os Intézet, 1999).

101. Sarotte, *1989*, 7.

102. A Külügyminisztérium feljegyzése [Memorandum by the Foreign Ministry], October 11, 1989, MNL OL, Küm, XIX-J-1-j, Anglia 1989 tük, 15. doboz, 00412. MNL OL, Küm, XIX-J-1-j, Anglia 1989 tük, 15. doboz, 00412.

103. Németh József jelentése [Németh's report], March 3, 1989, MNL OL, Küm XIX-J-1-j, EK 1989, 110. doboz, 00155/8.

104. A brüsszeli nagykövetség a Külügyminisztériumnak [The embassy in Brussels to the Foreign Ministry], July 24, 1989, MNL OL, Küm, XIX-J-1-j, EK 1989, 111. doboz. MNL OL, Küm, XIX-J-1-j, EK 1989, 111. doboz, 004275/2.

105. Memorandum of the president's conversation with NATO secretary general Manfred Woerner, April 12, 1989, http://bushlibrary.tamu.edu/research/memcons_telcons.php.

106. Memorandum of conversation with Woerner, October 11, 1989, https://bush

library.tamu.edu/research/memcons
_telcons.php.

107. A Külügyminisztérium V. Területi Osztályának feljegyzése (Horváth Gábor) a Bush látogatással kapcsolatos amerikai elképzelésekről [The Foreign Ministry's memorandum on the U.S. position regarding the Bush visit], May 11, 1989, MNL OL, Küm, XIX-J-1-j, USA tük 1989, 13-002245/2-1989.

108. Feljegyzés Kovács László washingtoni konzultációjáról [Kovács's consultation in Washington], November 8, 1989, ibid.; Paul Wolfowitz és Robert Blackwill közlései [Statements by Wolfowitz and Blackwill], MNL OL, Küm, XIX-J-1-j, USA tük 1989, 11. doboz, 135-004198-1989; A Külügyminisztérium Politikai Elemző és Tájékoztató Osztálya vezetőjének (Hajdu András) jelentése amerikai konzultációjáról [Report by the head of the Foreign Ministry Information and Political Analysis Department on consultations in the United States], November 24, 1989, ibid. 004198.

109. A Belügyminisztérium átirata Kovács László külügyminiszter-helyettesnek, a BM nemzetközi kapcsolatok osztályának feljegyzése Horváth István belügyminiszter és Mark Palmer amerikai nagykövet 1988. január 27-i megbeszéléséről [Memorandum of conversation between minister of the interior István Horváth and Mark Palmer], February 1, 1988, MNL OL, Küm, XIX-J-1-j, USA 1989 tük, 9. doboz, 001864.

110. Horn Gyula átirata Németh Miklósnak [Memorandum from Horn to Németh], May 12, 1989, MNL OL, Küm, XIX-J-1-j, USA tük, 1989, 11. doboz, 002244; the American ambassador in Budapest to the State Department, Horn-Cransten Meeting, August 24, 1989, NSAWDC, End of the Cold War Project, box 3.

111. Melega Tibor külkereskedelmi miniszter feljegyzése Kovács László külügyminiszter-helyettesnek [Memorandum from the deputy minister of foreign trade to the deputy foreign minister], April 18, 1989, ibid. 13. doboz, 001742.

112. Feljegyzés a Bush-látogatást előkészítő küldöttséggel (Bruce Swihart, Robert Hutchings) folytatott megbeszélésről [Memorandum of conversation with the U.S. delegation preparing the Bush visit], May 11, 1989, MNL OL, Küm, XIX-J-1-j, USA tük, 1989, 11. doboz, 002245/2.

113. Feljegyzés a képviselőház költségvetési bizottsága elnökének (Rostenkowski) 1989. március 27-29-i látogatásáról [Memorandum on the March 26-27 Visit by the chairman of the House Budget Committee], MNL OL, Küm, XIX-J-1-j, USA 1989 tük, 11. doboz, 001363/3/1989.

114. A washingtoni nagykövetség rejtjeltávirata [Telegram, embassy in Washington], April 12, 1989, MNL OL, Küm, XIX-J-1-j, USA 1989 tük, 9. doboz, 00625/5.

115. On May 8, ambassador Vencel Házi Vencel pleaded to Congressman Tom Lantos that if the United States approved of the changes, it needed to provide effective assistance and cited a figure of $1.5 to $2 billion. Otherwise, he claimed the economic situation could threaten or even impede political success. See A washingtoni nagykövetség számjeltávirata a Külügyminisztériumnak [Telegram by the embassy in Washington to the Foreign Ministry], May 5, 1989 MNL OL, Küm, XIX-J-1-j, 9. doboz.

116. A Külügyminisztérium V. Területi Főosztályának (Kiss Tibor) feljegyzése John Whitehead megbeszéléséről [Memorandum of conversation with Whitehead], ibid.

117. A Külügyminisztérium V. Területi Főosztályának tárgyalási javaslatai Németh Miklós számára Arlen Specter szenátorral, a szenátus igazságügyi és hírszerzési bizottsága tagjával folytatandó megbeszéléséhez [The Foreign Ministry's talking points for meeting with Arlen Specter], January 2,

1989, MNL OL, Küm, XIX-J-1-j, USA 1989 tük, 10. doboz, 0016/2.

118. For more detail see Ripp, *Rendszerváltás Magyarországon*, 277–86.

119. Kramer, "The Demise of the Soviet Bloc," 207–8. See also Savranskaya, "The Logic of 1989," 22–23.

120. Memorandum from Peter W. Rodman to Brent Scowcroft, March 14, 1989, BPL, Scowcroft files, USSR chronological files, Soviet power collapse in Eastern Europe files, 1665.

121. Memorandum from Condoleezza Rice to Brent Scowcroft through Robert Blackwill, March 30, 1989, BPL, Scowcroft Collection, USSR chronological file, box 12.

122. Memorandum from Peter W. Rodman to Brent Scowcroft, March 14, 1989, BPL, Scowcroft Collection, USSR chronological file, box 12.

123. See Waltz, "The Emerging Structure of International Politics," 166.

124. Thomas Simons, interview with the author.

125. Robert Hutchings, interview with the author.

126. Mark Palmer, interview with the author.

127. James M. Goldgeier and Michael McFaul, *Power and Purpose: U.S. Policy toward Russia After the Cold War* (Washington, D.C.: Brookings Institution Press, 2003).

128. Speech by Vice President Bush, September 19, 1983, BPL, White House Office of Speech Writing, Mark Davis files, subject file 1989–1991, box 5.

129. Memorandum of conversation, President Bush and Chancellor Vranitzky, May 5, 1989, https://bushlibrary.tamu.edu/research/memcons_telcons.php.

130. BPL, Condoleezza Rice Collection.

131. Brent Scowcroft, interview with the author.

132. Campbell Craig and Frederik Logevall, *America's Cold War: The Politics of Insecurity* (Cambridge, Mass.: Belknap Press of Harvard University Press, 2009), 342.

133. Stephen Cohen, "The Fate of the Soviet Union: Why Did It End?" in *Soviet Fates and Lost Alternatives: From Stalinism to the New Cold War*, ed. Stephen Cohen (New York: Columbia University Press, 2011), 112–40. For an interpretation that stresses economic crisis as a key element in the USSR's collapse, see Stephen Kotkin, *Armageddon Averted: The Soviet Collapse, 1970–2000* (Oxford: Oxford University Press, 2008).

134. Charles Gati, "Eastern Europe on Its Own," *Foreign Affairs* 68, no. 1 (Winter 1988/1989): 114.

135. A washingtoni nagykövetség számjeltávirata a Külügyminisztériumnak Gecse megbeszéléséről Helmut Sonnenfeldt-el [Report on Gecse's conversation with Sonnenfeldt], March 7, 1989, MNL OL, Küm, XIX-J-1-j, USA tük 1989, 9. doboz, 00625/3; A Külügyminisztérium rejtjeltávirata [Telegram by the Foreign Ministry], June 18, 1989, ibid. 00819; A New York-i főkonzulátus számjeltávirata Brzezinski Foreign Press Association beszédéről [The New York Consulate's telegram, Brzezinski's speech], May 24, 1989, ibid. 002543.

136. Address by James Baker to the Berlin Press Club, December 12, 1989, BPL, National Security Council (NSC), European and Soviet Directorate files, briefing books, box 1.

137. Memorandum of conversation with FRG president Richard von Weizsäcker, February 24, 1989, https://bushlibrary.tamu.edu/research/memcons_telcons.php.

138. Memorandum from Scowcroft to Bush, May 25, 1989, BPL, Scowcroft Collection, USSR chronological file, subseries SNF files, box 14.

139. Talking points for meeting with Defense Policy Board, May 1989, ibid.

140. Memorandum of conversation with Woerner, October 11, 1989, https://bushlibrary.tamu.edu/research/memcons_telcons.php.

141. Memorandum of Bush's conversation with Belgian prime minister Wilfrid Martens, May 28, 1989, ibid.

142. A washingtoni nagykövetség jelentése [Report, embassy in Washington], May 15, 1989, MNL OL, Küm, XIX-J-l-j, USA tük, 1989. 10. doboz, 002245.

143. Memorandum on the president's telephone conversation with Chancellor Kohl, May 5, 1989, https://bushlibrary.tamu.edu/research/memcons_telcons.php.

144. Memorandum of conversation between Bush and Vranitzky, May 5, 1989, https://bushlibrary.tamu.edu/research/memcons_telcons.php.

145. Memorandum from Condoleezza Rice through Robert Blackwill to Scowcroft, BPL, Condoleezza Rice collection.

146. A washingtoni nagykövetség rejtjeltávirata [Telegram, embassy in Washington], May 11, 1989. MNL OL, Kum, XIX-J-1-j, USA tük 1989, 9. doboz, 002245/3.

147. A washingtoni nagykövetség feljegyzése [Memorandum, embassy in Washington], May 15, 1989, MNL OL, Küm, XIX-J-1-j, USA tük 1989, 10. doboz, 0016/2.

148. A washingtoni nagykövetség feljegyzése [Memorandum by the embassy in Washington], May 15, 1989, MNL OL, Küm, XIX-J-l-j, USA tük, 1989.10. doboz, 002245/3.

149. Szovjet tájékoztatás a Külügyminisztériumnak [Soviet information for the Foreign Ministry], May 12, 1989, MNL OL, Küm, XIX-J-1-j, Szu tük 1989, 83. doboz, 001057/1.

150. Megjegyzések a Krasznaja Zvezda cikkéhez [Comments on article in *Krasnaia Zvezda*], June 30, 1989, MNL OL, Küm, XIX-J-1-j, Szu tük 1989, 86. doboz, 003062.

151. Jack Matlock, *Autopsy of an Empire: The American Ambassador's Account of the Collapse of the Soviet Union* (New York: Random House, 1995), 198.

152. The president's meeting with allies, September 25, 1989, https://bushlibrary.tamu.edu/research/memcons_telcons.php.

153. Memorandum from Condoleezza Rice, Adrian Basora, and Timothy Deal to Brent Scowcroft, June 14, 1989, BPL, Scowcroft files, USSR chronological files, Soviet power collapse in Eastern Europe files.

154. Memorandum from Scowcroft to the president regarding telephone call to Mitterrand, July 8, 1989, BPL, Scowcroft files, USSR chronological files, Soviet power collapse in Eastern Europe files.

155. Memorandum from Condoleezza Rice to Brent Scowcroft, June 28, 1989, ibid.

156. Memorandum from Eric Melby to Brent Scowcroft, July 5, 1989, ibid.

157. Memorandum of conversation, June 15, 1989, participants: Brent Scowcroft, Budomir Lončar, ibid., 5439.

158. Bush's closing remarks, Eastern Europe Symposium, July 6, 1989, BPL, Scowcroft chronological files.

159. Gregory Domber, "Skepticism and Stability: Reevaluating US Policy During Poland's Democratic Transformation in 1989," *Journal of Cold War Studies* 13, no. 3 (Summer 2011): 70.

160. The president's telephone conversation with Prime Minister Thatcher, June 6, 1989, https://bushlibrary.tamu.edu/research/memcons_telcons.php.

161. Domber, "Skepticism and Stability," 72.

162. Brent Scowcroft, Robert Hutchings, and Thomas Simons, statement to the author.

163. Memorandum of conversation, President Bush's Meeting with Jaruzelski, chairman of Poland, July 10, 1989, https://bushlibrary.tamu.edu/research/memcons_telcons.php.

164. Letter by Solidarity in Exile, BPL, Scowcroft chronological file, box 17.

165. Memorandum from Robert Hutchings to Brent Scowcroft, Jaruzelski's visit, September 10, 1990, BPL, Scowcroft files, USSR chronological files, Soviet power collapse in Eastern Europe files, 7185.
166. BPL, Condoleezza Rice collection.
167. Ripp, *Rendszerváltás Magyarországon*, 379–88.
168. Ripp, *Rendszerváltás Magyarországon*, 162–63.
169. Feljegyzés Bush látogatásáról [Memorandum on Bush's visit], July 15, 1989, MNL OL, M-KS 288. f. 11. cs., 4460. őe.
170. Hutchings, *American Diplomacy*, 66.
171. The president's bilateral meeting with Wojchiech Jaruzelski, July 10, 1989. https://bushlibrary.tamu.edu/research/memcons_telcons.php.
172. In Baráth and Rainer, *Gorbacsov tárgyalásai*, 194.
173. A Külügyminisztérium Nemzetközi Gazdasági Kapcsolatok Főosztályának feljegyzése a fejlett technológiák export liberalizálását célzó magyar-amerikai tárgyalások előkészítéséről [Foreign Ministry memorandum on the liberalization of export controls], September 13, 1989, MNL OL, Küm, XIX-J-j, USA tük 1989, 57-003520/1-1989.
174. A washingtoni nagykövetség rejtjeltávirata [Telegram, embassy in Washington], October 7 and 10, 1989, MNL OL, Küm, XIX-J-j, USA tük 1989, 5-003865-1989.
175. A Politikai Elemző és Tájékoztatási Főosztály (Kerékgyártó László) feljegyzése Kursch első beosztott látogatásáról [Memorandum on visit by Kursch], December 8, 1989, MNL OL, Küm, XIX-J-1-j, USA 1989 tük, 004422–1989.
176. NSC redraft, draft presidential statement, Poland, BPL, Scowcroft collection, USSR chronological file, box 12.
177. Memorandum from Robert Blackwill to Brent Scowcroft, July 3, 1989, BPL, Scowcroft files, USSR chronological files, Soviet power collapse in Eastern Europe files.
178. Domber, "Skepticism and Stability," 61.
179. Telephone conversation between President Bush and President Mitterrand, August 26, 1989, https://bushlibrary.tamu.edu/research/memcons_telcons.php.
180. Memorandum of conversation between President Bush and Foreign Minister Horn, New York, September 25, 1989, ibid.
181. Bush and Scowcroft, *A World Transformed*, 126.
182. Mark Palmer, statement to the author.
183. Barabás távirata Palmer közléseiről [Report by Barabás on statements by Palmer], July 25, 1989, MNL OL, Küm, XIX-J-1-j, Szu. 1989 tük, 83. Doboz, 001245/3.
184. Report to the Council of Ministers on the Bucharest meeting of the WTO Political Consultative Committee, July 8, 1989, MNL OL, Küm, Európa 1989, 107. doboz, 001367/12.
185. Memorandum of conversation between President Bush and Sergei Akhromeiev, undated, BPL, Condoleezza Rice collection, box 1.
186. Telegram by the embassy in Budapest, July 17, 1989, ibid.
187. Memorandum of conversation with Ruud Lubbers, July 17, 1989, https://bushlibrary.tamu.edu/research/memcons_telcons.php.
188. Az Országgyűlés elnöki titkárságának jelentése [Report by the Presidential Secretariat of the Parliament], September 26, 1989, MNL OL, Küm, XIX-J-1-k, USA admin 1989, 24. doboz, 4243-4/T.
189. Memorandum of conversation with Soviet foreign minister Eduard Shevardnadze, September 21, 1989, https://bushlibrary.tamu.edu/research/memcons_telcons.php.
190. Memorandum of conversation with FRG chancellor Helmut Kohl, May 31, 1989, https://bushlibrary.tamu.edu/research/memcons_telcons.php.

191. Bush's letter to Thatcher, September 22, 1989, BPL, Scowcroft collection, USSR files, Subseries, START files, box 16.
192. Memorandum of conversation between secretary of state James Baker and Van der Broek, September 25, 1989, https://bushlibrary.tamu.edu/research/memcons_telcons.php.
193. Kovács László levele [Open letter by Kovács], MNL OL, Küm, XIX-J-1-k, USA admin 1989, 24. doboz, 1-4979-23/1989.
194. This passage is based on Oplatka, *Egy döntés története*.
195. Ripp, *Rendszerváltás Magyarországon*, 176–77.
196. György Gyarmati, "A vasfüggüny és az állambiztonsági szervek alkonya Magyarországon 1989-ben," in *A Páneurópai Piknik és határáttörés húsz év távlatából*, ed. Gyarmati György (Budapest: L'Harmattan, 2010), 98.
197. Feljegyzés Somogyi Ferenc külügyminiszter-helyettes és Alexander Arnot NSZK nagykövet megbeszéléséről [Memorandum of conversation between Arnot and Somogyi], August 7, 1989, MNL OL, Küm XIX-J-1-j, NSZK tük 1989 002106/1/1989.
198. Imre Tóth, "A keletnémet menekültkérdés hatása a Berlin-Bonn-Budapest háromszög kapcsolatrendszerére," in *A Páneurópai Piknik és határáttörés húsz év távlatából*, ed. György Gyarmati (Budapest: L'Harmattan, 2010), 69.
199. Ibid., 87.
200. Angela Stent, *Russia and Germany Reborn: Unification, the Soviet Collapse and New Europe* (Princeton, N.J.: Princeton University Press, 1998), 84.
201. Ibid., 88.
202. Ripp, *Rendszerváltás Magyarországon*, 483.
203. Memorandum from Brent Scowcroft to the president, Jaruzelski's letter, July 8, 1989, BPL, Scowcroft files, USSR chronological files, Soviet power collapse in Eastern Europe files, 5386.

204. Memorandum from Deane E. Hoffmann to Brent Scowcroft, September 8, 1989, BPL, Scowcroft files, USSR chronological files, Soviet power collapse in Eastern Europe files, 7062; memorandum from Robert Blackwill to Brent Scowcroft, Strategy for Poland and Hungary, September 19, 1989, ibid., 7367.
205. Letter from Geoffrey Sachs to Brent Scowcroft, September 27, 1989, ibid., 7352.
206. Az Országgyűlés Elnöki Titkárságának jelentése a Szűrös Mátyás vezette küldöttség amerikai látogatásáról [Report on Szűrös's visit in Washington], September 26, 1989, MNL OL, Küm, XIX-J-1-k, USA admin, 1989, 24. doboz, 4243-4/T.
207. A washingtoni nagykövetség rejtjeltávirata a Külügyminisztériumnak [Telegram by the embassy in Washington], October 12, 1989, MNL OL, Küm, XIX-J-1-j, USA tük, 9. doboz, 003990.
208. Memorandum from Scowcroft to the president, meeting with Spanish foreign minister Gonzales, October 18, 1989, BPL, Scowcroft files, USSR chronological files, Soviet power collapse in Eastern Europe files, 8051.
209. Brent Scowcroft's statement to the author Robert Hutchings stated "that we had a pretty precise idea of the KGB's activities in Hungary."
210. Washingtoni rezidentúra, "Pagnon" jelentése [Pagnon's report], October 12, 1989, ÁBTL, USA, 1989.
211. Nagy Lajos távirata Biszku őrnagynak [Report to Major Biszku], November 28, 1989, ibid.
212. Bogye János vezérőrnagy főcsoportfőnök-helyettes távirata a külképviseleteknek [Major General Bogye's telegram to foreign representatives], November 27, 1989, ibid.
213. Theme paper on Eastern Europe drafted by the State Department Bureau of European Affairs, November 16, 1989, BPL, Condoleezza Rice collection.

214. A washingtoni nagykövetség rejtjeltávirata a Külügyminisztériumnak [Telegram by the embassy in Washington], October 12, 1989, MNL OL, Küm, XIX-J-1-j, USA tük, 9. doboz, 003990.
215. Stent, *Russia and Germany Reborn*, 92–93.
216. Sarotte, *1989*, 42–43, 64
217. BPL, Scowcroft chronological files, box 16.
218. Theme paper on Eastern Europe drafted by the State Department Bureau of European Affairs, November 16, 1989, BPL, Condoleezza Rice collection.
219. Rejtjeltávirat a Külügyminisztériumnak [Telegram to the Foreign Ministry], November 24, 1989, MNL OL, Küm, XIX-J-1-j, Európa, 97. doboz, 00275/129.
220. Sarotte, *1989*, 75–76.
221. Az MSZMP KB NKO javaslata a pártelnökség számára [Recommendation for the Party Presidium], June 30, 1989, MNL OL, M-KS 288. f. 59. cs. 1. őe.
222. As Horn put it, "[our] membership in the Warsaw Pact is not open to question." See Jelentés Aboimov látogatásáról [Report on Aboimov's visit], October 20, 1989, MNL OL, Küm, XIX-J-1-j, Szu tük 1989, 84. doboz, 003982.
223. Aboimov találkozója ellenzéki politikusokkal [Aboimov's meeting with the opposition], October 17, 1989, MNL OL, Küm, XIX-J-1-j, Szu tük 1989, 84. doboz, 003982.
224. A varsói nagykövetség távirata Sevardnadze látogatásáról [Telegram by the embassy in Warsaw regarding Shevardnadze's visit in Warsaw], October 27, 1989, ibid.
225. Telephone conversation between President Bush and Spanish prime minister Felipe Gonzales, November 25, 1989, https://bushlibrary.tamu.edu/research/memcons_telcons.php.
226. Letter from Gereben to George Bush, BPL, White House Office of Management Records (WHORM) subseries, subject files, foreign affairs, F0006-US-Soviet summit.
227. Telegram from the embassy in Moscow to the Foreign Ministry, Soviet view on East European developments, November 27, 1989, MNL OL, Küm, XIX-J-1-j, Szu tük 1989, 83. doboz, 00431.
228. Kramer, "The Collapse of East European Communism, part 3," 4, 7.
229. Memorandum from Scowcroft to the president, meeting with state minister Pozsgay, November 2, 1989, BPL, Scowcroft files, USSR chronological files, Soviet power collapse in Eastern Europe files, 8674.
230. Memorandum for G. Philip Hughes from Robert Blackwill, memorandum of conversation between the president and Imre Pozsgay, November 2, 1989, BPL, WHORM, subject files, foreign affairs, Malta.
231. Memorandum of conversation between Kamman and Kutuzov, November 25, 1989, NSAWDC, End of the Cold War project, box 4.
232. Memorandum from Edward Rowny to the secretary of state, Malta meeting, November 27, 1989, ibid., box 4.
233. NSC meeting, November 4, 1989, ibid.
234. The secretary of state to the ambassador in Moscow, Memorandum of conversation, participants: George Bush and Helmut Kohl, December 3, 1989, NSAWDC, End of the Cold War project, box 4.
235. Anatolij Chernaiev's memorandum on the Summit in Malta, NSAWDC, End of the Cold War project, box 4.
236. Jelentés a Minisztertanácsnak a Varsói Szerződés tagállamai vezetőinek tanácskozásáról [Report on meeting of WTO leaders], December 4, 1989, MNL OL, Küm, XIX-J-1-j, 177/HGY, 94. doboz.
237. Telegram by the secretary of state to all NATO capitals: Debrief of Malta meeting to allied ambassadors, December

7, 1989, NSAWDC, End of the Cold War project, box 3.

238. A washingtoni nagykövetség feljegyzése Várkonyi, Kamman, Hornblow és Swihart megbeszéléséről [Memorandum of conversation, Várkonyi, Kamman, Hornblow, Swihart], 1990, KIT, USA SZT 1990. 9. doboz, 0050.

239. Kramer, "The Collapse of East European Communism, part 3," 9–12.

240. Telephone conversation with President Mitterrand, September 16, 1989, https://bushlibrary.tamu.edu/research/memcons_telcons.php.

241. Statement by the press secretary; major excerpt from speech by Margaret Thatcher, November 13, 1989, BPL, Scowcroft collection, chronological file, box 17.

242. Memorandum from Robert Hutchings to Brent Scowcroft, United States Policy toward Eastern Europe, December 16, 1989, BPL, Scowcroft files, USSR chronological files, Soviet power collapse in Eastern Europe, 1015; handwritten note by Robert Blackwill on the margin: "Good thinking, keep it up."

243. Memorandum from Brent Scowcroft to the president, U.S. Policy in Eastern Europe in 1990, undated, ibid., 0192.

244. Memorandum from Brent Scowcroft to the president, U.S. policy toward the New Eastern Europe, May 11, 1990, ibid., 3562.

245. Memorandum from Lawrence Eagleburger to secretary of state James Baker, March 1, 1990, ibid., 1541.

246. Memorandum from Robert Hutchings to the secretary of state, August 16, 1990, ibid., 6578.

247. Memorandum from Brent Scowcroft to the president, meeting with Antall, October 17, 1990, ibid., 7791.

CONCLUSION

1. The literature includes Richard Breitman and Allen J. Lichtman, *FDR and the Jews* (Cambridge, Mass.: Belknap Press of Harvard University Press, 2013); David Wyman, *The Abandonment of the Jews* (New York: New Press, 2007); Martin Gilbert, *Auschwitz and the Allies* (New York: Holt, Rinehart and Winston, 1981).

2. Tim Cole, *Holocaust City: The Making of a Jewish Ghetto* (New York: Routledge, 2003).

BIBLIOGRAPHY

Archives

Archives diplomatiques du Quai d'Orsay
Arkhiv Vneshnei Politiki Rossiiskoi Federatsii
Állambiztonsági Történeti Levéltár
Bodleian Library
George H. W. Bush Presidential Library
Jimmy Carter Presidential Library
Library of Congress
Magyar Nemzeti Levéltár Országos Levéltára
Seeley Mudd Library
National Archives and Records Administration, Washington, D.C.
National Security Archive, Washington, D.C.
Országos Széchényi Könyvtár

Interviews

Robert Hutchings
Nagy, János
Mark Palmer
Brent Scowcroft
Thomas Simons
Somogyi, Ferenc
John Whitehead

Published Documents

Baráth, Magdolna, and István Feitl, eds. "Két összefoglaló a magyar-szovjet tárgyalásokról, 1958." *Múltunk* [Our Past], no. 4 (April 1993): 163–88.

Baráth, Magdolna, Lajos Gecsényi, and Gábor Máthé, eds. *Sub Clausula 1989: Dokumentumok az 1989-es rendszerváltozás történetéhez. A dokumentumokat válogatta és a jegyzeteket készítette.* Budapest: Magyar Közlöny, 2009.

Baráth, Magdolna, and M. János Rainer, eds. *Gorbacsov tárgyalásai magyar vezetőkkel: dokumentumok az egykori SZKP és MSZMP archívumaiból 1985–1991.* Budapest: 1956-os Intézet, 2000.

Békés, Csaba, and Malcolm Byrne, eds. *Political Transition in Hungary, 1989–1990: International Conference: A Compendium of Declassified Documents and Chronology of Events.* Budapest: 1956-os Intézet, 1999.

Békés, Csaba, Malcolm Byrne, and M. János Rainer. *The 1956 Hungarian Revolution: A History in Documents.* Budapest: Central European University Press, 2002.

Berle, Beatrice Bishop, and Travis Beal Jacobs, eds. *Navigating the Rapids, 1918–1971: From the Papers of Adolf A. Berle.* New York: Harcourt Brace Jovanovich, 1973.

Borhi, László. "Iratok a magyar-amerikai kapcsolatok történetéhez." *Történelmi Szemle* [Historical Review] no. 3-4 (1998).

Carter, Jimmy. *White House Diary*. New York: Farrar, Straus and Giroux, 2010.

Commission de publication des documents diplomatiques français. *Documents Diplomatiques Français, 1956. Tome III (24 octobre–31 dècembre)*. Paris: Imprimerie nationale, 1990.

Foreign Relations of the United States. Europe. Volume IV, 1945.

Foreign Relations of the United States. Eastern Europe, The Soviet Union. Volume VI, 1946.

Foreign Relations of the United States. Eastern Europe, The Soviet Union. Volume IV, 1947.

Foreign Relations of the United States. Eastern Europe; The Soviet Union. Volume IV, 1948,

Foreign Relations of the United States. Central and Eastern Europe; The Soviet Union. Volume IV, 1950.

Foreign Relations of the United States, Eastern Europe; Soviet Union; Eastern Mediterranean. 1952–1954. Volume VIII.

Foreign Relations of the United States: Diplomatic Papers: The Conferences at Cairo and Tehran 1943. Washington D.C.: Government Printing Office, 1961.

Foreign Relations of the United States. 1955–1957, Volume XXV.

Foreign Relations of the United States. 1958–1960, Volume X.

Foreign Relations of the United States: Diplomatic Papers: The Conferences at Malta and Yalta 1945. Washington D.C.: Government Printing Office, 1955.

Foreign Relations of the United States. 1961–1963, Volume XVI.

Foreign Relations of the United States. 1964–1968, Volume XVII.

Foreign Relations of the United States. 1969–1970, Volume XII.

Foreign Relations of the United States. 1971–1972, Volume 14 (Washington, D.C.: Government Printing Office, 2006).

Foreign Relations of the United States. 1973–1976, vol. E-15, pt. 1, Documents on Eastern Europe (Washington, D.C.: Government Printing Office, 2008).

Haraszti-Taylor, Éva, ed. *The Hungarian Revolution of 1956: A Collection of Documents from the British Foreign Office*. Nottingham: Astra Press, 1995.

Izsák, Lajos, and Miklós Kun, eds. *Moszkvának jelentjük: Titkos dokumentumok 1944–1948*. Budapest: Századvég, 1994.

Juhász, Gyula, ed. *Magyar-brit titkos tárgyalások 1943-ban*. Budapest: Kossuth Könyvkiadó, 1978.

Kecskés, D. Gusztáv, ed. *Magyar-francia kapcsolatok, 1945–1990: források*. Budapest: MTA Történettudományi Intézete, 2013.

Kimball, Warren F., ed. *Churchill and Roosevelt: The Complete Correspondence*. 3 vols. Princeton, N.J.: Princeton University Press, 1992.

Küsters, Hanns Jürgen, and Daniel Hofmann, eds. *Deutsche Einheit: Dokumente zur Deutschlandpolitik: Sonderedition aus den Akten des Bundeskanzleramtes 1989/90*. Digitale Bibliothek 21. Berlin: Directmedia, 2004.

Murashko, Galina P., et al., eds. *Vostochnaia Evropa v Dokumentakh Rossiskikh Arkhivov 1944–1953*. Vol. 1. Novosibirsk: Sibirskii Khronograf, 1998.

———, eds. *Vostochnaia Evropa v Dokumentakh Rossiskikh Arhivov 1944–1953*. Vol. 2. Novosibirsk: Sibirskii Khronograf, 1998.

Osterman, Christian, ed. *Uprising in East Germany, 1953: The Cold War, the German Question and the First Major Upheaval Behind the Iron Curtain*. Budapest: Central European University Press, 2001.

Petersen, Neil H., ed. *From Hitler's Doorstep: The Wartime Intelligence Reports of Allen Dulles, 1942–1945*. University Park:

Pennsylvania State University Press, 1996.
Romsics, Ignác, ed. *Amerikai béketervek a háború utáni Magyarországról*. Gödöllő: Typovent, 1992.
Rzheshevsky, Oleg, ed. *War and Diplomacy: The Making of the Grand Alliance; Documents from Stalin's Archives, Edited With a Commentary*. New History of Russia 2. Amsterdam: Harwood Academic Publishers, 1996.
Sand, G. W., ed. *Defending the West: The Truman-Churchill Correspondence, 1945–1960*. Westport, Conn.: Praeger, 2004.
Somorjai, Ádám, ed. *Mindszenty bíboros az amerikai nagykövetségen*. Budapest: Magyar Egyháztörténeti Enciklopédia Munkaközössége (METEM), 2008.
Urbán, Károly, and István Vida, eds. "Budapest 1941. május-1944. március. Részlet Barcza György Diplomata emlékeim című emlékiratának II. kötetéből." *Századok* [Centuries] 121, no. 23 (1987): 355–420.
Vass, István G. "Bakách-Bessenyey György tárgyalásai az Egyesült Államok megbízottaival Bernben 1943. augusztus 28. és 1944. március 19. között." *Levéltári Közlemények* [Archival Bulletin] 65, no 1–2 (1994): 153–205.
Volokitina, T. V. et al., eds. *Transilvanskii Vopros Vengero-Ruminskii territorialnii spor i SSSR, 1940–1946. Dokumenti*. Moscow: Rosspen, 2000.

Memoirs

Belovai, István. *Fedőneve – Scorpion*. Budapest: I. Belovai, 1998.
Brzezinski, Zbigniew K. *Power and Principle: Memoirs of the National Security Advisor, 1977–1981*. New York: Farrar, Straus, and Giroux, 1983.
Bush, George, and Brent Scowcroft. *A World Transformed*. New York: Vintage Books, 1998.
Dobrynin, Anatoly. *In Confidence: Moscow's Ambassador to America's Six Cold War Presidents (1962–1986)*. New York: Times Books, 1995.
Eisenhower, Dwight D. *Waging Peace, 1956–1961: The White House Years*. Vol. 2. Garden City, N.Y.: Doubleday, 1965.
Hillenbrand, Martin J. *Fragments of Our Time: Memoirs of a Diplomat*. Athens: University of Georgia Press, 1998.
Horn, Gyula. *Cölöpök*. Budapest: Zenit Könyvek, 1991.
Hutchings, Robert L. *American Diplomacy and the End of the Cold War: An Insider's Account of U.S. Policy in Europe, 1989–1992*. Washington, D.C.: Woodrow Wilson Center Press, 1997.
Kállay, Miklós. *Hungarian Premier: A Personal Account of a Nation's Struggle in the Second World War*. New York: Columbia University Press, 1954.
Matlock, Jack F. *Autopsy of an Empire: The American Ambassador's Account of the Collapse of the Soviet Union*. New York: Random House, 1995.
Montgomery, John Flourney. *The Unwilling Satellite*. New York: Devin-Adair Company, 1947.
Montgomery, John F., and Miklós Barabás. *Magyarország, a vonakodó csatlós*. Budapest: Zrínyi Kiadó, 2004.
Nyárádi, Nicholas. *My Ringside Seat in Moscow*. New York: Thomas E. Crowell, 1952.
Puhan, Alfred. *The Cardinal in the Chancery and Other Recollections*. New York: Vantage Press, 1990.
Rákosi, Mátyás. *Visszaemlékezések 1940–1956 Köt. 1*. Budapest: Budapest Napvilág Kiadó, 1997.
Szegedy-Maszák, Aladár, and László Csorba. *Az ember ősszel visszanéz: Egy volt magyar diplomata emlékiratából*. Budapest: Európa-História, 1996.
Thatcher, Margaret. *The Downing Street Years*. New York: HarperCollins, 1993.
Vogeler, Robert A. *I Was Stalin's Prisoner*. New York: Harcourt, Brace, 1951.

Secondary Sources

Ádám, Magda. *A Kisantant és Európa, 1920–1929*. Budapest: Akadémiai Kiadó, 1989.

Adamthwaite, Anthony P. *Grandeur and Misery: France's Bid for Power in Europe 1914–1940*. London: Arnold, 1995.

Applebaum, Anne. *Iron Curtain: The Crushing of Eastern Europe 1944–1956*. New York: Doubleday, 2012.

Aronson, Shlomo. *Hitler, the Allies and the Jews*. Cambridge: Cambridge University Press, 2004.

Balogh, Margit. *Mindszenty József (1892–1975)*. Budapest: Elektra Kiadóház, 2002.

Barker, Elisabeth. *British Policy in South-East Europe in the Second World War*. London: MacMillan, 1976.

———. "Problems of Alliance – Misconceptions and Misunderstanding." In *British Political and Military Strategy in Central, Eastern, and Southern Europe in 1944*, edited by William Deakin, Elisabeth Barker, and Jonathan Chadwick. London: Palgrave MacMillan, 1988.

Bart, István. *Világirodalom és könyvkiadás a Kádár-korszakban*. Budapest: Scholastica, 2000.

Bátonyi, Gábor. *Britain and Central Europe, 1918–1933*. Oxford: Clarendon Press, 1999.

Békés, Csaba. *The 1956 Hungarian Revolution and World Politics*. Cold War International History Project Working Paper no. 16. Washington, D.C.: Cold War International History Project, Woodrow Wilson International Center for Scholars, 1996.

———. "A Kádári külpolitika 1956–1968: Látványos sikerek – 'láthatatlan' konfliktusok." In *Európából Európába: Magyarország konfliktusok kereszttüzében, 1945–1990*, edited by Csaba Békés. Budapest: Gondolat, 2004.

———. *Az 1956-os magyar forradalom a világpolitikában: tanulmány és válogatott dokumentumok*. Budapest: 1956-os Intézet, 1996.

———. "Az Egyesült Államok és a magyar semlegesség 1956-ban." In *Az 1956-os Magyar Forradalom Történetének Dokumentációs és Kutatóintézete: Évkönyv* [Yearbook]: *1994*, edited by János M. Bak, B. András Hegedűs, and György Litván, 165–78. Budapest: 1956-os Intézet, 1994.

———. *Európából Európába: Magyarország konfliktusok kereszttüzében, 1945–1990*. Budapest: Gondolat, 2004.

———. *Hidegháború, enyhülés és az 1956-os forradalom. Évkönyv V* [Yearbook], *1996–1997*. Budapest: 1956-os Intézet, 1997.

———. "Magyar külpolitika a szovjet szövetségi rendszerben, 1968–1989." In *Magyar külpolitika a 20. Században: Tanulmányok*, edited by Ferenc Gazdag and J. László Kiss, 133–72. Budapest: Zrínyi Kiadó, 2004.

Beschloss, Michael R., and Strobe Talbott. *At the Highest Levels: The Inside Story of the End of the Cold War*. Boston: Little, Brown and Company, 1993.

Bischof, Günter. *Austria in the First Cold War, 1945–55: The Leverage of the Weak*. London: MacMillan, 1999.

Bischof, Günter, and Stephen E. Ambrose, eds. *Eisenhower: A Centenary Assessment*. Baton Rouge: Louisiana State University Press, 1995.

Bodzabán, István, Antal Szalay, and Endre Aczél, eds. *A puha diktatúrától a kemény demokráciáig*. Budapest: Pelikán, 1994.

Borbándi, Gyula. *Magyarok az Angol Kertben: A Szabad Európa Rádió története*. Budapest: Európa, 1996.

Borhi, László. *Hungary in the Cold War 1945–1956: Between the United States and the Soviet Union*. Budapest, New York: Central European University Press, 2004.

———. *Magyar-amerikai kapcsolatok, 1945–1989: források. Magyarország a szovjet zónában és a rendszerváltásban*. Budapest: MTA Történettudományi Intézete, 2009.

———. *Magyarország a hidegháborúban: A Szovjetunió és az Egyesült Államok között, 1945–1956*. Budapest: Corvina, 2005.

Bowie, Robert R., and Richard H. Immerman. *Waging Peace: How Eisenhower Shaped an Enduring Cold War Strategy*. Oxford: Oxford University Press, 2000.

Braham, Randolph L. *The Politics of Genocide: The Holocaust in Hungary*. 2 vols. New York: Columbia University Press, 1994.

Brands, H. W. *The Devil We Knew: Americans and the Cold War*. New York: Oxford University Press, 1993.

Breitman, Richard. *Official Secrets: What the Nazis Planned, What the British and Americans Knew*. New York: Hill and Wang, 1999.

Breitman, Richard, and Allen J. Lichtman. *FDR and the Jews*. Cambridge, Mass.: Belknap Press of Harvard University Press, 2013.

Brown, Anthony Cave. *Bodyguard of Lies*. Vol. 1. New York: Harper and Row, 1975.

Buckley, Mary. "The Multifaceted External Soviet Role in Processes towards Unanticipated Revolutions." In *The 1989 Revolutions in Central and Eastern Europe: From Communism to Pluralism*, edited by Kevin McDermott and Matthew Stibbe. Manchester: Manchester University Press, 2013.

Bull, Hedley. *The Anarchical Society: A Study of Order in World Politics*. New York: Columbia University Press, 1977.

Carruthers, Susan L. *Cold War Captives: Imprisonment, Escape, Brainwashing*. Berkeley: University of California Press, 2009.

Chen, Jian. *Mao's China and the Cold War*. Chapel Hill: University of North Carolina Press, 2001.

Cohen, Stephen F. "The Fate of the Soviet Union: Why Did It End?" In *Soviet Fates and Lost Alternatives: From Stalinism to the New Cold War*, edited by Stephen F. Cohen. New York: Columbia University Press, 2011.

Cohen, Warren I. *America's Response to China: A History of Sino-American Relations*. New York: Columbia University Press, 2010.

Cole, Tim. *Holocaust City: The Making of a Jewish Ghetto*. New York: Routledge, 2003.

Craig, Campbell, and Frederik Logevall. *America's Cold War: The Politics of Insecurity*. Cambridge, Mass.: Belknap Press of Harvard University Press, 2009.

Czettler, Antal. *A mi kis élethalál kérdéseink: a magyar külpolitika a hadba lépéstől a német megszállásig*. Budapest: Magvető, 2000.

Dallek, Robert. *Nixon and Kissinger: Partners in Power*. New York: HarperCollins, 2007.

De Santis, Hugh. *The Diplomacy of Silence: The American Foreign Service, The Soviet Union, and the Cold War, 1933–1947*. Chicago: University of Chicago Press, 1980.

Dobson, Alan P. *US Economic Statecraft for Survival 1933–1991: Of Sanctions, Embargoes, and Economic Warfare*. New York: Routledge, 2002.

Domber, Gregory F. "Skepticism and Stability: Reevaluating U.S. Policy During Poland's Democratic Transformation in 1989." *Journal of Cold War Studies* 13, no. 3 (Summer 2011): 52–82.

Edmonds, Robin. *The Big Three: Churchill, Roosevelt, and Stalin in Peace and War*. London: Hamish Hamilton, 1991.

Faure, Justine. *L'Ami Américain: La Tchécoslovaquie, enjeu de la diplomatie Américaine, 1943–1968*. Paris: Tallandier, 2004.

Felkay, Andrew. *Hungary and the USSR, 1956–1968: Kadar's Political Leadership*. New York: Greenwood Press, 1989.

Førland, Tor Egil. "Cold Economic Warfare: The Creation and Prime of CoCom, 1948–1954." PhD dissertation, University of Oslo, 1991.

———. "'Selling Firearms to the Indians': Eisenhower's Export Control Policy, 1953–54." *Diplomatic History* 15, no. 2 (April 1991): 221–44.

Földes, György. *Az eladósodás politikatörténete, 1957–1986.* Budapest: Maecenas, 1995.

———. "Kötélhúzás felsőfokon: Kádár és Brezsnyev." In *Ki volt Kádár? Harag és részrehajlás nélkül a Kádár-életútról*, edited by Árpád Rácz. Budapest: Rubin-Aquila-Könyvek, 2001.

Földesi, Margit. *A szabadság megszállása: a megszállók szabadsága: a hadizsákmányról, a jóvátételről, Szövetséges Ellenőrző Bizottságról Magyarországon.* Budapest: Kairosz, 2002.

Frank, Tibor. "Diplomatic Images of Admiral Horthy: The American Perspectives of Interwar Hungary." In *Ethnicity, Propaganda, Myth-Making: Studies on Hungarian Connections to Britain and America, 1848–1945*, edited by Tibor Frank. Budapest: Akadémiai Kiadó, 1999.

———, ed. *Gyarmatokból imperium: Magyar kutatók tanulmányai az amerikai történelemről.* Budapest: Gondolat, 2007.

Fülöp, Mihály. *A befejezetlen béke: A külügyminiszterek tanácsa és a magyar békeszerződés (1947).* Budapest: Héttorony, 1994.

Gaddis, John Lewis. *The Cold War: A New History.* New York: Penguin Press, 2006.

———. *The Long Peace: Inquiries into the History of the Cold War.* New York: Oxford University Press, 1987.

———. *We Now Know: Rethinking Cold War History.* Oxford: Clarendon Press, 1997.

Garadnai, Zoltán, and Thomas Schreiber. "A magyarországi rendszerváltozás a Quai d'Orsay szemével." *Külügyi Szemle* [Foreign Review], VII. 2008 nyár, 2. 129–149.

Garthoff, Raymond. "A magyar forradalom és Washington." In *Évkönyv V. 1996–1997*, edited by Hegedűs B., András et al., 214–27. Budapest: 1956-os Intézet, 1997.

———. *Détente and Confrontation: American-Soviet Relations from Nixon to Reagan.* Washington D.C.: Brookings Institution Press, 1985.

Gati, Charles. "Eastern Europe on Its Own." *Foreign Affairs* 68, no. 1 (Winter 1988/1989).

———. *Failed Illusions: Moscow, Washington, Budapest, and the 1956 Hungarian Revolt.* Stanford, Calif.: Stanford University Press, 2006.

Gellately, Robert. *Stalin's Curse: Battling for Communism in War and Cold War.* New York: Knopf, 2013.

Gilbert, Martin. *Auschwitz and the Allies.* New York: Holt, Rinehart and Winston, 1981.

———. *Road to Victory: Winston S. Churchill 1941–1945.* Boston: London: Heinemann, 1986.

Glant, Tibor. *A Szent Korona amerikai kalandja, 1945–1978.* Debrecen: Kossuth Egyetemi Kiadó, 1997.

———. *Emlékezzünk Magyarországra, 1956: Tanulmányok a magyar forradalom és szabadságharc amerikai emlékezetéről.* Budapest: Kiss József, 2008.

Goldgeier, James M., and Michael McFaul. *Power and Purpose: U.S. Policy toward Russia after the Cold War.* Washington, D.C.: Brookings Institution Press, 2003.

Gorodetsky, Gabriel. *The Grand Delusion: Stalin and the German Invasion of Russia.* New Haven, Conn.: Yale University Press, 1999.

Gough, Richard. *A Good Comrade: János Kádár, Communism and Hungary.* London: I. B. Tauris, 2006.

Grose, Peter. *Gentleman Spy: The Life of Allen Dulles.* Boston: Houghton Mifflin Company, 1994.

———. *Operation Rollback: America's Secret War Behind the Iron Curtain.* Boston: Houghton Mifflin Company, 2000.

Gyáni, Gábor. "Socio-Psychological Roots of Discontent: Paradoxes of 1956." *Hun-

garian Studies 20, no. 1 (June 2006): 65–74.

Gyarmati, György. "A vasfüggöny és az állambiztonsági szervek alkonya Magyarországon 1989-ben." In *A Páneurópai Piknik és határáttörés húsz év távlatából*, edited by György Gyarmati, 95–116. Budapest: L'Harmattan, 2010.

Hahn, Peter L. *The United States, Great Britain and Egypt, 1945–1956: Strategy and Diplomacy in the Early Cold War*. Chapel Hill: University of North Carolina Press, 1991.

Ham, Peter van. *The EC, Eastern Europe and European Unity: Discord, Collaboration and Integration Since 1947*. New York: Pinter Publishers, 1993.

Hanhimäki, Jussi. *The Flawed Architect: Henry Kissinger and American Foreign Policy*. New York: Oxford University Press, 2004.

Harbutt, Fraser J. *Yalta 1945: Europe and America at the Crossroads*. New York: Cambridge University Press, 2010.

Hargittai, István. *Judging Edward Teller: A Closer Look at One of the Most Influential Scientists of the Twentieth Century*. Amherst, N.Y.: Prometheus Books, 2010.

Harper, John Lamberton. *American Visions of Europe: Franklin D. Roosevelt, George F. Kennan, and Dean G. Acheson*. Cambridge: Cambridge University Press, 1994.

Harrington, Joseph F., and Bruce J. Courtney. *Tweaking the Nose of the Russians: Fifty Years of American-Romanian Relations, 1940–1990*. East European Monographs no. 296. Boulder, Colo.: East European Monographs, 1991.

Harrison, Hope M. *Driving the Soviets Up the Wall: Soviet-East German Relations, 1953–1961*. Princeton, N.J.: Princeton University Press, 2003.

Haslam, Jonathan. *Russia's Cold War: From the October Revolution to the Fall of the Wall*. New Haven, Conn.: Yale University Press, 2011.

Hazard, Elizabeth W. *Cold War Crucible: United States Foreign Policy and the Conflict in Romania, 1943–1953*. East European Monographs no. 442. Boulder, Colo.: East European Monographs, 1996.

Hixson, Walter L. *Parting the Iron Curtain: Propaganda, Culture, and the Cold War, 1945–1961*. London: MacMillan, 1997.

Holloway, David. "Nuclear Weapons and the Cold War in Europe." In *Imposing, Maintaining and Tearing Open the Iron Curtain: The Cold War and East-Central Europe, 1945–1989*, edited by Mark Kramer and Vít Smetana, 437–56. Lanham, Md.: Lexington Books, 2013.

Holloway, David, and Victor McFarland. "The Hungarian Revolution of 1956 in the Context of the Cold War Military Confrontation." *Hungarian Studies* 20, no. 1 (June 2006): 31–49.

Honvári, János. "Pénzügyi és vagyonjogi tárgyalások és egyezmények Magyarország és az Egyesült Államok között, 1945–1978." *Századok* [Centuries] 143, no. 1 (2009): 37–82.

Horváth, István, and István Németh. *És a falak leomlanak: Magyarország és a német egység (1945–1990): Legenda és valóság*. Budapest: Magvető, 1999.

Horváth, Sándor. "Hooligans, Spivs and Gangs: Youth Subcultures in the 1960s." In *Muddling Through the Long 1960s: Ideas and Everyday Life in High Politics and the Lower Classes of Communist Hungary*, edited by M. János Rainer and György Péteri. Budapest: Institute for the History of the 1956 Hungarian Revolution, 2005.

Hughes, Geraint. "British Policy Towards Eastern Europe and the Impact of the 'Prague Spring', 1964–68." *Cold War History* 4, no. 2 (2004): 115–39.

———. *Harold Wilson's Cold War: The Labour Government and East-West Politics, 1964–1970*. Royal Historical Society Studies in History, new series. Woodbridge, Suffolk, Rochester, N.Y.: Boydell Press, 2009.

Hunt, David. "British Military Planning and Aims in 1944." In *British Political and Military Strategy in Central, Eastern and South-eastern Europe in 1944*, edited by F. W. Deakin, Elisabeth Barker, and Jonathan Chadwick. London: MacMillan, 1988.

Huszár, Tibor. *Kádár: A hatalom évei, 1956–1989*. Budapest: Corvina, 2006.

———. *Kádár János politikai életrajza 1957. november –1989. június*. Budapest: Kossuth, 2003.

Iber, Walter M., and Peter Ruggenthaler, eds. *Stalin's Wirtschaftspolitik an der sowjetischen Peripherie: Ein Überblick auf der Basis sowjetischer und osteuropäischer Quellen*, Veröffentlichungen des Ludwig Boltzmann-Instituts für Kriegsfolgen-Forschung, Graz-Wien no. 19. Innsbruck: Studien Verlag, 2011.

Immerman, Richard H. *John Foster Dulles: Piety, Pragmatism and Power in U.S. Foreign Policy*. Wilmington, Del.: Scholarly Resources, 1999.

Jervis, Robert. *American Foreign Policy in a New Era*. New York: Routledge, 2005.

Johnson, A. Ross. *Radio Free Europe and Radio Liberty: The CIA Years and Beyond*. Washington, D.C.: Woodrow Wilson Center Press, 2010.

Joó, András. *Kállay Miklós külpolitikája: Magyarország és a háborús diplomácia 1942–1944*. Budapest: Napvilág, 2008.

———. "Világháborús intrikák: a magyar béketapogatózások és az isztanbuli színtér fontos mozzanatai." *Századok* [Centuries] 142, no. 6 (2008): 1421–64.

Juhász, Gyula. "A magyar-német viszony néhány kérdése a második világháború alatt." *Történelmi Szemle* [Historical Review] 27, no. 12 (1984): 269–79.

———. *Magyarország külpolitikája 1919–1945*. Budapest: Kossuth, 1988.

Kalmár, Melinda. *Ennivaló és hozomány: A kora kádárizmus ideológiája*. Budapest: Magvető, 1998.

Kamiński, Marek K. *Wobliczu sowieckego ekspansjonizmu: Polityka Stanów Zjednocznych I Wielkiej Britanii Wobec Polskii i Czechosłowacji, 1945–1948*. Warsaw: Instytut Historii PAN, 2005.

Kenez, Peter. *Hungary from the Nazis to the Soviets: The Establishment of the Communist Regime in Hungary, 1944–1988*. Cambridge: Cambridge University Press, 2009.

Kenney, Padraic. *A Carnival of Revolution: Central Europe 1989*. Princeton, N.J.: Princeton University Press, 2002.

Kent, John. "British Postwar Planning for Europe 1942–45." In *The Failure of Peace in Europe, 1943–48*, edited by Antonio Varsori and Elena Calandri. Cold War History Series. New York: Palgrave Macmillan, 2001.

Kertesz, Stephen D. *Between Russia and the West: Hungary and the Illusions of Peacemaking, 1945–1947*. Notre Dame, Ind.: University of Notre Dame Press, 1984.

Kieninger, Stephan. "Transformation versus Status Quo: The Survival of the Transformation Strategy during the Nixon Years." In *Perforating the Iron Curtain: European Détente, Transatlantic Relations, and the Cold War, 1965–1985*, edited by Poul Villaume and Odd Arne Westad. Copenhagen: Museum Tusculanum Press, University of Copenhagen, 2010.

Kissinger, Henry. *Diplomacy*. New York: Simon & Schuster, 1994.

Kornai, János. *A hiány*. Budapest: Közgazdasági és Jogi Könyvkiadó, 1980.

Kotkin, Stephen. *Armageddon Averted: The Soviet Collapse, 1970–2000*. Oxford: Oxford University Press, 2008.

Kovács Zoltán András. "A Janus arcú tábornok: Adalékok Ujszászy István vezérőrnagynak, a VKF 2 osztály és az Államvédelmi Központ vezetőjének az ÁVH fogságában írott feljegyzéseihez."

In *Vallomások a holtak házából*, edited by György Haraszti, 100–37. Budapest: Corvina K., 2007.

Kovrig, Bennett. *Of Walls and Bridges: The United States & Eastern Europe.* New York: New York University Press, 1991.

Kramer, Mark. "The Collapse of East European Communism and the Repercussions within the Soviet Union, part 2." *Journal of Cold War Studies* 6, no. 4 (Fall 2004): 43–64.

———. "The Collapse of East European Communism and the Repercussions within the Soviet Union, part 3." *Journal of Cold War Studies* 7, no. 1 (Winter 2005): 13–96.

———. "The Demise of the Soviet Bloc." In *The End of the Beginning: The Revolutions of 1989 and the Resurgence of History,* edited by Vladimir Tismaneanu and Bogdan C. Iacob, 171–255. Budapest: Central European University Press, 2012.

———. "The Early Post-Stalin Succession Struggle and the Upheavals in East-Central Europe: Internal-External Linkages in Soviet Decision-Making, part 3." *Journal of Cold War Studies* 1, no. 3 (Winter 1999): 3–55.

———. "New Evidence on Soviet Decision-Making and the 1956 Polish and Hungarian Crisis." *Cold War International History Project Bulletin* 8–9 (Winter 1996–1997): 358–84.

———. "Stalin, Soviet Policy and the Consolidation of a Communist Bloc in Eastern Europe, 1944–1953." In *Stalinism Revisited: The Establishment of Communist Regimes in East-Central Europe,* edited by Vladimir Tismaneanu, 53–100. Budapest: Central European University Press, 2009.

Laqueur, Walter. *Europe In Our Time: A History 1945–1992.* New York: Penguin Books, 1993.

Leffler, Melvyn. *For the Soul of Mankind: The United States, the Soviet Union, and the Cold War.* New York: Hill and Wang, 2007.

Levering, Ralph B., Vladimir O. Pechatnov, Verena Botzenhart-Viehe, and Earl C. Edmondson. *Debating the Origins of the Cold War: American and Russian Perspectives.* Lanham, Md.: Rowman & Littlefield, 2002.

Lévesque, Jacques. *The Enigma of 1989: The USSR and the Liberation of Eastern Europe.* Berkeley: University of California Press, 1997.

Lojkó, Miklós. "Conservative Realignment in British Policy on Central Europe and the Balkans During the Early Interwar Years." In *Európa, nemzet, külpolitika: tanulmányok Ádám Magda 85.születésnapjára,* edited by László Borhi and Attila Pók, 153–70. Budapest: Aura, 2010.

Lukes, Igor. *On the Edge of the Cold War: American Diplomats and Spies in Postwar Prague.* Oxford: Oxford University Press, 2012.

Lundestad, Geir. *The American Non-Policy Towards Eastern Europe 1943–1947: Universalism in an Area Not of Essential Interest to the United States.* Tromsö: Universitatsforlaget, 1978.

———. *The United States and Western Europe from 1945: From "Empire" by Invitation to Transatlantic Drift.* New York: Oxford University Press, 2003.

Magyarics, Tamás. "Az Egyesült Államok és Magyarország, 1957–1967." *Századok* [Centuries] 130, no. 3 (1996): 571–612.

Mark, Eduard. "American Policy Toward Eastern Europe and the Origins of the Cold War 1941–1946: An Alternative Interpretation." *The Journal of American History* 68, no. 2 (1981): 313–36.

———. *Revolution by Degrees: Stalin's National-Front Strategy for Europe, 1941–1947.* Working Paper (Cold War International History Project) 31. Washington, D.C.: Woodrow Wilson International Center of Scholars, 2001.

Mastny, Vojtech. *The Cold War and Soviet Insecurity: The Stalin Years*. Oxford: Oxford University Press, 1998.

———. "The Warsaw Pact as History." In *A Cardboard Castle? An Inside History of the Warsaw Pact, 1955–1991*, edited by Vojtech Mastny and Malcolm Byrne. Budapest: Central European University Press, 2005.

Matlock, Jack F. *Reagan and Gorbachev: How the Cold War Ended*. New York: Random House, 2005.

Max, Stanley M. *The Anglo-American Response to the Sovietization of Hungary, 1945–1948*. Ann Arbor, Mich.: East European Monographs, 1985.

Maynard, Christopher. *Out of the Shadow: George H. W. Bush and the End of the Cold War*. College Station: Texas A&M University Press, 2008.

McCauley, Brian. "Hungary and the Suez, 1956: The Limits of Soviet and American Power." *Journal of Contemporary History* 16, no. 4 (1981): 777–800.

Mitrovich, Gregory. *Undermining the Kremlin: America's Strategy to Subvert the Soviet Bloc, 1947–1956*. Ithaca, N.Y.: Cornell University Press, 2000.

Mong, Attila. *Kádár hitele: A magyar államadósság története, 1956–1990*. Budapest: Libri Kiadó, 2012.

Naimark, Norman. *The Russians in Germany: A History of the Soviet Zone of Occupation 1945–1949*. Cambridge, Mass.: Belknap Press of Harvard University Press, 1995.

Naimark, Norman, and Leonid Gibianski. *The Establishment of Communist Regimes in Eastern Europe, 1944–1949*. Boulder, Colo.: Westview Press, 1996.

Nye, Joseph S. Jr. *Soft Power: The Means to Success in World Politics*. New York: Public Affairs, 2004.

Okey, Robin. "Echoes and Precedents: 1989 in Historical Perspective." In *The 1989 Revolutions in Central and Eastern Europe: From Communism to Pluralism*, edited by Kevin McDermott and Matthew Stibbe. Manchester: Manchester University Press, 2013.

Oplatka, András. *Egy döntés története: Magyar határnyitás, 1989. Szeptember 11. nulla óra*. Budapest: Helikon, 2010.

Osgood, Kenneth. *Total Cold War: Eisenhower's Secret Propaganda Battle at Home and Abroad*. Lawrence: University Press of Kansas, 2006.

Pál, István. "A Vogeler-ügy." In *Gyarmatokból imperium: magyar kutatók tanulmányai az amerikai történelemről*, edited by Tibor Frank. Budapest: Gondolat, 2007.

Palasik, Mária. *Chess Game for Democracy: Hungary Between East and West, 1944–1947*. Montreal: McGill Queens University Press, 2011.

Papoušek, Vladimir. "Panslavism in the Work of Czech Writers in Wartime Exile." In *The Phoney Peace: Power, and Culture in Central Europe, 1945–1949*, edited by Robert B. Pynsent. London: School of Slavonic and East European Studies, University College London, 2000.

Porter, Anna. *Buying a Better World: George Soros and Billionaire Philanthropy*. Toronto: Tap Books, 2015.

Preussen, Ronald W. "John Foster Dulles and the Predicaments of Power." In *John Foster Dulles and the Diplomacy of the Cold War*, edited by Richard H. Immerman, 21–46. Princeton, N.J.: Princeton University Press, 1990.

———. "John Foster Dulles és Kelet Európa." In *Évkönyv V* [Yearbook], *1996–1997*. Budapest: 1956-os Intézet, 1997, 228–37.

Pruden, Caroline. *Conditional Partners: Eisenhower, the United Nations, and the Search for a Permanent Peace*. Baton Rouge: Louisiana State University Press, 1998.

Radványi, János. *Hungary and the Superpowers: The 1956 Revolution and Realpolitik*. Stanford, Calif.: Hoover Institution Press, Stanford University, 1972.

Rainer, János M. "The Sixties in Hungary: Some Historical and Political Approaches." In *Muddling Through the Long 1960s: Ideas and Everyday Life in High Politics and the Lower Classes of Communist Hungary*, edited by M. János Rainer and György Péteri, 4–26. Trondheim Studies on East European Cultures and Societies 16. Budapest: Institute for the History of the 1956 Hungarian Revolution, 2005.

———. "Döntés a Kremlben – Kísérlet a feljegyzések értelmezésére." In *Döntés a Kremlben, 1956: A szovjet pártelnökség vitái Magyarországról*. Budapest: 1956-os Intézet, 1996, 111–54.

Ripp, Zoltán. *Rendszerváltás Magyarországon, 1987–1990*. Budapest: Napvilág, 2006.

Romsics, Ignác. A brit külpolitika és a 'magyarkérdés', 1914–1946. *Századok* [Centuries] 130, no. 2 (1996): 273–339.

Sainsbury, Keith. *Churchill and Roosevelt at War: The War They Fought and the Peace They Hoped to Make*. New York: New York University Press, 1994.

Sakmyster, Thomas. *Hungary's Admiral on Horseback: Miklós Horthy, 1918–1944*. Boulder, Colo.: East European Monographs, 1994.

Sarotte, Mary. *1989: The Struggle to Create Post-Cold War Europe*. Princeton, N.J.: Princeton University Press, 2009.

Savranskaya, Svetlana. "The Logic of 1989: the Soviet Peaceful Withdrawal from Eastern Europe." In *Masterpieces of History: The Peaceful End of the Cold War in Europe, 1989*, edited by Svetlana Savranskaya, Thomas Blanton, and Vladislav Zubok. Budapest: Central European University Press, 2010.

Sayer, Ian, and Douglas Botting. *America's Secret Army: The Untold Story of the Counter Intelligence Corps*. New York: Franklin Watts, 1989.

Schreiber, Thomas. *Les Actions de la France á L'Est ou les Absences de Marianne*. Paris: L'Harmattan, 2000.

Sebestyen, Victor. *Revolution 1989: The Fall of the Soviet Empire*. New York: Pantheon Books, 2009.

Simándi, Irén. "A magyar forradalom a Szabad Európa Rádió hullámhosszán, I. rész." *Valóság* 45, no. 11 (2006): 36–61.

Sipos, Péter. "Az Egyesült Államok, a NATO és az 1968-as szovjet intervenció." *Történelmi Szemle* [Reality Historical Review] 50, no. 3 (2008): 383–406.

Sipos, Péter, and István Vida. "The Policy of the United States towards Hungary During the Second World War." *Acta Historica Academiae Scientiarum Hungaricae* 29, no. 1 (1983): 77–110.

Smetana, Vít. "Concessions or Conviction? Czechoslovakia's Road to the Cold War and the Soviet Bloc." In *Imposing, Maintaining and Tearing Open the Iron Curtain: The Cold War and East-Central Europe, 1945–1989*, edited by Mark Kramer and Vít Smetana. Lanham, Md.: Lexington Books, 2014.

Snyder, Timothy. *Bloodlands: Europe Between Hitler and Stalin*. New York: Basic Books, 2010.

Spalding, Robert, Jr. "'A Graduate and Moderate Relaxation': Eisenhower and the Revision of American Export Control Policy, 1953–1955." *Diplomatic History* 17, no. 2 (1993): 223–250.

Spohr-Readman, Kristina. "Conflict and Cooperation in Intra-Alliance Nuclear Politics: Western Europe, the United States and the Genesis of NATO's Dual-Track Decision, 1977–1979." *Journal of Cold War Studies* 13, no. 2 (2011): 39–89.

Spulber, Nicholas. "Problems of East-West Trade and Economic Trends in the European Satellites of Soviet Russia." In *The Fate of East Central Europe: Hopes and Failures of American Foreign Policy*, edited by Stephen D. Kertesz, 597–617. Notre Dame, Ind.: University of Notre Dame Press, 1956.

Stafford, David. *Britain and the European Resistance, 1940–1945: A Survey of the*

Special Operations Executive, With Documents. Oxford: St. Antony's College, 1980.

Stark, Tamás. *Magyar foglyok a Szovjetunióban*. Budapest: Lucidus, 2006.

Stent, Angela. *Russia and Germany Reborn: Unification, the Soviet Collapse and the New Europe*. Princeton, N.J.: Princeton University Press, 1998.

Sz. Bíró, Zoltán. "A szovjet végjáték." In *Megroppan a világrend, 1989–1991: célok, szereplők, következmények: az Egy Emberibb Világért Alapítvány által 2012. szeptember 28-án azonos címmel rendezett konferencia előadásai*. Budapest: Argumentum, 2013, 21–49.

Szemere, Anna. *Up from the Underground: The Culture of Rock Music in Postsocialist Hungary*. University Park: Pennsylvania State University Press, 2001.

Tischler, János. "The Hungarian Party Leadership and the Polish Crisis of 1980–1981." *Cold War International History Bulletin* 11 (Winter 1988): 77–89.

Tóth, Imre. "A keletnémet menekültkérdés hatása a Berlin-Bonn-Budapest háromszög kapcsolatrendszerére." In *A Páneurópai Piknik és határáttörés húsz év távlatából*, edited by György Gyarmati, 67–94. Budapest: L'Harmattan, 2010.

Trachtenberg, Marc. *Constructed Peace: The Making of the European Settlement, 1945–1963*. Princeton, N.J.: Princeton University Press, 1999.

Tudda, Christopher. *The Truth Is Our Weapon: The Rhetorical Diplomacy of Dwight D. Eisenhower and John Foster Dulles*. Baton Rouge: Louisiana State University Press, 2006.

Ungváry, Krisztián. *The Siege of Budapest: 100 Days in World War II*. New Haven, Conn.: Yale University Press, 2005.

Urban, George. *Radio Free Europe and the Pursuit of Democracy: My War within the Cold War*. New Haven, Conn.: Yale University Press, 1997.

Vida, István: "Az MSZMP Politikai Bizottságának 1958. január 15-i határozata a Külügyminisztérium munkájáról." In *Magyarország a (Nagy)hatalmak erőterében: Tanulmányok Ormos Mária 70. Születésnapjára*, edited by Ferenc Fischer, István Majoros, Mária Ormos, and József Vonyó. 629–50. Pécs: University Press, 2000.

Walt, Stephen. *The Origins of Alliances*. Ithaca, N.Y.: Cornell University Press, 1987.

Waltz, Kenneth. "The Emerging Structure of International Politics, 1993." In *Realism and International Politics*, edited by Kenneth Waltz. New York: Routledge, 2008.

———. *Theory of International Politics*. Reading, Mass.: Addison-Wesley Publishers, 1979.

Walzer, Michael. *Just and Unjust Wars: A Moral Argument with Historical Illustrations*. 3rd ed. New York: Basic Books, 2000.

Wettig, Gerhard. *Stalin and the Cold War in Europe: The Emergence and Development of East-West Conflict, 1939–1953*. Lanham, Md.: Rowman & Littlefield Publishers, 2008.

Wilentz, Sean. *The Age of Reagan: A History, 1974–2008*. New York: Harper, 2008.

Wyman, David. *The Abandonment of the Jews*. New York: New Press, 2007.

Zhai, Qiang. *China and the Vietnam Wars, 1950–1975*. Chapel Hill: University of North Carolina Press, 2000.

Zubok, Vladislav. *A Failed Empire: The Soviet Union in the Cold War from Stalin to Gorbachev*. Chapel Hill: University of North Carolina Press, 2007.

———. "Soviet Policy Aims at the Geneva Conference of 1955." In *Cold War Respite: The Geneva Summit of 1955*, edited by Günter Bischof and Saki Dockrill, 55–74. Baton Rouge: Louisiana University Press, 2000.

Zubok, Vladislav, and Constantine Pleshakov. *Inside the Kremlin's Cold War from Stalin to Khrushchev.* Cambridge, Mass.: Harvard University Press, 1997.

Unpublished Manuscripts

Marchio, James. "Rhetoric and Reality: The Eisenhower Administration and Unrest in Eastern Europe 1953–1956." PhD dissertation, American University, 1990.

Preussen, Ronald W. "Walking a Tightrope in the Twilight: John Foster Dulles and Eastern Europe in 1953." Unpublished paper prepared for the "Europe and the Cold War" conference in November 1998 at the Sorbonne, Paris.

Urbán, Károly. "Sztálin halálától a forradalom kitöréséig: a magyar-szovjet kapcsolatok története (1953–1956)." Unpublished manuscript. Budapest, 1996.

INDEX

Aboimov, Ivan, 378, 381, 424
Acheson, Dean, 67, 396
Ackerson, Garret, 158–159
Aczél, György, 283–284, 333–334
Adams, John Quincy, 404
Akhromeiev, Sergei, 412, 426
Alexander, Sir Harold, 27
Alföldy, György, 99
Allen, Dennis, 32
Ames, Aldrich, 361
Amin, Hafizullah, 324
Andropov, Yuri, 287, 327, 331, 340, 342
Antall, József, 412, 420, 424, 433
Antonescu, Ion, 18, 24
Arnot, Alexander, 417
Artajo, Alberto Martin, 124
Auschnitt, Max, 18

Badoglio, Pietro, 38, 45
Baibakov, Nikolai, 247
Bailey, George, 164
Bakách-Bessenyey, György, 17, 23–25, 37, 41
Baker, James, 359, 396, 398, 400, 402, 410, 413
Ball, George, 173
Bannantine, George, 79–82
Bányász, Rezső, 350
Baranyai, Lipót, 20, 47
Bárányos, Károly, 61
Barcza, György, 20, 47–48

Bárdossy, László, 14
Barnes, Spencer N., 96–97
Bartha, János, 176, 214, 334
Baumgartner, Ernst, 383
Bedell-Smith, Walter, 67
Békés, Csaba, 143, 377
Bella, Árpád, 418
Belovai, István, 361
Bender, David, 306
Beneš, Edvard, 4, 42, 54, 61
Berecz, János, 321, 338, 350
Bergsten, Fred, 260
Beria, Lavrenty, 93, 103, 113
Berle, Adolph, 18–19, 21, 34
Bernáth, Ernő, 206
Berry, Burton Y., 62
Bevin, Ernest, 70
Bianco, Jean-Louis, 390
Bibó, István, 126
Binder, David, 217
Bíró, József, 209, 286, 335
Bischof, Günter, 4
Bishop, Maurice, 343
Biszku, Béla, 159, 172, 258
Blackwill, Robert, 385, 397, 411, 421–422
Blot, Jacques, 390
Bodnăraş, Emil, 241
Bogdan, Corneliu, 239–240, 243
Bogomolov, Oleg, 347

Bogye, János, 336, 422
Bohlen, Charles, 54, 113, 121–123, 131, 224
Boland, Frederick, 172–173
Boldizsár, Iván, 257
Boldóczki, János, 106
Borbély, Sándor, 362
Borman, Frank, 255
Borsányi, György, 282
Borsányi, Julián, 134
Bowles, Chester, 173, 175
Brando, Marlon, 217
Brands, H. W., 132
Brandt, Willy, 230, 278
Brentano, Heinrich von, 130
Brezhnev, Leonid, 145–146, 210, 214, 223, 227–228, 241, 244, 247, 249, 255, 265, 267, 269, 271, 278, 286–288, 296, 320–324, 328–329, 370, 377, 382, 393, 401, 409, 428–429
Broek, Henri van der, 413
Brooke, Allan, 27, 32
Brzezinski, Zbigniev, 283, 301–302, 309, 311, 313–315, 317, 320–321, 325, 399
Buckley, James, 291
Buckley, Mary, 368
Bulganin, Nikolai, 115
Bullit, William, 26, 54–55
Bundy, McGeorge, 194
Burlakov, Matvei, 429
Bush, George H. W., 10, 137, 227, 326, 330, 340–343, 347, 351, 358, 364–365, 367, 376, 379, 382, 385–388, 390, 393, 396–398, 400–406, 408–413, 420–423, 425–431, 438
Butz, Earl, 299
Byrnes, James F., 64, 368

Cadogan, Alexander, 38
Carlos the Jackal, 246
Carr, E. H., 54
Carter, Jimmy, 145, 219, 227, 265, 287, 292–293, 300–302, 308–315, 317–321, 324–325, 329, 370
Casey, William, 338–339
Castro, Fidel, 181
Ceauşescu, Nicolae, 9, 168, 184, 188, 227, 239–243, 292, 302, 320, 331, 360, 374, 416
Chamberlain, Arthur Neville, 222

Chapin, Selden, 72–74, 82
Cheli, Giovanni, 263
Churchill, Winston, 22–23, 26–32, 35–36, 42, 47, 51, 53–54, 70, 323, 396
Cohen, Stephen, 399
Cole, R. Taylor, 33
Conrad, Clyde Lee, 360–361
Cornut-Gentile, Bernard, 125
Cranston, Alan, 387, 394
Craxi, Bettiono, 331
Cripps, Stafford, 54
Csornoky, Viktor, 69, 72
Csurka, István, 407
Cutler, Robert, 129

Dachy, Stephen, 283–284, 312
Daday, Ferenc, 226
Dálnoki Miklós, Béla, 59
Dam, Kenneth, 339
Davies, Richard T., 229, 261, 267
Davis, John R. Jr., 404
Davis, Nathaniel, 86
Davis, Richard H., 172, 181–182
Deak, Frances, 43
Deák, István, 282–284, 307
Debré, Michel, 222
de Gama, Saldanho, 23
Delors, Jacques, 392
De Michelis, Gianni, 384
Dent, Frederick, 275, 281
Dinnyés, Lajos, 72
Dixon, Sir Pearson, 121, 125
Dobrynin, Anatoly, 180–182, 209, 224, 227, 244, 268, 339, 379, 412
Domber, Gregory, 404
Donovan, William, 17, 34, 39
Dubček, Alexander, 222
Dudás, Sándor, 103
Duke, Florimont, 44–45
Dulles, Allen, 12, 16–18, 21, 23–24, 33–34, 37, 41, 43–45, 47, 133, 135, 148–149, 155
Dulles, John Foster, 95, 108–109, 111–115, 118–121, 123, 125–128, 130–131

Eagleburger, Lawrence, 337–338, 369, 397, 402, 421–423, 432
Eastland, James, 69

INDEX

Eckhardt, Tibor, 17
Eden, Anthony, 25, 27–29, 31, 33
Eisenhower, Dwight D., 27, 90–91, 108, 112, 118–122, 129, 131–133, 144, 147–149, 152, 154, 156, 160, 319, 365, 436
Esztergályos, Ferenc, 313

Faulkner, William, 333
Fehér, Lajos, 258
Fejti, György, 409
Fekete, János, 197, 246, 258
Feld, Nicholas, 164
Flossmann, Győző, 98–99
Fock, Jenő, 200, 202, 208–209, 215, 250, 281
Ford, Gerald, 287, 291–293, 295–300, 302
Franco, Francisco, 124
Frenkel, Max, 217
Frenzel, William, 319
Frischenschläger, Friedhelm, 383
Frost, Robert, 168
Fulbright, William, 210

Gaddis, John Lewis, 132, 367
Gates, Robert, 401, 411
Gati, Charles, 399–400
Geiger, Imre, 81
Genscher, Hans-Dietrich, 385, 416, 418
Gerő, Ernő, 62, 91, 93, 107
Gerth, Thomas, 304, 312–313
Gheorghiu-Dej, Gheorghe, 104, 158, 172
Ghika, György, 33
Ghyczy, Jenő, 25, 33, 48
Gierek, Edward, 238, 269, 302
Ginsberg, Allen, 333
Giscard D'Estaing, Valéry, 390
Goldgeier, James M., 398
Gomułka, Władysław, 127,–128
Gonzalez, Felipe, 425
Gorbachev, Mikhail, 10, 326, 347–348, 353–357, 360, 364–368, 371, 377–388, 390–391, 393, 396, 398, 400–403, 405–406, 409, 411–413, 421–423, 425–431, 438, 440
Gough, Richard, 250
Gray, Gordon, 94
Grechko, Andrei, 204, 210, 223
Greenspan, Alan, 359
Griffith, William, 134, 225

Gromyko, Andrei, 159, 324
Grósz, Károly, 353, 357–362, 374–375, 377, 389, 395, 407–408, 415
Groza, Petru, 62

Habsburg, Otto von, 37, 124, 417
Hackett, Charles, 308
Hackler, Károly, 172–173, 177
Haig, Alexander, 338–339
Halász, Béla, 98
Halász, László, 165
Halle, Louis, 113
Hanhimäki, Jussi, 290
Hansen, Lynn, 424
Harbutt, Frazer, 13
Harriman, Averell, 30–31, 35, 37, 54–56, 58, 88, 145, 152, 182, 320–321, 370
Harrison, W., 36, 38
Hartke, Vance, 294
Hartman, Arthur, 294, 311
Hatz, Ottó, 38–42
Havasi, Ferenc, 345, 347, 371
Házi, Vencel, 330, 343
Helmeczi, László, 106
Hennekine, Loic, 389
Hickerson, John, 66, 69
Hillenbrand, Martin, J., 207–209, 212, 214–218, 230, 245–246, 254, 256
Hitler, Adolf, 3, 13–15, 18–20, 22–23, 30, 32, 34–37, 39–41, 43, 45–48, 51, 54, 57, 121, 131, 186, 216–217, 222, 364, 424, 434, 439–440
Hollán, Sándor, 23–24
Honecker, Erich, 419, 423
Hoover, Herbert, 107, 123, 130
Horn, Gyula, 329, 344, 346, 350, 354, 365–366, 383, 386, 392, 394, 408, 410–411, 416, 418
Horthy, Miklós, 12, 14–16, 33, 38, 42, 158, 440
Horthy, Miklós Jr., 33
Horváth, Ede, 298
Horváth, István, 393
Horváth, Kálmán, 98
Höttl, Wilhelm, 45
Howe, Geoffrey, 391
Hoyer, Steny, 350, 353
Hughes, Geraint, 219, 224, 391
Hull, Cordell, 28–30, 33–34, 37, 55

Hutchings, Robert, 376, 388, 391, 393, 397, 405–406, 408–409, 432
Hyland, William, 310

Ingersoll, Robert, 288, 299

Jackson, C. D., 109
Jackson, Henry "Scoop," 296
Jacobsen, Israel, 81
Januzzi, Giovanni, 392
Jaruzelski, Wojciech, 327, 385, 398, 404–406, 413, 420, 425, 431
Jászi, Oszkár, 218, 251
Jensen, Bang, 172
Johnson, Alexis U., 267
Johnson, Lyndon B., 6, 184, 186–188, 193, 197, 209, 211, 222, 225, 248, 255
Jones, Brian, 217

Kádár, János, 6, 9, 119, 126, 136, 140, 142, 144–147, 154–156, 159, 163–164, 166, 171–172, 174–175, 177–178, 182–183, 192–196, 200–204, 207, 210–217, 238, 244, 246, 249–250, 253, 255–256, 258, 261, 265, 267, 269–272, 280, 286–289, 291, 293, 295–296, 300, 304, 308–309, 313, 316–318, 320–321, 323, 327–331, 340–341, 348, 350, 352–353, 357, 369–371, 374–375, 377, 382, 384, 391, 393, 398, 405, 410, 437
Kaiser, Philip, 303–304, 312–316, 321
Kállai, Gyula, 179, 200–201
Kállay, Miklós, 12, 14–15, 17, 19–20, 22–24, 33–34, 37, 39, 41, 46–48
Kamman, Curt, 427
Kampelman, Max, 331
Kassof, Alan, 284
Katzenbach, Nicholas, 224
Kefauver, Estes, 107
Kemenes, Ernő, 344, 389
Kennan, George F., 24, 54–55, 63, 83, 85, 131, 368
Kennedy, John F., 6, 144, 150, 152, 171, 173, 178, 180, 182, 186–187, 217
Keogh, James, 229
Kerouac, Jack, 333
Kershaw, Ian, 364
Kertay, György, 80
Kertész, Imre, 163

Khrushchev, Nikita, 115, 122, 128, 130, 144, 156–157, 159, 171–172, 174, 181–182, 193, 378, 440
Király, Béla, 281
Kiselev, Yevgeny, 96
Kiss, Károly, 201
Kissinger, Henry, 7, 131, 219, 225–228, 230, 234, 236, 239, 241, 243, 253, 260, 262, 268–270, 275–276, 278, 283, 287–288, 290–292, 296–297, 300, 302, 306, 311, 352, 396–397, 399, 440
Klein, Hans, 417
Klestil, Thomas, 383
Koch, Edward, 301
Kodály, Zoltán, 203
Kohl, Helmut, 331, 384–387, 389, 404, 413, 417–419, 421, 423–424
Komarek, Vladimir, 103
Komócsin, Zoltán, 258–259, 271
Komplektov, Viktor, 342
Konev, Ivan, 135, 154
König, Franz, 254, 263
Kornai, János, 370
Kornienko, Georgi, 251
Kós, Péter, 106–107, 121
Kosygin, Alexei, 186, 240, 247, 250, 328
Kovács, Béla, 65–68, 161
Kovács, László, 346, 362, 414, 422
Kovrig, Bennet, 136
Kramer, Mark, 368, 381
Kreisky, Bruno, 155, 180
Krenz, Egon, 423
Kriuchkov, Vladimir, 374, 377
Kuznetsov, Vasili, 169

Laird, Melvin, 7, 235–236
Lane, Arthur Bliss, 73
Lashchenko, Piotr N., 381
Latta, Delbart, 151
Lázár, György, 329, 341, 348
Leahy, William, 34
Leddy, John, 209, 211, 248–249
Leffler, Melvyn, 323, 366
Lékai, László, 312
Lesechko, Mikhail, 250
Lezsák, Sándor, 349
Lilienthal, David, 65
Lippmann, Walter, 55, 368

Litteráti-Loótz, Gyula (Patkó, Gyula), 134
Litvinov, Maxim, 28
Lodge, Henry Cabot Jr., 121, 124–126, 160, 169
Lončar, Budomir, 403
Lovett, Robert, 60
Lubbers, Ruud, 412
Luers, William, 309
Lugar, Richard, 379
Lukes, Igor, 74
Lundestad, Geir, 82–83

Major, John, 411
Malamud, Bernard, 333
Malița, Mircea, 292
Malone, George W., 157
Mănescu, Corneliu, 269
Maniu, Iuliu, 37
Mansfield, Mike, 245
Márai, Sándor, 58
Mardoniev, Nikolai, 295
Marjai, József, 288, 339, 356, 357
Marshall, George C., 66
Marton, André, 173
Masaryk, Jan, 54
Mason, George, 102
Matthews, Freeman, 34
Mazowiecki, Tadeusz, 425
McAuliffe, Eugene, 286, 288–289
McClintock, Robert, 69
McCullers, Carson, 333
McFarland, Lanning, 42
McFaul, Michael, 398
McNamara, Robert, 187
Mécs, Imre, 407
Meehan, Francis, 217
Méhes, Lajos, 200
Melby, Eric, 403
Merchant, Livingstone, 168
Mészáros, Ferenc, 417
Meyer, Cord, 133
Michael I of Romania, 62
Mikhalin, Ivan, 382
Mikoyan, Anastas, 51, 146
Mill, John Stuart, 132
Milleger, Joseph, 170
Miller, Arthur, 333
Mindszenty, József, 82, 86, 153–154, 156, 160–162, 169–170, 172, 178–181, 194–196,
206, 212, 253–254, 257–258, 262–264, 273, 295, 305–307, 312, 437
Mischnick, Wolfgang, 385
Mitterrand, François, 388–391, 411, 423, 425, 429
Mock, Alois, 365, 383, 416
Mód, Péter, 177
Molotov, Vyacheslav Mikhailovich, 30–31, 33, 42, 63, 70
Mondale, Walter, 236
Montgomery, Bernard, 27
Montgomery, John Flourney, 15–16
Moss, Frank, 281
Mudd, Robert C., 286, 293–294, 304, 311
Mulroney, Brian, 382
Münnich, Ferenc, 142, 146, 159
Munro, Sir Leslie, 160, 181, 183
Murphy, Robert, 126, 130
Muskie, Edmund, 236
Mussolini, Benito, 57

Nagy, Ferenc, 51, 54, 61, 64–66, 68–69, 72–73, 77, 112, 192, 305, 310
Nagy, Imre, 5, 104–106, 117, 119, 121, 123, 125–128, 134–135, 155, 159, 161, 222, 289, 348, 358, 373, 398, 407
Nagy, János, 248–249, 251, 259, 261, 283, 295–297, 314–316, 331
Namier, Lewis, 32
Nasser, Gamel Abdul, 123
Nehru, Jawaharlal, 136
Nemes, Dezső, 160
Nemes Nagy, Ágnes, 167–168
Németh, Károly, 258
Németh, Miklós, 358, 377, 379, 383, 387, 392–393, 395, 409, 415, 418
Nitze, Paul, 85
Nixon, Richard, 7, 62, 127, 146, 218–221, 225–227, 229–231, 233–244, 250, 253, 255–256, 261–272, 275–278, 281, 293–296, 300, 302, 306, 309, 311, 320, 352, 399, 405, 437
Norman, Montagu, 75
Nye, Joseph, 166
Nyers, Rezső, 202, 205, 215, 246, 258, 281, 377, 381, 386, 387, 395, 408, 409, 412

Oakar, Mary, 310, 315
Oatis, William, 87

Olti, Vilmos, 99
Orbán, Viktor, 406–408, 411
Ortutay, Gyula, 202

Pál, Losonczi, 314
Palmer, Mark, 346, 362, 376, 393, 398, 402, 411, 418, 436
Papp, Simon, 79–81
Patolichev, Nikolai, 274
Paul VI, 263, 305
Pedersen, Richard, 286, 294, 295
Pell, Herbert Clairborne, 15
Perle, Richard, 246
Péter, Gábor, 79
Péter, János, 174, 177, 195, 206, 207, 214, 215, 253, 259, 261–262, 264–265, 271
Pethő, Tibor, 216–217
Petkov, Nikola, 68
Petrovsky, Vladimir, 379–380
Pflüger, Friedberg, 387
Piros, László, 107
Pius XII, 161
Polgár, Dénes, 173, 178
Pompidou, Georges, 222
Ponomarev, Boris, 327
Pound, Ezra, 168
Pozsgay, Imre, 372, 379, 390, 392, 395, 415, 417–420, 426–427
Priesnitz, Walter, 417
Puhan, Alfred, 218, 229–230, 251, 253–265, 267–269, 271, 277, 280, 283
Puja, Frigyes, 215, 255, 270, 286–288, 294, 298–299, 303, 315, 317, 321, 330, 338, 414
Pushkin, Georgi, 51, 64–65

Radó, Zoltán, 81
Radványi, János, 173, 176–177, 180–182, 204, 206–207, 209, 248, 253
Rainer, M. János, 192
Rajk, László, 79, 85–86
Rajnai, Sándor, 342
Rákosi, Mátyás, 52, 58, 61, 64–65, 68, 80, 82–83, 92–93, 96, 101–102, 104–105, 107, 113, 127, 156, 216, 437
Rakowski, Mieczysław, 404
Ráth, Gedeon, 98–99

Ravndal, Christian, 106–107
Reagan, Ronald, 9–10, 227, 290, 323, 325–327, 338–343, 347–348, 350, 352, 354–359, 361, 367, 371, 397–398, 402, 407, 410, 428
Révai, József, 156
Ribbentrop, Joachim von, 45
Ribicoff, Abraham, 321
Rice, Condoleezza, 397, 403
Richardson, Elliot, 299
Ricoeur, Paul, 368
Ridgway, Rozanne, 326, 352
Ripp, Zoltán, 369
Rizhkov, Nikolai, 379
Roberts, F. K., 38
Robin, Okey, 367
Rodionov, N. N., 270
Rodman, Peter, 396
Rogers, William, 146, 226, 234, 235, 242, 251, 256, 257, 259, 264, 265, 267–273, 277, 278, 302, 307
Rómány, Pál, 332
Roosevelt, Franklin D., 15, 17, 23, 26–27, 29–32, 44, 53–55
Rowny, Edward, 427
Ruedemann, Paul, 79–82
Rühe, Volker, 386
Rush, Kennet, 279, 280, 283
Rusk, Dean, 173–174, 179–180, 186–188, 190, 195, 206, 223–225, 259
Ruttkay, Éva, 167

Sachs, Geoffrey, 420
Salgo, Nicholas, 344, 347, 351
Sarotte, Mary, 367
Savranskaya, Svetlana, 367
Schabowski, Günter, 416
Schifter, Robert, 362–363
Schlesinger, Arthur, 399
Schmidt, Helmut, 313, 370
Schoenfeld, Arthur, 60–61, 66–67, 72–73
Schreiber, Thomas, 388
Scowcroft, Brent, 227, 365, 398–403, 405, 408, 411, 413, 421, 426–427, 432
Serédi, Jusztinián, 20
Sergeev, Igor, 429
Serov, Ivan, 126

Shelton, Turner, 166, 177
Shepilov, Dmitri, 123
Shevardnadze, Eduard, 402, 413, 424–425
Shor, Francis, 164
Shultz, George, 235, 330, 339–342, 345, 347–349, 351
Sík, Endre, 101, 105, 158–159, 171–174
Simons, Thomas, 397, 405
Skorodenko, Petyr, 426
Skubiszewski, Krzysztof, 425
Smetana, Vít, 4
Smith, Kenneth, 348
Sobolev, Arkady, 121
Sokolov, Sergey, 355, 377
Somogyi, Ferenc, 417, 421
Sonnenfeldt, Helmut, 228, 233, 253, 269, 278–279, 283, 290–292, 298, 300, 306, 399
Soros, George, 336–337, 371
Späth, Lothar, 385–386
Specter, Arlen, 395
Springsteen, George, 280
Stalin, Joseph Vissarionovich, 5, 13–14, 18–19, 25–31, 42, 51–54, 58, 64–65, 67–68, 70, 85–87, 102–104, 109, 112–113, 354, 400, 440
Stans, Maurice, 234–236, 242, 263
Stassen, Harold, 120
Steinbeck, John, 333
Steinhardt, Lawrence, 61, 73–74
Stevenson, Adlai, 112, 172, 180
Stoléru, Lionel, 389–390
Stukalin, Boris, 378
Sudhoff, Jürgen, 417
Sulzberger, C. L., 290
Sung, Kim Il, 85
Sununu, John, 411
Sviridov, Vladimir, 66
Swank, Emory, 256, 306
Szabó, Károly, 265, 266
Szabo, Zoltan, 360
Szarka, Károly, 97, 105, 174–175
Szegedy-Maszák, Aladár, 17, 47, 68–69, 72
Székely, Mihály, 107
Szekér, Gyula, 298, 299, 309
Szemere, Anna, 201
Szent-Györgyi, Albert, 19–20

Szentmiklósy, Andor, 23
Szigeti, Károly, 107
Szilágyi, Béla, 204, 209–213, 215, 249, 251, 252, 256, 306
Szokai, Imre, 376
Szombathelyi, Ferenc, 39
Szurdi, Miklós, 215
Szűrös, Mátyás, 351–353, 413, 421

Teleki, Pál, 207
Thatcher, Margaret, 331, 385, 391–392, 404, 413, 420, 423, 425, 430
Thompson, Llewelyn, 131
Tikhonov, Nikolai, 329
Tildy, Zoltán, 60, 64, 66, 72
Timár, István, 77
Tito, Josip Broz, 26, 85, 99, 147, 224
Titov, Gherman, 167
Torbert, Horace G., 173–175, 178, 180
Trachtenberg, Marc, 365
Truman, Harry S., 4, 50–54, 59, 61–62, 64–65, 71, 74, 85, 152, 410–411, 435, 437
Tudda, Christopher, 108
Tyler, Royall, 23, 47

Ujszászy, István, 44
Ulbricht, Walter, 109
Ullein-Reviczky, Antal, 17, 33
Urban, George, 350
Ustinov, Vladimir I., 172

Vályi, Péter, 215, 263, 274–279, 286, 297
Vámbéry, Ármin, 73
Vámbéry, Rusztem, 73
Vance, Cyrus, 300–304, 309, 313–318, 321, 325
Vanden Heuvel, Frederick, 22, 48
Vanik, Charles, 150, 163, 303, 309, 311
Varga, Béla, 68, 192, 306
Várkonyi, Péter, 307, 350, 354, 391
Vas, István, 167
Vass, László, 389
Vedeler, Harold, 172, 178, 182
Veress, László, 22
Verity, William, 357–358, 361
Vígh, Gábor, 206
Vishinsky, Andrei, 62, 64

Vogel, Hans-Jochen, 387, 417
Vogeler, Robert, 53, 81–82, 86–87, 437
Voigt, Carsten, 418–419
Volpe, John, 230
Vörnle, János, 25
Voroshilov, Kliment, 52, 59–60, 66
Vranitzky, Franz, 383, 398

Wadsworth, James, 158
Wailes, Edward, 122, 127–128, 154–155
Wałęsa, Lech, 387, 404
Walzer, Michael, 132
Wegener, Henrik, 369
Weinberger, Caspar, 338–339, 344, 346
Weissengruber, János, 103
Weizsäcker, Richard von, 386
Whitehead, John, 326, 339–340, 344, 349–354, 356, 358–362, 394, 402
Whittome, John, 375

Wiley, Lance, 164
Williams, Tennessee, 333
Wilson, Charles, 297
Wilson, Harold, 222
Wisner, Frank, 124, 135
Wodianer, Andor, 17
Woerner, Manfred, 392, 393
Wolfowitz, Paul, 393
Wyszinski, Stefan, 269, 302

Yasyukov, M., 429
Yazov, Dmitri, 381

Zádor, Tibor, 156–157, 170, 172, 176, 178, 209, 211
Zágon, József, 263
Zarb, Frank, 296
Zhivkov, Todor, 385
Zhukov, Georgy, 120, 122–123

LÁSZLÓ BORHI

is the Peter A. Kadas Chair Associate Professor at the Department of Central Eurasian Studies at Indiana University. He is also Scientific Counsellor of the Institute of History Center for Humanities of the Hungarian Academy of Sciences. He is the author of *Hungary in the Cold War, 1945–1956: Between the United States and the Soviet Union* (2004) and the coauthor and coeditor of *Soviet Occupation of Romania, Hungary and Austria, 1944–1948* (2015), and several volumes in Hungarian. He is the recipient of the Gold Cross of Merit of the Hungarian Republic (2006), the Zoltán Bezerédj Prize of the Ministry of National Cultural Heritage of Hungary (2006), and the György Ránki Prize of the Hungarian Historical Association (1995).

Translator JASON VINCZ, a specialist in Anglo-American and Eastern European literature, holds degrees from Harvard College, the University of Iowa Writers' Workshop, and the Russian and East European Institute at Indiana University.